PENGUIN REFERENCE BOOKS

A DICTIONARY OF ART AND ARTISTS

Peter and Linda Murray were both trained as painters but turned to the history of art and went to the Courtauld Institute as students immediately after the war. They were married in 1947, in the middle of their Final examinations. They published their first joint work, a translation of Heinrich Wölfflin's *Classic Art*, in 1952. Since then they have collaborated on several translations as well as a book on the art of the Renaissance, but this was their first book. One wrote a complete entry which the other then picked holes in and rewrote; as a result they are now unable to tell who wrote which entries and must take joint responsibility for everything.

Linda Murray was for many years a lecturer in the Extra-Mural Department of the University of London. She has written books on the High Renaissance and Mannerism, a short book on Michelangelo and a second, longer work entitled *Michelangelo His Life, Work, and Times* (1984), and a novel, *The Dark Fire*, based on the life of Caravaggio. Peter Murray is Emeritus Professor of the History of Art at Birkbeck College, University of London. He has written a number of books on art and architecture, including a section of *A History of English Architecture* (Pelican, 1965) and an edition of Jacob Burckhardt's classic *Architecture of the Renaissance in Italy* (Penguin, 1987). He has also written several gallery catalogues.

PETER AND LINDA MURRAY

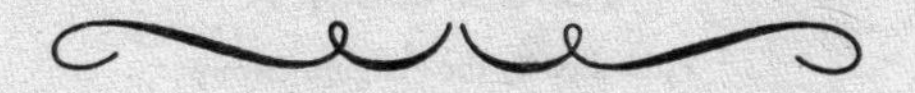

THE PENGUIN DICTIONARY OF ART AND ARTISTS

PENGUIN BOOKS

PENGUIN BOOKS

Published by the Penguin Group
Penguin Books Ltd, 27 Wrights Lane, London W8 5TZ, England
Penguin Books USA Inc., 375 Hudson Street, New York, New York 10014, USA
Penguin Books Australia Ltd, Ringwood, Victoria, Australia
Penguin Books Canada Ltd, 10 Alcorn Avenue, Toronto, Ontario, Canada M4V 3B2
Penguin Books (NZ) Ltd, 182–190 Wairau Road, Auckland 10, New Zealand

Penguin Books Ltd, Registered Offices: Harmondsworth, Middlesex, England

First published 1959
Reprinted with revisions 1960
Revised edition first published by Thames & Hudson 1965
Further revised edition published in Penguin Reference Books 1968
Third edition 1972
Fourth edition 1976
Fifth edition 1983
Reprinted with revisions 1986
Reprinted with revisions 1987
Sixthe edition 1989
Reprinted with revisions 1991
1 3 5 7 9 10 8 6 4 2

Printed in England by Clays Ltd, St Ives plc
Filmset in Monophoto Times

FOR OUR PARENTS

ABBREVIATIONS USED IN THE DICTIONARY

Acad.	Academy, Academia
Accad.	Accademia
Akad.	Akademie
ARA	Associate of the Royal Academy
b.	born
BC	Before Christ
Berks.	Berkshire
Bib.	Bibliothèque
BM	British Museum
Bucks.	Buckinghamshire
c.	*circa*, about
Cal.	California
Cath.	Cathedral
CBA	Center for British Art
cf.	*confer*, compare
Ch. Ch.	Christ Church
Col.	Colorado
Coll.	Collection, College
Conn.	Connecticut
d.	died
ed.	edition
e.g.	*exempli gratia*
Fdn	Foundation
ff.	following
Fitzwm	Fitzwilliam
Fla	Florida
Fr	French
Gall.	Gallery, Galleria
Ger.	German
Gk	Greek
Herts.	Hertfordshire
Hist.	Historical
Hosp.	Hospital
i.e.	*id est*, that is
Inst.	Institute
Ital.	Italian
K-H	Kunsthistorisches
Lat.	Latin
Lincs.	Lincolnshire
M of MA	Museum of Modern Art
Mass.	Massachusetts
Md	Maryland
Met. Mus.	Metropolitan Museum
Mich.	Michigan
Middx	Middlesex
Mo.	Missouri
MS, MSS	Manuscript, manuscripts
Mus.	Museum, Musée
N.	North
Nat. Marit. Mus.	National Maritime Museum
Naz.	Nazionale
NC	North Carolina
NG	National Gallery
NG of S	National Gallery of Scotland
NJ	New Jersey
NPG	National Portrait Gallery
nr	near
NSW	New South Wales
NY	New York
NZ	New Zealand
OED	*Oxford English Dictionary*
OM	Order of Merit
Pa	Pennsylvania
Pal.	Palais, Palace, Palazzo
PRA	President of the Royal Academy
RA	Royal Academy, Royal Academician
RAMC	Royal Army Medical Corps
RI	Rhode Island
Rijksmus.	Rijksmuseum
Royal Coll.	Royal Collection
RSA	Royal Scottish Academy
S.	Saint, San, Sankt, South
SC	South Carolina
S.M.	Santa Maria
SNPG	Scottish National Portrait Gallery
Soc.	Society
Span.	Spanish
SS.	Saints, Santissimo (a)
St	Saint
Sta	Santa
Staffs.	Staffordshire
Sto	Santo
Univ.	University
US	United States
USSR	Union of Soviet Socialist Republics
V&A	Victoria and Albert Museum
Va	Virginia
Wilts.	Wiltshire

LIST OF GENERAL (NON-BIOGRAPHICAL) ARTICLES

PREFACE TO THE FIRST EDITION

The purpose of this Dictionary is to act as a companion to the inquiring gallery visitor, and, we hope, to serve as a useful quick reference book. We have restricted the scope to the arts of painting, sculpture and engraving in Western Europe and North America, and to a period beginning about the year 1300 and continuing up to the present day. One good reason for this restriction is that we are almost totally ignorant of the arts of other periods and places; since writing this book we have come to realize that we have a restricted knowledge of the field we have undertaken to cover. Like the companion *Dictionary of Music* in this series we have to combine articles on technical terms and processes with biographies of as many artists as possible, and we decided to try to cover all the technical terms, processes and artistic movements as fully as we could, even at the expense of biographies. There have been many thousands of painters and sculptors in the last six centuries and most of them are in that monument of scholarship, Thieme and Becker's *Allgemeines Künstlerlexikon* in forty-odd large volumes.

There is one exception to our desire to give a definition for all technical terms, and that is when they are already adequately defined – even in the technical sense – in a normal English Dictionary (we have used the *Concise Oxford*): examples of this are 'Vignette', 'Diorama' or 'Retable'. Where a definition seemed to us not to cover a common usage in the arts we have given it here.

In the biographical articles our aim has been threefold. We have tried, first, to give dates of birth and death, or known activity, and such other dates as seemed important for an understanding of an artist's career. Next, we have tried to give the reader some idea of what his works look like, usually by relating them to other and perhaps better-known artists by means of frequent cross-references. Thirdly, we have given, in most cases, a list of museums which have pictures or sculpture by him. These lists are not intended to be exhaustive or critical. We have obviously tended to include museums in Great Britain or the United States and to omit those in Russia or, say, Bulgaria. For equally obvious reasons we have not mentioned pictures in private collections unless they are crucial to the artist's development, but this is very rare indeed. As far as we know, the pictures stated to be in a given museum are in that museum, but this is less simple than it sounds, for many museums are still recovering from the War and no modern catalogue is available, while others – such as the National and Tate Galleries in London – seem to play a constant game of musical chairs with their possessions. The Royal Collection comprises pictures in Hampton Court, Windsor, Buckingham Palace or any other Royal Palace. In nine cases out of ten they are on view permanently (at Hampton Court) or most of the time (Windsor Castle or Holyrood House), but it is not always possible to distinguish, and the pictures at Buckingham Palace are, of course, never visible except when lent to exhibitions or shown in the Queen's Gallery now attached to the Palace.

Cross-references. Capital letters are used to indicate cross-references, and we have made this systematic so that, by following up the cross-references, the reader can not only expand the information in the original entry but should also gain a better idea of X's relationship to his contemporaries. In any given entry several other names will occur in normal type: these may or may not have separate entries of their own, but we do not think that following them up will, in this case, add anything to the reader's knowledge of X.

Spelling. The spelling of names may present some difficulties, especially as de This or van That will be found under T, the prefixes being disregarded, while the Italian Giovanni di Paolo will be found under G and not P. In many cases we have given cross-references, but the best rule will be to look under everything possible before deciding that whoever it is has been left out.

Dates. Dates are given with as much precision as we can manage, and the distinction between 1520/5 and 1520–5 should be noted. The first means 'at some point in the period, but the exact point is unknown'; the second, 'beginning in 1520 and ending in 1525'. Authorities, of course, are not cited; we hope our fellow-professionals will find some amusement in spotting them, and to those who spot themselves we offer our grateful thanks.

London, September 1957

PREFACE TO THE SECOND PENGUIN EDITION

Since this Dictionary was published in 1959 it has been reprinted with a number of minor revisions, but in 1965 an edition was published by Thames & Hudson in London, and in America, which contained a revision of the original text and a considerable number of new articles. This edition was very fully illustrated and also contained two bibliographies. In this new Penguin edition the text is substantially the same as that of the illustrated edition with a small number of revisions and new entries. The principal difference between this and the original Penguin edition lies therefore in the larger number of biographies contained in this new edition, since the principal general articles are virtually unchanged and only a comparatively small number of new biographies of earlier artists will be found in this edition. We are inclined to feel that many 19th- and 20th-century artists are included in this edition because of their topical interest rather than their merits, but it is certainly true that there is a lively interest in their work and we have therefore provided an outline of their careers. From a historical point of view the book is now out of balance, but it may well be that this is justifiable on other grounds.

January 1968

PREFACE TO THE THIRD AND FOURTH PENGUIN EDITIONS

This Dictionary is becoming a bibliographical nightmare. The present, eighteenth, printing is either the third or fourth edition in the proper sense of the word: in fact, each printing has had small changes which distinguish it from its predecessors, but there have also been major re-settings, of which this is one, that can reasonably be called editions. We have taken the opportunity to add a great many small changes and a smaller number of entirely new entries, mostly of sculptors.

Christmas Day, 1974

PREFACE TO THE FIFTH PENGUIN EDITION

The opportunity offered by our publishers to prepare an entirely new and re-set edition has allowed us to make many changes and additions. Almost every entry has been modified in some way since the last major revision of 1976 and a considerable number of new entries, both general and biographical, has been added: we estimate that the book has been increased by something like twenty per cent. Many of the changes have been made necessary by the great volume of research and publication in recent years, and we have done our best to include these results; special thanks are due to Le and Helen Ettlinger, who read us with such close attention that we have had to revise many things.

June 1982

PREFACE TO THE SIXTH PENGUIN EDITION

Since the last major revision of 1982–3 we have acquired (and learned to use) a word processor. As a result, we have put the whole text of the Dictionary on disks, which means that every word has been scrutinized and therefore almost every entry has had an addition or deletion, if only of a few words. It has also given us the opportunity to add many completely new entries, so that over a ten-year period the book has been increased by almost a third.

Late in 1987 the Musée d'Orsay was opened in Paris, with a splendid collection of 19th-century works, not exclusively French, mainly transferred from the Louvre and other Parisian museums. We have done our best to record these changes, but it is likely that we have recorded some works in the Mus. d'Orsay which are still in their original locations, and vice-versa.

June 1988

A

ABBATE, Niccolò dell' (*c.*1512–71), was a Modenese painter whose style was founded on Mantegna's illusionism and especially on Correggio's softness. He painted frescoes in Modena (1546) and Bologna (1547: now in the University), and was in France by 1552, helping PRIMATICCIO with the decoration of the Royal château at Fontainebleau, but most of his work there has disappeared. He spent the rest of his life in France, where, with Primaticcio, he represents the end of the First School of FONTAINEBLEAU. He introduced the Mannerist landscape into France: there is a fine example in London (NG), and other works are in Detroit, Florence (Uffizi), Modena, Oxford (Ch. Ch.), Paris (Louvre), Rome (Borghese), Vienna and elsewhere.

ABBOTT, Lemuel Francis (*c.*1760–1803), was an English portrait painter, famous for his *Nelson*, of which many replicas and variants exist. These and other portraits are in London (NPG, Nat. Marit. Mus. and Tate).

ABSORBENT GROUND. A chalk-based ground, on canvas or panel, prepared without oil so that it will absorb oil from the paint layer, which then dries quickly with a matt surface.

ABSTRACT ART depends upon the assumption that specifically aesthetic values reside in forms and colours, entirely independent of the subject of the work of art. This view is of great antiquity and has resulted in much art of a semi-magical character, as well as pure decoration. It also prevails in Moslem countries, where representation of the human figure is frowned upon. The 'liberating' influence of the camera allowed the painter to neglect his social duty as a recorder of things and events, and, at the same time, late in the 19th century, Impressionism came to be regarded as a dead-end of naturalism, thus leading to an increased emphasis on formal values, and ultimately to CUBISM, CONSTRUCTIVISM, TACHISME and the rest. It is not synonymous with NON-OBJECTIVE ART.

The philosophical justification of abstract art may be found in Plato: 'I do not now intend by beauty of shapes what most people would expect, such as that of living creatures or pictures, but . . . straight lines and curves and the surfaces or solid forms produced out of these by lathes and rulers and squares . . . These things are not beautiful relatively, like other things, but always and naturally and absolutely' (*Philebus*).

ABSTRACT EXPRESSIONISM. A combination of ABSTRACT ART and EXPRESSIONISM which amounts to little more than automatic painting – i.e. allowing the subconscious to express itself (a SURREALIST idea) by the creation of involuntary shapes and dribbles of paint. Abstract Impressionism – which appears to be another name for the same thing – is supposed to derive from the intricate mesh of paint which forms the surface of MONET's last pictures, as, half-blind, he struggled to find pictorial equivalents for his optical sensations. Abstract Impressionism has been defined (by E. De Kooning, 1956) thus: 'Retaining the quiet uniform pattern of strokes that spread over the canvas without climax or emphasis, these followers keep the Impressionist manner of looking at a scene but leave out the scene'. *See also* ACTION PAINTING and TACHISME.

ABSTRACTION-CRÉATION. A loose association of abstract artists, many of them refugees from Nazi Germany, founded in Paris in 1931. They published an annual, *Abstraction-Création*, between 1932 and 1936.

ACADEMY. The name, derived from Plato's Academy, was used in Italy in the 15th century by groups of humanists meeting for discussion. The first academies of art are connected with LEONARDO da Vinci in his Milanese period and BERTOLDO in Florence. Little is known of the aims and activities of the 'Accademia Leonardi Vinci', as it was called, but Bertoldo was in charge of the statues and sculpture school in the Medici garden, fostered by Lorenzo de Medici, 'Il Magnifico' (*d.*1492), and had the distinction of helping the young Michelangelo. During the 16th century these groups acquired more formal aims and character, and the term was, by extension, applied to groups of artists meeting privately for study. Baccio BANDINELLI founded one in 1531 in the quarters granted him in the Vatican, and another in Florence *c.*1550. The first Academy of Fine Arts, properly speaking, was founded in 1563 in Florence by VASARI, under the patronage of the Grand Duke Cosimo and the absent and 88-year-old Michelangelo, who, by his personal prestige, had done more than anyone to raise the fine arts from the level of the mechanical to the equal of the liberal arts. Vasari's Accademia di DISEGNO was intended to be a teaching as well as an honorific body, for the main purpose of an Academy was always to raise the social status of the artist; but although almost every artist of repute in Italy became a member, its teaching programme was soon abandoned, and the apprentice system continued for many more years. The Accademia di San Luca, founded in Rome in 1593 with Federico ZUCCARO as its president, also had a similarly ambitious programme which came to nothing. Other such bodies were founded in Italy – notably in Bologna in 1598, where it became intimately associated with the CARRACCI – and the custom of artists meeting under the patronage of an enlightened nobleman or connoisseur, to draw from the nude, thus forming private teaching academies, was widespread by the middle of the 17th century.

The French Academy, charged with the study and preservation of the French language, was founded by Richelieu in 1634: the Academy of Painting and Sculpture, first founded in 1648, was closely modelled on the Italian examples, but did not reach its all-powerful position until 1661, when it came under the control of Colbert, who saw in it a golden opportunity to make the arts play a part in the aggrandizement of the monarchy. By 1664 he had obtained a new constitution for it, which made it primarily a teaching body, responsible for the training of artists capable of carrying out the artistic programmes he planned. He also founded the French Academy in Rome in 1666, as a school to which the most successful students (*see* ÉCOLE des Élèves Protégés) could be sent for further training. He intended POUSSIN to be its head, but he died in 1665. The French Academy reached perhaps its greatest power under LEBRUN, who became Director in 1683. The dual character of learned body, with a strict hierarchy of members graded according to the form of art they practised (history painters at the top, portraitists next, and so on down to landscape and genre), and with the exclusive privilege of public exhibition, combined with a state school, became the pattern for most of the Academies founded during the 17th and 18th centuries. The majority were not, however, successful until after the middle of the 18th century, when academies of all kinds were an established part of the pattern of intellectual life.

In England the autocratic constitution and the implications of state control of the arts under the French system were so unpopular that there was a long delay in founding an academy. Nevertheless, the need for a training school was recognized, and several private academies were set up, including two in St Martin's Lane, London, one of which was run first by THORNHILL and then by his son-in-law, HOGARTH.

The Royal Academy in London, founded in 1768 with provision for forty Academicians and (in 1769) twenty Associates, later increased to thirty, was one of the late-comers. It is an exception to the generality in that it was the outcome of private enterprise among artists, and, although it enjoyed royal patronage from the start (in fact, it owed its initial success to the keen interest of George III), it has never been subject to any state control, or had subsidies or monopoly of exhibitions. The efforts of its first President, REYNOLDS, established it as a school, and his personal prestige and intellectual attainments were reflected in the social status which membership conferred, while the open character of its yearly exhibitions ensured a flow of new talent. The first American Academy, founded in Philadelphia in 1805, grew out of a private institution (the PEALE Museum), and the National Academy of Design was founded in New York in 1826, under MORSE, who had been trained in London and exhibited at the RA.

It was mainly during the reign of late-19th-century conservatism that Academies became the centres of opposition to all new ideas in art, with results that have brought nothing but discredit on themselves, so that the term 'academic' has become a synonym for dullness, conventionalism, and prejudice. This cleavage between official bodies and the mass of artists outside the academic fold has bedevilled the relations between artists and public, fostered unfortunate extremes of taste, and rendered the fair appreciation of academic art difficult and the criticism of art particularly unfruitful. There are, however, signs that it is now realized, inside and outside the academies, that this cleavage is to the detriment of all.

ACADEMY FIGURE. A painting, statue, or drawing, generally about half life-size, of a nude figure executed solely for purposes of instruction or practice, and not intended as a work of art.

ACRYLIC paint – properly acrylic vinyl polymer emulsion paint – is a recent synthetic paint which allows a combination of the traditional techniques of oil and watercolour. It is a plastic emulsion which is soluble in water, so that very thin, transparent washes can be applied, as in classical watercolour. It is also possible to apply a very thick impasto, as in ALLA PRIMA oil-painting, and there is also a special polymer medium with a function similar to that of oil in oil-painting. The synthetic substances are said to be permanent and to adhere to almost any surface, but it is perhaps too early to judge this.

ACTION PAINTING. Splashing and dribbling paint on canvas. The basic assumption is that the Unconscious will take over and produce a work of art. The technique is claimed to go back to Leonardo da Vinci, who suggested using stains on walls as a starting-point for designing (cf. BLOT): the essential difference is that Leonardo used the method solely as a means of stimulating the creative imagination, and not as an end in itself. Action Painting should not be confused with the intellectual type of Abstract art in which some thought is necessary, but its advocates claim that the beauty of the 'calligraphy'

– i.e. the movements of the artist's wrist – constitutes its justification, as well as distinguishing it from TACHISME. *See* POLLOCK *and* TOBEY.

ADAM, Lambert-Sigisbert (1700–59), a French sculptor, went to Rome in 1723 and there won the competition for the Trevi Fountain (1731), which he did not execute. He returned to Paris in 1733 and was received into the Academy on his *Neptune Calming the Waves* (1737: Louvre), which is derived directly from Bernini while his *Neptune* at Versailles is also markedly Baroque; yet he also published a collection of Greek and Roman sculpture, the 'Recueil des sculptures antiques . . .', Paris, 1754, i.e. at the moment of the shift to NEO-CLASSICISM.

AD VIVUM (Lat. from the life), that is, a portrait taken from a living sitter and not from a death-mask, as was often the case, or from earlier portraits.

AERTSEN, Pieter (1508/9–75), was a painter, born in Amsterdam, who continued the tradition of peasant genre established by BRUEGEL, and was unaffected by the ROMANISTS. He settled in Antwerp *c.*1535, where he married and entered the Guild, but he returned to Amsterdam in 1556, possibly on account of religion. Many of his pictures were destroyed in the religious troubles of 1566, but there are many survivors, mostly with kitchen or genre scenes in the foreground and a religious scene (such as Christ in the House of Martha and Mary) in the background. His still-life painting was important in the development of the genre in the Netherlands and even in Italy, and it has been argued that he influenced both CARAVAGGIO and VELÁZQUEZ. It is difficult to see how they could have known his work, and BASSANO is a more likely source, at least for Caravaggio. His surviving religious pictures, while less influential, show the straightforward realistic tradition of Netherlandish art. His wife's nephew, Joachim BUECKELAER, was his pupil. There are works by Aertsen in Amsterdam, Antwerp (Mus. and Mus. Mayer van den Bergh), Berlin, Birmingham, Brussels, Copenhagen, Cracow, Genoa, Leningrad, Pisa, Rotterdam, Rouen, Stockholm, Uppsala (Univ.) and Vienna.

AFRO (1912–76) was an Italian abstract painter whose real name was Afro Basaldella. He lived in Rome and worked a good deal in the US, but his style derived from Picasso and Braque. There are murals by him in the Banco Nazionale del Lavoro, Rome, and the UNESCO building in Paris.

AGOSTINO di Duccio (1418–81), sculptor, was born in Florence. He became a mercenary soldier in 1433, and did not return to Florence until after 1442, by which date he had executed the altar in Modena Cathedral, accepted as his earliest independent work. Its figures in deep relief against a plain background suggest that he was probably a pupil of Jacopo della QUERCIA, who worked at S. Petronio, Bologna, from 1425 to 1438. By 1446 he had again left Florence, accused, with his brother, of theft from a church. From about 1450 until 1457 he worked on his masterpiece – the tombs and the extensive series of low reliefs forming the sculptural decoration of the interior of the Tempio Malatestiano in Rimini, reconstructed by Sigismondo Malatesta, who employed ALBERTI as his architect and PIERO della Francesca as his painter. Agostino worked on the façade of the Oratory of S. Bernardino, Perugia, until 1462, and in 1463 he returned to Florence, where he entered the Guild, and began work on a block of marble, which he spoiled: it was later used by Michelangelo for his *David.* In 1473 he went back to Perugia and remained there until his death. Agostino's marble reliefs are usually of an even flatness, and his decorative, intensely linear style has none of the illusionistic effects used by DONATELLO or the ROSSELLINO brothers. There are further examples in Florence (Bargello), London (V&A), Paris (Louvre) and Washington (NG).

AIKMAN, William (1682–1731), was a Scottish portrait painter, pupil of MEDINA, to whose business in Edinburgh Aikman succeeded, but after KNELLER's death in 1723 he migrated to London, where he had many literary friends, including Pope and Swift. Allan Ramsay, the poet and father of the painter, was portrayed by him; the picture is inscribed: 'Here painted on this canvas clout By Aikman's hand is Ramsay's snout.' He is chiefly remarkable for having studied in Rome (1707–10) before this became common; after this he went to Constantinople and Syria. There are self-portraits in Edinburgh (NG) and Florence (Uffizi). He continued Medina's series of portraits in the Royal College of Surgeons, Edinburgh (one is dated 1715).

ALBANI, Francesco (1578–1660), was a Bolognese painter contemporary with Guido RENI, whose fellow-pupil he was, first under the Mannerist CALVAERT and then, *c.*1595, at the CARRACCI Academy. He also had strong links with DOMENICHINO and the paintings in the Oratory of S. Colombano, Bologna, may have been worked on by all three, 1600–1. Albani went to Rome with Reni in 1601/2, but, while Reni struck out on his own, Albani and Domenichino worked for Annibale Carracci; in particular, on a series of important landscapes with small figures of sacred subjects (now in Rome, Pal. Doria). These were among the earliest landscapes painted in Rome by Italian artists (but *see* BRIL), and, although Carracci was certainly the designer of the whole series, both Albani and Domenichino learned much from them. After Annibale Carracci's death in 1609 Albani worked in Rome and Bologna, returning to Bologna in 1625, where he worked less and less; but he did produce many replicas of small mythological subjects which influenced French painters of the 18th century: the Louvre and Fontainebleau have good examples, but most of his works are in Rome and Bologna.

ALBERS, Josef (1888–1976), was born in Germany and studied at Berlin, Essen and Munich, where he worked under F. von Stuck, who had taught KLEE and KANDINSKY. Albers subsequently studied and taught at the BAUHAUS until its closure in 1933, when he emigrated to the USA, where he became principal of the Yale School of Design in 1950. His geometric art is summed up in his series called Homage to the Square (1949 onwards: one painting is in the Tate, London). He also wrote a book on colour, to which he attached an importance equal to that of form, *Interaction of Color* (1963), and his *Despite Straight Lines* was published posthumously. There are large murals by him in the Graduate Center, Harvard University (1950), and the Time-Life Building, New York (1961).

ALBERTI, Leon Baptista (*c.*1404–72), was a Florentine humanist, principally famous as an architect, but who is also known to have practised as a painter and sculptor. The only work attributable to him in these arts is the plaque, said to be a self-portrait, in Washington (NG). His importance in the arts of painting and sculpture is on account of his theoretical writings, *De Sculptura* and especially *Della Pittura* (1435), which gives the first exposition in the Renaissance of the theory of PERSPECTIVE and of the COSTRUZIONE LEGITTIMA, as well as of History Painting.

ALBERTINELLI, Mariotto (1474–1515), was a Florentine painter who collaborated with Fra BARTOLOMMEO from before 1500, and was taken into partnership in 1508 in the S. Marco workshop. After three years he abandoned painting for innkeeping, which he said was less exacting and less open to criticism, declaring, so the story goes, that he was 'sick of this everlasting talk of perspective'. His best work is the *Visitation* (1503), in the Uffizi, Florence, but there is a charming example in London (Courtauld Inst.). There is a *Madonna and Saints*, signed and dated 1506, in Toulouse, which is said to have been begun by Filippino LIPPI and completed by him.

ALDEGREVER, Heinrich (1502–55/61), was a German engraver of religious subjects in the manner of DÜRER, popular scenes and ornamental patterns adapted from Italian arabesques. *See* KLEINMEISTER.

ALGARDI, Alessandro (1595 or perhaps 1598–1654), was a Bolognese sculptor who worked in Rome and represented the classicism of the Bolognese Academy in opposition to BERNINI. He was a pupil of the painter Lodovico CARRACCI and worked in the Carracci Academy in Bologna before going to Rome *c.*1625, where he became a friend of DOMENICHINO, also a Bolognese Carracci pupil. He was, however, also a friend of PIETRO da Cortona, a much more Baroque figure. His early works – the tomb of Cardinal Millini (*d.*1629) in S. M. del Popolo, and the Frangipane portrait busts in S. Marcello – show his marked dependence on antique portrait types. His *S. Philip Neri* (S. Maria in Valicella), an imaginary portrait of the saint (canonized 1622), is another example of his skill in portraying people he never set eyes on; but his *Cardinal L. Zacchia* (1626/37, Berlin) shows what he could do when working from life. A terracotta bust of Cardinal P. E. Zacchia (*d.*1605) dates from very late in Algardi's career (?1654): it is now in London (V&A), and the marble made from it is in a private collection in Florence. However, it is probably by an assistant, since Algardi grew so fat in his last years that he was apparently unable to carve. The bust of Bracciolini, also in London (V&A), formerly attributed to him and now given to Finelli, is one of several which have been attributed first to Bernini and then to Algardi. On the whole, Algardi's are graver in deportment and have greater inward characterization than Bernini's highly extrovert portraits. There can be no doubt, however, that Algardi borrowed from Bernini, whose portrait statue of Urban VIII underlies Algardi's *Innocent X*, begun in 1645 for the Conservatori Palace in Rome as a companion to Bernini's *Urban*; while the tomb of Leo XI (St Peter's, 1634–52) is a chastened and plain white marble version of Bernini's polychrome tomb of Urban VIII. Algardi's leadership of the classical opposition to Bernini was recognized in 1640 by his election as Principe of the Academy of St Luke, but his real success came under Innocent X (1644–55), when Bernini was in disgrace. His only important relief also dates from this period: the *Attila* in St Peter's of 1646–53, which is a piece of technical virtuosity, but is less a relief than a Carracci altarpiece in marble. The full-size terracotta *modello* was exhibited in St Peter's in 1950; one of the few of its kind to have survived, it is now in the Biblioteca Vallicelliana, Rome, and a bronze reduction of it is in Vienna (K-H Mus.). There are other works elsewhere in Rome and in Bologna (S. Paolo), Cleveland Ohio, Detroit, Hamburg, Manchester, Minneapolis, New York (Met. Mus.), Paris (Louvre), Ravenna and Yale.

ALLAN, David (1744–96), sometimes called 'the Scottish Hogarth', was, more accurately, a painter of genre and portraits anticipating WILKIE. He lived in

Rome *c.*1767–*c.*1777 and won a medal for a history picture in 1773. He studied under Gavin HAMILTON and was influenced by NEOCLASSICAL ideas. There are works in Aberdeen, Edinburgh and Glasgow.

ALLA PRIMA (Ital. at first) describes the technique, general since the 19th century but considered freakish and slapdash before then, of completing the picture surface in one session in full colour and with such opacity that neither previous drawing nor underpainting – if these exist – modifies the final effect. *Au premier coup* is the French equivalent.

ALLORI, Cristofano (1577–1621), was the son of a Florentine Mannerist painter, Alessandro (1535–1607), and the great-nephew of BRONZINO. He was in Rome in 1610 and was influenced by Caravaggio, as may be seen in his masterpiece, *Judith with the Head of Holofernes*, said to portray the artist's unkind mistress and himself as the dead Holofernes. The original is probably the picture, signed and dated 1613, in the Royal Coll., but another in Florence (Pitti) may also be AUTOGRAPH: there are numerous replicas and copies. Allori was also a fine portraitist, as shown by the painting of his friend, Count Davanzati Bostici, in Oxford (Ashmolean), which has recently also acquired a portrait by his father Alessandro.

ALLSTON, Washington (1779–1843), was the first important American landscape painter. He was trained in London (1801–3) under WEST and travelled in Europe before returning to America. He made a second visit to Europe in 1810 and was elected ARA in 1818, the year in which he returned to America. His early works were Italianate landscapes in the Claude manner, but his intensely Romantic outlook caused him to admire FUSELI and TURNER, and ultimately to imitate the hyper-romanticism of MARTIN. Most of his works are in America, especially Boston, but his portrait of his life-long friend, the poet Coleridge, is in London (NPG) and Birmingham has an extravagant landscape attributed to him. *See* HUDSON RIVER SCHOOL.

ALMA-TADEMA, Sir Lawrence (1836–1912), was a Dutch painter of genre scenes set in Greece, Rome and Ancient Egypt, who settled in England in 1870 and became naturalized. His early work followed that of the Baron Leys in Belgium in scenes of medieval history, but a visit to Naples and Pompeii in 1863 changed his subject matter to a form of classicizing genre in which he was successful and popular (it has been described as similar to Hollywood epics). He became an ARA in 1876, and RA in 1879, and was knighted in 1899. His works were numbered in Roman numerals from 1850, reaching *Opus CCCCVIII*, and have a detailed surface and particularization of marble, drapery and flesh similar to the confections of Lord LEIGHTON. There are works in Baltimore (Walters), Boston, Cambridge Mass. (Fogg), Cardiff, Dordrecht, The Hague (Mesdag), London (Tate, V&A and Guildhall), Philadelphia and Washington (Corcoran).

ALTARPIECE *see* ANCONA, PALA, POLYPTYCH and REREDOS.

ALTDORFER, Albrecht (*c.*1480–1538), a Bavarian painter, worked in Regensburg (Ratisbon), becoming city architect and a councillor. In 1511 certainly, and probably earlier, he travelled along the Danube and visited the Austrian Alps where the scenery moved him to become the first landscape painter in the modern sense. His earliest dated paintings (1507, Berlin and Bremen) show the influence of CRANACH and DÜRER, but the landscape is already very significant, and by 1510 the figures are quite unimportant – only the rustle of the trees beside the mountain lake matters. The figures in his pictures are the complement of his romantic use of landscape (*St George in the Forest*, Munich), and their gestures and facial expressions, as well as their colour, show his use of subjective distortion for dramatic and emotional ends. He also made many drawings and etchings of pure landscape, the importance of which makes him the head of the DANUBE SCHOOL and also of the KLEINMEISTER. His major works are the *S. Florian Altar* (1518, mostly still in S. Florian's Monastery, near Linz) and *Alexander's Victory* (1529, Munich). Other works are in Basle, Cleveland Ohio, Cologne, Florence (Uffizi), London (NG), Nuremberg, Ratisbon and Vienna.

ALTICHIERO was a Veronese painter of the late 14th century, whose style was formed on Giotto's frescoes in Padua. With his helper Avanzo he painted frescoes in Padua (Il Santo, and, 1379–84, Oratorio di S. Giorgio), and, at the end of the century, he founded the School of Verona with his frescoes in Sant' Anastasia.

ALTO-RILIEVO *see* RELIEF.

'ALUNNO DI DOMENICO', i.e. 'Pupil of Domenico' (GHIRLANDAIO). A name invented by Berenson for the Florentine painter to whom he ascribed most of the designs for Florentine woodcut book-illustrations of the late 15th century. This wholesale attribution has not won general acceptance, but the actual pupil and assistant of Ghirlandaio postulated by Berenson has been identified as Bartolommeo di Giovanni, who was commissioned to paint the predella of Ghirlandaio's *Adoration* in the Foundling Hospital, Florence, in 1488.

AMANNATI is the correct form of AMMANATI.

AMBERGER, Christoph (*c.*1500–61/2), was an Augsburg portrait painter whose works resemble those of Holbein, but with a strong Venetian influence, perhaps due to Paris BORDONE, who may have visited Augsburg in 1540. There is a signed altarpiece of 1560 in S. Anna, Augsburg, but the only signed portrait by him seems to be the *Emperor Charles V* (Berlin). There are works in Augsburg, Birmingham (Barber Inst.), Glasgow, Munich, Philadelphia (Johnson), Toledo Ohio, Vienna and York.

'AMICO DI SANDRO' (Friend of Sandro, i.e. Botticelli) was the name given by Berenson to the artist he invented as the painter of several pictures which seemed to lie between the styles of BOTTICELLI and Filippino LIPPI; e.g. two Filippinos in London (NG) and a Botticelli also in London (V&A). His creator later repudiated him and the pictures have been redistributed, although an attempt has been made to resuscitate him.

AMIGONI (Amiconi), Jacopo (1682?–1752), was a Venetian history and portrait painter who worked all over Europe in a more or less international style, the Venetian Rococo, with elements compounded from Sebastiano RICCI and French Rococo, and, later, TIEPOLO. He worked for some years for the Elector of Bavaria and then came to London in 1730, where he painted several decorative cycles (e.g. Rickmansworth, nr London, Moor Park Golf Club) and portraits; though these, according to VERTUE, were 'not his inclination – nor Talent'. In 1739 he returned to Venice with a small fortune, and it was he who persuaded Canaletto to visit London (1746). In 1747 he went to Madrid as Court painter: Vertue records that news of his death there reached London just as his finest works – in St James's Square – were destroyed. The altarpiece of Emmanuel Coll., Cambridge, is his: other works are in Darmstadt, London

(NPG – an allegorical portrait of Queen Caroline – and Tate), Madrid, Schleissheim, Sheffield, Venice and York.

AMMANATI (more properly, Amannati), Bartolommeo (1511–92), was a Florentine sculptor influenced by Michelangelo and Sansovino. His best-known work is the *Neptune* on the fountain (1563–75) in the Piazza della Signoria at Florence, of which a contemporary said: 'Ammanato, Ammanato, che bel marmo hai rovinato!' (what fine marble you have ruined!). Of the bronze figures surrounding the fountain he probably executed only the bearded marine god; it is possible that some of the others were by Giovanni BOLOGNA. In his old age, affected by Counter-Reformation austerity, he is said to have destroyed some of his secular works. He also wrote an important letter (published in 1582) setting out his ideas on decency and on the sculptor's responsibility for his work, which is a major document of Mannerist art theory after the Council of Trent. His chief claim to fame rests on his work as an architect. In 1550 he married Laura Battiferri, who was well-known as a poet.

AMORINO (Ital. little love). A small Cupid or PUTTO.

ANAMORPHOSIS (Gk. distortion of form). Prominent in the foreground of HOLBEIN's *Ambassadors* (1533, London, NG) is an extremely elongated and distorted representation of a skull which can only be recognized by viewing it through a special lens or at an extreme angle. Such a representation – not unlike the reflection in a distorting mirror – is called an Anamorphosis. They are rare as serious works of art, and no convincing explanation for the skull has so far been proposed, but there is a similar, contemporary, *Edward VI* (1546, London, NPG).

ANCONA (Ital.). A large altarpiece composed of several compartments, made in one piece with the frame. *See* PALA and POLYPTYCH.

ANDREA del Castagno *see* CASTAGNO.

ANDREA del Sarto (1486–1530) was, with Fra BARTOLOMMEO, the most important painter working in Florence at the time when Michelangelo and Raphael were active in Rome. He was the best painter (as opposed to draughtsman) in 16th-century Florence, and had more feeling for tone and colour than any of his contemporaries south of Venice. He was the first Florentine to depart from the coloured-drawing approach in favour of composition by coloured patches of light and shade, although his actual draughtsmanship is derived from Michelangelo. He also borrowed from the newly-arrived prints by Dürer. As a fresco painter he made his name with a series of grisailles in the cloister of the Scalzi in Florence, depicting the story of the Baptist (1511–26), and the *Miracles of S. Filippo Benizzi* (1509–10) in SS. Annunziata. These were followed by his most famous frescoes, epitomizing the High Renaissance style in Florence, the *Birth of the Virgin* (1514) and the *Madonna del Sacco* (1525), both also in the Annunziata. Andrea went to France in 1518/19 at the invitation of Francis I and was well received there, but he broke his contract in order to return to his wife, who, in the opinion of contemporaries, ruined him. Browning's poem is probably the best explanation of his failure to live up to his early promise, but his works are of great importance in the evolution of Florentine painting, especially the *Holy Families*, often in half-length. The *Madonna delle Arpie* (1517, Florence, Uffizi), is a purely classical work comparable with Raphael's Madonnas: Sarto is, however, a starting point for MANNERISM, since his pupils included PONTORMO, ROSSO and VASARI.

Outside Florence there are works by him in the Royal Coll. and in Berlin, Cleveland Ohio, Dresden, Edinburgh (NG), London (NG and Wallace Coll.), Madrid, New York (Met. Mus.), Paris (Louvre, including some painted in France), Philadelphia, Vienna, Washington (NG) and elsewhere.

ANGELICO, Fra (*c.*1387 or perhaps *c.* 1400–55). Fra Giovanni da Fiesole, known as Beato Angelico and now officially beatified, was a Dominican friar who was a friend of S. Antoninus and knew Popes Eugenius IV and Nicholas V. As a member of the Order of Preachers he used his art for didactic rather than mystic purposes and the style he evolved was correspondingly simple and direct; conservative, and yet based on the largeness of form of Giotto and Masaccio, so that the general development of his style begins with a Gothic quality akin to LORENZO Monaco and runs counter to the trend of Florentine painting in the 1440s as shown by Fra Filippo LIPPI (both Lorenzo Monaco and Lippi were monks), but there is a mysterious *tondo* in Washington which is said to have been started by Angelico and finished by Lippi. Stylistically, this is quite feasible. He entered the convent at Fiesole and shared in its vicissitudes at Cortona and Foligno, but he does not seem to have painted much before 1428, although he seems to have been both a layman and a painter in 1417. An altarpiece in the S. Marco Mus., Florence, is probably of 1425/8. The new theory that he was not born until about 1400 would go a long way towards explaining this. The first certainly datable work by him is the *Linaiuoli Madonna* (Florence, S. Marco), commissioned by the Linen Guild in 1433, with a stone frame commissioned in 1432/3 from GHIBERTI, an artist very similar to Angelico in style. The convent of San Marco was taken over by his Order in 1436 and he decorated it with a series of about fifty frescoes, mostly in the friars' cells and intended as aids to contemplation, rather than as factual representations. At the same time – *c.*1440 – he painted the altarpieces for S. Marco and two other convents: these show the Madonna surrounded by Saints and are important in the development of the type of altarpiece known as the SACRA CONVERSAZIONE. He was called to Rome, probably by Eugenius IV, to decorate a chapel in the Vatican (*c.*1446–9), which still exists. In 1447 he painted two frescoes in Orvieto Cathedral as part of a *Last Judgement*, a scheme which was finished by Signorelli after 1499. He was elected Prior of Fiesole in 1449 and probably returned to Rome after his three-year term expired to paint the Chapel of the Sacrament in the Vatican, now destroyed. He died in Rome in 1455 and was buried in the Dominican church of Sta Maria sopra Minerva. The biggest collection of his works is in his own convent of S. Marco in Florence: others are in Assisi (S. Francesco), Cortona, Fiesole, Florence (Uffizi), Fort Worth Texas, Perugia and the Vatican, as well as Berlin, Boston (Mus. and Gardner), Cambridge Mass., London (NG), Madrid, Paris (Louvre), Munich, New York (Met. Mus.) and elsewhere. His most important pupil was Benozzo GOZZOLI.

ANGUISSOLA (Anguisciola), Sofonisba (1532/5–1625), claimed to be 96 when van Dyck visited her in Palermo in 1624. He drew a portrait of her in his sketchbook and noted that although blind she was still mentally alert. She was the eldest daughter of a Cremonese nobleman (her five sisters also painted) and received a good education, painting being only one of her accomplishments. She studied under local artists and practised a portrait style based on MORETTO and MORONI: she painted a few religious subjects, but most of her work consists of portraits of herself and her family. Her first dated work is the *Self-portrait* of 1554 (Vienna). In 1557 her father thanked Michelangelo for his help and advice, and in 1559 she went to Spain as a lady-in-waiting to the Queen, remaining there at least ten years. She was twice married. Though not important as a painter, she was the first Italian woman artist to win international fame and she opened the way for later women painters, most of whom were the daughters of painters and therefore of lower social standing. There are works by her in Bergamo, Budapest, Florence (Uffizi), Naples and Siena.

ANNIGONI, Pietro (*b.*1910), is an Italian painter. He works in a highly realistic and dramatic style, and in a deliberate revival of traditional Renaissance techniques in oil, tempera, fresco and drawing, exemplified in his two portraits of Queen Elizabeth II, one of which is in the NPG, London. Other works are in Florence (Uffizi Print Room), Milan (Gal. d'Arte Mod.) and frescoes in Florence (S. Martino) and Pistoia (Madonna del Consiglio).

ANONIMO (Ital. anonymous). Often applied to any unidentified Italian artist, but specifically it refers either to the Anonimo Morelliano (i.e. Marcanton Michiel), a writer on the art of Venice and N. Italy in the first half of the 16th century, or to the Anonimo Magliabechiano (or Gaddiano), a Florentine writer of the same period who was one of VASARI's predecessors.

ANTELAMI, Benedetto, was the chief Italian sculptor before the PISANI. In 1178 he signed and dated a relief of the *Deposition* in Parma Cathedral; the Baptistry at Parma, begun in 1196, and some of the sculpture at Fidenza (formerly called Borgo San Donnino) are attributed to him.

ANTI-CERNE (Fr. *cerne*, outline). A contour managed by leaving a white line of bare canvas between two or more areas of colour. It is the opposite of a black outline and was a favourite device of the FAUVES.

'ANTICO', Pier Jacopo Bonacolsi called (*c.*1460–1528), was Court Sculptor to the Gonzagas at Mantua. He was influenced by Mantegna and Donatello, whose Paduan works he may have known. He is recorded as a medallist in 1479 and was in Rome in 1497, where he may have been on other occasions. His nickname (*cf.* MODERNO) derives from his bronze statuettes after antique originals, always highly worked and often with gold and silver inlays and rich gilding. He also restored antiques for Isabella d'Este. The largest collection of his small copies is in Vienna (K-H Mus.): original works are very rare. Other museums with examples include Boston, Florence (Bargello), London (V&A), Modena, New York and Venice (Ca d'Oro).

ANTOLÍNEZ, José (1635–75), was active 1658–73 in Madrid, where he was the equivalent of MURILLO in Seville. In his genre scenes the influence of VELÁZQUEZ, as well as that of Murillo, is evident – e.g. the *Studio* (Munich), but his style derives from the Venetians and from Rubens. He specialized in the typically Spanish subject of the Immaculate Conception, of which at least twenty-five versions by him are known. He also painted portraits. There are works in Amsterdam, Barnard Castle (Bowes Mus.), Copenhagen, Dublin, Madrid, Oxford (Ashmolean) and Seville.

ANTONELLO da Messina (*c.*1430–79) was the only major S. Italian painter of the 15th century, and the only Italian decisively influenced by the minute oil-technique associated with the EYCKS. He may have been a pupil of the half-legendary Colantonio in Naples (where he could have seen Flemish paintings) and there is no reason to suppose that he actually visited Flanders. His mature style combines Flemish detail and technique with Italian breadth of form. In 1475/6 he was in Venice, where he painted the S. Cassiano altarpiece (now known only from copies and fragments in Vienna): this was contemporary with the altarpiece by PIERO della Francesca (Milan, Brera) and the one (now destroyed) by Giovanni BELLINI for SS. Giovanni e Paolo, Venice. One of these three was the first great SACRA CONVERSAZIONE to treat the picture-space as a continuation of the real space – like a chapel opening out of the church – so that the spectator is drawn into the scene in active participation. Antonello's virtuoso technique also influenced the Venetians, especially Giovanni Bellini's portraits, which show traces of the Flemish type of design favoured by Antonello. Apart from the Vienna fragments there are works in London (NG: *Salvator Mundi*, 1465, the first dated work, and others); Paris (Louvre) and Antwerp which both have works dated 1475, presumably painted in Venice; Berlin, Bucharest, Messina, Munich, New York, Philadelphia, Rome (Borghese), Washington and elsewhere.

ANTWERP MANNERISTS. A term used to describe a group of Antwerp painters, mostly unidentified, working in the early 16th century (*c.*1510–30), and who, strictly speaking, have nothing to do with MANNERISM proper. Their style is characterized by affected poses and florid ornament, some of which is Italianate in type. ISENBRANDT is related to this group. *See also* ITALIANIZERS and ROMANISTS.

APPEL, Karel (*b.*1921), is a Dutch painter, born in Amsterdam, who works in Paris. He exhibited with the group known as Cobra (i.e. Copenhagen, Brussels, Amsterdam) from 1949. In 1951 he painted a mural for the Stedelijk Museum, Amsterdam, and he has also produced some book-illustrations, but most of his works are in immensely thick layers of frenziedly moulded oil paint, Abstract Expressionist in type and similar to the work of the American KOONING. There are examples in Antwerp, Auckland NZ, Brussels, Buffalo, Cologne, Copenhagen, The Hague Liège, London (Tate), Manchester (Whitworth), New York (Guggenheim), Ottawa, Pittsburgh (Carnegie), Sheffield and Utrecht.

APPIANI, Andrea (1754–1817), was the leading Lombard Neoclassical painter, comparable with DAVID. He learned fresco-painting and his first big commission was for frescoes in Sta Maria sopra S. Celso, Milan (1792–5). Napoleon made him his Court Painter in Italy and employed him extensively on frescoes (largely destroyed in 1943) in the Royal Palace in Milan (*Apotheosis of Napoleon*, 1808), as well as at the Villa Reale (now Mus. d'Arte Mod., Milan). His masterpiece is the *Parnassus* (1811) in the Villa Reale. He also painted many portraits, most of which are in Milan, but there are two splendid ones in Versailles and others in Birmingham and Rome (Accad. and Mus. d'Arte Mod.). He was incapacitated by a stroke in 1813.

APT, Ulrich the Elder (*d.*1532), was active in Augsburg in 1481. He painted many portraits, mostly in the style of Hans Holbein I, and several have been confused with HOLBEIN the Younger's. There are pictures by him in Augsburg, Florence (Uffizi), Munich and Vienna, and there are two replicas of *A Man and his Wife*, 1512, in the Royal Coll. and New York (Met. Mus.).

AQUATINT *see* ENGRAVING.

ARABESQUE. A flowing linear decoration. *See* GROTESQUE.

ARCHIPENKO, Alexander (1887–1964), was a Russian-American abstract sculptor. He went to Paris in 1908 and met MODIGLIANI and GAUDIER-BRZESKA, and there he developed a form of Cubist sculpture in which convexities were replaced by concavities and solids by voids. He exhibited at the SECTION D'OR in 1912, but immediately afterwards claimed to have abandoned Cubism. He went to America in 1923. There are works by him in Cardiff, Detroit, London (Tate), New York (M of MA), Strasbourg and elsewhere.

ARCHITECTONIC in the sense in which it is used in art criticism means 'possessing the massive stability and calm grandeur of noble architecture'. A handy synonym for MONUMENTAL.

ARCIMBOLDI, Giuseppe (1527–93). A Milanese painter of fantastic heads composed of fragments of landscape, vegetables, flowers etc.; he was much overrated in his own day (and now) and claimed as an ancestor by the Surrealists. He worked in a normal manner for Milan Cathedral (1549–58) and designed tapestries for Como (1558). Court Painter at Prague (1562–87), his bizarreries appealed to the Hapsburgs, especially Rudolf II, who made him a Count Palatine. Several pictures painted for Rudolf are in Vienna (K-H Mus.); other works are in Brescia, Cremona, Graz, Hartford Conn. (Wadsworth Atheneum) and Innsbruck.

ARETINO *see* SPINELLO.

ARMATURE. A metal skeleton, usually of flexible lead piping, used to support clay or wax in the making of a piece of sculpture.

ARMITAGE, Kenneth (*b.*1916), is a British sculptor who now works almost exclusively in modelled plaster, subsequently cast in bronze. His figures are exceedingly thin and sail-like, with much attention given to the effect of movement. In 1956 he won a competition for a war memorial at Krefeld, and in 1958 he was the British representative at the Venice Biennale. There are works by him in Antwerp (Middelheim Park), Brussels, Buffalo, Leeds, London (Tate and V&A), New York (Brooklyn and M of MA), Paris, Rome and elsewhere.

ARMORY SHOW. Held in 1913 in a regimental armoury in New York, this exhibition was the principal means of introducing 'Modern' – i.e. Post-Impressionist – art to the United States.

ARNOLFO di Cambio (*d.* probably 1302). Italian architect and sculptor, and designer of Florence Cathedral (1300). A pupil of Nicola PISANO, Arnolfo worked on his master's Shrine of S. Dominic, Bologna (1264–7), and pulpit at Siena (1265–8), before going to Rome in 1277, where he made a portrait of Charles of Anjou (Rome, Conservatori Mus.), which is one of the first modern portrait statues. His tomb of Cardinal de Braye (*d.*1282) in San Domenico at Orvieto, now much altered, fixed the type of wall-tomb for more than a century, with its arrangement of the effigy of the dead man lying on a bier below the Madonna and Child in glory, all set in a vertical architectural frame. He also made a tomb and a bust of Boniface VIII, as part of that Pope's campaign of artistic propaganda, and built ciboria in S. Paolo fuori le Mura (1285) and Sta Cecilia (1293), both in Rome. The famous bronze statue of St Peter in St Peter's is attributed to him. The remains of his sculptural decoration for Florence Cathedral are in the Cathedral Museum and other works are in the Bargello in Florence, Boston and London (V&A).

ARP, Jean (Hans) (1887–1966), was born in Alsace and studied in Paris, but also knew Ernst, Klee and Kandinsky, and exhibited in the second Blaue Reiter exhibition. In Zürich in 1916 he was one of the co-founders of DADA, and later, after settling in France, he became a Surrealist, which may explain the evident sexual symbolism of his forms. There are works in Edinburgh, Grenoble, Leeds, London (Tate), New York (M of MA) and Strasbourg. His *On My Way*, a selection of essays and poems, 1912–47, has been published in English. His Swiss wife, Sophie Taeuber-Arp (1889–1943), collaborated with him. She was also associated with the Zürich Dada group.

ARPINO, Giuseppe Cesari, called Cavaliere d'Arpino (1568–1640), was 'the last melancholy champion' of conservative and anaemic MANNERISM in opposition to CARAVAGGIO's naturalist revolution (he employed Caravaggio and outlived him by thirty years), and was patronized by the Vatican and the Roman Princes. He designed the mosaics of the dome of St Peter's, painted the frescoes in S. Martino, Naples (1589–91), and painted huge and dull histories in the Conservatori Palace, Rome, the earliest of 1591 and the latest of 1636. Most old galleries have examples, including Glasgow, Hull, London (Wellington Mus.), Oxford (Ashmolean and Ch. Ch.), the Vatican and Vienna.

ARRICCIATO (ARRICCIO) *see* FRESCO.

ARS MORIENDI (Lat. the art of dying). One of the most famous BLOCK-BOOKS, printed in Germany *c*.1466. It is a devotional work, like the *Biblia Pauperum*, and is based either on a Netherlandish block-book of *c*.1450 (in London, BM) or on a set of engravings (Oxford) by the anonymous Master E. S. *See* E. S.

ART BRUT *see* DUBUFFET.

ART NOUVEAU was a 'new art' which spread across Europe and America in the 1890s. It was principally a style of architecture and interior decoration (followed by e.g. Horta, van de Velde) and flourished especially in Belgium and Britain, using flat patterns of writhing vegetable forms based on a naturalistic conception of plants rather than a formalized type of decoration. Cast-iron lilies and copper tendrils are still with us, as is furniture with heart-shaped holes in it. ENSOR was associated with the creators of the style in Belgium, but he is much less typical than MORRIS, whose Arts and Crafts movement may be the progenitor of Art Nouveau. Better still, perhaps, was BEARDSLEY, whose drawings appeared in the first issue of *The Studio* (1893), a periodical which helped to spread the style. The posters of MUCHA popularized the style commercially (and still do). In Germany and Austria (*see* KLIMT) the movement was called *Jugendstil*, after a magazine *Jugend* (Youth), first published in 1896; in Italy, where it had a great vogue, particularly in ironwork and decoration – especially in Milan, Turin, Genoa and Mantua – it is known as *Stile Liberty*, after the famous London department store. The Spanish centre was Barcelona, where the young PICASSO was influenced by it.

ART UNIONS. Characteristic 19th-century institutions for disseminating a love of the arts and broadening the basis of patronage of living artists, especially among the middle classes. A Union organized an annual exhibition, and members paid a subscription which entitled them to a print from an engraving specially commissioned by the Union, as well as a chance to win one of the works in the exhibition, bought by the organizers and offered as a prize in a lottery. This sometimes caused difficulty with anti-gambling laws, and not everyone agreed with the principle. Lady Eastlake noted in 1843: 'These Art Unions have been most pernicious things – in other words, a cabal for encouraging trumpery painters. There might as well be a club for encoring bad singers . . .' The first Art Union, the Berlin KUNSTVEREIN, was formed in 1814, but the first in the English-speaking world seems to have been the London one in 1836, followed by Edinburgh (1837, reorganized 1842) and Glasgow (1841), but the idea was also popular in America – the American Art-Union seems to date from 1839, and by 1849 had nearly 19,000 members; but in 1852 it had trouble with the New York State lottery laws. Other states copied the idea, but the Unions seem to have petered out, although the Glasgow Art Union was still active in the late 1930s. A monthly magazine, *The Art-Union*, was published in London 1844–8, renamed *The Art Journal* from 1849, and was widely influential.

ASAM, Cosmas Damian (1686–1739) and Aegid Quirin (1692–1750), were German architects who were trained in Rome. Cosmas was also a painter, and Aegid a sculptor, so they were able to undertake the complete decoration of all their buildings, e.g. their own house and church in Munich. Their style shows the move away from the dramatic seriousness of Italian Baroque towards a lighter and more elegant treatment of religious themes – often nevertheless deeply emotional – which is typical of German 18th-century art, ROCOCO rather than Baroque.

ASCRIPTION *see* ATTRIBUTION.

ASHCAN SCHOOL. A group of 19th/20th century American 'realist' painters and illustrators, whose interest in the sordid side of city life (especially in New York) provoked the nickname. The best-known were HENRI and BELLOWS, although Bellows was not one of the original Group of Eight who exhibited in 1908.

ASSELYN, Jan (1610/15–52). A Dutch Italianate landscape painter, probably a pupil of E. van de VELDE, but whose style was formed on the Arcadian landscapes of CLAUDE, and on the Roman Campagna: hence his work resembles that of BERCHEM, BOTH and DU JARDIN. He spent about ten years in Italy *c.*1634–44. His best-known picture is a political allegory of Dutch independence, *The Angry Swan* (Amsterdam), but *Beggars at a Monastery* (1647, Dresden) is more typical. There are works in Berlin, Brussels, Cambridge (Fitzwm), Cardiff, Edinburgh, Paris and several in Vienna (Akad.).

ATELIER (Fr. studio). The *atelier libre* is a common feature of the continental art world. It is a studio, open freely but not free, which provides a nude model in fixed sessions, but no tuition or control. The most famous was opened *c.*1825–30 in Paris by a model called Suisse, and was used by Delacroix, Courbet, Manet, Monet, Pissarro, Cézanne and other Impressionists. The Atelier Julian, opened in Paris in 1860, was not strictly an *atelier libre*, since it provided a teacher, though it was more liberal than the official École des Beaux-Arts, for which it often served as a forcing ground or alternative. Most of the NABIS worked at the Julian, as did MATISSE, Derain and Léger. Sometimes these *ateliers libres* are called *Académies*.

ATTRIBUTION. When a work of art is signed or recorded in a document there can be little doubt that it is by the artist to whom it is attributed; 'attribution', however, usually means assigning a work to an artist on the grounds of its likeness to works known to be his. This, which involves STYLE CRITICISM, can range from moral certainty to mere guess-work, depending on such factors as the number of certain works known to the person making the attribution, as well as the degree of his intimacy with them. For this reason, a conscientious cataloguer gives at least the main reasons for his decisions, and it is desirable to use phrases like 'Attributed to . . .' 'Ascribed to . . .' 'Circle of . . .' or 'Studio of . . .' with some precision. In normal English usage there is no distinction between Attributed and Ascribed, but it may be suggested that a useful terminology would be to keep 'Ascribed to . . .' to imply a slightly greater degree of dubiety than 'Attributed to . . .' The distinction between 'Studio of . . .' and 'Follower of . . .' maintained in the catalogues of the National Gallery, London, is similar, 'Follower of . . .' not implying any direct contact with the artist himself. A Follower may be considerably later, whereas an Imitator is self-explanatory.

AUDUBON, John James (1785–1851), an American naturalist and traveller of French extraction, who studied in Paris under DAVID, before going to America in 1803. His most famous works are the illustrations for 'The Birds of America' (1827–38), the original drawings for which are in New York (Historical Soc.), and the *Quadrupeds of N. America* (1845–8). There are oils and watercolours in Liverpool (Univ.).

AU PREMIER COUP (Fr. at the first shot) *see* ALLA PRIMA.

AUTOGRAPH. A painting or other work of art is said to be autograph when it is thought to be entirely from the hand of the artist to whom it is attributed. In the case of frescoes or other very large undertakings it can hardly be expected that the artist should execute every part with his own hand, but the expression 'Studio of . . .' in connection with smaller works indicates a desire not to suggest that the work is a copy. In some cases, especially that of RUBENS, one often finds that the original sketch or MODELLO is autograph and the execution of the finished, large, canvas was entrusted to assistants overseen by the master, who usually added the final touches.

AUTOMATISM. Doodling. Shut your eyes and draw, the subconscious will do the rest. A favourite SURREALIST technique.

AVANZO, Jacopo. A 14th-century painter who was the pupil and apparently inseparable partner of ALTICHIERO.

AVED, Jacques (1702–66). A French portrait painter trained in Amsterdam and influenced by Rembrandt, who became a friend and collaborator of CHARDIN, whose splendid portrait of Aved is now in the Louvre. There are portraits by Aved in Paris (Louvre), Versailles and other French museums, as well as Amsterdam (Rijksmus.), Cleveland Ohio and The Hague.

AVERCAMP, Hendrik (1585–1634). A landscape painter, born in Amsterdam, but influenced by BRUEGEL the Elder and CONINXLOO, making the transition to the realistic Dutch landscape of the 17th century. He was dumb and spent his life in the isolated little town of Kampen. He specialized in ice scenes and there are works in Amsterdam (Rijksmus.), Edinburgh (NG), London (NG), Manchester, Rotterdam, St Louis, Toledo Ohio and Vienna. Barent Avercamp (1612–79) was his nephew, pupil and imitator.

B

BABUREN, Dirck van (*c.*1590–1624), was one of the three principal painters of the UTRECHT SCHOOL. He was in Rome 1617–20/2 and there painted the *Deposition* (S. Pietro in Montorio) which is derived from CARAVAGGIO's (now in the Vatican). His career was very short, but he brought the low-life naturalism of Caravaggio and MANFREDI to the Netherlands. Only a handful of pictures survive, others being in Amsterdam, Boston, Kansas City, New York (Met. Mus.), Oslo, Utrecht, Vienna and York.

BACICCIO (Baciccia) Giovanni Battista Gaulli (1639–1709), was a Genoese whose early contact with works by Rubens and van Dyck influenced him deeply. After the plague of 1657 killed the rest of his family he went to Rome, where he studied with a Frenchman, thought to have been Gaspard POUSSIN. He met BERNINI and his rise thereafter was rapid. His portraits were as highly prized as his decorations (he painted seven Popes), and a visit to Modena in 1669, which enabled him to study Correggio in Parma, led to a heightened illusionism in his decorations and an increased tenderness of sentiment and colour in his easel pictures. His most famous decoration is the ceiling of the Gesù in Rome (1672–83), where, with a Rubensian warmth of colour and a staggering illusionism, far exceeding PIETRO da Cortona's and approached later only by POZZO, he merges painted figures into painted and modelled stucco ones which burst out of the frame and into the plane of the spectator. There are *modelli* for the Gesù ceiling in Cleveland Ohio and Rome (Pal. Spada). Some of his later portraits have a quieter, almost Marattesque, quality. There are many works by him in churches, museums and palaces in Rome, as well as in Fermo (Carmine), Florence (Uffizi), Genoa (Doria), Manchester, New York (Met. Mus.), Oberlin Ohio and São Paulo.

BACKER, Jacob Adriaensz (1608–51), was a pupil of Rembrandt in about 1632 and painted portraits in Amsterdam. Occasionally he crossed the influence of Rembrandt with that of HALS, particularly in his use of light colour. Amsterdam, The Hague, and London (Wallace Coll.) have good examples.

BACKHUYSEN, Ludolf (1631–1708), was a Dutch marine painter, a pupil of A. van EVERDINGEN. He is well represented in London (NG, Nat. Marit. Mus. and Dulwich) and his *Boats in a Storm* (Dulwich) may well have been one of the sea-pieces that influenced Turner.

BACON, Francis (*b.*1909), is a self-taught painter who destroys a large part of his output, so much so that virtually nothing of his early work has survived. Through his highly personal subject matter, which concentrates chiefly on dogs, carcasses and evocations of men, including elderly tycoons and Velázquez's *Innocent X*, caged in plate glass and screaming in a silent world of horror, dissolution and fear, he expresses with energy and singleness of aim all the gradations of emotion from pity and disgust to horror, traumatic revulsion and the unbalance of panic. His work, which can be interpreted as an attempt to evoke an essentially partial, since incomplete, catharsis in the spectator, raises in its most acute form the problem of the relationship between art and pleasure. There are pictures by him in Aberdeen, Batley, Belfast, Birmingham, Buffalo NY, Chicago, Detroit, London (Tate), Manchester (Whitworth), New York (M of MA), Ottawa and Yale.

BACON, John (1740–99), began by modelling china figures. He also worked in Coade's artificial stone, and for Wedgwood and the Derby porcelain factory. He became an RA in 1770. He was a fashionable sculptor who executed many tombs, including the huge Chatham Monument in Westminster Abbey (1779) and the one to Dr Johnson in St Paul's Cathedral (1796). He was considered the best sculptor of his day for tombs, as BANKS was for history pieces and NOLLEKENS for busts and he prided himself on his Christian sentiment: he was 'pious and zealously attached to Methodism . . . yet knowing in the ways of the world . . . and eager among stock-brokers'. His son John (1777–1859) was his pupil and finished his equestrian *William III* in St James's Square, London, and also executed a large number of tombs.

BAGLIONE, Giovanni (1571–1644), worked principally in Rome, but was in Naples 1609/10. He came from the circle of ARPINO, and is known, not so much for his mediocre frescoes in the Vatican Library, or even for his competent but uninspired altarpieces in Roman churches, as for his connection with CARAVAGGIO, under whose influence his art briefly reached another plane. In 1603 he sued Caravaggio for libel, and achieved the supreme revenge of being his first biographer. His 'Vite de' Pittori . . .' (Rome, 1642) also has his own biography, added by the printer. His masterpiece was the lost *Tabitha* (once in St Peter's). Apart from his works in Rome there are others in the Royal Coll. and Berlin.

BALDINUCCI, Filippo (*c.*1624–96), succeeded VASARI as historiographer of Florentine art, his 'Notizie de' Professori . . .' appearing in many volumes, 1681–1728. He made greater use of documents than his predecessor, and the vast collection of drawings in the Uffizi is due to his appreciation of their importance in the study of paintings.

BALDOVINETTI, Alesso (*c.*1426–99), was a Florentine painter and worker in mosaic and stained glass who was influenced by DOMENICO Veneziano. His experiments with the technique of fresco painting were unfortunate, witness the frescoes in SS. Annunziata (1460/2) and S. Miniato (1466), in Florence. He painted three panels in the series on the doors of the Silver Cupboard of SS. Annunziata (now in the Museo di S. Marco, Florence) which had been begun by Fra ANGELICO. There are other works by him in Florence, as well as in London, Paris and elsewhere.

BALDUNG, Hans (1484/5–1545), called Grien, was a Strasbourg painter and designer of woodcuts and stained glass. His woodcuts, in particular, show the influence of DÜRER, in whose shop he may have worked before 1505 (*see* KLEINMEISTER). His principal picture is the altarpiece in Freiburg Cathedral (1512–16), but his favourite theme was the female nude, often in horrible allegories such as the *Death and the Woman* (1517, Basle). Outside Germany and Austria there are pictures in the Royal Coll. and in Cleveland Ohio, The Hague, Liverpool and London (NG).

BALLA, Giacomo (1871–1958), painted subjects in the Roman Campagna and portraits. He was in Paris 1900–1, and was strongly influenced by DIVISIONISM (already experienced in Rome). In 1910 he signed the FUTURIST Manifesto, and exhibited with the group from 1912, painting the only amusing picture produced by that dreary movement – the *Dog on a Leash* – before returning to a more traditional use of a free Divisionist technique for subjects of social comment. There are works from his Futurist phase in London (Tate) and New York (M of MA), and of his Divisionist style in Rome (Gall. Naz. d'Arte Mod.).

BALTHUS (Balthasar Klossowski de Rola, *b.*1908) is a French painter, the son of a Polish painter and writer, who was encouraged by Derain and Bonnard. In 1961 he became Director of the French Academy in Rome. His early works are mainly street scenes and interiors derived largely from the influence of the artists who first encouraged him, and painted in heavy, earthy colours. His later, post-Rome, works are more consciously poetic and colourful with distinctly erotic overtones of *Jeunes filles en fleur*. There are examples in Chicago, Minneapolis and Paris (Mus. d'Art Moderne).

BAMBINO (Ital. baby) – usually specifically the Christ Child.

BAMBOCCIATA (Ital.). The name given to low-life and peasant subjects, generally small, with small figures, of the type painted by Dutch and Flemish artists in Italy in the 17th century, mainly between 1625 and 1650. These were popular even in Italy (though frowned on by theorists of the Grand Style such as Bellori) as well as in the North. The name probably derives from BAMBOCCIO, although it also means 'jest, triviality'. The French form *bambochade* is also used. The painters themselves are often called Bamboccianti.

BAMBOCCIO (Ital. puppet). A BENTNAME, on account of his deformity, given to Pieter van Laer (*c.*1592–1642 or later), a Dutch painter from Haarlem who lived in Rome *c.*1625–38, where he was a friend of Poussin, Claude and SANDRART. In 1638 he returned to Haarlem, where he died. His pictures of everyday life with peasants, soldiers and brigands became popular in Italy (though officially disapproved of by the theorists of Ideal Art), and were much imitated by other Northern artists who made the journey to Italy. Ultimately they derive from CARAVAGGIO's naturalism. Unfortunately many of his paintings have now darkened, but there are examples in the Royal Coll. and in Amsterdam, Budapest, Dresden, Florence (Uffizi), Gateshead, Hartford Conn., Munich, New York (Met. Mus.), Oxford (Ch. Ch.), Paris (Louvre), Rome (Gall. Naz. and Spada), Vienna (Akad.) and elsewhere.

BANCKET (Banquet) PIECE (Dutch, Bancketgen). A still-life painting developed from the BREAKFAST PIECE, showing a table covered with a carpet or fine linen, rich foods, gold and silver dishes, and flagons or glasses of wine. Van BEYEREN and KALF produced typical examples.

BANDINELLI, Baccio (1493–1560), was a Florentine sculptor, goldsmith and painter whose constant efforts to outdo Michelangelo generally rebounded on his own head. He was the rival of CELLINI, who hated him both on his own account and on behalf of Michelangelo, but he enjoyed the favour of the Medici, and through them he got the commission for the *Hercules and Cacus* (1534, Florence, Piazza della Signoria), made in direct emulation of Michelangelo's *David*. It was not much liked and Cellini and Bandinelli had a highly public quarrel over it. His best works are the reliefs in the choir of Florence Cathedral, but his greatest importance lies in the part he played in the development of ACADEMIES. There are works in London (V&A), Oxford (Ashmolean) and Paris (Louvre).

BANKS, Thomas (1735–1805), was one of the first British sculptors to be influenced by Neoclassic ideals. He went to Rome in 1772 on a scholarship from the RA and remained there seven years: while there he carved the *Thetis* (London, V&A). He spent 1781–2 in St Petersburg but in 1786 was elected RA and worked for the rest of his life on busts and monuments, the most famous of which was the dead child, *Penelope Boothby* (Ashbourne, Derbyshire), which moved Queen Charlotte to tears when it was exhibited at the RA in 1793. There are works in London (NPG, RA, Soane Mus., Westminster Abbey and St Paul's), Stratford-on-Avon (a relief formerly on the Shakespeare Gallery, 1789) and elsewhere.

BAPTISTE *see* MONNOYER.

BARBARI, Jacopo de' (*d.c.*1515/16), is said to have been a Venetian painter, but from 1500 he worked in Germany and the Netherlands; in about 1501 he wrote a curious letter to the Elector of Saxony called *De la eccelentia de la pittura.* He influenced DÜRER and was also influenced by him – certainly his engravings fit into the development of German graphic art. Perhaps more importantly, he inspired Dürer's theoretical studies ('I can find none who has written about a canon of human proportions, save one, Jacopo by name, born at Venice, and a charming painter . . .'). There is a portrait of Pacioli, the mathematician and pupil of Piero della Francesca, with another man, signed and dated 1495 (Naples), but this is sometimes held to be the work of a different painter; on the other hand, he certainly painted the first modern STILL-LIFE, the *Dead Bird*, of 1504, in Munich. The reason for the doubt over the attribution of the *Pacioli* is that it is signed 'Jaco. Bar. vigennis P. 1495' – i.e. the painter was in his twenties and thus born *c.*1475, which accords ill with an application for a pension (1511/12) which describes him as 'old and weak'. Both documents may well be correct. Berlin, Dresden, London (NG), Paris, Philadelphia (Johnson), Verona and Weimar also have works by him.

BARBIZON SCHOOL. A mid-19th-century group of landscape painters centred on the village of Barbizon in the Forest of Fontainebleau, some thirty miles from Paris. Its chief members were MILLET, Théodore ROUSSEAU, and DIAZ, their aims being an exact and unprettified rendering of peasant life and scenery, painted on the spot. This last makes them the precursors of IMPRESSIONISM, although the major influences upon them were COROT, MICHEL, Dutch 17th-century landscape painters such as Hobbema and Ruisdael, and, to a lesser degree, CONSTABLE and BONINGTON. Only Millet seems to have had consciously socialist intentions in his peasant scenes. There are good collections of their work in Boston and London (V&A), as well as Paris (Mus. d'Orsay) and many other French museums.

BARISANUS of Trani was a bronze-founder and sculptor working in S. Italy in the last quarter of the 12th century. There are three large pairs of bronze doors by him at the cathedrals of Trani, Ravello and Monreale. Those at Trani have a self-portrait and a signature and are thought to date from *c.*1175. The doors at Ravello are dated 1179, but are not signed. Those at Monreale are signed and are thought to be contemporary with the other set of doors made for the same cathedral by the Pisan BONANUS in 1185. The difference in style is considerable and emphasizes the much greater dependence of Barisanus upon Byzantine models – in some cases he even retains Greek inscriptions – as well as his far greater interest in decorative forms. Many of Barisanus's figures are repeated, even on the same door, and were thus cast from a single mould. His doors are made of plates of bronze nailed on to an oak framework, since the technique of bronze-casting in the 12th century was still comparatively rudimentary.

BARLACH, Ernst (1870–1938), was a German EXPRESSIONIST sculptor and illustrator of great tragic power. His pessimistic art was condemned by the Nazis and many of his works destroyed: survivors are now in German museums and there is a small Barlach Museum near Lüneburg. His best works are perhaps the woodcarvings of single figures of peasants, beggars and similar subjects, many of them inspired by a visit to Russia (cf. KOLLWITZ). His woodcarving technique was closely based on German Late Gothic work, and his woodcarvings (e.g. Edinburgh) are his most characteristic works: other techniques include ceramics (e.g. two in Harvard Univ., Busch-Reisinger Mus.).

BARNA was a Sienese painter, active *c.*1350/6, who was the greatest of Simone MARTINI's followers. In the Collegiata at S. Gimignano he painted a fresco cycle of the Life of Christ, and he is said to have died as a result of a fall from the scaffolding, leaving the series unfinished. The *Christ Carrying the Cross* (New York, Frick Coll.) is attributed to him.

BARNABA da Modena (active 1362–83) was a N. Italian painter who combined an almost purely Byzantine tradition with some Giottesque elements. There are dated works in Berlin (1369), Turin (1370, Sabauda Gall.), London (1374) and elsewhere.

BAROCCI, Federico (*c.*1535–1612), was, after Raphael, the most important painter of Urbino. His soft, colouristic and emotional art is a perfect expression of one aspect of the Counter-Reformation, and it is not surprising that St Philip Neri regarded him highly. He was also a sensitive portrait painter. He was in Rome in the mid-1550s, when Michelangelo is said to have encouraged him, and he returned in 1560, making his name with the decorations in the Casino of Pius IV (1561–3, Vatican). Most of the rest of his life was spent in Urbino, working for only two hours a day and crippled by ill-health (though he lived to extreme old age). He became a Tertiary of the Order of St Francis in 1566 and his greatest patron was the austere and pious Duke of Urbino, although he is better known for his connection with St Philip. Many drawings made as studies for his carefully-prepared paintings survive – e.g. the finished MODELLO in Oxford (Ashmolean) for the *Madonna of the Rosary* (*c.*1589–93, Senigallia, Bishop's Pal.), for which at least twenty-seven other drawings and studies are known. Apart from the numerous works in Urbino, there are others in Brussels, Copenhagen, Florence (Uffizi, including the big *Madonna del Popolo*, 1575–9), London (NG), Madrid, Milan (Brera), Munich, Paris (Louvre), Perugia (Cath., 1567, a *Descent from the Cross*, showing the influence of PONTORMO and CORREGGIO), Rome (Borghese and churches), Stuttgart, the Vatican, Vienna and Weimar.

BARONZIO, Giovanni, was a Riminese painter, working in 1345 and earlier, who was much influenced by CAVALLINI and GIOTTO. He was dead by 1362. He is the best evidence for Giotto's activity in Rimini, recorded in old sources. There are two pictures dated 1345 in Urbino and Mercatello, near Urbino (but the attribution of this is open to doubt), and frescoes in Ravenna and Tolentino. Other works are in Baltimore, Berlin, Birmingham (Barber Inst.), Munich, New York (Met. Mus.), Paris (Jacquemart-André), Rimini, Rome, Venice and elsewhere.

BAROQUE. The style that succeeded MANNERISM and lasted, though with profound modifications, until well into the 18th century. At the beginning of the 17th century, as a direct result of the Council of Trent (1545–63), there was an upsurge of spiritual confidence and a new direction in religious art which combined with a fresh approach to the Antique to create a new style. The flaccid forms and narrative confusion of late Mannerism gave place to the simple subject matter, the unidealized naturalism, the uncomplicated iconography, the direct emotional appeal and strong chiaroscuro of CARAVAGGIO. The return to Raphael's clarity of composition, balance and harmony and Correggio's softness of handling was expressed in the nobility of form and the directness of meaning and imagery of Annibale CARRACCI, DOMENICHINO, Guido RENI and GUERCINO. The style is seen at its purest in the so-called 'High Baroque', which is virtually confined to Italy (to Rome even) and to the period *c.*1630–80, that is, roughly, the maturity of its greatest exponent, BERNINI. The High Baroque, at its best and fullest, is a union of the arts of architecture, painting and sculpture acting in concert on the emotions of the spectator; inviting him, for example, to participate in the ecstasies of the saints. Its blend of illusionism, light, colour and movement is calculated to overwhelm the spectator by a direct emotional appeal. Owing to its essential links with Counter-Reformation Catholicism, pagan antiquity and the Mediterranean generally, many Northerners are – or were until recently – queasy about it. Of the painters of the High Baroque, LANFRANCO, PIETRO da Cortona, BACICCIO and, at the end of the century, Padre POZZO, specialized in the florid and exuberant illusionism which is one of the characteristics of the style, while Bernini pushed to their furthest limits the use of painterly effects in sculpture, notably through the use of coloured marbles and bronze, the dissolved contour, the rendering of movement by means of flickering light, to express profound and passionately felt religious emotion. Some artists in Rome, such as SACCHI, MARATTA and ALGARDI, were always more restrained. POUSSIN, who lived and worked in Rome for most of his life, developed the classical and intellectual aspects of the Baroque almost to the exclusion of its emotional side. Outside Italy, astute politicians like Colbert, Louis XIV's great minister, were quick to see that the religious style could easily be made to subserve autocratic regimes, by the glorification of the monarch, but in this process a good deal of pompous inflation was superimposed on the original religious fervour; and the French exponents of the Baroque, LEBRUN and his team, replaced its emotional qualities with a self-conscious and frigid use of the Antique. Even RUBENS, the greatest Northern Baroque artist, sometimes allowed himself to be used in this way. The style lasted longest in Catholic Germany and Austria, and had the least influence in Protestant countries – Britain, Scandinavia and Holland, although there are aspects of REMBRANDT which place him among the greatest artists of the Baroque, and there is certainly such a thing as English Baroque (e.g. THORNHILL). In the North it is still possible to use the term as one of simple abuse (e.g. non-Gothic, unRuskinian), but this is now confined to the very old or the very unsophisticated. A more dangerous misuse is as a synonym for '17th Century', and the use of the word in musicology is very different. Late Baroque merges almost imperceptibly into ROCOCO, and the Age of Reason finally rejected both and produced NEOCLASSICISM.

BARRY, James (1741–1806), was an Irish painter who was brought to London by Edmund Burke in 1764. He was encouraged by Reynolds to persist in grand-manner historical painting, and Burke paid his expenses to Italy in 1765–71.

In Rome from 1766 he studied Raphael and, especially, Michelangelo, with more enthusiasm than discretion. He was however, like Reynolds, also influenced by Titian. In Rome he met NOLLEKENS and other English Neoclassical artists and on his return to London was made ARA in 1772 and RA in 1773. In 1775 he published 'An Inquiry into the Real and Imaginary Obstructions to . . . the Arts in England'. From 1777 to 1783/4 he worked on a huge decoration in the Great Room of the Society of Arts in London, consisting of six pictures (two are 42 feet long), representing *The Progress of Human Culture*. He received almost no payment for his work, but when they were exhibited in 1783 Dr Johnson said of them: 'Whatever the hand may have done, the mind has done its part. There is a grasp of mind there which you find nowhere else.' He was elected Professor of Painting at the RA in 1782, but by 1799 he had so alienated some other members by his bitter attacks on them and on the memory of Reynolds that they persuaded the King to expel him – the only case so far. In fact, he painted only four historical pictures between 1783 and his death, and much of his time was spent in controversial writing. He lived and died in great poverty and squalor. BLAKE was an admirer: his projected poem 'Barry' exists only as a fragment which is a diatribe against Reynolds. He represents, with HAMILTON, FUSELI and HAYDON, another instance of the failure of British patrons to appreciate history painting on a gigantic scale and on heroic themes, based on a studious adaptation of the Italian Grand Style, as advocated (but seldom practised) by Reynolds. His portraits are very fine, but he could only rarely be persuaded to demean himself to paint one: his prints were his principal source of income and are perhaps his best memorial. He made only one lithograph, in 1803, of King Lear, based on his own painting, and it is one of the earliest examples of the use of the new medium for purely artistic ends. There are paintings by him in Bath, Bologna, Cork, Dublin (NG), London (Tate: *King Lear Weeping Over the Body of Cordelia*, 1786–7, NPG and V&A), Manchester, New Brunswick (*Death of Wolfe*, 1776 – cf. WEST), Sheffield and Yale (CBA).

BARTOLO di Fredi was a Sienese who died in 1410, but who was still working in the style of the LORENZETTI and of BARNA.

BARTOLOMMEO di Giovanni *see* 'ALUNNO di Domenico'.

BARTOLOMMEO della Porta, Fra (*c.*1472–1517), was born in Florence and apprenticed to Cosimo ROSSELLI in 1484. Vasari stresses the influence on him of Leonardo da Vinci, but Leonardo's cartoon for the *Battle of Anghiari* was not begun until 1503. In 1498 the convent of San Marco, where Savonarola was Prior, was stormed and Savonarola was dragged off to prison (and, later, execution): Fra Bartolommeo was in the convent at the time and vowed then to become a monk, which he did in 1500. He was by then active as a painter and his earliest extant work, the *Last Judgement*, now in S. Marco, was begun in 1499 and was partly finished by Mariotto ALBERTINELLI in 1501. It is in bad condition, but enough remains to show that it influenced the young RAPHAEL. From 1500 for about four years he did no painting, but in 1504 he became head of the monastery workshop, a position once held by Fra Angelico. He visited Venice in 1508, where he saw the great *Sacre Conversazioni* by Giovanni BELLINI. After his return he took Albertinelli into partnership. He was in Rome in 1514 and there painted a *St Peter* and a *St Paul*, dated 1514 and both now in the Vatican. He left the *St Peter* incomplete and it was finished by Raphael, then at the height of his fame. Vasari suggests that Raphael's fame discouraged Fra Bartolommeo and caused his early return to Florence; nevertheless, his visits were important for the development of his ideals of simplicity and balance in composition, decorum of presentation, the use of telling gestures and rapt expressions, the exclusion of picturesque detail, and the adoption of sober and rather generalized settings. He introduced figures in strong *contrapposto* for its own sake, and was among the first to replace contemporary costume with nondescript drapery in his religious figures, in order to stress the gulf between divine and earthly. All these ideas mark the change from the style of the 15th century to that of the 16th – the High Renaissance, of which he was one of the first representatives in Florence. His *God the Father With Saints* (1509, Lucca) is contemporary with the beginning of Raphael's Stanze and is comparable in many ways. His influence was spread by his huge output of drawings, including some very fine landscapes, forty of which were rediscovered in the 1950s. He is also said to have invented the LAY-FIGURE. After his death the S. Marco workshop petered out. There are pictures in Berlin, Besançon (Cath.), Cambridge Mass. (Fogg), Florence (Accad., Pitti, Uffizi and Mus. di S. Marco), London (NG), Los Angeles, Lucca (Mus. and Cath.), Paris (Louvre), Philadelphia (Johnson), Rome (Gall. Naz.), Stuttgart, Vienna and Washington.

BARYE, Antoine-Louis (1796–1875), the son of a Parisian goldsmith, served in the Napoleonic armies 1812–14 and began to study sculpture only in 1816. He worked for a goldsmith from 1823 to 1831 in the Jardin des Plantes, making models of the animals, and from then on devoted himself almost exclusively to animal sculpture – he was certainly the greatest of the so-called *animaliers*. In 1848 he went bankrupt, but was appointed Keeper of Casts at the Louvre (1848–50) and later taught zoological drawing at the Natural History Museum in Paris. His first major work of a non-animal subject was the *Napoleon dominating History and the Arts* (1855–7), a pediment on the Pavillon de l'Horloge of the Louvre, and in 1860 he made the equestrian *Napoleon* for Ajaccio, Napoleon's birthplace. He was one of the major Romantic artists of the 19th century and his choice of violent – even sadistic – subjects (tigers, jaguars and other carnivores, often shown devouring other animals or even human beings) gives him a certain affinity with DELACROIX, although Barye was never able to invest the human figure with Romantic overtones. Some of his small figure-groups, such as the *Theseus*, show strong influence from archaic Greek sculpture, for which he was criticized at the time. There is a large collection of his works in the Louvre and over 140 in Washington (Corcoran). He also painted landscapes in the Barbizon manner (e.g. London, NG).

BASAITI, Marco (*c.*1470–1530), was a Venetian painter much influenced (*c.*1500–10) by Giovanni BELLINI and then by GIORGIONE. There is a signed *Madonna* in London (NG) which shows him using Bellini's types. 'Pseudo-Basaiti' is probably only a name for one aspect of Bellini.

BASCHENIS, Evaristo (*c.*1617–77), was a priest in Bergamo who painted still-life pictures of musical instruments which are unique in the 17th century. The detail reminds one of contemporary Dutch still-life, but there is a dramatic effect of light, as well as a concentration on geometry, which reflects the influence of Caravaggio and foreshadows Cézanne. Most of his works are in Bergamo.

BAS-RELIEF *see* RELIEF.

BASSANO. This was the name of a family of Venetian painters, of which there were four main members. The first, Francesco da Ponte the Elder (*c.*1475–1539), worked in Bassano (hence their name) and was a modest provincial follower of the Bellini. His son Jacopo (*c.*1510/18–92) was the most considerable artist of the family. He was a pupil in Venice of BONIFAZIO de' Pitati, and was independent by the early 1530s. Although he worked almost entirely in Bassano he was by no means a provincial painter, and his works show successive waves of influence, proving him to have been in constant and sensitive touch with Venice, and perhaps Parma as well. His was a highly personal style, robust and energetic, with stocky figures in strong chiaroscuro and heavy impasto, with at least one kneeling figure with the soles of his feet towards the spectator, almost as a sign-manual. He pioneered the large rustic genre scene depicting the seasons, or the trades, with many figures and animals, often set in a mountainous and stormy landscape, and favoured religious subjects which allowed him to introduce peasants and animals (in which he was one of the first to be interested) and heaped-up STILL-LIFE of fruit, game, vegetables and utensils (cf. AERTSEN, BUECKELAER).

Jacopo had three painter sons. Francesco the Younger (1549–92) ran the Venetian branch of the workshop. His paintings are often based on his father's drawings and closely, but rather weakly, follow his style. He committed suicide a few months after his father's death. Leandro (1557–1622) worked in the Venetian studio under Francesco, and after the latter's death took over the workshop. He was the chief portrait painter of the family, and his portraits are closely allied to those of TINTORETTO. Gerolamo (1566–1621) entered the workshop under Leandro. There are works by members of the family in the museums and churches of Bassano and Venice, in the Royal Coll., and in Bergamo, Berlin, Budapest, Cambridge (Fitzwm) and Cambridge Mass. (Fogg), Chicago, Cleveland Ohio, Copenhagen, Detroit, Dresden, Dublin, Edinburgh (NG), Florence (Uffizi and Pitti), Greenville SC, Grenoble, London (NG and V&A), Madrid (Acad., Prado), Manchester, Mantua, Memphis Tennessee, Milan (Brera, Ambrosiana and Castello), Munich, Naples, New York (Met. Mus. and Frick Coll.), Nîmes, Oxford (Ashmolean), Paris (Louvre), Pasadena Cal., Philadelphia (Johnson), Prague, Rome (Gall. Naz., Borghese and Capitoline), Rouen, Stockholm, Toronto, Turin, Vienna and elsewhere.

BASTIEN-LEPAGE, Jules (1848–84), exhibited at the Salon from 1870 until the end of his short life. Most of his exhibits were portraits, but he is now remembered for his rustic genre scenes – his masterpiece, *The Haymakers* of 1877, is in the Louvre – and there was much contemporary discussion of his truthfulness to the Lorraine countryside. By comparison with the REALISM of MILLET he seems sentimental, which may explain his popularity in Scotland (pictures in Aberdeen, Edinburgh and Glasgow), and he probably influenced the GLASGOW SCHOOL. Zola percipiently identified his type of picture as Impressionism sweetened into popularity. There are other works in Dublin, The Hague, Moscow, New York (Met. Mus.) and French provincial museums.

BATONI (Battoni), Pompeo (1708–87), was the principal rival of MENGS in Rome, but, although he was an enthusiast for Raphael and the Antique, he was less whole-heartedly Neoclassic. The minute delicacy of his handling won him many foreign patrons and the greater part of his output must consist of portraits of Princes, *milordi* and other Grand Tourists who sat to him in Rome. He painted three Popes and most European princes; but the idea of a portrait of an educated man, seen against a background of classical antiquity (e.g. the Colosseum), seems to be Batoni's speciality and was well suited to the travelling Englishman. Many such portraits still exist in private collections, and there is a famous one of *General Gordon* (1766, Fyvie Castle, Aberdeenshire, National Trust) which shows him in full Highland dress with a claymore, posturing in front of the Colosseum (the claymore is also at Fyvie). Reynolds was more influenced by these portraits than he cared to admit, and in his 14th Discourse he goes out of his way to praise Gainsborough at the expense of Mengs and Batoni. From 1735 Batoni had a great many commissions for altarpieces, as well as historical and mythological pictures: in 1760–61 he painted an altarpiece for St Peter's, but it was not very successful and is now in Sta Maria degli Angeli, Rome. More importantly, he is believed to have been the first to represent the new subject of the Sacred Heart (*c.*1780, Rome, Gesù). Other works are in Roman churches and galleries, and in Berlin, Birmingham, Cardiff, Dresden, Dublin (NG), Edinburgh (NG and NPG), Florence (Uffizi and Pitti), Frankfurt (Städel), Greenville SC, Hartford Conn., Leeds, London (NG, NPG, V&A and Kenwood), Madrid (Acad. and Prado), Milan (Brera), Minneapolis, Munich, New York (Met. Mus.), Oxford, Paris (Louvre), St Louis, Toledo Ohio and Vienna.

BATTISTELLO *see* CARACCIOLO.

BAUGIN. There appear to be two French 17th-century painters of this name. Lubin Baugin (*c.*1610–63), sometimes called 'le petit Guide' (i.e. Guido RENI), was a painter of religious pictures who was influenced not only by Reni but also by Raphael, Correggio and Parmigianino. The *Holy Family* (London, NG) is characteristic. The other Baugin, whose Christian name is unknown, was a painter of austere still-life subjects (cf. MOILLON and STOSKOPFF), who was perhaps closest to the Spaniard MELENDEZ.

BAUHAUS, The. This was the most famous school of architecture, design and craftsmanship of modern times, and has had an inestimable influence on art-school training all over the world. It was founded in 1919 at Weimar, in Germany, by the architect W. Gropius. It moved to Dessau in 1925 and then to Berlin, where, in 1933, it was closed by the Nazis. Its great importance lay in the fact that its teachers included ALBERS, FEININGER, KLEE and KANDINSKY, and it attempted to face the problem of machine production, which MORRIS had evaded. The influence of DOESBURG, DE STIJL and SCHLEMMER may be seen in this. The New Bauhaus was at Chicago, opened by MOHOLY-NAGY in 1937.

BAUMEISTER, Willi (1889–1955), was a German abstract painter who began as a Constructivist. He was in Paris in 1912 and 1914 and was first influenced by Lautrec, Gauguin and Cézanne, but was later decisively influenced by the mechanical forms of LÉGER. He was dismissed from his teaching post in 1933 for 'degeneracy', but, unlike most others, he remained in Germany and was, in due course, reinstated. From *c.*1936 his works were entirely abstract: examples are in Cologne and Frankfurt (Städel).

BAXTER PRINTS are colour prints reproducing oil-paintings by a process invented by George Baxter (1804–67) and patented by him in 1835. An engraved or etched outline was used as the key, with superimposed wood or metal blocks printing in oil-colours. The process died out in about 1865 and was never of artistic significance. *See also* BOYS.

BAYEU, Francisco (1734–95), was a Spanish painter who worked under MENGS on the decoration of the Royal Palace in Madrid, but is better known as GOYA's master (1766–*c*.1771) and brother-in-law. There is a portrait of him by Goya in the Prado, Madrid, which also has some of his own works; others are in Castres and London (NG). His brother Ramón (1746–93) was also a painter and worked with Goya.

BAZAINE, Jean (*b*.1904), denies that he is an abstract painter, but since 1945 he has produced non-figurative pictures as well as stained glass and mosaics (churches at Assy, 1950, Audincourt, 1951, and for the UNESCO building in Paris). In 1948 he published 'Notes sur la peinture d'aujourd'hui' (2nd edn 1953). He was in Spain in 1953–4. There is a painting by him in Paris (Mus. d'Art Moderne), and glass in S. Severin, Paris.

BAZILLE, Frédéric (1841–71), was a pupil of the academician GLEYRE at the same time as Renoir, through whom he came into close contact with most of the Impressionists and with Manet. His chief aim was the study of figures painted out of doors, relating the tones of the flesh to those of the landscape. He was killed in the Franco-Prussian War when still on the threshold of his career. Most of his pictures are in Paris (Mus. d'Orsay) and his native Montpellier.

BEALE, Mary (1633–99), was the daughter of a clergyman and married Charles Beale, an artist's colourman who had LELY among his customers. Lely gave her some help, and after his death in 1680 she made many copies of his works. She became a professional portrait-painter *c*.1654 and 'great numbers of persons of good rank sat to her, especially the greatest part of the dignified clergy of her time', but little is known for certain before 1671, when her husband began to record the works of his 'deare heart', listing about 140 Lely-style portraits in ten years. There are examples in London (NPG, a *Self-portrait*; Geffrye Mus., her own *Family*, *c*.1663/4; and Dulwich).

BEARDSLEY, Aubrey (1872–98), was an illustrator whose highly-wrought, stylized black and white drawings exude a typically *fin-de-siècle* atmosphere of decadence and express perfectly the ART NOUVEAU of which they were an ingredient. He is best known for his work on the 'Yellow Book' in 1894, and for illustrations to Wilde's 'Salome', and Pope's 'Rape of the Lock'. There are drawings in London (V&A and Tate).

BECCAFUMI, Domenico (1484/6–1551), was, with PARMIGIANINO, the most interesting of the non-Florentine Mannerist painters, and the last of the great Sienese. A member of the High Renaissance generation, his years in Rome (1510–12) saw the painting of Raphael's Stanze and Michelangelo's Sistine Ceiling, both of which influenced him. In such works as the *St Catherine receiving the Stigmata* (*c*.1514, Siena, Accad.) he appears also to have been affected by Fra BARTOLOMMEO, whose work was known in Siena. Soon after his return to Siena in 1513 his highly personal style displays characteristics usually associated with the Mannerism of the following decade; his use of strong effects of perspective and *contrapposto*, his intensity of emotion, and his use of subtle, shot colour, as well as of lurid effects of light, are all stylistic features of central Italian painting of the 1530s and 1540s, which he probably knew as a result of the dispersal of Roman artists after the Sack of 1527. Most of his best works are in Siena, but there are others in Baltimore, Berlin, Birmingham (Barber Inst.), Boston, Cambridge (Fitzwm), Detroit, Dresden, Dublin, Florence (Uffizi, Pitti and Horne Mus.), Hull, Leicester, London (NG, V&A and Wallace Coll.), Munich, Naples, Paris, Pisa (Cath.), Rome (Gall. Naz., Borghese and S.M. Maggiore), Sarasota Fla, Washington (NG), Yale, York and elsewhere.

BECKER, Paula Modersohn *see* MODERSOHN.

BECKMANN, Max (1884–1950), was one of the leading German EXPRESSIONIST painters. He met MUNCH in 1906, exhibited with DIX and GROSZ and other NEUE SACHLICHKEIT painters and taught in Frankfurt until 1933, when he was dismissed as 'decadent'. Just before the opening of the Nazi-sponsored Degenerate Art exhibition in 1937 he emigrated to Holland, moving to America in 1947, where he died. His nine *Triptychs*, painted from 1932 onwards, show that the main influences on him were Bosch and the German primitives, apart from his own contemporaries. He is represented in American museums (e.g. Harvard Univ. and St Louis), and now in Germany as well. There is a work in London (Tate).

BEECHEY, Sir William (1753–1839), was a portrait painter of far less skill than LAWRENCE, but he may have had a more truthful eye, and he was certainly more sober in approach. He was elected ARA in 1793 and made Portrait Painter to the Queen; in 1798 he exhibited the huge *George III and the Prince of Wales reviewing Troops* (Royal Coll.) for which he was knighted and elected RA. He was a very careful craftsman and most anxious to ensure the durability of his pictures. There are examples in London (Tate, NPG, Dulwich, Soane Mus. and Courtauld Inst.), Ottawa and many American museums.

'BEFORE ALL LETTERS' *see* PROOF.

BEGGARSTAFF BROTHERS *see* NICHOLSON, William.

BEHAM, Hans Sebald (1500–50) and Bartel (1502–40), were brothers, born in Nuremberg and greatly influenced by DÜRER: Bartel may have been his pupil. After 1527 Bartel worked in Munich and Landshut, but he died in Italy. His engravings show an attempt to graft Italian Renaissance ideas on to the Dürer tradition. He also painted portraits (Schleissheim). Hans Sebald was particularly active as a designer of woodcuts (over 1,000), and both brothers were important KLEINMEISTER.

BELL, Vanessa (1879–1961), was a British painter, sister of Virginia Woolf. She studied at the RA and under Sargent, and lived with Virginia and her two brothers in the house in Gordon Square, London, which became the nucleus of the Bloomsbury group of writers and painters. In 1907 she married the art critic Clive Bell, and she worked with Roger FRY in the Omega Workshops 1913–19. Her style reflects the influence of Cézanne, the FAUVES, and Picasso's Blue Period. Later it became more abstract, possibly as a result of her design work and her fifty-year association with Duncan GRANT. There are works in London (Tate, V&A and Courtauld Inst.) and Yale (CBA, *Self-portrait*).

BELLANGE, Jacques (active 1602–17), was a French Mannerist working in Lorraine, who is recorded as painting portraits and decorations for the Dukes. Nothing is now known of these, except from engravings, and his work consists of drawings and some extraordinary etchings, so close to PARMIGIANINO in feeling that it is supposed that he went to Italy in the late 16th century, rendering the ecstatic religious atmosphere of the time in a style similar to Parmigianino's on the one hand, and Northerners like GOLTZIUS on the other. He influenced CALLOT.

BELLECHOSE, Henri, *see* MALOUEL.

BELLINI. There were three painters in this Venetian family: Jacopo, and his sons Gentile and Giovanni.

Jacopo (*c.*1400–70/1) was a pupil of Gentile da Fabriano, with whom he was working in Florence in 1423, when he was prosecuted as a result of an affray with a youth who threw stones into the workshop yard. Only four pictures are known to be certainly his, all rather stiff and hieratic in pose and treatment; yet in 1441 he defeated PISANELLO in a competition portrait of Lionello d'Este of Ferrara, but this portrait cannot be identified with certainty. His major surviving works are his two sketchbooks (BM and Louvre), which were the source of many ideas and designs used by his sons and by his son-in-law, MANTEGNA. The four signed works are in Lovere, near Bergamo; Milan (Brera), Venice (Accad.) and Verona. Other, attributed, pictures are in Florence (Uffizi), Milan (Poldi-Pezzoli), Padua, Verona and elsewhere.

Gentile (*c.*1429/30–1507) probably worked in the family shop until his father died (an altarpiece said to have been signed by all three and dated 1460 is recorded), but he had achieved sufficient fame to be ennobled by the Emperor in 1469, though nothing is known of the work that procured him this honour. In 1479–81 he was in Constantinople, painting portraits for the Sultan, Mahomet II. He worked on the cycle of history pictures in the Doge's Palace in 1474, and again on his return from Turkey, but all were burnt in the fire of 1577. His series depicting the processions and ceremonies of two major charitable foundations in Venice became the standard type for this kind of picture, full of portraits and views of the city. His large *St Mark preaching at Alexandria* (Milan, Brera) was unfinished at his death, and he bequeathed one of his father's sketchbooks to his brother on condition that he finished it. He also bequeathed to two of his pupils his sketchbook of Roman drawings (now lost), which may be evidence for his having visited Rome. There are works in Berlin, Birmingham, Boston (Gardner), Budapest, Chicago, Istanbul (University), London (NG), Milan (Brera), New York (Frick Coll.), San Francisco, Venice (Accad., Correr and S. Marco Mus.) and elsewhere.

Giovanni (*c.*1430–1516) is usually thought to be the younger son, but his birthdate is pure conjecture. There is some evidence that he was independent by 1459, but he can be presumed to have been connected with the family workshop until Jacopo's death. His early work derives mainly from his father's, but, like Gentile, he was strongly influenced by Mantegna, who married their sister Nicolosia in 1454. The chronology of his works is difficult because he became the main teacher of his generation, the main source of new ideas and forms, with a large shop of pupils and assistants, so that 'OP. IOH. BELL.' is not only a signature but a trademark, the sign of the workshop rather than the artist. His pupils included Giorgione, Titian, Palma Vecchio and Sebastiano del Piombo, and he influenced directly or indirectly all the painters of his own and the next generation, even when they were the pupils of his brother or the VIVARINI; Cima, Catena, Basaiti, Montagna and

Carpaccio are examples of this. Dürer wrote home from Venice that he was 'very old, but still the best in painting'. He became the greatest of the Venetian *Madonnieri*, or Madonna painters, evolving a succession of designs and types of unparalleled imaginativeness and versatility for official commissions, such as the votive offerings of the Doges, large altarpieces and small devotional works. He was influenced by ANTONELLO, and from the latter's S. Cassiano altarpiece and one of his own, painted for SS. Giovanni e Paolo (and burnt in 1867), stem the great SACRE CONVERSAZIONI painted for S. Giobbe (*c*.1483/5, now in the Accad.) and S. Zaccaria (1505, still in the church) and the later developments of the form, notably those by Giorgione and Titian. His compositions of the *Pietà*, particularly those with the dead Christ supported in the tomb by angels or by the Virgin and St John, derive ultimately from Donatello and Jacopo Bellini, and were intended more as private devotional works than for churches. He frequently included landscape as a background, and in the *Agony in the Garden*, painted in emulation of Mantegna's similar work (both in London, NG), he combines observation of nature with rare poetic feeling, but naturalistic details are never allowed to overwhelm the figures. In 1479, when Gentile went to Turkey, he took over the work in the Doge's Palace and eventually became chief painter to the State, a position he held until his death, in spite of Titian's attempts to displace him. The loss of these history paintings, together with those by Pisanello and Gentile da Fabriano, in the fire of 1577 means that the early style of Venetian history painting can only be guessed at. His official duties included painting portraits of the Doges – the *Doge Loredano* (*c*.1501, London, NG) is the finest of these – and his portraits, many of which adapt the Flemish type of the three-quarter view against a landscape background, are simple, sensitive and compelling. His last works break new ground. His *S. Jerome* (1513, Venice, S. Giovanni Crisostomo), with its spatial device of the saint seated in a landscape and seen through an arch, before which the other life-size figures stand, is an entirely new invention. He had painted Christian and classical allegories before, but never a mythology on such a scale as the *Feast of the Gods*, painted in 1514 for the Duke of Ferrara (now in Washington, NG), which depicts a rustic Olympian picnic in a mildly erotic pastoral vein. Titian later repainted the landscape background to make it suit his own mythologies painted for the same room. The *Lady at her Toilet* (1515, Vienna), a semi-mythological subject which possibly started as a portrait, combines the composition used for his late Madonna pictures with genre detail and a nude figure. These three works show the old Bellini coming to terms with the new century. Technically, he learned much from Antonello; stylistically, he digested Mantegna, yet survived as an independent personality; iconographically, he was the most inventive painter North Italy produced. There are works in the Royal Coll., Baltimore (Walters), Bergamo, Berlin, Besançon (a very late *Noah*), Birmingham (Mus. and Barber Inst.), Boston (Gardner), Bristol, Cambridge Mass. (Fogg), Detroit, Dresden, Florence (Uffizi), Glasgow (Mus., Burrell), Houston Texas, Kansas City, Los Angeles, London (NG and Courtauld Inst.), Milan (Brera and Poldi-Pezzoli), Naples, New Orleans, New York (Brooklyn, Frick Coll., Met. Mus. and Morgan Library), Ottawa, Oxford, Padua, Paris (Louvre and Jacquemart-André), Pasadena Cal. (Simon), Pesaro, Philadelphia (Johnson), Rimini, Rome (Borghese, Capitoline Mus.), San Diego Cal., San Marino Cal.

(Huntington), Stuttgart, Toledo Ohio, the Vatican, Venice (Accad., Correr, Cà d'Oro, Doge's Palace, Querini-Stampalia and churches), Verona, Vienna, Washington (NG) and elsewhere.

BELLOTTO, Bernardo (1721 (1720 Venetian style)–80), was the nephew and pupil of CANALETTO, and is sometimes confusingly so called (especially in E. Europe): he himself started the custom, doubtless because it paid. They appear to have separated by 1746, perhaps after a quarrel, for Canaletto came to London and Bellotto began travels in N. Italy before leaving for Dresden in 1747. Before then he had visited Rome (probably in 1742) and Florence, Lucca, Lombardy (1744) and Turin (1745). He became Painter to Frederick Augustus II in 1748 and painted many views of Dresden, Pirna and Königstein for him. He also visited Vienna and Munich before going to Poland in 1767. Although nominally on his way to Russia, he settled in Warsaw and worked for King Stanislas Poniatowski until his death. His *vedute* of Warsaw are of great topographical exactness, and were used to help with the reconstruction of the city after 1945. In general, his style is very similar to that of his uncle, but his colour is colder and there is often blackness in the shadows; on the other hand, he has a feeling for landscape and a certain humour in his figure groups lacking in Canaletto's work. Almost all his best works are still in Dresden and Warsaw, but there are examples in Boston, Cambridge (Fitzwm), Dublin, Glasgow, London (NG), Manchester (a fine pair of views of Königstein), New York (Met. Mus.), Powis Castle Wales, Vienna, Zurich and elsewhere.

BELLOWS, George (1882–1925), was an American illustrator and painter of city life, who was influenced by the ASHCAN SCHOOL and was one of the organizers of the ARMORY SHOW. His *Cave Dwellers* (1913, Los Angeles), showing slum life in New York, is a good example of his Ashcan realism. He also painted a number of fine portraits in a bold style, e.g. *Mrs. T., No. 2* (Minneapolis).

BENEDETTO da Maiano (1442–97), was a Florentine sculptor of the post-Donatello generation. His major work is the pulpit in Sta Croce, Florence (*c.*1475), with scenes from the life of S. Francis, three *bozzetti* of which are in London (V&A). He also made several fine portrait busts, examples being those in Florence (Bargello), London (V&A), Paris (Louvre) and Washington (NG). A Giovanni da Maiano, perhaps from the same family, worked in England for Cardinal Wolsey at Hampton Court (terracotta roundels *c.*1521).

BENTNAME (Dutch), the nickname given to Dutch and Flemish members of the *Schildersbent*, or group of painters working in Rome. They were also called *Bentvueghels* (birds of a flock) because they formed a group in 1623, partly in solidarity against the Italians and against the law, but ostensibly to defy the dues levied by the Roman Academy of St Luke. The founders included BABUREN and BOR, but most of the members painted BAMBOCCIATE (Bamboccio was the Bentname of Pieter van Laer). As more Northerners flocked to Rome the Bentvueghels got more rowdy and held huge drinking parties ending in Sta Costanza, where scores of their names are still scratched on the walls (many of the names are of completely unknown artists). Their riotousness and mock baptisms caused the Pope finally to suppress them in 1720.

BERCHEM, Nicolaes (Claesz.) (1620–83), was born in Haarlem, the son of P. CLAESZ., and studied under an assortment of masters, but his style was really formed in Italy, where he went with J. B. WEENIX 1642–5. He painted a few religious subjects (e.g. *The Angel appearing to the Shepherds*, 1656, Bristol) and allegorical subjects and some portraits, as well as some realistic Dutch landscapes (e.g. *Winter Scene, Haarlem*, 1647, Amsterdam, Rijksmus.). Indeed, one of his early teachers was Jan van GOYEN, so he was brought up in the naturalistic tradition, and he also travelled to the German border with RUISDAEL in 1650. Nevertheless, his most characteristic works are Italianate landscapes, seen through a golden haze and peopled with travellers and their mules, or Arcadian shepherds and their flocks. The ruins and taverns blend to a nicety the spirit of Antiquity and the spirit of BAMBOCCIO, and it is not surprising that he and his chief rival, BOTH, were the principals among the popular ITALIANIZERS, the landscape painters influenced by CLAUDE and, above all, by a nostalgic longing for the South. This Romantic vision of Italy made him very popular with English 18th-century collectors and many of his works are still here. He may have returned to Italy 1653/6, but he settled in Amsterdam in 1677. Not only did he paint many pictures of his own but he also added the figures (*staffage*) for others, including Hobbema and Ruisdael. He also made a number of etchings. There are representative works in London (NG, Wallace Coll. and Dulwich). HOOCH and DU JARDIN were his pupils.

BERCKHEYDE (Berck Heyde), Gerrit (1638–98), was a Haarlem painter of town views. He was the pupil of HALS (with whom he can have had little in common) and of his own brother Job (1630–93), and was influenced by his older Haarlem contemporary SAENREDAM, the greatest of all Dutch architectural painters. After 1660 he went to Germany and painted views of Cologne, Heidelberg and Bonn; on his return he painted views in Amsterdam and The Hague, but he often rearranged the buildings to improve the composition – in other words, he painted VEDUTE IDEATE long before the Italians. For this reason, as well as the similarity of name, he can be confused with Jan van der HEYDEN. There are good examples in London (NG), and a fine *Canal Scene* by Job is in The Hague.

BERGOGNONE *see* BORGOGNONE.

BERLINGHIERO was active in Lucca from *c.*1215, and died in 1242 or earlier. His signed crucifix in Lucca is of the old-fashioned CHRISTUS TRIUMPHANS type, which was to be superseded by those of GIUNTA Pisano. Berlinghiero's three sons were all painters, and one, Bonaventura, painted the *St Francis* (1235, Pescia), which is one of the earliest altarpieces dedicated to the saint (canonized 1228). Attributed works are in Cleveland and Toledo Ohio. The Berlinghiero family exerted considerable influence on Florentine painting before CIMABUE.

BERMEJO, Bartolomé (active 1474–95 or later), was a Spanish painter who was much influenced by the Flemings and was one of the first to practise oil-painting in Spain. In 1474 he painted the *S. Dominic of Silos* (Madrid, Prado), which is very close to Jan van EYCK. From 1475 his contracts stipulate the use of oil, but the *Pietà* of 1490 in Barcelona Cathedral is less Eyckian and reflects some influence from later Flemish, and perhaps also French, painters. There are other works by him in Berlin, Boston (Gardner), and Luton Hoo (Wernher Coll.), nr Luton.

BERNARD, Émile (1868–1941), was the friend of GAUGUIN, van Gogh and Cézanne. He experimented with Signac's POINTILLISM, *c.*1886, but subsequently quarrelled with Signac and destroyed all the works of this type. He then went to PONT-AVEN, where he met Gauguin in 1886, and he evolved a style known as *Cloisonnisme* from its resemblance to *cloisonné* enamels; this was a method of painting strong, flat forms in strong, flat colours with blue or black contours separating the colour-patches. It was to lead eventually to a quarrel with Gauguin, who got all the credit. Bernard subsequently travelled in Spain, Egypt and Italy (1893–1900); his later works are reactionary in style and often vitiated by a sentimental religiosity. There are good examples in Paris. *See also* SYMBOLISM.

BERNINI, Gianlorenzo (1598–1680), was born in Naples, the son of Pietro Bernini, a Tuscan sculptor in the late Mannerist style, who moved to Rome *c.*1605 to work for Pope Paul V. The young Bernini early attracted the patronage of the Pope's nephew, Cardinal Scipione Borghese. His first known work, the *Goat Amalthea* (*c.*1615, Rome, Borghese) long passed as an antique, and the *Aeneas and Anchises* (1618–19, Borghese) shows him working, perhaps with his father's help, within the Mannerist tradition – the group has no fixed viewpoint and the spectator is encouraged to walk round it, thus obtaining a varying silhouette, which, coupled with the slipping movement and the strongly emphasized details of muscles, veins and joints, creates the impression of uncertainty and strain. The *Neptune and Triton* (1620, London, V&A) shows this uncertainty resolved into energy and movement, though still within the tradition of the multiple viewpoint; but in the group of works executed for the Cardinal (*Rape of Proserpine*, 1621–2; *David*, 1623; *Apollo and Daphne*, 1622–4: all in the Borghese Gall.) Bernini adopts a single frontal viewpoint and the indecisions are resolved into a clearcut expression of supreme energy, coupled with a psychological insight and a delicacy of finish that established him as the greatest sculptor since Michelangelo.

The roots of his style are not only in Michelangelo and the Antique, but also in contemporary painting, for his attitude to the Antique is conditioned by his admiration for Annibale CARRACCI, his naturalism is stimulated by CARAVAGGIO, and his gestures and facial expressions are influenced by Guido RENI. He rejected Michelangelo's concept of the figure adhering closely to the block, just as he rejected the Mannerist multiple silhouette, and he evolved the new concept of the figure with a single action and viewpoint freed from the limitations of the block and infringing the limits of its own space by breaking into that of the spectator, who is thus drawn into the action. This new concept lay at the root of the BAROQUE, of which Bernini was the virtual creator and the greatest exponent. His search for a means of expressing different realms of the divine, the mystical and the earthly led him to imaginative mixtures of white and coloured marbles, bronze, stucco, stone, painting and even coloured light filtered through stained glass. The combination of these materials has often been condemned by Puritan and uncomprehending critics as tasteless overdecoration. The finest examples of this use of mixed media are in the Cornaro Chapel (1645–52, Rome, Sta Maria della Vittoria) with the *Ecstasy of St Teresa*, and the tombs of Urban VIII and Alexander VII in St Peter's. The latter is a dramatic conception in white and coloured marbles, with a bronze figure of Death writing the Pope's name in his book.

Bernini's busts prove his insight into character, and his religious statues and groups show his passionate concern with the expression of states of mind and soul, while his feeling for the unity of sculpture and its setting led him to become the architect who most fully expressed the upsurge of religious confidence and militant faith that characterize the Counter-Reformation. He was a man of difficult and stormy temperament – his son, Domenico, described him as *'terribile nell' ira'* – but of deep piety, who regularly practised the Spiritual Exercises of St Ignatius Loyola, the founder of the Jesuits.

Papal patronage provided him with enormous architectural commisions (in and around St Peter's and the Vatican, tombs, fountains and churches), which demanded the participation of numerous assistants, and of these MOCHI, BOLGI, RAGGI and CAFFÀ were the best of his frequent helpers, while DUQUESNOY was a friendly, and ALGARDI a bitter, rival. His usual practice was to make several BOZZETTI in terracotta, which could be enlarged and worked up by his skilled helpers – several of these small *bozzetti* are in Cambridge Mass. (Fogg). Louis XIV invited him to Paris to redesign the Louvre in 1665; the French architects effectively sabotaged the plan, but one result was a magnificent bust of the King (Versailles) and a later equestrian statue of him (1669–77), which, when it arrived in Versailles in 1685, was so disliked by him that GIRARDON was employed to convert it into a garden ornament. This only too truly fulfilled Bernini's own prediction that after his death his reputation would decline. It is hardly possible to appreciate his work outside Rome, and on no city has one man left a stronger imprint. There are also works in Birmingham, Bologna (Mus. Civico), Bordeaux (S. Bruno), Copenhagen, Detroit, Edinburgh (NG), Florence (Bargello and Contini Coll.), London (V&A), Modena, New York (Met. Mus.), Paris (Louvre and Jacquemart-André) and Washington (NG). Several paintings have been attributed to him, including a *Self-portrait* in Florence (Uffizi), *Two Saints* (London, NG), and others in Glasgow (Univ.) and Oxford.

BERRETTINI *see* PIETRO da Cortona.

BERRUGUETE, Alonso (*c.*1489?–1561), was the son of Pedro Berruguete and became the major Spanish sculptor of the 16th century. He was trained in Italy and brought back Italian Mannerist ideas, both in sculpture and in painting. He went to Florence about 1504, where he saw and copied Michelangelo's lost cartoon for the *Battle of Cascina* (he is even mentioned in Michelangelo's letters). He may have been in Rome before returning to Florence for about 5 years before his final return to Spain in 1517. He was, therefore, acquainted with the early work of PONTORMO and ROSSO at the very beginning of Mannerism. His own work as a painter is close to Rosso, and he probably finished the *Coronation of the Virgin* (Paris, Louvre) which was left incomplete by Filippino LIPPI at his death in 1504. He was active in Spain principally as a sculptor on such works as the altar of the Irish College, Salamanca (1529–32) and especially the choir stalls in Toledo Cathedral (on the Epistle side), executed 1539–43. These works, like his paintings, show a combination of the influences of LEONARDO da Vinci, ANDREA del Sarto and RAPHAEL. He had an extremely successful career, being made Painter to the King on his return from Italy and ennobled in 1559. Other works attributed to him are in Arezzo, Budapest, Florence (Uffizi), Munich and Rome (Borghese). An engraving, possibly unique, is in London (BM).

BERRUGUETE, Pedro (*c.*1450–1503/4), was Court Painter to Ferdinand and Isabella of Spain. He was a Castilian who worked at Avila and in Toledo

Cathedral from 1483. At some date before this he may have been in Italy since it is often held that he painted some of the pictures in the Palace at Urbino, usually given to the Fleming JOOS van Gent. This problem is much confused by a document, purporting to be of 1477, which says that 'Pietro Spagnuolo' – Peter the Spaniard – was working in Urbino: unfortunately, nobody has set eyes on this document since 1822. On the other hand, a 16th-century Spanish writer says that the *Famous Men* at Urbino were by an unspecified Spanish painter. Some further evidence in favour of the attribution may be found in works by Berruguete at Avila and in his native village, Paredes de Nava; and also in the fact that his son Alonso studied in Italy. Other works by Pedro are in Madrid (Prado) and Paris (Louvre), these latter being part of the disputed series from the Palace at Urbino.

BERTOLDO di Giovanni (*d.*1491) was the pupil and assistant of DONATELLO (whose pulpits in S. Lorenzo he finished) and the teacher of Michelangelo, since he was employed by Lorenzo de' Medici, Il Magnifico, as keeper of his sculpture garden, which was one of the earliest modern ACADEMIES. There he carved a *Battle* based on an antique sarcophagus, and probably also made the small bronzes of classical subjects – e.g. *Bellerophon*, Vienna. This was in the 1480s, and Bertoldo was said to be 'old'; but he is first recorded as Donatello's assistant in 1460, so the date of his birth may be later than *c.*1420, which is the current guess – he may have been a Medici bastard. There are works by him in Florence (Bargello), Modena and Paris (Louvre).

BERTRAM von Minden, Master, was a German painter working in Hamburg from 1367 to *c.*1415. The most important picture attributed to him is the *Grabow Altar* (*c.*1379/83, Hamburg, Kunsthalle). Others are in Hanover, Paris (Mus. des Arts Décoratifs) and London (V&A). He was a precursor of the realistic Flemish approach of the 15th century, and also of the SOFT STYLE, and he may have had some contact with THEODORIC of Prague and with French art.

BEUCKELAER *see* BUECKELAER.

BEWICK, Thomas (1753–1828), was the father of modern wood-engraving, abandoning the practice of cutting the block along the grain (*see* ENGRAVING) and using the end-grain of boxwood to give far greater delicacy, detail and gradation of tone. He was born near Newcastle and apprenticed at 14 to Ralph Beilby, trade-engraver and jeweller, the brother of the famous glass-enamellers, William and Mary Beilby. From Ralph he learned both wood- and metal-engraving. He visited London in 1776, but returned to Newcastle and entered into partnership with Ralph Beilby until 1797. The success of his 'General History of Quadrupeds' (1790) encouraged him to begin the 'History of British Birds' (1797, 1804) and the 'Fables of Aesop' (1818), all illustrated with exquisite miniatures of birds and beasts and appropriate human beings. He also illustrated other books and made a few larger engravings, such as the *Chillingham Bull* (1789) and the tragic dying horse, *Waiting for Death*, which he was working on at his own death. There are preparatory drawings in London (BM and Courtauld Inst.) and Newcastle (Natural History Soc.). His autobiography was first published (incompletely) in 1862, and more fully in 1975.

BEYEREN, Abraham van (1620/21–90), though not successful in his lifetime is now regarded as one of the finest Dutch 17th-century painters of still-life, equal to De HEEM, who inspired him. He was born in The Hague and entered the Guild there in 1640. He began as a painter of fish, but turned to other forms of still-life, especially BANCKET and VANITAS pieces, as well as flowers. There are several examples, including a fish piece, in Oxford (Ashmolean), as well as Amsterdam and The Hague and several American museums.

BIBIENA. A family of Bolognese stage-designers and architects active from the 1670s to the 1780s in most European countries. They were the most famous exponents of the elaborate perspectives and settings for theatrical productions and state occasions. The Opera House at Bayreuth was their work, and about 200 engravings exist, some of which influenced PIRANESI.

BIEDERMEIERSTIL is the name given to the style, roughly corresponding to Early Victorian, in furniture and decoration in Austria and Germany *c.*1815–48. It is a bourgeois style, clear and simple, and is often extended to cover painting and sculpture of the same period (cf. SPITZWEG). The name derives from two fictitious characters, Biedermann and Bummelmeier, who were supposed to represent genuine German Philistines.

BIERSTADT, Albert (1830–1902), was born in Germany, but emigrated with his family to the US in 1832. He went back to Germany in 1853 to study in Düsseldorf, returning to America in 1857, where he specialized in Far Western landscapes, with or without Indians, such as *The Rocky Mountains* (1863, New York, Met. Mus.). Other works are in Boston (twenty-seven), Mount Holyoke and Smith College Mass. and in Washington (Corcoran and NG).

BIJLERT *see* BYLERT.

BILL, Max (*b.*1908), is a Swiss abstract sculptor who is also active as a painter, architect and writer. He was trained in Zürich and at the BAUHAUS in Dessau (1927–9), and was a member of ABSTRACTION-CRÉATION. In 1951 he went to Ulm to teach for six years, exerting considerable influence on young German artists. His writings include essays on the mathematical elements in modern art and on KANDINSKY.

BINGHAM, George Caleb (1811–79), was an American painter of the great settlements in the Far West in the 19th century. Bingham was the most important of the so-called Frontier Painters, but he had no real training, apart from a few months in Philadelphia in 1837–8. He worked for a time in Washington, but returned to Missouri *c.*1844 and painted scenes of everyday life which were widely engraved. The most famous was also one of the earliest, *Fur Traders on the Missouri River* (1845, New York, Met. Mus.), but similar subjects exist elsewhere, e.g. in Detroit. In 1856 he went to Düsseldorf (*see* BIERSTADT) and was much influenced by the sentimental German art of the period, but in 1859 he returned to America and wasted most of the rest of his life in politics. Many of his works are in St Louis Mo.

BIOMORPHIC ART is a form of Abstract Art which purports to take its abstract forms from living organisms rather than from the geometrical basis of such abstract movements as CONSTRUCTIVISM. MIRÓ and KANDINSKY were the chief influences.

BIRD, Francis (1667–1731), was born in London, but went to Brussels at the age of 11, and from there to Rome. When he returned to London *c.*1689, he could hardly speak English. He worked under CIBBER and GIBBONS and then went back to Rome for nine months. On his return, *c.*1700, he made the *Henry VIII* for St Bartholomew's Hospital, London (1702/3), and then, from before 1706 to 1721, he executed most of the statues for St Paul's Cathedral (including the main pediment relief of the *Conversion of St Paul*, for which he received £620 in 1706). He also made the statue of Queen Anne outside, which has been replaced by a poor Victorian copy. There are other works by him in Oxford and monuments in Westminster Abbey.

Bistre (Fr.). A brown pigment made from charred wood, used as ink or chalk, or, principally in the 17th century, as a wash. Rembrandt's drawings are mostly in bistre.

Bitumen. A rich brown pigment made from asphaltum. Its use, though pleasant, is very dangerous, since it never dries completely. It was popular during the late 18th and early 19th centuries, especially in England, and has been the cause of severe damage in many paintings of that time.

Lake, William (1757–1827), earned a meagre living working for publishers as an engraver, usually of other men's designs, but between his bread-and-butter work he produced his own poems in books which he made and published himself, engraving the text and surrounding it with an illustration which he coloured by hand. In this way he issued 'Songs of Innocence' (1789) and 'Songs of Experience' (1794), and his various 'Prophetic Books' (1783–1804). His greatest works are the twenty-one large watercolours illustrating the Book of Job, the first set of which was probably made *c.*1818/20, and a second set commissioned by Linnell and produced from 1821 and engraved in 1823–5; 102 illustrations to Dante (also suggested to him by Linnell), six of which were engraved at Blake's death; and his colour-printed drawings, which include *Nebuchadnezzar*, *Hecate* and *Elijah in the Chariot of Fire*. These were made by printing off a design prepared in distemper on millboard, and then finishing each individually. Most of his designs were carried out in normal watercolour technique, but his so-called 'frescoes' are in a highly unorthodox form of tempera which has deteriorated badly. His early work was within the current Neoclassical style, but as his verse and philosophy acquired a more visionary quality, so he turned to forms and ideas evolved from medieval and Mannerist examples, abandoned logical arrangement in space, and developed a purely subjective use of colour, light and form to give substance to his visions. Whatever his sources, he always transmuted everything by the power of his imagination: this is his salient quality and marks the sharpest reaction against the Age of Reason and is the dawn of Romanticism.

In 1800 he moved to Felpham, near Bognor, where he lived uneasily for three years in the circle of the poet Hayley, which included Flaxman and Romney. His difficulties with the engraver Cromek over his illustrations to Blair's 'Grave' (1808), and his painting and engraving of the *Canterbury Pilgrims* (1810), are reflected in one of his typically pungent epigrams: 'A petty sneaking knave I knew – Ah! Mr Cromek, how d'ye do?' His detestation of Reynolds's theory was expressed in his annotation to a copy of the 'Discourses' – 'This Man was Hired to Depress Art'. He was also of the opinion that all the parts of the 'Discourses' with which he found himself agreeing were actually due to Barry or Fuseli. In his last years he was helped by Linnell, and his circle of friends included Varley, Richmond, Calvert, Palmer and Fuseli, who admitted that he found Blake 'damned good to steal from'. The Tate Gallery, London, has a fine collection of his work, and there are also examples in Aberdeen, Boston, Brighton, Cambridge (Fitzwm), Cambridge Mass. (Fogg), London

(BM and V&A), Manchester (City Gall. and Whitworth), Melbourne, New York (Met. Mus., Morgan Library and Brooklyn), San Marino Cal. (Huntington), Yale (CBA) and elsewhere.

BLANCHARD, Jacques (1600–38), was born in Paris, but was in Rome 1624–5 and moved to Venice in 1626, where he saw the work of LISS. He then went to Turin, where he worked for the Dukes of Savoy, before returning to France in 1628. The principal influence on him was Veronese, whose blond and silvery colour and limpid light he used most effectively in his small religious and mythological subjects. The several versions of *Charity*, depicted as a young woman with two or three children, are excellent examples of his tenderness of colour handling, and of a softness of sentiment nearer to the 18th than the 17th century. He was also a sensitive portrait painter, and played a leading part in French painting of the 1630s. There are examples in Amsterdam (Rijksmus.), London (Courtauld Inst.), New York (Met. Mus.), Paris (Louvre and Notre-Dame), Toledo Ohio, Venice (Accad.) and in French provincial museums.

BLAUE REITER, Der (Ger. The Blue Rider), was the name given to a group of Munich artists in 1911 by the two most important members, KANDINSKY and MARC. According to Kandinsky, they invented the name because they both liked blue, Marc liked horses, and Kandinsky liked riders . . . MACKE and CAMPENDONK were also members. The group was later joined by KLEE and, with the BRÜCKE, was the most important manifestation of modern art in Germany before 1914. Munich now has the largest collection of their works.

BLAUEN VIER, Die (Ger. The Blue Four), *see* JAWLENSKY.

BLECHEN, Karl (1798–1840), was a German Romantic painter influenced by FRIEDRICH, whom he probably met in Berlin in 1823. Blechen worked for the Berlin Theatre, and went to Italy in 1828–9. On his return he became Professor of landscape painting at the Berlin Academy (1831). He visited Paris in 1835. His later works are more realist and show him moving away from his early Romanticism. Most of his pictures are in Berlin, but there are others in Hanover, Karlsruhe and Vienna.

BLOCK-BOOK. An early form of illustrated book, of a popular devotional character, in which the text and illustrations are cut together from the same block. Oddly, the earliest block-books seem to date from *c.*1460, after the invention of movable type (though this is controversial), and are contemporary with books printed with movable type and illustrated with separately cut blocks. Nevertheless, recent research seems to show that 'Apocalypse I' (Manchester, Rylands Library) dates from 1451/2 – i.e. somewhat earlier than Gutenberg. The influences of Roger van der WEYDEN and MEMLINC seem to confirm dates in the 1460s. Some early examples are the 'Biblia Pauperum' (1465), the 'Song of Songs' (1466), and the ARS MORIENDI (1466).

BLOEMAERT, Abraham (1564–1651), was an Utrecht Mannerist. He was in Paris 1580–83 and returned to Utrecht to paint elaborate history and genre subjects, bright in colour and with an exaggerated figure style reminiscent of WTEWAEL. He was important in the formation of the UTRECHT SCHOOL because he was the teacher of so many other painters, including BOTH, J.G. CUYP, HONTHORST, TERBRUGGHEN, WEENIX and others. He himself came strongly under the influence of Caravaggio (although he never visited Italy) in the early 1620s, just when his pupil Honthorst returned from Italy with the new ideas. His son, Hendrick (*c.*1601–72), was also a painter and his pupil. There are works by Abraham in the Royal Coll. and in Amsterdam, Barnard Castle (Bowes Mus.), Berlin, Brunswick, Brussels, Cape Town, Copenhagen, Dublin, Frankfurt, Grenoble, Haarlem, The Hague, Hamburg, Leamington Spa, Leyden, London (V&A (Ham House) and Blackheath), Nottingham, Ottawa, Paris (Louvre), Stockholm, Toledo Ohio, Utrecht and Vienna (K-H Mus.).

BLOT DRAWING was the name given by Alexander COZENS to the practice of evolving a composition from the forms suggested by allowing a few blobs of ink or colour to fall at random on a sheet of paper, if necessary folding the paper to create further blots. The method seems to have been known to Leonardo da Vinci, who advocated the study of stains on a wall, or the shapes in the fire, as a stimulus to the creative imagination. Cozens's advocacy of the method as a means of teaching his numerous pupils led to his being dubbed 'Blotmaster to the Town': at the end of his life he published his system as 'A New Method of Assisting the Invention in Drawing Original Compositions of Landscape' (*c.*1785). It was reprinted in 1952.

BLUE FOUR *see* JAWLENSKY.

BLUE RIDER, The, *see* BLAUE REITER, Der.

BOAST (usually pronounced 'boost'). To shape a statue roughly; hence boaster, a broad chisel or a pointed hammer (*boucharde*) used for blocking out a stone carving.

BOCCIONI, Umberto (1882–1916), was strongly affected by BALLA's DIVISIONISM after 1901, but by 1907/8 had veered in the direction of SYMBOLISM, and in 1910 he became one of the original FUTURISTS, signing the Manifesto and issuing the Manifesto of Futurist Sculpture in 1912. He also wrote a book about it (1914). He volunteered for the War in 1915 and died as the result of an accident, after being wounded. He had been the most active of the Futurists and the group never recovered from his death. His work realized, in attempting to render movement, two of the clauses of the Manifesto: 'Universal dynamism must be rendered in painting as a dynamic sensation ... Motion and light destroy the materiality of bodies'. His *Unique Forms of Continuity in Space* is in London (Tate).

BÖCKLIN, Arnold (1827–1901), was, with HODLER, the major Swiss painter of the 19th century, and he exerted a great influence on the German-speaking countries through the expression of a heightened Romanticism and poeticism. He was trained in Germany, Flanders and Paris, and spent seven years in Rome (1850–57), where he transformed his early naturalistic landscapes, more or less in the manner of COROT, into symbolic subjects with figures epitomizing the mood of the landscape. In the 1860s he visited Pompeii, where the ancient Roman frescoes led him to attempt classical history subjects, often harsh in colour. He was in Munich 1871–4, where he met THOMA, but, like other German artists of the period, (e.g. his friends FEUERBACH and MARÉES) he spent much of the rest of his life in Italy, where he died. The work by which he is best known, *The Island of the Dead*, was first painted when he was living in Florence (1874–85) and was repeated in many versions. It has a curiously haunted quality which can be felt even in the reproductions in elementary German grammars, where many people first see it: the same quality can be found in his *Pan* (which also exists in several versions) and in some other landscapes. Most of his works are in his native Basle, where the Museum has a frescoed staircase, and in Munich and other German museums, New York

(Met. Mus.: a good version of the *Island of the Dead*), Paris (Mus. d'Orsay) and Washington (NG).

BODEGÓN (Span. tavern). Kitchen scenes in which the interest in still-life predominates. Typical examples are Velázquez's pair in Edinburgh and London (NG), but even in Spanish it is often only a synonym for STILL-LIFE.

BODY COLOUR is WATERCOLOUR mixed with white pigment to make it opaque. It is identical with GOUACHE. Body colour is often used in drawings done on tinted paper, or on watercolours to heighten the contrast with the transparency of pure watercolour, to give highlights or to accent strong passages of local colour. Turner was the greatest master of this technique.

BOL, Ferdinand (1616–80), was a pupil of Rembrandt before 1640, and for many years imitated his master so closely that many of his works have passed as Rembrandt's – e.g. the *Lady* in London, Kenwood. By about 1660, when Rembrandt's portraits were less in demand, Bol adapted his style to a more fashionable French manner, lighter and more courtly. He painted several big group portraits, such as the *Governors of the Leper Hospital* (1649, Amsterdam, Rijksmus.). In 1669 he married a rich widow and gave up painting.

BOLDINI, Giovanni (1845–1931), was a fashionable portrait painter, the Italian equivalent of SARGENT, whom he knew. He was born in Ferrara, but in 1867 went to Paris and was swept off his feet by MANET, whose virtuosity he imitated, but without Manet's impeccable taste. He visited London before settling in Paris *c.*1872, where he spent the rest of his life. Whistler and the Impressionists also influenced him, but he is best remembered as the recorder of Paris in the Belle Époque. There is a Boldini Museum in his native town, and other works are in Paris, as well as Florence, London and New York (Brooklyn: *Whistler*).

BOLGI, Andrea (1605–56), an Italian sculptor, was a pupil of BERNINI. His best-known work is the *S. Helena*, one of four huge statues in the crossing of St Peter's in Rome; the others are by MOCHI, DUQUESNOY and Bernini himself. A bust of Laura Frangipane is signed and dated 1637 (Rome, S. Francesco a Ripa). He was in Naples in 1645, and the De Caro monument in S. Lorenzo Maggiore is a late work there, and perhaps his masterpiece.

BOLOGNA, Giovanni (da), or Giambologna, Jean de Boulogne (1529–1608), the most famous sculptor in Florence after the death of Michelangelo, was born in Douai and trained in Flanders before arriving in Italy *c.*1555. After a period in Rome he settled in Florence, where he competed with AMMANATI and CELLINI for the commission for the fountain in the Piazza della Signoria. Ammanati won, but Giambologna assisted him and later made his own *Neptune* fountain in Bologna (1563–7). His *Rape of the Sabines* (1579–83, Loggia de' Lanzi, Florence) shows the fully-developed Mannerist principle of sculpture to be seen from all points of view equally, by walking round it instead of regarding it from a single, fixed viewpoint. All his marbles are in Florence except *Samson slaying the Philistine* (London, V&A, begun *c.*1565). The best known of his bronzes are the *Mercury* (Florence, Bargello, 1564; Vienna; and many other versions, e.g. Oxford, Ch. Ch.) and the equestrian statues of the Grand Dukes Cosimo I (1594, Florence, Piazza della Signoria) and Ferdinando (Piazza dell'Annunziata). Small bronze replicas of his works were produced in huge quantities in his shop. There are four wax models (London, V&A and Brisbane) for the bronze reliefs in Genoa University chapel (*c.*1580).

BOLTRAFFIO, Giovanni Antonio (1467–1516), was the best of LEONARDO's Milanese followers. Most of his works are in Milan, but others are in Berlin, Budapest, Cambridge Mass. (Fogg), Florence (Uffizi), London (NG), New York (Met. Mus.), Paris (Louvre and Jacquemart-André) and Philadelphia (Johnson). An interesting portrait by him is at Chatsworth, Derbyshire, and another, in Washington (NG), may have been worked on by Leonardo.

BOLUS GROUND. Canvas or panel is primed with a dark red or brownish earth ground (*bole*). Eventually, the colour of the ground shows through the paint-layers and upsets the colour-balance of the painting. It is particularly noticeable in 17th/18th century pictures, e.g. by PIAZZETTA. *See* BITUMEN.

BONACOLSI, Piero *see* 'ANTICO'.

BONANUS made the bronze doors of Pisa Cathedral in 1179, but they were destroyed in 1595. The side door of the Cathedral (Porta di S. Ranieri) is attributed to him, as it is identical in style with the bronze doors of Monreale Cathedral, signed by him and dated 1185 (New Style). The other bronze doors at Monreale are by BARISANUS.

BONDIEUSERIE (Fr. good Goddery). Now a recognized term for nauseatingly sentimental religious art, usually produced in quantity in Belgium and France. MURILLO has much to answer for in the origins of *bondieuserie*.

BONE, Sir Muirhead (1876–1953), was an architectural draughtsman and etcher, whose *Demolition of St James's Hall* (1905) was the first major work in a field he made his own. There are many drawings and etchings of the First World War by him in the Imperial War Museum, London, and in the Second World War he produced the huge *Ruins of London from St Bride's, Fleet Street*, showing the devastation of the City in 1940.

BONHEUR, Rosa (1822–99), was, with LANDSEER, the most famous animal painter of the 19th century, but her works are free from anthropomorphic sentimentality. The huge *Horse Fair*, exhibited at the Salon of 1853, established her reputation. She made studies at the Marché aux Chevaux in Paris dressed as a man, and received formal police *permission de travestissement*. The original, offered to her native Bordeaux and refused, was bought by an English dealer and is now in New York (Met. Mus.). In order to facilitate the engraving (by Landseer's brother Thomas) she had a reduced version – still over 8 feet wide – made by her friend Natalie Micas, which she then finished herself: it is now in London (NG). She enjoyed great popularity in Britain and was, like Landseer, fascinated by the Highlands of Scotland, which she visited in the 1850s. In 1894 she became the first woman Officer of the Legion of Honour. There are no works by her in the Louvre, but there is a Musée Bonheur at Fontainebleau, good examples in the Wallace Coll., London, and a *Self-Portrait* in Florence (Uffizi).

BONIFAZIO de' Pitati (Bonifazio Veronese) (1487–1553), was born in Verona but trained under PALMA Vecchio and ran a large workshop in Venice. His style was greatly influenced by Giorgione and Titian, and to some extent his name is used to cover works which the owner dare not quite attribute to either of them, but there is a fine picture in Birmingham which is closer to BASSANO. Other examples are in Adelaide, Boston, Dresden, Florence (Pitti, Uffizi), London (NG), Milan (Brera and Ambrosiana), San Francisco, Venice and Vienna. There are also many *cassoni* and furniture decorations attributed to him.

BONINGTON, Richard Parkes (1802–28), was an English landscape painter who went to France as a boy and was trained there. He was a friend of DELACROIX as well as a pupil of GROS, and first exhibited in 1822. He returned to England in 1825 and 1827, and went to Italy in 1826. His historical pictures were much influenced by the Venetians, but Delacroix's remark that Bonington was carried away by his own skill is truer of them than of his landscapes. There are works by him in his native Nottingham and in Birmingham (said to be his last work), Budapest, Cambridge (Fitzwm), Edinburgh (NG), London (BM, V&A, Tate Gall., Courtauld Inst. and especially Wallace Coll.), Muncie Indiana (*Venice*, 1827), Ottawa, Paris (Louvre) and Yale (CBA).

BONNARD, Pierre (1867–1947), became a painter after selling a poster to a champagne house in 1889. In 1890 he shared a studio with VUILLARD and DENIS, which was a meeting-place for the NABIS, with whom he was associated until the group broke up in 1899. Until then his work was strongly influenced by Japanese prints and based on flat decoration and asymmetrical composition. It was subdued, even dark, in colour. After 1900 his palette became richer, he used heavier impasto and more strongly modelled forms, and his – and Vuillard's – more Impressionist technique and choice of subjects became known as *Intimisme*. His subjects were limited: domestic interiors, many with a woman bathing, dressing or sleeping, family scenes round a table, and sunlit landscapes, all increasingly brilliant in light and colour, which made his work so influential on later painters. Marthe, whom he met in 1893 and married in 1925, was usually the model for his domestic scenes and seems never to have aged. He also made many lithographs in colour and black-and-white, some as book-illustrations. Most museums of modern art have a work by him.

BONNAT, Léon (1833–1922), was born in Bayonne and brought up in Spain, receiving his first training in Madrid. Early impressions of RIBERA and Caravaggio were succeeded by the influence of the Bolognese during a stay in Italy (1858–60). There is a certain similarity to COUTURE in some of his sketches, but he does not seem to have shared MANET's Spanish interests. In the latter part of his career he became an enormously successful portrait painter (of Victor Hugo, and many Presidents of the Third Republic and American millionaires). He also painted murals in the Hôtel de Ville, Palais de Justice, the Panthéon and many churches in Paris, but his memorial is the Musée Bonnat in Bayonne, which contains his own splendid collection of drawings. There are numerous works in museums in Paris, and in Boston, Lille, New York (Met. Mus.), Poitiers and other French museums.

BOR, Paulus (*c.*1600–69), was born in Amersfoort, Holland, and went to Rome *c.*1620/23, where he was one of the founders of the BENT. He returned to Amersfoort by 1628 and painted at first in a manner deriving from the young Rembrandt, but the influence of Caravaggio – whose works he must have seen in Rome – seems to have grown on him and he became a member of the UTRECHT SCHOOL. There are works in Amersfoort, Amsterdam (Rijksmus.), Liverpool, London (Courtauld Inst.), New York (Met. Mus.) and Utrecht.

BORCH, Gerard ter, *see* TER BORCH.

BORDONE, Paris (1500–71), was a Trevisan painter who spent most of his life in Venice, but probably visited France (1538? and 1559?), and also Augsburg – a portrait in the Louvre is signed and dated 1540 and inscribed 'Augusta', so he was probably in Augsburg in that year, and the Venetian influence on AMBERGER may well come from this visit. Vasari says that he was apprenticed to Titian, but set himself to imitate GIORGIONE. There are works by him in the Royal Coll. and in Augsburg, Baltimore, Bergamo, Birmingham Alabama, Boston (Mus. and Gardner), Caen, Cologne, Dublin, Edinburgh, Florence (Uffizi and Pitti), Genoa, Glasgow, Hamburg, London (NG, Courtauld Inst.), Milan (Brera), Munich, Paris, Philadelphia (Johnson), Raleigh NC, Rome (Borghese), Toronto, Treviso, Vaduz, the Vatican, Venice, Vienna and Washington.

BORGOGNONE, Ambrogio (*c.*1450/60–1523), was a Milanese painter, influenced by FOPPA and not by Leonardo, whose best works are in the Certosa at Pavia, including some *trompe-l'oeil* frescoes of monks looking through windows. Other works are in Bergamo, Birmingham, London (NG) and Milan (Brera).

BOSBOOM, Johannes (1817–91), was a Dutch painter specializing in church interiors, preferably Gothic. His very detailed handling slowly became looser, but his colour tended to retain a warm and glowing tonality, derived – as he said himself – from his admiration for Rembrandt. He travelled extensively in France, Germany and the Netherlands, in search of suitable subjects, often incorporating figures in 17th-century costume into his compositions. There are works in Amsterdam (Rijksmus. and Stedelijk), Edinburgh (NG), Glasgow, Groningen, The Hague (where he lived and died), London (NG), Montreal, Munich, Paris (Louvre) and Rotterdam.

BOSCH, Hieronymus (Jerome) (*c.*1450–1516), perhaps the greatest master of fantasy who ever lived, is first recorded in 's Hertogenbosch in 1480/1. He may have been born there and his name probably derives from it: certainly he spent his life there and died there. His obsessive and haunted world is that of Gothic twilight and is the best surviving expression of some aspects of the waning of the Middle Ages, but it is now largely incomprehensible. The Surrealists have claimed him as a sort of Freudian *avant la lettre*, but it is certain that his paintings had a very definite significance and were not merely ramblings of the unconscious mind. For example, the *Hay Wain* (Madrid, Prado) once belonged to Philip II of Spain and is obviously an allegory on the general theme 'All flesh is grass', just as the *Ship of Fools* (Paris, Louvre) is a well-known late medieval allegory. About 1600 a Spanish writer apparently thought it necessary to defend Bosch's memory against imputations of heresy, which seems to show that even then the real meaning of his pictures had been lost. In recent years there has been an elaborate attempt to 'explain' many of the pictures – in particular, the *Earthly Paradise* (Madrid, Prado) – as altarpieces painted for a heretical cult addicted to orgiastic rites. Not only is there no evidence for this, but it also fails to explain why so many of Bosch's pictures belonged to people of unimpeachable orthodoxy, such as Philip II. The problem of Bosch's patrons resembles that of BRUEGEL's, and there is much in common between the two, although Bosch's fantasy is always far more inventive and seems to plumb deeper levels of symbolism, even in what appear to be purely erotic scenes. It is also worth nothing that, according to a mid-16th-century Spanish writer, there were already forgeries in circulation, apparently signed by Bosch: he cites the *Seven Deadly Sins* (Madrid, Prado) as an example, but it is now universally accepted as authentic. The chronology of Bosch's pictures is far from clear, but it is probably safe to assume that the *Crucifixion* (Brussels) is his earliest known work, on the grounds that it is closer to the styles of BOUTS and Roger van der WEYDEN – the dominant styles in the Netherlands *c.*1480 – than any others by him. His master is unknown, and the origins of his style are very obscure, but are probably to be found in popular woodcuts and devotional prints. Other early works are probably the *Christ Mocked* (London, NG), the *Cure for Madness* (Madrid, Prado), and the *Seven Deadly Sins*; the later works seem to be those with greater numbers of small-scale figures, painted in pale, bright, transparent colours on a very white ground. There are examples in Antwerp, Berlin, Boston, Chicago, Cologne (Wallraf-Richartz), Denver Col., the Escorial, Frankfurt (Städel), Ghent, Lisbon, Munich, New York (Met. Mus.), Philadelphia (Johnson), Princeton NJ, Rotterdam (Boymans), S. Diego Cal., Valenciennes, Venice (Doge's Pal.), Vienna (Akad. and K-H Mus.), Washington (NG), Yale and elsewhere.

BOTH, Andries (*c.*1612–41) and Jan (*c.*1618–52), were Utrecht painters who, according to SANDRART, worked together, with Andries painting the figures in Jan's landscapes, until one day Andries fell into a canal in Venice on his way home from a party. Andries and Jan were in Rome by 1635, and both were there in 1639–41. Jan returned to Utrecht after his brother's death. No joint works are known which can be recognized as having figures by Andries, and it is difficult to date any of Jan's landscapes before 1641: signed works by Andries such as the *Boors Carousing* (1634, Utrecht) or the *Card Players* (Amsterdam, Rijksmus.) show Andries as a painter of BAMBOCCIATE in a style closer to Brouwer than to his brother's idyllic landscapes. Jan was profoundly influenced by the works of CLAUDE in the period 1638–41. He became one of the leading ITALIANIZERS, and, like his chief rival, BERCHEM, painted Claudian landscapes with a golden light falling on the picturesque peasantry. The treatment of light in CUYP's work owes much to him. Both brothers were pupils of the Utrecht Mannerist BLOEMAERT, and in their several ways they show the new directions taken by Dutch painting in the 17th century. Jan is represented in most older galleries; there are typical works in Amsterdam, Detroit, Edinburgh, Indianapolis, London (NG, Wallace Coll., Dulwich), Toledo Ohio and Worcester Mass.

BOTTEGA (Ital. shop). The workshop or studio of an artist; specifically, that part in which the pupils and assistants worked on productions commissioned from, and often signed by, the master. An *opera di bottega* or 'shop work' is one produced in the shop of a master, but hardly touched by him.

BOTTICELLI, Sandro (*c.*1445–1510), was the most individual, if not the most influential, painter in Florence at the end of the 15th century. He was probably a pupil of Fra Filippo LIPPI, but was influenced by the POLLAIUOLI for a short time around 1470, when he painted a *Fortitude* to go with a set of six other *Virtues* by Piero Pollaiuolo (all seven now in the Uffizi). The chronology of his work is difficult to establish, since it ranges between the vigorous realism of the 1470 *Fortitude* and the langorous and anti-naturalistic ecstasy of his last dated (and only signed) work, the *Mystic Nativity* (1500, London, NG). It seems certain that the Victorian interpretation of his style as progressively more naturalistic (and more Pre-Raphaelite) is topsy-turvy: we know that he was neurotic, much troubled by the religious crisis of the late Quattrocento and yet ambiguous in his attitude to Savonarola, and that he was at any rate accused of pederasty (this charge seems to have been made as freely in 15th-century Florence as that of Communism in modern America, and on about the same evidence). His extreme dependence on outline as a means of emotional expression is a summary of Florentine tendencies in the 15th century, but his style seems nevertheless to have been deliberately archaic; just as his most celebrated mythological pictures – the *Primavera* and the *Birth of Venus* (both in the Uffizi) – have very involved allegorical meanings. These were probably painted for a member of the Medici family, then ruling Florence, but we know almost nothing about the commissioning or his relationship with the Medici and their humanist circle. In 1481/2 he was in Rome, painting frescoes in the Sistine Chapel along with Ghirlandaio, Rosselli, Signorelli and Perugino, but these do not seem to have been particularly successful (he painted few frescoes). During the last twenty years of the 15th century he ran a large shop for the production of *Madonnas* of a gently devout kind, well suited to the piety of the age: these made him prosperous and many of them are repetitions by different hands from cartoons by him. They were also extensively forged during the 19th century, but these are now beginning to look strangely Victorian. By about 1500 his style was so obviously opposed to the new ideas of Leonardo da Vinci and Michelangelo that he suffered a decline in popularity, and the last ten years of his life are mysterious. It is probable that the clumsy, almost hysterical, style of works like the *Pietàs* in Milan (Poldi-Pezzoli) and Munich, the ruined *Crucifixion* in Cambridge Mass. (Fogg), or the S. Zenobius series in London (NG), Dresden and New York (Met. Mus.) is that of his last period, i.e. after the 1500 *Mystic Nativity*, rather than works of his youth. Probably in the 1490s he made a series of splendid outline drawings illustrating Dante (Berlin and the Vatican), which show his sensitive feeling for contour at its most subtle. Other works by him are in Avignon, Bergamo, Berlin, Birmingham, Boston (Mus. and Gardner), Chicago, Detroit, Edinburgh (NG), Florence (Accad., Uffizi, Pitti, and Ognissanti and other churches), Frankfurt, Glasgow, London (NG, V&A and Courtauld Inst.), Milan (Ambrosiana), New York (Met. Mus.), Ottawa, Paris (Louvre and Jacquemart-André), Philadelphia, Rome (Borghese), the Vatican, Washington (NG) and elsewhere. Filippino LIPPI was his pupil; *see also* AMICO di Sandro.

BOTTICINI, Francesco (*c.*1446–97), was a Florentine painter who imitated many others, including Botticelli. The most interesting picture ascribed to him is the *Assumption* (*c.*1474/6, London, NG), which is the only Quattrocento picture known to have been painted to illustrate a heresy: Matteo Palmieri, the donor, held that human souls are the angels who remained neutral when Lucifer rebelled.

BOUCHARDE *see* STONE CARVING.

BOUCHARDON, Edmé (1698–1762), was a French sculptor who worked under G. COUSTOU I and then went to Rome (1723), where he remained for 9 years and enjoyed considerable fame. He worked at Versailles, but is best remembered for his Fontaine de Grenelle, Paris (1739–45), his *Cupid* (1750, Louvre), and his equestrian statue of Louis XV, designed as the centrepiece of the Place de la Concorde, Paris, but destroyed during the Revolution. It had *Virtues* by PIGALLE which evoked the epigram:

Oh! la belle statue! Oh! le beau piédestal!
Les vertus sont à pied et le vice à cheval!

BOUCHER, François (1703–70), was the most typical ROCOCO decorator, and the friend and protégé of Mme de Pompadour. One of his best portraits is of her (1758, London, V&A – others are in the Wallace Coll. and Edinburgh NG). He began as an engraver of Watteau, won the Prix de Rome in 1723, but did not go to Italy until 1727; there he admired little but Tiepolo, the greatest decorator of the age. He returned to France in 1731, became an Academician in 1734, and Director in 1765. He made many tapestry designs and painted charmingly indelicate mythological scenes, ultimately inspired by Veronese, Rubens and Watteau. He was censured for these on moral grounds by DIDEROT. Reynolds, who visited his studio, was scandalized by his working without a model: 'He said, when he was young, studying his art, he found it necessary to use models; but he had left them off for many years.' The best collection of his works is in London (Wallace Coll.) – especially the large tapestry designs of the *Rising* and *Setting of the Sun* (1753). There are others in Boston, Cambridge (Fitzwm), Detroit, London (NG and Kenwood), Manchester, New York, Paris, Waddesdon Bucks. (National Trust) and Washington.

BOUDIN, Eugène (1824–98), was a direct precursor of Impressionism. He was born at Honfleur, son of a pilot, and he painted seascapes and harbour scenes with luminous skies taking up much of the picture space. These skies are the link between his friend COROT and his younger friends, the Impressionists, especially MONET. He exhibited at the first Impressionist Exhibition, 1874. There are eight typical works in Edinburgh (NG) and he is well represented in museums of modern art.

BOUGUEREAU, Adolphe William (1825–1905), won the Prix de Rome in 1850 and spent four years in Italy. He painted 'Renaissance-type' nudes, rather cloying religious subjects, and portraits of photographic verisimilitude: this probably explains why Renoir, on being fitted with new glasses to correct his myopia, threw them on the floor, crying: 'Bon Dieu, je vois comme Bouguereau!' There are works in Birmingham, Bordeaux, Dijon, La Rochelle, Paris (Mus. d'Orsay) and in many US museums, especially Williamstown Mass., where his nudes make an instructive comparison with those by Renoir in the same collection.

BOURDELLE, Émile Antoine (1861–1929), was a pupil of RODIN, but soon reacted against his loose and impressionistic modelling and began to study early Greek and Gothic sculpture for its more stylized forms. He did both sculpture and decorative paintings in the Théâtre des Champs-Élysées, Paris, but his major work is the *Virgin of Alsace*, an enormous statue on a mountain in the Vosges, the sketch for which is in Edinburgh. There is a Musée Bourdelle in Paris, and other works in the Mus. d'Orsay.

BOURDON, Sébastien (1616–71), was born in Montpellier and spent his early years in Paris and Bordeaux. He served in the army until 1634, when he went to Rome; there he imitated current styles – the landscapes of CLAUDE, the genre subjects of CASTIGLIONE, and BAMBOCCIATE, the speciality of Dutch and Flemish painters in Italy. One such subject, a KORTEGAARDJE, is in London (Dulwich). In1637 he returned to Paris, visiting Venice on the way, and continued along the same lines before turning to large religious and classical subjects in a more Baroque manner, with a Venetian richness of handling, though the influence of POUSSIN eventually subdued their exuberance. In 1652 he went to Sweden as Court portraitist to Queen Christina, and after her abdication and his return to Paris in 1654 he continued to paint portraits with great success. The years 1659–63 were spent in Montpellier, but he was finally compelled to leave through the jealousy of local artists, and he passed his remaining years in Paris. His late works show strong influence from Poussin, but with tenderness, charm and cool colour. There are pictures in Amsterdam, Cambridge (Fitzwm), Greenville SC (Bob Jones Univ.), The Hague, Hartford Conn. (Wadsworth), Lawrence Kansas, London (NG), Madrid (Prado), Montpellier, Montreal, Munich, Paris (Louvre), Providence RI, Sarasota Fla (Ringling), Stockholm and elsewhere.

BOUTS, Dieric (*c.*1415–75), was a Netherlandish painter, born in Haarlem, but active in Louvain – where he died – by 1457, and probably before 1448. His rather skinny figures are stiff and unemotional, but his treatment of light and landscape is of great beauty and delicacy, especially in colour. With Roger van der WEYDEN, who influenced him strongly , he was a major influence on German 15th-century painting. The only works certainly by him are a series of *Mystic Meals* (1464–8, S. Pierre, Louvain) and the large pair of *Justice Scenes* (Brussels), one of which was unfinished at his death and may have been completed by Hugo van der GOES. An *Entombment* (London, NG) is painted in tempera on linen, a technique known to have been used in the Netherlands, but of which very few examples have survived, since such works are far more delicate than oil paintings on panel. In 1957 a large *Crucifixion* (now in Brussels), in the same technique, was discovered and it seemed likely that there would have been three more small scenes to go with the London *Entombment*, forming wings to the central *Crucifixion*. Since then, a *Resurrection* (Pasadena Cal., Simon Mus.) and an *Annunciation* (Getty Mus., Malibu) have appeared, and an *Adoration of the Magi* is said to be in Switzerland. Doubts have been expressed about the authenticity of these, and the situation is still (in 1988) unclear. Bouts had a great influence – like his fellow Dutchmen OUWATER and the MASTER OF THE VIRGO INTER VIRGINES – on the beginnings of woodcut book-illustration. He was also a fine portrait painter, as is shown by the *Man* (1462, London, NG). Other works are in Bruges, Lille, Madrid, New York (Met. Mus.), Paris (Louvre), Philadelphia and elsewhere.

His two sons, Dieric II (*c.*1448–90/1) and Aelbrecht (*c.*1460–1549) were also painters. Nothing is known for certain by Dieric II, but a fine altarpiece known as *The Pearl of Brabant* (Munich) has been attributed to him, as well as to his father. Aelbrecht's principal work is an *Assumption* in Brussels.

BOYD, Arthur (*b.*1920), is an Australian Expressionist painter. He was born in Australia and worked with his family, including running a workshop for ceramic sculpture, until 1959, when he settled in England. He is represented in several Australian galleries.

BOYS, Thomas Shotter (1803–74), was a topographical draughtsman and the first artist to exploit chromolithography. He was born in London, but went to Paris in 1823, where he became a friend of BONINGTON, who influenced him in making topographical drawings in watercolour: both men were influenced by GIRTIN's 'Picturesque Views in Paris', published posthumously in 1803.

Boys learned the new technique of lithography in Paris in the 1830s before returning to London in 1837. He made many architectural lithographs for picturesque travel books, but his major achievements were 'Picturesque Architecture in Paris, Ghent . . .', (1839) in which lithographs were printed in oil-colours from multiple stones in a process called chromolithography (cf. BAXTER Prints), and 'London As It Is' (1842), for which he reverted to monochrome lithography with a few examples hand-coloured. There are works in Cambridge (Fitzwm), Liverpool, London (BM, Tate, V&A and Courtauld Inst.), Paris (Carnavalet) and elsewhere.

BOZZETTO (Ital. sketch), or MAQUETTE. Usually applied to models for sculpture, but can also be used for painted sketches, though these are more often called MODELLI.

BRAMANTE (1444?–1514), the greatest architect of the High Renaissance in Rome, and the rival of Michelangelo and Raphael, began as a painter. He was trained by PIERO della Francesca and MANTEGNA, and his earliest works, a ruined fresco in Bergamo (1477), an engraving of 1481 and some fresco fragments in Milan (Brera), reflect these influences. A *Christ at the Column* (Milan, Brera) is also attributed to him.

BRAMANTINO, Bartolomeo Suardi called (*c.*1465–1530), was a Milanese painter who married a rich wife in 1504 (and is thus recorded in many fiscal documents), but whose artistic career is obscure. He worked in the Vatican in 1508, possibly on some project before Raphael arrived, and in Milan for the Trivulzio and Sforza families. He was briefly exiled by the French in 1525, but after their expulsion he returned to work for the Sforzas. The similarity of his nickname to that of BRAMANTE makes it likely that there was some connection: indeed, the surviving fragments of Bramante's paintings, and their links with Mantegna, find echoes in Bramantino's highly personal art, which is deliberately anti-LEONARDO, and therefore singular in 16th-century Milan. There are works in Milan and in Lombard churches as well as Boston, Cologne, London (NG) and elsewhere.

BRANCUSI, Constantin (1876–1957), was a Romanian sculptor, whose most successful works are often simple, highly-polished shapes. He settled in Paris in 1904 and was influenced by RODIN, but by 1907 was more concerned with abstract shapes: he was a friend of MODIGLIANI and induced him to turn to sculpture. He exhibited at the ARMORY SHOW in New York in 1913, and was involved in a notorious case in 1926–8, when the US Customs refused to admit a work of his as sculpture, claiming it to be turned metal and thus dutiable. In 1937 he began a column, some 90 feet high, at Tirgu Jiu, near his birthplace in Romania, where he subsequently made three more very large monuments. This group is said to constitute his masterpiece. On his death he bequeathed many works to France, on condition that his studio be kept intact: it has been reconstituted in the Musée d'Art Moderne in Paris. There is also a large collection of his works in Philadelphia, and others in London (Tate) and the Museums of Modern Art in New York and Paris.

BRANGWYN, Sir Frank (1867–1956), was a Welsh painter of huge mural decorations, usually with many figures executed in a brilliantly colourful handling. He became an RA in 1919, and was knighted in 1941. There are examples of his decorations in the City of London (Skinners' Hall, Royal Exchange, Lloyd's Register), Cleveland Ohio (the Court House), Missouri State Capitol and New York (the Rockefeller Center, replacing one by RIVERA). After many troubles his projected decorations for the House of Lords ended up in the Guild Hall, Swansea. Most British museums have an example of his paintings or his large and important etchings (he was unusual in using zinc, rather than copper, plates). Bruges (his birthplace) and Orange in the South of France have museums devoted to his work.

BRAQUE, Georges (1882–1963), learned to paint as an apprentice in his family firm of decorators, which gave him a good grasp of technique. He was at the École des Beaux-Arts in Le Havre and, later, in Paris, but preferred to work on his own. He was friendly with Dufy and Friesz (both were from Le Havre) and by 1906 was in the FAUVE circle; by 1909 he knew PICASSO well, and with him had started to work out the basis of a new approach to painting which developed into CUBISM. By the outbreak of war in 1914 this close collaboration was at an end. Braque was called-up immediately, severely wounded in 1915, and was unable to resume painting until 1917, when he tried to pick up Synthetic Cubism where he had left off. Picasso, meanwhile, as a Spaniard not liable for military service, had gone his own way. By 1920/1 Braque had evolved a less arbitrary spatial composition and an acknowledgement of the real world which led to the ample and vigorous still-life and figure compositions, with a complete balance and harmony between colour and design, which he continued to develop for the rest of his life. In 1952–3 he was commissioned to paint three ceilings in the Etruscan Room of the Louvre. He also executed a certain amount of sculpture, incised plaster plaques and plaster reliefs. There is a small body of graphic work – between forty and fifty lithographs, some woodcut book-illustrations and some etchings for which the drawings were originally produced in 1931 as illustrations for Hesiod's 'Theogony'. There are works in Basle, Buffalo NY, Chicago, Cleveland Ohio, Copenhagen, Detroit, Edinburgh, Frankfurt (Städel), Glasgow, Le Havre, Los Angeles, London (Tate), New York (M of MA and Guggenheim), Ottawa, Oxford, Paris (Mus. d'Art Moderne and Petit Pal.), Philadelphia, Prague, San Francisco, Stockholm, Toledo Ohio, Washington (NG and Phillips) and many French museums.

BRAY, Jan de (*c.*1626/7–97), was the son and pupil of Salomon. He worked in Haarlem, and was much influenced by HELST, as well as by HALS. His best works are portraits and portrait groups, such as the *Regents of the Children's Hospital* (1663, Haarlem), which clearly shows the influence of similar group portraits by REMBRANDT (e.g. the *Staal Meesters*, 1662), and Hals, but is much less free in handling. He also painted some more consciously poetical works, such as *Antony and Cleopatra* (1669, replicas in the Royal Coll. and Nuremberg). These works show him, like LIEVENS and MAES, aping the Grand Manner of contemporary French historical painting. Other works are in Amsterdam (Rijksmus.), Edinburgh (NG), London (NG) and Worcester Mass.

BRAY, Salomon de (1597–1664), was an Amsterdam painter, poet and architect, who settled in Haarlem *c.*1625. He was the pupil of GOLTZIUS, whose manner he occasionally imitated, but his portraits, like those by his son Jan, are often close to HALS. There are works by him in Bristol, Dresden, The Hague (1651, decorations for the House in the Wood) and London (V&A).

BREAKFAST PIECE. A form of Netherlandish STILL-LIFE developed mainly in

Haarlem *c.*1620, in which a table is laid with a snack (*Ontbijt*) of bread, cheese, beer or wine in a glass, and similar simple fare. The type was developed notably by CLAESZ. and HEDA; later, more elaborate meals with nautilus shells, lobsters, silver dishes and goblets are known as BANCKET (Banquet) PIECES, and the climax of ostentatious display is reached with a *Pronkstilleven* (Dutch, showy still-life).

BREENBERGH, Bartholomeus (1599/1600–57), was a Dutch landscape painter who went to Italy *c.*1619/20 and spent several years in Rome, where he knew Paul BRIL and was influenced by ELSHEIMER. His paintings are usually small, with small figures, often mythological, in a landscape dotted with Roman ruins; he also made etchings of similar subjects. He had returned to Holland by 1633. There are works in Amsterdam (Rijksmus.) Antwerp, The Hague, London (NG and Dulwich), Munich, Paris and elsewhere.

BREGNO, Andrea (1421–1506), was a North Italian sculptor, born near Como, who from the 1460s became the most popular sculptor of his day in Rome, with a large workshop (which included MINO da Fiesole) producing principally grand WALL-TOMBS, which make up in the quality of their execution for their stereotyped design. The chief examples, all in Rome, are in S.M. in Aracoeli, S.M. sopra Minerva, S.M. del Popolo and SS. Apostoli.

Antonio Bregno (active 1425 to after 1457) also came from near Como, and, after executing sculpture in the Ca' d' Oro in Venice in 1425–6, he apparently joined the BUON workshop. He was largely responsible for the Arco Foscari on the Doge's Palace, and the Foscari Tomb (S.M. dei Frari, *c.*1457) with Antonio RIZZO.

BRETON, André (1896–1966), trained as a doctor and discovered Freud's theories of the unconscious while working with psychiatric cases in the First World War. He evolved a theory of art and literature based on psychoanalysis which had great influence through the Surrealist Manifestoes of 1924, 1930 and 1942. *See* SURREALISM.

BREU, Jörg (*c.*1475–1537), was a painter and designer of woodcuts who worked in Austria 1496–1502, but settled in Augsburg in 1502 and came under the influence of HOLBEIN the Elder and BURGKMAIR. There are works by him in Augsburg, Basle, Berlin, Herzogenburg in Lower Austria (an altarpiece dated 1501), London (Courtauld Inst.), Melk, Munich, San Diego Cal. and Vienna.

BREUGHEL *see* BRUEGEL.

BRIL (Brill), Mattheus (1550–83) and Paul (1554–1626), were brothers, born in Antwerp, who both worked in Rome and painted landscapes which form the link between the panoramic views of PATENIER or even Bruegel, and the ideal landscape evolved by Poussin and Claude. Mattheus was in Rome by about 1570 and painted several large frescoes, including the *Seasons* in the Vatican, but he died young and much of his work was completed by Paul, who also succeeded him in the Papal favour. Paul seems to have followed his brother to Italy *c.*1574, and was certainly in Rome in 1582. He also painted frescoes, including the landscapes in the Casino Rospigliosi, Rome, accompanying Guido RENI's *Aurora*; but he is best known for his small easel pictures on copper, many of which are deeply influenced by ELSHEIMER (at whose wedding in 1606 Bril was a witness). TASSI, later to become Claude's master, was probably his pupil. His influence was also widely spread by his engravings. Among his pictures (some of which are signed with a pair of spectacles – *brille*) are examples in Amsterdam, Antwerp, Basle, Berlin, Birmingham, Bradford, Brussels, Dresden, Dunedin NZ, Edinburgh, Florence (Uffizi and Pitti), Glasgow, Leeds, London (NG and Wellington Mus.), Milan, Munich, Paris (Louvre), Rome (Gall. Naz. and Borghese), Stockholm, the Vatican and Vienna.

BROAD MANNER *see* FINE MANNER.

BROEDERLAM, Melchior (active 1381–*d.*1409 or later), was a painter in Ypres who became Painter to Philip the Bold, Duke of Burgundy, in 1385 and was in Paris 1390/3. In 1392 he was commissioned to paint two wings for an altarpiece, which he completed in 1399 (Dijon): this is probably the earliest example of INTERNATIONAL GOTHIC.

BRONZE was used as a material for sculpture in ancient Greece and Rome, as well as in Africa and China, but the art of casting seems to have become almost lost in the Middle Ages, when effigies were made by hammering thin plates of bronze on to a wooden core. The *St Peter* (Rome, St Peter's), attributed to Arnolfo di Cambio, is one of the earliest modern cast bronzes on a big scale, but by the early 15th century the craft was well established in the hands of masters like Ghiberti. Modern bronzes are made either in sand moulds or by the *cire perdue* method, both these techniques being very ancient. Sand casting is done by simply making a mould of special sand from the original PLASTER model, inserting a core, and pouring in the molten bronze. *Cire perdue* (Fr. lost wax) is economical of bronze because it employs a model which is a few millimetres smaller in all directions than the enclosing mould, the space between being filled with wax and with vent-pipes inserted at various points. The outer side of the wax is exactly what the finished bronze should look like, and molten bronze is poured through the top vent, taking the place of the wax which has previously been melted out. The quantity of wax run out serves as a guide to the amount of bronze needed. Any number of such casts can be made. In Renaissance times it was usual to work on the casts with files and chasers, polishing and engraving the surface as well as removing flaws, but it is now the fashion to prefer a rough surface, showing the thumb-marks of the original clay model. Patina is the lovely greenish tint and matt surface which age and chemical reaction have imparted to Greek bronzes, but which is now artificially created by chemical means: a peculiarly vivid green patina is characteristic of Epstein's work.

BRONZINO, Agnolo (1503–72), was a Florentine painter who was the pupil and adopted son of PONTORMO. He is traditionally said to be the boy sitting on the steps in Pontormo's *Joseph in Egypt* (London, NG), and he certainly seems to have looked after Pontormo in his neurotic old age, as well as completing his frescoes in S. Lorenzo, Florence, in 1556–8. Bronzino became Court Painter to Cosimo I de' Medici, the first Grand Duke of Tuscany, and was one of the most important Mannerist portrait painters, concentrating on expressing an inhuman elegance and self-restraint in his sitters, totally unlike the nervous sensibility of Pontormo. He was influenced by Michelangelo – like everyone of his generation – but he learned from him little but tricks of foreshortening. His few religious works are highly-wrought and devoid of any kind of feeling; but his *Venus, Cupid, Time and Folly* (London, NG) has a kind of icy obscenity. Most of his works are still in Florence; others are in

Antwerp (Mayer van den Bergh), Berlin, Boston (Gardner), Budapest, Chicago, Cincinnati, Cleveland Ohio, Detroit, London, Madrid, Milan, New York (Met. Mus. and Frick), Ottawa, Oxford, Paris, Pisa (S. Stefano), Rome (Gall. Naz. and Borghese), Toledo Ohio, Vienna, Washington and Worcester Mass.

BROOKING, Charles (1723?–59), was an early British marine painter (but cf. SCOTT), influenced by such earlier Dutch painters as Willem van de VELDE I and II. His large painting of all the ships of the Royal Navy (1754) is in London (Coram Fdn) and others are in Glasgow, Hull and London (Tate and Nat. Marit. Mus.).

BROUWER, Adriaen (1605/6–38), was the link between Flemish and Dutch genre painting. He was born in Flanders, but spent some time in Holland, and may have been a pupil of Frans Hals. His pictures, apart from a few landscapes, represent sordid tavern scenes, usually with boors carousing. He himself lived like that, and has been compared with Villon in consequence. His earliest works may start from the village scenes of BRUEGEL, and he may have known one of Bruegel's sons before going to Amsterdam in 1625, and on to Haarlem, where he met Hals. In 1631/2 he was in the Guild in Antwerp and came under the influence of Rubens, who in turn admired him. His political activities led in 1633 to imprisonment, where the prison baker was Joos van Craesbeck who became his pupil and imitator. Brouwer's best works are comparable with those of STEEN and David TENIERS II (both of whom were influenced by him), and have a delicacy of colour combined with a breadth of handling that compensate for his subjects, in which his most fervent admirers see an almost Rembrandtesque pathos. The best collection of his works is in Munich; others are in Amsterdam, Antwerp, Berlin, Brussels, Dresden, Frankfurt, Haarlem, The Hague, Leipzig, London (N G, V&A, Wallace Coll., Wellington Mus. and Dulwich), Madrid (Prado), New York (Met. Mus.), Paris (Louvre and Petit Pal.), Philadelphia (Johnson), Rotterdam, Vienna (Akad.) and York.

BROWN, Ford Madox (1821–93), was born in Calais, and studied in Belgium, Paris (1840–4) and Rome (1845–6), where he met OVERBECK and other NAZARENE artists, and was strongly influenced by their use of clear colour and medieval subject matter, which reinforced the teaching he had received in Belgium. He came to England in 1846, and his *Wycliffe* (Bradford, with preparatory sketch) of 1847–8 so impressed ROSSETTI that he asked to become his pupil. This brought Brown into the orbit of the PRE-RAPHAELITE BROTHERHOOD; although he never became a member of the Brotherhood he had much in common with them, notably painting out of doors and developing an interest in contemporary genre subjects, such as his evocative *The Last of England* (1852–5, Birmingham), inspired by the emigration to the Colonies in the mid-19th century. In 1852–65 he executed the large *Work* for Manchester Town Hall, saying of it: 'The British excavator . . . in the full swing of his activity . . . appeared to me . . . at least as worthy of the powers of an English painter as the fisherman of the Adriatic, the peasant of the Campagna, or the Neapolitan *lazzarone*.' There are other works in Liverpool, London (Tate, V&A), Melbourne, Sydney (*Chaucer Reading His Poems to Edward III*, one of the several versions of his painting for the Houses of Parliament, 1848 onwards) and Yale (C B A).

BROWN, Mather (1761–1831), was born in Boston and studied under STUART in 1773, during Stuart's visit to America. Brown arrived in London in 1781 and then studied under WEST, exhibiting at the RA from 1782 until he died in 1831. He painted George III and Queen Charlotte, but was never very successful, as he was overshadowed by his fellow-Americans, West and COPLEY. There are examples in London (NPG), New York (Met. Mus.) and other US museums.

BRÜCKE, Die (The Bridge), was the name taken by a group founded in 1905 in Dresden by E. L. KIRCHNER, K. SCHMIDT-ROTTLUFF, Erich HECKEL and F. Bleyl. There was no particular programme, but the name was chosen to indicate their desire to link like-minded artists. The group style, however, was that of EXPRESSIONISM and was manifested in forms very close to those of FAUVISM, since they admired the works of Gauguin, van Gogh, Munch and MATISSE. The group broke up in 1913, but it had exerted considerable influence on public taste, and was particularly important in the revival of woodcut and other graphic arts. *See also* BLAUE REITER, Der.

BRUEGEL, Jan I (1568–1625), called 'Velvet Bruegel', was the younger son of Pieter I and brother of Pieter II. Like his father, he visited Italy. He was in Naples in 1590, met BRIL in Rome in 1591, and worked for Cardinal Borromeo in Milan in the 1590s before returning to Antwerp in 1596. He was Court Painter to the Regents Albert and Isabella and was a successful painter of landscape and still-life in a highly detailed style which was much admired by contemporaries. Rubens collaborated with him and painted a portrait of him and his family (London, Courtauld Inst.). There are pictures in London (NG and Wellington Mus.), Madrid, New York (Met. Mus.), Oxford and many other museums. His son, Jan II (1601–78), was also a painter.

BRUEGEL (Brueghel, Breughel), Pieter I (*c.*1525/30–69), sometimes also called 'Peasant Bruegel', was the most important satirist in the Netherlands after BOSCH and one of the greatest of landscape painters. The date of his birth may be guessed at from the fact that he became Master in the Antwerp Guild in 1551: immediately after this he went to France and Italy (*c.*1552), travelling as far south as Sicily. He was in Rome in 1553 and returned over the Alps, probably in 1554. The Alps, and to a lesser extent the scenery of Italy, made a deep impression on him, as may be seen from the drawings he made on the journey and also from the whole development of his landscape style. The art of Italy seems to have made little impact on him. On his return he began to make drawings for engravers, very much in the manner of Bosch and dealing with the same subjects. His earliest dated painting is of 1553, and in the last ten or twelve years of his life he produced the genre scenes and the religious subjects set in vast landscapes which are his finest works. The old nickname 'Peasant Bruegel' is misleading if it is held to mean that he was himself a peasant: on the contrary, he was highly cultivated and is known to have enjoyed the friendship of humanists and the patronage of the Emperor's representative, Cardinal Granvella. Later, many of his finest works belonged to Rudolf II. His attitude, and that of his patrons, is hard to define since it is not simply condescending but seems to show a real interest in village customs coupled with a satirical approach to drunkenness, gluttony and other sins of the flesh. Some pictures – for example the *Massacre of the Innocents* – have been held to be veiled allusions to the Spanish Fury and the subjection of the Netherlands in general, and it has also been suggested that Bruegel's move from Antwerp to Brussels *c.*1563 was due to his membership of a heretical sect and fear of persecution. Yet he was certainly patronized by Cardinal Granvella, and Brussels was the centre of orthodoxy and of government. The great series of the *Months* (or *Seasons*) consists of five pictures (now in Vienna, Prague and New York), all but one dated 1565. They have no moral message comparable with his earlier works, such as the *Fall of the Rebel Angels* or the *Dulle Griet*, but they are among the great landscape paintings of the age, influenced by PATENIER and even Titian, but surpassing both in their feeling for nature and the unity of man and his surroundings. The best collection of his works is in Vienna (K-H Mus.), but there are others in the Royal Coll. and in Antwerp (Musée van den Bergh), Berlin, Boston, Brussels, Budapest, Darmstadt, Detroit, London (NG and Courtauld Inst.), Madrid (Prado), Munich, Naples, New York (Frick Coll.), Paris (Louvre), Philadelphia, Rome (Doria), Rotterdam, Upton House nr Banbury (National Trust) and Washington (NG).

BRUEGEL, Pieter II (*c.*1564–1638), called 'Hell Bruegel', was the son of Pieter I and elder brother of Jan. He frequently copied his father's works and was the master of SNYDERS and, presumably, of his own son, Pieter III.

BRUGGHEN, H. ter, *see* TERBRUGGHEN.

BRUNELLESCHI, Filippo (1377–1446), trained as a goldsmith and sculptor in Florence, making various figures and reliefs (the Silver Altar, *c.*1399, in Pistoia Cath., has been attributed to him). He was deeply interested in PERSPECTIVE, and is credited with the invention of the COSTRUZIONE LEGITTIMA. He competed in 1401 for the second pair of doors for the Baptistry in Florence, but the commission went to GHIBERTI. His competition piece, the *Sacrifice of Isaac*, is believed to be the one in the Bargello in Florence, together with Ghiberti's. After this, he went to Rome (possibly with the young DONATELLO), and was inspired to turn to architecture, becoming the major architect of the Early Renaissance in Florence.

BRUSHWORK. With the development of the technique of oil-painting it soon became clear that the use of stiff bristle brushes charged with sticky oil paint and applied to a grainy surface such as canvas gives a special texture and quality of handling which is aesthetically pleasing in itself, independently of its function in representing form. A painter's brushwork is as personal as his handwriting (and is sometimes so referred to) – and it is even harder to imitate. The encrustations of Rembrandt, the frenzied drama of the actual strokes of van Gogh's brush, the thin films of Gainsborough, the gem-like luminosity of Vermeer's small dabs of paint: all these are possible in one and the same medium, so that brushwork is one of the painter's most powerful tools in the creation of his own world. In some cases it becomes the end rather than the means, as in certain forms of Abstract Impressionism, where the word can perhaps hardly be legitimately applied to paint trickled, rather than brushed, onto the ground.

BRUSTOLON, Andrea (1662–1732), was the leading Venetian woodcarver of the 18th century. Most of his elaborate altarpieces are in churches in and around his native Belluno, but there is a complete altarpiece, together with the original terracotta *bozzetto* in London (V&A).

BRUYN, Barthel (1492/3–1555), was a Cologne painter, chiefly of portraits. His religious works are much influenced by Netherlandish painters of the late 15th century, and his portraits, which are grimly realistic representations of unaristocratic sitters, are very close to those of JOOS van Cleve. In 1515–16 he is documented as a painter of altarpieces, and the Xanten Altar was commissioned in 1529. His career, 1515–55, invites parallels with HOLBEIN and LUCAS van Leyden, although a beautiful *Nativity* of 1516 (Frankfurt) is closer to GEERTGEN. There are works in Cologne (Mus. and churches), churches in Essen and Xanten, and in Antwerp, Basle, Berlin, Brussels, Cambridge Mass. (Busch-Reisinger), Copenhagen, Dresden, Frankfurt (Städel), Göteborg, Gotha, The Hague, Hanover, Leipzig, London (NG, Courtauld Inst.), Munich, New York (Met. Mus.), Oberlin Ohio, Ottawa, Paris (Louvre), Prague, Siena, Toronto, Vienna, York and several other German museums.

BRZESKA *see* GAUDIER.

BUECKELAER (Beuckelaer), Joachim (*c.*1530/35–1573/4), was the nephew by marriage and pupil of AERTSEN, and painted very similar still-life pictures with ostensibly religious subjects. He often worked as a journeyman for other artists, but became a master in the Antwerp Guild in 1560. His first dated work is of 1561. There are works in Amsterdam (Rijksmus.), Antwerp (Mus. and Mus. Mayer van den Bergh), Brussels, Florence (Uffizi), Genoa, Hull, Paris (Louvre), Stockholm, Vienna and York (The Treasurer's House).

BUFFET, Bernard (*b.*1928), is a French painter of extreme precocity who made his name as early as 1948. During the 1950s he was put forward as the principal figurative painter in Paris, and was much influenced by the 1940s movement known as *Misérabilisme*, of which GRUBER was also an exponent. Sad greys, thin spiky forms, and an obtrusively angular signature characterize his style. In later years he has painted views of London, Paris and New York, as well as a series of *Toreadors* and *St Joan of Arc*. There are works in Cincinnati, London (Tate), New York (Brooklyn), Paris (Mus. d'Art Moderne) and Toronto.

BUON, Bartolommeo (*c.*1374–1464/7), was the son of a sculptor, Giovanni (*d.*1443). Between them they ran the leading Venetian sculpture workshop of the first half of the Quattrocento. Bartolommeo worked at the Ca' d' Oro 1422–34, and made the tympanum of the Scuola di San Marco in 1437. His work was strongly influenced by South German sculpture, and most of it is in Venice (e.g. Porta della Carta, Doge's Palace), but there is a *Madonna della Misericordia* (1441–5) in London (V&A).

BURGKMAIR, Hans (1473–1531), was an Augsburg painter who was not influenced by Dürer but, like him, formed his style by contact with Venetian art. He soon surpassed the elder Holbein and also had a good connection with publishers, designing woodcuts (*see* KLEINMEISTER). He was patronized by the Emperor Maximilian. There are works in Augsburg, Cologne, Munich, Nuremberg, Vienna and elsewhere.

BURIN or Graver. The principal tool used in ENGRAVING on wood or metal to plough the lines out of the surface of the plate or block.

BURNE-JONES, Sir Edward (1833–98), was one of the painters in the circle round William MORRIS and ROSSETTI, by whom he was greatly influenced. He travelled in Italy in 1859, and was in Milan and Venice in 1862 with Ruskin, for whom he copied works by Tintoretto: he himself had considerable influence on Italian painters of the turn of the century, mainly through his decorations (including mosaics) in S. Paolo entro le Mura, Rome. He produced many designs for William Morris's firm for tapestries and stained glass (e.g. S.

Martin's, Brampton, Cumbria, or Middleton Cheney church, Northants., which also has glass by Morris and F. M. BROWN). These and his paintings evoke a dreamy, romantic, literary never-never land of Botticelli and Mantegna, executed in a flat technique and a colour aptly described by the phrase 'greenery-yallery Grosvenor Gallery'. He was made a baronet in 1894. There is a large collection of his works in his native Birmingham (including four of *Pygmalion*), and a room, including the *Perseus* series, in Stuttgart. Other works are in Cardiff, London (Tate), Paris (Mus. d'Orsay), Sarasota Fla, and Yale (CBA), as well as many English provincial museums.

BURR *see* ENGRAVING 2(b).

BURRI, Alberto (*b*.1915), an Italian abstract painter, began by practising medicine, but started painting in a prisoner-of-war camp in Texas in 1944. He settled in Rome in 1945, exhibited in New York in 1954, and received a prize at the Venice Biennale in 1960. His works are not so much paintings as compositions in patched sacking with an occasional blob of colour. There are examples in London (Tate) and New York (Guggenheim).

BUSHNELL, John (*d*.1701), fled from England because of matrimonial troubles and went to Rome. He worked in Italy, France, and Flanders before settling in Venice, where he made the huge monument to Alvise Mocenigo in S. Lazzaro dei Mendicanti. He returned to England after twenty-two years, but his impossible pride and conceit suggest that he had become mentally unbalanced. He executed a number of tombs, including two in Westminster Abbey and one in Mid Lavant church, Sussex, and a bust of Mrs Pepys (St Olave's, in the City of London), but his work is very uneven in quality. A terracotta bust of Charles II (Cambridge, Fitzwm) is attributed to him.

BUTLER, Reg (1913–81), one of the leading 20th-century British sculptors, was originally an architect and also worked as a blacksmith, 1941–5. Most of his work is in metal, either forged or cast. He won the 1953 competition for a monument to the Unknown Political Prisoner, and produced another version in 1957. His first one-man show was in 1949. The works of this period were all Constructivist, but in the late 1950s he returned to figurative work with a series of highly realistic female nudes, the latest of which were in painted bronze with real hair. He also wrote a short book on the processes of artistic creation ('Creative Development', 1962). There are works in Aberdeen, Cologne, London (Tate), New York (M of MA) and Ottawa.

BYLERT (Bijlert), Jan van (1597/8?–1671), was an UTRECHT painter who was the pupil of BLOEMAERT and then went to France and Italy (he was in Rome in 1621), returning to Utrecht by 1625. His work between 1620 and 1630 is based directly on Caravaggio's in subject and handling; after *c*.1630 he used much lighter and brighter colours and chose subjects which have a certain pastoral prettiness, as well as painting some portraits. There are works in Amsterdam (Rijksmus.), Belfast, Berlin, Brunswick, Budapest, Cardiff, Cassel, Greenville SC, London (NG), Lyons, Oslo, Rotterdam, Sydney, Utrecht (Mus.) and elsewhere.

C

CABINET PICTURE. A small easel painting, usually of a genre subject, still-life or landscape, not more than about 3 feet across, and often less. The minor Dutch and Flemish masters were the principal painters of this best kind of furniture picture.

CAFFÀ, Melchiorre (1635–67), was born in Malta (where his name is given variously as Cafà or Gafà). He was the pupil and assistant of Ercole FERRATA, and was never either a pupil or assistant of BERNINI, yet his style is similar in its astonishing virtuosity in the expression of religious ecstasy. His marble reliefs and figure groups display an exalted sensibility which exceeds even Bernini's own, and his masterpiece, the *Ecstasy of St Catherine of Siena* (Rome, S. Caterina a Monte Magnanapoli) is obviously based on Bernini's *St Teresa.* Caffà's very short life – only 10 working years – meant that many of his works were finished by others. There are also works in Roman churches (S. Agostino and S. Agnese in Piazza Navona), in Lima Peru and in Malta. A signed bronze bust of *Alexander VII* is in New York (Met. Mus.).

CAILLEBOTTE, Gustave (1848–94), was an engineer and amateur painter who met MONET and RENOIR at Argenteuil in 1874. He adopted Impressionist ideas, and helped materially by buying pictures; at his death he left sixty-five works to the state. Renoir was his executor, and, despite Caillebotte's provision that the bequest must be accepted as a whole, he was forced to agree to partial acceptance only, to avoid a total rejection. Eight out of sixteen Monets, seven of eighteen Pissarros, six of eight Renoirs, six of nine Sisleys, two of three Manets, two of four Cézannes, but all seven Degas, were eventually accepted. This was the first entry of Impressionist works into a State museum, and as late as this an academic painter could still refer to Impressionist pictures as 'filth'. There are now four paintings by Caillebotte himself in the Musée d'Orsay, Paris, but his masterpiece is the *Paris Street* (1877, Chicago).

CALDER, Alexander (1898–1976), was an American sculptor, abstract painter, and illustrator of children's books. He was originally an engineer, and his main inventions – STABILES (so named by ARP) and MOBILES (so named by DUCHAMP) both dating from 1931/2 – can be regarded as a marriage between engineering and sculpture. His paintings were influenced by MIRÓ. He said that he wanted to make 'moving MONDRIANS'. Most of his works are in America, but there is a large one in the UNESCO building in Paris (1945) and a Stabile was made for the Montreal Expo in 1967; two large works in the US are at Kennedy Airport, New York, and in Washington (NG). There is a Mobile of 1959 in Leeds, and others in Edinburgh (NG) and London (Tate).

CALLCOTT, Sir Augustus Wall (1779–1844), was born only four years after Turner, whose chief follower and imitator he became, especially in the Dutch-inspired landscapes and seapieces (*see also* STANFIELD). He entered the RA Schools in 1797, became an ARA in 1806 and RA in 1810. He was in Paris in 1815, visited the Continent in 1818 and 1824, and in 1827–8 he spent his honeymoon in Germany and Italy, his wife being Maria Graham. She was herself an artist (drawings in the BM) and a prolific writer on art and travel. She wrote the first monograph on Poussin in English (1820), and in 1826 had published three volumes on 'Rome in the Nineteenth Century'.

Together they studied the works of art and met most of the artists of the day, including CORNELIUS, FRIEDRICH and OVERBECK. Callcott was also a friend of DYCE, and sat on the Schools of Design Board, but failed to become PRA in 1830, on the death of Lawrence. He was knighted in 1837 and became Surveyor of the Royal Collection in 1843. Towards the end of his life he painted historical and genre subjects, but his earlier Turneresque landscapes are his best works. There are examples in Coventry, Hamburg, Leeds, London (RA, Tate, V&A and Soane Mus.), Manchester (Whitworth), Nottingham, Yale (CBA) and York.

CALLIGRAPHIC is an adjective applied to an artist's HANDLING. In drawing it means freely and rhythmically treated, with pen squiggles like handwriting – calligraphy is literally 'beautiful handwriting'. In painting it means free and loose BRUSHWORK.

CALLOT, Jacques (1592/3–1635), was one of the greatest of etchers and produced some 1,500 plates. He was born in Lorraine, at Nancy, and went to Rome at some time between 1608 and 1611, when he went to Florence. There he made many etchings of fairs and festivals, as well as of courtiers, beggars and hunchbacks, many of them based on *Commedia dell' arte* types. In 1621 he returned to Nancy, where his work took a more serious turn, culminating in his masterpiece, the *Grandes Misères de la Guerre* of 1633, which was at least partly inspired by Richelieu's invasion of Lorraine. It is a terrifying record of the savagery of the Thirty Years War, comparable with Goya's later *Desastres*.

CALRAET, Abraham van (1642–1722), was a Dordrecht painter, who may have been a pupil of CUYP. The close similarity between some of Calraet's small pictures and those of Cuyp has led to a great deal of confusion and misattribution, some of it deliberate. The initials AC apply equally to both, but the still-life pictures so signed are certainly Calraet's and many of the stable-scenes are probably his. There are pictures in London (NG, Dulwich) which are signed AC and were previously attributed to Cuyp.

CALVAERT, Dionisio (Denis) (*c*.1545–1619), was an Antwerp painter who went to Italy *c*.1562. He eventually set up an Academy in Bologna and became the first master of RENI, ALBANI and DOMENICHINO; his Academy seems to have inspired the CARRACCI one. There are works by him in Bologna and other Italian museums, and in Edinburgh, Hull, Vienna and Worcester Mass.

CALVERT, Edward (1799–1883), joined the Navy as a young man and first exhibited at the RA in 1825. He met PALMER there in 1826, who described him as 'a prosperous, stalwart country gentleman . . . redolent of the sea, and in white trousers'. Between 1827 and 1831 he was deeply influenced by BLAKE and Palmer, but he lost his innocent eye and spent the rest of his long life absorbed in anti-Christian mythological musings. There are works by him in London (Tate) and Yale (CBA).

CAMAÏEU (Fr.). A form of GRISAILLE, defined in French as a painting imitating a bas-relief, painted in a single colour but in varied tones. *See also* CHIAROSCURO.

CAMBIO, Arnolfo di, *see* ARNOLFO.

CAMDEN TOWN GROUP. A small secession from the NEW ENGLISH ART CLUB, which later developed into the LONDON GROUP. GILMAN and GORE were the major figures in it, but the inspiration was SICKERT (the name comes from a district in N. London, where Sickert had a studio). The group is usually said to have introduced Post-Impressionism into England. Their works are well represented in Brighton, Exeter, Huddersfield, Leeds and Leicester, as well as London (Tate).

CAMERA OBSCURA, LUCIDA. A mechanical means of securing accuracy in drawing, particularly of topographical detail. The *camera obscura* (Lat. dark room) was invented in the 16th century, and consists of an arrangement of lenses and mirrors in a darkened tent or box. The view seen by the lens is reflected through the mirrors on to a sheet of paper, so that the draughtsman need do no more than trace round the outlines. CANALETTO is known to have made use of the machine in making studies for his VEDUTE, and its use was undoubtedly widespread – CARLEVARIS also used it. Drawings made in this way are sometimes recognizable by the distortions at the edges due to primitive lenses. A *camera lucida* is a more sophisticated optical instrument, incorporating a prism. Examples of these mechanisms can be seen in the Science Mus., London.

CAMPENDONK, Heinrich (1889–1957), was the youngest member of the BLAUE REITER, which MARC and KANDINSKY invited him to join in 1911. He emigrated to Holland in 1933 and taught in Amsterdam. Most of his works are woodcuts, but his paintings are rich in colour with small, puppet-like figures reminiscent of Chagall and the Russians.

CAMPIGLI, Massimo (1895–1971), was a Florentine painter who studied in Paris (1919–23), where he was influenced by the art of SEURAT, PICASSO and LÉGER. He was also influenced by archaic art – Cretan, Etruscan and Pompeian – and by Greco-Roman and Early Renaissance painting. The effect of Etruscan art changed his style, causing him to abandon perspective and the representation of volume, placing his silhouetted figures side by side or in rows one above the other without light and shade. His portraits and scenes of modern life were treated decoratively in pallid colours, with a dry surface texture like fresco. In Milan (1939–49) he executed mosaics, frescoes and lithographs. There are works in Rome (Gall. d'Arte Mod.) and other Italian museums.

CAMPIN, Robert (*c*.1375–1444), is known to have been a painter active in Tournai from 1406. No pictures are known certainly to be his, but he had two pupils, Jacques DARET and (probably) Roger van der WEYDEN: he may therefore be identical with the MASTER OF FLÉMALLE.

CAMPIONESI, Maestri. The artists grouped under this heading were Lombard sculptors, builders and stonemasons from the 12th century to the end of the 14th. They included masters of various families which appear to have been trained originally in the Provençal workshops of Arles (S. Trophime) and S. Gilles-du-Gard before spreading across N. Italy, into Switzerland and Austria, and as far south as Tuscany. Their style was strongly realistic and solid, with reminiscences of Late Roman and Early Christian art, largely derived from sarcophagi. Though some worked in Fidenza they remained independent of ANTELAMI; others working in Tuscany imperfectly assimilated forms derived from ARNOLFO. In the later part of the 14th century the most notable artist of the group was Bonino da Campione, who executed the tomb of Cangrande della Scala in Verona, *c*.1376.

CAMUCCINI, Vincenzo (1771–1844), was the leading Roman painter in the Neoclassical style in the early 19th century. He was the successor of MENGS in history painting and of BATONI in portraiture, and his emulation of DAVID makes him the later, Roman, equivalent of SUVÉE. His history-pictures of the *Death of Caesar*, 1798, and *Death of Virginia*, 1804, brought him fame. At the end of the century he painted a ceiling in the Villa Borghese, Rome, and in 1802 he was made a member of the Accademia di S. Luca, becoming Principe as early as 1806. He worked in Florence as well as Rome, and went to Munich and Paris during the Napoleonic period. There are works in Naples, Prague and Rome (including St Peter's).

CANALETTO, (Giovanni) Antonio (1697–1768), Venetian *vedutista*, went to Rome *c.*1719 (and probably again *c.*1740), where he was influenced in some not clearly definable way by PANINI. He had already worked as a scene-painter with his father, and was back in Venice by 1720, where he is recorded in the Guild (*Fraglia*) from 1720 until 1767. The earliest signed and dated work, recently discovered in a private collection in Milan, is a very large and very stagey *Architectural Capriccio* of 1723, which clearly reflects this training. In 1725–6 he painted four views of Venice for Stefano Conti of Lucca (private coll., Montreal), which are the first datable examples of the Venetian views for which he was to become famous. These have the strong contrasts of light and shade which made his name at the expense of CARLEVARIS (who may have been his master, though this is not likely). It is clear that these *vedute* were extremely unusual in that they were painted from nature, instead of from drawings, although he later abandoned this practice and returned to the traditional method of working from drawings made on the spot (*'dal vero'*), some of which were probably made with the help of a CAMERA OBSCURA; occasionally he even worked from etchings by Carlevaris. By 1726 he was already working for the English market, and by about 1730 he had come to an agreement with Joseph Smith, later British Consul in Venice, who had the pick of his output, arranged other sales, and probably forwarded his visit to England, which, with short intervals in Venice, lasted from 1746 until *c.*1756. He returned to Venice in 1750/1 and perhaps again in 1753, and was last recorded in England in 1755. During these years he painted many London views and some of other English scenes, notably Warwick Castle and Eton College, and also CAPRICCI. On his arrival he had some difficulty in establishing himself in London, and VERTUE observed that 'on the whole of him something is obscure or strange, he dos not produce work so well done as those of Venice or other parts of Italy . . . especially his figures in his works done here, are apparently much inferior to those done abroad, which are surprizeingly well done and with great freedom and variety – his water and skys at no time excellent or with natural freedom, and what he has done here his prospects of Trees woods or handling or pencilling of that part not various nor so skillful as might be expected . . . which has much strengthened a conjecture that he is not the veritable Cannalleti of Venice'. As a counter to this damaging gossip he advertised in a London newspaper in July 1749: 'Signor Canaletto hereby invites any gentleman . . . to see a picture done by him, being *A View of St James's Park*, which he hopes may . . . deserve their approbation . . .' The confusion was perhaps partly due to BELLOTTO's use of his uncle's name. During and after his English period Canaletto's style, as Vertue observed, became harder and tighter, losing much of the breadth and freedom of his earliest works. These later works were much imitated by English painters such as SCOTT and MARLOW (who also seems to have forged Bellottos). It should be noted, however, that the six pictures painted as late as *c*.1754 for Thomas Hollis (London, NG and Dulwich, and elsewhere) are all of excellent quality.

The Royal Coll. has the largest and best collection of Canaletto's works, with more than fifty paintings and over 140 drawings from Joseph Smith's collection. Most galleries, and several English country houses, have one or more examples. About 1741/4 he issued his etched *Vedute* . . . with a dedication to Smith.

CANO, Alonso (1601–67), was one of the leading painters and sculptors of Seville. He was the son of a sculptor who specialized in the construction of elaborate altars and he himself continued the business (he worked for MONTAÑES 1620–5), but became a master painter in 1626. His early works were influenced by ZURBARÁN, but his style later became softer in handling. In 1636 he was imprisoned for debt; in the following year he was in trouble for duelling, and in 1638 he left Seville for the Court in Madrid, where he may have been invited by VELÁZQUEZ, who had been his fellow-apprentice under PACHECO. In 1644 his young second wife was found stabbed to death: he was arrested but subsequently freed. He returned to Madrid in 1645, but obtained the stipend of a Prebendary at Granada Cathedral and was ordained in 1658, although he does not seem to have been very satisfactory to his ecclesiastical superiors. He designed the façade of Granada Cathedral *c*.1664. A contemporary records his systematic use of prints, even the crudest street ballads, as a means of stimulating his imagination. Most of his polychrome sculpture is in Granada, but there are paintings and some carved wooden figures in Berlin, Budapest, Dresden, Dublin, Kansas City, London (Wallace Coll.), Los Angeles, Madrid (Prado and Acad.), Munich, New York (Hispanic Soc.), Paris (Louvre), Seville, Stockholm, Worcester Mass. and York.

CANOVA, Antonio (1757–1822), was brought up as a mason and already had his own studio, in Venice, by 1774. He became the most famous NEOCLASSIC sculptor, whose international reputation surpassed even those of FLAXMAN, THORWALDSEN and GIBSON. His early work is still very much in the 18th-century tradition, and reminiscent of French portrait sculpture (e.g. HOUDON) in its liveliness, but by 1779 he had been converted to Neoclassic theory and this was confirmed by his visit to Rome and Naples in 1780 and his residence in Rome from 1781. He is said to have been influenced by Gavin HAMILTON. In 1782 he received his first major commission, the Monument to Pope Clement XIV (1782–7, Rome, SS. Apostoli), followed by that to Clement XIII (1787–92, St Peter's). The French invasion caused him to go to Vienna in 1797, and there he got the commission for the Monument to Maria Christina in the Augustinerkirche. In 1802, pressed by the Vatican, he accepted Napoleon's invitation to Paris; although he did not approve of the French looting of works of art from Italy he became an admirer of Napoleon and made a bust of him from life. This was followed by many others and in the years 1806–8 he began several, including an equestrian bronze for Naples and two gigantic standing figures of the Emperor, stark naked. One of these, in bronze, is in Milan (Brera); the other, in marble, is now in the Wellington

Museum, London – the restored Bourbons, having no use for it, sold it off cheaply to the British Government, which presented it to Wellington. In 1807 he also began (but abandoned) a Nelson Monument. His best-known work is the portrait of Napoleon's sister, *Pauline Bonaparte Borghese as Venus* (1808, Rome, Borghese), one of several statues of members of Napoleon's family based on classical prototypes. In 1815, after the fall of Napoleon, Canova was sent by the Pope to Paris to try to secure the return of the works looted by the French. With English help, he succeeded in large measure and he visited London on his way home. There he studied the Elgin Marbles, bought after much controversy for the British Museum in 1816, but they had little effect, at that stage in his career, upon the fundamentally Roman (rather than Greek) basis of his art. For his part in securing the return of the Italian treasures the Pope created him Marchese d'Ischia. In 1817 he transformed his equestrian *Napoleon*, destined for Naples, into *Charles III Bourbon*, and in the same year he adapted his colossal *Religion* into a smaller figure for a Brownlow Monument in Belton Lincs., where it is said to represent *Protestant Faith*. Two years later, at the expense of George III, he made the *Monument to the Stuarts*, now in St Peter's, Rome. In 1820 he made a *Washington* for N. Carolina (now destroyed). He seems to have been an extremely kind and generous man, spending his large fortune freely in helping young students and sending patrons to struggling sculptors. Like BACON, he seems to have made innovations in POINTING, but his reliance on such mechanical methods makes his handling somewhat insensitive: to counteract this he often spent much time on finishing himself. There is a large collection of casts of his works in his native village, Possagno, near Treviso; other works are in Bassano, Bergamo, Berlin, Florence (Pitti and Sta Croce), Forlì, Genoa (Pal. Bianco), Leeds (a version of the *Venus de' Medici*), Liverpool (a *Self-portrait*), London (V&A), Milan (Ambrosiana), Munich, Naples (Mus. Nazionale and Filangeri), Ottawa, Padua, Paris (Louvre), Parma, Rome (Mus. Capitolino, Napoleonico, and churches), Treviso, Turin, the Vatican, Venice (Accad., Correr, Mus. dell'Arsenale, Querini-Stampalia and Seminario Arcivescovile) and Vienna (K-H Mus.).

CAPPELLE, Jan van de (*c*.1624/5–79), was an Amsterdam painter of calm seas and fleecy white clouds. He also painted a few winter landscapes. His style was based on that of Simon de VLIEGER, of whose work he owned nine paintings and 1,300 drawings. Cappelle seems to have been wealthy, since his collection also included 500 Rembrandt drawings, and portraits of him were painted by Rembrandt, Hals and Eeckhout; unfortunately, none of them is now identifiable, although the Rembrandt may be the portrait in Buscot Park, Oxfordshire (National Trust). There are works by Cappelle in many Dutch museums, and in Antwerp, Berlin, Birmingham (Barber Inst.), Brussels, Chicago, Detroit, Dublin, Glasgow, London (NG and Kenwood), Munich, New York (Met. Mus. and Frick Coll.), Ottawa, Toledo Ohio, Vienna, Washington (NG) and elsewhere.

CAPRICCIO (Ital. caprice). Any fantasy, but usually applied to architectural and topographical subjects made up of elements from various sources, or purely imaginary; or VEDUTE IDEATE such as MARLOW's *St Paul's, London, with the Grand Canal, Venice* (London, Tate). *Capricci* were often used for decorative pictures such as SOPRAPORTE. *Los Caprichos* is the title of a set of highly phantasmagoric etchings by Goya.

CARACCIOLO, Giovanni Battista, called 'Battistello' (1578–1635), was one of the first Neapolitan painters to be influenced by CARAVAGGIO. Nothing can be positively ascribed to him before the arrival of Caravaggio in Naples in 1606, but he may have been in Rome before *c.*1615 and have seen pictures by Caravaggio then. He was in Florence in 1618, and in Rome again late in 1618 and early in 1619, but his chronology is obscure until 1622, when he painted his masterpiece, *Christ Washing the Disciples' Feet* (Naples, S. Martino). His later works are more classicizing, in the Bolognese manner, and by the late 1620s or early 1630s he had abandoned any influence from Caravaggio. During the early part of the century, however, he exerted a decisive influence in Naples towards Caravaggism. There are works in Berlin, Cambridge Mass. (Fogg), Dundee, Florence (Uffizi and Pitti), Hartford Conn. (Wadsworth), Lausanne, Leningrad, Los Angeles, Milan (Brera), Naples (Capodimonte and many other museums and churches), Newmarket (St Mary's), New York (Met. Mus. and Columbia Univ.), Palermo, Prato, Rome (Gall. Naz.), Sarasota Fla., Versailles, Vienna (K-H Mus.) and elsewhere.

CARAVAGGIO, Michelangelo Merisi da (1571–1610), was so called from the Bergamasque town near Milan, from which his family came. Recently discovered documents provide fairly convincing evidence that he was born, not in 1573, as was long believed, but in 1571. In 1584 he was apprenticed for four years to Simone Peterzano, a Bergamasque working in Milan, who claimed to have been a pupil of Titian. After his apprenticeship ended Caravaggio appears to have gone to Rome, but his early years are very obscure, and there is some evidence in his works that he may have been in Venice, since he was, through his Bergamasque origins, a Venetian citizen. It is not known when he arrived in Rome, nor exactly when he worked for the Cavaliere d' ARPINO. His earliest works were still-life subjects and small dramatized self-portraits of a distinctly Northern and vaguely Venetian character, with strong chiaroscuro and detailed execution. During the 1590s he worked for Cardinal del Monte, who commissioned several genre subjects, and it was probably through him that he obtained in 1599 the commission to decorate the Contarelli Chapel in S. Luigi dei Francesi, the French church in Rome, with three scenes from the life of St Matthew. This – his first public work – was finished only after many difficulties, including the rejection of the original altarpiece of *St Matthew and the Angel* on the grounds of indecorum, and radical repainting of the *Martyrdom of St Matthew* on one of the side walls, probably occasioned by unfamiliarity with working on such large canvases and with problems caused by the scale of the figures compared with those in the *Calling* of the Saint on the opposite wall. The present altarpiece was substituted for the original one (destroyed in Berlin in 1945). With the extensive repaintings, the work may well have lasted until 1603, although the chapel was opened in 1601.

During these years he also painted the *Martyrdom of St Peter* and the *Conversion of St Paul* for the Cerasi Chapel in Sta Maria del Popolo (1600–1), but these also seem to have been rejected and then replaced with new renderings of the subjects. These are smaller pictures than those in S. Luigi, with fewer figures much larger in scale, but with an even more dramatic chiaroscuro. Three further altarpieces were bitterly criticized: the *Madonna di Loreto*, the *Virgin and Child with St Anne*, and the *Death of the Virgin*. Basically, the objections were on the grounds of indecorum – the sweaty headcloth and dirty feet of the pilgrims in the *Madonna di Loreto*, the nakedness of the Child and the peasant appearance of the Virgin and St Anne, and the coarse peasant types and the bloated figure of the dead Virgin, reputed to have been painted from a drowned strumpet fished out of the Tiber. These accusations, and the opposition to his works among the later Academic Mannerists such as ZUCCARO, were founded on his vivid realism, his use of contemporary costumes and settings, his rejection of idealization, the immediacy and simplicity of his approach, and the novelty of his use of strong chiaroscuro with a wealth of detail which, though appearing to conform to the new ideas favoured by Counter-Reformation artistic theory, were radically opposed to the forms and ideas expressed by the CARRACCI. Yet all his rejected works found ready buyers among cardinals and noblemen against whom no accusations of insincerity or sensationalism can be made. His reputation as a stormy petrel was probably added to by the libel action brought against him in 1603 by BAGLIONE (his denigratory biographer in 1642) because of scurrilous verses which Baglione accused him of circulating, and by the many fracas with the police caused by his violent temper. His career in Rome was brought to an inglorious end in 1606 by just such an outburst: during a game of racquets he quarrelled with his opponent and stabbed him. He fled first to Zagarolo and then to Naples, where he painted several works before going on to Malta in 1607. Here he was well received by the Grand Master of the Order of St John, of whom he painted a portrait (which may be the one in the Louvre, although there are doubts). He was made a Knight of Grace – the lowest grade – and commissioned to paint two works still in Malta, one of which, the *Decollation of the Baptist* in the Oratory of St John, is his only signed work, and a superb example of his use of dramatic lighting as an extension of the actual lighting in the chapel. After assaulting a Knight Justiciary (the highest grade) he was imprisoned, but escaped and fled to Sicily in 1608. He was expelled from the Order, and though it is commonly said that he was pursued by its agents this is difficult to believe, since in Syracuse and Messina there were houses of the Order, and Palermo was the seat of the government of the Viceroy. This would have made it easy for the sovereign Order to extradite him had the authorities in Malta wished, but no move was ever made against him. There is even some evidence that he worked for the Order in Messina. Finally, in 1609, he returned to Naples, where in a tavern, the haunt of German mercenaries and cut-throats, he was seriously wounded in a brawl and his death was reported. Meanwhile in Rome efforts were being made to obtain a pardon, but, not daring to return to Rome until he was sure of it, he left Naples by sea for Port'Ercole, a Spanish enclave on the Tuscan coast. Here he was imprisoned by mistake, and was released in time to discover that the felucca which he believed still had all his goods on board had sailed. His efforts to overhaul the vessel brought on an attack of fever, and in a few days he died in a tavern. After his death, the Spanish Viceroy in Naples sent to Port'Ercole for his effects, which were in fact in the customs house in the port.

His last works in Malta and Sicily are very dark and somewhat damaged, but their direct iconography, their inspired simplicity and poignancy, embody a new intensity of dramatic feeling. His technical methods were revolutionary, and brought him into endless controversy. He is recorded as painting directly on to the canvas from a model, instead of working from the customary sketches and squared-up preparatory drawings. Apart from Naples, his methods and ideas had little lasting effect in Italy, where his principal followers were Orazio GENTILESCHI and his daughter Artemisia, MANFREDI, Borgianni, SARACENI (who painted the replacement for the rejected *Death of the Virgin*), and a number of lesser men who imitated his manner without catching more than his realism and light effects. He had some passing influence on Guido RENI and GUERCINO, and a decisive one on the UTRECHT SCHOOL and in Naples. The realism of RIBERA and MAINO links him with the early work of VELÁZQUEZ and MURILLO, and in France LA TOUR and the LE NAIN brothers show the spread of his ideas. RUBENS was also another profound admirer of Caravaggio, with first-hand experience of his works in Rome, and much of REMBRANDT's work stems from him. There are pictures in Berlin, Cleveland Ohio, Cremona, the Escorial, Florence (Uffizi and Pitti), Forth Worth Texas (the recently rediscovered *Card Sharps*), Hartford Conn., Kansas City, Leningrad, London (NG), Madrid (Prado), Messina, Milan (Brera, Ambrosiana), Naples (S. Domenico Maggiore and Misericordia), Nancy, New York (Met. Mus.), Paris (Louvre), Rome (Gall Naz., Borghese, Capitoline, Corsini, Doria Galls. and churches), Rouen, Valletta Malta, the Vatican and Vienna. The *Nativity* in the Oratory of S. Lorenzo, Palermo, stolen in 1969, has not yet been recovered.

CARIANI, Giovanni Busi called (active 1509 to after 1547), was a Bergamasque, but worked principally in Venice. He was perhaps a pupil of Giovanni BELLINI and PALMA Vecchio, but was also influenced by Giorgione, Titian and Lotto. In turn, some of his works foreshadow his fellow-Bergamasque, Caravaggio (e.g. *A Concert*, private coll., Switzerland). Some frescoes have recently been discovered in the citadel, Bergamo. Other works are in the Royal Coll. and in Bergamo, Edinburgh (NG), London (NG), Milan (Brera), New York (Met. Mus.), Ottawa, Rome (Gall. Naz., Borghese and Pal. Venezia), Venice, Vienna and Washington (NG).

CARICATURE (Ital. caricatura, from caricare, to load). The word was first used in English in 1748, in the time of HOGARTH, one of the principal exponents. His engraving *Character and Caricatura* (1743) neatly summarizes the essence of caricature, which is to seize upon some trait of appearance – usually facial – and to exaggerate it, but not so much as to lose likeness. The idea of exaggerating characteristics is very ancient and is, perhaps, inseparable from portraiture itself. In the usually accepted form, however, the invention is ascribed to that upholder of the Grand Style, Annibale CARRACCI, who certainly made drawings *c.*1600 which are recognizably caricatures, and who defended his position by comparing it with the ideals of classicism – to see and bring out the lasting truth beneath the accidents of outward appearance. P. L. Ghezzi (1674–1755) was perhaps the first to make a living out of caricature, which, in his case, consisted of exaggerated portraiture, but Bernini and both Giambattista and Domenico Tiepolo also made drawings of this type, and even REYNOLDS painted some caricature-portraits of English visitors in Rome, until he realized that it might harm his future as a portrait painter. ROWLANDSON, Gillray, and above all DAUMIER, used it as a political weapon – Daumier's famous caricature of Louis Philippe as a pear is a well-known example. It is not clear how the word CARTOON came to be connected with satire and caricature (the Oxford English Dictionary gives 1863 as the earliest use in this sense).

CARLEVARIS, Luca (1665–1731), was the precursor of CANALETTO as the painter of Venice, and his *Vedute*, 103 etchings, were published in 1703. A sketchbook with preparatory drawings for these is in London (BM), and a volume of fifty-three oil sketches is in the V&A. The large picture of *Lord Manchester's Embassy to Venice in 1707* (Birmingham) was probably the cause of his patronage by the English. There are other paintings in the Royal Coll., Detroit, Dresden, New York (Met. Mus.), Venice and elsewhere.

CARLONE. A family of painters in Genoa in the 17th century, the best-known being the brothers Giovanni Andrea, called 'Il Genovese' (1590–1630) and Giovanni Battista (1592–1677), and Giovanni Battista's son Andrea (1639–97). Andrea was a pupil of his father before working in Rome under MARATTA. He travelled extensively in Italy and was much influenced in Venice by Veronese. He lived for several years in Perugia and also worked in Rome (Chapel of St Francis Xavier in the Gesù) before returning to Genoa in 1686. There are works by all three in the churches and galleries of Genoa.

CARO, Anthony (*b.*1924), English sculptor, was an assistant to Henry MOORE 1951–3. He visited the US in 1959, and subsequently began to work in welded steel, brightly coloured or allowed to rust, in a CONSTRUCTIVIST idiom. These are often very large, but from *c.*1966 he began to make 'table-top' sculptures, intended to be seen from higher up. In 1978 he was commissioned to make a sculpture for the National Gallery in Washington. Other works are in Cleveland Ohio, London (Tate), and New York (M of MA).

CAROLSFELD, Schnorr von *see* SCHNORR.

CARON, Antoine (*c.*1520–*c.*1599), is first recorded in the 1540s at FONTAINEBLEAU, where he worked under PRIMATICCIO and was much influenced by Niccolo dell' ABBATE. In 1599 he became Court Painter to Queen Catherine de' Medici. He was an exponent of the most exaggerated and sophisticated Mannerist court art, executing works based on court ballets and festivities, which he was employed to design. His use of strange colour-schemes, especially yellows, oranges and pinks, and lurid skies, and his fantastic architecture peopled by wildly gesticulating figures of extraordinarily elongated proportions blend peculiarly with some of his depictions of battles and massacres suggested by the Wars of Religion. There are works in Beauvais, Blois and Paris (Louvre), and drawings in Edinburgh and Florence.

CARPACCIO, Vittore (*c.*1460/5–1523/6), was probably a pupil, and certainly a follower, of Gentile BELLINI. He was also influenced by Giovanni Bellini, whose assistant he was in 1507, and perhaps also by Giorgione. His best work is the cycle of large pictures of the *Legend of St Ursula*, in Venice (Accad.), the earliest of which is dated 1490. In 1511 he offered to sell a *View of Jerusalem*, from which it has been inferred, perhaps rashly, that he had been there. His *Knight in a Landscape* (Lugano, Thyssen Coll.) is dated 1510, and may be the earliest full-length portrait, preceding CRANACH and MORETTO: if so, it clearly derives from pictures of saints, such as the S. Liberale in Giorgione's *Castelfranco Madonna*. Other works by Carpaccio are in Berlin, London (NG), Milan (Brera), New York (Met. Mus.), Paris (Louvre and Mus. Jacquemart-André), Philadelphia (Johnson), Rome (Borghese) and Washington.

CARPEAUX, Jean-Baptiste (1827–75), was the principal French sculptor of his day and is, in some ways, parallel to Delacroix. He was a pupil of RUDE, whose influence he combined with the Romanticism of BARYE; he was also a precursor of Rodin and Medardo Rosso in the importance he attached to chiaroscuro in sculpture. He went to Italy in 1854 and made his name with a dramatic statue of *Ugolino*, before returning to Paris in 1862. His most famous works were a pediment for the Pavillon de Flore of the Louvre, begun in 1863, and the *Dance*, begun in 1865 for the new Opera House in Paris. This caused a great sensation, and was attacked on moral grounds – it was even suggested that the group should be removed. The outbreak of the Franco-Prussian War in 1870 prevented this, but the original is now in the Mus. d'Orsay and has been replaced by a copy on the Opéra. A variant of the principal figure is now in Detroit. Carpeaux worked in England in 1871, to avoid the Commune. His last years were clouded by persecution mania and he died of cancer at 48. He was a painter as well as sculptor, and his native Valenciennes has a museum of his works; others are in Paris (Petit Pal.), and in Birmingham (a painting), Cardiff, Copenhagen, Glasgow, London (Tate), Manchester, New York, Providence RI and Washington.

CARR, Emily (1871–1945), was the most famous Canadian woman artist. She was influenced by the Group of SEVEN and also by motives taken from West Coast Indian folk-art. In France in 1910/11 she probably met her New Zealand contemporary, Frances HODGKINS. Her autobiography was published posthumously (1946). Ottawa (NG), Toronto, Vancouver and other Canadian galleries have examples.

CARRÀ, Carlo (1881–1966), was one of the original FUTURISTS, but his study of Giotto (1915) convinced him that the Italian tradition was not yet exhausted. In 1917, while serving in the army, he met CHIRICO in Ferrara and they evolved PITTURA METAFISICA. He was associated with MORANDI in a quest for a heightened realism, thus departing entirely from his original Futurism. There are works in Italian galleries and in New York (M of MA).

CARRACCI. There were three important members of this Bolognese family: Lodovico, and his cousins Agostino and Annibale, who were brothers.

Lodovico (1555–1619), as eldest, probably took the lead in establishing the workshop and the family style. He seems to have entered the Bologna Guild in 1578, but had already been to Parma and Venice, where he was influenced by CORREGGIO and TINTORETTO respectively. His first surviving signed and dated work is of 1588 (Bologna, Pinacoteca), but by 1585/6 he had founded, with his cousins, the teaching Academy in Bologna which became the most celebrated of its kind and was responsible for the training of most major Bolognese painters of the next generation, including DOMENICHINO, RENI and GUERCINO. He ran the academy alone after his cousins left Bologna (except for a period in Rome, 1602–*c.*1605), but after this there was a notable falling-off in his work, and he dwindled into a painter of large, rather sentimental and didactic Counter-Reformation altarpieces, with none of the originality that his cousins, particularly Annibale, had stimulated in him. Such an altarpiece, dated 1619, was once in Notre-Dame, Paris, but now seems to be lost.

Agostino (1557–1602) was principally an engraver who executed many plates after works by High-Renaissance, and particularly Venetian, artists. He visited Venice and North Italy in 1580–81 and was in Parma with Annibale *c.*1585. His wide knowledge of North Italian painting reinforced the trend away from the dying forms of Roman Mannerism and towards a fresh evaluation of the part to be played by the High Renaissance and classical tradition in the creation of the new and revitalized painting which culminated in the Baroque. He was in Rome in 1597–9, working with Annibale on the Farnese Gallery, but by 1600 had moved to Parma and was working for the Farnese family there when he died. His major altarpiece, *The Last Communion of St Jerome* (Bologna), greatly influenced Domenichino.

Annibale (1560–1609), was a pupil of Ludovico, and was by far the greatest artist of the three. He may have travelled in Tuscany *c.*1583–4, was in Parma with Agostino and almost certainly visited Venice *c.*1585/6. He participated with Ludovico and Agostino in the Academy, and they all shared in the decoration of the Fava (1584) and Magnani (1588–91) Palaces in Bologna. In 1595 he went to Rome to work for Cardinal Farnese on the decoration of the Farnese Palace, and for this he first executed the 'Camerino', with an elaborate ceiling with subjects from classical mythology in fresco surrounding an oil-painting of *Hercules at the Crossroads* (now in Naples). The Gallery, which he undertook next, is a room some 66 feet long by 22 feet wide, with a high barrel-vault for which he designed an elaborately illusionistic arrangement of mythological pictures supported by herms against an open colonnade, with, seated above the cornice, nude male figures reminiscent of those in Michelangelo's Sistine ceiling. The Farnese Gallery ranks with Raphael's decorations in the Stanze and the Farnesina and Michelangelo's Sistine ceiling as one of the great decorative schemes. In its illusionism and imaginative scope it has a lightness of touch, a sense of humour, and a freshness of vision and fancy transcending his other works, where the conscious recreation of the grander aspects of High Renaissance painters such as Raphael, Correggio, Andrea del Sarto and the Venetians is more readily perceptible. He was helped in the Gallery by Agostino until 1599, and by Domenichino (particularly in the landscapes) and Albani. It was finished by 1604, and in 1605 Annibale was first attacked by the illness which virtually prevented him from working and eventually killed him.

The term Eclectic, now abandoned, was formerly applied to the Carracci as an imputation that their use of Renaissance and Classical traditions involved a deliberate policy of selection and combination of the forms and concepts, often mutually incompatible, characterizing the style of their predecessors. There is no evidence of any such specific programme underlying either the teaching in their Academy or their own works, which illustrate the truism that all art is nourished by tradition.

Antonio (*c.*1583–1618), an illegitimate son of Agostino, and Francesco, an illegitimate brother of Agostino and Annibale, were also painters and worked as assistants.

There are works by one or more of the Carracci in the Royal Coll., and in Amsterdam, Berlin, Birmingham, Bologna (Mus. and churches), Boston, Brussels, Cambridge (Fitzwm), Dresden, Florence (Uffizi), Indianapolis, Leicester, London (NG, V&A and Dulwich), Milan (Brera), Modena, Munich, Naples, Oxford (Ch. Ch. – a rare genre subject, *The Butcher's Shop*), Paris (Louvre), Parma, Rome (Borghese, Capitoline, Colonna, Doria and Spada Galls), Sheffield, the Vatican, Venice (Accad.), Vienna and elsewhere.

CARREÑO de Miranda, Juan (1614–85), was a member of a Spanish noble family, whose studies in the royal collection in Madrid caused him to be influenced by Rubens and Titian. In 1669 he was made a Painter to the King and in 1671 Court Painter. He produced several religious pictures, but was chiefly a portrait painter, adapting the styles of Velázquez and van Dyck. There are works in Barnard Castle (Bowes Mus.), Madrid (Prado and Galdiano Mus.), Paris (Louvre) and elsewhere.

CARRIERA, Rosalba (1675–1757), was a Venetian woman pastellist who had a great vogue in Venice, chiefly among British tourists, in Paris (1720–21), and Vienna (1730). She painted snuff-boxes for the tourist trade with miniatures on ivory, a technique she seems to have pioneered as against the earlier use of card as a ground. She was painting miniatures by 1700, and her earliest pastels are of *c.*1703. In 1705 she was made an 'accademico di merito' by the Accademia di San Luca in Rome, a title reserved for non-Roman artists. She achieved immense popularity, and made pastel portraits of notabilities from all over Europe. She also had great success with her near-pornographic *demi-vierges*, much earlier examples of the genre than those by GREUZE. She went blind at the end of her life, which provoked a mental collapse. There are 157 of her pastels in Dresden, and others in the Royal Coll., London (V&A) and elsewhere.

CARRIÈRE, Eugène (1849–1906), was taken prisoner in the Franco-Prussian War (1870), and thus had the opportunity to see, in Dresden, some pictures by Rubens which influenced his style at the beginning of his career – the 'mistiness' which is so characteristic of his works (giving many of them the appearance of a smudgy sepia-print) dates from his later years. His famous portraits of Daudet and his daughter, of Verlaine (both 1891), and of Edmond de Goncourt on his death-bed (1896), are all in Paris (Mus. d'Orsay), along with many others. Another *Verlaine* is in Boston and there are works in Avignon, Cardiff and Toulon.

CARSTENS, Asmus (Erasmus) Jakob (1754–98), was Danish-born, but was the most *ernst* of the German Neoclassic artists; his difficult temperament prevented him from obtaining due recognition. He made his first Italian journey in 1783, but money soon gave out and he had to return. He was helped to settle in Berlin in 1787 and became a professor at the Academy in 1790, but in 1792 he was able to go back to Rome, where he died. In 1796 he wrote to the Prussian Minister repudiating his obligations and asserting the duty of the artist to fulfil his personal destiny. He produced almost no paintings, and his work consists of large cartoons in black and white chalk, very much influenced by Michelangelo, so that the combination of Neoclassical rectitude with Mannerist form is curiously reminiscent of BARRY and BLAKE. There are examples in Berlin and Copenhagen and, especially, Weimar. His works became better known through the publication of engravings, 1864–84.

CARTELLINO (Ital. a little paper). A small scroll or piece of paper painted on a picture to appear like a real scroll affixed to the background or the small foreground parapet, which is often supplied to limit the front of the foreground plane and provide something for the *cartellino* to be stuck to. The commonest use for a *cartellino* is to take the painter's signature, as in the works of Giovanni Bellini and Antonello da Messina, but it sometimes carries a religious invocation, or the motto of the sitter in a portrait. *Cartellini* are also found in engravings and on reliefs.

CARTOON. Nowadays this normally means a drawing with a humorous or satirical intent, but the original meaning (from Ital. *cartone*, a big sheet of paper) is quite different. A cartoon in this sense is a full-size drawing for a painting, usually worked out in detail and ready for transfer to canvas, wall or panel. The cartoon was rubbed on the back with chalk or charcoal, and the main lines were then gone over with a stylus, thus transferring them to the ground; sometimes the main lines had their contours pricked through in a series of small dots, through which fine charcoal dust could be 'pounced', or a SPOLVERO was used to preserve the cartoon itself. The procedure for FRESCO was more complex but the same in essence. Several cartoons still survive, and it is possible to tell which were actually used for transfer, from the presence of prickings or the indentation of the lines. An Auxiliary Cartoon – largely confined to Raphael's workshop – is a detail, e.g. a head, transferred from the main cartoon and then worked out in greater detail before final painting (an example is the *St James* in London (BM) for the Vatican *Coronation of the Virgin*). The most famous of all cartoons, however, are those by Raphael for the Vatican tapestries (Royal Coll., on loan to the V&A), which were not transferred in this way.

CASSATT, Mary (1844–1926), was born in Pittsburgh, the daughter of a banker who offered little encouragement to her desire to be a painter. In 1868, after travelling widely in Europe, she settled in Paris to study under Chaplin, a typical academic painter, but was far more interested in Courbet, Manet and the Impressionists. In 1877 she met Degas, who invited her to exhibit with the Impressionists, which she did in 1879, 1880, 1881 and 1886. She bought Impressionist paintings for herself and her family, tried to get other Americans to do so, and helped their dealer, Durand-Ruel, in some of his more difficult moments. She was partly blind by 1912, and totally so at her death. In 1914 she was awarded the Gold Medal of Honor of the Pennsylvania Academy, where she had studied 1861–6. Degas became a close friend and portrayed her on several occasions, notably in two etchings showing her in the Louvre. She herself made several fine coloured etchings, intended to make original works available at reasonable prices. These are mostly of domestic scenes, and show a combination of Japanese colour-printing techniques with the vision of Degas and Renoir: they are a unique and significant (though still undervalued) contribution to Impressionism and probably influenced BONNARD and VUILLARD. They also show how she was able to treat the mother and child theme with tenderness, but not sentimentality. There are works in Birmingham, Boston, Detroit, Los Angeles, New York (Met. Mus.), Paris (Mus. d'Orsay), Washington (NG) and other US museums.

CASSONE is an Italian word for a special kind of coffer, used as a marriage-chest and containing the bride's household linen. They were often very richly decorated, with carved and gilt mouldings and painted panels at the front and sides, and sometimes also inside and outside the lid. The great age of *cassone* painting was from the 14th to the 16th century, and the subjects were usually mythological, of the *Rape of Helen* type, or from classical antiquity. The exact significance of some of the paintings inside the lids is still not clear, and may have been quasi-magical. Many panels from the fronts of *cassoni* are now framed and hung as Old Masters, although most of the original painters were not regarded as more than craftsmen by their contemporaries: Uccello and

Botticelli are exceptions. A panel from a *cassone* is nearly always recognizable on account of its shape – some 4–6 feet wide by about 12 or 18 inches in height.

CASTAGNO, Andrea del (1419/21–57), was one of the most influential Florentine painters of the generation after Masaccio. The date of his birth is now thought to be as late as 1419/21, although it was formerly put at 1412 or even in the 14th century. He seems to have been precocious: traditionally he painted some effigies of rebels hanged by the heels, *c.*1440, from which he derived the nickname Andreino degli Impiccati (of the hanged men). He was certainly in Venice in 1442, when he signed and dated some frescoes in S. Zaccaria; but these do not give an unequivocal picture of his style in his youth, since they were painted in collaboration with the otherwise unknown Francesco da Faenza. He was back in Florence in 1444, designing a stained glass window for the Cathedral (still there), and soon after this (*c.*1447) he must have painted his frescoes of *Passion Scenes* and the *Last Supper* (Florence, S. Apollonia, now the Castagno Mus.). These were his first famous works and show the influence of Masaccio's scientific realism. In 1449–50 he painted an *Assumption* for S. Miniato fra le Torri (now in Berlin), which is far closer to the International Gothic style; and, for the last 7 years of his short career, Castagno broke with the style of Masaccio (whom he could not have known) in favour of one based on the emotional and linear style of DONATELLO (who was alive and very famous): in fact, Castagno translated Donatello's sculpture into pictorial terms and thus influenced all 15th-century Florentine painters. The major examples of the Donatellesque style are the *Famous Men and Women*, painted for a villa at Legnaia, near Florence (now in the Uffizi). His last dated work was the fresco equestrian portrait of *Niccolò da Tolentino* in the Cathedral, a pendant to Uccello's *Hawkwood*. This is of 1456 and shows a more dynamic style than Uccello's (1436), and is based in part on Donatello's *Gattamelata*. In recent years a number of Andrea's SINOPIE have been recovered, justifying the praise lavished on him by contemporaries as a draughtsman. There are other works by him in Florence (SS. Annunziata), and in Edinburgh (NG), London (NG), New York (Met. Mus. and Frick Coll.), Venice (S. Marco) and Washington (NG).

CASTIGLIONE, Giovanni Benedetto (*c.*1610–63/5), was a Genoese and a pupil of van DYCK, in whose studio in Genoa he worked from 1621. He was – for an Italian – much influenced by foreigners, for his style was formed by Flemish painters and Rembrandt's etchings; later, he was much influenced by POUSSIN and Rubens. Like Bassano, he was a great animal painter. He was in Rome by 1634, when he was in the Academy of St Luke, and he remained there until at least 1650, with visits to Naples and Genoa. It was at this time that he was influenced by Poussin. About 1648/50 he began to work for the Mantuan Court, which perhaps explains the influence of Rubens, who had worked there some forty years earlier. His latest works have a deep mystical fervour, but he is principally remembered as the inventor of a kind of drawing in thin washes of oil-paint, and, more important, of the MONOTYPE. He may also have invented soft-ground Etching (*see* ENGRAVING (*c*)), of which he was certainly an early exponent. Excellent examples of both drawings and monotypes are in the Royal Coll. at Windsor, and other works are in Bergamo, Cambridge (Fitzwm), Dresden, Dublin, Genoa, Hartford Conn., Los Angeles,

Madrid, Montpellier, Munich, Ottawa, Paris (Louvre), Rome (Doria), Rouen and Turin.

CASTILLO, Antonio del (1616–68), was a Spanish painter active in Cordova, who was a pupil of his uncle Juan (1584–1640), who had himself been a pupil of ZURBARÁN and was the master also of MURILLO. Antonio was therefore much influenced by Zurbarán's dramatic sobriety, as well as by Netherlandish engravers such as BLOEMAERT, whose genre treatment of religious themes influenced Castillo. His earliest work (*St Jerome*, Madrid, Prado) is dated 1635. He also painted portraits and landscapes, and was the master of VALDÉS Leal. There are works in Cordova, Madrid (Prado and Acad.) and Munich.

CASTING *see* PLASTER and BRONZE.

CATALOGUE RAISONNÉ *see* OEUVRE.

CATENA, Vincenzo (*c.*1480–1531), was a Venetian painter who began as an imitator of Giovanni BELLINI and CIMA, but who entered into some kind of partnership with GIORGIONE by 1506, according to an inscription on the back of Giorgione's *Laura* in Vienna: it is now known that there is a Catena-type *Madonna* below the self-portrait sometimes attributed to Giorgione in Brunswick. Nevertheless, the influence of Giorgione did not make itself felt until after his death in 1510, as in Catena's *Sta Cristina* (Venice, S.M. Mater Domini), or the *Adoration of the Shepherds* (New York, Met. Mus.). In the last twenty years of Catena's life he was also influenced by Palma Vecchio, Titian and others. There are works by him in Berlin, Boston (Gardner), Budapest, Dresden, Edinburgh, Frankfurt (Städel), Glasgow, Liverpool, London (N G), Madrid (Prado), Milan (Brera), Ottawa, Paris (Louvre), Venice (Accad., Correr and Querini-Stampalia), Vienna (K-H Mus.), Washington (N G) and elsewhere.

CATTANEO, Danese (*c.*1509–Dec. 1572/Jan. 1573), was a Tuscan sculptor and a pupil of Jacopo SANSOVINO in Rome; after the Sack (1527) he accompanied his master to Venice, where he worked on tombs, some figures on the Library, and the right-hand panel of the Loggetta. His earliest Venetian work was the *St Jerome* in S. Salvatore (*c.*1530). He was a good portraitist, although his mild, tender style lacks energy. His tomb figures include busts of *Bembo*, 1547, and *Alessandro Contarini*, 1555 (both Padua, Santo); the Fregoso Altar (1565, Verona, Sant' Anastasia); the Loredan Monument (*c.*1572, Venice, SS. Giovanni e Paolo, with Campagna). His statue of *Girolamo Fracastoro* (1559) is now on the arch flanking the Loggia del Consiglio, Verona. His best bronze bust is the *Lazzaro Bonamico* (*d.*1552, now Bassano, Mus.), and there are bronzes in Cardiff, Florence (Bargello), New York (Met. Mus.) and Vienna.

CAVALLINI, Pietro (active 1273–1308), was the great representative of the Roman School slightly before GIOTTO. He painted fresco cycles and designed mosaics in a purely classical style which forms the link between the painting of antiquity and the revived forms introduced principally by Giotto. The mosaics in Sta Maria in Trastevere in Rome are recorded as having been signed and dated 1291 (but the evidence is very unsatisfactory); the fragmentary *Last Judgement* fresco in Sta Cecilia, also in Rome, is probably of 1293. He was in Naples in 1308 and the frescoes in Sta Maria Donna Regina are probably his. A *Head of an Angel*, a fragment of a mosaic in S. Paolo fuori le Mura, Rome, has recently been attributed to him.

CAVALLINO, Bernardo (1616–*c.*1656), was a short-lived Neapolitan painter of small-scale figures set against a murky background, which have something in common with the Northern BAMBOCCIANTI. He was the major Neapolitan painter of the 1640s and early 1650s until his death in the great plague of 1656. There are about eighty pictures ascribed to him, of which eight are signed or initialled and only one is dated: this is the *S. Cecilia* of 1645, now in the Pal. Vecchio, Florence (there is a sketch in Naples, Capodimonte). The influence of Rubens and van Dyck can be seen in these works. Signed pictures are in Cleveland Ohio, Molfetta Apulia, Moscow, Rome and Stockholm, and other works are in Barnard Castle (Bowes Mus.), Birmingham (Barber Inst.), Boston, Brunswick, Budapest, Detroit, Florence (Uffizi), Hartford Conn. (Wadsworth), Houston Texas, Kansas City, Liverpool, London (NG), Lyons, Madrid, Malibu Cal., Melbourne, Milan (Poldi-Pezzoli), Munich, New York (Met. Mus.), Ottawa, Puerto Rico, Rotterdam, Sarasota Fla., Verona, Vienna (K-H Mus.) and York.

CAVO-RILIEVO *see* RELIEF.

CECCO del Caravaggio. Mancini, in his 'Considerazioni sulla Pittura' of *c.*1620, mentions a 'Francesco detto del Caravaggio' as an admirer and imitator of CARAVAGGIO. In a document of 1619 a 'Cecco' – an abbreviation of Francesco – is recorded among French artists working with TASSI at Bagnaia in 1613–15. He is therefore believed to be French (or at least Northern), which is supported by his hard, coarsely realistic style, with exaggerated facial expressions and elaborate still-life attributes, not unlike FINSON. His works may include *Christ driving the Money-Changers from the Temple* (Berlin), *The Resurrection* (Chicago), *Guardian Angel with two Saints* (Kansas City), *Musician* (London, Wellington Mus. – also given to Finson); all datable *c.*1610. Another *Musician* (Oxford, Ashmolean), attributed to Finson, may also be his.

CELLINI, Benvenuto (1500–71), Florentine sculptor, goldsmith and amorist, is best-known for his 'Autobiography' (1558–62: several English editions exist). This is one of the great autobiographies and gives us a glimpse of the processes of artistic creation, as well as an insight into the troubled Italy of the years following the Sack of Rome in 1527: Cellini's love-life also features in considerable detail, not all of it entirely credible. In 1519 he refused an invitation to go to England with TORRIGIANO, on the grounds that he could not do anything with the man who had broken the divine Michelangelo's nose. Instead, he went to Rome, and, according to his own account, played a heroic part in the defence of the city during the siege. He also claims to have killed Charles de Bourbon, one of the Imperial commanders in an attack. As an artist, Cellini was first influenced by the pupils of Raphael but later came very much under the shadow of Michelangelo, and his *Perseus* (1545–54, Florence, Loggia dei Lanzi) stood fittingly near Michelangelo's *David* and Donatello's *Judith*, its other main prototype. It is a curious fact that he and VASARI, the other great idolater of Michelangelo, hated each other. In 1537 and again in 1540–5 Cellini went to France to work for Francis I, for whom he made a salt-cellar (1540–3, now in Vienna) and the *Nymph of Fontainebleau* (1543–4, Paris, Louvre), whose sophisticated elegance and elongatedly Mannerist forms sum up the whole of the Second School of FONTAINEBLEAU. Imprisoned in 1556, apparently for immorality, in 1558 Cellini took the first steps towards becoming a priest, but in 1560 obtained his release from his vows. He also designed coins and medals, and there are other works by him in Boston (Gardner), the Escorial, Florence (Bargello) and Oxford.

CENNINI, Cennino, wrote, *c.*1390 or a little later, the earliest Italian treatise on painting, 'Il Libro dell' Arte', which is the source of most of our knowledge of TEMPERA technique. He says in it that he was a pupil of Agnolo GADDI – and could therefore trace his artistic descent back to Giotto – but no works by him are known.

CERANO *see* CRESPI, G.B.

CERUTI, Giacomo (1698–1767), like CIPPER, was one of the so-called Lombard Painters of Reality (i.e. low-life). He is now known to have been born in Milan, where he died, but by 1721 he was in Brescia and his earliest work (1724) is a signed portrait of a Brescian patrician: his portraits are influenced by his elder contemporary GHISLANDI. He frescoed the staircase of the Palazzo Grassi in Venice *c.*1740 and was back in Milan by 1757. His present fame is based on his groups of working-class sitters, ranging from lacemakers to destitute vagabonds, painted in a technique similar to Ghislandi's, but the subject matter is far closer to the LE NAIN brothers, and ultimately derived from Caravaggio's realism. None of these works is dated, and few are yet in museums, but there are examples in Belfast, Bergamo, Brescia, London (NG), Milan (Brera) and New York (Met. Mus.).

CÉSAR (*b.*1921) was born César Baldacchini in Marseilles, but has lived in Paris since 1943. He is a sculptor who works with characteristic 20th-century materials, mostly crushed motorcars and similar industrial debris. He has three workshops, one in a foundry, so that material is always handy, and he can then weld the crushed scrap into assemblages that often take their titles from the location of the workshop, e.g. *Man of Saint-Denis* (London, Tate).

CÉZANNE, Paul (1839–1906), was probably the greatest painter of the last century. He was born in Aix-en-Provence, the son of a wealthy banker and tradesman, and was educated at the Collège Bourbon, where he became friendly with Zola. The friendship, which meant a great deal to Cézanne, lasted until the publication of Zola's *L'Oeuvre* in 1886: the character of Claude Lantier seemed a travesty of Cézanne, and not only to Cézanne. In 1861, after abandoning the study of law, Cézanne went to Paris, where he met PISSARRO and from 1862 he devoted himself to painting, living in Paris until 1870. The Franco-Prussian War drove him to L'Estaque (and Pissarro to London) and they met again at Pontoise in 1872. In the 1860s his ardent Southern temperament expressed itself in a series of more or less erotic and melodramatic pictures, such as the *Rape* (1867), or the *Murder* (Liverpool), of similar date. These were, not unnaturally, received with no enthusiasm. While he was closely associated with Pissarro Cézanne began to paint landscapes in an Impressionist technique, and he exhibited at the first IMPRESSIONIST Exhibition in 1874. One of his pictures was among those which incurred the greatest public displeasure. This was the most extraordinary of all his erotic fantasies, the *Modern Olympia* (now in the Mus. d'Orsay, Paris), so called as a rather dubious compliment to MANET: it represents a fat, squatting female being disrobed by a negress, while a man (very like Cézanne) watches with interest. In the midst of the chaste Impressionist landscapes the effect must have been unnerving, particularly as these pictures are painted with great violence, and the colour is often piled on with a palette-knife. During the 1870s Cézanne digested the theories of colour and light which the Impressionists were then developing: in the third Impressionist Exhibition (1877) he showed sixteen pictures, and one critic praised them highly. Gradually he calmed down the exuberant Romanticism of his temperament and abandoned a Delacroix-like technique, to which he was not really suited. His great achievements lay in the direction of an ever more subtle analysis of colour and tone, totally different from the Impressionists' analysis in that they sought to capture the surface – the impression – and therefore painted quickly. Cézanne's analysis was infinitely prolonged and laborious because he sought to use colour as a means of modelling, and as the ultimate expression of the underlying forms of visible objects. In this he was simply following classical prototypes, and some of his recorded sayings are of great importance. He said that he wanted 'to do Poussin again, from Nature' and that he wanted 'to make of Impressionism something solid and durable, like the art of the Museums'. This was clearly because Impressionism was lacking in formal qualities, but 'when colour has its greatest richness then form has its plenitude': in particular, the basic ideas of CUBISM have been claimed to be implicit in his teaching that the painter ought to look for the cone, the sphere and the cylinder in Nature. Cézanne himself was no theorist, and constant insults from critics and public made him very chary of exposing himself. When his father died in 1886 he found himself rich and able to live in seclusion in his native Provence, mainly at the Jas de Bouffan, near Aix, a house his father had bought, and which once contained some very early decorations by Cézanne (now in Paris, Petit Pal.). In 1890 he was invited to exhibit in Brussels by Les XX; in 1895 he had his first big show; and from about 1900 his genius was fairly widely recognized. In the last years of his life he returned to some of his favourite early themes – in particular the big compositions of *Bathers*, with nude figures in a landscape setting. His great contribution was to show that colour and tone values must be considered as one thing and not two; in doing this he made Impressionism into something solid, like Poussin. Because his analysis was pursued with agonizing care many of his paintings were never finished – he is said to have abandoned a portrait of Vollard, the dealer, after more than a hundred sittings, with the remark that he was not displeased with the shirt-front! Naturally, still-life and landscape offered the greatest freedom in this respect and most of his flower-pieces were probably painted from artificial flowers. His few portraits were of himself or of people – his wife, his gardener – whose sittings could be protracted almost indefinitely.

There are pictures by him in Amsterdam (Stedelijk), Basle, Berlin, Berne, Boston, Budapest, Cambridge (Fitzwm) and Cambridge Mass., Cardiff, Chicago, Cleveland Ohio, Columbus Ohio, Detroit, Edinburgh, Essen, Fort Worth Texas, Glasgow (Mus. and Burrell), The Hague (Gemeente Mus.), Hamburg, Helsinki, Kansas City, Leningrad, London (NG, Tate and Courtauld Inst.), Los Angeles, Mannheim, Merion Pa (Barnes), Minneapolis, Montreal, Moscow, Munich, New York (Met. Mus., M of MA, Brooklyn and Guggenheim Mus.), Northampton Mass. (Smith Coll.), Oslo, Ottawa, Paris (Mus. d'Orsay), Philadelphia, Prague, Providence RI, San Francisco, St Louis, São Paulo, Sheffield, Stockholm, Toledo Ohio, Washington (NG and Phillips) and Zurich.

CHADWICK, Lynn (*b.*1914), is a British abstract sculptor who works in welded iron and steel, copper, bronze, metal compositions, plaster and glass. Like his contemporary, BUTLER, he was trained as an architect. After war service he turned to sculpture and produced mobiles under the influence of CALDER (he made three big mobiles for the 1951 Festival of Britain), but later evolved 'Balanced Sculptures' which do not attempt to exploit the quality of movement. He was awarded a prize at the 1956 Venice Biennale and is now represented in museums in Adelaide, Bradford, Brighton, Bristol, Brussels, Chicago, London (Tate and V&A), Manchester (Whitworth), Montreal, New York (M of MA), Ottawa, Paris (Mus. d'Art Mod.), Pittsburgh, Rome, Rotterdam, and Turin.

CHAGALL, Marc (1887–1985), was born in Vitebsk and trained (1908) in St Petersburg, where he came under the influence of Bakst and the Ballet. He was in Paris 1910–14 and was influenced by CUBISM; in 1917, after the Russian Revolution, he became Commissar of Fine Arts in Vitebsk and founded an Academy. After disagreements with MALEVICH he resigned and worked for theatres in Moscow, returning to Paris in 1923. By then his highly imaginative style was fully formed, and he was painting recognizable objects in unusual juxtapositions, floating rather insecurely in space. His colour was very rich, and most of his subjects were poetic evocations of Russian-Jewish village life, increasingly religious in sentiment. His fantasies influenced the SURREALISTS. In 1941 he was invited to America by the Museum of Modern Art in New York, and he remained in the US until 1948. A visit to Chartres was the occasion of a series of stained-glass windows: Assy, 1957; Metz and Reims Cathedrals, 1960s and 1974; the *Twelve Tribes of Israel* for a synagogue near Jerusalem, as well as mosaics and tapestry for the Knesset, 1960–69; in 1964 he painted a ceiling for the Paris Opéra, and followed it with decorations for the Metropolitan Opera, New York, in 1966. He also made windows for Tudely Church, Kent (1966–78), and Chichester Cathedral (1978). His Musée Biblique, containing religious works, is at Cimiez, Nice, and there are paintings in most museums of modern art. He published an autobiography, 'Ma Vie', in 1931, and an English translation appeared in 1965.

CHAMPAIGNE, Philippe de (1602–74), was born in Brussels and received his first training there as a landscape painter. He went to Paris in 1621, and worked with POUSSIN on the decoration of the gallery in the Luxembourg Palace which was to house Rubens's series of the life of Marie de' Medici. In 1628 he became Painter to the Queen Mother, Marie de' Medici, and also worked for Louis XIII and Richelieu, painting for the Cardinal the dome of the Sorbonne church, a full-length portrait, and a triple portrait similar to the one by van Dyck of Charles I of England made for the same purpose – to be sent to Rome as a model for Bernini to make a portrait bust. About 1643 he began to work for the Jansenists of Port Royal. This austere Catholic sect deeply influenced him and accentuated his tendency, observable as early as the middle 1630s, towards a form of classicism parallel to that then being developed independently in Rome by Poussin. His early portraits show his links with Rubens and van Dyck, who were fellow-Flemings, but there is no strong Baroque feeling in his later works – no ecstasies, radiances or visions. All is kept clear and lucid, to appeal to reason rather than to the emotions, with severe composition, frequently of the frieze type used by Poussin, cool, strong colour, and an unexaggerated though strict naturalism. His portraits of lawyers and merchants, and the group portraits of the sheriffs of Paris, show his humane and sensitive grasp of character, and are as grave and sober as his sitters. His finest portraits are those in the votive picture made on the recovery of his daughter, a nun at Port Royal, who was stricken with paralysis and cured in 1661 by the prayers of the community (Paris, Louvre). There are works in the Royal Coll. and in Alençon, Amsterdam, Barnard Castle (Bowes Mus.), Berlin, Birmingham (Barber Inst.), Boston, Brighton, Brussels, Detroit, Florence (Pitti and Uffizi), Greenville SC, The Hague, Hull, Le Mans, London (NG and Wallace Coll.), Lyons, New York (Met. Mus.), Paris (Louvre), Rome (Gall. Naz.), Rouen, São Paulo, Toledo Ohio, Toulouse, Versailles, Vienna and Washington.

CHANTREY, Sir Francis (1781–1841), was an English sculptor, born near Sheffield, celebrated for his portrait busts and monuments. He had little formal training, being apprenticed to a woodcarver, and, after trying portrait painting, he turned to sculpture. In 1802 he was in London, studying intermittently at the RA, but he worked mostly in Sheffield, where in 1805 he received his first important commission, a bust of the *Rev. J. Wilkinson* (Sheffield Cath.), his first work in marble. In 1809 he settled in London with a moneyed wife and from 1811, when he exhibited his bust of *Horne Tooke* (Cambridge, Fitzwm) he never looked back. He visited France in 1815, and Italy in 1819, but remained unenthusiastic about Italian art – he thought Michelangelo's unfinished *Madonna* in Florence 'a work of wonderful promise' – but by then his own style was fully formed. He became an ARA in 1816, RA in 1817 and was knighted in 1837. His large fortune was bequeathed to the RA for the purchase of 'works of Fine Art of the highest merit . . . executed in Great Britain'. The choice of many works has, however, been sharply criticized.

Chantrey's style was naturalistic, with strong characterization. Some of his monuments, such as the *Robinson Children* (1817, Lichfield Cath.) are deeply affecting, but some verge on the sentimental (Pike Watts monument, Ilam, Staffs., 1817–25). He used a *camera lucida* to make preparatory drawings, often making a cast of a sitter's mouth, and then his assistants prepared the marble with a POINTING MACHINE before Chantrey himself finished the work in a final sitting. Over 100 busts are known, many in several versions – the *Walter Scott* (Abbotsford, 1820) in forty-five, as well as countless pirated ones. There are also scores of monuments all over England, as well as works in the Royal Coll. and in Birmingham (Gall. and Handsworth), Edinburgh (NPG and Parliament House), London (NPG, V&A, Soane Mus., RA, Houses of Parliament, Westminster Abbey and St Paul's), Oxford (Ashmolean: a large collection of models from his studio), Salisbury (Cath.) and Yale (CBA).

CHAPUS *see* MASTER OF THE AIX ANNUNCIATION.

CHARCOAL is made from twigs of willow or vine which have been charred away from the air. Each twig will then make a blackish mark that is easily rubbed off if necessary. Charcoal is sometimes used for drawing on paper, but its principal use is for making the preliminary drawings on walls or canvas as the first stage of a painting.

CHARDIN, Jean-Baptiste-Siméon (1699–1779), the finest 18th-century French painter of still-life and genre, became a member of the Academy in 1728, and was its treasurer and hung its exhibitions for over twenty years. His early works are not so much inspired by similar Dutch paintings as extensions of the Netherlandish cabinet pictures so popular in France in the 18th century: they take up the modest size and restricted range of subjects, adapting them to French tastes and feeling. His still-lifes, composed of the simplest elements – kitchen utensils, vegetables, game, baskets of fruit, fish and similar domestic materials – are exceptional in their impasted technique and solid colour, with great depth of tone achieved by extreme delicacy of touch and the subtle use of dragged and scumbled pigment. They have a straightforward honesty of vision and truth of representation untainted by mere verisimilitude. His genre scenes are small in format, with small figures in homely interiors, redolent of the simple domesticity of everyday bourgeois life, unsentimentalized and un-idealized, but not rendered picturesque by any concessions to low life, or titillating by excursions into modish society. In the 1775 Salon he exhibited two self-portraits and one portrait of his wife in pastel (all now in the Louvre) which are masterpieces of acute analysis, breadth of vision and technique, far excelling LATOUR's more fashionable pastel portraits. Fragonard was his pupil for a short time.

There are works in Amiens, Angers, Baltimore, Berlin, Besançon, Boston, Cambridge Mass. (Fogg), Carcassonne, Chartres, Chicago, Cleveland Ohio, Detroit, Dublin, Edinburgh, Fort Worth Texas, Frankfurt, Glasgow (Hunterian and Burrell), The Hague, Hartford Conn., Indianapolis, Kansas City, Karlsruhe, Leningrad, London (NG), Merion Pa. (Barnes Fdn), Minneapolis, Moscow (Pushkin), New York (Met. Mus. Frick Coll.), Oberlin Ohio, Ottawa, Oxford, Paris (Louvre, Jacquemart-André), Pasadena Cal. (Simon), Pittsburgh, Potsdam, Princeton NJ, Rotterdam, St Louis, Springfield Mass., Stockholm, Toronto, Washington (NG, Corcoran and Phillips) and Williamstown Mass.

CHARONTON *see* QUARTON.

CHASSÉRIAU, Théodore (1819–56), was a pupil of Ingres who was much influenced by Delacroix – the only artist of his time to make this difficult synthesis with any success. He used subject matter from the repertory of both, often with erotic overtones (though these were frequent in both Ingres and Delacroix) – illustrations to the Bible or Shakespeare, scenes from North African life, reconstructions of antiquity, religious and allegorical decorations, and portraits in pencil, like Ingres. He is well represented in Paris and in French museums.

CHAVANNES, Puvis de, *see* PUVIS.

CHIAROSCURO (Ital. light-dark). As generally used, chiaroscuro (or Fr. *clair-obscur*) means the balance of light and shade in a picture, and the skill shown by the artist in the management of shadows. The word tends to be used mainly of painters like Rembrandt or Caravaggio, whose works are predominantly dark in tone (but *see* CUYP). A *chiaroscuro woodcut* is a woodcut, linocut or other similar relief engraving printed from several blocks, in exactly the same way as a colour print, in imitation of a drawing in several shades of monochrome wash, each shade being cut on a separate block: intermediate tones are obtained by careful overprinting of two or more blocks. The first Italian artist to specialize in this technique was Ugo da Carpi (*c.*1480–*c.*1525), and many designs for such woodcuts go back to PARMIGIANINO. Ugo claimed to have invented the process, in an application to the Signoria of Venice for privilege, 1516; but the first dated example is of 1518, and there are some German prints which may be datable 1508/9.

CHIRICO, Giorgio de' (1888–1978), was an Italian painter born in Greece of Italian parents, who trained in Athens and Munich until 1908, and then in Italy and Paris (1911), where he met Picasso and Apollinaire. He returned to Italy in 1915 and served in the army during the First World War. In hospital in Ferrara he met CARRÀ and together they founded the quasi-Surrealist movement PITTURA METAFISCA in 1917, when he produced hallucinatory views of uninhabited cities, of great emotional power and painted in dark, earthy tones. In the 1930s he suddenly abandoned his 'modern' ideals and began a sort of imitation of the Old Masters. There are works by him – mostly from the more esteemed 'unregenerate' period – in Rome (Gall. d' Arte Mod.), Chicago, Detroit, London (Tate), New York (M of MA) and elsewhere. An English translation of his autobiography appeared in 1971.

CHRISTUS PATIENS and CHRISTUS TRIUMPHANS are the names given to the two main types of the very large painted crucifixes which normally stood on the rood-screens of medieval churches. Very few still exist in their original positions, most of the surviving examples having been cut down in size and transferred to chapels or sacristies. The Christus Patiens (Suffering Christ) represents Christ as dead on the Cross, whereas the Triumphans type represents Him with open eyes and outstretched arms standing on (rather than hanging from) the Cross. The dramatic emphasis of the Patiens type is certainly to be connected with the influence of St Francis of Assisi. An early example is provided by the work of GIUNTA Pisano.

CHRISTUS (Cristus), Petrus (*d.*1472/3), was the major master in Bruges after the death of Jan van EYCK (1441). Christus settled there in 1444, but he is sometimes said to have been Jan's pupil: two pictures – a *St Jerome* (1442, Detroit) and a *Madonna* (probably finished 1443, New York, Frick Coll.) – have been claimed as works by Jan finished by Christus. His own dated works range from 1446 to 1452 (or 1457 – the date is not clear), the latter being a *Madonna* in Frankfurt (Städel) which has some of the characteristics of a *Sacra Conversazione* in the manner of contemporary Italians such as Fra Angelico or Domenico Veneziano. This is signed; there is also a portrait in Los Angeles which is very similar in style to ANTONELLO da Messina, but it is not signed and may not be his. Certainly, however, Antonello was aware of contemporary Flemish painting, and these two pictures have been taken with a document in the Sforza archives in Milan, of March 1456, which refers to 'Antonellus sicilianus' and 'Piero di Burges' to endow Petrus with an Italian period and an influence on Antonello. However, the document does not specify them as painters (and may refer to soldiers), and 'Burges' may not mean 'Bruges' (the Italian for which is 'Bruggia'). It may be Burgos, or it has even been suggested that it refers to Piero dal Borgo – i.e. PIERO della Francesca. In any case, Antonello was certainly in Sicily in 1455 and 1457 and there is no evidence of Christus ever having left the Netherlands. His style is a simplification of Jan van Eyck's with very smooth, rounded forms, but he also painted two versions of the *Lamentation* (Brussels and New York, Met. Mus.) which both derive more or less from Roger van der WEYDEN's Escorial *Deposition*. The New York picture is simpler, and the two are put at opposite ends of Christus's career; early or late depending on individual choice of the moment of maximum Eyckian influence. There are other pictures by him in Berlin, Birmingham, Copenhagen, Dessau, Kansas City, London (NG), Madrid (Prado) and Washington (NG).

CHROMOLITHOGRAPHY *see* ENGRAVING (3).

CIBBER, Caius Gabriel (1630–1700), sculptor to William III, carved the bas-relief at the base of the Monument to the Great Fire of London in 1673–5, while imprisoned for debt. He worked at Hampton Court (1692–4) and at St Paul's Cathedral (1698–1700), but his best-known works are *Melancholy* and *Raving Madness* (inspired by Michelangelo's Medici Tombs) formerly over the gate of Bedlam and now in the Bethlem Royal Hospital, Beckenham, Kent.

CIMA da Conegliano, Giovanni Battista (1459/60–1517/18), was a Venetian painter much influenced by Giovanni BELLINI and also by ANTONELLO. He was in Venice by 1492 and spent most of his life there, mainly producing imitations of Giovanni Bellini, especially his *Madonnas* (e.g. the signed ones in London, NG, and Washington, NG). Later, he was also influenced by GIORGIONE. There are works by him in Amsterdam, Baltimore (Walters), Berlin, Birmingham, Bologna, Boston (Mus. and Gardner), Cambridge (Fitzwm), Cleveland Ohio, Conegliano near Treviso (Cath. and S. Fiore), Detroit, Dresden, Edinburgh, Florence (Uffizi), Frankfurt (Städel), London (NG, Wallace Coll. and Courtauld Inst.), Milan (Brera, Poldi-Pezzoli and Ambrosiana), New York (Met. Mus.), Paris (Louvre), Parma, Philadelphia (Johnson), Vicenza and York, and a large number in Venice.

CIMABUE (*c*.1240–1302?) is generally put at the beginning of modern art, as the teacher of GIOTTO (which he may in fact have been). The basis of his fame is due to Dante's choice of him as an example of the transitory nature of earthly glory: 'Cimabue thought that he held the field in painting, but now Giotto is acclaimed and Cimabue's fame is obscured' (*Purgatorio* xi, 94–6). The early commentators drove home the moral by insisting that Giotto was Cimabue's pupil, and he is consequently credited with the introduction of a more naturalistic style into the Byzantine formulae current in Tuscan Dugento painting. In fact, Cimabue is known to have been in Rome in 1272 and may well have been influenced by the classical current which is represented by CAVALLINI; but the sole securely documented work by Cimabue is the *St John*, part of a large mosaic in Pisa Cathedral on which he was working in 1302. This affords only the most tenuous grounds for stylistic generalizations, but there are also several works attributed to him on what seem good traditions. These include the ruined frescoes in the choir of the Upper Church at Assisi, and the repainted *Madonna of St Francis* in the Lower Church, as well as the very large and impressive *Sta Trinita Madonna* (Florence, Uffizi), which can reasonably be compared with the *Ognissanti Madonna* by Giotto, or the *Rucellai Madonna* attributed to DUCCIO (both in Florence: the latter was once attributed to Cimabue). Other works attributed to him are in Arezzo (S. Domenico), Bologna (S.M. dei Servi), Florence (Baptistry, Sta Croce – a Crucifix very badly damaged in the 1966 flood – and S.M. Novella), Paris (Louvre) and Washington (NG).

CINQUECENTO (Ital. five hundred). The 16th century, i.e. the fifteen-hundreds.

CIONE, Nardo and Jacopo di, *see* ORCAGNA.

CIPPER, Giacomo Francesco (active *c*.1705–*c*.1736), also called Todeschini, was probably of German origin ('tedesco' or 'todesco' is Italian for German). Like CERUTI, he was one of the leading Lombard Painters of Reality: they seem to have influenced each other, although Cipper is recorded as working earlier, since there is a genre scene by him dated 1705. There is a group (perhaps including a self-portrait) in the Royal Coll., which is signed and dated 1736, as well as three other signed pictures. The V&A, London, has a genre scene, and there are two pictures in the NG which may be his.

CIRE PERDUE *see* BRONZE.

CLAESZ., Pieter (*c*.1597–1660), was born in Germany, but married in Haarlem in 1617 and worked there for the rest of his life (his earliest dated picture is of 1621). With HEDA he was the greatest exponent of the so-called monochrome BREAKFAST PIECE, a form of still-life almost restricted to Haarlem in the 1620s. Properly speaking, they are not monochromes, but are painted in subdued greys, browns and greens with a peeled lemon often giving a touch of colour, as well as a white table-cloth or crumpled napkin providing an opportunity for virtuoso management of half-tones. He also painted a few VANITAS still-lifes (New York, Met. Mus. 1623; Oxford, Ashmolean). He was the father of BERCHEM. Other works are in Amsterdam, Boston, Bristol, Cambridge (Fitzwm), Chicago, Dublin, Haarlem, The Hague, London (NG), Paris (Louvre), Toledo Ohio and Vienna (K-H Mus.).

CLASSIC, CLASSICAL, ROMANTIC. In addition to the meanings given in any standard dictionary, the following occur in writings on art. *Classic* usually means an established standard of excellence (cf. classic car, classics of literature), and *classicism* a form of art derived (or believed to be derived) from the study of Antique exemplars, which are, by definition, *classic*. This became a fixed dogma in the mid-18th century, though prevalent enough from the 16th century, or even earlier. The 18th-century form is better referred to as NEO-CLASSICISM, and with its inflexible rules and passion for Academies it soon led to a marked reaction, Romanticism. It is a curiosity of history that the French Revolution fostered both ideals simultaneously, but the Romantic movement, with its unbridled expression of the passions, its love of the exotic, and its occasional absurdities, reached its apogee about 1830 in France, Britain and Germany. In France the situation was clarified by the presence of INGRES and DELACROIX as living embodiments of the two approaches to life and art, and indeed the dichotomy is still apparent in CUBISM and SURREALISM, the antithesis between form and content (or subject). The culmination of 19th-century art can be seen in CÉZANNE, who began as a positively orgiastic follower of Delacroix, and ended as one of the great classic French artists, like Poussin.

CLAUDE Gellée, or Claude Lorrain(e) (1600–82), was born in Lorraine, near Nancy, and, according to SANDRART, was originally trained as a pastry-cook. By *c*.1613 he was in Italy, working as a *garzone* for the Cavaliere d'ARPINO and the landscape painter Agostino TASSI. From 1618 until 1620 he was probably in Naples, then he settled in Rome as Tassi's pupil and assistant. In 1625 he returned to Nancy, but was back in Rome by 1627; there are no works by him certainly datable before 1630, but by the end of the 1630s he had a big reputation as a landscape painter and his popularity has remained undimmed ever since. The 195 drawings in his LIBER VERITATIS (London, BM), begun *c*.1635, were his own record of his paintings, made to guard against copies and forgeries.

The obvious comparison is with POUSSIN, but while the latter derived his heroic landscapes from Titian and Annibale Carracci, Claude's sources lie chiefly in the romanticized poetic landscapes of the later Mannerists such as Tassi, and the Northerners ELSHEIMER and the BRILLS. Like them, Claude used the later Mannerist traditions of the division of the picture into areas of dark greenish-brown foreground, light-green middle distance, and blue far distance, with the composition set out in COULISSES to create a sense of infinite distance, and tree forms treated as feathery fronds in silhouette. He also developed Elsheimer's landscape of mood created by poetic lighting effects, though not so much with strong chiaroscuro as by looking into the sun in a blaze of golden light. His composition remains virtually constant: a large mass of trees on one side counter-balanced by a smaller mass on the other, a middle distance with some small features such as a bridge or a farm, and a far distance of mountains, rivers or the Roman Campagna, in the most delicately atmospheric handling. In his sea-pieces and port scenes the additive detail of shipping, masonry, rigging and merchandise lying on quays does not really alter this arrangement of the parts, and allows him to concentrate on the magical effect of sunlight shimmering on water. He also uses small figures (possibly sometimes by other artists) not for themselves, but as a part of Nature, the drama of their action absorbed into immensities of light and space. His working drawings, loose and free in their handling, exemplify his way of looking at landscape by gradations of tone rather than colouristically, and his poetic rather than formal vision. Sandrart describes Claude's working methods and claims (perhaps wrongly) to have persuaded him to paint, as well as draw, in the open air. He also claims to have gone on sketching parties with Claude, Poussin, and BAMBOCCIO. Claude's influence was particularly strong in England, where his works were eagerly collected in the 18th and 19th centuries: most older galleries have examples and he is now also well represented in the US.

CLAW CHISEL *see* STONE CARVING.

CLEVE, Joos van *see* JOOS.

CLICHÉ-VERRE *see* ENGRAVING (2*c*).

CLODION. Claude Michel, called Clodion (1738–1814), was a French sculptor who won the Rome Prize in 1759 and went there in 1762. In 1767 he left the French Academy in Rome, but stayed on in the city working for Catherine II of Russia and other patrons until he was sharply reminded that he had been sent to Rome at the King's expense for the glory of France. He went home in 1771, but did not become an Associate of the Academy until 1793; never became a full Academician; and never received official commissions, other than the *Montesquieu* for the King (1779–83, the marble in the Institut, Paris). His works were almost entirely small figures of nymphs, satyresses and similar subjects treated in a frankly sensual way and he was nearly ruined by the Revolution and Republican Virtue. He rallied, however, and adopted the Greek taste so successfully that he was able to get work on the Colonne de la Grande Armée (1806–10) and the Arc de Triomphe du Carrousel (1806–9). There are works in London (V&A and Wallace Coll.), Paris (Louvre), Versailles and other French museums.

CLOISONNISME *see* BERNARD *and* SYMBOLISM.

CLOUET, François (*d.*1572), was the son of Jean II Clouet, whom he succeeded as Court painter in 1541. Like his father, he was sometimes called 'Janet', and Ronsard, his contemporary as Court Poet, called him 'Janet, honneur de notre France . . .'. He worked as a portraitist and on general decorative work normal for Court artists, such as the funeral of Francis I (1547). His earliest signed portrait is the *Pierre Quthe* (1562, Paris, Louvre), which suggests that he had visited Italy, since it shows knowledge of Italian portraits of the BRONZINO type. He is also believed to have painted the *Francis I* (Louvre), based on a drawing by his father, and the full-length *Charles IX* (Vienna, K-H Mus.), which is of the hieratic type current in Mannerist Court portraits internationally popular in the later 16th century. There is also a *Lady in her Bath* (Washington, NG; copy at Azay-le-Rideau), clearly representing a royal mistress, which appears linked to a number of similar erotic portraits of Venetian–Florentine Mannerist type, possibly connected with Bronzino's *Venus, Cupid, Time and Folly* (London, NG), which may be the picture Vasari says was sent to Francis I. Clouet also executed a series of portrait drawings, most of which are now in Chantilly (Mus. Condé). There are paintings in the Royal Coll. and in Florence (Uffizi and Pitti), Rouen, Versailles and Worcester Mass.

CLOUET, Jean II ('Janet') (*d.*1540/41), was probably the son of the Fleming Jean Clouet, painter to the Duke of Burgundy. Jean II is first recorded in a poem of 1509, where he is referred to along with Leonardo and others. He later became Court Painter in France, and was succeeded by his son François in 1541. He made a number of portrait drawings (mostly in the Mus. Condé, Chantilly) which are comparable to those of Holbein as records of a Court, though quite different in style. Paintings ascribed to him are in the Royal Coll. and in Antwerp, Edinburgh (NG), New York (Met. Mus.) and elsewhere.

COBRA *see* APPEL.

COELLO, Claudio (1642–93), was, like Velázquez, of Portuguese descent, but became the last great painter of the School of Madrid. The principal influences on his work seem to have been RUBENS, van DYCK and TITIAN – that is, he used his opportunities to study the Spanish Royal collection, which had masterpieces by all of them. He also studied in Italy at some time 1656/64 and was influenced by contemporaries such as DOLCI. He became Painter to the King in 1683, and was promoted Pintor de Cámara in 1686. His pictures tend to be overcrowded and rather complicated, and are reminiscent of Neapolitan Rococo. His masterpiece is *Charles II adoring the Blessed Sacrament* (1685–90: Sacristy of the Escorial), the space of the actual sacristy being continued in the picture, which contains the portraits of many priests and courtiers. There are other works by him in Castres, Frankfurt, London (Wellington Mus.), Madrid (Prado, Acad. and churches), Munich and Toledo Ohio.

COELLO, Sánchez, *see* SÁNCHEZ.

COLD COLOUR, TONE: COOL COLOUR, TONE. Those colours and tones which are blue, blue-green or blue-violet in general effect. The opposite of HOT or WARM.

COLE, Thomas (1801–48), was the principal member of the HUDSON RIVER SCHOOL of American landscape painters. He was born in England and worked as an engraver before emigrating to the US in 1818. In 1819 he went to the West Indies and was deeply impressed by the beauty of the scenery. His efforts as a landscape painter met with little success until he settled in New York in 1825, when he began to be recognized (e.g. by DUNLAP and

DURAND), and in 1826 he was one of the founders of the National Academy of Design. He returned to England in 1829 and went to Italy in 1831, where he lived in a studio that had traditionally been Claude's; Cole admired Claude (and therefore also Turner) more than any other painter, but his works are far more dramatically Romantic than theirs, and are perhaps closer to his contemporary MARTIN. The sheer immensity of the American wilderness gives many of his works – especially the series *The Voyage of Life* – a visionary quality. He returned to America in 1832, but made another trip to Europe in 1841–2. There are several of the *Voyage of Life* paintings in Utica, NY, a *View of Florence*, 1837, painted from drawings made in 1831, in Cleveland Ohio and an extraordinary fantasy, *The Architect's Dream*, 1840, in Toledo Ohio. Other works are in Boston, Hartford Conn., Los Angeles, Minneapolis, New York (Met. Mus. and Hist. Soc.), Oberlin Ohio, Providence RI, Washington (NG and Corcoran) and Yale.

COLLAGE (Fr. *coller* to stick). A composition built up wholly or partly from pieces of paper, cloth or other materials stuck on to a support. The device was much used by the early Cubists, who stuck pieces of newspaper on to canvases otherwise painted in a normal way, and by the Dadaists, such as SCHWITTERS. It is an unfortunate fact that newsprint has a very short life. In his last years Matisse used pieces of coloured paper as a complete substitute for painting. *See also* FROTTAGE.

COLLANTES, Francisco (1599–1656), was the leading Spanish landscape painter of the 17th century. He was born in Madrid, but was influened by Ribera and the Neapolitans, and also by the Venetian painters of the 16th century, especially in his landscape settings for Old Testament subjects. There are works in Bonn, Madrid (Prado and Acad.), New York (Hispanic Soc.), Paris (Louvre) and Providence RI.

COMPLEMENTARY COLOUR. Red, blue and yellow are called Primary Colours, and a Complementary Colour is obtained by mixing the other two – red has green as its complementary (blue and yellow). It is part of Impressionist theory that a primary-coloured object casts a shadow containing its complementary; thus, a yellow object has violet in the shadows.

COMPOSITION. The art of combining the elements of a picture or other work of art into a satisfactory whole: in art the whole is very much more than the sum of the parts. A picture is well composed if its constituents – whether figures or apples or just shapes – form a harmony which pleases the eye when regarded as two-dimensional shapes on a flat ground. This is the sole aim of most abstract painting, but in more traditional forms the task is made more difficult by the need to project the forms in an ordered sequence into an imaginary depth or picture space without losing their effectiveness as a pattern. The word is often used loosely to mean a work of art, a group, etc.

CONCA, Sebastiano (1680–1764), was a belated Baroque decorator. He was born near Naples and trained under SOLIMENA before moving to Rome in 1706. He was much employed in churches and also had a great reputation (like Solimena) as a teacher. In 1751 he was commissioned to decorate the church of Sta Chiara in Naples (totally destroyed in the Second World War) and he spent the rest of his life there. There are works by him in Augsburg, Brighton, Dresden, London (NG), Parma, Rome (Accad., Borghese, Gall. Naz. and churches), Sarasota Fla and elsewhere.

CONCRETE ART. A rigid form of abstraction exemplified by KANDINSKY, KUPKA, MALEVICH and MONDRIAN, and formulated in the Manifesto of Concrete Art by DOESBURG in 1930. Later, it was associated with the ABSTRACTION-CRÉATION group and with BILL. The forms employed are strictly non-natural in origin.

CONEGLIANO *see* CIMA.

CONINXLOO, Gillis van (1544–1607), was an important link in the chain of landscape painters between Bruegel and the early 17th-century Dutch realist painters such as E. van de VELDE, van GOYEN and S. van RUYSDAEL. Coninxloo travelled in France and Germany as well as his native Flanders, before settling in Amsterdam, where he died. His type of landscape has much realist detail, especially in the trees and foliage, but is combined with fantasy of shape and viewpoint, as well as adhering closely to the 'three-tone' scheme – warm brownish foreground, green middle distance, and blue distance. There are works in Brussels, Dresden, Graz, Rouen and Vienna.

CONSTABLE, John (1776–1837), was, with TURNER, the major English landscape painter of the 19th century. He first exhibited in 1802, but achieved only limited recognition, not becoming an ARA until 1819 (RA 1829). His comment on the Suffolk countryside, 'These scenes made me a painter', takes little account of his skill in composition and his brilliant use of chiaroscuro as a unifying factor. In 1806 he travelled in the Lake District, but he was happiest with the vivid, dewy greens of water-meadows and mills, under fresh, windy skies, his deep knowledge of which he owed, not only to his early life as a miller's son, but to the sky studies made under the influence of Luke Howard's 'The Climate of London' (1818–20). In 1824 his *Haywain* (shown at the Academy in 1821; now London, NG) and a *View on the Stour* were awarded a Gold Medal at the Paris Salon, and the great success of these and other works imported into France had an appreciable effect on the development of the BARBIZON SCHOOL, and on the painting of the Romantic Movement – Delacroix, for instance, was greatly impressed by them. He left few successors. The greatness of his art lies in the fact that it appears to be a spontaneous and immediate transcription of the scene before him (cf. Impressionism), whether in Suffolk, on the Dorset coast, at Salisbury or on Hampstead Heath, but it is actually a deeply pondered reconstruction of nature, modified by his close study of Claude and of the tradition inherited from Dutch 17th-century landscape painters such as RUISDAEL, and by his admiration for GAINSBOROUGH's view of nature, both in the early, Dutch-inspired *Cornard Wood* period, and the later, poetic, *Market Cart* type. He was the last great painter in this tradition, except, perhaps, Wilson STEER. After him, Turner's 'airy visions, painted with tinted steam' – the description is Constable's – and the meticulous detailing of the Pre-Raphaelites exploited different, and contradictory, attitudes to nature. Two of his sons, John and Lionel (1825–87), also painted, and some of their landscapes have become confused with their father's, although these are now being re-attributed. George Constable, an amateur of Arundel, did not disdain to profit from the accidental similarity of name. A large collection of Constable's works was bequeathed to the V&A, London, by his daughter, and this is the touchstone for all attributions. There are other examples in Boston, Cambridge (Fitzwm) and Cambridge Mass.

(Fogg), Chicago, Cincinnati, Detroit, Dublin, Dunedin NZ, Edinburgh (NG), Hartford Conn., Leeds, Le Mans, London (NG, BM, RA, Tate, Guildhall and Courtauld Inst.), Manchester, Montreal, New York (Met. Mus.), Ottawa, Oxford (Ashmolean), Philadelphia (Mus.), San Marino Cal., Toledo Ohio, Toronto, Washington (NG, Corcoran and Phillips), Worcester Mass. and Yale.

CONSTRUCTIVISM was principally a Russian movement which grew out of COLLAGE. Vladimir TATLIN in Moscow developed this into hanging and relief constructions, abstract in conception, and made of a variety of materials, including wire, glass and sheet metal. He later turned to architectural and engineering schemes such as the projected monument to the Third International – a leaning spiral about 1,300 feet high with counter-rotating central sections. The styles of PEVSNER and his brother GABO evolved from Cubism, but only after returning to Moscow in 1917 did they become abstract Constructivists, publishing in 1920 – the year of the big Constructivist exhibition – their 'Realistic Manifesto', in which they restated the ideas of Archipenko and Boccioni that only movement in space, and not volume, was important in art. By 1921 the movement was dead in Russia for political reasons, and its practitioners turned to furniture design, the stage, typography – anything, in fact, but painting and sculpture. Pevsner went to Paris in 1923, and Gabo worked in Germany until 1932. Constructivist ideas have had considerable influence on architecture and decoration, and their manifestations include abstract sculpture employing non-traditional materials such as perspex and other plastics, and industrial methods such as welding.

CONSULAR DIPTYCH *see* DIPTYCH.

CONTÉ. A proprietary name for synthetic black, red or brown chalk, as opposed to naturally coloured chalks. Nicolas Conté invented the modern 'lead' PENCIL in 1790.

CONTINUOUS REPRESENTATION. In many medieval and Early Renaissance – and some Mannerist – pictures there are representations of several successive incidents in the same story shown as taking place in different parts of the same picture or relief. For example, a painting of the martyrdom of a saint may show his miracles dotted about in the background, although they obviously took place before and after the actual martyrdom.

CONTOUR (Ital. *contorno*). The outline which, in drawing or painting, forms the boundary of one shape, defining it in relation to another, so that the outline of a head against a wall is at once the pattern made by the head at that particular position against the wall, and also the shape as if it were cut out of the wall by the impingement of the head. Contour means slightly more than outline or silhouette, because an attentive study of any good drawing – especially one by INGRES – will reveal that the modulation of the contour traced by the point of the pencil can express the fullness and recession of forms and even the variety of texture and surface between bony structure and fatter tissue. *See also* ANTI-CERNE.

CONTRAPPOSTO. An Italian word used to mean a pose in which one part of the body is twisted in the opposite direction from the other – usually with the hips and legs in one way and the chest and shoulders twisted on the opposite axis. Michelangelo's fantastic virtuosity in this (e.g. the *Ignudi* on the Sistine Ceiling) led to a sort of mania in the 16th century (with e.g. TIBALDI and VASARI) to see who could invent the most elaborate and improbable *contrapposto* for a figure supposedly performing some quite simple action.

CONVERSATION PIECE. A special kind of genre picture consisting of two or more small portraits of people in informal, usually domestic, surroundings. It is a group portrait, but with the sitters engaged with each other rather than the spectator. The type probably began in the Netherlands – COQUES, for example – but became an established English form in the hands of MERCIER and HOGARTH, DEVIS and ZOFFANY and it also passed into common use in the American Colonies, perhaps as a result of the importation of engravings. WATTEAU was the greatest French exponent, but it was not a popular form, and his pictures lack the specific portrait interest which normally distinguishes Conversation Pieces from straight genre subjects.

COOL COLOUR *see* COLD.

COOPER, Samuel (1609–72), was an English miniaturist who enjoyed a European reputation. Aubrey called him 'the prince of limners' and his prices were not far short of LELY's. Unlike HILLIARD he regarded the miniature as a painting, not a drawing or piece of goldsmith's work, and he modelled his heads in light and shade. Horace Walpole said: 'If a glass could expand Cooper's pictures to the size of Vandyck's they would appear to have been painted for that proportion. If his portrait of Cromwell could be so enlarged, I do not know but Vandyck would appear less great by the comparison . . .' The *Cromwell* is the best-known image of the Protector (private coll.; replica in the Royal Coll.). Evelyn's *Diary* for 10 January 1662 records: 'Being called into his Majesties Closet, when Mr Cooper (the rare limner) was crayoning of his face and head, to make the stamps by, for the new *mill'd* mony, now contriving, I had the honour to hold the Candle whilst it was doing; choosing to do this at night & by candle light, for the better finding out the shadows . . .' A few days earlier, Pepys had been disappointed in his hopes of meeting Cooper; later, however (30 March 1668), he visited Cooper's house and saw his work 'which is all in little, but so excellent as, though I must confess I do think the colouring of the flesh to be a little forced, yet the painting is so extraordinary, as I do never expect to see the like again . . . Being infinitely satisfied with this sight, and resolving that my wife shall be drawn by him . . .' In fact, this miniature of Mrs Pepys cost him £30, and another £8 3*s*. 4*d*. for its crystal and gold case, a large sum of money. Samuel Cooper's elder brother, Alexander (*d*.1660), was also a miniaturist who worked in Holland, Sweden and Denmark. Both were pupils of their uncle, John HOSKINS, who probably anticipated them in treating a miniature like an oil painting. There are works in the Royal Coll., The Hague, London (V&A) and Yale (CBA).

COPLEY, John Singleton (1738–1815), was a Boston painter, almost self-taught, who evolved a distinguished and direct portrait style for his New England clients. In 1774 he left America for good, and visited Italy and much of Europe before settling in London, where competition with Reynolds and WEST profoundly altered his style – in later life he carried on a feud against West and the Royal Academy. In spite of his Grand Manner aspirations his portraits of children retain an engaging vivacity. His *Brook Watson and the Shark* (1778, Washington NG and Boston), the *Death of Chatham* (1780, London, Tate) and *Death of Major Pierson* (1783, Tate) are notable for being among the first large pictures of contemporary history (cf. West's *Wolfe*) and grand-scale genre subjects, of a type later common in France during the Napoleonic period and the Romantic movement. There are examples in the Royal Coll., Cambridge Mass. (Fogg and Harvard), Cleveland Ohio, Detroit (a version of the *Shark*, 1782), Dundee, Hartford Conn. (a religious subject), London (NPG, Nat. Marit. Mus., RA and Guildhall), Los Angeles, New York (Met. Mus. and Brooklyn), Philadelphia (Hist. Soc.), Providence RI, Raleigh NC, Washington (NG and Corcoran) and Yale (CBA). The American museums contain most of his early portraits, of which there are many in Boston (Mus. and public buildings).

COQUES, Gonzales (1614 or 1618–84), was born and worked in Antwerp. His name seems to have been Cockx, but he used the Spanish form, probably for prestige. He did not become a Master in the Antwerp Guild until 1640/41 and he may have spent some time in England before then, possibly working for Charles I; in any case, he was aware of the work of van DYCK, which he adapted to his own small CONVERSATION PIECES of bourgeois family groups, often in opulent settings, which were very influential on later painters in the Netherlands. There are works by him in the Royal Coll. and in Antwerp, Barnsley, Berlin, Brussels, Budapest, Dublin, London (NG, V&A and Wallace Coll.) and elsewhere.

CORINTH, Lovis (1858–1925), was, like LIEBERMANN, one of the leading German Impressionists. He worked in Paris 1884–7 and painted in an Impressionist style until 1911, when he was crippled by a stroke. He forced his hand to work, and from then on painted in a more violent and pessimistic way: some of his later works are crude and harshly Expressionist. There is a museum in Tapiau, East Prussia (his birthplace), and he is well represented in German museums; other works are in Basle, Belgrade, London (Tate), New York (M of MA), Pittsburgh, Vienna and Zurich.

CORNEILLE de Lyon (active 1533/4–74), was a painter of small-scale portraits – almost miniatures – who was born in The Hague and settled in Lyons, where he was naturalized in 1547, and where he and his family, who were Huguenots, became Catholics in 1569. In 1540 he was made Painter to the Dauphin (later Henri II), and in 1551 the Venetian Ambassador described a visit to his studio, where he saw many small portraits of courtiers. After the death of Henri II in 1559 Corneille continued to work for the Court. The only definite attribution is a portrait of an unknown man in a French private collection, which is inscribed on the back as having been painted in 1533 by 'Corneille de La Haye' – i.e. Corneille from The Hague. All other attributions of his distinctive little half-length portraits, usually of men in black, very delicately modelled, against a green or blue background, are based on this single work, which is nearer to the larger portraits by JOOS van Cleve than to anything being produced in France or the Low Countries. There are examples in Amsterdam, Boston, Cleveland Ohio, Edinburgh (SNPG), London (NG and Wallace Coll.), Paris (Louvre) and New York (Met. Mus.).

CORNELISZ., Cornelis, van Haarlem (1562–1638), travelled in France and the Netherlands, but not, apparently, in Italy, before returning to Haarlem by 1583, where he spent the rest of his life. With the other 'Haarlem Mannerists', van MANDER and GOLTZIUS, he founded the Haarlem Academy, which was a school for drawing from the nude, providing material for his religious and mythological pictures, influenced by SPRANGER, which made him one of the last Dutch Mannerists. At the beginning of his career he painted two very large group portraits of the Haarlem militia, which influenced HALS, and he continued to paint portraits later in his career. Apart from Haarlem, there are works in Amsterdam, Antwerp, Baltimore, Brunswick, Budapest, Cambridge (Fitzwm), Dresden, Hartford Conn., Karlsruhe, London (NG), Ottawa, Oxford (Ashmolean), Paris (Louvre), Philadelphia, Utrecht, Valenciennes, Vienna and elsewhere.

CORNELIUS, Peter von (1783–1867), went to Rome in 1811 and there worked with OVERBECK and the NAZARENER until 1819. He then returned to Munich and became head of the so-called Munich School, which sought to revive monumental fresco painting. Most of his works are in Munich, but, like DYCE, he was also important as a teacher and administrator.

COROT, Jean Baptiste Camille (1796–1875), was born in Paris. His early training, from 1822 onwards, was with the classicizing landscape painters Michallon and Bertin, and in 1825 he went to Italy, via Switzerland, for two years. He spent most of his time in and around Rome, where he developed, through painting on the spot, his sensitive treatment of light, form and distance in terms of tonal values rather than by colour and drawing. In this he resembled MICHEL (whom he knew), but never to the point of abandoning, for works to be exhibited, the traditional classical or religious subject; this he used as a disguise for his unconventional vision, although these carefully composed landscapes have little of the spontaneity of his sketches from nature. He travelled widely in France 1827–34, and returned to Italy for several months in 1834 and 1843, his journeys being recorded in his drawings or his *pochades*, which are small and very freely handled, and remarkable for the justness of their tonal values and the freshness of their colour. By the early 1850s the tide of official and public favour had turned, possibly because by then he had developed for his Salon exhibits a fuzzy, woolly, poeticizing manner entirely different from the directness and keenness of observation found in his sketches. This muzzy treatment of the landscape and trees in soft, grey-green tones became immensely popular, and has assured him the most notoriously prolific of all posthumous productions (it has been said that Corot painted 1,000 pictures, of which 1,500 are in America). His very late figure studies and portraits are entirely free from the blurred and formless approach of his public manner, and show that in his 70s he was able to absorb the ideas of younger men, such as Courbet and Manet. His personal prestige with the younger generation was very great, and he did all in his admittedly limited power to soften the rigours of the Salon jury towards the works of unacademic artists. He was a man of great simplicity and generosity and extremely charitable, as witness his support of Daumier in his blindness, Millet's widow, and his benefactions during the Franco-Prussian War. There are examples of his art – autograph or attributed – in almost every museum of any size all over the world (there are sixteen in the NG, London, alone). The works of Caruelle d'Aligny (1798–1871) and Édouard Bertin (1797–1871), who were his companions in Rome in 1825–7 on many of his painting expeditions, can all too easily be confused with his.

CORREGGIO, Antonio (probably 1489–1534), worked mostly in Parma in a style that looks forward to the Baroque and even, in its softness, to the French 18th century (cf. *Venus, Mercury, and Cupid*, London, NG). His earliest works show the combined influences, oddly disparate, of MANTEGNA, whose pupil he traditionally was, and of LEONARDO (who influenced most early 16th-century painters in N. Italy). From Leonardo he developed a very soft painterly style, extolled by 18th-century critics as MORBIDEZZA, or the 'Corregiosity of Correggio'. This softness, which in works like the *SS. Placid and Flavia* (Parma) is allied to a virtually Baroque movement and emotion, is characteristic of all his oil-paintings and achieves in his mythologies a tender and voluptuous quality. His frescoes show so much of the influence of Michelangelo and Raphael as to make a visit to Rome before 1520 fairly certain. He is first documented as a painter in 1514, and his first set of frescoes was painted about 1518: these are the decorations in the Camera di S. Paolo, Parma, which derive partly from the SOTTO IN SÙ perspective of Mantegna's Mantuan frescoes and his *Madonna della Vittoria*, and partly from Leonardo. His major frescoes in Parma are the cupolas of S. Giovanni Evangelista (1520–23) and the Cathedral (documented from 1522, but probably executed 1526–30). Both these have extremely illusionistic effects as seen from below, and anticipate the ceilings and domes of the 17th century, particularly those of LANFRANCO. The dome of the Cathedral, representing the *Assumption*, is composed of ascending concentric circles of flying figures and is said to have been described unkindly (but not altogether unreasonably) by one of the canons as 'a hash of frogs' legs'. Apart from Parma there are no other frescoes, but there are fresco fragments in London (NG), and oil-paintings in the Royal Coll. and Berlin, Boston (Gardner), Budapest, Chicago, Detroit, Dresden, Florence (Uffizi), Frankfurt (Städel), London (NG, Wellington Mus. and Courtauld Inst.), Los Angeles, Madrid (Prado and Acad.), Milan (Brera and Mus. Civico), Modena, Munich, Naples, New York (Met. Mus.), Paris (Louvre), Philadelphia (Johnson), Pavia, Rome (Borghese), Vienna and Washington (NG).

CORTONA, Pietro da, *see* PIETRO.

COSMATI. A name given to the marble and mosaic workers in Rome from the 12th to the 14th centuries, many of whom were of the same family. They made many pavements, pulpits, tombs and other church furnishings in marble with inlays of coloured stones and glass, mosaic and gilding. Towards the end of the period they also produced sculpture. 'Cosmati work' is thus a generic term for work in coloured stones – for example, the Tomb of Henry III in Westminster Abbey.

COSSA, Francesco del (1435/6–probably 1477), worked in Ferrara from 1456 as a follower, to some extent, of Cosmè TURA; but his style was probably first formed in Florence, and his *Crucifixion* (Washington, NG) although probably a late work shows clear traces of the style of Castagno. Like all the other Ferrarese of the 15th century he was basically influenced by MANTEGNA and also by Piero della Francesca, whose lost frescoes in Ferrara may well have influenced Cossa's best-known works, the fresco-cycle of the *Months* in the Palazzo Schifanoia at Ferrara. These were completed in 1470 and Cossa – who did not paint all of the cycle – was so ill-satisfied with his pay that he left the city and spent the rest of his life in Bologna. The Schifanoia frescoes are charming and mildly lascivious, but they can hardly rank with the Camera degli Sposi at Mantua, in which Mantegna also depicted the daily life of a Court, nor (presumably) would they have compared with the lost Pieros. Parts of the Schifanoia frescoes are lost, parts are by pupils, and one – *September* – is possibly the earliest work of Ercole ROBERTI. There are works by Cossa in Berlin (Schloss Mus.), Bologna (Pinacoteca and churches), Dresden, Forlí, London (NG), Milan (Brera) and Paris (Jacquemart-André).

COSTA, Lorenzo (*c.*1460–1535), was trained in Ferrara and brought up in the style of TURA, COSSA and ROBERTI. He moved to Bologna by 1483 and worked there for the Bentivoglio Court, becoming the partner of Francesco FRANCIA and tempering the ferocity of his Ferrarese style with Francia's Umbrian softness. In 1506 he was appointed Court Painter at Mantua in succession to Mantegna and painted two *Allegories* for Isabella d' Este (now in Paris, Louvre); later in life, however, ill-health led to his eclipse by GIULIO Romano. There are works by him in the Royal Coll. and in Amsterdam, Berlin. Bologna (Pinacoteca, S. Giacomo Maggiore and other churches), Boston, Dresden, Dublin, Florence (Uffizi), London (NG), Lyons, Mantua (S. Andrea), Milan (Brera), New York (Met. Mus.), Paris (Louvre and Jacquemart-André), Toledo Ohio, Vaduz (Liechtenstein Coll.) and Washington (NG).

COSTA, Nino (i.e. Giovanni) (1826–1903), pioneered the introduction of realistic landscape into 19th-century Italy, becoming one of the precursors of the MACCHIAIOLI (especially FATTORI) when, for political reasons, he lived in Florence (1859–70). He was a life-long friend of LEIGHTON and knew BÖCKLIN, as well as the work of COROT and the BARBIZON painters. He often visited Paris and London, and organized exhibitions in Rome which included the works of Leighton, Alma-Tadema, Burne-Jones and other foreigners. There are works in Milan (Gall. d' Arte Mod.) and Rome (Gall. d' Arte Mod.).

COSTRUZIONE LEGITTIMA. A modern term for an early system of PERSPECTIVE, described in the treatise on painting, 'Della Pittura', written *c.*1435 by the architect, humanist and aesthetic theorist ALBERTI. The theory was derived ultimately from the practice of the architect BRUNELLESCHI, but, since his demonstrations are lost, Alberti's written description is the earliest evidence we have. The system is based on a geometrically constructed picture-plane, in which the height of a figure in the foreground becomes the unit on which the proportions of the whole are calculated. The horizon is fixed at the eye-level of this figure and becomes the Vanishing Point, to which all lines that recede into the picture are made to converge. Lines parallel to the picture-plane have no point on which to converge, since they remain perpetually parallel; thus introducing an element of distortion, since, for example, a house in the picture will seem to have one side vanishing according to the laws of perspective, while the side parallel to the spectator remains unaffected. Examples of this type of perspective can be found in e.g. UCCELLO's *Deluge*.

COSWAY, Richard (1742–1821), was a fashionable miniaturist of great charm and ability. He became an RA in 1771, was a collector of Old Master drawings, dealt in pictures as a side-line, and was a famous fop and a friend of the Prince of Wales (later George IV). In 1781 he married Maria Hadfield, who had been born and brought up in Florence, and was also a miniaturist, though not in her husband's rare class. They entertained lavishly in London, perhaps imprudently in view of the scandalous rumours which circulated about their house. After her husband's death Maria Cosway returned to Italy, where she ran a girls' school at Lodi until her death in 1838. There are examples of Richard's works in the Royal Coll., and in London (NPG, Tate, V&A and Wallace Coll.) and a landscape in oil in Cambridge (Fitzwm).

COTÁN *see* SANCHEZ-COTÁN.

COTES, Francis (1726–70), first made his mark in 1748 as a pastellist. He was a pupil of KNAPTON, but used brighter colour than his master, and shows the influence of Rosalba CARRIERA and LIOTARD. During the 1760s he worked more in oils, adopting Reynolds's portrait style – e.g. *Two Ladies as Diana and Companion* (York) – in contrast to the more conservative patterns of Knapton. He was Reynolds's most serious competitor before the arrival of Gainsborough in London in 1774 (after Cotes's early death), but his portraits have neither Reynolds's inventiveness nor Gainsborough's charm, though at his best – e.g. in his portrait of the watercolour painter Paul Sandby (London, Tate) – he is fine indeed. He was a Founder-Member of the RA (1768). His house and studio in Cavendish Square were later taken over by another rival of Reynolds, George Romney. There are examples in the Royal Coll., Cardiff, Edinburgh (NPG), Leeds, Leicester (a pastel dated 1747: the earliest dated work), London (NPG, Tate, RA and Coram Fdn), New York (Met. Mus.), Oxford (Ch. Ch.), Yale (CBA) and elsewhere.

COTMAN, John Sell (1782–1842), was a painter in watercolour and oil, whose austere sense of design produced some of the finest English landscape paintings of the early 19th century, comparable with the works of Constable and Turner. He was born in Norwich but worked in London, partly with Dr MONRO, and exhibited at the RA 1800–06. He then returned to Norwich, where he first exhibited in 1807, becoming the leading member of the NORWICH SCHOOL along with CROME. While living in East Anglia he began to make etchings for 'The Architectural Antiquities of Norfolk' (sixty plates, 1811–18), and, unlike Crome, print-making became a major part of his work. He visited Normandy in 1817–18 and again in 1820, making drawings for Dawson Turner's 'Tour of Normandy' (1820), and, more importantly, for Cotman's own large etchings for 'The Architectural Antiquities of Normandy' (1822). In 1834 he returned to London. From 1831 he used watercolour mixed with rice-paste, producing an impasted and richly-wrought surface which (to modern taste) is rather vulgar and totally different from his earlier work, which depends solely on simple flat washes of colour and clearly defined, almost geometric, planes. There are many works by him in Norwich and in London (BM, NG, Tate, V&A and Courtauld Inst.) and others in Birmingham, Hull, Kendal, Leeds, Port Sunlight (Lady Lever Gall.), and Yale (CBA). His sons Miles Edmund (1810–58) and John Joseph (1814–78) were also painters, and are well represented in Norwich. John Thirtle of Norwich was also greatly influenced by him.

COULISSE (Fr.). The side-pieces at either side of the stage, so arranged as to give room for exits and entrances. The idea has been extended to describe the type of composition in which the effect of recession into space is obtained by leading the eye back into depth by the overlaps, usually alternately left and right, of hills, bushes, winding rivers and similar devices. *See* REPOUSSOIR.

COUNTERPROOF. A mirror-image reproduction, made by damping an original drawing or engraving, laying a damp sheet of clean paper on it, and then running both through a press. This is sometimes done by the artist himself, in order to bring a fresh eye to the work (which looks quite different when reversed), but it is also the commonest and simplest method of faking 'original' drawings. Fortunately, such elementary fakes are easy to detect, since right hands become left and the normal right-handed direction of shading is reversed. An offset is the same thing, but has a rather wider meaning, e.g. in printing, when the not-quite-dry ink prints off on the next page.

COURBET, Gustave (1819–77), was born at Ornans, near the Swiss border of France. He was in Paris by 1839, working under a minor painter, in the so-called ATELIERS LIBRES and in the Louvre, copying Dutch, Flemish, Venetian and Spanish pictures, as well as works by Delacroix and Géricault. Much later – characteristically – he claimed to have been self-taught. He exhibited at the Salon regularly only after the State bought his *After Dinner at Ornans* (1849, Lille), when the award of a medal exempted him from the jury system, until the privilege was abolished in 1857. He often exhibited in the provinces, which were generally less acidly critical than Paris, and he made many trips to Belgium, Holland and Germany between 1846 and 1868, exhibiting there with more success than in France. He evolved a vigorous naturalism, tinged with the influence of Caravaggio and the Venetians, and painted scenes of everyday life, portraits (particularly self-portraits), nudes, still-life, sea- and landscapes, and flowers. The landscapes are often of mountain scenery round Ornans, and include hunting scenes or deer in the snow. His scenes from everyday life range from the depiction of abject poverty (as in the *Stonebreakers*, 1850, formerly Dresden, destroyed 1945), social comment (the *Young Women of the Village*, 1851, Leeds; or the *Young Women by the Seine*, 1856–7, Paris, Mus. d'Orsay) to the representation of a peasant funeral with more than fifty life-size figures in the *Burial at Ornans* (1850, Paris, Mus. d'Orsay). He also painted a quasi-philosophical manifesto in the huge *Painter in his Studio* (1855, Paris, Mus. d'Orsay).

In 1853, Alfred Bruyas, a rich collector, bought the *Bathers* and the *Spinner* and sat for his portrait. Their unlikely friendship endured until Courbet's death, and Bruyas was his most devoted patron, host and admirer, portrayed in the *Bonjour, Monsieur Courbet* of 1854. All the Bruyas pictures are now in Montpellier, Mus. Fabre. In 1855 and 1867, on the occasion of International Exhibitions in Paris, he held large private exhibitions of his works in an attempt to offset official neglect. Both attracted more adverse than helpful comment, but they established the precedent of private exhibitions, later followed by Manet and the Impressionists (cf., however, ROSA). Courbet was intransigent in his political attitudes, articulately Republican and anti-Imperialist, a friend of the socialist philosopher Prudhon, and rabidly anti-clerical. His *Return from the Conference* (1862), depicting drunken priests, was rejected both by the official Salon and the Salon des Refusés, earned him general abuse, and was bought by a strict Catholic who destroyed it. After the restoration of Republican government, following the disasters of the Franco-Prussian War, he proposed the demolition of the Vendôme Column, which celebrated the victories of the first Napoleon, although he does not appear to have had a hand in the actual demolition in April 1871. At the overthrow of the Commune he was arrested and sentenced to 6 months' imprisonment for his part in the destruction of the column; but in 1873 he was re-tried and condemned to pay for its restoration, estimated at over Fr.323,000. Faced with total ruin, he fled to Switzerland. He set up a picture factory, employing hacks in what was virtually a production-line for Swiss landscapes, which have damaged his reputation. His technique was imperfect; reworkings and bitumen have played havoc with many works, and his brushwork and use of the trowel-shaped palette knife are often as insensitive as his colour, although in his best works this can be extraordinarily rich, his chiaroscuro and his vivid, unconventional approach dramatically exciting. Many of his nudes range from the mildly to the highly erotic, but his painting of bare flesh is always superb. He had a certain influence on Whistler, although the American indignantly repudiated this. He was of inordinate vanity, with an unendearingly caustic tongue, and led a flamboyantly Bohemian life; eventually he developed dropsy and died in exile on the last day of 1877.

There are works in Baltimore, Basle, Berne, Birmingham, Boston (Mus. and Gardner), Bristol, Budapest, Cambridge (Fitzwm), Cambridge Mass. (Fogg), Chicago, Cincinnati, Cleveland Ohio, Cologne (Mus.), Columbus Ohio, Detroit, Dublin, Edinburgh (NG), Glasgow (Mus. and Burrell), Hartford Conn., Kansas City, Liverpool, London (NG, Tate and V&A), Manchester, Mannheim, Minneapolis, Montreal, New York (Met. Mus. and Brooklyn), Northampton Mass. (Smith Coll.), Ornans, Ottawa, Paris, Philadelphia (Mus. and Acad.), Portland Oregon, Providence RI, Rochester NY, St Louis, Toledo Ohio, Toronto, Washington (NG, Corcoran and Phillips), Yale and French provincial museums.

COUSTOU, Guillaume I (1677–1746), was one of a family of French sculptors. He was a pupil of his uncle COYSEVOX and went to Rome, where his sister married LEGROS. He became Director of the Academy and worked for the Crown from 1707; his masterpieces, the *Chevaux de Marly*, were made for the Royal park at Marly 1740/5 and are based on the antique *Horse-Tamers* in Rome. They now stand at the entrance to the Champs-Élysées in Paris. Liverpool has a fine bust by him of his brother Nicolas (1658–1733), who was also a sculptor. Guillaume's son, Guillaume II (1716–77), became an Academician in 1742 and produced much sculpture for churches and public buildings. There is a bust by him in London (V&A) and his *Vulcan*, made for the Academy, is in Paris (Louvre).

COUTURE, Thomas (1815–79), was a French history and portrait painter whose best-known work is the *Romans of the Decadence* (1847, Paris, Mus. d'Orsay), which united the soft colour of the 18th century to the contemporary classic strictness, but is in fact a 19th-century orgy picture of a recognizable type. He was a pupil of GROS and was a good portrait painter (e.g. Glasgow, Burrell), with a bold attack, and is now remembered as an outstanding teacher, whose pupils included FEUERBACH as well as MANET. His *Etex* (Birmingham) shows his influence: much of the so-called Spanish influence on Manet's early work is in fact derived from Couture's freedom of handling and sharp tonal contrasts. Outside France there are pictures in Boston, Bristol, Budapest, Cambridge (Fitzwm), Cambridge Mass. (Fogg: a sketch for the *Decadence*), Cleveland Ohio, Edinburgh, London (NG and Wallace Coll., including the first idea for the *Decadence*, dated 1843), New York (Met. Mus.), Philadelphia, Providence RI, Toledo Ohio and Washington (Corcoran).

COX, David (1783–1859), was a watercolour painter who studied for a while under VARLEY (1804) and first exhibited at the RA in 1805. He lived by teaching and published several books, of which the best-known is the 'Treatise on Landscape Painting and Effect in Watercolours' (1813–14, reprinted 1922). His favourite painting ground was North Wales, but he visited Holland and Belgium in 1826 and France in 1829 and 1832. His effects are extremely broad, with a vigour of handling that sometimes appears forced, as if for exhibition. In 1836 he discovered accidentally a kind of cheap wrapping paper made in Dundee, which exactly suited his style, since the rough, slightly tinted paper absorbed the washes quickly. A similar kind of paper is now sold as 'Cox Paper'. In 1840 he took lessons in oil painting from MÜLLER, but his watercolours have always been more prized. The best collection of his work is in his native Birmingham, but other works are in Cardiff, London (BM, V&A, Tate and Courtauld Inst.), Manchester (City Gall. and Whitworth), Yale (CBA) and elsewhere. His son David (1809–85) was also a painter.

COYPEL, a dynasty of French painters active in the 17th and 18th centuries. The founder was Noël (1628–1707) whose career began in 1646 and who painted in a style derived from POUSSIN. He decorated the Invalides in Paris (*c.*1700–07), worked for the Gobelins tapestry factory from 1674 and had a distinguished career in the Academy. He became a Member in 1663, Professor in 1664 and Director in 1695. The influence of LEBRUN got him the appointment as Director of the French Academy in Rome, 1672–4. Some of his writings were published posthumously. There are pictures by him in Paris (Louvre), Madrid, and many French provincial museums.

His son, Antoine (1661–1722), was the most famous of the family. He began his training under his father in Rome in 1672 and was made a Member of the Academy in Paris in 1681, becoming Director in 1714 and Rector in 1716. In 1717 he was ennobled. His works are evidence of the triumph of RUBÉNISME by the 1690s, but the vast ceiling of the chapel at Versailles (1708) is much more reminiscent of Roman High-Baroque illusionism, as practised by BACICCIO at the Gesù. There are works by him in Berlin, Dublin, Florence, Madrid, Paris (Louvre) and many French provincial museums.

Antoine's half-brother, Noël-Nicolas (1690–1734), was also a painter and pastellist, and became a Member of the Academy in 1720. Antoine's son, Charles-Antoine (1694–1752), also had a distinguished academic career, becoming First Painter to the King in 1743 and Director of the Academy in 1747. He was widely read and himself wrote forty pieces for the stage; Voltaire wrote an epigram on him: 'On dit que notre ami Coypel/ Imite Horace et Raphaël./ A les surpasser il s'efforce;/ Et nous n'avons point aujourd'hui/ De rimeur peignant de sa force,/ Ni peintre rimant comme lui'. His huge output included book-illustrations and tapestry designs as well as religious pictures, portraits and writings on art. He was the originator of the idea of the ÉCOLE des Élèves Protégés. There are works by him in Paris (Louvre, Jacquemart-André and Gobelins Mus.), Senlis Cath. and other French museums, and in Berlin, Cleveland Ohio, Hartford Conn., Minneapolis, New York (Met. Mus.), Philadelphia and Sarasota Fla.

COYSEVOX, Antoine (1640–1720), was the chief sculptor to Louis XIV of France, and worked much at Versailles, in a vigorous Baroque style derived ultimately from Bernini. His chief rival there was the more classicizing GIRARDON. He arrived in Paris in 1657, became sculptor to the King in 1666, and was received into the Academy in 1676, his diploma work being the splendidly Berninesque bust of Charles Lebrun (the original terracotta, 1676, is in the Wallace Coll.,

London, and the finished marble, 1679, is in the Louvre). He made several tombs, including that of Cardinal Mazarin (1689–93, now in the Louvre), and a portrait bust for the monument to Matthew Prior (London, Westminster Abbey). COUSTOU was his nephew and pupil.

COZENS, Alexander (1717–86), was born in Russia (though the picturesque story that his father was Peter the Great is not now credited). He went to England as a child, but returned to Russia and then went to Rome in 1746. He was back in England by 1749, and seems to have made another journey to the Continent in 1764, but most of his time was spent as a drawing master. He is best known for his system of 'BLOT drawings' – in 1781 he was described by Beckford as 'almost as full of systems as the Universe' – which developed an idea adumbrated by Leonardo da Vinci. A blot or blots made haphazardly on a sheet of paper would suggest a landscape or other composition, which could then be worked out in full. This system was set out in his 'Essay to Facilitate the Inventing of Landskips . . .', 1759, and his 'New Method of Assisting the Invention in Drawing Original Compositions of Landscape', 1785/6, and several other books. There are drawings and blottings by him in London (BM, V&A, Tate and Courtauld Inst.), and in Bedford, Birmingham, Manchester (Whitworth) and Yale (CBA).

COZENS, John Robert (1752–97), the son of Alexander, was, according to Constable, 'the greatest genius that ever touched landscape' and 'Cozens is all poetry'. His entire work consists of landscapes in watercolour, and only one oil painting, of 1791 and traditionally attributed to Richard Wilson, is known (in a private collection). Another, exhibited at the RA in 1776, of *Hannibal crossing the Alps*, is now lost, but Turner admired it greatly and painted his own version of the subject. Cozens went to Switzerland and Italy with the famous connoisseur Richard Payne Knight in 1776–9, when his style seems to have been modified by contact with Swiss watercolourists, notably DUCROS, who was said to be an innovator in technique. He returned to Switzerland and Italy, going as far south as Naples, in 1782–3, this time in the train of William Beckford, the eccentric millionaire author of 'Vathek'. On these journeys Cozens discovered the grandeur of the Swiss Alps, as well as the better-known beauties of the classical Italian landscape; his gentle and poetic landscapes are muted in colour and soft in lighting, being predominantly blue-green or blue-grey in tonality. Some time in 1793 his mind gave way, and early in 1794 he was under the care of Dr MONRO, who regarded him as incurable. He died in 1797 without recovering. He exercised an enormous influence on the next generation, since both Turner and Girtin worked for Dr Monro and copied drawings by Cozens. There are watercolours by him in the Royal Coll. and in Aberdeen, Birmingham, Cambridge (Fitzwm), Leeds, London (BM, V&A, Tate and Soane Mus.), Manchester (Whitworth: seventeen drawings and seven sketch-books), Oxford (Ashmolean), Yale (CBA) and elsewhere.

CRAESBECK *see* BROUWER.

CRANACH, Lucas I (1472–1553), painter, etcher and designer of woodcuts, was in Vienna in 1503 and had probably been there since 1500. In 1505 he went to Wittenberg to become Court Painter to the Electors of Saxony and there he met Luther, became his friend and designed propaganda woodcuts for him. His earliest works are religious subjects in which the landscape plays a great part; they are therefore linked with the ideas of the DANUBE School. In

Wittenberg his style changed considerably, partly on account of the large shop he set up. He seems to have invented the full-length portrait as an independent work of art, for the splendid pair of *Henry the Pious of Saxony* and his *Duchess* (1514, both in Dresden, and probably originally on one panel) certainly ante-date the Italian examples by MORETTO and others, and probably ante-date other German examples: only CARPACCIO's *Knight* has a claim to be earlier. All his life Cranach continued to paint splendid portraits, including a large number of versions of Luther, but at the same time he developed a new kind of highly erotic female nude, usually full-length, painted with a glossy, enamel-like finish and purporting to represent Lucretia, Venus or some other mythological character. They usually wear elaborate hats and jewellery, but not much else. From about 1505/9 he made a number of woodcuts, much influenced by Dürer, and from about 1520 he designed many more, often rather crudely executed, to illustrate the Bible, or the writings of the Reformers. Most of his pictures are signed with a winged snake and the monogram LC, but it is very difficult to distinguish his own works from those produced in his shop or by his sons Hans (*d.*1537) and Lucas II (1515–86). One of the most interesting lost masterpieces must be his portrait of TITIAN, painted in 1550 at Augsburg. There are pictures by him in the Royal Coll., and in Augsburg, Basle, Berlin, Boston, Bristol, Brunswick, Brussels, Budapest, Cincinnati, Cologne (Wallraf-Richartz), Darmstadt, Detroit, Dresden, Edinburgh (NG), Florence (Uffizi), Frankfurt (Städel), Glasgow (Burrell), Kansas City, Karlsruhe, Knightshayes Court Devon (Nat. Trust), Leipzig, Leningrad, Lisbon, Liverpool, London (NG and Courtauld Inst.), Milwaukee, Munich, New York (Met. Mus.), Nuremberg, Oslo, Ottawa, Paris (Louvre), Philadelphia, Sarasota Fla, Stockholm, Toledo Ohio, Vaduz (Liechtenstein), Vienna (K-H Mus., Akad. and Albertina), Weimar, Wroclaw (Mus. and Cath.), Yale and many other museums.

CRAQUELURE (Fr. cracking). The network of fine cracks which covers the surface of an old oil painting, caused by shrinkage of the paint film, movement of the ground and varnish deterioration. There are characteristic crack-formations for each type of ground and paint film, and they also vary with age and with the technical skill of the original painter. *Craquelure* remains one of the principal means of detecting forgery, although really high-class forgers use elaborate electrical and chemical means to counterfeit the effects of time.

CRAYON. (i) In ordinary English usage, a mixture of dry, powdered colour with a wax binder, giving an effect not unlike PASTEL, but greasier and much less easily rubbed. It is familiar from the drawings of small children. (ii) In French, *crayon* is what in English is lead-pencil, but (iii) *crayon électrique* (properly *crayon de charbon de lampe électrique*) is a carborundum arc-lamp element which can be used as a sort of drypoint: DEGAS was the only major engraver to exploit its possibilities. *See also* TROIS CRAYONS.

CREDI, Lorenzo di (*c.*1458–1537), was a Florentine painter who was the fellow-pupil of LEONARDO under VERROCCHIO, whose principal assistant on the painting side of the business he became. He was in Verrocchio's shop in 1480/1 and was still there in 1488, when Verrocchio died. His style is technically admirable, but is otherwise an insensitive and highly-coloured version of Leonardo's earlier works. There are several pictures by him in Florence, and others in Berlin, Boston (Gardner), Cambridge Mass. (Fogg), Cleveland Ohio,

Dresden, Liverpool, London (NG), Naples, New York (Met. Mus.), Oxford, Paris (Louvre), Philadelphia (Johnson), Princeton NJ, San Marino Cal., the Vatican, Worcester Mass., Yale, York and elsewhere.

CRESPI, Daniele (*c.*1598–1630), was probably related to G. B. CRESPI and was certainly much influenced by him. His career was cut short by the plague of 1630, but, like G. B. Crespi, he expressed Counter-Reformation piety, and his best-known work is *St Charles Borromeo's Lenten Meal* (*c.*1628) in S. Maria della Passione, Milan, which has many other paintings by him. His *St Bruno* cycle in the Certosa at Garegnano, Milan, of 1629, shows the influence of Rubens and van Dyck, and was followed by a similar (less good) cycle in the Certosa at Pavia. There are works in Milanese museums and churches, and also in Berlin, Budapest, Florence (Uffizi), Madrid (Prado), Munich, Piacenza (S.M. di Campagna), Vienna (K-H Mus.) and Wellesley College Mass.

CRESPI, Giovanni Battista 'Il Cerano' (*c.*1575–1632), was the major Lombard Mannerist of the early 17th century. He was born at Cerano, near Novara, and visited Rome and Venice; as a result, the main influence on his early style, Gaudenzio FERRARI, was overlaid by the influences of BAROCCI, Tintoretto and Veronese. He settled in Milan *c.*1598 and worked for Cardinal Federigo Borromeo, contributing to the scenes from the life of St Charles Borromeo, painted for Milan Cathedral between 1602 and St Charles's canonization in 1610. In 1620 he was appointed first Director of the painting school in the Cardinal's new Accademia Ambrosiana, and in 1629 he became head of the sculpture workshop of the Cathedral (his designs for sculpture are in the Cath. Mus.). His paintings reflect the piety of the age of St Charles (*d.*1584), and are Mannerist principally on account of their emotional quality and their pale, clear tonality, with a favourite lemon, grey and pink colour scheme. With MORAZZONE and G. C. PROCACCINI he was the leading Milanese painter of the early 17th century, and a curious *Martyrdom* (Milan, Brera), painted before 1625, shows all three collaborating in what is called 'the three-handed picture'. There are works in many Milanese churches and in the Ambrosiana, Brera, and Castello Museums, and also in Bristol, Detroit, Florence (Uffizi), Pavia (Certosa), Princeton NJ, Turin, Varese (S. Vittore), and Vienna. A drawing in New York (Met. Mus.) is a study for a statue, 70 feet high, of St Charles Borromeo, on a 42-foot pedestal, at Arona, the saint's birthplace on Lago Maggiore. It was designed by Crespi, but not erected until 1697.

CRESPI, Giuseppe Maria (1665–1747), was a Bolognese painter, trained in the academic tradition, which he came to loathe. In his youth, Bologna was still the Mecca of foreigners studying in Italy, but he predicted its end as a School and lived long enough to see it replaced by Rome. He developed a vivid genre style: dark shadows and very strong lights – time has accentuated the contrasts – and a passion for effects of light, which often involved a surrender to anecdote, and gives the details of his settings an almost Dutch character, although they are in fact derived from the Caravaggesque tradition. He influenced PIAZZETTA, who used his low tones, rich greys and light effects. P. LONGHI was his pupil. He died blind. There are works in Birmingham, Bologna, Boston (Mus.), Cambridge Mass. (Fogg), Chicago, Dresden (the *Seven Sacraments*, his best-known works), Florence (Uffizi and Pitti), London (NG and Courtauld Inst.), Munich, Paris (Louvre), St Louis, the Vatican, Vienna, Washington (NG) and elsewhere.

CRISTUS, Petrus, *see* CHRISTUS.

CRITZ *see* GHEERAERTS.

CRIVELLI, Carlo (*d.*1495/1500), was a Venetian painter, probably trained in the VIVARINI workshop, imprisoned in Venice for adultery in 1457. Some Paduan training is also likely, since his strongest stylistic affinities are with SQUARCIONESQUE painters like Schiavone, and his hard, wiry style is powerfully influenced by MANTEGNA. In 1465 he was recorded in Zara (now Zadar) in Dalmatia, and soon afterwards he must have moved to the Marches of Italy, where he is documented from 1468, mostly in Ascoli Piceno. Though he always signed himself as a Venetian, he never returned to Venice. In 1490 he was knighted, a rare distinction for an artist. All his pictures are of religious subjects, and old-fashioned in type since he did not use the SACRA CONVERSAZIONE form until it had been current in the rest of Italy for some thirty years; he also used, until the 1480s, the old-fashioned device of raised plaster details, such as crowns or saints' attributes, giving a three-dimensional quality to his linear and highly stylized forms in which there is a strong element of Late Gothic fantasy. His iconography is very elaborate, and the gourds and garlands of fruit, and other complicated details, all further the inner significance of his hieratic images. Vittorio Crivelli, possibly a younger brother, worked in a similar style, but was less accomplished. Many of Carlo's works are still in the churches for which they were painted, but twelve pictures are now in London (NG), and the Brera in Milan also has important examples.

CROME, John (1768–1821), was, with COTMAN, the major artist of the NORWICH SCHOOL. He began life as an errand boy, but apprenticed himself to a sign painter, and is said to have taught himself by being allowed to copy pictures by Gainsborough and Hobbema in the collection of Thomas Harvey of Catton, who was his patron from 1790 (although little is known of his work before 1805). Certainly the Dutch 17th century is the principal influence on his style, together with that of Wilson – a perceptive contemporary described him as 'combining Ruisdael with Gainsborough'. His observation of Norfolk scenery has the same freshness as Hobbema and Ruisdael, while Cuyp and Wilson influenced his sense of design and light. He founded the Norwich Society of Artists in 1803 and exhibited there regularly. In 1814, along with many other British artists, he went to Paris to see the pictures looted by Napoleon, and on the way he visited Belgium. He made a number of etchings, but almost all were 'finished' by others after his death, so that his graphic work is less important than Cotman's. He is well represented in Norwich and other works are in Boston, Edinburgh, London (NG, Tate and Courtauld Inst.), New York (Met. Mus.), Ottawa, Yale (CBA) and elsewhere. He was often called 'Old Crome' to distinguish him from his son, John Berney Crome (1794–1842), who imitated him. The large picture of the *Yarmouth Water Frolic* (London, Kenwood) is at least partly by the younger man, but the sketch for it (private coll.) is certainly by the elder. There are other works by J. B. Crome in Norwich. James Stark was also a pupil of Old Crome.

CROQUIS *see* SKETCH.

CROSS-HATCHING *see* HATCHING.

CUBISM is the parent of all modern abstract movements although itself an avowedly realist movement. It grew out of the efforts of PICASSO and BRAQUE to replace the purely visual effects of Impressionist preoccupation with the surface of objects with a more intellectual conception of form and colour. Their starting-point was Cézanne, who had striven towards the same ends, but Cubism carried much further the ideas of the unity of the two-dimensional picture surface, and the analysis of forms and their interrelation, since they deliberately gave up the representation of things as they appear in order to give an account of the whole structure of any given object and its position in space. This meant, in practice, combining several views of the object all more or less superimposed, expressing the idea of the object rather than any one view of it. The first exhibition of such pictures was in 1907 in Paris. The name Cubism, like Impressionism, was derisive and it excited much opposition, like the then recent FAUVISM. Cubism was much influenced by Negro art, by Picasso's interest in Iberian sculpture, and by reaction from the pattern-making of Fauvism. GRIS, LÉGER, DELAUNAY and DERAIN were among the early adherents, and the new aesthetic was soon preached by two practising Cubist painters, Gleizes and Metzinger, whose book 'Du Cubisme', was published in 1912 and soon translated into English. The poet Apollinaire followed in 1913 with 'Les Peintres Cubistes'. The first phase, under the influence of Cézanne, lasted from 1906 to 1909; the second, sometimes called High or Analytical Cubism, lasted from 1909 to 1912 and excluded interest in colour or handling while concentrating on the breaking down of forms; finally, Late or Synthetic Cubism (1912–14) allowed a re-emergence of tactile qualities, colour and handling. ORPHIC CUBISM is a derivative.

CURRIER, Nathaniel, published in 1840, three days after the disaster, a highly-coloured print of the burning of the steam-boat *Lexington* in Long Island Sound. The edition went like wildfire, and established him as the most important publisher of 'Colored Engravings to the People'. James Ives joined the firm in 1852, and it became Currier and Ives in 1857. The prints were lithographs, hand-coloured on a mass-production system of one girl to each colour, and for 50-odd years they published about three new prints each week on every aspect of American life – views, portraits of notabilities, Wild West, Indian, sporting and pioneering scenes, disasters (such as the *Great Fire of Chicago*, 1871), the Civil War, temperance and other tracts – which reached into the farthest confines of the land, and also had a considerable export sale. The largest collection is in the City Museum of New York.

CUYP, Aelbert (1620–91), was a Dordrecht painter, principally of landscapes and animals, but also of sea-pieces, still-life and portraits, such versatility being rare in the Dutch School. There is a fine signed portrait of 1649 in London (NG) and two still-lifes in Oxford. He was the son and pupil of Jacob Gerritsz. Cuyp (1594–1651/2), a painter of portraits (Edinburgh, fragments of *Family Group*) and landscapes. In his earlier works Aelbert was influenced by van GOYEN and S. van RUYSDAEL, painting landscapes with the same fidelity to nature (Besançon, 1639 – the earliest dated work – and London, Dulwich, *c.*1640), but, after Jan BOTH returned from Italy in 1641 Cuyp became more interested in the play of light. From the mid-1640s he began to experiment with the golden glow which the Italianate Dutch landscape painters had learned from CLAUDE, but he never went to Italy himself. In 1658 he married a rich widow, became a landowner, and was a magistrate 1680–2; although free to devote himself to his art he painted little in the last twenty-five years of his life. The light in his pictures is always poetic in feeling: Constable said of him,

'Chiaroscuro is by no means confined to dark pictures: the works of Cuyp, though generally light, are full of it. It may be defined as that power which creates space'. Nearly all his best works were bought by British collectors in the 18th and early 19th centuries, and he exerted an incalculable influence on British art of the 18th and 19th centuries. The finest collection is perhaps that in London (Dulwich), and other works are in the Royal Coll., Edinburgh (NG), Glasgow (a rare religious work), London (NG, Wallace Coll. and Kenwood), as well as Amsterdam, Antwerp, Berlin, Brussels, Cambridge (Fitzwm), Cape Town, Cardiff, Dordrecht, Dublin, Frankfurt (Städel), The Hague, Karlsruhe, Munich, New York (Met. Mus.), Paris (Louvre), Philadelphia, Rotterdam, Toledo Ohio, Toronto, Vienna (K-H Mus.), Waddesdon Bucks. (National Trust) and Washington (NG). Many pictures signed with the initials A C, once thought to be his, are now given to Abraham CALRAET.

Benjamin Gerritsz. Cuyp (1612–52), was Aelbert's father's half-brother, and painted genre scenes in the manner of OSTADE, with some influence from the young Rembrandt. There are examples in Cardiff, Dessau, Gateshead, Glasgow and Paris (Louvre). The Rijksmuseum, Amsterdam, has works by all three Cuyps.

D

DADA is a French word for a child's hobby-horse, said to have been chosen at random from a dictionary and used as a label by a group of artists and writers who were refugees from World War I in Switzerland. It was a nihilistic precursor of SURREALISM and lasted from about 1916 to 1922, spreading from Zurich to Paris, Cologne and New York. It was deliberately anti-art and anti-sense (and, unlike Surrealism, anti-politics as well), intended to shock and outrage. Its most characteristic production was the reproduction of the *Mona Lisa* with a beard and moustache and the obscene caption LHOOQ (i.e. *elle a chaud au cul*) 'by' DUCHAMP and, perhaps, PICABIA. Other manifestations included 'Readymades', i.e. any object at hand, such as the bottle-drier and bicycle wheel signed by Duchamp, or the urinal which he signed R. Mutt and tried, unsuccessfully, to exhibit in New York; ARP's COLLAGES of coloured paper cut up and shuffled at random; and Picabia's drawings of bits of machinery with incongruous titles. An exhibition held in an annexe to a café lavatory in Cologne in 1920 provided a chopper for visitors to use on the works displayed. The movement was always strongly literary, and may have been invented by the poet Tristan Tzara.

DADDI, Bernardo (*c.*1290–1349/51), was a pupil of Giotto, but was influenced by the LORENZETTI; that is, he attempted to fuse the plastic qualities of Giotto with some aspects of Sienese art, and in this he represents the generation after Giotto, both in Florence and in Siena. His triptych of 1328 (Florence, Uffizi) is typical; other works are in Florence and in the Royal Coll., and Baltimore, Berlin, Boston (Mus. and Gardner), Cambridge Mass. (Fogg), Edinburgh, London (Wallace Coll. and Courtauld Inst.), New York (Met. Mus. and Hist. Soc.), Paris (Louvre and Mus. des Arts Décoratifs), Philadelphia (Johnson), Utrecht (Archiepiscopal Mus.), the Vatican, Washington (NG) and York.

DAHL, Michael (1659?–1743), was a Swedish painter who was KNELLER's only serious rival in London. He probably arrived in London about 1682, made a Grand Tour in 1685, travelling through Paris, making a long stay in Rome, and visiting Naples and Venice before returning via Frankfurt to London, where he decided to settle in 1689 and where he had a long and successful career. His style is softer than Kneller's, warmer and less forced but perhaps with less character. There are works in London (NPG, Nat. Marit. Mus. and Dulwich), British provincial museums, New York (Met. Mus.), Stockholm and Yale (CBA).

DALI, Salvador (1904–89) was originally a Spanish Cubist, but went to Paris in 1928 and in 1929 was welcomed into the SURREALIST group by André BRETON, who in 1938 expelled him for rejecting the Marxist connections of the movement while retaining the Freudian overtones. His is the nightmare world of man-size ants and limp pocket watches, meticulous in realistic detail, haunting in the inescapability of the horrific, and even in his later religious works – the Glasgow *Crucifixion* or the *Last Supper* in Washington – unable to avoid crude and wilful sensationalism. Perhaps his best works, in their extraordinary mixture of wild imagery and precise execution, are his pieces of jewellery, where the fantastic is enhanced by being allied successfully to precious materials. He was in the US between 1940 and 1955, after which he returned to Spain. He also made films with Buñuel. He wrote two autobiographies and is buried in his own museum in Figueras, N.-E. Spain. Many works are in US museums.

DALMAU, Luis (active 1428–60), was a Spanish painter, first recorded in Valencia in 1428. He became Court Painter to Alfonso of Aragon, who sent him to Flanders in 1431. By 1437 he was back in Valencia and his only certain work, the *Virgin of the Councillors* (Barcelona, Mus.), is signed and dated 1445. It is an almost literal imitation of Jan van EYCK and is therefore important as showing not only the significance of Flanders for Spanish 15th-century painting, but also the direct influence of Jan van Eyck (rather than Roger van der Weyden) outside Flanders.

DANCE OF DEATH (Ger. *Totentanz*). A typically macabre late medieval fantasy, in which Popes, Emperors, Lords and so on down to Artisans and Beggars are shown being whirled off in a dance with skeleton Popes, Emperors and so on, and not enjoying the experience. The most celebrated of these cycles were in cemeteries (e.g. Paris, 1424/5) and, especially, the woodcut series by HOLBEIN the Younger, designed in Basle *c.*1523/6 and published in Lyons in 1538, which was almost certainly based on paintings in Basle cemetery.

DANCE, Nathaniel (1735–1811), was trained under HAYMAN *c.*1749, but went to Rome in 1754 and immediately came under the influence of Neoclassicism, and BATONI in particular. He remained in Rome until 1765, and his *Death of Virginia* (1761, lost, but known from an engraving) has been claimed as the first British fully Neoclassic history painting (but cf. Gavin HAMILTON). His portraits, in Rome and London, are much influenced by Batoni. He was a Founder-Member of the RA (1768), but he gradually gave up painting, married a very rich widow, became an MP and, in 1800, was created a baronet (Sir Nathaniel Dance-Holland). He was the brother of George Dance the Younger, the architect, and the two made a number of portrait-drawings which cannot be attributed separately. Nathaniel's *Timon*, a history painting of 1767, is in the Royal Collection and there are portraits by him in London (NPG, Tate and Science Mus.).

DANTI, Vincenzo (1530–76), was a Perugian sculptor much influenced by Michelangelo. His first work was the bronze *Julius III* (1556, Perugia), which was probably based on Michelangelo's bronze *Julius II* (destroyed in 1511). After this he worked mainly in Florence, where he completed SANSOVINO's *Baptism of Christ* and made his own *Decollation of the Baptist*, both on the Baptistry. Other works are in Florence (Bargello and Pal. Vecchio) and London (V&A). In 1567 he published a treatise claiming Michelangelo as the greatest painter, sculptor and architect who had ever lived.

DANUBE SCHOOL (Ger. *Donauschule*, *Donaustil*). This is really only a name for the pre-eminence of the Danube region in the formation of modern landscape painting: the romantic effects and the emotional sympathy between landscape and human action found in ALTDORFER's pictures are the principal examples, but other major painters of the 'School' are the young CRANACH and Wolf HUBER.

DARET, Jacques (*d.* after 1468), was a painter in Tournai who, in 1427, became an apprentice of CAMPIN. He painted an altarpiece for S. Vaast, Arras, 1433–5 (now in Berlin, Lugano (Thyssen Coll.) and Paris (Petit Palais)), which is documented as his, and which shows very strongly the influence of the

MASTER OF FLÉMALLE: hence the identification of Flémalle with Campin receives considerable support, and light is also cast on the stylistic origins of Roger van der WEYDEN.

DAUBIGNY, Charles (1817–78), was a French landscape painter much influenced by the BARBIZON School, who worked mostly in the Paris region. He went to Italy in 1836 and also visited England, Spain and Holland. He was a friend of Corot and was admired by Monet: he thus forms a link between the Barbizon painters and the Impressionists. There are pictures by him in Aberdeen, Berwick, Birmingham, Boston, Budapest, Edinburgh (NG), Glasgow, London (NG, Tate and Courtauld Inst.), Montreal, New York (Met. Mus.) and Washington, as well as many French museums.

DAUMIER, Honoré (1808–79), worked as a cartoonist on 'La Caricature', founded in 1830, and was imprisoned in 1832 for representing King Louis Philippe as Gargantua. After the suppression of 'La Caricature' in 1835 he joined 'Charivari', and made for it, and other similar journals, some 4,000 lithographs, mostly of the aptest and bitterest social and political satire. His watercolours and drawings of scenes in the Courts of Justice, and of everyday life, are untouched by any romantic feeling for picturesque poverty, and his large oil-paintings, many on the theme of Don Quixote, are loosely handled, with calligraphic brushwork and intense light and shadow. In his old age he became blind, and was rescued from desperate poverty by Corot. He also made some sculpture, including a series of thirty-six heads used for his drawings, many of which, in painted clay, are now in Paris (Mus. d'Orsay) and a complete set, cast in bronze, is in Washington. There are works in Baltimore (Mus. and Walters), Boston, Cambridge Mass. (Fogg), Cardiff, Glasgow, London (NG, BM, V&A, Tate and Courtauld Inst.), Montreal, New York (Met. Mus. and Brooklyn), Ottawa, Paris (Petit Pal.), Philadelphia (Mus.), Washington (NG, Corcoran and Phillips) and elsewhere.

DAVID, Gerard (*d.*1523), was born in Oudewater in Holland, but was in Bruges by 1484. He was the last master of the Bruges School, painting gently pious pictures in a 15th-century style, which was superseded in his own lifetime by the new, Italianate, Antwerp style, just as the commercial prosperity of Bruges faded before the rise of Antwerp. David seems to have gone to Antwerp and joined the Guild there in 1515, but he was certainly back in Bruges by 1521 and he died there. His only documented picture is a *Sacra Conversazione* (1509, Rouen), but two *Justice Scenes* of 1498 (Bruges) are certainly his. Many pictures are ascribed to him in Antwerp, Berlin, Brussels, Chicago, Cleveland, Denver Col., Detroit, Dublin, Edinburgh (NG), the Escorial, Florence (Uffizi), Frankfurt (Städel), Granada, Greenville SC, London (NG), Madrid (Prado), Munich, New York (Met. Mus. and Frick Coll.), Paris (Louvre), Pasadena Cal. (Simon), Philadelphia (Johnson), St Louis, Stockholm, Toledo Ohio, Vienna, Washington (NG), Worcester Mass. and elsewhere.

DAVID, Jacques Louis (1748–1825), was distantly related to BOUCHER, who recommended his being placed under VIEN, in 1765. He won the Prix de Rome in 1774, and went there with Vien in 1775, remaining until 1781 (*see* SUVÉE). He abruptly forsook Boucher's Rococo in favour of the new NEO-CLASSICISM and at the same time adopted the strong chiaroscuro of the Caravaggesques. In 1782 he became an Academician and in 1784 he returned to Rome to paint the *Oath of the Horatii* (1785, Paris, Louvre), which was acclaimed in Rome and again in Paris at the Salon of 1785. It is perhaps the most important French Neoclassic picture, simple, severe and uncompromising in its subordination of colour to drawing. It was also highly political in its topical republican implications; and it was followed by other large paintings extolling classical and republican virtues. During the Revolution David became a Deputy and voted for the execution of Louis XVI. He became dictator of the arts, designed huge propaganda processions – such as the 'Feast of Reason' – abolished the Academy in 1793, and helped to found the Institut which replaced it: he also painted memorial portraits of the martyrs of the Revolution, Lepelletier de Saint-Fargeau and Marat. After the fall of Robespierre he was imprisoned. His release was due to the intercession of his pupils and his wife, who had divorced him because of his revolutionary activities, but who now remarried him and lived happily with him for another 31 years. The *Sabine Women* was begun in 1798, partly in recognition of her devotion, partly as a manifesto of his attachment to the Antique. In the same year he met Napoleon and promptly became an ardent Bonapartist. Napoleon fully appreciated the usefulness of a great painter for propaganda purposes. As part of the Napoleonic Saga David painted *Napoleon crossing the Alps* (1801), and worked 1805–7 on the huge *Coronation of the Emperor Napoleon*, containing over a hundred portraits. This was followed by *The Emperor distributing Eagles* (1810). After Napoleon was crushed at Waterloo David fled to Switzerland, and, in 1816, to Brussels, where he died. Several contradictory strains combine in David's art. From the stern Neoclassicism of his youth he moved, in the Napoleonic pictures, towards a Venetian understanding of light and colour; yet contemporary and later paintings of classical subjects show a concentration on drawing and a rigid antiquarianism at variance with everything Venetian. His portraits are always supremely well designed and full of realism, yet his later classical subjects betray a progressive sweetening of style, perhaps caused by the stultifying influence of his self-imposed exile, cut off from the stimulating conflict of ideas resulting from the rise of Romanticism. He was a great teacher, whose many pupils included GÉRARD, GIRODET, GROS, NAVEZ and INGRES. Most of his major pictures are in Paris (Louvre, Petit Pal., Jacquemart-André and École des Beaux-Arts); others are in Aix-en-Provence, Algiers, Angers, Avignon, Berlin (Charlottenburg), Besançon, Boulogne, Buffalo NY, Cambridge Mass. (Fogg), Cherbourg, Chicago, Cincinnati, Cleveland Ohio, Detroit, Hartford Conn., Kansas City, Le Mans, Lille, London (NG), Lyons, Montauban, Montpellier, New York (Met. Mus. and Rockefeller Inst. for Medical Research), Northampton Mass. (Smith Coll.), Rome (Museo Napoleonico), Rouen, Springfield Mass., Toledo Ohio (a version of *The Horatii*, perhaps by Girodet), Troyes, Versailles, Vienna (Belvedere) and Washington (NG).

DAVID d'Angers, Pierre-Jean (1788–1856), was a French sculptor called after his birthplace to distinguish him from the painter J-L. David. The son of a sculptor, he won the Prix de Rome in 1811 and was in Rome until 1816, when he returned to France via London, in order to see the Elgin marbles (which had just been bought for the British Museum) and to meet FLAXMAN, to whom he carried a letter of introduction from CANOVA. Canova was the main influence on him and his rather chilly classicism is redeemed by his great technical skill. His Bourcke and Foy monuments (1821 and 1825, both in Père Lachaise cemetery, Paris), the bloodless *Racine* (1827, La Ferté Milon, Racine's birthplace), and the bombastic *Philipoemen* (1837, Louvre) are examples of the POMPIER style, against which younger painters (though not sculptors) were already rebelling. After the 1848 Revolution he was imprisoned and then exiled to Brussels. He visited Greece in 1852, but was horrified by the neglect of ancient monuments, the total absence of any surviving artistic impulse, and by the vandalism perpetrated upon his *Greek Girl Mourning* (1827), which he had given as a monument to the patriot Botzaris, who had died with Byron at Missolonghi. He was allowed to return to Paris in 1853, but ill-health prevented further work. His most important works are the 500-odd portrait medallions, representing almost every major figure of the time. He presented a cast of each, with casts of his other works, to his native Angers. Many other French museums have works: there is a portrait bust of Jeremy Bentham in the Senate House of the University of London.

DAVIES, Arthur B. (1862–1928), was an American painter who visited Europe in 1893 and was influenced by the frescoes at Pompeii, as well as by contemporaries such as BÖCKLIN, PUVIS de Chavannes, and possibly REDON. Davies's own works were highly Romantic and simplified in style, but he nevertheless exhibited with the Group of Eight – the ASHCAN School – in 1908 and was one of the organizers of the ARMORY Show in 1913, after which he was temporarily influenced by Cubism. From 1925 he designed tapestries for the Gobelins factory. There are paintings in Detroit, New York (Met. Mus. and Whitney) and other US museums.

DAVIS, Stuart (1894–1964), was an American painter who exhibited at the ARMORY Show. He was influenced by Cubism, but later moved from flat, low-toned townscapes (many of Paris) to simple loud-coloured patterns in which letters and words are major elements. Paintings of commercial artefacts and packages – *Lucky Strike*, 1921; *Odol*, 1924 – are more than prototypes for POP ART; they are Pop *avant la lettre*. He is represented in New York (M of MA and Whitney).

DEAD COLOUR *see* LAY-IN.

DEËSIS (Gk). A group of Christ enthroned in Majesty, with the Virgin and St John on either side. The idea is Byzantine, but is central to the Ghent Altar (*see* EYCK). It is often used as the central group in a Last Judgement.

DEGAS, Edgar (1834–1917), was born in Paris of a wealthy family. He studied at the École des Beaux-Arts under a pupil of INGRES, whom he knew and greatly admired. His early works – family portraits and some history pictures – suggest that he was to develop into an academic painter in the Ingres tradition. By the late 1860s, however, he had begun to develop a deceptively casual composition, probably influenced by Manet and possibly also by Whistler, and certainly by snapshot photography. He knew Manet well, as he did Bazille, Berthe Morisot and Tissot, and was a frequent member of the circle which gathered round Manet, where he also met Fantin-Latour, Renoir, Constantin Guys, Cézanne, Monet, Sisley and Pissarro. During the Franco-Prussian War he remained in Paris and in 1872–3 he visited relations in New Orleans. There he painted only a few pictures, but these – and those executed after his return to Paris – show him using unusual viewpoints and purely contemporary subject matter, e.g. the Cotton Exchange in New Orleans. He ceased exhibiting at the Salon in 1870, and in 1874 he took part in the first Impressionist Exhibition, as he did in six of the subsequent seven. His works could only be seen in public at these group exhibitions, always received with hostility and ridicule, or at the dealer, Durand-Ruel, whose patient and persevering faith in Impressionism nearly ruined him. Like Manet, Degas was a *grand bourgeois* with a private income, and he was less than understanding towards others in the group – e.g. Renoir – over their defections from the exhibitions which he largely organized, in order to send works to the Salon in an endeavour to attract purchasers.

His first pictures of dancers were painted about 1873, and from then on ballet girls, laundresses, models dressing and bathing, and cabaret singers became his principal subjects. He recorded the manners and movements of a society which he observed almost as if it were another world, treating the figures as the material of his investigations into light, colour and form, as much as the pastel or paint he used. Technically, he was one of the greatest experimenters and innovators. His sound knowledge of the traditional technique of oil-painting enabled him to make endless trials of various media and mixtures such as oil paint thinned with turpentine after the oil has been partly extracted with blotting-paper (*peinture à l'essence*), pastel used in superimposed layers, or with watercolour or spirit-thinned oil paint, or thinned with water, gouache, egg-tempera, etching, drypoint, monotype, lithography, aquatint and drawing in every kind of material. In later life, he used pastel more than any other medium, and as his eyesight weakened his handling became broader and freer. There are also seventy-four pieces of sculpture – late works – including ballet dancers and figures in movement, originally executed in wax, but now generally cast in bronze. The most unusual is the large figure of the little ballet girl wearing a real tutu (London, Tate). There are works in Baltimore (Walters), Berlin, Berwick on Tweed, Birmingham, Boston (Mus., Gardner), Cambridge Mass. (Fogg), Chicago, Cleveland Ohio, Columbus Ohio, Copenhagen, Detroit, Dumbarton Oaks, Edinburgh, Frankfurt (Städel), Glasgow (Burrell), Hartford Conn., Leicester, Liverpool, London (NG, Tate, V&A and Courtauld Inst.), Los Angeles, Lyons, Malibu Cal. (Getty), Minneapolis, Moscow, New York (Met. Mus., M of MA, Brooklyn and Frick Coll.), Northampton Mass., Ottawa, Paris (Mus. d'Orsay and Mus. Moreau), Pau, Philadelphia (Mus.), Rochester NY, São Paulo, St Louis, Stockholm, Toledo Ohio, Toronto, Vienna, Walsall, Washington and elsewhere. London (Tate) and New York (Met. Mus.) have good collections of the sculptures.

DE HEEM *see* HEEM.

DEL., DELIN. (Lat. *delineavit*, he drew it) after a name on an engraving or drawing is an assertion of authorship.

DELACROIX, Eugène (1798–1863), was the major painter of the Romantic Movement in France. He was the pupil of Baron Guérin (who also taught GÉRICAULT), whose lack of artistic authority made his studio tolerant of new ideas. Delacroix was the ardent admirer rather than an intimate friend of Géricault, but in the grim year which preceded his death was a frequent visitor to his studio. To Géricault's influence is probably due Delacroix's interest in English art and in animal painting, and his revolt from the classicizing forms and classical literary subjects which still dominated French painting in the early 19th century. He admired GROS, studied Rubens and Veronese, and was a friend of Bonington and an admirer of Constable. He was in England in 1825 and was much impressed by the charm of English colour and freshness of handling, particularly in landscape, and the predominance of medieval and anecdotal subject pictures.

His first Salon exhibit, *Dante and Virgil Crossing the Styx* (1822, Paris, Louvre), was well received, but subsequent ones – the *Massacre at Chios*, 1824, or *Sardanapalus*, 1829 (both now in the Louvre) were bitterly attacked for his use of brilliant colour, contemporary and exotic literary subjects, and free handling, which was seen as showing the influence of Géricault and English art, and as a rejection of traditional French classicism. In 1832 he visited North Africa and this opened a whole new field of subjects: scenes from Arab and Jewish life, animal subjects, innumerable combinations of illustrations to Byron and allusions to the Greek wars against the Turks abound in his gigantic *oeuvre* after this, and share the honours with Scott and Shakespeare as constant sources of inspiration. From the mid-1830s he was in official favour, receiving commissions for large-scale decorations in which INGRES, his greatest rival and inveterate opponent, was unsuccessful. His principal decorations were the *Justice of Trajan* for Rouen Town Hall (1840, now Rouen Mus.), the ceiling of the Salon d'Apollon in the Louvre (1849), and works in S. Sulpice (1857–60), and the Hôtel de Ville (destroyed in 1870). Nevertheless, the works he was happiest with are small, freely handled, colourful subjects – battles, hunts, animals in combat, and portraits of intimate friends such as Chopin (1838, Louvre). His diary, kept from 1822 to 1824, and again from 1847 to 1863, is a precious source for his life and work, and as a commentary on the social, intellectual and artistic life of Paris. Delacroix only occasionally took pupils, and never taught in the sense that Ingres did, though he had assistants for his large decorations. He left no artistic succession, for the essence of Romanticism is its personal quality. His contribution to the struggle of the non-conforming artist against entrenched classicism is reflected in his long wait for election to the Institut (1857), the frequent battles over the admission of his works to the Salon, and the veneration in which he was held by younger artists. There are works in Baltimore (Walters), Birmingham, Bordeaux, Boston (Mus. and Gardner), Bristol, Budapest, Buffalo, Cambridge (Fitzwm), Cambridge Mass. (Fogg), Chantilly, Chicago, Cincinnati, Cleveland Ohio, Dublin, Edinburgh, Fort Worth Texas, Glasgow, Hartford Conn. (Wadsworth), Lille, London (NG and Wallace Coll.), Los Angeles, Melbourne, Metz, Minneapolis, Montpellier, Montreal, Munich, New York (Met. Mus. and Brooklyn), Northampton Mass. (Smith), North Carolina (Univ.), Ottawa, Paris (Mus. d'Orsay and Carnavalet), Philadelphia (Mus. and Johnson), Princeton (Univ.), Reims, São Paulo, St Louis, Toledo Ohio, Toronto, Toulouse, Versailles, Vienna, Washington (NG, Corcoran and Phillips) and elsewhere.

DELAROCHE, Paul (1797–1856), was a French painter, an exact contemporary of Delacroix, who achieved great fame in his lifetime as a painter of historical subjects, but his melodramatic Romanticism shows the decline of history painting into illustration. This happened in England and Germany, as well as France, during the 19th century. He studied under GROS in 1818, and was elected to the Institut in 1832, in sharp contrast to Delacroix, and he became a professor at the École des Beaux-Arts in 1833, inheriting Gros's studio after his suicide in 1835. Delaroche visited Italy in 1834–5, marrying Horace VERNET's sister in Rome, and was again in Italy in 1838 and 1843. Between 1837 and 1841 he painted the hemicycle in the École des Beaux-Arts in Paris, depicting the history of art from Antiquity to the 18th century by means of a huge group of artists, based on more or less authentic self-portraits (or frankly imaginary ones). His early fame rested on the series of English and French historical subjects – *The Death of Queen Elizabeth*, 1827, and *The Little Princes in the Tower*, 1831 (both in the Louvre); *The Execution of Lady Jane Grey* (1833, London, NG); *Murder of the Duc de Guise* (1835, Chantilly, and water-colour replica London, Wallace Coll.) – and much of his success derived from the lucrative sale of engravings after these subjects. He was also a fine portrait painter. Other works are in French museums and in Baltimore (Walters) and Cambridge Mass. (Fogg).

DELAUNAY, Robert and Sonia. Robert (1885–1941), was the inventor of ORPHIC CUBISM. He was mainly concerned with the emotional effects of pure colour, which may have grown out of his early preoccupation with Impressionism. In 1911 he exhibited with the Independents in the Cubist Room, and was also invited by KANDINSKY to exhibit with the BLAUE REITER group. Delaunay began to paint a series of the city of Paris and the Eiffel Tower in 1910–12, and he returned to these themes in 1924, after a seven-year stay (1914–21) in Spain and Portugal. In 1912 he also began a series *Disques* and *Formes circulaires cosmiques*, which are among the earliest non-objective paintings. In 1937 he was commissioned to paint vast murals – one was 9,000 square feet – for the Universal Exposition in Paris. There are works by him in Amsterdam (Stedelijk), Dijon, Grenoble, London (Tate), Lyons, Minneapolis, Montpellier, New York (Guggenheim), Paris (Mus. d'Art Moderne) and Toledo Ohio.

Sonia Terk (1884–1979), was a Russian who went to Paris in 1905, where she was influenced by Gauguin. She married Delaunay in 1910, after having been married to the German art critic Uhde (*see* SÉRAPHINE). She seems to have painted pure abstractions before her husband, but some of her best work was done long after his death. Like him, she painted a huge mural for the Paris Exposition of 1937. There are 523 of her designs in the Musée des Tissus at Lyons, and other works are in Grenoble and Lyons. Their joint writings on art were published in New York as 'The New Art of Colour' in 1978.

DELVAUX, Laurent (1696–1778), was a Flemish sculptor who came to London in 1717 to work with his fellow Fleming SCHEEMAKERS. In 1728 they went to Italy together, where Delvaux spent several years, on and off, before returning to Brussels, where he got a Court appointment in 1733. In Brussels he made a large number of statues for churches, several important pulpits (e.g. Ghent Cathedral, 1745), and a number of tombs; he worked on two tombs in Westminster Abbey with Scheemakers, and there are works, including terracotta models, in London (V&A and RA) and Brussels.

DELVAUX, Paul (*b.*1897), is a Belgian painter, trained in Brussels, who was first influenced by the Expressionism of PERMEKE and SMET, but under the influence of MAGRITTE and CHIRICO turned to Surrealism in the 1930s. He visited Italy in 1939 and was deeply impressed by Roman architecture, so that a typical Delvaux consists of a meticulously detailed representation of a full-breasted Rubensian nude contemplating a Roman temple in the company of a man in a bowler hat. He is well represented in Brussels, and there is a characteristic *Venus Asleep* in London (Tate).

DENIS, Maurice (1870–1943), was a co-founder and principal theorist of the NABIS. In Paris in 1888 he met BERNARD, BONNARD, VUILLARD and SÉRUSIER, who knew Gauguin. In 1900 he painted his celebrated group portrait, *Homage to Cézanne* (Paris, Mus. d'Art Moderne). He made several trips to Italy and particularly studied the decorative style of Giotto, Fra Angelico and Piero della Francesca; in 1903 he accompanied Sérusier to Beuron, the German Benedictine monastery which was a centre of religious art, and from 1910 he painted many religious works, including the decoration of St Paul, Geneva (1914). In 1919 he founded the Ateliers d'Art Sacré. His interest in subject matter seems to run counter to his famous dictum (1890) that a picture is essentially a flat surface covered with colours assembled in a certain order, but the contradiction is more apparent than real. Denis was a prolific writer on art, his best-known works being 'Théories' and 'Nouvelles Théories'. There are paintings by him in Paris (Mus. d'Orsay and Mus. des Arts Décoratifs).

DERAIN, André (1880–1954), was one of the original FAUVES. In Carrière's studio he met Matisse, who persuaded Derain's parents to allow him to become a painter. His early works, influenced by Matisse, are bright in colour and painted in a pointillist technique; he was also much influenced by VLAMINCK, by van Gogh and, later, by Cézanne. As the impetus of Fauvism petered out, he became more traditionalist and evolved a style of landscape and still life based on browns and olive greens. He was also a successful portrait painter. There are works in Paris (Mus. d'Orsay and Mus. d'Art Moderne) and in Avignon, Birmingham, Calais, Chicago, Cleveland Ohio, Detroit, Glasgow, Grenoble, Leeds, Liverpool, London (Tate), Manchester (Rutherston), Nancy, New York (M of MA), Oxford, Washington (NG) and elsewhere.

DESCO da Parto (Ital. birth plate). In medieval Italy there was a charming custom of visiting a woman who had just given birth to a child, and carrying sweets or small gifts on a special tray – these *deschi da parto* were sometimes painted with appropriate subjects, e.g. a visit to a lady in childbed by ladies carrying gifts, as in the famous example in Berlin, sometimes attributed to Masaccio.

DESIDERIO da Settignano (1428/30–64) was probably the most promising sculptor among the followers of Donatello. He adopted the technique of very low relief (*rilievo schiacciato*) which had been invented by Donatello, but Desiderio used it for purposes of extreme delicacy of effect quite different from the heroic style of Donatello. Desiderio's sensitive treatment of women and children is best seen in his busts: examples are in Berlin, Florence (Bargello), London (V&A), Paris (Louvre), Philadelphia, Toledo Ohio, Washington (NG). His major monumental work is the tomb of Carlo Marsuppini (*d.*1453) in Sta Croce, Florence, which derives from Donatello and the ROSSELLINI.

DESIGN. Roughly the same, in normal usage, as COMPOSITION. It may mean part of a composition considered in isolation, as 'The design of the left-hand group in Mr Blank's composition . . .'. The arts of design are the visual arts, but in recent years there has been a tendency to use the word as a genteel synonym for what used to be called Commercial Art or Industrial Design; the word graphic (or, now, graphics) has similarly come down in the world. For the distinction between Design and Disegno *see* DISEGNO.

DE SMET *see* SMET.

DESPIAU, Charles (1874–1946), was a French sculptor who was influenced by RODIN from 1903 and worked for him 1907–14. Despiau's *Paulette* of 1907 (Paris, Mus. d'Art Moderne), his earliest major work, attracted Rodin's attention, but later Despiau rejected the softness and vagueness of Rodin's forms and, like MAILLOL, returned to the simplicity and formal severity of antique sculpture, particularly of the archaic period. His only large-scale work was the war memorial for his native Mont-de-Marsan (Landes), of 1920–22, but he was a sensitive and famous portraitist. There are works in Buffalo, Detroit, London (Tate), New York (M of MA), Philadelphia and Rotterdam, and several in Paris (Mus. d'Art Moderne).

DESPORTES, Alexandre François (1661–1743), was a French painter trained in the Flemish tradition by a pupil of SNYDERS. He was in Poland, painting royal portraits, in 1695–6, and on his return to France became the official painter of hunting scenes to Louis XIV and XV, also painting dogs, the animals in the royal menagerie, and profuse still-life subjects. He worked on decorations for the royal palaces, and, like OUDRY, made cartoons for the Gobelins tapestry factory. His small landscape studies made for the backgrounds of his hunting scenes are early examples of direct painting from nature. His rich still-life and animal pictures helped turn French taste from an exclusive concentration on Italian art to a greater interest in Flemish painting (*see* RUBÉNISME). He visited England *c.*1712/13. There are examples in Compiègne, London (Wallace Coll.), Munich, Paris (Louvre) and elsewhere.

DE STIJL *see* STIJL.

DETROY *see* TROY.

DEVIS, Arthur (1712–87), was a successful painter of small portraits and conversation pieces of great charm, cool delicate colour and high finish. His solid middle-class sitters are usually portrayed in their gardens or parks, or in very sparsely furnished interiors (often of a grandeur beyond their actual houses). They are stiffly posed and it is known that he used small dolls, about 30 inches high, as an aid to composition (there are clothes for a mannikin which belonged to him in the Preston Museum). He was trained under the Fleming Tillemans and MERCIER influenced these groups as well as HOGARTH. His half-brother, Anthony (1729–1816) was a minor landscape painter, and his son, Arthur William (1762–1822), was also a painter and topographical draughtsman in the service of the East India Company. Their native Preston has works and others by Arthur are in Chicago, Hull, Leicester, Liverpool, London (Tate and V&A), Manchester, Upton nr Banbury (National Trust), Yale (CBA and Univ.) and elsewhere.

DE WINT, Peter (1784–1849), was born at Stone, Staffs., of Dutch-American descent. He was trained in London, and, through Dr MONRO, was influenced by GIRTIN. He was also helped by VARLEY. Apart from a visit to France in 1828 and to North Wales in 1829, he painted only the English landscape, especially the flat country round Lincoln, which lends itself to his favourite format, very wide in comparison to its height. In breadth of handling he sometimes approaches Cox, but his washes are simpler and more liquid, and the whole atmosphere calmer. There are examples in Birmingham, Cambridge (Fitzwm), Dublin, Edinburgh, Leeds, Lincoln, London (BM, Tate and V&A), Manchester, Yale (CBA) and elsewhere.

DIAZ de la Peña, Narcisse Virgile (1807/8–76), was a French landscape painter of the BARBIZON SCHOOL, but his earlier works were Romantic compositions in the manner of Delacroix. There are pictures by him in Birmingham, Boston, Edinburgh, Glasgow, London (NG, Tate, Wallace Coll. and Courtauld Inst.), New York (Met. Mus.) and many French museums.

DIDEROT, Denis (1713–84), was the most important 18th-century French writer on art, and a precursor of the modern art-critic. He wrote informative and penetrating accounts of the SALONS in 1759–71, 1775 and 1781, which circulated widely in Grimm's privately subscribed *Correspondance Littéraire*. His plays, the earliest examples of the *comédie larmoyante*, by their emphasis on tableaux and on incident rather than character, explain his admiration for GREUZE's development of narrative bourgeois genre.

DIPTYCH. A picture or relief consisting of two parts, usually hinged together like the pages of a book: a POLYPTYCH in two parts. A *Consular Diptych* is a pair of ivory reliefs commemorating a Consulship of the Roman Empire, mostly of the 5th century AD and later. There are several extant examples of Flemish 15th-century diptychs which consist of a portrait of the owner, represented in prayer, facing the Madonna and Child on the other (right-hand) panel. These were intended as objects of private devotion and as memorials.

DISEGNO. An Italian word, capable of a variety of meanings, the simplest of which is 'drawing' and the next simplest, DESIGN. The *arti del disegno* are the visual arts in general, including architecture, not just drawing alone, and the 16th-century usage became more and more complicated as the MANNERISTS evolved theories about design which perhaps reached a climax in the anagram *Disegno, segno di Dio* – i.e. design is the sign-manual of God. This clearly has links with the theological 'argument from design'. In this involved theory the idea of *disegno interno* plays an important part; the artist is thought of as having a Platonic Idea of an object in his mind, implanted by God, so that the perfect idea of a human figure which exists in the painter's mind is what he has to realize, not contenting himself with the mere copying of any figure which happens to be in front of his eyes. This theory, explicit in Mannerists like Federico ZUCCARO, is implicit in all theories of IDEAL ART and is at the back of most anti-naturalistic modern movements. In its purest 16th-century form it has much in common with the Counter-Reformation, a fact which might well surprise some of its more recent exponents. In 1548, in reply to a question about the relative importance of painting and sculpture, PONTORMO wrote to Benedetto Varchi that the nobility of both arts lay in *disegno*, which was fundamental to both. This is similar to, but not quite the same as, INGRES's reference to drawing as *la probité de l'art*.

DISTEMPER. A painting technique in which the powdered colours are mixed with glue-size. As anyone who has ever done home-decorating will know, it is easy and cheap, but very impermanent; for this reason alone it should not be confused with TEMPERA.

DIVISIONISM *see* OPTICAL MIXTURES.

DIX, Otto (1891–1969), learned to paint in Dresden. His experiences in the German army in 1914–18 and in the inflation after the War led him to paint with a bitter realism, even in portraits, although it was never quite so caricatural as the works of GROSZ. He was one of the leaders of the NEUE SACHLICHKEIT group, and his portrait of his parents (1924, Hanover) is one of the masterpieces of the movement. He was persecuted by the Nazis, and 260 of his works were removed from German galleries, but he was nevertheless conscripted in 1945 and was, for a short time, a prisoner of war in France. During the 1920s and 1930s he was much influenced by early German painters – e.g. Baldung and Cranach – but after 1946 he painted large religious and allegorical pictures in a rather Expressionist style. Many of his works are now back in German galleries, especially Stuttgart, and others are in Detroit, New York (M of M A) and Paris (Mus. d'Art Moderne).

DIXON, Robert (1780–1815) *see* NORWICH SCHOOL.

DOBELL, William (1897–1970), was an Australian painter who studied in London and Holland before returning to Australia in 1939. He won a prize for portrait painting in 1943, but the award was contested on the ground that his picture overstepped the limits of portraiture and became a caricature: Dobell won the ensuing lawsuit. In 1954 he exhibited at the Venice Biennale with NOLAN and DRYSDALE. All Australian State Galleries have examples.

DOBSON, William (1611–46), was born in London. He was described by his contemporary Aubrey as 'the most excellent painter England hath yet bred', and as such he succeeded van DYCK as Court Painter in 1642 and to some of the position of van Dyck, whose assistant he may have been. It is, however, not certain that he was van Dyck's pupil (an early *Self-Portrait* is markedly Rembrandtesque), or even that he was appointed Serjeant Painter. His impasted and robust style is more Italianate than van Dyck's, and may have been formed on a study of the superb Titians and other Venetian pictures in Charles I's collection. He first appeared in 1642, in Oxford, where the Civil War had driven Charles and his court; between then and his early death he painted many of the Royalists, as well as the king and the royal children. He seems to have been imprisoned for debt in 1646, and his 'loose and irregular habits' may have contributed to his premature death. There are works in the Royal Coll., and in Birmingham, Dunedin NZ, Edinburgh (SNPG), Hull, Liverpool, London (Tate, NPG, Nat. Marit. Mus. and Courtauld Inst.), Yale (CBA) and elsewhere.

DOELENSTUK, Schutterstuk. Dutch words meaning group portraits of the Civic Guards formed in Dutch towns during the Wars of Independence. HALS and REMBRANDT painted the most celebrated examples, but most of the late-16th- and early-17th-century portrait painters received commissions.

DOESBURG, Theo van (1883–1931), was born in Utrecht and began his career as a painter (there are pictures in Amsterdam, London (Tate) and The Hague), but in 1917, with MONDRIAN, he founded the magazine De STIJL and most of the rest of his life was spent as a publicist. He had some influence on BAUHAUS ideas. Just before he died, he issued (1930) the Manifesto of CONCRETE ART. 'Principles of Neo-Plastic Art' was published in English in 1969.

DOLCI, Carlo (1616–86), was the leading painter in Florence in the mid-17th century, and an exponent of the restrained style of Late Baroque comparable with SACCHI's Roman works. Dolci was extremely precocious and one of his finest pictures is the portrait, painted when he was 16, of Fra Ainolfo dei Bardi (1632, Florence, Pitti). Nevertheless, he later became very neurotic and felt himself to be professionally inadequate. Most of his later works are small devotional pictures, often painted on copper in an extremely finicky and detailed manner. When GIORDANO was in Florence in 1682 he said jokingly that his own virtuoso style had brought him a fortune of 150,000 scudi, but that by spending so much time on his works Dolci would starve; an idea that preyed on Dolci's mind. One of his best works is the *Martyrdom of St Andrew* of 1646 (Florence, Pitti), for which there is a sketch of 1643 in Birmingham. There are also two splendid portraits in Cambridge (Fitzwm). Other works are in Glasgow, London (NG, V&A, Wallace Coll. and Dulwich) and Oxford.

DOMENICHINO (1581–1641), one of the chief pupils of the CARRACCI, was an assistant to Ludovico in Bologna before he joined Annibale in Rome in 1602 to work in the Farnese Palace. He exemplified the Carracci doctrine of a return to the Antique and to Raphael, and was also, with Annibale Carracci and the Northerners Elsheimer and the Brills, one of the pioneers of landscape painting. In 1621 he returned to Rome from Bologna, where he had been since 1619, to work as Papal architect for the newly-elected Gregory XV, but his main work of this period was the decoration of the choir and pendentives of Sant' Andrea della Valle (1624–8), the dome being by LANFRANCO. The bitter enmity between them was exacerbated by Domenichino's neurotic temperament and his jealousy at having to share the commission. In 1631 he went to Naples to decorate the chapel of S. Gennaro in the Cathedral, a commission that had been hawked around because of the difficulty of getting any major Roman artist to brave the hostility of the Neapolitan artists, before whom the Cavaliere d'Arpino prudently retired, and Guido RENI fled, after the murder of one of his assistants. Domenichino's acceptance of this ungrateful task was prompted by the increasing unpopularity of his style in Rome, where the day was being carried by the more exuberant Baroque of Lanfranco and PIETRO da Cortona. Domenichino also had trouble with the Neapolitan faction and worked reluctantly and not very successfully, with several flights, and again in bitter competition with Lanfranco, until his death there. His most famous altarpiece is the *Last Communion of St Jerome* (1614, Vatican). Outside Rome and Naples (where there are too many to list) examples may be found in the Royal Coll., and in Berlin, Béziers, Bologna, Bristol, Cambridge (Fitzwm), Chatsworth, Darmstadt (a self-portrait of 1603), Detroit, Edinburgh (NG), Florence (Uffizi and Pitti), Genoa (Pal. Rosso), Glasgow (Univ.), Grottaferrata nr Frascati (frescoes of 1609/10), Hartford Conn., Leeds, Leningrad, London (NG), Madrid (Prado), Malibu Cal. (Getty), Milan (Brera), Montpellier, Munich, Newcastle (King's Coll.), New York (Met. Mus.), Oxford (Ashmolean and Ch. Ch.), Paris (Louvre), Raleigh NC, Vicenza, York and Zurich.

DOMENICO VENEZIANO (*d.*1461) was probably a Florentine painter, although his name implies Venetian origin. The date of his birth is unknown, but he is first recorded in 1438, in Perugia, when he wrote to the Medici in Florence asking for a job. He may have been successful in this, for he was working in Sant' Egidio (S.M. Nuova) in Florence 1439–45, on frescoes which are now lost. One of his helpers was PIERO della Francesca, and Domenico's greatest influence on the future was probably through Piero rather than in Florence proper. His main concern was with the mutation of colour by light, a subject that hardly interested the Florentines, obsessed as they were by drawing. In recent years there have been attempts to represent Domenico as the most important influence after Masaccio, but there are only two signed pictures by him and barely half a dozen plausibly attributed. What is probably his earliest surviving work is the *Carnesecchi Madonna* and two *Saints* from the same street tabernacle (London, NG); these fresco fragments are in bad condition, but the *Madonna* is signed. The other signed picture is his masterpiece, the *St Lucy Altarpiece*, painted for Sta Lucia de' Magnoli in Florence and now dispersed. The main panel is still in Florence (Uffizi), but the *predelle* are in Berlin, Cambridge (Fitzwm) and Washington (NG): the main panel, of the Madonna and Child with Saints, is one of the earliest SACRE CONVERSAZIONI. The date is unknown, but it has been suggested that Domenico had painted, before this, the lower half of Angelico's *Coronation of the Virgin* (Paris, Louvre), and after the *St Lucy Altar* he was sufficiently influenced by CASTAGNO to paint the *Baptist and St Francis* (Florence, Sta Croce): there is no compulsion to believe either of these theories. One of the few things known with certainty about him is that he died in 1461, and therefore could not have been murdered by Castagno, who died in 1457. Nevertheless, this story was current in Florence in the late 15th century. Other works attributed to him are in Berlin, Boston (Gardner), Bucharest, New York (Met. Mus.) and Washington (NG).

DONATELLO (*c*.1385/6–1466) was not only the greatest Florentine sculptor before Michelangelo; he was the most individual artist of the 15th century. Much of the later 15th-century painting in Florence stems from him, as does the whole Paduan School, while, through MANTEGNA and the BELLINI, his influence was felt even in Venice. Practically every later sculptor, including Michelangelo, was deeply indebted to him; while the heroic types he invented have coloured our whole conception of Renaissance Florence. He was apprenticed to GHIBERTI and worked on the First Doors in 1403, but had left by 1406, when he was working with NANNI di Banco on the Cathedral; he continued to work for the Cathedral on and off for the next 30 years. In 1408/9 he carved his marble *David* (reworked 1416, Florence, Bargello): this shows him as still very influenced by Gothic formal ideas, but his own heroic style is first seen in the *St Mark* (1411–12, Florence, Orsanmichele) and the *St John Evangelist* (1413–15, Cathedral) which made his reputation. In both these he created a new kind of humanity, slightly larger than life, and exemplifying those qualities of will and *virtù* that were so highly prized in the Early Renaissance. The knowledge of ancient Roman sculpture shown in these works makes it likely that he had visited Rome in 1409/11. In 1415 he began his series of statues for the Campanile and from 1416 to *c*.1420 he worked on his *St George* for Orsanmichele (now in the Bargello). The saint is a portrayal of the Christian hero, but perhaps even more significant was the relief below (still on Orsanmichele) of St George killing the dragon. This is the earliest surviving datable example (*c*.1417) of the new science of perspective being used to create a defined, measurable, space for the figures to inhabit: it was probably only slightly later than the theoretical studies by BRUNELLESCHI, Donatello's friend, and precedes the work of MASACCIO by several years. About 1425 Donatello entered into partnership with the sculptor and architect MICHELOZZO, with whom he produced a series of works, including the tomb of the Antipope John XXIII (Florence, Baptistry) and the tomb of Cardinal Brancacci (Naples, S. Angelo a Nilo), both of which were being worked on in 1427, in which year he also finished the *Salome* for the Baptistry Font in Siena. The tomb of John XXIII established a type of wall-tomb, with the dead man lying on a bier, which derived from much earlier examples (e.g. by ARNOLFO di Cambio), but which was decisive for the later Florentine examples (e.g. those by the ROSSELLINI or DESIDERIO). Both the marble relief from the Brancacci Tomb and the bronze one of *Salome* show Donatello exploiting the dramatic possibilities of a combination of very low relief (*rilievo schiacciato*) with the new perspective effects, and these mark his full maturity as a tragic artist. The relief of the *Ascension and the giving of the Keys to Peter* (London, V&A) is another example of about the same date, and may have come from the Brancacci chapel in Florence. In 1431–3 he was in Rome, probably with Brunelleschi, and there he seems to have produced little, presumably because he was absorbed in the study of antiquity. Certainly his later works are saturated in the spirit of Roman classical art and architecture, which he understood more profoundly than any other 15th-century artist, with the possible exception of Mantegna. Properly speaking, he was as much influenced by Early Christian art as by pagan Roman, but he would not have regarded the distinction as valid. It was probably after his return to Florence that he made the very classical bronze *David* (Bargello), one of the earliest of Renaissance independent nude statues. He was also commissioned to carve the Cantoria, or Singing Gallery, for the Cathedral (1433–9, Cath. Mus.) to match the one already begun by Luca della ROBBIA. During these years he also made the external pulpit for Prato Cathedral (still in partnership with Michelozzo), and carried out the elaborate decorations for the Old Sacristy of S. Lorenzo, Florence. These include two bronze doors, much less ambitious than Ghiberti's, but which far surpass his in the interpretation of human character. From 1443 to 1453 Donatello was in Padua, where he made the High Altar of the Santo (now altered) and the equestrian monument to Gattamelata, the first reworking in modern times of the ancient Roman type, and clearly owing much to the most famous antique example, the *Marcus Aurelius* in Rome. He also made a wooden statue of the Baptist for the Frari in Venice, now known to be dated 1438, much earlier than previously believed. His works in Padua were models for all North Italian artists.

On his return to Florence he explored new possibilities of romantic distortion and religious emotion by following his wooden *Baptist* with another carved and painted wooden figure, of the Magdalen (Florence, Baptistry), which shows the dramatic impact of extreme ugliness. This, which was perhaps his last statue in the round, was of great importance in the development of Florentine painting, for it has the qualities of expressive contour and tense drama that painters like Castagno or, later, Botticelli sought. At his death he left two unfinished pulpits in S. Lorenzo with reliefs that show the extreme distortion he was prepared to practise in his old age. They were completed by his pupil BERTOLDO. Other works by or attributed to Donatello are in Berlin, Boston, Faenza, Florence (Sta Croce Mus. and Piazza della Signoria), Lille, Pisa, Rome (St Peter's and Aracoeli), Siena (Cath.) and Washington (NG).

DONNER, Georg Raphael (1693–1741), was the leading Austrian Baroque sculptor and a pupil of PERMOSER. He probably went to Italy before 1715, although the evidence for such a journey is purely stylistic. The influence of Michelangelo is very marked in his works, as well as that of his own contemporaries. He worked in Salzburg 1725–8, in Pressburg (now called Bratislava) 1728–38, and then in Vienna. Most of his best works are in lead (e.g. the

St Martin of 1735 in Pressburg Cath.), but the lead figures for the fountain in the Mehlmarkt, Vienna (now in the Barockmus.), of 1737–9, had to be replaced by bronze copies. This was his masterpiece, and in the opinion of some critics it shows him moving away from Baroque exuberance.

DORÉ, Gustave (1832–83), was the most productive and celebrated designer of wood-engraved book-illustrations of the 19th century. He began by supplying lithographs for a weekly paper in Paris, but soon turned to making drawings which could be engraved on wood by teams of skilled craftsmen: in this way he soon achieved international fame (there was even a special Doré Gallery in London). His books included Rabelais, Balzac, Dante's *Inferno* and 'the Doré Bible', and his engravings of the squalor of London life still provide material for social historians. He produced a few paintings and some sculpture in his later years: Grenoble has a *Scottish Loch in a Storm*, there is a huge landscape in Boston, Northampton Mass. (Smith) has *Rossini on his Deathbed*, and Wellesley Coll. nr Boston has sculpture. He is well represented in Britain and America, and French museums include Paris (Mus. d'Orsay) and Bayonne, Montpellier, Reims, Rouen, Troyes and Versailles.

DOSSI, Dosso (*c.*1479/90–1542), was the last of the Ferrarese painters, much influenced by GIORGIONE and Titian, and also by Raphael. He is first recorded in Mantua in 1512, but had presumably already been in Venice. His most famous work, the *Circe* (Rome, Borghese), shows the unearthly light which plays about his fantastic landscapes inhabited by gorgeously dressed actors. His conception of Circe, however, owes at least as much to his Ferrarese contemporary Ariosto's *Orlando Furioso* as to Homer: indeed, it probably represents Ariosto's Melissa rather than Circe. Giorgione's influence on the idyllic pastoral has now become full-blooded Romanticism in landscape. There are works in the Royal Coll. and in Baltimore, Birmingham (Barber Inst.), Cleveland Ohio, Detroit, Dresden, Ferrara, Florence (Uffizi and Pitti), Glasgow, Hartford Conn., London (NG), Malibu Cal., Modena, Naples, New York (Met. Mus.), Ottawa, Oxford, Parma, Philadelphia (Johnson), Rome (Capitoline), Trent, Vienna (K-H Mus.), Washington (NG), Worcester Mass. and elsewhere.

His brother, Battista Dosso (*d.*1548), was his helper, but pictures in Modena and Dresden may be by Battista alone.

DOTTED PRINT. Among the earliest forms of ENGRAVING were prints made from metal plates treated as relief blocks, the white lines being cut out of the metal. The surface was extensively ornamented with dots made by using punches to produce a decorative effect, often regardless of the design as a whole.

DOU, Gerard (1613–75), a portrait and genre painter of Leyden, was a pupil of the young REMBRANDT from 1628 until Rembrandt left Leyden in 1631/2, although it is difficult to see any trace of Rembrandt's handling (or intellectual powers) in the elaborately wrought small scenes of everyday life that made Dou one of the highest-paid of Dutch painters and were so popular in the 18th and 19th centuries that every major gallery possesses at least one. Nevertheless, the *Parable of the Treasure* (Budapest) and the *Tobit* (London, NG) are reasonably attributed to Rembrandt and Dou jointly: he collaborated with others also – e.g. the portrait group in Amsterdam, Rijksmus., is signed by him and by Berchem (who painted the landscape). He was the founder of the Leyden school of *fijnschilders* ('fine painters'), and the extreme minuteness of his handling may be connected with his horror of dust – he would sit motionless in his studio waiting for it to settle before beginning work. SANDRART visited his studio with BAMBOCCIO and admired the finish of a broomstick, but Dou asserted that it still needed three days' work. Many of his still-life details are VANITAS symbols, and the *Lady at a Clavichord* (London, Dulwich) may have been the inspiration for VERMEER's *Lady at the Virginals* (London, NG). METSU was his pupil.

DOWNMAN, John (1750–1824), travelled in Italy with WRIGHT of Derby in 1773–5, and made a number of landscape drawings, but on his return to London he turned to small portraits in oil (often on copper), and was particularly successful with pencil and charcoal drawings delicately tinted with watercolour. He became an ARA in 1795. There are examples in London (Tate, NPG and Wallace Coll.), and many of his portrait drawings are in Cambridge (Fitzwm).

DRAPERYMAN. An essential member of every portrait-painter's studio in the 18th and 19th centuries. He was a specialist who concentrated on clothes, curtains, and similar accessories, often supplying pattern-books from which the painter or sitter could choose. The drawings from RAMSAY's studio (Edinburgh, NG) give a good idea of this. Hogarth is said to have made a satirical drawing of the funeral in 1749 of Joseph Vanaken, with all the portrait-painters in London following the coffin in deep distress – Vanaken worked for Hudson, Ramsay, Reynolds and many others, except Gainsborough, who was almost unique in painting all his own pictures. 'Mr Vanaken having an excellent, free, genteel and florid manner of pencilling silks, satins, velvets, gold lace, etc., has worked hard for several painters . . . which without his help and skill would make but a poor figure . . . It is a great addition to their work, and indeed puts them so much on a level that it is difficult to know one hand from another' (VERTUE).

DRILL *see* STONE CARVING.

DROUAIS, François-Hubert (1727–75), was a French portrait painter who studied under his father and BOUCHER, and others. His father painted actresses and so did he: his *Mme Favart* (1757, New York, Met. Mus.) is a good example. He became a serious rival to NATTIER and worked for Mme du Barry and the royal family, being particularly successful with children. In 1771, however, his large semi-nude portrait of Mme du Barry as a Muse had to be withdrawn from the Salon. There are works in London (NG), New York (Met. Mus. and Frick Coll.) and Paris (Louvre).

DRYPOINT *see* ENGRAVING (2*b*).

DRYSDALE, Sir Russell (1912–81), was born in England, but went to Australia as a child. He returned to London in 1938 to study British and French painting, before settling in Sydney in 1940 to paint the Australian outback, inspired by the semi-Surrealism of NASH and SUTHERLAND. With NOLAN and DOBELL he represented Australia at the Venice Biennale of 1954. There are works in London (Tate), New York (Met. Mus.) and many Australian museums.

DUBUFFET, Jean (1901–85), was inspired by *graffiti* on walls ('the art of the ordinary man') and produced works, called *pâtes*, which are not painted but made of junk – tar, sand, glass and so on – which has been scratched, coloured and manipulated into shapes resembling human beings, e.g. aggressively female women, as in the series *Corps de Dames*. He preferred amateur spontaneity to professional skill, and collected the works of psychotics, calling it *art brut* – he was a wine merchant for many years before becoming a full-time painter in 1942, and presumably the term means 'unsweetened', like champagne. He travelled extensively and worked for a time in America, where he produced *Bowery Bums*. There are works in Amsterdam, Belfast, Edinburgh (M of MA), London (Tate) and New York (M of MA), as well as in France. His writings were published in 1967.

DUCCIO di Buoninsegna (*c*.1255/60–in or before 1319, probably 1315/18) was the first great Sienese painter, and he stands in relation to the Sienese School as GIOTTO does to the Florentine; yet without the powerful naturalism that makes the art of Giotto so revolutionary. Rather, Duccio sums up the grave and austere beauty of centuries of Byzantine tradition and infuses it with a breath of the new humanity which was being spread by the new Orders of SS. Francis and Dominic. Duccio is first recorded in 1278 and 1279, working for the Commune, and then in 1280 he was heavily fined for an unspecified offence, probably political: it was the first of many fines to be inflicted on him, but the others were all much smaller. In 1285 a large *Madonna* was ordered from him for the Florentine church of Sta Maria Novella: this was almost certainly the *Rucellai Madonna* (now in the Uffizi), but the picture is sometimes called a work of the 'Master of the Rucellai Madonna', and Vasari, in one of his patriotic moods, ascribed it to the Florentine Cimabue. The picture was probably painted in Siena, where Duccio is recorded at intervals 1285–99, when he was again fined for refusing to swear fealty to the Capitano del Popolo, a civic official. In 1296 and 1297, however, a 'Duche de Siene' is recorded in Paris, which may explain the Gothic influence in some of his works and in those of his followers. In 1302, in Siena, he was fined again, probably for debt, but he also received the commission to paint a *Maestà* for Siena Town Hall, now lost. He was also fined again, this time for refusing military service, and yet again for some activity apparently connected with sorcery. This last accusation cannot have been very serious, since in 1308 Duccio achieved the consummation of his career with the contract for the huge *Maestà* for the High Altar of the Cathedral. The work was finished in 1311 and carried in solemn procession from his workshop to the Cathedral. Most of it is still in Siena (Cath. Mus.), but a few small panels are missing, and the other panels, all small ones from the *predelle*, are in Fort Worth Texas, London (NG), the Thyssen Coll. in Lugano, New York (Frick Coll.) and Washington (NG). An *Angel* is in Mount Holyoke College, Mass. In its original form the *Maestà* proper – that is, the Enthroned Madonna and Child surrounded by Saints and Angels – occupied the whole of the main panel facing the congregation. Above and below were scenes from the Life of Christ and the Virgin, with small figures of Saints. Most of these smaller scenes would have been visible only to the officiating priest. The whole of the back of the main panel was taken up by twenty-six scenes from the Passion, while above and below, as on the front, were smaller panels with scenes from the Life of Christ. While the front is principally an icon for devout contemplation, the narrative cycle may have been visible only to those in the sanctuary, or perhaps the ambulatory. For this reason, the narrative may act as a commentary on Scripture. From the artistic point of view both sides show Duccio as a profound innovator, for the front has figures of greater weight and solidity, and more characterization, than had been seen previously in Siena; while the back shows him as a master of narrative, equal to Giotto in his power of story-telling though less fresh in iconographical invention, for Duccio was content to use the old Byzantine models for most (though not all) of his scenes from the New Testament. The superb craftsmanship, the use of gold as a decoration and a compositional feature at the same time, the rich and subtle colour which is made into an aesthetic feature in its own right, rather than treated (as in Giotto's works) as explaining the forms, and above all the use of varied and elegant outlines as a surface pattern as well as a description of form: all these features characterized the Sienese School for nearly two centuries. In the next generation artists as profoundly different as Simone MARTINI and the LORENZETTI started from aspects of Duccio's work, although the influence which Giovanni PISANO's sculpture had had on Duccio himself was also a potent factor in the development of the Lorenzetti.

Other works by or ascribed to Duccio are in the Royal Coll. and in Badia a Isola near Siena (a *Madonna* often ascribed to the Badia a Isola Master rather than to Duccio himself), Berne, Boston, Budapest, Cambridge Mass. (Fogg), London (NG), Manchester (Gall.), New York (Met. Mus. and Frick Coll.), Perugia, Philadelphia (Johnson), Siena (Pinacoteca, Opera del Duomo and the cathedral itself – stained glass, also ascribed to Cimabue) and Utrecht (Archiepiscopal Mus.).

DUCHAMP, Marcel (1887–1968), brother of R. DUCHAMP-VILLON and J. VILLON, was one of the original Dadaists even though he had gone to New York in 1915, before the invention of DADA. In the ARMORY SHOW he exhibited his *Nude Descending a Staircase* (two versions, 1911 and 1912, both in Philadelphia). This was a relatively straightforward Cubo-Futurist work, but it was soon to be succeeded by ready-mades (i.e. anything that comes to hand). The first ready-made, a bottle-rack, was exhibited in 1914 and was followed by a urinal, entailed *Fountain* and 'signed' R. Mutt, 1917. His version of the *Mona Lisa* was made in 1919, but his major work is *The Large Glass*, or *The Bride Stripped Bare by her Bachelors, Even* (1915–23, Philadelphia). This is not a painting, but a transparent construction made of wire and painted foil sandwiched between carefully dirtied plate glass. The original version (1915, unfinished) was broken by accident in 1926 and was repaired by Duchamp himself, retaining the cracks, so that the work could be considered 'by chance'. He published a complete documentation of all this, but the last forty years of his life were largely devoted to chess. Duchamp has been hailed as the most inventive, liberating force in modern art, as the creator of 'conceptual art' and the supreme exponent of the idea that there is no borderline between life and art. This extreme nihilism and contempt for the actual production of works of art seems to result in a dead end. Most of his works are in Philadelphia, but there is one in London (Tate).

DUCHAMP-VILLON, Raymond (1876–1918), was the elder brother of Marcel DUCHAMP and younger brother of Jacques VILLON. From 1898 his sculpture was under the influence of RODIN, but he later came to sympathize with Cubist ideals, and, with his brothers, exhibited at the SECTION D'OR. From 1912 to 1914 there is a series of *Horses* which have something of the quality of a Cubist manifesto, combined with BOCCIONI's interest in movement. He was gassed in 1916 and died two years later. There is one of the *Horse* series (1914) in Paris (Mus. d'Art Moderne) and another work in London (Tate).

DUCROS (Du Cros), Louis (1748–1810), was a rather mysterious Swiss landscape painter, mainly in watercolour, who was credited by Sir R. Colt Hoare in 1822 with having revolutionized watercolour by turning it from drawing into painting. Ducros was in Italy by *c.*1770 and lived in Rome for thirty-odd years, returning to Switzerland *c.*1805/6. He was in Rome while J. R. COZENS was there, but there is no real evidence of his supposed influence on British landscape painters. He visited Malta, and there are several oil paintings of Maltese scenes in the Valletta Mus. Other works are in Lausanne and in Berne, London (BM, V&A and Courtauld Inst.) and Manchester (Whitworth).

DUFY, Raoul (1877–1953), worked in a sub-Impressionist manner until 1905, when the impact of the FAUVE movement (particularly of Matisse's *Luxe, Calme et Volupté*) impelled him to adopt simplified forms and bright colour. He designed textiles and ceramics and developed a light-hearted decorative style, eminently suited to his range of subjects – esplanades, race-courses, regattas etc. – and used odd tricks of technique, such as white patches ('neutrals') for shadows, and a rapid, modish, calligraphic draughtsmanship. There are examples in London (Tate and Courtauld Inst.), New York (M of MA), Paris (Mus. d'Art Moderne), and large collections at Le Havre and Nice.

DUGENTO (*Duecento:* Ital. 200). The 13th century, i.e. the twelve-hundreds.

DUGHET, Gaspard, *see* POUSSIN.

DU JARDIN, Karel (1621/2–78), was born in Amsterdam. He was a pupil of BERCHEM, and went twice to Italy. He painted chiefly Italianate landscapes with figures, occasional religious subjects, and an exceptionally fine group portrait of the *Regents of the Women's Prison in Amsterdam* (1669, Rijksmus.). He returned to Italy in 1674/5 and died in Venice. There are examples in the Royal Coll. and in Berlin, Brussels, Cambridge (Fitzwm), Dresden, Edinburgh (NG), The Hague, Hartford Conn., Leningrad, London (NG, Wallace Coll. and Dulwich), Munich, Oxford (Ashmolean), Paris (Louvre), Vienna, Yale, York and elsewhere.

DUNLAP, William (1766–1839), was an American painter of portraits – for example, the one of himself showing his parents his *Hamlet* (New York, Hist. Soc.) on his return from studying in London, 1788. He was also a playwright and kept thirty volumes of diary (1786–1834), of which eleven survive and have been published; above all, he wrote 'A History of the Rise and Progress of the Arts of Design in the United States', 1834, which is the best source-book on early American painting.

DUNOYER de Segonzac *see* SEGONZAC.

DUQUESNOY, François (1597–1643), known in Italy as 'Il Fiammingo' (the Fleming), was born in Brussels and worked in Rome 1618–43. He was the most famous non-Italian sculptor of his day (cf. Giovanni da BOLOGNA), and, like ALGARDI, represented a more classical tendency than the exuberant Baroque of BERNINI (by whom he was nevertheless influenced, particularly in portraiture). In his poverty-stricken early days in Rome he made small carvings in ivory and wood, but from 1621 he worked for some of the greatest patrons of the day. He was a great friend of Poussin, the most classical painter of the age, and was also intimate with SANDRART. In 1639 Poussin was offered the post of *peintre ordinaire* to Louis XIV in Paris, and shortly afterwards Duquesnoy was invited to become the King's sculptor; he did not accept at once, but in 1641 he had developed a neurotic condition which needed treatment in Paris. He actually left Rome in 1643, but he died in Leghorn on the way to Paris. His major works were the *St Andrew* (1628–40, St Peter's: *see* BOLGI), the *S. Susanna* (1629–33; Rome, S.M. di Loreto), the relief in SS. Apostoli, Naples (1642), and two monuments in S.M. dell' Anima, Rome, both of which have groups of his much admired *putti*. Numerous smaller works spread his fame outside Italy; there are examples in Berlin, Dublin, London (V&A), Paris (Louvre), Vaduz (Liechtenstein Coll.) and elsewhere.

DURAND, Asher B. (1796–1886), began as an engraver whose reputation was established in 1820 with his engraving after TRUMBULL's painting of *The Declaration of Independence*. As early as 1830 he projected a serial publication of engravings devoted to the American landscape, but it was not successful and had to be suspended after the first issue. By this time he had turned to painting portraits and landscapes, and he eventually became one of the leading landscape painters of the HUDSON RIVER SCHOOL. In 1840–1 he made a trip to Europe and copied old masters; on his return he was elected President of the National Academy of Design (1845–61), being one of the first landscape painters in the world to receive such recognition. Unlike his friend COLE, he worked out-of-doors, and the artless realism of his landscapes is their chief attraction: nevertheless, he was much influenced by Dutch 17th-century painters such as Hobbema, as well as by Claude (who greatly influenced Cole and other Hudson River painters). His later works strive after the sublime, and, as a deeply religious man, he regarded landscape as a manifestation of the divine. There are pictures by him in many US museums – Boston, Cambridge Mass. (Fogg), Cleveland Ohio, Detroit, New York (Met. Mus.) among others – but there do not seem to be any outside America.

DÜRER, Albrecht (1471–1528), was the son of a goldsmith who settled in Nuremberg in 1455, and in 1467 married his master's daughter. The young Albrecht was first apprenticed to his father, and was then bound for three years to the painter Michael WOLGEMUT, whose large workshop also produced woodcut book-illustrations for the printer Anton Koberger, Dürer's godfather. He travelled for four years from Easter 1490, visiting Colmar (intending to work under SCHONGAUER), Basle and Strasbourg, and in May 1494 he returned to Nuremberg and married. In the autumn of the same year he went to Venice (his great friend, the humanist Willibald Pirckheimer, was then a student at Padua) and returned home by spring 1495: it has, however, been suggested that the evidence for this Venetian journey is inadequate. Late in 1505 he certainly went to Venice via Augsburg, and stayed until February 1507. During this visit he met Giovanni BELLINI, whom he greatly admired, and painted several works, including the *Madonna of the Rose Garlands* (Prague, NG: now very damaged) for the German merchants in Venice, and the *Christ among the Doctors*, which shows some knowledge of Leonardo. On his return to Germany he intensified the learned side of his art and personality; he studied mathematics, geometry, Latin and humanist literature, and sought the company of scholars rather than that of his fellow artisans. This departure in mode of life and thought is directly traceable to the influence of Leonardo and Mantegna and the example of Bellini, and although it was common enough in

Italy it was unprecedented in Germany. In 1512 he became Court Painter to the Emperor Maximilian, and in July 1520 he journeyed to the Netherlands to obtain from Maximilian's successor, Charles V, the ratification of his post and pension. He saw the coronation of the new Emperor at Aachen and was confirmed in his office, after which he visited Antwerp, Brussels, Malines, Cologne, Middelburg, Bruges and Ghent, honoured and feted all along the route. He returned home in July, 1521, and despite ill-health resulting from fever, probably contracted in the swamps of Zeeland, where he had ventured in the hope of seeing a dead whale, he worked unremittingly until his death.

His enormous œuvre consists of woodcuts and copper engravings, paintings, preparatory and independent drawings, as well as treatises on measurement (1525), fortification (1527), proportion and artistic theory (1528) and the detailed diary of his Netherlands journey. He was the main channel through which Italian Renaissance forms and ideas were introduced into the North, and he combined these with the individualism normal in German art, inherited from the Gothic tradition. His greatest influence was through his graphic work. He is one of the supreme masters of woodcut and copper engraving, and these easily transportable models carried his technique, subject matter, designs and style all over Europe, and even had a considerable influence in Italy (cf. PONTORMO). He extended the range of woodcut and copper engraving by perfecting the technique of both, and raised the standard of graphic art by the training he gave to the craftsmen who executed his designs (*see* KLEINMEISTER). His main works in woodcut were series such as the *Apocalypse* (1498), the *Great Passion* (1498–1510), and the *Little Passion* (1509–11), the *Life of the Virgin* (1501–11), and single prints such as the *Men's Bathhouse* (1497); and in engraving the *Engraved Passion* (1507–12) and the many single plates such as the *Sea Monster* and the *Prodigal Son* (1497), the *S. Eustace* (*c.*1501), the *Great Fortune* (1501/2), the *Adam and Eve* (1504), the *Knight, Death, and the Devil* (1513), *St Jerome* and the *Melencolia* (1514). The *Apocalypse* was the first book to be entirely the work of an artist (apart from the text) – Dürer was his own illustrator, printer and publisher. The text was available in either Latin or German. All his works combine vivid imagery, technical refinement, expressiveness and masterly draughtsmanship with deeply thought-out, and often involved, iconography which must be read, layer upon layer, before the meaning of the design becomes clear, although its visual impact is immediate. He shared in the Emperor Maximilian's commissions for the huge woodcut *Triumphs*, and executed some blocks for them, but they added little to his fame.

Compared with his graphic work, his paintings are few in number; they are more traditional in type and usually less packed with significance. One of his greatest contributions is his watercolour and gouache landscapes, some made during his Italian journeys, for they are among the most evocative expressions of mood and atmosphere in landscape painting (cf. DANUBE SCHOOL). In October 1526 he presented to his native city, as a memorial of himself, the *Apostles* (Munich), probably designed as part of a *Sacra Conversazione* on the Italian model, but which was not executed on account of the Reformation. In form, the Saints owe much to Bellini's in the Frari Altar (Venice), and their significance is bound up with the spiritual conflicts of the Reformation, which affected him deeply. Melancthon was a close friend, and he knew and admired both Luther and Erasmus. Despite his large workshop he left no succession; his art was too universal and yet too personal to breed imitators. There are works in Augsburg, Berlin, Boston (Gardner), Budapest, Cassel, Cologne (Wallraf-Richartz), Dresden, Florence (Uffizi), Frankfurt (Mus. and Städel), Lisbon, London (NG), Madrid (Prado), Munich, New York (Met. Mus.), Nuremberg, Ober St Veit nr Vienna, Paris (Louvre and Bib. Nat.), Toledo Ohio, Vienna, Washington (NG), Weimar and elsewhere.

DYCE, William (1806–64), painter, scientist and art administrator, was born in Aberdeen and studied in London and Rome (1827–9). There he was much influenced by the NAZARENER and he is said to have painted a *Madonna* in 1828 (now lost), which may have helped to transmit the new German ideas to the Pre-Raphaelite Brotherhood (founded in 1848). He was very important in the development of art education in Britain, sharing the ideals of Prince Albert, who helped him. There are works in the Royal Coll. (including a beautiful Peruginesque *Madonna* of 1845, bought by Prince Albert), and in Aberdeen, Edinburgh (NG), Liverpool and London (Tate).

DYCK, Sir Anthony van (Antoon van Dijk, Vandyke) (1599–1641), was born in Antwerp. He became an independent master as early as *c.*1615/16 and was a member of the Guild in 1618. He was RUBENS's chief assistant while still in his teens, his forte being for subjects requiring pathos rather than movement. He visited England in 1620 (James I wanted to employ him as Court Painter), but after 4 months he returned to Flanders and in 1621 went to Italy where, except for a visit to Flanders in 1622 when his father died, he remained for 6 years. He visited Rome, Florence, Venice and Palermo, but stayed mostly in Genoa, where he laid the foundations of his career as a portrait painter and evolved the repertory of patterns which he later used in Antwerp and London. He was not at his best in Rome, where he quarrelled with his fellow-Flemings, the BENTVUEGHELS, although he painted two of his most striking portraits there, in 1622, of *Sir Robert* and *Lady Shirley* in Persian costume (Petworth, Sussex, National Trust). At that time Rome was full of brilliant artists – Bernini, Domenichino, Guercino, Pietro da Cortona – and the Baroque that Rubens had seen coming to birth was fully developed. He was in Palermo in 1624, where he painted the Viceroy (London, Dulwich) and began his most important Italian commission, the *Madonna of the Rosary* (Palermo, Congregazione del Rosario), but the outbreak of plague caused him to flee back to Genoa. He returned to Antwerp *c.*1627 and tried to obtain the patronage of the Regent Isabella, as well as working for the House of Orange. Between then and his departure for England he produced most of his finest portraits; for, less forceful as a personality than Rubens, he was more sensitive to the individuality of his sitters, and he expressed it with an unfailing sense of style that reflects something of his own introspective melancholy. In religious works he leaned heavily on Rubens and on Titian and Correggio, though he digested these Italian influences less successfully than Rubens had done. Technically, his paint is thinner than Rubens's vigorous impasto, drier, more dragged, and with a greyer underpainting, less limpid and free in handling. His years in England – from 1632 until his death – were outwardly successful, with immense prestige at the Court of Charles I, a knighthood, and an enormous practice as a portrait painter, for he supplanted MYTENS, and overshadowed JOHNSON. Nevertheless, his efforts to re-establish himself on the Continent in 1634 and again in 1640, to succeed Rubens (cf. JORDAENS), and then to get the commission for the decoration of the gallery in the Louvre which, when he arrived in Paris, had already been given to Poussin, suggest that he realized how precarious Charles I's position had become, and how limiting was the patronage of the English Court. By now, he was very ill and he returned to England in 1641, only to die. His nine years in England were prolific, but involved the constant repetition of his Genoese types, with varying success, according to whether he himself or a studio hand executed the work. None of his helpers was of any significance, and he lacked Rubens's ability to control a large workshop. Among the most famous of his English portraits are the equestrian ones of Charles I, the triple portrait of the King sent to Bernini to serve as the model for a bust, the groups of the royal children, and the great family group at Wilton House, nr Salisbury. All these became models for English portrait painters for centuries to come, through DOBSON, Lely, Reynolds and GAINSBOROUGH, to Lawrence and beyond. Although he died young he was very productive and most older galleries have examples: Antwerp, Brussels, Edinburgh, London (NG, Wallace Coll., Dulwich, Courtauld Inst. and Kenwood), and the Royal Coll. being exceptionally rich. The following American and Canadian museums also have examples: Baltimore, Boston (Mus. and Gardner), Chicago, Cincinnati, Cleveland Ohio, Columbus Ohio, Denver, Detroit, Hartford Conn., Indianapolis, Kansas City, Los Angeles (Mus. and Univ. of S. California), Louisville, New York (Met. Mus. and Frick), Ottawa, Raleigh NC, St Louis, San Diego, San Francisco, Toledo Ohio, Toronto, Washington (NG, Corcoran and Nat. Coll.) and Yale.

E

EAKINS, Thomas (1844–1916), was an American painter, principally of portraits. He went from Philadelphia to Paris in 1866, where he came under the influence of MANET's realism. After a visit to Spain in 1869 he went back to Philadelphia and became a successful teacher, whose quest for realism led him to attend medical classes to improve his knowledge of anatomy and led indirectly to his *Gross Clinic* (1875), with its representation of a surgeon operating, which caused an uproar, as did his *Agnew Clinic*. These Rembrandtesque subjects were treated in the 'Spanish' style of Manet, which had itself caused uproar in Paris rather earlier. He is well represented in US museums, especially Philadelphia.

EARDLEY, Joan (1921–63), was trained in Glasgow and painted subjects from Glasgow slum life until, in 1950, she discovered Catterline, a fishing village south of Aberdeen, where she painted landscapes of that stormy coast. The Tate Gallery has *Salmon Net Posts*, 1963.

EARL, Ralph (1751–1801), was an American portrait painter who is first recorded in 1775, making sketches for engravings of the Revolution. He worked in England 1778–85, exhibiting at the RA 1783–5, and probably coming into contact with the Loyalist WEST. In 1785 he returned to New England and painted portraits there until his death; he was twice married and deserted both wives, and from 1799 his work deteriorated because of the alcoholism which eventually killed him. His *Roger Sherman* (*c.*1775/7, Yale) has a gaunt Yankee quality which seems preferable to the pastiche of fashionable English painting apparent in his later works. Many American museums have works by him: the only ones outside the USA appear to be the *Admiral Kempenfelt* (1783, London, NPG) and one in the American Museum, Bath.

EASEL painting/picture. Any painting not a WALL-PAINTING. An easel-painting may be quite large – much bigger than a CABINET picture.

EASTLAKE, Sir Charles (1793–1865), was a pupil of HAYDON and exhibited at the RA from 1827. Like Dyce he was more successful as an administrator than as a painter, and he became President of the RA in 1850 and Director of the National Gallery in 1855, holding both posts until his death. He was largely responsible for making the National Gallery one of the world's best collections. His wife Elizabeth (1809–93), whom he married in 1849, was a considerable writer on art and also translated many important art-historical works from German, e.g. Waagen's 'Treasures of Art in Great Britain'.

EAU-FORTE. French for etching (*see* ENGRAVING).

ECKERSBERG, Cristoffer (1783–1853), was a Danish neoclassical painter of portraits, landscapes and marines. He was trained in Copenhagen (1803–10) but went to Paris and studied under DAVID (1811–13) before going to Rome in 1813, where he remained until 1816. There he met Ingres and became a friend of THORWALDSEN. His portraits are greatly influenced by David, but the landscapes of the Roman campagna are similar to – but much earlier than – those of COROT. He was an important teacher at the Copenhagen Academy: KØBKE was his pupil. He is well represented in Copenhagen.

ECLECTIC *see* CARRACCI.

ÉCOLE de Paris *see* PARIS, School of.

ÉCOLE Royale des Élèves Protégés was a special school set up by the French Academy in 1748, under its head, Charles COYPEL, on the insistence of the Surintendant, Mme de Pompadour's uncle. It was thought to be necessary to give instruction to young artists, since the quality of the ROME Prize competitors had for some years been too poor to make an award. Only the prize-winners in the Academy of Painting and Sculpture were admitted, three of each, and students had to remain in the school for three years before they were allowed to go to Rome. In 1771 the number was reduced to two students, who had to remain only a year, and in 1775 the school was abolished, because of the hostility of the Academy, which saw it as a reflection on its teaching. Instruction was not greatly concerned with technique – entrants had already proved themselves competent – but rather with Greek and Roman history and mythology. Outside students were admitted to the lectures.

EECKHOUT, Gerbrand van den (1621–74), was an Amsterdam painter who was the pupil, friend and close imitator of Rembrandt. In about 1655 he painted a number of scenes in the totally different manner of TER BORCH. There is a fine portrait group (1657) in London (NG).

EIDOMETROPOLIS, EIDOPHUSIKON *see* GIRTIN and LOUTHERBOURG respectively.

ELIASZ., Nicolaes, called Pickenoy (1590/1–1654/6), was an Amsterdam portrait painter of the generation before Rembrandt. His *Company of Captain Jan van Vlooswijck* (Amsterdam, Rijksmus.) was painted in 1642, the year of Rembrandt's *Night Watch*: his *Company of Captain Jacob Rogh* (1645, Rijksmus.) seems to be influenced by the *Night Watch*. Birmingham has a *Lady* (1630) of the early-Rembrandt type.

ELLE, Ferdinand I (*c.*1580–1649), was a Flemish portrait painter active in Paris at the same time as Frans II POURBUS. Poussin worked with him for a time, but otherwise little is known of him. His son, Louis (1612–89), worked for Louis XIV and was a Founder-Member of the Academy.

ELSHEIMER, Adam (1578–1610), was a German landscape painter whose most important work was done in Italy. He was in Venice *c.*1598 and in Rome by 1600, where he spent the rest of his short life. His landscapes are among the first ideal ones, in which the figures have a considerable but not overwhelming part to play, and in which the effects of light are studied with great care. He probably learned the effectiveness of a variety of points of light from Tintoretto and Caravaggio (his contemporary in Rome) and many of his small landscapes have several sources of light – e.g. a warm sunset with the cold light of the moon in another part of the picture, and the light of a torch elsewhere. His works are small; always on copper (sometimes silvered), and executed with great precision. They had great influence on his friend Rubens and on younger men such as Rembrandt and Claude. The works of Paul BRIL are very similar. Rubens, in a letter of 14 January 1611, refers to Elsheimer's death as causing him great grief, saying 'I pray that God has forgiven Signor Adam his sin of sloth, by which he has deprived the world of most beautiful things, caused himself much misery and finally, I believe, reduced himself to despair; whereas with his own hands he could have built up a great fortune and made himself respected by all the world'. He then goes on to offer to sell any of Elsheimer's pictures on behalf of the widow – a Scotswoman who claimed to be a refugee from heresy and who married him in 1606, Bril being a witness –

for considerable sums of money: 'and if the painting should not be sold immediately, we shall in the meantime find a way to advance her a good sum of money on it without prejudice to the sale'. SANDRART, however, says that Elsheimer was afflicted by melancholia and could not work, so that he was exploited by his own pupil Goudt, who eventually had him imprisoned for debt. There are pictures by him in the Royal Coll., and in Berlin, Bonn, Brunswick, Cassel, Cambridge (Fitzwm), Copenhagen, Dresden, Edinburgh, Florence (Uffizi), Frankfurt (Städel), The Hague, Leningrad, London (NG and Wellington Mus.), Madrid, Munich, Paris (Louvre), Venice (Accad.), Vienna (K-H Mus.), Yale and elsewhere; there are eight small *Saints* at Petworth Sussex (National Trust) and a ninth in Montpellier.

ENCAUSTIC WAX was a painting technique apparently practised in antiquity with success, but since fallen into disuse. The principle seems to have been to work on a wall with colours mixed with soft wax, which, when heated with irons or similar means, were driven into the wall itself. Pliny's 'Natural History' (before AD 79) gives an account of the method, and this probably inspired LEONARDO's disastrous attempt at reviving it (1503–5) as well as later attempts in the 19th century. The technique was also used, with success, for the small, vivid portraits made for mummy-cases. Many of these have survived from Fayoum, an oasis near the Nile, and date from the 1st century AD onwards. There are examples in London (BM).

ENGELBRECHTSZ., Cornelis (1468–1533), was the leading artist in Leyden in the early 16th century and the master of LUCAS van Leyden. His strong colour and fancy costumes were influenced by the ANTWERP Mannerists and in turn influenced Lucas. There are works in Amsterdam, Ghent, Leyden, Munich, New York (Met. Mus.), Stockholm, Utrecht and Vienna.

ENGRAVING. A generic title often used to cover all the methods of multiplying prints, although strictly the word should apply only to the second of the processes described below. The first distinction to be drawn is between Reproductive and Original Engravings, a reproductive engraving being a means of divulgating an idea expressed in a painting, drawing, statue or other medium, invented by an artist other than the engraver. An original engraving is an independent work of art invented and executed by the engraver himself. Before the invention of photography reproductive engravings, executed by very skilled craftsmen, were the chief means of disseminating information of all kinds, and, in particular, works of art produced in other times or places. The three main types of engraving may be classified as (1) Relief or cameo, (2) Intaglio, and (3) Surface or planar. Each of these types corresponds to one or more of the main techniques, but they are distinguished by the fact that each has its own special method of printing.

(1) Relief. The main techniques are woodcut and wood-engraving, linocut, and its simpler forms, such as potato cuts. A plain block of wood, if covered with printing ink and pressed on to a sheet of paper, would print as a solid black rectangle; but if channels were cut into the surface with a gouge these would not catch the ink, and would therefore print as white patches. The basic idea of a woodcut is thus to leave the black lines or patches untouched, cutting away only those parts intended to print as white. This means that a single black line has to have the wood cut away on both sides, which is done with special knives and gouges. Woodcuts are done on blocks of soft wood,

cut plank-fashion, and will give hundreds, or even thousands, of impressions before wearing out. Lino or plastic is often used nowadays, as it is easier to work, but its life is shorter. Colour prints are produced by cutting a special block for each colour, as well as a key-block, usually in black, which carries the linear structure (*see* CHIAROSCURO woodcut), and these blocks have to be printed 'in register', so that the blocks do not overlap: the exception is when two colours, e.g. blue and yellow, are deliberately overprinted, to give green. The earliest woodcuts are now thought to date from the end of the 14th century, but wood-engraving hardly occurs before the mid-18th century, and found one of its greatest exponents in Thomas BEWICK, who revived white-line engraving. Wood-engraving is very similar to engraving on copper, using the same kind of tool, called a graver or burin, but differs in the printing process. The main difference between woodcut and wood-engraving is in the block itself, which is boxwood, cut across the grain, in wood-engraving. On this smooth, grainless surface the sharply pointed graving tools can plough very fine furrows, each of which prints as a fine white line. Clearly, it is easier to think in terms of fine white lines on a predominantly black ground, and the great modern revival (since about 1920) of wood-engraving has been of the white-line or Xylographic type, which offers a means of stylized design.

(2) Intaglio (Ital. cut into). The intaglio techniques are all forms of engraving on metal – normally copper, but also zinc, pewter or steel – and they are distinguished from the other techniques by the method of printing. When the plate has been engraved by one or more of the processes described below (and several processes may be used in combination) the plate is dabbed all over with a thin kind of printing ink, which is then rubbed off again with muslin or the palm of the hand, leaving the ink in the furrows. A sheet of paper is then dampened to soften it, laid on the plate, and both are then passed through a heavy press not unlike a mangle. The damp paper is forced into the engraved lines and picks up the ink which has been left in them: when dry the engraved lines stand up in relief. This explains the great difference between a copper-engraving, or any other intaglio print, and a wood-engraving which has been cut in a very similar way – the ink lies on the surface of the wood-engraved block instead of being forced into the lines cut (*intagliate*) into the metal plate. A wood-engraving cannot be printed in the intaglio manner as it would break under the great pressure. The main intaglio processes are: (*a*) line or copper engraving, (*b*) dry-point, (*c*) etching, including soft-ground etching, (*d*) stipple and crayon engraving, (*e*) mezzotint, and (*f*) aquatint and related processes.

(*a*) *Line-engraving*. The sharp graver is pushed into the copper, exactly like a plough into the earth, throwing up small shavings and leaving a line which has a V-section. This is the earliest of the intaglio techniques, as the earliest dated print is of 1446, but it is also the one demanding the greatest discipline and precision of hand, since the sharp tool has to be pushed ahead of the hand – and polished copper is very slippery. DÜRER is incomparably the greatest artist in this medium, which was later mainly used for reproducing pictures and other works of art or didactic diagrams. Seventeenth-century engravers (especially French ones) brought the art to the pitch of perfection as a didactic medium.

(*b*) *Dry-point*. This is the simplest technique, since it consists of drawing on the metal plate with a 'pencil' made of steel, or steel tipped with diamond, ruby or carborundum (*see* CRAYON ÉLECTRIQUE). The great quality of dry-point lies in the burr, which is the shaving of metal turned up at the side of the furrow. When burr occurs in line-engraving it is scraped off, but it is left in a dry-point because it catches the ink and prints with a richness which adds to the directness of the artist's work. Unfortunately, it is soon crushed by the pressure of printing, so that less than 50 good impressions can be taken, and sometimes even fewer. Dry-point is often used to reinforce etching or even engraving: Rembrandt, in particular, combined it with etching.

(*c*) *Etching*. Here the metal plate is covered with a resinous ground, impervious to acid, and then the etcher draws on the ground with a needle, exposing the copper wherever he wants a line to print. The plate is put in an acid bath, which eats away the exposed parts, but subtlety is given by taking the plate out of the acid as soon as the faintest lines are bitten. These faint lines are then 'stopped-out' with varnish and the plate is re-bitten until the medium-dark lines are stopped-out in their turn, and so on. The first dated etching is of 1513 (by Urs GRAF), but Dürer was making etchings on iron at about the same time. The great period came with the 17th century, culminating in Rembrandt, and the process has been popular ever since. *Soft-ground etching* looks like a pencil or chalk drawing, because the ground is mixed with tallow, and has a sheet of thin paper laid on it, on to which the etcher draws directly with a pencil; part of the ground sticks to the paper giving a grainy effect when the plate is bitten. CASTIGLIONE may have invented the process. A *photographic etching* or *cliché-verre* is made by drawing with a stylus on a grounded glass plate which is then treated like a photographic negative and printed on photographic paper. More than sixty such 'etchings' were made by Corot from *c.*1853, but the technique never became popular, even though it permits of limitless prints.

(*d*) *Stipple*, *crayon engraving* and *colour printing* were popular 18th-century techniques. Stipple and crayon engraving were used for the reproduction of portrait drawings, giving an effect remarkably similar to that of a chalk drawing. It is obtained by a combination of etching and engraving techniques, stippling dots over a grounded plate with the point of an etching needle, or, more usually, by the use of special tools: a *roulette* is a spur-like wheel which gives an effect similar to the grainy quality of chalk, and it can be combined with a *mattoir*, which is an instrument like a tiny club with sharp points projecting from the head. These points produce a grained effect on the bare copper which prints as black, chalk-like dots. Occasionally the effect of two-colour chalks is obtained by printing from two plates, usually black and red. Colour engravings of the 18th century fall into two main categories, English and French. The finest English prints are usually based on the aquatint process (*see* (*f*) below), and are made by a single printing from a plate coloured in the appropriate areas. Some English prints are, in fact, monochrome aquatints hand-coloured in watercolour: both GIRTIN and TURNER earned a living colouring engravings at the beginning of their careers.

The French technique, sometimes called *manière de lavis*, is an imitation of a wash drawing or a watercolour obtained by the use of a great number of *roulettes*, *mattoirs* and gravers. The use of these tools gave the tones, but the actual colours were printed from four separate plates – yellow, red, blue and black, printed in that order, the black being the most important since it defined the contours. The most difficult part of this technique is to ensure that one plate is printed exactly on top of another – 'in register'. This method – originally in three colours only – was invented by the German Jacob Le Blon (1667–1741) before 1720, when he was in London trying to exploit it. He went bankrupt, and died in Paris still working on it.

(*e*) *Mezzotint*. This was the great reproductive process of the 18th century (though invented in the 17th, traditionally by Prince Rupert of the Rhine). It was especially successful in England, where the portraits of Reynolds, Gainsborough, Romney and others were normally reproduced by it. The plate is first covered with a mesh of small burred dots, made by a toothed chisel-like instrument called a rocker, since it is rocked back and forth to produce the dots. In this state the plate would print as a solid, rich black. The half-tones and lights are obtained by scraping off the burr with a scraper, or polishing the plate smooth again with a burnisher so that the ink may be wiped off the highest lights. The technique is rarely practised now, since photographic methods have superseded it for reproduction.

(*f*) *Aquatint*. Like mezzotint, aquatint is a tone process rather than a line method, but it is admirably adapted to the rendering of transparent effects, such as watercolour gives. It is basically a form of etching, but using a porous ground which the acid can penetrate to form a network of fine lines. Any pure whites are stopped out in the usual way before biting begins, then the palest tints are bitten and stopped-out, and so on, as in etching. Variations of texture can be obtained by pressing a piece of sandpaper on the grounded plate, mixing sugar with the ground, or attacking the plate with sulphur ('sulphur-tint'). Paul SANDBY was the first imaginative artist to use the process, followed by the greatest of all aquatinters, GOYA, but it was revived by John Piper in the 1930s, and Picasso used the sugar process for his illustrations to Buffon.

(3) Surface (or Planar) Printing. The one major process which involves no cutting into the plate or block (and therefore no 'engraving' in the strict sense), is lithography, formerly executed on a thick slab of limestone, but now usually on zinc or even plastic, which are cheaper and lighter (although still called 'the stone'). The whole technique, invented in 1798 by Alois Senefelder, is based on the fact that water runs off a greasy surface. The design is drawn or painted on the stone with a greasy chalk or ink, and then the stone is wetted. When greasy printers' ink is rolled on to the stone it will not 'take' on the wet parts, but sticks to those parts which are already greasy – i.e. the drawing. The new process was quickly taken up by several 19th century artists, including Delacroix, Goya, Géricault, Daumier, Manet and others, and it is still a popular medium. Senefelder came to London in 1800 to obtain patents, and he persuaded several artists to try his new 'pen-lithography', i.e. drawing with a pen and greasy ink; Fuseli (1802), Barry (1803) and West were among them. Lithography is used extensively for posters and other forms of commercial art, since it can produce many thousands of prints. The scraper-type printing press is much less damaging to the stone than the presses used for relief or intaglio printing and there is therefore almost no limit to the number of prints obtainable. Chromolithography, to give it its full name, can be used for colour printing, with one stone for each colour, printed in register. The first major work produced by this method was BOYS's 'Picturesque Architecture' in 1839. *See also* SERIGRAPHY.

ENSOR, James (1860–1949), was a Belgian painter whose father was English. Apart from his training in Brussels Ensor spent his life in Ostend. He had a peculiarly macabre outlook, taking the subjects of Callot, Bosch or Bruegel and treating them in the technique of Manet, Courbet and Rubens. He frequently used masks and skeletons for Expressionist purposes before EXPRESSIONISM was invented. In 1884 he exhibited with Les XX, who, in 1889, rejected his *Entry of Christ into Brussels in 1889* (1888, Malibu Cal., Getty) and voted for his expulsion. His best work was done by 1900: in 1929 he was made a Baron. There are pictures in Antwerp, Brussels, Detroit, London (Tate), New York (M of M A) and Paris (Mus. d'Orsay).

EPSTEIN, Sir Jacob (1880–1959), was born in New York and went to Paris in 1902; from 1905 he lived in England. In 1907 he was commissioned to carve eighteen statues for the British Medical Association building. They were erected in 1908 and caused great scandal: after that, it became customary for any new imaginative work of his to be greeted with uproar – e.g. the *Rima* in Hyde Park (1925) or the stone carvings on the London Transport Building in Westminster (1928–9). His stone-carvings are technically deficient, but his portraits in bronze have an over-lifesize quality, partly due to the rugosity of the handling, reminiscent of Rodin, and are generally admired. The last example was the official commission of *Smuts* outside the Houses of Parliament. Like many of his bronzes it has a distinctive green patina. There are collections in Bolton and Walsall (given by his widow), and other works are in Aberdeen, Auckland N Z, Birmingham, Coventry (Cath., *Archangel Michael* in bronze), Edinburgh, Hull, Leeds (*Maternity*, a large stone-carving), Liverpool, Llandaff Cath., London (Westminster Abbey, St Paul's, Tate, Imperial War Mus. and Heythrop College, Cavendish Sq.), Manchester, New York (M of M A), Oxford (New Coll.), Paris (Cemetery of Père Lachaise, Tomb of Oscar Wilde, 1912) and elsewhere.

ERCOLE de' Roberti *see* ROBERTI.

ERHART (Erhaert), Gregor (*d.* probably 1540), was a German sculptor, born in Ulm, who worked in Augsburg from 1494 until his death. There are no documented works by him, although he is known to have made a stone crucifix in 1498, and in 1509 he was working on an equestrian monument for the Emperor Maximilian. Nothing is known of his later work, but he seems to have been an important sculptor of the transitional period, whose work was influenced first by MULTSCHER, the leading Ulm artist, and later by RIEMENSCHNEIDER. The most important attributions to Erhart are the altarpiece at Blaubeuren (1493–4), and *Madonnas* in Berlin (1502–4, destroyed 1945) and Frauenstein, Austria (*c.*1515). Other works attributed to him are in Cleveland Ohio, Detroit, London (V&A) and Paris (Louvre).

ERNST, Max (1891–1976), met ARP, who became his lifelong friend, in 1914. Ernst introduced the DADAIST movement into Cologne in 1919, but he settled in Paris in 1922 and was associated with the Surrealists from 1924, making *collages* and *frottages* and writing *collage* novels. From 1941 to 1949 he lived in the U S. There are works in Edinburgh, Grenoble, Hartford Conn., Karlsruhe, London (Tate), Manchester, New York (M of M A) and Strasbourg.

E.S., The Master, was a Rhinelander or Swiss, active *c.*1450–67, who was the most important engraver in the years after 1450, and whose style has been compared with that of the sculptor GERHAERT. He produced more than 300 prints (*see* ARS MORIENDI), eighteen of which bear the initials ES. He was the first engraver to use this form of signature, and he also invented systematic cross-hatching, paving the way for SCHONGAUER. He was probably originally a goldsmith.

ESQUISSE is French for sketch.

ETCHING *see* ENGRAVING.

ETTY, William (1787–1849), was one of the very few English artists to paint the nude almost exclusively. This he did in a manner derived from Titian and Rubens, and therefore glowing and sensual, but subject to the requirements of IDEAL ART. Many of his pictures consist of extremely faithful studies from the nude, done in the Academy Life School which he frequented all his life, presented as mythological characters. He made several journeys to the Continent and met DELACROIX in 1825, so he must have been aware of the French Romantic movement. In 1828 he defeated CONSTABLE in the RA elections: Constable avenged himself by referring to Etty's *Youth on the Prow and Pleasure at the Helm* (1832, London, Tate) as 'Etty's Bum-Boat' (it represents a boat with a number of naked women in it or clinging to it – in 19th-century naval usage a bumboat was a small boat offering supplies or luxuries to a larger ship in harbour). He also alluded sarcastically to the purity of landscape by comparison with 'the shaggy posteriors of satyrs'. The best collection of Etty's work is in his native York, but there are other pictures in Boston, Edinburgh, Leeds, London (Tate), Manchester, New York (Met. Mus.), Oxford, Port Sunlight (Lever Gall.), Preston, Scarborough and elsewhere.

EUSTON ROAD was the name given to an English group, founded in the late 1930s, which was so called after the Euston Road in London (near the Slade School, where most of the members were trained). They sought to return to a more realistic conception of painting, neither abstract nor Surrealist. The principal members were Coldstream, Gowing, Rogers and PASMORE (who later became an abstract painter). There are examples of their work in London (Tate). They had considerable influence on English painting in the post-war period, as Sir William Coldstream was head of the Slade School for many years.

EVERDINGEN, Allart and Caesar Boëtius van. Allart (1621–75), was a Dutch landscape painter who visited Scandinavia (1643–4) and returned to Holland with a new type of romantic mountain landscape, with pine forests and waterfalls, which was novel and successful. His type of scenery influenced some of the later works of Jacob van RUISDAEL. There are pictures by Allart in many Dutch and German galleries, London (NG and Wallace Coll.) and elsewhere. He also produced over 100 landscape etchings.

His elder brother, Caesar Boëtius (1617–78), was a figure painter in Alkmaar and Haarlem, who was much influenced by Caravaggio and was therefore a sort of offshoot of the UTRECHT SCHOOL. There are pictures by him in Alkmaar, Amsterdam, Barnsley, Dresden, Haarlem, The Hague, Rouen, Southampton and Stockholm.

EWORTH, Hans, who signed his pictures HE, was an Antwerp painter, probably identical with Jan Euworts, who was recorded in the Antwerp Guild in 1540. Eworth worked in London from 1549 (or perhaps 1545) until 1574. His first work with both HE and a date is the *Turk on Horseback* of 1549, but he painted chiefly portraits, sometimes allegorical, such as the *Sir John Luttrell* of 1550, or straightforwardly Holbeinesque, such as the *Mary Tudor* (1559, London, Soc. of Antiquaries). His style is sensitive and nervous, employing a great deal of delicately rendered detail, but ultimately dependent on HOLBEIN (who preceded him as Henry VIII's Court Painter), yet without his robustness. The *Queen Elizabeth confounding Juno, Minerva and Venus* (1569, Royal Coll.) is an example of the unsubtle flattery expressed in highly sophisticated and involved Mannerist imagery which was typical of Elizabeth's Court, especially in literature. The style of this picture, however, and also the form of the monogram differ from those of the portraits, and it has been suggested that it is the work of a different painter; on the other hand, a picture of 1570 (Copenhagen), of a similar subject, may be held to bridge the gap. The *Lord Darnley and his Brother* (1563, Royal Coll.) is a straightforward portrait, but equally introspective and elegant, with the pallid complexions typical of Eworth's figures. There are several of the HE pictures still in private collections and others attributed to him are in the Royal Coll. and in Antwerp, Cambridge (Fitzwm), Edinburgh (SNPG), London (NPG, Tate and Wallace Coll.), Ottawa, Oxford, Wellington NZ and Yale (CBA).

EXC., EXCUDIT (Lat. he executed it) on an engraving usually refers to the publisher, who was often identical with the engraver.

EXPRESSIONISM. The search for expressiveness of style by means of exaggerations and distortions of line and colour; a deliberate abandon of the naturalism implicit in Impressionism in favour of a simplified style intended to carry far greater emotional impact. In this general sense of emotional force Expressionism is a feature of non-Mediterranean art in general, GRÜNEWALD being the standard example. In the more limited context of modern art, the Expressionist movement may be said to spring from van GOGH's use of drastically simplified outline and very strong colour. In France, this has clear affinities with FAUVISM, but the principal exponents, apart from Toulouse-Lautrec, were mostly German (or at least 'Nordic', like the Norwegian MUNCH, whose hysterical art is one of the foundations of the movement). The BRÜCKE and the BLAUE REITER are two of the principal sub-groups, while some of the major individual artists are BECKMAN, ENSOR, NOLDE, KOKOSCHKA, ROUAULT and SOUTINE. The nature of their subject matter and the emphasis placed on outline are two reasons for the important part played by Expressionist graphic art. The Rifkind collection (now in Los Angeles Mus.), of some 6,000 drawings and engravings is one of the finest collections of Expressionist graphics.

EX VOTO. A votive offering. *See* MAI.

EYCK, van. On the frame of the huge polyptych of the *Adoration of the Lamb* in S. Bavo, Ghent, is a Latin quatrain containing a chronostich giving the date 1432; a rough translation is 'The painter Hubert van Eyck, than whom none was greater, began it; Jan, second in art, having completed it at the expense of Jodocus Vyd, invites you by this verse on the 6th May to contemplate what has been done.' On the problems raised by the meaning of this verse, more ink has been spilt than on any other problem in the history of art, except perhaps the frescoes at Assisi. Only four facts can reasonably be assumed to apply to Hubert van Eyck: in 1424/5 a Master Luberecht was paid by the Ghent magistrates for two designs for an altarpiece, and in 1425/6 a Master Ubrechts was visited by the magistrates in his workshop; in 1426, a 'Master Hubrechte the painter' had in his workshop a statue and other works connected with an altarpiece, and later in that year the heirs of Lubrecht van Heyke (not specified as a painter) paid inheritance tax on his property. Except for two copies said to have been made of the epitaph on his tomb before its destruction in 1578, and according to which he died on 18 September 1426, that is all that is known of Hubert.

By comparison, Jan van Eyck is well documented. From 1422 to 1424 he was working for Count John of Holland at The Hague, and around, or before, this date was perhaps connected with the HOURS of Turin. In 1425 he was appointed Court Painter and 'varlet de chambre' to Philip the Good, Duke of Burgundy, and from then until late in 1429 he lived in Lille. He moved to Bruges, probably in 1430, bought a house there in 1431/2, and lived there until he died in 1441. Between 1426 and 1436 he made several secret journeys on the Duke's business, two of which – concerned with marriage negotiations – took him to Spain in 1427 and to Portugal in 1428. Many records testify to his presence and activity in Bruges (payments of salary, a visit by the town councillors to his workshop in 1432, and one by the Duke himself in 1433) until the final record of his burial in July 1441. In addition to the documented facts there are a number of signed and dated pictures: the portrait of a man, inscribed 'Tymotheos Leal Souvenir 1432', the *Man in a Red Turban*, 1433, bearing the painter's challenging motto 'Als ich kan' (As I can) on the frame, and the Arnolfini Marriage Group, 1434, with the declaration of his own participation as a witness – 'Johannes de Eyck fuit hic' (. . . was here) – all in London (NG); the *Madonna and Child* in Melbourne, 1433, but, although the inscription appears to be authentic, many scholars reject the attribution; the *Madonna of Canon van der Paele*, 1436, in Bruges; the *St Barbara*, an elaborate drawing on a gesso ground for a painting never completed, 1437, and the Dresden *Madonna*, which recent cleaning has revealed to be dated 1437; the *Madonna of the Fountain*, 1439, in Antwerp; the *Portrait of his Wife*, 1439, in Bruges. In all these works the stupendous Eyckian technique is a major factor. For centuries the brothers were credited with the invention of oil-painting, and, although this is no longer a tenable idea, it is clear that Jan perfected an oil medium and varnish which has enabled his brilliant colour to survive almost unchanged, and which was fluid enough to allow him to achieve the subtlest effects of light and the most detailed rendering of objects. It is through his detailed analysis of surfaces that he reached a larger understanding of form and space; from his capacity to observe the minute he achieves a complete expression of the whole, and his technique is the perfect servant of his realistic, unidealizing and unemotional attitude.

The Ghent Altar is a very large and complex polyptych. It consists of two superimposed rows of paintings, which do not appear to have been designed to go together, as there are great discrepancies in the shapes of the panels and the relative scales of the figures. Most panels are painted on both sides, and on the back there are obvious gaps which have been filled by specially painted interior scenes. On the front, the upper row has *Christ the King*, flanked by the Virgin and St John Baptist to form a DEËSIS. The insides of the wings have *Musician* and *Singing Angels*, and *Adam* and *Eve*. The theme is a combination of the Book of Revelation and St Augustine's 'City of God', but Adam and

Eve are not part of such a scheme. The theme of the lower row is again largely from Revelation, and is the Adoration of the Lamb (the altar is inscribed *Ecce Agnus Dei*): this forms the whole of the central part, with the wings consisting of panels of the faithful coming to adore the Lamb, in the form of four groups of *Judges*, *Knights, Hermits* and *Pilgrims* (the *Judges* panel is a copy of the original, stolen in 1934). When open, the altarpiece is about 12 feet by 18, and the whole consists of twenty separate panels. The outside of the wings, in the upper row, have an *Annunciation*, with *Micah*, *Zechariah* and two *Sibyls* as part of the complex iconographical scheme. In the lower row are grisailles imitating statues of the two Saints John and portraits of the donor and his wife. This huge and heterogeneous work is rendered even more difficult to interpret by the extensive restorations and repaintings disclosed by recent scientific investigations. The quatrain with the date 1432 would make it – with the *Leal Souvenir* portrait – the earliest of Jan's dated works, but it is impossible to decide how many or what parts are due to an earlier hand, which may or may not be identifiable as Hubert's. The theory has been advanced that the quatrain is a later forgery, and Hubert a legendary figure to whom no works or participation in the Ghent Altar can be allowed. This is certainly going too far, since the inscription appears to be genuine, and there exist a few works – the *Three Maries at the Sepulchre*, Rotterdam, and the so-called *Friedsam Annunciation*, New York, Met. Mus. – which are related to known works by Jan, but not to the point of being attributable to him, and which also possess characteristics from which his own style might have developed. Other works attributed to Jan with some degree of certainty include the *Virgin in a Church* (Berlin) and the *Annunciation* (Washington, NG), both of which have the same elaboration of iconography found in the Ghent Altar, and the *Madonna and Donor*, formerly at Warwick Castle; the *Madonna with Chancellor Rolin*, Paris, Louvre; the *Madonna*, Frankfurt, Städel; and the so-called '*Cardinal Albergati*', Vienna, the preparatory drawing for which, in Dresden, is the only surviving silverpoint unanimously attributed to Jan. Besides the works already mentioned there are others in Berlin, New York (Met. Mus.), Philadelphia (Johnson), Turin and Vienna.

Jan's ability and inventiveness make him easily the major artist of the Early Netherlandish School, and his position is challenged only by the MASTER OF FLÉMALLE. In Jan, the opulent, politically opportunist and aristocratic Burgundian Court found its complete artistic expression. The Ghent Altar was extremely influential throughout the 15th century, and the technique evolved by Jan became the accepted Flemish one, spreading to the Rhineland and, later, to Italy and Spain. Jan's formal influence, however, was less in the succeeding years than that of Roger van der WEYDEN, due to the greater appeal of Roger's warmer and more emotional approach. Jan's chief follower was Petrus CHRISTUS, who is believed to have completed the *Madonna and Child with Saints* (New York, Frick Coll.) commissioned in 1441, a few months before Jan died, as well as the *St Jerome* (Detroit), and who probably took over Jan's workshop and something of his position as the principal Bruges painter of his time.

Margaret van Eyck, said to have been a sister of Jan and a miniaturist, is pure fiction.

F

F., FEC., FECIT (Lat. he made it) frequently follows a name on paintings, engravings or drawings as an assertion of authorship.

F.F. is an abbreviation of *fieri fecit* (Lat. he caused to be made), and should not be confused with a signature: *Johannes Smith FF* means that John Smith paid for the picture, not that he painted it.

FABRIANO *see* GENTILE da Fabriano.

FABRITIUS, Barent (1624–73), was the younger brother of Carel. Like Carel, he was probably a pupil of Rembrandt *c.*1640, but unlike Carel he remained a Rembrandt imitator all his life. He painted portraits and Biblical and mythological subjects, examples of which are in Amsterdam, Bergamo, Berlin, Boston, Cambridge (Fitzwm), Chicago, Frankfurt, Haarlem, Hartford Conn., Hull, Leningrad, London (NG), New York (Met. Mus.), Munich, San Francisco, Vienna and York.

FABRITIUS, Carel (1622–54), was the finest of Rembrandt's pupils, whose brilliant promise was cut short by the great Delft explosion of 12 October 1654, which killed him as he was working on a portrait. He was in contact with Rembrandt about 1641–3 and was himself perhaps the master of VERMEER; the extraordinary gap between Rembrandt and Vermeer being bridged by Fabritius's reversal of Rembrandt's practice, in that he painted dark objects against a light background (e.g. the *Self-portrait*, Rotterdam). Several Rembrandtesque portraits have recently been attributed to him, but the few known works – only five are dated, and only eight are undisputed – do not seem to confirm these attributions, and there is still considerable confusion with his brother's work. The *Goldfinch* (1654, The Hague) is almost unique in Dutch art, but it has much more in common with Vermeer than with Rembrandt. There are pictures in Amsterdam (Rijksmus., one apparently dated 1640, but probably either 1648 or 1649), Groningen, The Hague, Innsbruck, Liverpool, London (NG, dated 1654) and Warsaw.

FACTURE, FATTURA are the French and Italian equivalents of HANDLING.

FAKES and FORGERIES. The nature of these is really self-evident, but there exist grey areas which do not fall quite into the same category as the deliberate and intentional fraud. Instances are disputed ATTRIBUTIONS. An amateur painter called George Constable introduced himself to John Constable and became a friend of his. Pictures by George Constable have become confused into the true Constable oeuvre, not entirely innocently, and in fact George Constable himself has been accused of assisting the confusion. Often genuine REPLICAS – for instance, those made by John Dunthorne, whom Constable employed as a copyist and assistant – have been known to travel under the name of the greater man, and have been distinguished from his works partly on the evidence of quality, and partly by pedigree or PROVENANCE. This type of confusion is even easier to create where the major artist maintained a large and prolific studio. Rubens is one example, where innumerable sketches, projects and versions were produced by very skilled and experienced assistants, and the tendency is to sail them all under the master's colours. Another example is Rembrandt, who had many pupils, who, at one time or another, endeavoured to imitate their teacher's handling, colour and style, and whose works must now be distinguished from the true products of Rembrandt's own hand. To the generality of collectors, and even more so to dealers, the temptation to see the geese as swans is almost irresistible, and as much for motives of prestige as for merely pecuniary ones. There also exists a whole category of repainted, over-restored pictures, where no satisfactory determination of authorship can really be made, and which depend upon the eye of faith to discern their genuineness. On the whole, the art historian distinguishes these without difficulty; the real problems occur when 'certificates of authenticity' are being sought by a hopeful, and often generous, owner, though nowadays the provision of these doubtful passports is only solicited by the unsophisticated and supplied by the cynical. They are, in fact, totally worthless. Some forgeries are difficult to distinguish – for instance, the drawing copied by the COUNTERPROOF method, where only the recognition of the direction of the stroke which converts a right-handed artist into a left-handed one, may sometimes betray the spurious nature of an otherwise perfect-seeming example; or the false cast, of a bust, or a medal, or a figurine, detectable only by careful analysis with scales and callipers, and with a genuine example for comparison. Some intentional fakes are betrayed by the inclusion of colours – Prussian blue, Viridian, the Cadmium reds and yellows – which were invented long after the putative date of the picture; some by their being painted on supports which were not available at the date at which they appear to have been made – mahogany panels, for instance, before the mid-18th century; or by their having a CRAQUELURE which gives rise to suspicion. But these are cases of detective work done by museum laboratories for the specific purpose of nailing a forgery which has usually suggested itself as spurious because of some inexplicable dissonance between genuine, irreproachable examples and an irrational or irreconcilable divergence. Most forgeries 'fall out' after about 50 years or so; in other words, they conform to the popular image of the artist held at the time the fake was made – an instance of this is the Botticelli forgeries made during the Burne-Jones period. Later generations, who see the artist quite differently, distinguish between the true appearance of his work and the ideas held about him by an earlier generation of admirers and smugly wonder how their fathers could have been so easily deceived.

FALCONET, Étienne-Maurice (1716–91), worked under J. B. LEMOYNE and was accepted into the Academy in 1744. In 1757 he was appointed Director of Sculpture at the Sèvres Porcelain Manufactory, where he remained until 1766, supervising the production of many pieces from his own models. He also worked for Mme de Pompadour. Through Diderot the Empress Catherine II invited him to Russia in 1766 to make a bronze equestrian monument to Peter the Great at St Petersburg: this is his masterpiece and a great feat of technique, as the horse rears up on its huge plinth of rough granite with both forelegs unsupported. He left Russia in 1779, before the statue was unveiled, returning to France in 1781. A stroke in 1783 forced him to stop working. He also wrote on sculpture and was notorious for his opinion that the warmth and softness of the human body were better rendered by his own contemporaries than by the Ancients (*Réflexions sur la sculpture*, 1761); most of his own works are of Venus, nymphs and similar subjects tending to warmth and softness. His more formal *Milo of Croton* (1754, made for the Academy) is in the Louvre, and the *maquette* for the *Peter the Great* is in the Hermitage, Leningrad; the Wallace

Coll. and V&A, London, and the Frick Coll., New York, have more characteristic works.

FANTIN-LATOUR, Henri (1836–1904), was a French painter of romantic figure subjects, portrait groups and still-life. He exhibited at the Salon regularly from 1861, but found himself in the SALON des Refusés in 1863, and, for all that he seems a straightforward Salon painter, he was friendly with most of the advanced artists of the day, including Manet and Whistler, and also admired the Pre-Raphaelites. He painted several portrait groups, the best-known being the *Hommage à Manet* (*L'Atelier aux Batignolles*) (1870, Paris, Mus. d'Orsay), but his Romantic imagination and, later, a passion for Wagner, led him to paint some extraordinary figure subjects. In England he has always been popular for his still-life and flower paintings, executed in a meticulous 'Dutch' manner totally unlike his sub-Delacroix fantasies. There are pictures in Birmingham, Boston, Cambridge (Fitzwm), Cardiff (a figure subject), Cleveland Ohio, Dublin, Edinburgh (NG), Glasgow (Burrell Coll. and Univ.), Grenoble, Kansas City, London (NG, Tate and V&A), Manchester, Ottawa, Oxford, Port Sunlight (Lever Gall.), Toledo Ohio, St Louis, Washington (NG and Phillips) and elsewhere.

FAP (Federal Art Project), *see* WPA.

FARINGTON, Joseph (1747–1821), was a topographical draughtsman of no great ability who became an RA in 1785 and whose talent for intrigue gave him an enormous influence in that institution. He kept a very full diary which is one of the principal sources for the history of English art (and the RA) in the last years of the 18th and the early 19th centuries: extracts from it have been published and a complete edition is in preparation. The original text is mostly at Windsor Castle, but some parts have been dispersed. Farington's drawings are in London (BM and V&A), Yale (CBA) and elsewhere.

FAT. Pigment is said to be fat when it is mixed with oil to make an oleaginous paste, giving a rich IMPASTO. Lean paint has been thinned with turpentine or other spirit, which helps to make it dry quicker. A studio maxim used to be: 'Start lean and finish fat'.

FATTORI, Giovanni (1825–1908), was one of the leading members of the MACCHIAIOLI. He was trained in Florence and then joined in the struggle for independence 1848–9: in 1861 he won a prize with his *Battle of Magenta* (1861–2, Florence, Gall. d'Arte Moderna). This was followed by other military subjects as well as landscapes and scenes of peasant life. He visited Paris in 1875, the year after the first Impressionist Exhibition, but was little influenced by them. There are works by him in Florence, Leghorn, Milan, Rome and Venice, as well as about 200 etchings (a technique unusual in 19th century Italy).

FATTURA *see* HANDLING.

FAUVE. At the Paris Salon d'Automne of 1905, the works of a number of painters were hung together in one room: these were MATISSE, MARQUET, DERAIN, VLAMINCK, ROUAULT, Manguin, Camoin, Jean Puy and Othon Friesz. Their works, full of distortions and flat patterns and painted in violent colour, created a furore, and a critic dubbed them collectively '*Les Fauves*' (the wild beasts). They were not, until then – or even afterwards – a particularly coherent group. Matisse came to be regarded as their leader, possibly because he was older and not unwilling, but the parts of the group had various origins. Matisse, Marquet, Rouault and Camoin had all been pupils of Gustave

MOREAU at the École des Beaux-Arts; Matisse and Marquet had often worked together, strongly influenced by EXPRESSIONISM; the others adhered temporarily, mostly out of rebellion against the academic system and because their brightly coloured works could be hung in no other company. In 1906 DUFY, and in 1907 BRAQUE and METZINGER, exhibited with them, but by 1908 the Fauves had fallen apart as a group and a number of its members had seceded to CUBISM.

FAYDHERBE, Luc (1617–97), was one of a family of sculptors and architects in the Malines area of Belgium. He went to Antwerp in 1636 and worked for Rubens, who became his friend. After Rubens's death, he settled in Malines (1640) and was the only major Baroque Flemish sculptor who never went to Italy (cf. DUQUESNOY). From the 1660s he was active as an architect. There are sculptures by him in Malines (Mus. and churches) and in Brussels.

FEININGER, Lyonel (1871–1956), was born and died in New York, but was really a German Cubist. He went to Germany in 1887 and finally returned to America only in 1937; he was trained in Germany and was in Paris in 1892–3. From 1911 he was interested in Cubism, and DELAUNAY was the main influence on his painting. In 1912 he met the members of the BRÜCKE group and in the following year exhibited with the BLAUE REITER. He was particularly close to KLEE and KANDINSKY, and taught at the BAUHAUS. After his return to the US his works became more abstract. Many German and American museums have examples, as have Edinburgh (NG Modern Art) and Leicester.

FEKE, Robert (*c.*1705–51/67), was the first major painter born in N. America. His first documented work is the *Royall Family* (1741, Harvard), which is based on SMIBERT's *Berkeley Family* (Yale). He married in 1742 and settled in Rhode Island, and his recorded activity is 1741–51, but his works are so close to such British contemporaries as HUDSON and RAMSAY that he must have visited London – he is known to have worked as a seaman. There are pictures in Boston, Cleveland Ohio, Detroit, New York (Met. Mus.), Providence RI and Toledo Ohio.

FERGUSON, William Gouw (1632/3–95?), was born and died in Scotland, but worked in England, France, Italy and especially in Holland. He was in The Hague by 1660 and became a painter of still-life so much in the Dutch manner that he is often confused with painters like Jan WEENIX. He also worked in Amsterdam and Utrecht. His last dated paintings are of 1695. According to VERTUE (1725) 'he livd several years abroad some part in France came to England & livd & dyed here – ye latter part of his time to get bread he painted still life particularly dead fowl hanging against a bord & such other things very natural. & very cheap'. There are four pictures by him in Edinburgh (NG) and others in Aberdeen, Amsterdam, Barnsley, Berlin, Glasgow, London (Tate and V&A at Ham House), Manchester, Paris (Louvre) and elsewhere.

FERNELEY, John (1782–1860), was an English sporting painter whose works became widely popular in reproduction. He worked in Ireland 1809–10. His *Bay Horse* (1826, London, Tate) is typical, but the *Boy and Girl beside a Hurdy-Gurdy* (1847, Leicester) is unusual.

FERRARI, Gaudenzio (1471/81–1546), was a Lombard painter who combined the influence of Leonardo with that of both Perugino and Correggio and sometimes added a strong dash of German art. His earliest works (1507) were for Varallo, near the Swiss border, and his principal fresco cycles are in Lombardy; in the Sacro Monte, Varallo (begun 1517), in S. Cristoforo, Vercelli (1529–32) and in Saronno (1534–6). The Sacro Monte frescoes, which contain an element of overcrowding derived from German examples, are further complicated by the addition of large groups of painted terracotta figures, to add to the illusion. In all, there are forty-five small chapels with tableaux, containing 600 statues and over 4,000 frescoed figures, and Gaudenzio had many helpers over many years, including TIBALDI and Galeazzo Alessi in the architecture, and MORRAZONE and TANZIO da Varallo for the paintings. From 1539 he worked in Milan. There are pictures by him in Amsterdam, Bergamo, Berlin, London (NG), Milan (Brera, Poldi-Pezzoli, Castello, and churches), Paris (Louvre), Sarasota Fla, Turin and elsewhere.

FERRATA, Ercole (1610–86), was an Italian Baroque sculptor who worked in Naples and Aquila before going to Rome, probably in the late 1640s, accompanied by his pupil CAFFÀ. In 1647 he was working for BERNINI in St Peter's, and in 1653 with RAGGI on Bernini's Pimentel Tomb (S.M. Maggiore). Ferrata continued the work in S. Nicola da Tolentino which ALGARDI had left unfinished at his death, and he also worked in S. Agnese in Piazza Navona (*S. Agnes*, 1660, and *S. Emerenziana*, 1660, but finished after his death). Despite the connection, he never assimilated Bernini's style, retaining the classicism of Algardi and Bolognese painting. Cambridge (Fitzwm) has a terracotta *bozzetto*.

FERRI, Ciro (1628/34–89), was the closest follower of PIETRO da Cortona, some of whose frescoes he completed in the Pitti Palace, Florence and elsewhere. He worked mainly in Rome, Florence and Bergamo and he also made many designs for engravers. There is a *Holy Family* by him in Liverpool.

FETI (Fetti), Domenico (*c*.1588/9–1623), was born in Rome and began as a follower of Caravaggio's followers and an admirer of ELSHEIMER. He was taken to Mantua in or before 1613 by Cardinal Ferdinando Gonzaga (who became Duke of Mantua) and worked there as Court Painter until he went to Venice in 1621. In 1622 he settled there and is recorded as gravely ill early in 1623. In Mantua he saw the Rubens portraits and was also influenced by Venetian painting, and these influences, together with his early admiration for Elsheimer, led him to produce smallish genre pictures, usually representing one of the Parables, which are very broadly treated and rich in colour. He painted some frescoes in Mantua, but they are less successful. There are examples in the Royal Coll. (a series at Hampton Court) and in Baltimore, Birmingham (Barber Inst.), Dresden, Florence (Uffizi and Pitti), Frankfurt (Städel), Kansas City, London (Courtauld Inst.), Manchester, Mantua (Palazzo and Cath.), Munich, New York (Met. Mus.), Paris (Louvre), Prague, Venice (Accad.), Vienna, Washington (NG) and York.

FEUERBACH, Anselm (1829–80), was, like BÖCKLIN, a German Romantic painter who came under the spell of Italy and Italian art (in his case, Raphael). He was trained in Germany and Antwerp before going to Paris and working in COUTURE's studio (1852–3); he was also simultaneously influenced by Delacroix and Courbet. In 1855 he went to Italy and spent most of the rest of his life there except for three unsuccessful years (1873–6) teaching in Vienna. He painted some fine portraits, 16th-century Italian in feeling, especially those of Nanna, whose features obsessed him from 1860 to 1865. Karlsruhe has a whole room of his works and most German galleries possess examples.

FIAMMINGO *see* DUQUESNOY.

FIJNSCHILDER *see* DOU.

FILARETE. Antonio Averlino, called Filarete (Gk 'lover of virtue') (*c.*1400–69), was a Florentine sculptor and architectural theorist. His major surviving work in sculpture is the pair of bronze doors for St Peter's in Rome, which include scenes from the life of Pope Eugenius IV. His fellow-Florentine, Vasari, criticized these: 'If Pope Eugenius IV, when he resolved to make the bronze doors for San Pietro in Rome, had been diligent in seeking for men of ability to make them – and he would easily have found them then, when Brunelleschi, Donatello, and other rare craftsmen were alive – it would not have been carried out in the deplorable manner we see . . .' and of Filarete's architectural treatise Vasari says it was 'mostly ridiculous, and perhaps the most stupid book that was ever written'.

FILDES, Sir Luke (1844–1927), started as an illustrator and began painting in 1870, treating themes which combined realism and genre, concentrating on subjects illustrating poverty and deprivation. *Waiting for Admission to the Casual Ward* (Royal Holloway College, Egham, Surrey), exhibited at the RA in 1874, derives from one of his illustrations in 'The Graphic' (1869); and his *The Doctor* was one of the first pictures in the Tate Gallery.

FINE MANNER. Early Florentine engravings, of the mid- and later 15th century, are divided into two classes – the Broad and Fine Manners. The Fine Manner is so called because it uses fine lines, often cross-hatched, to give a general effect not unlike a wash drawing. The Broad Manner uses bolder lines, parallel but further apart, often with small hooks at the end, the general effect being similar to a bold pen drawing. MANTEGNA, although not a Florentine, was influenced by the Broad Manner.

FINIGUERRA, Maso (1426–64), was a Florentine goldsmith, possibly a pupil of GHIBERTI, who was credited by Vasari with the invention of engraving. Unfortunately, no documented engravings by him are known, and the book of drawings called the Florentine Picture Chronicle (London, BM) is no longer attributed to him. There are, however, some NIELLI and some *intarsie* which are probably his and seem partially to confirm Vasari's statement.

FINSON (Finsonius), Ludovicus (before 1580–1617), was a rather mysterious Caravaggesque who was born in Bruges, died in Amsterdam, formed his style in Naples and seems to have worked principally in Aix-en-Provence. He was in Naples certainly in 1608, and probably *c.*1606/7, and was in Aix in 1610, but his *Annunciation*, still there, is signed and inscribed '1612 in Naples', and another version is in Naples Mus. He seems to have been in Paris *c.*1615. His style was closely modelled on Caravaggio's Neapolitan followers (cf. the UTRECHT SCHOOL) and he actually owned a part-share of Caravaggio's *Madonna of the Rosary*: he could have known Caravaggio in Naples. There are two pictures of 1613 in Marseilles, and the *Martyrdom of St Stephen* (1614) is in Arles Cathedral; another, also dated 1614, is in St Trophime, Arles, and recalls Veronese. Most of his works are in S. France, especially Aix, but there are attributed pictures in Chicago, London (Wellington Mus.) and Oxford. *See also* CECCO del Caravaggio.

FIXATIVE. A kind of thin varnish sprayed on to drawings and pastels to prevent their being rubbed.

FLAXMAN, John (1755–1826), was an English NEOCLASSIC sculptor with an enormous European reputation in his own day. He first exhibited in 1767 and became friendly with ROMNEY early in his career. He went to the RA Schools in 1770 and met BLAKE at about this time: much of his sympathy for Gothic art is probably due to this friendship. In 1775 he began to work for Wedgwood, who was then popularizing Neoclassical designs in his new 'Etruscan' ware. With Wedgwood's help he went to Italy in 1787, where he remained until 1794, looking at a great variety of works of all periods. A sketchbook in the V&A, London, shows the catholicity of his tastes, for it includes drawings after Bernini although he loathed everything he stood for. His dislike of the Baroque was probably partly religious in origin, reflecting his Low Church sympathies; and it is interesting that BACON was a Methodist and BANKS an atheist, and all employed only generalized Christian symbolism – non-Catholic – in their funerary sculpture, although Flaxman prided himself on Christianizing monumental sculpture. After he returned from Italy Flaxman devoted himself almost exclusively to monuments, two of his most famous having been begun in Rome. These are the *Mansfield*, erected in Westminster Abbey in 1795, and the *Collins* of the same year in Chichester Cathedral. While still in Rome he had also begun the book-illustrations which brought him the greatest fame on the Continent and influenced later generations – INGRES and the NAZARENER among them. These are pure outline drawings of strictly Neoclassical simplicity, which give the impression of being sketches for relief sculpture: they include long series of plates for the 'Odyssey' and the 'Iliad', Aeschylus, Hesiod and Dante, as well as Milton and Bunyan drawings. He became an RA in 1800 and was made Professor of Sculpture in 1810, his lectures being published posthumously in 1829. Among his few statues in the round which are not monuments are the *Fury of Athamas* (1791–2, Nat. Trust, Ickworth House) and *St Michael Overcoming Satan* (1821) and the *Pastoral Apollo* (1824, both National Trust, Petworth). University Coll., London, has a large collection of his drawings and models, and the Soane Mus., London, also has models. Other works are scattered as far as Madras and Quebec and include works in Bath, many in Chichester Cath., Copenhagen, Edinburgh (NPG), Glasgow, Gloucester, London (NPG, V&A, RA, Westminster Abbey and St Paul's), and many other English churches and cathedrals.

FLINCK, Govaert (1615–60), was a pupil of REMBRANDT, and imitated him until the mid-1650s, though always with a greater striving for elegance, which brought him a successful practice as a portrait painter. He had ambitions, however, as a historical painter, and was commissioned by the City Council of Amsterdam to decorate the interior of the new Town Hall with large historical works, but he died before executing the work, which was then divided among different artists – including Rembrandt. There are works in Amsterdam (Rijksmus.), Antwerp, Berlin, Birmingham (Barber Inst.), Boston (Mus.), Brunswick, Cape Town, Dresden, Dublin, London (NG, Wallace Coll.), Leningrad, Liverpool, Munich, New York (Met. Mus.), Paris (Louvre), Rotterdam, Vienna and elsewhere.

FLORIS, Frans (Frans de Vriendt) (*c.*1518/20–70), was a Flemish painter who went to Italy, probably *c.*1542/7, after entering the Antwerp Guild in 1540. He was particularly influenced by Michelangelo's *Last Judgement* (unveiled in 1541) as well as by Raphael and the Antique, so that he became, on his return, one of the leading ITALIANIZERS. Apart from his very large religious and mythological compositions – painted with the help of numerous assistants – he was also a fine portrait painter. There are works in Amsterdam (Rijksmus.), Antwerp, Berlin, Brunswick, Brussels, Caen, Cambridge (Fitzwm), Dresden, Florence (Pitti), The Hague, Madrid (Prado), Oxford (Ch. Ch.), Paris (Louvre), Prague Castle, Vienna and elsewhere. His son, Frans II (*b.c.*1545/7), was also a painter who worked in Rome.

FONTAINEBLEAU, First and Second Schools of. The First School of Fontainebleau is the name given to the combination of Mannerist painting and stucco decoration created by the Italians ROSSO, PRIMATICCIO and Niccolò dell' ABBATE for the Royal Palace of Fontainebleau, under the patronage of François I. The style begins in 1530, with Rosso's arrival in France, and continues to *c.*1560 under Niccolò dell' Abbate. The extreme elegance of Parmigianino's art is characteristic of this First School. The Second School of Fontainebleau represents an attempt at a similar decorative tradition in the second half of the 16th century, mostly under Henri IV. The palaces decorated by him have suffered greatly, but the Salle Ovale at Fontainebleau is an example of the revival. The names usually associated with the Second School are not illustrious: Ambroise Dubois (1542/3–1614), Toussaint Dubreuil (1561–1602) and Martin Fréminet (1567–1602).

FONTANA, Lavinia (1552–1614), was the daughter and pupil of Prospero Fontana (1512–97), and began her career in Bologna. She painted portraits and religious pictures, her earliest recorded work being the *Holy Family* of 1575 (Dresden), In 1577 she married a rich pupil of her father's, G. P. Zappi, who became her assistant. Despite having eleven children she enjoyed a successful career, working in a style close to Correggio and Parmigianino in her religious works (often of considerable size), and to the Florentine Mannerists in her portraits. She moved to Rome in 1603, at the invitation of Pope Clement VIII, and died there. There are works in Bordeaux, Dublin, the Escorial, Florence (Uffizi), and in churches in Bologna, Cento and Rome.

FOPPA, Vincenzo (1427/30–1515/16), was the leading painter of the Milanese School before it was transformed by the influence of Leonardo da Vinci. He was born near Brescia and may have been a pupil of the Paduan SQUARCIONE, who was Mantegna's master: in any case his first dated work, the *Crucifixion* (1456, Bergamo), shows the influence of Jacopo Bellini, and Foppa's later works amply prove that he knew the work of Jacopo's son Giovanni and son-in-law Mantegna. From 1456 to 1490 he worked in Pavia and was employed a good deal by the Dukes of Milan. There are works by him in Milan (Brera, Castello, Poldi-Pezzoli and S. Eustorgio), and in Baltimore (Walters), Bergamo, Berlin, Brescia (Accad. and Carmine), London (NG and Wallace Coll., all that is left of the frescoes in the Medici Bank, Milan), New York (Met. Mus.), Pavia, Philadelphia (Johnson), Washington (NG) and Worcester Mass.

FORAIN, Jean Louis (1852–1931), was a draughtsman and illustrator working for satirical papers in Paris from 1876 onwards. He was greatly influenced by Rembrandt and Goya, by DAUMIER, who preceded him in his chosen field, and by Manet. He was a friend and follower of Degas, and exhibited four times with the Impressionists between 1879 and 1886. Until *c.*1909 his subjects were chiefly scenes from Parisian life, with occasional cartoons on political scandals, e.g. the Panama Canal; after 1909 he turned to the depiction of social misery and the callousness and inhumanity of the processes of justice. He also illustrated the New Testament. Most of his drawings are in limpid watercolour washes of sepia on a loose and evocative outline, full of movement and luminosity, highly reminiscent of Daumier. There are works in Boston (Mus.), Chicago, Dresden, London (Courtauld Inst. and Tate), Paris (Louvre), Washington and elsewhere.

FORESHORTENING is perspective applied to a single object. An arm pointing directly at the spectator so that little more than the hand can be seen is said to be strongly foreshortened. Extreme foreshortening can have emotional overtones, as is best demonstrated by Mantegna's *Dead Christ* (Milan, Brera). (*See also* SOTTO IN SÙ). The work of Uccello is sufficient proof that a mastery of foreshortening is not necessarily accompanied by the ability to construct coherent perspective systems.

FORGERIES *see* FAKES.

FOUND OBJECT (*Objet trouvé*). In SURREALIST theory an object of any kind, such as a shell found on a walk, can be a work of art; and such 'Found Objects' have been exhibited. If a little judicious touching-up has been indulged in, the object is known technically as a 'Found Object Composed'.

FOUQUET, Jean (*c.*1420–in or before 1481), was the major French painter of the 15th century. He went to Italy and was in Rome at some time between 1443 and February 1447, since he is said to have painted a portrait of Eugenius IV and two attendants: this, however, depends on the identification of Jehan the Frenchman with *Giachetto francoso*, which is not self-evident, but is due partly to Filarete and Vasari. He may have gone to Rome with a French embassy in 1446, or he may have gone to get a dispensation to enter the priesthood, since there is a letter of 1449 from Nicholas V to 'Johanni Fouquet Juniori clerico . . .'. By 1448 he was back in his native Tours, where he soon began to work for Charles VIII. He was appointed Painter to the King in 1475. He is known to have designed sculpture and to have worked for the Order of S. Michel, but the only documented works extant are the miniatures in a copy of *Les Antiquités Judaïques* (Paris, Bibliothèque Nationale). On grounds of style several other MSS. and some easel pictures are attributed to him: they include works in Paris (Louvre (portraits of *Charles VII* and *Jouvenel des Ursins*) and Bib. Nat.), Antwerp and Berlin (the two halves of the Melun diptych: *Étienne Chevalier* and a *Madonna*), Chantilly (Mus. Condé), London (BM), Munich (Staatsbibliothek), Nouans Indre-et-Loire (parish church, *Deposition*), and Tours (*Head of a Monk*).

A very fine portrait of a young man, dated 1456, in the Liechtenstein Coll., Vaduz, used to be attributed to Fouquet but is now generally given to the Master of 1456, and another portrait, *Man with a Glass of Wine*, in the Louvre, has also been attributed to him, but is now officially catalogued as 'Portuguese School, 15th century', perhaps because of its affinity with GONÇALVES. Vienna (K-H Mus.) has a *Portrait of Gonella, Jester at Ferrara*, once attributed to Bruegel and now given to Fouquet.

FRAGLIA. The Venetian painters' GUILD.

FRAGMENT. In sculpture, this has two possible meanings: (1) the piece or pieces which survive after an accident or a disaster, and which – preserved or perhaps excavated centuries later – are valued not only for themselves but also because of the beauty or significance of that of which they are the surviving pieces; (2) a piece of sculpture created deliberately in a fragmentary state, because concentration on a part rather than on the whole is more attractive to the artist from an aesthetic standpoint – examples are Ivan Meštrovič's *Torso of a Hero* (London, Tate), or some of Rodin's works, in which parts of a figure appear to be emerging from the block. Michelangelo's fragments are never so sophisticated: in his oeuvre they occur when he abandoned a work incomplete, not because he was using partial execution for emotive purposes. *See also* NON-FINITO.

FRAGONARD, Jean Honoré (1732–1806), was the typical painter of gallant and sentimental subjects in the reign of Louis XV during the ascendancy of Mme du Barry, and during the reign of Louis XVI. He was a pupil of Chardin for a few months in 1750 and then went to BOUCHER until 1752, when he won a Rome Prize with *Jeroboam sacrificing to the Golden Calf* (Paris, École des Beaux-Arts). He did not go directly to Rome, however, but worked under Carle van Loo 1753–6, in the ÉCOLE des Élèves Protégés: his *Psyche* (1753, London, NG) shows him working in the Grand Manner. From 1756 until 1761 he worked at the French Academy in Rome, where he studied the living TIEPOLO more than any of the Old Masters. He also went, with Hubert ROBERT, to the South under the patronage of the Abbé de Saint-Non, who later wrote a book about the trip. In 1761 Fragonard returned to Paris and made his name in 1765 with his *High Priest Coresus sacrificing himself to save Callirhoe* (Paris, Louvre), a piece in the very Grand Manner. He soon abandoned history (having been elected *Agréé* of the Academy) and turned to more congenial subjects, such as *The Swing* (*c.*1766, London, Wallace Coll.). This was originally commissioned from a serious history painter by the Baron de St Julien: 'I desire', he said, 'that you should paint Madame (pointing to his mistress) on a swing which is being set in motion by a Bishop. You must place me where I can have a good view of the legs of this pretty little thing . . .'. The serious history painter could think of nothing else to say except to recommend M. Fragonard as a more suitable executant. He continued in this lighthearted and sometimes frankly erotic vein with great success, being commissioned by Mme du Barry to paint a series of the *Progress of Love* for her new house at Louveciennes (1771); unaccountably, however, she rejected them and Fragonard took them back to his native Grasse when he fled there during the Terror. They are now in New York (Frick Coll.). In 1773 he went to Italy again, returning via Austria and Germany. He may also have visited Holland, as, like his contemporary Gainsborough, he painted some landscapes in the Dutch manner (e.g. *Return of the Herd*, Worcester Mass.). The Revolution put an end to his patrons and to the demand for his kind of art, which was entirely superseded by the high-mindedness of DAVID and Republican Virtue. In desperate poverty, he returned to Paris from Grasse, and it was David who got him a job in the Museums Service. He died in Paris, almost totally forgotten. There are works by him in Besançon, Paris (Louvre and Banque de France), and other French museums; outside France the best collection is in London (Wallace Coll.), and there are others in Boston, Cambridge Mass. (Fogg), Cincinnati, Cleveland, Detroit, St Louis, New York (Met. Mus.), Toledo Ohio, Washington (NG) and elsewhere. Splendid examples of his *portraits de fantaisie*, based on Rembrandt and Tiepolo, are in Barcelona, Liverpool and Williamstown Mass.

FRANCESCO di Giorgio Martini (1439–1501/2), was a Sienese painter, sculptor, architect and military engineer (he is credited with inventing the landmine). He was the pupil of VECCHIETTA, and is first recorded as a painter and sculptor in 1464. His sculpture was influenced by Donatello and his paintings by Fra Filippo Lippi, but they remain close to the Sienese tradition. There is a documented altarpiece of 1475 in Siena; other paintings are in Avignon, Cambridge Mass., London (NG), New York (Met. Mus.) and Washington (NG) (which have parts of the same altarpiece), and sculpture in Siena, Paris (Louvre), Perugia and Washington (NG). As an architect he worked on the Palace at Urbino, collaborated with Leonardo da Vinci in giving advice on Milan Cathedral, and wrote an important treatise.

FRANCIA, Francesco (*c.*1450–1517/18), was a Bolognese goldsmith who is first recorded as a painter in 1486. It used to be thought that a *Madonna* (London, NG) of 1492 was his earliest known dated work; this is now regarded as a forgery, and the earliest picture would now seem to be the large *Felicini Madonna* (signed and dated 1494, Bologna, Pinacoteca), which shows a blend of the style of PERUGINO with that of COSTA and the Ferrarese – COSSA and ROBERTI – and almost no personal character. Until 1506, when Costa went as Court Painter to Mantua, they worked in partnership, but after that date Francia was more and more influenced by Raphael and the soft style of Perugino and the Umbrians. Raphael's *St Cecilia* is supposed to have caused him to die of depression at his own inferiority. There are works by him in the Royal Coll., and in Berlin, Bologna (Pinacoteca, Mus. Civico and several churches), Boston (Gardner), Budapest, Chantilly, Dresden, Dublin, Ferrara (Cath.), Florence (Uffizi), Glasgow, London (NG), Milan (Brera, Poldi-Pezzoli), Munich, New York (Met. Mus.), Paris (Louvre), Philadelphia (Mus. and Johnson), Pittsburgh (the undated original of the NG painting), Rome (Gall. Naz., Capitoline and Borghese), San Marino Cal. (Huntington), Turin, Vienna (K-H Mus. and Akad.), Washington (NG), Worcester Mass., Yale and elsewhere.

FRANCIA, François Louis Thomas (1772–1839), was born in Calais, but went to England as a boy, where he worked for Dr MONRO and knew GIRTIN. He exhibited at the RA 1795–1822, although he returned to Calais in 1817. He taught BONINGTON and was visited by British artists on their way to the Continent, so that he formed a bridge between the pure watercolour tradition of the English and contemporary French ideas.

FRANCIABIGIO (*c.*1482/3–1525), was a Florentine painter who was the assistant of ANDREA del Sarto and a pupil of ALBERTINELLI. Franciabigio's best works are his rather introspective portraits, and he is a characteristic representative of the generation between Andrea del Sarto and Fra BARTOLOMMEO, as may be seen in his frescoes in the Chiostro dello Scalzo, Florence, of about 1518. There are works by him in Florence (Uffizi, Pitti and churches) and in the Royal Coll., Barnard Castle (Bowes Mus.), Berlin, Brussels, Detroit, London (NG), Munich, New York (Met. Mus.), Oxford, Paris (Louvre), Rome (Borghese and Gall. Naz) and Vienna.

FRANCIS, Sam (*b.*1923), is a Californian Tachiste painter. He served in the US Air Force 1943–5, and, after a long spell in hospital, became an abstract painter in 1947. In 1950 he went to Paris, joining the circle of American painters around the French-Canadian RIOPELLE. He has painted murals for the Kunsthalle, Basle (1956–8) and, on a visit to Japan in 1957, for a School of Flower Arrangement there. His technique of dribbling paint differs from the more 'calligraphic' style used by many Americans (cf. POLLOCK). There are paintings by him in London (Tate) and New York (M of MA).

FRANCKE, Master (active *c.*1405–after 1424), was the most important Hamburg painter after Master BERTRAM, but was (like KONRAD von Soest) an exponent of the SOFT STYLE. He was probably in France about 1405, since his style owes much to French illuminated MSS. His major work was the *St Thomas à Becket Altar*, painted for the merchants trading with England, of which only fragments are known (begun 1424, Hamburg). Other works are in Hamburg, Helsinki and Leipzig.

FRESCO (Ital. fresh). Wall-painting in a medium like watercolour on plaster. *Fresco secco*, painted on dry plaster, gives an effect not unlike an ordinary distempered wall and suffers from the same defect of the paint scaling off, but true fresco, or *buon fresco*, practised in Italy from the 13th century and perfected in the 16th, is one of the most permanent forms of wall decoration known. The wall is first rough-plastered and then a coat, known as the *arricciato* (or *arriccio*), is applied. On this the SINOPIA is drawn, or the CARTOON is traced, so that the whole composition is transferred to the wall, and then an area sufficient for one day's work is covered with the final layer of plaster, called the *intonaco*. The cartoon is redrawn over this, joining up with the parts still uncovered, and the damp plaster is then painted with pigments mixed with plain water or lime-water, allowance being made for the fact that the colours dry much lighter. Because the plaster is still damp a chemical reaction takes place and the colours become integrated with the wall itself, so that scaling cannot occur. The use of a detailed, full-size cartoon means that several assistants can work simultaneously on different parts of the wall, provided that all work is done from the top downwards so that the splashes fall on the unpainted parts. At the end of the day all the unpainted *intonaco* is cut away, to be re-laid next day, so that the working surface is always damp: careful examination of a fresco reveals the joins in the plaster and from these the number of days (*giornate*) taken to paint the whole can be estimated approximately. *Fresco secco* may legitimately be employed to retouch or to add accents, but during the 16th century it was almost obligatory to work entirely in *buon fresco*, and some of the finest examples of the technique are Raphael's decorations in the Stanze of the Vatican. Climatic conditions outside Central Italy are not always favourable and the Venetian preference for oil-painting is usually ascribed to this. Attempts to revive the technique in London for the decoration of the House of Lords, early in the 19th century, were not successful, although RIVERA and OROZCO practised a form of fresco in Mexico in the present century.

FRIEDRICH, Caspar David (1774–1840), was the most purely Romantic of German landscape painters, and in his vision of the great forests one of the purest of European Romantics. He was trained in Copenhagen and never went to Italy – he said that he was afraid he would never want to return if he ever saw Rome. He was particularly interested in the expression of effects of light and of the seasons, but his feeling for the haunted silence of the woods has no parallel outside Altdorfer. DAVID d'Angers, who met him in Dresden in 1834, said he 'discovered the tragedy of landscape'. In 1808 he exhibited the

Cross in the Mountains (Dresden), which was painted as an altarpiece for a private chapel, although it has no specifically religious subject matter. It started a debate over the suitability of landscape for religious purposes: in fact, all Friedrich's pictures of this kind are landscapes with pantheistic implications, and not 'religious' subjects at all. He spent most of his life in Dresden, where he knew RUNGE. Most of his works are in German museums, especially Dresden, but others are in Leningrad (Hermitage), London (NG), Paris (Louvre) and Vienna.

FRITH, William Powell (1819–1909), was the son of an innkeeper in Harrogate, who virtually forced him to become an artist. He started as an itinerant portrait painter, and after 1840 specialized in costume history and genre subjects, becoming one of the most successful painters of contemporary life. *Ramsgate Sands* (1853, Royal Coll.), *Derby Day* (1858, London, Tate) and *The Railway Station* (1862, Royal Holloway College, nr Windsor) depict with minute detail an enormous variety of anecdotal incidents, which made his works so popular that barriers had to be erected at the Royal Academy to protect them from the crush of admirers. He travelled a good deal in Holland, and visited Italy. He published three volumes of memoirs, recounting in the most matter-of-fact way the sources of his subjects, and the details of his phenomenal success.

FROMENT, Nicholas (active 1450–90), worked in the South of France and was painter to René of Anjou. There are two documented works by him: the unusual subject of *Mary in the Burning Bush* (1476, Aix-en-Provence, Cath.), an allegory of the Virgin Birth, and the *Raising of Lazarus* (1461, Florence, Uffizi). A diptych of René and his wife, attributed to Froment, is in Paris (Louvre).

FROTTAGE (from Fr. *frotter*, to rub). Most people know the parlour game which consists of putting a piece of plain paper over a penny and rubbing a soft pencil over it, causing an image of the monarch's head to appear on the paper. This simple device, dignified by the name of *frottage*, has frequently been used to obtain effects of texture in abstract or semi-abstract painting. It is normally done by making a *frottage* on a piece of paper and then applying one or more of these to a canvas as COLLAGES. Max ERNST frequently used the method, employing the floorboards and other wooden surfaces.

FRUEAUF, Rueland I and II, were Austrian painters from Passau. Rueland I (*c*.1440/5–1507) worked in Passau and Salzburg from 1470 in a style derived from Flemish painters such as Jan van Eyck and the Master of Flémalle. There are four *Passion Scenes* of 1490–91 by him in Vienna (K-H Mus.). His son Rueland II (*c*.1470/5–1545 or later) was a citizen of Passau before 1497, a Councillor in 1533 and was still active as an artist in 1545. He painted a series of scenes from the life of St Leopold, some of which are signed RF and dated 1507, for Klosterneuberg, near Vienna, as well as a *St Anne with the Virgin and Child* (1508, Vienna, K-H Mus.). Other works by father or son are in Boston, Budapest, Cambridge Mass. (Fogg), Detroit, Munich, Prague and Venice (Correr).

FRY, Roger (1866–1934), started as a painter but became an art historian and influential critic. He was Director of the Metropolitan Museum, New York, 1905–10, but returned to London to edit the 'Burlington Magazine' and organize an exhibition, in 1910, of POST-IMPRESSIONISM, and a second in 1912. In 1913 he founded the Omega Workshops, producing furniture, textiles and decorative objects of modern design (Vanessa BELL and Duncan GRANT worked there), and during the 1920s he was associated with the LONDON Group. His paintings are less important than his lectures (which were famous) and his books, including the first book in English on Cézanne (1927). There are works in London (Tate and Courtauld Inst., which has a large collection of Omega products).

FULLER, Isaac (*d.*1672), was probably trained in France and was working in Oxford in 1644, at the same time as DOBSON. He seems to have been a very Bohemian character, and his few surviving works are all painted with a fierce bravura and an impasto distantly reminiscent of Rembrandt. His series of paintings illustrating the escape of Charles II after the battle of Worcester, formerly in the Irish Houses of Parliament, is now in a private collection. His altarpiece in All Souls College, Oxford, now lost, was described by Evelyn as 'too full of nakeds for a chapell' (*Diary*, 1664). He died in London. There are works in London (Tate, NPG and Dulwich) and Oxford (*Self-portrait*, in the Bodleian Library and a version in Queen's College).

FUSELI, Henry (1741–1825), was Swiss by birth, his name, Füssli, being modified to suit the Italian tongue. His father, a painter and art historian, forced him to become a clergyman, and he was ordained in 1761, but his exposure of a dishonest magistrate ended his career as a Zwinglian minister. In 1763 he began studying art in Berlin and later came to England to work as a hack translator of French, German (WINCKELMANN, as early as 1765) and Italian books, and occasional illustrator. He was encouraged by Reynolds to become a painter, and in 1770 went to Rome for eight years, where he taught himself, mainly by copying Michelangelo in the Sistine Chapel. On his return to England he began exhibiting works of imaginative power, executed in a deficient technique, his first success being *The Nightmare* (1781, Detroit), a picture redolent of Romantic horror. He then worked for Boydell's Shakespeare Gallery, became an ARA in 1788 and an RA in 1790, and began a series of huge paintings illustrating Milton (forty-six in all) to which public and patrons remained indifferent. He was made Professor of Painting at the Academy in 1799 and Keeper in 1804. He had to resign as Professor in 1805, but the statutes of the RA were altered in 1810 to allow him to hold both posts, in spite of the inadequacy of his technical knowledge (his paintings have suffered badly from his poor procedures). Among his pupils were Etty, HAYDON, Mulready, Leslie, Constable and Landseer; and the artistic memoirs of the period are full of anecdotes of his eccentricities and sarcasms. Fuseli's art, with its extravagance of movement and gesture, its distortions and stylizations of form (particularly in his often erotic drawings of women), its exploitation of the murky layers of horror and fear in the imagination, is the antithesis of Reynolds's classicism and Gainsborough's charm, but is a less dedicated form of the visionary quality which inspired BLAKE, whom he first met *c.*1787, and of whom he said that 'Blake was damned good to steal from'. He also knew DAVID (in Rome 1775/8) and GÉRARD. In 1831 a 'Life' was published with an edition of his writings. There are works in Auckland NZ, Birmingham, Cambridge (Fitzwm), Cardiff, Frankfurt (Goethe Mus.), London (Tate and Courtauld Inst.), Weimar, Yale (CBA), Zürich and elsewhere. (*See also* BARRY.)

FUTURISM. This word, sometimes used to mean any art more recent than 1900, has in fact a precise meaning. It was the only important modern movement before the New York School to be largely independent of Paris (for which reason it is not popular in France), and it can be dated from 20 February 1909 to its virtual demise in the First World War (*c*.1915). It was actually born in Paris, in an article in 'Le Figaro' by MARINETTI, poet, dramatist, mountebank and future friend of Mussolini, in which he announced '. . . a new beauty . . . a roaring motorcar, which runs like a machine-gun, is more beautiful than the *Winged Victory of Samothrace* . . . We wish to glorify war . . .'. This general Manifesto was followed by a 'Manifesto of Futurist Painting' (1910) and a 'Technical Manifesto' (also 1910), which is the key to the aesthetics of Futurism. They wished to represent machines or figures actually in motion – 'We proclaim . . . that universal dynamism must be rendered as dynamic sensation; that movement and light destroy the substance of objects.' The 'Manifesto of Futurist Painting' was signed by BOCCIONI, CARRÀ, Russolo, BALLA and SEVERINI; Boccioni also issued a Manifesto of his own, on sculpture, in 1912. In that year the Futurist Exhibition was held in Paris and caused a great scandal; from Paris it went on to London and Berlin and eventually all over Europe, causing riots and general excitement. Nevertheless, Futurism as an aesthetic force died early in the First World War and all the major Futurists who survived subsequently returned to a more traditional method of expressing their ideas.

G

GABO, Naum (1890–1977), was born in Russia and was the younger brother of PEVSNER. He abandoned a medical career and began to study in Munich under the great art historian Heinrich Wölfflin. In 1910 he met KANDINSKY and in 1913/14, while visiting his brother, then a Cubist painter in Paris, he met other artists and made his first construction in 1915. On returning to Russia in 1917, he found himself involved in art and politics. He and his brother opposed TATLIN and in 1920 issued their 'Realistic Manifesto', which begins: 'We deny volume as an expression of space . . .'. Inevitably, he had to leave Russia and he spent the years 1922–32 in Berlin, leaving when the Nazis came to power. He had met Ben NICHOLSON and Barbara HEPWORTH in Paris, so he came to England and settled at St Ives in Cornwall. He spent many years there, broadcasting for the BBC during World War II, but in 1946 he settled in America. His first public monument was a 50-foot sculpture in Rotterdam (1957), but his works are mostly small constructions in glass, perspex, wire and similar materials. His gift to the Tate Gallery, London, includes many *maquettes* and also a large *Fountain* (1972), in the grounds of St Thomas's Hospital, London. Other works by him are in New York (Met. Mus.) and other US museums. His 'Of Divers Arts' was published in 1962.

GADDI, Taddeo (*d.*1366), was one of the most faithful of the followers of GIOTTO, for whom he is supposed to have worked for twenty-four years – thus transmitting, through his son Agnolo, the Giotto tradition to the very end of the Trecento, and even, through Agnolo's pupil Cennini, into the Quattrocento. Since Giotto died in 1337 Taddeo must have been apprenticed to him not later than 1313, but by 1332 he took an important independent commission to paint the fresco cycle of the *Life of the Virgin* in the Baroncelli Chapel in Sta Croce, Florence, where Giotto himself painted four chapels. These frescoes were completed in 1338 and form his most important work; they show a strong dependence on Giotto and also a certain desire to break away, which is confirmed by the signed and dated triptych (1334, Berlin) which shows an affinity with the art of Bernardo DADDI. Several other dated works are known, and in 1347 his name heads the list of famous painters who might be employed to paint a polyptych for S. Giovanni Fuorcivitas, Pistoia. He was given the commission, and the altarpiece (dated 1353) is still in the church. He also painted a series of scenes from the Life of Christ and of St Francis on the panels of a Sacristy cupboard door (now in Florence (Accad.), Berlin and Munich): these are often adapted from Giotto's frescoes in Sta Croce and Assisi. Other works are in Avignon, Berne, Bristol, Esztergom, Florence (Uffizi, Accad., Horne Mus., Bargello and churches), New York (Met. Mus.), Pisa (S. Francesco), Yale (Univ.) and elsewhere.

His son, Agnolo (*d.*1396), was working in the Vatican as an assistant to his brother Giovanni in 1369 and seems to have had a very prosperous career, founding the fortunes of the Gaddi family. He painted a series of frescoes in Sta Croce, so that his style is easily compared with that of both Giotto and his own father: the most important of his frescoes is the cycle of the *True Cross* in the choir (perhaps of the early 1380s). There are documented frescoes in Prato Cathedral (1392–5) and panels in S. Miniato al Monte, Florence (1393–6).

Other works are in Florence and in Berlin, London (NG and Courtauld Inst.), Montreal, Munich, Paris (Louvre), Perugia (Cath.), Washington (NG), Yale and elsewhere.

GAINSBOROUGH, Thomas (1727–88), was born in Sudbury, Suffolk, but went to London in 1740, where he worked for the next few years under GRAVELOT and probably met HAYMAN, then working on his Vauxhall decorations. The connection with Hayman is not very clear, but it is certain that many of the small portrait-groups, with the figures set in a realistic landscape, which Gainsborough painted at the beginning of his career are markedly dependent on Hayman, and perhaps also on the earlier small portraits by HOGARTH. One of the principal influences on him at this stage, however, was Dutch 17th-century landscape painting. In London he seems to have copied and restored such pictures for the dealers, and it is certain that he thought of himself as a landscape painter in this style. His earliest landscapes, painted in Suffolk, are very close to the example of Wynants, Ruisdael, and Hobbema as may be seen from the most famous of them, the *Cornard Wood* (finished 1748, London, NG), of which Gainsborough himself wrote: '... as an early instance how strong my inclination stood for Landskip, this picture was actually painted at Sudbury in the year 1748: it was begun *before I left school*; – and was the means of my Father's sending me to London ...'. All his life he was to regard landscape as his real bent, but he painted portraits for a living and set up in Sudbury *c.*1748. He moved to Ipswich *c.*1750 and remained there until he moved to Bath at the end of 1759. In Suffolk he continued to paint landscapes as well as the little portrait groups, like conversation pieces in a park, which distantly echo Watteau – perhaps through the French influence of Gravelot as well as from Hayman. A pair of early landscapes at Woburn Abbey (1755) are also French in style. His move to Bath, then a highly fashionable town, was probably in order to find more sitters. This he did, and he remained the most sought-after painter there until his final removal to London in 1774. His Bath period is characterized by a loss of the ingenuous quality of his early work, which gives way to a sense of fashionable elegance, now often displayed in full-length portraits, life-size, set against an imaginary landscape background. The influence of van Dyck, whom he now had opportunities to study, is very apparent in such pictures as the *Blue Boy* (San Marino, Cal.) and some others in which he actually dresses the sitter in van Dyck costume. He continued to paint landscapes, but they are now more Arcadian in quality, obviously composed rather than observed, although the finest of them, such as the *Harvest Wagon* (Birmingham, Barber Inst.), have a new richness of colour. He began to exhibit in London (at the Society of Artists) in 1761 and was sufficiently well-known there to be among the original members of the Royal Academy when it was founded by George III in 1768. He was later elected to the Council of the Academy but his relations with it were always uncertain: in 1773 he quarrelled with the hanging of his pictures and did not exhibit again until 1777; after another dispute in 1784 he ceased to exhibit there. His move to London in 1774 was in order to match himself against Reynolds, and most people relished the rivalry. Their styles are utterly different and Gainsborough, who was fortunate in seizing a likeness much better than Reynolds could, is often empty and mechanical in his later portraits: yet he has always, as Reynolds has not, a superb handling of paint. The rivalry was rendered all the more piquant by the fact that Reynolds was knighted and the head of the King's own Academy – yet all the Royal Family preferred Gainsborough to paint them, although RAMSAY was Painter to the King until his death in 1784, when Reynolds succeeded to the title but not the favour. From about 1780 Gainsborough painted several 'Fancy Pictures', more or less in imitation of Murillo, of a poetic quality which was an extension of his interest in landscape. His later landscapes are much influenced by Rubens and were composed of 'broken stones, dried weeds and pieces of looking-glass . . . magnified and improved into rocks, trees and water'. The *Watering Place* (RA 1777, Tate) was described by Horace Walpole: 'the landscape in the style of Rubens is the most beautiful which has ever been painted in England and equal to the great masters'.

Contrary to normal 18th-century practice Gainsborough painted all his pictures himself and never employed a drapery man. His technique was, he realized, an essential part of the effect he sought and he made it a beauty in its own right. It is best described in the noble tribute paid by his rival Reynolds in an obituary 'Discourse' (the 14th) at the RA in which he says, 'all those odd scratches and marks which, on a close examination, are so observable . . . and which even to experienced painters appear rather the effect of accident than design: this chaos, this uncouth and shapeless appearance, by a kind of magic, at a certain distance assumes form . . .'. He seems to have used very long brushes and to have diluted the paint with turpentine to the consistency of watercolour. As a result, his works have lasted much better than those of almost any other 18th-century British painter. His wife's nephew Gainsborough Dupont (*c.*1755–97) was his pupil and imitator. There are pictures by Gainsborough in almost every major museum and in many English country houses.

GALGARIO, Fra, *see* GHISLANDI.

GARZONE is an Italian word for a boy apprentice, less skilled than an assistant or JOURNEYMAN. When a part of a picture is apparently ill-executed it is usual to blame the *garzone*.

GASPAR. The usual English 18th-century form of Gaspar(d) POUSSIN.

GAUDIER-BRZESKA. Henri Gaudier (1891–1915) was a French sculptor who lived in London (Brzeska was the name of a Polish woman he lived with). He was associated with the Vorticist movement, but he joined the French Army in 1914 and was killed before he had time to develop as a sculptor: he is perhaps at his best in the calligraphic drawings made in the Zoo, where the taut pen line perfectly expresses the grace of a puma or a jaguar. He is well represented in Cambridge (Kettle's Yard) and the Tate Gallery, London, and also in Birmingham, Cardiff, Chicago, Hull (Univ.), Liverpool, Manchester, New York (M of MA), Southampton, Yale (CBA) and elsewhere.

GAUGUIN, Paul (1848–1903), was born in Paris. Part of his childhood was spent in Peru, whence his mother's family came, and from 1865 to 1871 he was at sea. He became a stockbroker in 1871, and a Sunday-painter who collected the works of the Impressionists and joined in their exhibitions (1881–6). He gave up his job in 1883, and after many vicissitudes separated from his family and went to live in Brittany at PONT-AVEN and Le Pouldu, where he worked from 1886 to 1890, except for visits to Paris, a trip to Panama and Martinique in 1887 and a disastrous stay of two months with van Gogh in Arles in 1888.

In 1891 he went to Tahiti, returned to Paris in 1893 for lack of money, but went back to the South Sea Islands in 1895. His health was failing and he had been seriously hurt in a brawl with sailors in Brittany in 1894. His remaining years were spent in poverty, illness, and continual strife with the colonial authorities through his championing of native causes. He died at Atuana in the Marquesas.

His early works may be ranged with those of the Impressionists, particularly with Pissarro and Cézanne, but after 1886 when his works hung in the eighth and last Impressionist Exhibition with those of Seurat he endeavoured to introduce more colour and this tendency became more marked after his voyage to Martinique. In 1888 at Pont-Aven he met SÉRUSIER and BERNARD, whose knowledge of medieval art joined with Gauguin's own interest in primitive sculpture, Romanesque, and Far and Near Eastern art, to encourage him to abandon Impressionism and all attempts at the representation of nature in favour of SYNTHETISM. His rejection of Western civilization led to his departure for Tahiti, and to his efforts to express, through an art free from the conventions of the naturalistic tradition, the simplicity of life among primitive and unspoiled peoples. His influence has been enormous, since he is one of the main sources from which non-naturalistic 20th-century art has emanated (cf. EXPRESSIONISM). There are works, including sculpture, in Baltimore, Basle, Birmingham (Barber Inst.), Boston (Mus.), Brussels, Budapest, Buffalo, Chicago, Cleveland Ohio, Cologne, Detroit, Edinburgh (NG), Essen, Glasgow, Grenoble, Hartford Conn., Indianapolis, Kansas City, London (Tate and Courtauld Inst.), Los Angeles, Manchester (City Mus.), Minneapolis, Moscow, Munich, Newcastle, New York (Met. Mus. and M of MA), Northampton Mass., Oslo, Ottawa, Paris (Mus. d'Orsay), Prague, Reims, Stockholm, Toledo Ohio, Washington (NG and Phillips) and elsewhere.

GAULLI *see* BACICCIO.

GEDDES, Andrew (1783–1844), studied from 1807 onwards in the RA Schools, where he met WILKIE, whose lifelong friend he became. He painted portraits in Edinburgh from 1810 to 1814, when he removed to London although he frequently returned to Edinburgh. In 1828 he travelled in France, Germany and Italy, and was elected ARA in 1832. He died soon after a visit to Holland. His portraits, direct and in a solid technique with a skilful use of grey, owe much to RAEBURN and have great charm; his subject paintings tend to be sentimental and vaguely NAZARENE in type. He is well represented in Edinburgh (NG).

GEERTGEN tot Sint Jans (i.e. 'little Gerard of the Brethren of St John') was a Dutch painter active in the late 15th century. He was born at Leyden and is said to have died at about 28, perhaps *c.*1485/95. He was a pupil of Albert van OUWATER and the only works which can reasonably be connected with his name are two very large panels in Vienna (K-H Mus.), originally back and front of a single panel from an altarpiece in the Monastery of St John at Haarlem, for which Geertgen worked. They represent the *Lamentation over the Dead Christ* and *Julian the Apostate Burning the Bones of St John Baptist, with Members of the Order Saving Some Relics.* The curious egg-shaped heads make it easy to group some other works around these two, but a picture of the Cathedral at Haarlem (in the Cathedral) which is traditionally his shows no characteristics in common. The principal pictures attributed to him are in

Amsterdam (Rijksmus.), Berlin, Cleveland Ohio, Leipzig, Leningrad, London (NG), Milan (Ambrosiana), Paris (Louvre), Prague and Utrecht.

GELDER, Aert de (1645–1727), was a pupil of Rembrandt in the 1660s and continued his late style well into the 18th century, giving it a Rococo flavour by lightening Rembrandt's palette and using pinks and violets. He painted principally Biblical subjects and portraits, and his Old Testament scenes are often markedly Rembrandtesque in their strong, warm colour as well as in their use of Oriental types and costume; indeed, his *Jacob's Ladder* (London, Dulwich) was for much of the 19th century the most popular 'Rembrandt' in the gallery. He also probably provided Rembrandt's first biographer with information. There is a series of New Testament scenes, of *c.*1715, in the galleries of Aschaffenburg and Munich and other pictures are in Amsterdam, Berlin, Birmingham (Barber Inst.), Boston, Brighton, Cambridge (Fitzwm), Chicago, Dordrecht, Dresden, Frankfurt, The Hague, Melbourne, Paris (Louvre) Providence RI, Rotterdam, Vaduz (Liechtenstein Coll.) and Vienna.

GENRE (Fr. kind, variety). A type of picture, usually small in size, depicting not so much a subject as everyday life and surroundings, though the opportunity for narrative content leads easily into subdivisions such as moralities and the conversation piece, which is a form of genre portrait. The important thing is that it should not represent idealized life. Small touches of genre – interest in setting, in objects – can be found in 14th- and 15th-century Italian painting and in early Flemish painting, but not so strongly developed as to affect its status as religious art. Although genre appears in Italy in e.g. CARPACCIO and, later, in CARAVAGGIO, G. M. CRESPI and CERUTI, it plays a minor role until the 18th century when Pietro LONGHI devoted his whole life to it. It is in the North that it first gains a strong hold and appears as a distinct form, as in the engravings of the MASTER OF THE HOUSEBOOK and in the *Bankers* of Massys and MARINUS. In 17th-century Holland the absence of patronage for religious and decorative painting stimulated the development of genre, and OSTADE, STEEN, METSU, TER BORCH, VERMEER and de HOOCH produced little else, each specializing in sub-varieties such as peasant and tavern scenes, musical or genteel drinking parties, with displays of glittering satin, or simple interiors with dazzling effects of light. In 18th-century France CHARDIN imbued his humble subjects with supreme dignity and beauty; in England the main forms were the moralities of HOGARTH, the 'fancy pictures' of GAINSBOROUGH, and the rustic scenes of MORLAND. In the 19th century the genre subject became the commonplace anecdotal painting of Victorian narrative painters like MULREADY; and the PRE-RAPHAELITES, with their mixture of costume-history and religious subjects and scenes from contemporary life, blurred further the line dividing genre from history painting. MANET used the form occasionally and so did the IMPRESSIONISTS, RENOIR and DEGAS, and it survives into our own times with SICKERT and the Camden Town Group, the Euston Road painters, and even the new Realists and Pop, for much the same reasons as caused its enormous development in Holland.

GENTILE da Fabriano (*c.*1370–1427) is first recorded in 1408, when he was in Venice. In 1409 he was working on historical frescoes in the Doge's Palace which were later finished by PISANELLO but were subsequently destroyed. From 1422 to 1425 he was in Florence where he completed, in May 1423, the resplendent altarpiece of the *Adoration of the Magi*, now in the Uffizi. This was one of the masterpieces of the INTERNATIONAL GOTHIC style and exerted enormous influence on Florentine art; it was followed by the *Quaratesi Altarpiece*, completed in May 1425, of which the *Madonna* is now in the Royal Coll. and the remainder divided between the Uffizi, the Vatican and Washington. In 1425 he left Florence and worked in Siena and Orvieto, and by 1427 he was working on frescoes in the Lateran Basilica in Rome, which have also been destroyed. His art is the charming, elegant, and courtly art of the International Gothic style; he shows little or no interest in the intellectual problems of space and volume which exercised MASACCIO, who was working in Florence at precisely the same time (cf. Gentile's *Madonna* in the Royal Coll. with Masaccio's Pisa Polyptych *Madonna*, in the NG, London). There are other pictures by him in Berlin, Ferrara, Florence (Pitti and I Tatti), Malibu Cal. (Getty Mus.), Milan (Brera and Poldi-Pezzoli), New York (Met. Mus. and Frick Coll.), Orvieto, Paris (Louvre: part of the Uffizi *Adoration*), Perugia, Pisa, Velletri, Vienna, Washington (NG) and Yale (Univ.).

GENTILESCHI, Orazio (1563–1639), was a follower of CARAVAGGIO who worked in Paris *c.*1623/4 and came to London as Court Painter to Charles I in 1626, i.e. before the arrival of van Dyck and Rubens. He remained in England until his death and was – with HONTHORST – one of the first practitioners of Caravaggism in England. The ceiling painted by him for Inigo Jones's Queen's House at Greenwich is now in Marlborough House, London. There are works by him in the Royal Coll. and in Berlin, Birmingham, Cleveland Ohio, Dublin, Fabriano (Cath. and churches), Florence (Pitti), Hartford Conn., Madrid, Milan, Paris (Louvre), Prague, Rome (Corsini and churches), St Louis, Turin (Mus. Civico and Sabauda), Urbino, Vienna (K-H Mus.) and Washington (NG).

His daughter Artemisia (*c.*1597–1651/3) was also a Caravaggesque, one of her most popular subjects being a particularly violent rendering of Judith killing Holofernes (versions in Florence, Uffizi and Pitti). In 1612 her father sued Agostino TASSI, under whom she was then studying, for raping her 'many times' and Tassi was imprisoned. She accompanied her father on his wanderings but later settled in Naples where, except for a visit to her dying father in London in 1638/9 she spent the rest of her life. There are works by her in Berlin, Bologna, Columbus Ohio, Madrid (Prado), Naples, New York (Met. Mus.), Pozzuoli (Cath.) and a ceiling in the Casa Buonarroti in Florence. The Royal Coll. has her *Self-Portrait as Painting*: it and Detroit are among the few collections to have works by both father and daughter (the Detroit Orazio is said to be a portrait of Artemisia).

GÉRARD, Baron François (1770–1837), was born in Rome. While he was a pupil of DAVID – from 1786 onwards – he worked for engravers to earn a livelihood and during the Revolution, to evade military service, he obtained through David's influence a position on a Revolutionary tribunal, but contrived to be continuously ill so as to avoid its dreadful duties. His reputation as a portrait painter was made in 1795, and during the first Empire he rivalled David in court favour. It was Gérard who suggested to David that in his huge *Coronation of Napoleon* the Emperor should crown Josephine rather than himself. Later there was bitter animosity between them, and also between him and GROS, whom he defeated both in the speed with which he turned his political coat and in his efforts to secure the Court appointment to the restored Bourbons. He was ennobled by Louis XVIII, and kept a large studio of assistants to help with his glossy, showy, superficial portraits that compete with Lawrence for facility and charm, but lack the vision and solidity which make David's portraits outstanding. There are works in Paris (Louvre and Carnavalet), Fontainebleau (Mus. Napoleon), and Versailles, as well as Barnard Castle (Bowes Mus.), Dublin (NG), London (Wellington Mus.), Oxford (two good portraits in the Examination Schools) and elsewhere.

GERHAERT, Nicolaus (von Leyden or Leyen) (active 1462–73/8), was the last great German Gothic sculptor in the realist tradition – at least if he was not Dutch, as the 'Leyden' often added to his name would imply. He is first recorded in Trier in 1462, when he signed and dated the Tomb of Archbishop von Sierck (Diocesan Mus.), but he was in Strasbourg from 1463 until 1467 (a tomb in Strasbourg Cath. is signed and dated 1464). In 1467 he carved the Baden-Baden Crucifix and went to Vienna to work on a Tomb for Friedrich III (Vienna, S. Stephan). He seems to have died in Vienna between 1473 and 1478. Other works by him are in Chicago, Frankfurt, New York (Met. Mus.), Passau Cath., and Ranshofen. A fine *Madonna* formerly in Berlin was destroyed 1939/45.

GÉRICAULT, Théodore (1791–1824), was born in Rouen of well-to-do parents. In 1808 he became the pupil of Carle VERNET, but left him after two years ('One of my horses would have devoured six of his', he said) for Guérin, in whose studio DELACROIX was also a pupil. He was strongly influenced by GROS, particularly in his painting of horses, and his choice of contemporary subjects. His technical innovations, too, are noteworthy: he abandoned the use of detailed preparatory drawings and squared-up studies, painting directly on to the final canvas from models posed according to a painted sketch. During the Hundred Days (of Napoleon's return from exile, 1815), he was so disgusted by the desertion of the troops of Louis XVIII back to Napoleon that he joined the Musketeers and accompanied the fleeing King to the Belgian frontier. Later, he regretted this and sided with the liberal opponents of the Restored Monarchy, an alignment reflected in many of his drawings (scenes from the Greek Wars of Independence, anti-slavery subjects, the ending of the Inquisition) and particularly in his most celebrated work, the *Raft of the 'Medusa'*, a shipwreck which was a political scandal of the day (1819, Louvre). In 1816 he visited Italy for a year, and in 1820–22 he was in England, where his *Raft* was shown in a travelling exhibition. During this long stay, he made many lithographs of horses and scenes of the poverty in the London streets, as well as small paintings of horses and racing subjects. His influence on the development of the Romantic movement exceeded what might have been expected from his total of no more than three exhibited works, a few portraits and horse pictures, and his lithographs and drawings. But his art, as much as that of GROS and Rubens, was one of the starting points for the young Delacroix, who admired him deeply: Géricault's copy of Titian's *St Peter Martyr* (then temporarily in the Louvre) later belonged to Delacroix (it is now in Basle).

In 1822–3 he painted a series of ten movingly realistic portraits of inmates of the Paris asylum of the Salpêtrière, of which only five survive (Ghent, Louvre, Lyons, Springfield Mass. and Winterthur). They were inspired by his friend, the alienist Georget, a follower of Pinel in the humane treatment of the insane, but the idea behind them – that certain types of physiognomy accompany certain kinds of insanity – has now been abandoned; they may have been intended to be engraved as illustrations for a treatise by Georget. There are works in Alençon, Baltimore (Walters), Bayonne, Berwick-on-Tweed, Buffalo, Cambridge (Fitzwm), Cambridge Mass. (Fogg), Glasgow (Burrell), London (Wallace Coll.), Montpellier, Munich, New York (Met. Mus.), Northampton Mass. (Smith Coll.), Paris (Louvre), Providence RI, Richmond Va., Rouen, Stockholm (gruesome *Heads of Guillotined Men*), Washington (NG), Zürich and elsewhere.

GESSO is the name given to the ground used in TEMPERA painting and in certain types of oil painting. It is a dense and brilliantly white ground with a rather high degree of absorbency (in Italy it was usually gypsum, but in N. Europe usually chalk). In Italian practice it was usual to prepare a panel with several coats of *gesso grosso*, which is simple gesso mixed with size, like white distemper. This is highly absorbent. The panel was then given ten or more coats of *gesso sottile*. This is plaster of Paris slaked in water for a month or more, so that all the setting power goes out of it. It is then made into a silky smooth mixture with size and painted on over the *gesso grosso*. The result is a smooth, brilliant white surface with a pleasantly crisp 'feel' and low absorbency.

GHEERAERTS. The Gheeraerts, the de Critzes and Isaac OLIVER were all Huguenot refugees in England who inter-married and were probably members of a single workshop, to which most English portraits of the later Elizabethan period tend to be attributed. John de Critz (1555–1641) was well established in England by 1598 and was Sergeant Painter to the Crown from 1605 until his death, at a great age, in 1641. He probably originated the pattern of the full-length *James I*, seen in Cambridge (Univ.), London (Dulwich), Madrid, and other examples. His sister, Susanna, married in 1571 Marcus Gheeraerts the Elder, a decorative painter from Bruges who fled from the Alvan persecution in 1568 and was in England 1568–77: he died before 1604. He made a signed engraving of the *Garter Procession* in 1576 and may have painted the *Queen Elizabeth* (Coll. the Duke of Portland), which is signed MGF (but this may also be his son's signature). Marcus Gheeraerts the Younger (*c*.1561–1636) was a child of an earlier marriage and himself married, in 1590, Magdalen de Critz, his stepmother's younger sister. No works can be attributed to John de Critz, and there is not much evidence for Marcus Gheeraerts I as a portrait painter, but a *Winter Landscape*, signed and dated 1587, at Burghley House, Lincs., may be by him. Marcus the Younger is documented as a portrait painter and as working for the Crown: the *Duke of Württemberg* (Royal Coll.), is of *c*.1608 and is signed 'Gerardi Brugiense'. There are other works, notably in Oxford (Bodleian), in the Duke of Bedford's Coll., and at Penshurst, which are certainly by him. The *Capt. Thomas Lee* (1594, London, Tate) is neither signed nor documented, but is usually regarded as his masterpiece. The portraits and allegories (there were few other possible subjects) which usually sail under the Gheeraerts colours are full or half-length, life-sized effigies of noblemen and women in full dress with heavy curtains, a table or chair, or a Turkey carpet as accessories. They have a formal, heraldic air and, when clean, are bright in colour. The portraits of Queen Elizabeth in English country houses are usually lumped together under the name Gheeraerts (when not called 'ZUCCARO'), but the *'Ditchley' Elizabeth* (London, NPG) may be his.

Emmanuel de Critz (*d.*1665) was a younger son of John. He is usually credited with the fine de Critz and Tradescant family portraits (one is dated 1645) in the Ashmolean Mus., Oxford, but no convincing reason can be adduced in support.

GHENT ALTAR *see* EYCK.

GHIBERTI, Lorenzo (1378–1455), was the Florentine sculptor who made two of the three bronze doors of the Baptistry in Florence. He was younger than Brunelleschi but older than DONATELLO or Masaccio, and in spite of his collection of antique sculpture and his desire to be regarded as a humanist he was not really like the Masaccio–Brunelleschi–Donatello triumvirate and had only a superficial feeling for classical art, at least in the earlier stages of his career, although it deepened in his later years. In 1401 a competition was announced for a bronze door for the Baptistry, to match the one by Andrea PISANO, but to consist of Old Testament scenes. The competition was won by Ghiberti in 1402, against Brunelleschi (who subsequently devoted himself to architecture), Jacopo della QUERCIA, and four others: according to his own account, 'The palm of victory was conceded to me by all the experts and by all my fellow-competitors. By universal consent and without a single exception the glory was conceded to me . . .'. Up to this time Ghiberti had been active as a goldsmith and painter, but the rest of his life was principally devoted to his first Doors (1403–24) and to the second pair commissioned immediately afterwards (1425–52). The competition reliefs, of the *Sacrifice of Isaac*, submitted by Ghiberti and by Brunelleschi survive (Florence, Bargello), but all the others are lost. When the commission was given to Ghiberti in 1403 (and renewed in 1407) the subjects were changed from Old to New Testament, but the doors remained very close to the type established by Andrea Pisano, with high reliefs enclosed in Gothic frames, the figures being gilt and set against a neutral ground. Ghiberti established a large workshop to carry out this great undertaking, and this shop was the principal training ground for the next generation of artists – including Donatello as well as painters like MASOLINO and UCCELLO.

In spite of a restrictive clause in his contract Ghiberti made several other works during the period 1403–24. Two large statues – the *St John Baptist* (1414) and the *St Matthew* (1419–22, but dated 1420 and recast in 1422) – made for the church of Orsanmichele, show the movement of his style away from Gothic linear rhythms towards a graver and more antique treatment. Between 1417 and 1427 he made two reliefs for the Font of the Baptistry in Siena, where the pictorial treatment of the relief foreshadows his own second Doors, but was probably derived from Donatello's contribution to the Font. Finally, in 1418 Ghiberti was paid for a model of the dome of Florence Cathedral, thus proving that he was also involved in the greatest architectural enterprise of the day: his share in the dome as built by Brunelleschi is still controversial.

After a trip to Venice in 1424 Ghiberti returned to Florence and was commissioned in 1425 to make the remaining (third) pair of doors. Such had been the success of his first pair that he was allowed to exercise his own judgement. He altered the whole layout and reduced the number of Old Testament scenes to ten (against twenty-eight New Testament scenes on the earlier doors), allowing each rectangular field to appear like a picture in a frame, with the plane of the background representing the sky or the ground, and not simply a neutral foil as in the earlier doors. The perspective is carefully calculated and depended on the recent researches of Brunelleschi and Donatello: Ghiberti himself described the doors thus, 'There were ten scenes, each framed so that the eye measures them from a distance and they appear in relief. The relief is very low and figures are so disposed on the planes that those which are nearest are seen to be larger than those further off, just as happens in reality. The whole work is based on these principles.' These doors were very richly gilded, thus adding to the painterly effect, but the gold was completely obscured by time and dirt until the doors were taken down during the Second World War and cleaned (though some panels suffered in the flood of 1966). This pair is often called the Door of Paradise – the *Porta del Paradiso* – because Michelangelo is said to have called them worthy to be the gates of Paradise.

During the period 1425–52 Ghiberti also made the bronze shrine for the Three Martyrs (1428, Florence, Bargello) and the bronze Reliquary of St Zenobius (1432–42, Florence Cath.) as well as another statue, the *St Stephen*, for Orsanmichele (1428). There are other works by him in Florence (Sta Croce, S. Egidio, and S.M. Novella) and he also designed a number of stained glass windows for the cathedral.

In the last years of his life Ghiberti wrote his *Commentarii* – already quoted from – the second of which is the principal source of our knowledge of Trecento art in Florence and Siena and also includes Ghiberti's autobiography, the earliest by an artist to survive. His interest in the art of the Trecento links him firmly with his Gothic predecessors: his consciousness of his own individuality in his autobiography shows him to have been also a man of the Renaissance, and perhaps the vital link between the two worlds.

GHIRLANDAIO, Domenico (1449–94), was the best fresco executant of his generation in Florence, whose main claim to fame is that he had Michelangelo as an apprentice. With his brother Davide (1452–1525) and other relatives he ran an extensive and well-organized studio, but he himself preferred fresco to tempera, and he never attempted oil-painting. He worked in the Sistine Chapel in the Vatican (1481–2), along with Botticelli and others, and his contribution is notable for the fact that it is nearest in spirit to Masaccio – i.e. it was old-fashioned in the 1480s – and that the nominal subject, the *Calling of the First Apostles*, is half-swamped in the rows of life-like portraits of prominent Florentines living in Rome. His essentially prosaic mind and the naturalistic detail in all his works made him very popular in his own day and in the late 19th century, but it is significant that he received only one commission (now lost) from the Medici family and none from any other cultivated patron. His frescoes are, of course, of great historical interest. Most of them are in Florence: the *St Jerome* (1480, Ognissanti) shows strong Flemish influence in the treatment of detail, and the two major cycles are those in the Sassetti Chapel, Sta Trinità (completed 1485), and the choir of S.M. Novella (completed 1490). Outside Florence, there are works of his in Berlin, Cambridge (Fitzwm), Cambridge Mass. (Fogg), Detroit, London (NG), Munich, New York (Met. Mus.), Paris (Louvre), Philadelphia (Johnson), Washington, and elsewhere.

His son Ridolfo (1483–1561) was much influenced by his friend Raphael and was a portrait painter of distinction. He is well represented in Florence, and there are portraits by him in Chicago, London (NG), Philadelphia (Johnson), Washington (NG), Worcester Mass. and Yale.

GHISLANDI, Vittore, called Fra Galgario (1655–1743), was an Italian portrait painter, active mainly in Bergamo, who was trained in Venice and whose portraits reflect the best qualities of Late Baroque Venetian painting in their solid handling and strong but subdued colour. His sitters are usually simple people and he represents them in informal poses, often with a strength of light and shade indicating a knowledge of Rembrandt. He has lately been connected with the Realist tendency (*see* CERUTI) in Lombard painting of the early 18th century, but the closest parallels among his contemporaries seem to be Hogarth's portraits, although his best-known work, the *Boy Painter* (Bergamo), in some ways anticipates GREUZE. Sir Marmaduke Constable, on his Grand Tour, visited Bergamo specially to have his portrait painted (it is now lost). His works are best represented in Bergamo, but there are others in Cambridge (Fitzwm), Hartford Conn., Milan, Minneapolis and Venice.

GIACOMETTI, Alberto (1901–66), was a Swiss sculptor, painter and poet. He was trained in Italy 1920–22 and then spent three years in Paris under BOURDELLE, but he was also much influenced by BRANCUSI and became a Surrealist in the 1930s. The sculpture of this period has been called 'still-life' or 'magic objects', and the most famous is *The Palace at 4 a.m.* (1932–3, New York, M of MA). Later he returned to more realistic single figures, extremely emaciated in form, usually built up by working directly in plaster of Paris on a wire foundation. A characteristic example is the *Man Pointing* (1947, London, Tate). He was also active as a painter, especially towards the end of his life.

GIAMBOLOGNA *see* BOLOGNA.

GIAMBONO, Michele, was a Venetian painter and mosaic worker. He is recorded in 1420 as a married man and is last recorded in 1462. He came of a family of painters, but his Venetian workshop tradition was profoundly influenced by the International Gothic style imported into Venice in the first half of the 15th century by GENTILE da Fabriano and PISANELLO in their major works in the Doge's Palace (destroyed in the 16th century, and known to us mainly from reflections in the style of artists like Giambono). He worked on the mosaics in the Mascoli Chapel in St Mark's from 1444 and his *Coronation of the Virgin*, ordered in 1447, is probably the painting now in Venice (Accad.) which was copied from an earlier picture of the same subject. There are other works by him in Bassano, Oxford (Ashmolean), Rome (Gall. Naz.) and Venice.

GIAQUINTO, Corrado (1703–65), was a Neapolitan painter who was a pupil of SOLIMENA until 1723, when he went to Rome and began to work under CONCA, who had also been a Solimena pupil. Giaquinto worked with Conca in Rome and Turin. He was elected to the Academy of St Luke in Rome in 1740 and became President in 1750. In 1752 he was invited to Madrid to succeed AMIGONI as Court Painter. He arrived in 1753 and became Director of the Academy, but in 1761 Charles III summoned MENGS to Madrid, and Giaquinto, whose Neapolitan Rococo style was the antithesis of Mengs's Neoclassicism, at once returned to Italy. One of his most important works is the huge *Birth of the Virgin* in Pisa Cathedral (1751/2) for which several sketches exist, one in Oxford (Ch. Ch.). There are pictures in Madrid and sketches in London (NG) for a ceiling in a palace in Palermo (now in Rome) and Roman churches.

GIBBONS, Grinling (1648–1721), was born in Rotterdam of English parents, but came to England by 1670/1. He was one of the most skilful woodcarvers who ever lived, as witness such virtuoso performances as the wooden cravat in the V&A, London. With the help of John Evelyn the diarist he was introduced to Charles II and became Master Carver in Wood to the Crown. Evelyn's Diary (18 Jan. 1671) describes how 'I this day first acquainted his Majestie with that incomparable young man, whom I had lately found in an Obscure place, and that by meere accident, as I was walking neere a poore solitary thatched house in a field in our Parish . . . looking into the Window I perceiv'd him carving that large *Cartoone* or *Crucifix of Tintorets* . . . I saw him about such a work, as for the curiousity of handling, drawing, and studious exactness, I never in my life had seene before in all my travells . . .'. This is probably the carving now at Dunham Massey, Cheshire (National Trust). Apart from his mastery of woodcarving Gibbons is also supposed to have made the bronze *James II*, now outside the National Gallery, London, but it is probable that most of it is by others. He worked with Arnold QUELLIN on the Chapel at Whitehall Palace (1685–6) and it is likely that Quellin actually modelled the *James II*, although Gibbons was paid for it. The *Stoning of St Stephen* (London, V&A) is a virtuoso woodcarving.

GIBSON, John (1790–1866), was apprenticed to a mason in Liverpool in 1804 but contrived to get to Rome in 1817 and spent the rest of his life there ('I thank God for every morning that opens my eyes in Rome'). He worked under CANOVA and THORWALDSEN and enjoyed a reputation little below theirs, revisiting England only in 1844 and 1850, on both occasions to work for the Queen: his monument to her is in the House of Lords (1854). His principal innovation was to re-introduce the tinting of marble, which, although certainly practised by the Greeks, seemed to a contemporary 'a dangerous departure from true art'. Many stories are told of his simplicity: a woman pupil said of him that 'he is a god in his studio, but God help him out of it', and to a puzzled railway porter he is said to have replied, 'No, I am not a foreigner, I am a sculptor'. Nevertheless, he left a large fortune and his bequest to the Royal Academy (to which he was elected in 1838) paid for most of the building of the Diploma Gallery, which contains works by him: there are others in the Royal Coll. and in Cambridge (Fitzwm), Cardiff, Durham (Cath.), Liverpool (which has his rediscovered *Tinted Venus*), London (NG, NPG, Tate, V&A, Wellington Mus. and Westminster Abbey) and Yale (CBA).

GIGANTE, Giacinto (1806–76), was a Neapolitan *veduta* painter. He studied with PITLOO, and worked for the tourist trade producing picturesque views of Rome and Naples before establishing himself as the major artist of the School of Posillipo. The artists in this group, which developed from Pitloo, specialized in local views executed on the spot. They were all influenced by foreign artists – 18th-century ones such as J. R. COZENS, WRIGHT of Derby, DUCROS, HACKERT, and 19th-century *plein-air* painters such as Corot and Turner. Gigante developed a freedom of handling reminiscent of Turner, whose works he probably saw in Rome in 1828: he made several visits to Rome and was in Paris in 1869. Most of his works are in Naples (Mus. di S. Martino).

GILL, Eric (1882–1940), English engraver, letter-cutter, sculptor, typographer and writer. The *Stations of the Cross* (Westminster Cath.) and *Prospero and Ariel* (Broadcasting House) are his best-known carvings; others are in the Tate Gallery. He will probably best be remembered as the designer of the lettering known as Gill Sans-serif, and many other fine alphabets, and for his wood-engravings and book-illustrations.

GILMAN, Harold (1876–1919), was trained at the Slade School, met GORE, and joined SICKERT's circle, against which he subsequently reacted violently, coming under the influence of van Gogh. He was a member of the CAMDEN TOWN GROUP and became the first President of the LONDON GROUP on its foundation in 1913. He is represented in Cardiff, Ipswich, Leeds, Liverpool, London (Tate), Manchester (Whitworth), Ottawa and Yale (CBA).

GILPIN, Sawrey (1733–1807), was an English animal painter with Romantic ambitions. He was the younger brother of the Rev. William Gilpin, the celebrated writer on the PICTURESQUE. Sawrey studied in London from 1749 under SCOTT. His work is less sensitive than that of STUBBS and is somewhat marred by anthropomorphism. This may be seen in his *Election of Darius* (York) – according to legend the election was influenced by the neighing of Darius's horse – but most of his works are straightforward sporting pictures. He exhibited at the RA from 1786, and was elected RA in 1797.

GINNER, Charles (1878–1952), was a painter of townscapes and a friend of SICKERT, GILMAN and GORE. He was a member of the CAMDEN TOWN GROUP (1911) and the LONDON GROUP (1913), and was elected ARA in 1942. He is well represented in the Tate Gallery, and in Brighton and other Camden Town collections, as well as Yale (CBA).

GIORDANO, Luca (1632–1705), was a Neapolitan painter known as 'Luca fa presto' (*Luke, paint quickly*) from the alleged habit of his father in urging ever greater speed and facility. Certainly he was able to paint in an amazing variety of styles, which has earned him praise and disdain in about equal measure. He was probably a pupil of RIBERA in Naples but went on to Rome, where he was influenced by the lighter style of PIETRO da Cortona, and to Florence and Venice, where the influence of Venetian art was instrumental in getting away from the darkness of Ribera's style. In Florence he painted a chapel, and, in 1682–3, the huge ceiling of the Ballroom of the Pal. Medici-Riccardi. His great renown led Charles II to summon him in 1692 to Spain, where his ceilings in the Escorial are probably his masterpieces. He returned to Naples in 1702 and spent his last years there. He was the most important Neapolitan painter of the second half of the 17th century, and his lighter and more colouristic style marks a great change from the Neapolitan painting of the first half of the century. His output was huge and most older galleries have examples of his easel paintings. London (NG) has a characteristic *Perseus*.

GIORGIONE (*c.*1476/8–1510) was a Venetian painter, a pupil of Giovanni BELLINI, who was ranked by Vasari with Leonardo da Vinci as one of the founders of modern painting. He was the first exponent in Venice of the small picture in oils, intended for private collectors rather than for churches, and frequently mysterious and evocative in subject. Many of his contemporaries were unable to interpret the subject of such a picture as the *Tempest* (Venice, Accad.), of which we can say only that it appears to be the first 'landscape of mood', expressing the heat and tension of an approaching thunderstorm. His career is almost entirely mysterious. In 1506 he shared a studio with, of all people, CATENA; recent X-rays seem to show a Catena-type *Madonna* below the picture in Brunswick which has been called a self-portrait and attributed to Giorgione. In 1507/8 he was working in the Doge's Palace, but these works are lost; in 1508 he was painting frescoes on the outside of the Fondaco dei Tedeschi, the headquarters of the German merchants in Venice, and TITIAN was also working there in a subordinate capacity. Only faded fragments of these frescoes now exist, but the link with Titian is important, for it seems to prove that it was Giorgione, and not Titian, who was the great innovator. This would be less controversial if we had more knowledge of Giorgione's style, but no extant pictures can be regarded as completely documented and there are only about half a dozen which are generally agreed to be attributable to him on adequate evidence. The problem is much complicated by the fact that he died, of the plague, in 1510 and several pictures seem to have been completed by Titian and SEBASTIANO del Piombo, both of whom were, at that date, profoundly influenced by him; nevertheless, optimistic attributions to him continue to be made. The *Castelfranco Madonna* (Castelfranco Veneto – his birthplace – S. Liberale) is derived from the large altarpieces of Giovanni Bellini, and is therefore probably an early work: it is universally accepted as Giorgione's. Other works, in Dresden, Leningrad, Venice and Vienna (K-H Mus.), including the *Laura* in Vienna which is dated 1506, are almost beyond controversy, but the debate continues over works in the Royal Coll. and in Berlin, Boston (Gardner), Budapest, Florence (Uffizi and Pitti), Glasgow, London (NG and Courtauld Inst.), Madrid, Oxford, Paris (Louvre), San Diego Cal. and Washington as well as other less likely candidates. The portrait in San Diego has a 16th-century inscription attributing it to 'Zorzon' (the Venetian form of his name) and a date which has been read as 1508 and 1510, but may be neither. The *Adoration* in Washington is very controversial but may be an early work. The ruined *Judgement of Solomon* (Kingston Lacy, Dorset, National Trust) has been much argued over, but is now thought to be by Sebastiano del Piombo, *c.*1511, rather than Giorgione.

GIORNATA (Ital. day – i.e. a day's work) *see* FRESCO.

GIOTTESCHI, Giottesques. The name given to a number of 14th-century painters working in the shadow of GIOTTO. Many of them are anonymous, others are known by names like the MASTER OF S. CECILIA, while others again are distinct personalities such as DADDI, GIOTTINO, Taddeo GADDI or MASO di Banco.

GIOTTINO, active in the mid-14th century, probably painted the *S. Remigio Deposition* in Florence (Uffizi) which was regarded as a work of MASO by Vasari and earlier writers. The distinction of hand is evident, but it is by no means certain that Giottino was identical with a Giotto di Maestro Stefano who was painting in the Vatican in 1369, who in turn cannot be reconciled with Vasari's Maso/Giottino figure. No other work can reasonably be attributed to the painter of the Uffizi *Deposition*, unless one accepts the attribution of it to ORCAGNA's brother Nardo di Cione.

GIOTTO (1266/7 or less probably, 1276–1337) was a Florentine, who, with CIMABUE, is generally regarded as the founder of modern painting, since he broke away from the stereotyped forms of Italo-Byzantine art and tried to give his figures the maximum solidity and naturalism. He gave passion and imagination to his scenes, just as Giovanni PISANO had done slightly earlier in sculpture. His dramatic power can be felt in his frescoes of scenes from the lives of SS. Joachim and Anne and the Virgin, and of the Life and Passion of Christ, in the Arena Chapel, Padua. These were completed by 1313, perhaps *c.*1306. Before then Giotto had probably designed the fresco cycle of the Legend of St Francis in the Upper Church at Assisi, although his authorship is denied by many critics on stylistic grounds. These frescoes are imbued with the humanity which St Francis himself had brought into the religious life of the 13th century, and which was so potent an influence on the arts.

Probably just after 1300 Giotto designed the *Navicella*, a huge mosaic of the Ship of the Church, in St Peter's, but this has been so reworked that his hand is no longer discernible in it. Much later, perhaps in the 1320s, he decorated four chapels in Sta Croce, Florence, of which two chapels (Bardi and Peruzzi: *Life of St Francis* and *Lives of St John Baptist and Evangelist*), and an *Assumption* (doubtfully attributed) from a third chapel, survive. A slight influence from Gothic sculpture is perceptible in them. Giotto also worked in Naples (1329–33), but all his work there is lost. There are several panel pictures – some of them signed – attributed to him: in Bologna, Florence (Sta Croce), London (NG), Munich, Paris (Louvre), Raleigh NC, Upton Park (National Trust) near Banbury, Washington and elsewhere, but all of these are held to be works of his school or shop, and even the signed ones are, as it were, trade-marked rather than signed in the modern sense. This is true even of the *Stefaneschi Altar* in the Vatican, which is mentioned as his in a document of 1342; on the other hand, the *Ognissanti Madonna* (Florence, Uffizi) is universally accepted as his although it is neither signed nor documented. Other works with a good claim to be considered as his include the *Dormition of the Virgin* (Berlin) and a Crucifix in S.M. Novella, Florence.

On account of his great fame – he and Cimabue are both mentioned by Dante – Giotto was appointed supervisor of Florence Cathedral in 1334, and he began work on the Campanile ('Giotto's Tower'), but his design was altered later. Nearly all Florentine and many Sienese painters of the mid-14th century were influenced by him (the Giotteschi), but his influence waned in the later 14th century, to be revived in MASACCIO and even in Michelangelo.

GIOVANNI d'Alemagna *see* VIVARINI.

GIOVANNI da Bologna *see* BOLOGNA.

GIOVANNI da Milano (active 1346–69), in spite of his name, worked in Florence, where he is first documented in 1346, becoming a member of the Guild in 1363 and a Florentine citizen in 1366. His *Pietà* (Florence, Accad.) is signed and dated 1365, the year in which he signed the contract for the decoration of the Rinuccini chapel in Sta Croce. In 1369 he was working in the Vatican, but the paintings are now lost. His style was formed by Giotto's followers in North Italy, reinforced in Florence by that of ORCAGNA. There are works in Amsterdam, Bordeaux, Florence (Accad., Uffizi and Cath. Mus.), London (NG), New York (Met. Mus.), Prato, Rome (Gall. Naz.), the Vatican and Williamstown Mass.

GIOVANNI di Paolo (1403–82/3) was, with SASSETTA, the leading Sienese painter of the 15th century. There are documented works from 1426 down to about 1475 and it is likely that he ceased painting towards the end of his long life. His style is a rather more archaic and tortured version of Sassetta's, with a certain influence from GENTILE da Fabriano (who was in Siena 1424/6): his later works seem to show that he had visited Florence. Nevertheless, like Sassetta, he seems always to be looking back over his shoulder to the masters of the Trecento. There are works in Altenburg,

Baltimore (Walters), Berlin, Boston (Mus. and Gardner), Cambridge (Fitzwm), Cambridge Mass. (Fogg), Chicago, Cleveland Ohio (a copy of Gentile's *Adoration*), Cologne (Wallraf-Richartz and Rheinisches Mus.), Florence (Uffizi and Bargello), London (NG), Minneapolis, Modena, Mount Holyoke Coll. Mass., Münster, New York (Met. Mus. and Frick Coll.), Oxford (Ashmolean and Ch. Ch.), Paris (Louvre), Philadelphia (Johnson), Rochdale (a fine early *Crucifixion*), Siena (Pinacoteca, Cath. Mus. and churches), Utrecht, the Vatican, Vienna (Akad.), Washington (NG) and Yale (Univ.).

GIRARDON, François (1628–1715), was the most classical of the sculptors working at Versailles for Louis XIV. He was in Rome 1645/50 and on his return collaborated with LEBRUN at Versailles. His *Apollo and the Nymphs*, commissioned in 1666 for the Grotto of Thetis and now much altered by the regrouping of the figures, is severely classical in style and based on the Apollo Belvedere and on Poussin, whose type of composition it translated into sculpture. His *Rape of Proserpine*, in the gardens, though full of movement, consciously avoids both the Mannerism of Giovanni da Bologna's group, and the Baroque movement in depth of Bernini's group of the same subject: indeed, he was chosen to alter BERNINI's over-Baroque equestrian *Louis XIV*. He made a bronze equestrian *Louis XIV* of his own in 1699 for Paris; it was destroyed in 1792 and only a fragment – the left foot – survives in the Louvre. It is, however, known from what may be the original model (Paris, Carnavalet) and from many bronze reductions (e.g. London, Wallace Coll.). His great rival at Versailles was the younger COYSEVOX.

GIRODET de Roucy-Trioson, Anne-Louis (1767–1824). He became a pupil of DAVID in 1785 and won the Prix de Rome in 1789. He was in the French Academy in Rome when in 1793 David's order to replace the Royal arms by the Republican ones touched off the riot in which the mob wrecked the Academy and murdered the French agent. Girodet escaped to Naples, but there found his republicanism dangerous and after a gruelling flight through Italy arrived, very ill, in Genoa where he was succoured by GROS. His *Endymion*, sent from Rome in 1793, reflects not only his Romantic temperament but also the drift from David's classicism towards more poetic and Romantic themes. David disapproved of him, and of GÉRARD, declaring that they had debased the art by their pandering to poetry and portraiture: indeed, his notorious *Danäe* of 1799 (now in Minneapolis) was a portrait of a well-known *demi-mondaine*, with her current protector recognizably represented as a turkeycock. In 1812 Girodet inherited a large fortune and abandoned painting to compose unreadable poems on aesthetics, writing in a house shuttered against daylight. There are works in Leipzig, Malmaison, Montpellier, Northampton Mass. (Smith: *Mme Trioson*, 1804), Orleans, Paris (Louvre), Versailles and elsewhere.

GIRTIN, Thomas (1775–1802), was the friend and contemporary of TURNER, but all his important work was done in watercolour and in his short life he revolutionized landscape painting in that medium. With Turner he worked for Dr MONRO and also copied Canaletto drawings, from which he learned much about topographical drawing. In 1801–2 he went to Paris where he made a series of soft-ground etchings of views of Paris, published posthumously in 1803 (cf. BOYS). On his return from Paris he resumed his enormous PANORAMA of London (*The Eidometropolis*) which he exhibited in 1802. The

Panorama is lost, but half a dozen sketches for it are in the BM. In his watercolours Girtin bridged the gap between the 18th-century stained drawing and the 19th-century watercolour painting: the *White House at Chelsea* (1800, London, Tate), one of his finest works, shows this transition and the poetic spirit which informs his work. He made several technical innovations, including the use of rather absorbent off-white cartridge paper (cf. COX), but his most radical change was the abandonment of the older monochrome underpainting in favour of a richer handling, with broad washes of strong colour often offset by dark blobs. There are works by him in Bedford (Higgins Mus.), Birkenhead, Birmingham, Brighton, Bristol, Cambridge (Fitzwm), Cardiff, Dublin, Edinburgh, Leeds, Lincoln, London (BM, Tate, V&A, Guildhall and Courtauld Inst.), Manchester (Whitworth), Newcastle, New York (Met. Mus.), Ottawa, Oxford, Sheffield, Swansea, Victoria NSW, Yale (CBA), York and elsewhere.

GISANT (Fr. recumbent). A recumbent figure on a tomb, usually representing the dead body of the person commemorated. In France in the 15th and 16th centuries these figures were often represented as decaying, with or without worms.

GISLEBERTUS was a French Romanesque sculptor who worked *c.*1125–35 at Autun cathedral in Burgundy, where he carved a tympanum *Last Judgement* (conspicuously signed), and also executed many capitals. His figures are characterized by vivid imagery, and by minutely pleated drapery in rhythmic folds and flutters. The fragments of the N. transept door include the famous *Eve*. There are affinities between the work at Autun and some of the sculpture at Vézelay, which suggest that he may have worked there before going to Autun, and his iconographic dependence on Cluny suggests close links with the Abbey there. Other places in Burgundy have works deriving from Autun, probably by his workshop.

GIULIO Romano (1492 or 1499–1546). Painter and architect and one of the creators of MANNERISM. From about 1515 until RAPHAEL's death in 1520 Giulio was his chief assistant and was working on the frescoes in the Sala dell' Incendio in the Vatican, a fact which makes it unlikely that he was born in 1499. Before going to Mantua in 1524 Giulio completed some of Raphael's unfinished works, including the *Transfiguration* and the Vatican frescoes (Sala di Costantino), and he also painted an altarpiece for S.M. dell'Anima, Rome, and the *Stoning of St Stephen* for Sto Stefano, Genoa (1523). All these works show an exaggeration of Raphael's style and also a melodramatic invention coupled with the influence of MICHELANGELO. These qualities are carried further in the frescoes in the Palazzo del Tè, designed by him for the Gonzaga of Mantua. The *Fall of the Giants*, occupying the whole of one room, is a piece of brutal illusionism deliberately designed to overwhelm the spectator, who finds himself involved in the crushing of the Giants by the thunderbolts of Jove in the sky above. The whole of the room is painted from floor to ceiling to increase the illusion, and Vasari – who admired it greatly – tells us that the flames in the fireplace were intended to add to the effect of general destruction. This series was painted 1532–4, and there are other frescoes by him in Mantua. Giulio left Rome hurriedly, as a result of a series of engraved illustrations designed by him for Pietro Aretino's obscene sonnets (1523), known as 'Aretino's Postures'. Edinburgh (NG), Florence, London (NG), Naples, Paris, Rome and Vienna also have works. *See also* PARMIGIANINO.

GIUNTA PISANO was, with BERLINGHIERO, one of the earliest Italian painters known to us as individuals. Giunta was active in Pisa *c.*1229–*c.*1254 and is known from three surviving crucifixes in Assisi, Pisa and Bologna. He is also known to have painted a crucifix in Assisi, dated 1236 but now lost, and he may have painted the dramatic *St Francis* (Pisa). His style is more consciously realistic than that of Berlinghiero and he uses the modern CHRISTUS PATIENS type of crucifix.

GLASGOW SCHOOL, The. Unlike Italy, where such regional schools as Florence, Naples or Venice are very different, yet each has an inner coherence, there have been only three regional schools in Britain: NORWICH, NEWLYN and Glasgow, all of them short-lived. The Norwich School was dominated by two major artists, Cotman and Crome, and therefore has a stylistic unity, but the Newlyn School and the 'Glasgow Boys' (they were all young) had far less in common. They were both influenced by the naturalistic *plein-air* landscapes of the BARBIZON SCHOOL – some of them had been trained in Paris – and by the similar works of the HAGUE SCHOOL, as well as by BASTIEN-LEPAGE. The Glasgow Boys were well acquainted with these pictures because several Glasgow dealers took a lead in exhibiting them. In England there is a parallel with the NEW ENGLISH ART CLUB. Whistler was an influence on both. From about 1880 the Glasgow Boys exhibited together and had a great success with a group exhibition in London and Munich in 1890, but by *c.*1895 the disparate tendencies of the group became evident: Lavery (1856–1941), for example, moved to London and became a society portrait-painter. The other main members (there were about twenty in all) were Guthrie (1859–1930), Hornel (1864–1933) and Henry (1859–1943), with Melville (1855–1904) in Edinburgh.

GLAZING is the process of applying a transparent layer of oil paint over a solid one, so that the colour of the first is profoundly modified. Thus, a solid blue which has been allowed to dry, if glazed over with transparent crimson, will give effects of purple to mulberry, depending on the thickness of the glaze and the intensity of the pigments used. It is thus the opposite of SCUMBLING and is impossible in direct, or ALLA PRIMA, painting, The use of glazing is now rather rare, as it implies a deliberation and a craftsmanly approach to painting which is often thought to be inconsistent with inspiration: by a paradox, the principal exponents of glazing are probably now the TACHISTES. The exact use made of glazes by different Old Masters is a highly controversial subject, since every time a picture is cleaned someone will claim that 'the Master's final glazes have now irretrievably vanished'; occasionally this is true, but it usually means that the dirty varnish layer has been regarded as a glaze in its own right. There is an added complication in that some glazes were undoubtedly put on with fugitive colours, and have therefore vanished of their own accord. This has affected many pictures by Reynolds, as may be seen in the deathly pallor of his *Countess of Albemarle* (1757/9, London, NG), where the pink glazes of the flesh tones have faded, leaving only the monochrome under-painting.

GLEIZES, Albert (1881–1953), was overwhelmed by CUBISM in 1910, and in 1912 published with METZINGER 'Du Cubisme', the first book on the subject (English translation 'Cubism', 1913). He was one of the flat-pattern Cubists, and also produced abstract works. He was also a founder-member of

SECTION D'OR and exhibited in the ARMORY show. In 1917, when in America, he turned to religion, and many of his later works are a marriage of traditional Catholic themes with Cubist ideas. He also wrote on religion and art. There are works in London (Tate), Paris (Mus. d'Art Moderne), New York (M of M A) and Toronto.

GLEYRE, Charles (1806–74), was born in Switzerland but went to the École des Beaux-Arts in Paris in the mid-1820s. He became friendly with Bonington, whom he met at the Atelier Suisse. He was in Italy 1828–33, where he was impressed by the NAZARENES and became a lifelong admirer of Raphael. He was in the Middle East 1834–7, painting landscapes for an American patron. On his return to Paris in 1838 he met DELAROCHE, who managed to get him a commission to decorate the Château de Dampierre, but the Duc de Luynes had the paintings destroyed on completion (1842) to make way for new ones by Ingres (which were never completed). The disaster embittered Gleyre, but his *Illusions Perdues* had a great success in the 1843 Salon, and, when Delaroche closed his teaching studio in that year most of the students transferred to Gleyre. His encouragement of *plein-air* landscape painting, his insistence on the importance of the sketch as a first idea, on drawing from memory, and on the primacy of personal expression and originality made him admired as a teacher, particularly by the young men who were to become the Impressionists: Monet, Bazille, Sisley and Renoir. He closed his studio in 1864, because of failing sight and money problems. There are works in Baltimore (Walters), Basle, Cambridge Mass. (Fogg), Lausanne, Montpellier, Paris (Louvre) and elsewhere.

GLOVER, John (1767–1849), was born in Leicestershire and began to paint in 1805, moving to London, where he soon became a fashionable drawing-master. He was President of the Old Watercolour Society (1815) and a founder-member of the Society of British Artists (1824), but in 1830 he decided to emigrate to Australia, and, in 1831, settled in Tasmania, where he became one of the most important influences on Australian art: just before he left England, Constable wrote that 'Lord N– . . . esteems "our own Glover" too much to like our *disowned* Constable. One picture he had of Glover, the foreground of which consisted of 100 flower pots all in a row . . . the sun was shining bright, but they cast no shadow.' This is an accurate, though biased, description of the PALMER-like sharpness of vision of *Glover's House and Garden* (N G of S. Australia). He is represented in Australian museums, as well as Birmingham, Dublin, Leicester, London (V&A, Tate), Nottingham, Paris (Louvre) and Yale (C B A).

GLYPTIC *see* SCULPTURE.

GOES, Hugo van der (*d.*1482), was the most important Ghent painter in the period after Jan van Eyck, and one of the most gifted of all the early Netherlandish painters. He was probably born at Ghent and was in the Guild there in 1467, becoming Dean in 1473/4 and 1475. About 1475 or a little later he completed the *Portinari Altarpiece* (Florence, Uffizi) for a Florentine resident in the Netherlands: the picture went direct to Florence and had little influence in the Netherlands, but it made a considerable impression on several Florentines, notably Ghirlandaio. It is unusual in Flemish work in that it is on a huge scale (over 8 ft high), and the great size is a positive gain to Hugo's composition, whereas to any other Flemish painter it would have been an embarrassment. The cool but rich colour and the virtuosity of the oil technique must also have been regarded with wonder in Florence. About 1475 (or perhaps 1477/8) Hugo joined his brother as a lay-brother in the Augustinian monastery at Roode Clooster, near Brussels; but he continued to paint, to receive noble visitors, and apparently to travel, since he went to Louvain to value the estate of Bouts in 1479/80 and, about 1481, went to Cologne. On this journey he was seized by madness (from a contemporary description, a form of religious melancholia) and he died, still insane, the following year. The *Portinari Altar* is rather exiguously documented as his, but all other attributions are based on it; his dramatic, almost *exalté* style is easily recognizable. There are two other very large pictures by him, both in Berlin, and other works in Baltimore, Bruges (Mus. and S. Sauveur), Brussels, Cassel, Edinburgh (NG, on loan from the Royal Coll.), Frankfurt (Städel), Leningrad, New York (Met. Mus.), Oxford (Ch. Ch.), Philadelphia (Johnson), Vaduz (Liechtenstein Coll.), Venice (Correr), Vienna and Wilton House Wilts.

GOGH, Vincent van (1853–90), was the son of a Dutch pastor. He was first employed in The Hague, London, and Paris by the picture dealers for whom his brother Theo worked. He then taught in two English schools, worked in a bookshop in Holland, began studying for the Church, and became a missionary in the coalmining district of the Borinage in Belgium, where he shared the poverty and hardships of the miners. He did not begin to become an artist until he was living in great poverty after his dismissal from the mission in 1880, and from then until 1886 he lived variously at Brussels, Etten, The Hague, Drenthe, Huenen and Antwerp, teaching himself to draw and paint, with occasional lessons in Brussels, from his relation Anton MAUVE, a member of the HAGUE SCHOOL, in The Hague, and at the Academy in Antwerp, which appear to have contributed little to his development. In 1886 he joined Theo in Paris and immediately came into contact with the works of the Impressionists, which Theo endeavoured to sell in the gallery devoted to modern art that he directed. He met Toulouse-Lautrec, Pissarro, Degas, Seurat and GAUGUIN, and in 1888 went to Arles where he was later joined by Gauguin. In December 1888 he became insane, and from then until his death suffered intermittent attacks of mental trouble. During the intervals between them he continued to paint, both in the asylums at Arles and S. Rémy and after his removal to Auvers, where, in July 1890, he shot himself. His brother Theo, to whom most of his long and revealing letters were addressed, and who was his constant support, moral and financial, died six months later.

Van Gogh's Dutch period is characterized by his use of dark colour, heavy forms and subject matter chiefly drawn from peasants and their work. He ignored Theo's advice to lighten his palette as the Impressionists were doing, but during his short stay in Antwerp he became more interested in Japanese prints and the work of Rubens. After his arrival in Paris a complete change took place in his palette and subject matter; he adopted the Impressionist technique, leaning briefly towards the pointillism of Seurat, and turned to flowers, views of Paris, and portraits and self-portraits which enabled him to experiment with these new ideas. After he went to Arles, he painted many landscapes and portraits in heightened colour and with a vivid, passionate expression of light and feeling, and after the arrival of Gauguin his work shows the influence of SYNTHETISM in the greater simplification of his forms and his use of less modulated colour. His paintings done at S. Rémy and Auvers are vivid in colour and with writhing, flame-like forms in the drawing, completely expressive of his tormented sensibility. His greatest influence was on MUNCH and the German Expressionists.

He left a vast volume of work, all painted 1880–90, most of which is in a special van Gogh Mus. in Amsterdam (more than 200 paintings and 600 drawings), and in the Kröller–Müller Museum at Otterlo in Holland. There are also works in Amsterdam (Stedelijk Mus.), Baltimore, Boston (Mus.), Cambridge Mass. (Fogg), Chicago, Copenhagen, Edinburgh (NG), Essen, Glasgow, London (NG, Tate and Courtauld Inst.), Minneapolis, Moscow, New York (Met. Mus., M of MA and Brooklyn), Paris (Mus. d'Orsay and Mus. Rodin), São Paulo, Washington (NG and Phillips) and many other museums.

GOLDEN SECTION (Golden Mean) is the name given to an irrational proportion, known at least since Euclid, which has often been thought to possess some aesthetic virtue in itself, some hidden harmonic proportion in tune with the universe. It is defined as a line which is divided in such a way that the smaller part is to the larger as the larger is to the whole (AB cut at C, so that CB:AC = AC:AB). In practice it works out at about 8:13 and may easily be discovered in most works of art. *See also* SECTION D'OR.

GOLTZIUS, Hendrik (1558–1617), was a Haarlem engraver and painter, who, with SPRANGER, BLOEMAERT and WTEWAEL, was a leading Mannerist. With CORNELISZ. van Haarlem and van MANDER he founded a school for drawing from life in Haarlem in 1583, but did not begin to paint until 1600, under Italian influence – he had been in Italy in 1590–91, where he met Federico ZUCCARO (a signed and dated drawing of him by Goltzius is in Berlin, Dahlem). About 1593 he made a series of six engravings called 'Masterpieces' of the Life of the Virgin, imitating the styles of Barocci, Raphael, Dürer, Lucas van Leyden, Bassano and Parmigianino. His *Venus and Adonis* (1614, Munich) is based on Titian, but also seems to reflect Rubens. His portraits, both painted and engraved, have a sober realism and grasp of character quite different from his fancy subjects, and occasionally they seem to foreshadow Hals, his fellow-townsman. His engravings, executed by himself or by others to his designs, are very numerous and of superb technique. He was also the first to use colour wood-blocks for landscape prints, and he made a number of CHIAROSCURO woodcuts of figure subjects. There are paintings in Amsterdam, Arras, Baltimore (Walters), Basle, Haarlem, The Hague, Leningrad, Los Angeles, Paris (Louvre), Philadelphia, Providence RI, Rotterdam and Utrecht.

GONÇALVES, Nuno (active 1450–72), was the most important Portuguese painter of the 15th century. His *S. Vincent Altar* for Lisbon Cathedral was destroyed in 1755, but another, of six panels dedicated to the same Saint (now in Lisbon Mus.), is reasonably attributed to him. It contains many portraits and may be dated *c.*1465–7: the style is ultimately Flemish, based on BOUTS, but simpler and more austere. The influence of wood-carving is discernible in the treatment of the heads. *A Man with a Wine-Glass* in the Louvre, formerly ascribed to the circle of FOUQUET, is now thought to be Portuguese and resembles the work of Gonçalves.

GONCHAROVA, Natalia (1881–1962), was a Russian painter strongly influenced by Gauguin, Cézanne and Matisse from 1906 onwards. She was closely associated with Mikhail Larionov, the inventor of RAYONISM. She combined motives from Russian peasant art with the thick outlines, simplified forms and strong colour of Fauve painting, becoming more abstract as she moved towards Rayonism. She worked with Larionov as a designer for Diaghileff's Ballet 1914–29. There is a painting by her in New York (Guggenheim).

GONZÁLEZ, Julio (1876–1942), was, with LAURENS and LIPCHITZ, a Cubist sculptor. He was born in Barcelona, into a family of metalworkers. The family moved to Paris in 1900 and González soon came in contact with Picasso, whom he had already met in Barcelona: in 1930–2 he taught Picasso the technique of ironworking. For many years a painter, González worked in the Renault factories during the First World War and subsequently devoted himself to sculpture in iron. He was influenced by ARCHIPENKO and produced a form of Cubist sculpture: in turn, his work has had great influence on British and US sculptors (e.g. Butler). His masterpiece is the *Montserrat* (1936–7, Amsterdam, Stedelijk Mus.) made for the Spanish Pavilion at an International Exhibition, but it is more naturalistic than most of his works – e.g. the *Woman doing her Hair* (1936, New York, M of MA). Many of his works are in Paris (Mus. d'Art Moderne); others (including many drawings) are in London (Tate).

GORE, Spencer Frederick (1878–1914), was strongly influenced by SICKERT and late Impressionist painting, and from 1910 (when Roger Fry organized the first POST-IMPRESSIONIST Exhibition in London) he was (like GILMAN) deeply influenced by Cézanne and Gauguin. In 1911 he was the first president of the newly founded CAMDEN TOWN GROUP. There are works by him in Exeter, Manchester, London (Tate), Plymouth and Yale (CBA).

GORKY, Arshile (1904–48), was born Vosdanig Adoian in Turkish Armenia, fled before the Turks in 1915 and finally arrived in the US in 1920. His life began in tragedy – his mother starved to death – and ended in suicide following a cancer operation in 1946 and a car crash in which he broke his neck. He worked in New York from *c.*1925 and began to paint Cubist pictures in 1927: his earliest works are imitations of Cézanne, later of Picasso and finally of MIRÓ. His *Artist and his Mother* (*c.*1926–36, New York, Whitney Mus.) is an able pastiche of Picasso's figure style of *c.*1920. In 1935 and 1939 he painted two large murals on the theme of aviation, but both are lost. In 1940 he met MATTA, who inspired him with Surrealist ideas similar to those of Miró. Other American museums with pictures by Gorky include Baltimore, Buffalo, Chicago, New York (M of MA), Oberlin Ohio, San Francisco, Tucson Ariz. (Univ.) and Utica NY (Munson–Williams–Proctor). There is also one in London (Tate).

GOSSAERT or Gossart, Jan, *see* MABUSE.

GOTHIC is a term normally used to describe the architectural style of N. Europe from the early 12th century until the 16th, and, as such, has no place in this Dictionary. It is, however, often used to describe the other arts of the same period, particularly when emphasizing their transcendental qualities in contradistinction to Renaissance art. The phrase 'Late Gothic' is useful in this connection, since it means that artists such as NOTKE, HOLBEIN the Elder and even GRÜNEWALD continued to practise a style which was not affected by Renaissance ideas, as late as the end of the 15th century and into the 16th. The genuine Gothic art of France in the 14th century influenced some Italians, notably Simone MARTINI, and the result of this was the stylistic offshoot known as INTERNATIONAL GOTHIC.

GOTTLIEB, Adolph (1903–74), was born in New York, and studied there and in Paris, Berlin and Munich. With his close friend ROTHKO, he became known as an abstract painter, exploring myth-laden and subconscious mental states through automatic painting. During the 1950s he developed his 'pictographs' – panels divided first into chequerboard compartments, and later into bands, containing Red Indian magic symbols (hands, eyes, snakes, arrows). In 1956 he evolved his symbols of the cosmos and chaos: large disks of colour over explosive black blots. He also made a huge stained-glass façade for the Steinberg Memorial Center, New York (1952).

GOUACHE is opaque watercolour paint (known to many people as Poster Paint). With gouache effects very similar to those obtainable in oil-painting may be got with less trouble, so that it is a useful means of making studies for a large picture in oils; although, like its kin DISTEMPER and TEMPERA, it has the defect of drying much lighter in tone than it seems when wet. The medium lacks the peculiar charm of pure watercolour, but has always been popular on the Continent. Paul SANDBY was one of the few British artists to use it extensively. *See also* BODY COLOUR.

GOUJON, Jean (active 1540–62), was a French sculptor who is also recorded as an architect. His elegant, elaborately draped figures derive from the First School of FONTAINEBLEAU and CELLINI, but these influences are so completely assimilated that he achieves a striking personal style, showing the influence of classical sculpture (possibly known through a visit to Italy before 1540). He first appears in Rouen where he made capitals in S. Maclou: the tomb of Louis de Brézé (Cath.), husband of Henri II's mistress Diane de Poitiers, is reasonably attributed to him in view of the links between caryatides on the tomb and those (now much restored) in the Salle des Caryatides in the Louvre. He worked in Paris on the rood-screen for S. Germain l'Auxerrois (from 1544, Louvre) and on the *Fontaine des Innocents* (1547–9; most of the reliefs now in the Louvre), and on exterior sculpture on the Lescot wing of the Louvre (begun 1546). He disappears from sight in 1562. According to an (ambiguous) document he may have left France, as a Huguenot, in 1563 and died *c.*1568.

GOWER, George (*d.*1596), was a fashionable London portrait painter by 1573 and Sergeant Painter to Elizabeth I in 1581: in this capacity he attempted, with HILLIARD, to get a monopoly of Royal portraits. Two of the three known documented works are in London (Tate). Attributed works are in Adelaide, Indianapolis, Manchester and York. The so-called 'Armada' portrait of Queen Elizabeth at Woburn Abbey (Duke of Bedford) has recently been attributed to Gower.

GOYA, Francisco de G. y Lucientes (1746–1828), was born near Saragossa and studied there until (apparently) his amours and knifings caused him to leave; in 1763 he was in Madrid working under BAYEU, whose sister he married. He was in Italy *c.*1770 and was in Rome in 1771, but was back in Saragossa later in the year, working in the Cathedral. By 1775 he was in Madrid and from 1776 began producing tapestry cartoons for the Royal manufactory; this started his successful career and he became Deputy Director of the Academy in 1785, *pintor del rey* 1786, *pintor de cámera* 1789, and *primer pintor de cámera* (i.e.

Principal Painter to the King) in 1799, so that his contemporaries certainly recognized his genius. In 1792, however, he was very ill and became deaf, which undoubtedly made him still more introspective, so that we find Goya the official portrait painter also producing works which, he said, were 'to make observations for which commissioned works generally give no room, and in which fantasy and invention have no limit'. This fantasy was typified in the series of etchings called *Los Caprichos*, produced 1796–8 and announced for sale in 1799 (eight more were added in 1803). These are savagely satirical attacks on manners and customs and on abuses in the Church, yet in 1798 he painted the frescoes of the cupola of S. Antonio de la Florida in Madrid (technically fascinating, because apparently executed with sponges in dabs and wipings of colour). The dilemma in which Goya and other liberal Spaniards found themselves became acute in 1793 when Charles IV declared war on the new French Republic; for Charles was very reactionary and most liberals were then partly in sympathy with France. In 1808 the troops of Napoleon invaded Spain and drove out Ferdinand VII (who had succeeded Charles IV in 1808), replacing him with Joseph Bonaparte. Many Spaniards welcomed his liberalism, yet hated the foreigners – in particular the French troops, who behaved with almost 20th-century savagery. These atrocities were recorded by Goya in the series of etchings called *The Disasters of War* (1810–13: first published in full in 1863) and, above all, in the two paintings called *2 May* and *3 May 1808* (*c.*1814, Madrid, Prado). The French were driven out with the aid of Wellington (whom Goya painted in 1812) and in 1814 Ferdinand VII was restored. Goya was pardoned for having worked for Joseph Bonaparte and continued to work for the Spanish Court until 1824 when there was a fresh wave of reaction and he went to Paris and then settled in voluntary exile in Bordeaux. What seems difficult to understand is how the Bourbons could continue to employ him, for his portraits of Charles IV and his family have been described as making them look like prosperous grocers; but in fact these portraits, and those of Ferdinand VII, make them appear brutish, moronic and arrogant.

From 1819 Goya began to practise the new art of lithography and he produced some bull-fighting scenes (*The Bulls of Bordeaux*) as well as single prints and several more etchings and aquatints. There are good examples of his prints in the BM, London, in Madrid, and in New York (Hispanic Soc.).

As a painter Goya began his decorative works very much under the influence of Tiepolo's Spanish frescoes, while his portraits are influenced by Mengs and, oddly, by English 18th-century portraits (he is known to have owned engravings); an intensive study of Velázquez, his predecessor as Court Painter, led to a breadth of style which ends as a kind of Impressionism. He had great influence on 19th-century French painting, especially on Manet, and he has been called the last of the Old Masters and the first of the moderns (whatever that may mean). There are pictures in Agen, Amsterdam (Rijksmus.), Baltimore, Barnard Castle, Bayonne, Berlin, Besançon, Boston (Mus.), Budapest, Castres, Chicago, Cincinnati, Cleveland Ohio, Detroit, Dublin, Edinburgh, Hartford Conn., Houston Texas, Kansas City, Lille, London (NG, Courtauld Inst. and Wellington Mus.), Madrid (Prado, Acad. and S. Antonio de la Florida), Minneapolis, Montreal, Munich, New York (Met. Mus., Frick Coll., Brooklyn Mus. and especially Hispanic Soc.), Northampton Mass. (Smith

Coll.), Ottawa, Paris (Louvre), St Louis, San Diego Cal., São Paulo Brazil, Seville, Toledo Ohio, Valencia, Washington (NG and Phillips) and Worcester Mass.

GOYEN, Jan van (1596–1656), was, with Salomon van RUYSDAEL, the most important Dutch landscape painter of the realist school before Jacob van RUISDAEL. He spent a year in France as a young man and then worked under E. van de VELDE in Haarlem *c.*1617 before settling in The Hague in 1634. He travelled extensively in Holland and also went to the neighbourhood of Antwerp and Brussels (a sketch-book exists of his Belgian trip): many of his pictures represent identifiable places. He speculated all his earnings on tulips and houses and died insolvent, in spite of his huge production, but a portrait of the family by his son-in-law, Jan STEEN, shows a very prosperous-looking group, complete with negro page. His earliest works, up to *c.*1630, show the influence of Esaias van de Velde, with rather crowded compositions and strong local colours. About 1630 a marked change is observable in his style. His composition is simplified, with the horizon set very low in the picture, and a great breadth of handling and tonality is obtained by the use of near-monochrome, with the light green and yellow-brown which is typical of him (Houbraken, writing before 1718, said that the blues had faded out of his greens, leaving yellows – cf. PYNACKER). At this stage it is often difficult to distinguish his pictures from those of S. van RUYSDAEL (a Ruysdael of 1631 in London, NG, passed for years as by van Goyen, and reasonably so). Later on his colour becomes richer again, until, at his death, the poetic imagination of Jacob van Ruisdael carried Dutch landscape painting to fresh heights. Van Goyen made some etchings as well as very numerous drawings, some of which were certainly made for sale as independent works of art. He painted his own figures in his landscapes, the earliest of which dates from 1620 (a picture in the Fitzwm Mus., Cambridge, signed and dated 1618 is now thought to be falsified). About 1,200 paintings are recorded, so that he is well represented in museums.

GOZZOLI, Benozzo (*c.*1421–97), was the assistant of Fra ANGELICO, but was entirely secular in outlook. His numerous frescoes give a picture of 15th-century life, the most famous being the *Medici Family as the Magi* (*c.*1459, Florence, Medici Pal.). His other famous fresco-cycle, begun 1467, in Pisa was largely destroyed in the Second World War. A typical panel is the altar-piece of 1461 in London (NG).

GRAF, Urs (*c.*1485–1527/8), was a Swiss draughtsman, engraver and goldsmith. He painted only one picture, *War* (*c.*1515, Basle), and possibly one other, the *St George*, which is also in Basle. He was a vile man who frequently went off as a mercenary soldier, and his drawings of the life of these brutes have a morbid fascination, enhanced by the sweeping rhythms of the pen stroke. He disappeared from Basle in 1527 – perhaps to take part in the Sack of Rome – and his wife remarried in 1528. His *Woman Washing Her Feet* (1513) is probably the first dated etching (*see* ENGRAVING (2*c*). He also worked as an engraver for silversmiths. In 1519 he engraved eight panels with scenes from the Life of St Bernard for the Cistercian monastery near Lucerne; four of the panels are now in Zurich (Landesmuseum) and the others, three signed with his monogram and one dated 1519, are now on loan to the British Museum, which also has many of his prints. Most of his drawings and engravings are in Basle.

GRAFF, Anton (1736–1813), was born in Switzerland, but was the leading German portrait painter of the 18th century. He was a younger contemporary of Reynolds, with whom he is often compared, but Graff really belongs to a later generation, since most of his portraits lack the trappings of the Grand Style, and he worked almost into the BIEDERMEIER period. He was in Augsburg by 1756 and removed to Dresden in 1766 to teach at the newly founded Academy. He recorded himself as having painted some 1,240 portraits in his long career and his sitters included many of the most famous of his contemporaries – Lessing, Herder, Schiller (whom he records as having fidgeted the whole time). He also made some 322 portrait drawings in silver point, a very rare technique in the 18th century. Some fragments of an autobiography were posthumously published in Zurich in 1815. There are pictures in many German museums, including Berlin, Dresden and Leipzig.

GRAFFITO *see* SGRAFFITO.

GRANACCI, Francesco (1469/70–1543), was a Florentine painter of the generation immediately preceding MICHELANGELO whose friend he was from early youth. Like Michelangelo, Granacci was a pupil of Domenico GHIRLANDAIO, whose assistant he later became. Granacci was one of the assistants engaged by Michelangelo in 1508 for the beginning of the Sistine ceiling but, like the others, was dismissed after about one month. On his return to Florence Granacci fell under the influence of Fra BARTOLOMMEO, and his later works have elongated figures in an attempt at monumentality. The Dublin *Holy Family*, which is usually attributed to him, has also been attributed to Michelangelo and shows the approximation of their styles. Basically, however, Granacci was a Quattrocento artist and is thus very similar to such transitional painters as Ridolfo Ghirlandaio and FRANCIABIGIO. There are works by him in Florence and in Baltimore (Walters), Berlin, Cardiff, Greenville SC (a version of the Dublin *Madonna*), London (V&A), Munich, Oxford, San Francisco, Sarasota Fla and Washington.

GRANDI, Ercole di Giulio Cesare, *see* ROBERTI.

GRANT, Duncan (1885–1978), was a British painter who travelled in Italy and worked in Paris, where he also met Matisse and Picasso. In London he was associated with Bloomsbury, being a cousin of Lytton Strachey, and a close friend of Clive and Vanessa BELL, Virginia Woolf, Maynard Keynes and Roger FRY. His early work was based on Cézanne, Matisse and Picasso, but after 1918 he turned from abstraction to a renewed interest in nature, although he also worked for the Omega Workshops (founded in 1913 by Fry), designing pottery, textiles, interior decoration and stage sets. There are works in Aberdeen, London (Tate and Courtauld Inst., which has a large collection of Omega products), Manchester and Yale (CBA).

GRAPHIC ARTS. The phrase is an importation into English from the German *Graphik*, and is used to mean those arts which depend mainly for their effect on drawing and not on colour; in other words, the arts of drawing and engraving in all their forms. The word Graphics – often in the singular – is a recent coinage, as in 'Television Graphics', for the production of expository diagrams: it is what used to be called Commercial Art and is not confined to monochrome.

GRAVELOT, Hubert (1699–1773), was a French book-illustrator and engraver. He came to London in 1733 after studying in Paris under BOUCHER, and returned to Paris in 1746, after having been Gainsborough's master. He came back to London and remained till 1755 and then finally returned to Paris: he is the most important link between the French School – especially the Watteau followers – and the British in the mid-18th century. He illustrated most of the important books published in London during the years he lived in England. His paintings – which influenced HAYMAN, among others – are rare, but there is a fine one at Marble Hill, Twickenham, London. One in York is, perhaps, a copy.

GRAVER *see* BURIN.

GRAVURE. Originally this was the French word for engraving (or engraved prints), but it has come to be extended to mean a combination of engraving techniques, as in the influential book *New Ways of Gravure* by S. W. Hayter. It has also been taken over – by extension from the photogravure process – to be a genteelism for a reproduction of a print.

GREAVES, Walter (1846–1930), was born in Chelsea, the son of a Thames boat-builder. He and his brother Henry used to row WHISTLER on the Thames (as their father had Turner) and became his studio assistants. His early, naive, *Hammersmith Bridge on Boat-Race Day* (*c.*1862, London, Tate) is probably his masterpiece. By the late 1870s Whistler had become jealous of him, and Greaves had a very difficult time for many years, until in 1911 an exhibition revived his fame briefly. This, however, was crushed by Pennell, Whistler's self-appointed champion, and in 1922 Greaves was able to secure a place in the Charterhouse (a charitable foundation in the City of London), where he died.

GRECO, Domenikos Theotocopoulos (1541–1614), called El Greco, was born in Crete and probably received his early training there. In 1987 a signed icon, a very early work by Greco, was discovered on Syros, a Greek island. Crete then belonged to Venice, but it was a centre of the survival of Byzantine art in the 16th century, and it would be natural for a young artist who wished to receive further training to go to Venice for it, as Greco did. The references to his Italian years are very scanty, the most important being the letters of his friend, the illuminator Giulio Clovio. One, written in 1570, seeks the patronage of Cardinal Farnese for him: 'There has arrived in Rome a young Candiot, a pupil of Titian, who seems . . . to have a rare gift for painting.'

One early 17th-century source, not very reliable, records him as working in Rome during the Pontificate of Pius V (1566–72) and says that he had studied under Titian, coming to Rome at a propitious moment and with a great opinion of himself – saying, when Pius proposed to cover the nudities in Michelangelo's *Last Judgement* (eventually done by Daniele da Volterra), that if the whole thing were demolished he would paint another as good and decorous into the bargain. This caused such resentment that Greco was forced to go to Spain, where he had to compete for Court favour with established painters such as TIBALDI, ZUCCARO and others, whose intrigues caused him to retire and die in obscurity. There is an element of truth in all this, including his lack of success at Court, and he is known to have owned a copy of VASARI's *Lives* in which he wrote slighting comments on Michelangelo and Florentine art in general.

Greco's early works show his wide range of sources: Titian, Michelangelo, Bassano, Raphael, Dürer, the MANNERISTS of Central Italy, such as Pontormo and Parmigianino, and underlying all these, his Byzantine heritage. It is not known why he went to Spain, but he is recorded in Toledo from 1577 until his death. Soon after his arrival he received his first major commission – the High Altar and two transept altars in Santo Domingo el Antiguo (1577–9). The High Altar has been dispersed but the transept altars remain. It astonishes by the completeness with which he has assimilated all the varied elements of his style and also by its great scale – *The Trinity* (now in Madrid, Prado) is nearly 10 feet high and the *Assumption* (now in Chicago) is over 16 feet. His next major commission (also 1577–9) was for the *Disrobing of Christ* (*El Espolio*), for Toledo Cathedral: it was rejected and he had to bring a lawsuit, but the verdict of the assessors was enthusiastic and may explain the number of repetitions (e.g. a small one at Upton House, Banbury, National Trust). Soon after this he made a bid for Court favour with his *Dream of Philip II of Spain* (in the Escorial; sketch or repetition in London, NG), a sort of counterpart to Titian's *Gloria, or Vision of Charles V*. It represents the Adoration of the Name of Jesus, and is an allegory of the Holy League against the Turks. This was painted *c.*1580, and in 1581 Philip commissioned the *Martyrdom of St Maurice and the Theban Legion*, delivered in 1584, and immediately refused by the King, whose secretary wrote: 'The picture does not please His Majesty, and that is no wonder, for it pleases few, although it is said that there is much art in it and its author understands much for there are excellent things of his to be seen.' Philip was devoted to the balanced, serene art of Titian and this highly Mannerist work, asymmetrical, violent in scale changes, disturbing, and acid in colour, was bound to clash with the King's tastes. Philip tried hard to attract major artists into his service, but he got only feeble exponents of a style one of whose greatest masters he rejected out of hand. Greco passed the remainder of his life in Toledo, where one of his major masterpieces, *The Burial of Count Orgaz* (S. Tomé), was painted in 1586. His ecstatic and passionate style becomes heightened with time, often increasing with successive repetitions of a subject, and so personal that his pupils and assistants do not even attempt to follow his example except for occasional weak imitations by his son Jorge Manuel. In Italy the development of Mannerism was conditioned by the Sack of Rome and the Counter Reformation; in Spain the background to Greco is in the Wars with the Netherlands and in the long tragedy of the Expulsion of the Jews and the Moriscos from 1585 to 1609, which ruined Toledo and left whole districts desolate, with grass growing in the streets. It lies also in the *Spiritual Exercises* of St Ignatius, the founder of the Jesuits, which insist upon immediacy of experience, even of the events of the Passion, for the person practising the devotions. Greco's use of colour, often eerie and strident, with sharp contrasts of blue, yellow, shrill green and a livid mulberry pink, the elongated limbs and nervous tension of his figures, the feeling that the draperies swathing them have a life of their own – all these suggest the intensity of the painter's mystical experience and the catharsis he found in his art. His last works include the mysterious *Laocöon*, (1608–14, Washington, NG) with its extraordinary view of Toledo, and the *View and Plan of Toledo* (1610–14, Toledo), and some of his most impressive portraits, such as the *Fray Hortensio Pallavicino* (*c.*1619, Boston). The finest collections of El Greco's works are in Spain: in the Escorial, the Prado in Madrid, and in the museums and churches of Toledo. There are others in Barnard Castle (Bowes Mus.), Boston, Budapest, Cadiz, Cambridge Mass. (Fogg), Chicago, Cincinnati,

Cleveland Ohio, Copenhagen, Detroit, Dresden, Edinburgh (NG), Glasgow (Pollok House), Hartford Conn. (Wadsworth Atheneum), Kansas City, London (NG), Los Angeles, Milan, Minneapolis, Modena, Montreal, Munich, Naples, New York (Met. Mus., Frick Coll. and Hispanic Soc.), Oslo, Ottawa, Palencia (Cath.), Paris (Louvre), Parma, Philadelphia, Princeton, Providence RI, Rochester NY, St Louis, San Diego Cal., San Francisco Cal., Saragossa, Sarasota Fla, Seville, Stockholm, Strasbourg, Toledo Ohio, Villanueva y Geltrú, Washington (Dumbarton Oaks, NG and Phillips) and Worcester Mass.

GRECO, Emilio (*b*.1913), is a Sicilian sculptor. As a boy he worked for a tombstone maker, but while in the army managed to attend art school in Palermo. His first one-man show in Rome in 1946 brought him immediate success. His principal works are bronze portrait busts and life-size bronze female figures, tall, slender, posturing with great elegance, and often in sharp and witty parody of classical statues. In 1964 he completed the bronze doors of Orvieto Cathedral, and in 1987 his fountain in Carlos Place, London, was given by the Italian State to London. His pen drawings express form through hatchings, with only an occasional fine contour.

GREENHILL, John (*c*.1640/45–76), was a pupil and assistant of LELY. He set up on his own *c*.1665 as a portrait painter, but soon 'fell into a loose and unguarded Manner of Living' and died as the result of falling into a gutter while drunk. His *Self-Portrait*, showing him holding a drawing of himself by Lely, and other portraits in London (Dulwich), are the basis of all attributions to him, e.g. in Cardiff.

GREUZE, Jean Baptiste (1725–1805), made his name in the Salon of 1755 with *A Grandfather Reading the Bible to His Family*, a piece of Dutch-inspired narrative genre painting, extolling the simple virtues of the poor. Enormously popular works such as *L'Accordée de Village* (1761, Louvre) and the *Paralytic tended by His Children* (1763, Leningrad, Hermitage) exploit this Rousseauish field with skill and determination, winning him extravagant praise from DIDEROT, who later came to a more just appreciation of Greuze's talent. His excessive vanity so antagonized his fellow-artists that his attempt in 1769 to secure election to the Academy as a history painter with the inadequate and ill-drawn *Septimius Severus reproaching Caracalla* (now in the Louvre) met with a deservedly humiliating rebuff, and caused his withdrawal from all further Salons. He exhibited his works privately, enjoying a great vogue during the 1770s when much of his fame derived from the popularity of engravings after his works, fully exploited by a number of engravers, and, less profitably, by the artist, whose wife embezzled most of the proceeds. During these years a severe and Poussinesque composition and a more restrained use of accessory detail were combined with turgid colour, strong chiaroscuro, and a heightened rendering of the gamut of the passions, displayed in vivid facial expressions and gestures and in a mountingly high moral tone. He also painted some excellent portraits and charmingly tender studies of children. During the late 1770s and in the 1780s, to offset his dwindling popularity, adversely affected by Neoclassicism, he produced increasing quantities of titillating semi-draped figures of young girls, grossly deficient in drawing and of mawkish sentimentality, and numerous 'Expression Studies' arbitrarily named 'Sorrow' or 'Innocence' and so on. His life was embittered by his disastrous marriage to the pretty model of his early pictures who later degenerated into a sleazy drab, whom he eventually divorced. After the Revolution, which ruined him, he endured poverty and neglect, occasionally relieved by a charitable commission from Napoleon and his circle. He died unnoticed, having – like FRAGONARD – outlived his time and his reputation. The largest collections of his pictures are in the Louvre, London (Wallace Coll.), and Montpellier. His native Tournus has a Musée Greuze which contains two very early portraits and some drawings as well as a room devoted to his life. This has interesting comparative material ranging from Poussin to Hogarth. There are paintings in most French provincial museums and in the Royal Coll. and Baltimore, Berlin, Berne, Brighton, Budapest, Dublin, Edinburgh, Glasgow, Hartford Conn., Leningrad, London (NG), Malibu Cal. (Getty Mus.), Minneapolis, Moscow, Munich, New York (Met. Mus.), Rotterdam, Stockholm, Vienna, Waddesdon Bucks. (National Trust), Washington (NG), Worcester Mass. and York. There are also many drawings in Russia, where he was very popular.

GRIEN, Hans Baldung, *see* BALDUNG.

GRIMSHAW, Atkinson (1836–93), was born and died in Leeds. His early landscapes were influenced by the PRE-RAPHAELITE BROTHERHOOD's ideals of painstaking detail, but he later developed a special kind of industrial landscape, lit by moonlight or gaslight, or both. Like LOWRY in the 20th century, these urban scenes were very popular with the public, less so with the official art world. There are works by him in London (Tate), and in Gateshead, Harrogate, Leeds, Preston and Scarborough.

GRIS, Juan (1887–1927), left Madrid in 1906 and settled in Paris, living near PICASSO. At first he broke up the objects in his pictures into many-faceted planes, but by 1911 he was using the analytical form of Cubism, and later used collage and synthetic forms, with an understanding and an originality that preserve him from inclusion among the more obvious Picasso followers. He did some work for Diaghileff in 1922–3, but found the world of ballet too hectic. His 'Possibilités de la peinture' was given as a paper at the Sorbonne in 1924. There are works in New York (M of MA), Paris (Mus. d'Art Moderne) and many other museums.

GRISAILLE (Fr. *gris*, grey) is a painting executed entirely in monochrome, in a series of greys. Strictly speaking, a monochrome painting is one executed in any one colour, red, yellow, blue or black; a *grisaille*, as its name implies, is in neutral greys only. A *grisaille* may be executed for its own sake as a decoration, or as a model for an engraver to work from, or it may be the first stage, or LAY-IN, in building up an OIL-PAINTING.

GROS, Baron Antoine Jean (1771–1835). His parents were both minor artists, and he became a pupil of DAVID in 1785. In 1793 he was in Italy and was introduced by Josephine into the entourage of Napoleon (whom he painted) in Milan after the Italian campaign; he was one of the committee which selected the looted works of art taken from Italy to France. His strength lay in large pictures illustrating the Napoleonic Myth, such as *Napoleon visiting the Plague-stricken at Jaffa* (1804, Louvre) and battlepieces full of movement and colour. He was David's closest friend and fervent admirer, and after his death in 1825 Gros assumed the leadership of the classicist school. He was made a Baron by Charles X for his dome of the Panthéon, which he had originally planned as an apotheosis of Napoleon and had to convert into an apotheosis of the Restoration Bourbons. His late classicist pictures were received with derision, and partly in despair at his failure, partly because of his miserable married life, he drowned himself. His influence on GÉRICAULT and DELACROIX was important for the development of the Romantic Movement. There are works in Algiers, Besançon, Bordeaux, Chartres, Cleveland Ohio, Detroit, Grenoble, Malmaison, Moscow, Paris (Louvre, Carnavalet and Invalides), Toulouse, Valenciennes, Versailles and elsewhere.

GROSZ, George (1893–1959), was the leading German satirical draughtsman of this century. He was trained at the Dresden Academy from 1909 and served in the army from 1914, but his dislike of authority resulted in a court martial for insubordination and he was nearly shot. In 1918 he was one of the founders of DADA in Berlin and in 1920 produced a book of satirical drawings – *Gott mit uns* – as a result of which he was fined for insulting the German Army. In 1923 he was again fined for an insult to morality, and in 1928 for blasphemy. Fortunately for him, he began to exhibit in America in 1931 and in 1933 he went to New York, remaining in America until he revisited Germany in 1951. His years in the US took the edge off his satire. He returned to Berlin, with the intention of staying there, in 1959, but died soon after his arrival. His autobiography has been published in German and English: the German version (1955) is called *Ein Kleines Ja und Ein Grosses Nein* – 'A small yes and a big no', being a pun on his own name. There are examples of his work in Berlin, Cologne and Stuttgart, as well as Boston, Cambridge Mass. (Fogg), Chicago, London (Tate) and New York (M of MA).

GROTESQUE in its technical sense has nothing to do with its normal usage. It refers to the kind of ornament, sometimes also called Arabesque (though this is not really identical), which was used as a decoration in antiquity. This consists of medallions, sphinxes, foliage and similar elements, and the name Grotesque derives from the fact that these classical ornaments were rediscovered in places like the Golden House of Nero, in grottoes, and were thus named *Grotteschi*. Raphael was one of the first modern artists to use these motives, particularly in the Loggie of the Vatican. The word *grottesco* is first recorded in 1502, in the contract for PINTORICCHIO's Piccolomini frescoes in Siena – with which Raphael may have been concerned.

GROUND is the surface on which a painting is made. If on canvas, the ground is usually white oil-paint, sometimes with a tinted layer on top; on panel the ground may be the same or GESSO. Some incompetent artists do not use a ground and paint direct on to the support – i.e. the bare canvas or wood. On canvas this practice is always, eventually, fatal. *See also* BOLUS GROUND and ENGRAVING (2*c*).

GROUP OF EIGHT *see* ASHCAN SCHOOL.

GROUP OF SEVEN *see* SEVEN, Group of.

GRUBER, Francis (1912–48), was a French painter connected with the movement known as *Misérabilisme*, current during the 1940s and 1950s. At the 'Salon de la Libération', the first Salon d'Automne held in Paris in 1944 after the liberation of Paris, he exhibited the *Job* (Tate) which symbolized in its colour and dejection the sufferings of Europe during the years 1939–44. His interest in straightforward figurative art makes this, and others such as the *Artist's Studio*, as well as works by fellow *Misérabilistes* such as BUFFET, the antithesis of the hermetic imagery and distortions of Picasso at the same period, and an attempt to break away from the artistic language of the then bygone age. Gruber was a friend of Friesz and Giacometti. His life was gravely affected and eventually shortened by asthma.

GRÜNEWALD, Mathis Neithardt-Gothardt, called Grünewald (*c.*1470/80–1528), was a contemporary of Dürer, and his exact opposite. Little is known of his life – he is first documented in 1501 in Seligenstadt – but he may have been in Aschaffenburg before then and was perhaps born in Würzburg. From 1508 to 1514 he was Court Painter to the Archbishop-Elector of Mainz and then to Cardinal Albrecht, Elector of Mainz; but (like Dürer) he seems to have had Lutheran sympathies and in 1526 he was in Frankfurt and 1527 in Halle, where he died. By then, he may have developed more extreme Protestant opinions. Unlike most of his German contemporaries he seems never to have designed any woodcuts or made etchings or engravings, and relatively few drawings by him have survived. The first datable work is the *Mocking of Christ* (formerly dated 1503, Munich) but his masterpiece is the huge *Schnitzaltar* or folding altar for a hospital for skin diseases in Isenheim (finished *c.*1515/16, Colmar, Musée). This old-fashioned REREDOS has carved and painted figures (by Niklaus Hagenauer, *c.*1505) as the basis (they were reinstalled in 1984), and it shows how completely his outlook differed from that of Dürer. Dürer attempted to learn Italian technical methods in order to penetrate into the serene world of the Italian and classical tradition; Grünewald seems to have been well acquainted with Renaissance ideas in, for example, perspective and the definition of a given space, but he uses these Renaissance technical means simply to heighten the emotional impact made by his essentially Late Gothic religious imagery. The terrible figure of the Crucified Christ in the *Isenheim Altar* is anti-Renaissance in its intensity, but the altarpiece as a whole combines a passionate expression of the Visions of St Bridget with an Italian (or rather Renaissance) feeling for drawing, light and colour. His few paintings are in Basle, Donaueschingen, Frankfurt (Städel), Freiburg i. B., Karlsruhe, Munich, Stuppach in Württemberg and Washington (NG).

GUARDI, Francesco (1712–93), was a Venetian VEDUTA painter, whose free handling and atmospheric effects now appeal more than CANALETTO's meticulous views of Venetian architecture, which were the more highly valued until the Impressionists taught us to see transient effects of light. Most of Guardi's views of Venice – he painted little else – were produced as souvenirs for tourists, and a contemporary diarist records him as a disciple of Canaletto, working for an Englishman. He worked with his elder brother, Giovanni Antonio (1699–1760), and collaborated with him on some religious pictures, but Francesco's activity as a figure painter has only recently been clarified by the discovery of such works as the altarpiece at Roncegno in Valsugana, of *c.*1777, and five large decorative panels (one in Hull). Two *Allegories* (Liverpool) may be by either Francesco or Giovanni Antonio and in this they represent a large class. The only certain (and very mediocre) work by Giovanni is *The Death of St Joseph* (E. Berlin): this was thought to have been destroyed in 1945, but reappeared (rather mysteriously) in 1965. Francesco's *vedute*, for which he got only about half Canaletto's prices, were produced in great numbers and have also been imitated ever since the 18th century, The vivacity and bravura of his little figures, and his pale, bright colour, may owe something to his brother-in-law, TIEPOLO. Most large galleries have works by him, but the following are dated sets of pictures: *Election of Doge Alvise IV Mocenigo*, 1763, based on engravings after drawings by Canaletto; in the Louvre (seven), Brussels, Grenoble, Nantes (two), and Toulouse; *Pius VI's Visit to Venice*, 1782, in Oxford and private collections; *Fêtes for the Archduke Paul of Russia and Maria Feodorowna* (*'I Conti del Nord'*), 1782, in Munich and private collections. Other dated pictures include *Faith* and *Hope*, in the Ringling Mus., Sarasota Fla: *Hope* was signed by Francesco and dated 1747 – but both signature and date disappeared during cleaning and doubts have been expressed, perhaps wrongly, concerning their authenticity. There are also two signed views of Venice of exceptional size, unique in his work, at Waddesdon, Bucks. (National Trust).

GUARIENTO di Arpo (recorded 1338–70), was the leading Paduan follower of GIOTTO. His frescoes (now partly destroyed) in the Eremitani Chapel in Padua show how Giotto's frescoes in the Arena Chapel there transformed the Veneto–Byzantine style. There is a signed Crucifix in Bassano (Mus.) which is also very Giottesque. In 1365–8 he worked on the huge fresco of the *Coronation of the Virgin* in the Doge's Palace, Venice, but it was badly damaged by fire and was replaced by Tintoretto's *Paradise*. Fragments are still in the Palace and other works are in Padua and Cambridge Mass. (Fogg), London (Courtauld Inst.), Mount Holyoke Coll. Mass., New York (Met. Mus.), Raleigh NC, and Vienna (Czernin, dated 1344).

GUERCINO (1591–1666) was born at Cento, near Bologna. His nickname means 'squint-eyed', his real name being Francesco Barbieri. He was first strongly influenced by Ludovico CARRACCI, but early overlaid his Carraccesque training with the strong chiaroscuro associated with the Caravaggesques, which he invested with a charm and softness unknown to its originator, though he later abandoned it for an even, characterless illumination more suitable for the didactic, mechanical Counter-Reformation altarpieces of his late Bolognese period. In 1621 he was in Rome working for Pope Gregory XV, and his masterpiece is the *Aurora* on the ceiling of the Casino Ludovisi, one of the finest Baroque illusionistic decorations. In the landscape parts he was helped by TASSI and the BRILS. He returned to Cento on the death of the Pope in 1623, and set up a studio, where, in 1629, he was visited by VELÁZQUEZ. After the death of RENI – who loathed him, and accused him of fishing in his ideas and copying his handling – he moved to Bologna *c.*1644, and took over the Reni religious picture factory. His account-book for the years 1629–66 (the year of his death) has survived, with details of his patrons and payments, and summaries of his earnings at the end of each year. There are examples in the Royal Coll. (rich in fine drawings), Bologna (Mus. and churches), Berlin, Birmingham, Brussels, Budapest, Cambridge (Fitzwm), Cento, Cleveland Ohio, Detroit, Dresden, Dublin, Edinburgh, Florence (Uffizi and Pitti), Genoa, Greenville SC, Hartford Conn., Leningrad, London (NG, Dulwich, Lancaster House and Wellington Mus.), Madrid (Prado), Milan (Brera), Minneapolis, Modena, Munich, Naples, New York (Met. Mus.), Ottawa, Oxford (Ch. Ch.), Parma, Paris (Louvre), Piacenza, Providence RI, Rome, Rouen, Sarasota Fla, Toulouse, Vaduz (Liechtenstein Coll.), Vicenza and Vienna.

GUIDI, Domenico (1625–1701), was an Italian sculptor, who worked in Naples, but fled after Masaniello's revolt (1647) and settled in Rome, where he worked with ALGARDI. He was never in the Bernini studio, but he worked with

RAGGI and FERRATA, and Bernini did employ him on one of the angels – the *Angel with the Lance* – on the Ponte S. Angelo, 1670–71. He was twice Principe of the Accademia di S. Luca and was a friend of LEBRUN, through whose influence he became an Honorary Member of the French Academy (1676), was appointed Sculptor to the King (1680) and executed *Fame* for Versailles (1686). This was not liked and was consigned to the gardens. In return for French favour he kept an eye on the young sculptors in the French Academy in Rome, and his rather crude style marks the transition to Late Baroque. He employed many assistants and produced numerous works, mostly in Italy but also in France (La Vrillière tomb, Châteauneuf-sur-Loire; model in Berlin) and Bratislava Cath. (1698, with Ferrata).

GUIDO da Siena was the all but mythical founder of the Sienese School. He signed a picture in the Pal. Pubblico, Siena, and dated it 1221, but there are other pictures, also in Siena, associable with him which are datable 1262 and in the 1270s. There are therefore two schools of thought: (i) that 1221 is correct, in spite of the evidently repainted surface of much of the picture. In this case (*a*) Siena precedes Florence in the development of Dugento painting, and (*b*) the other pictures mentioned are by Guido's followers, not by Guido himself. (ii) The other school (which contains few Sienese) holds that 1221 is an old tampering with an original date *c*.1261 – perhaps MCCXXI was altered from MCCLXI – and the other pictures are therefore his and contemporary. Recent X-rays give no grounds for believing this. Another theory, more reasonable, assumed that the picture was painted perhaps 1260/70, but was a copy and replacement of an older image, and the date 1221 was copied faithfully from this older image.

GUILD. In the Middle Ages tradesmen formed themselves into guilds for economic, religious and social purposes, and often several different trades would unite in a single guild; at Florence, for example, painters belonged to the Doctors' and Apothecaries' Guild (*Medici e Speziali*), St Luke being the patron saint of both artists and physicians, and painters, like druggists, being dependent on imported gums and pigments. Much of our knowledge of early painting comes from guild records, since all painters had to join unless they were in the personal service of the ruling prince. Only a Master could set up in business, take pupils and employ JOURNEYMEN, and to become a Master it was necessary to submit a masterpiece to the guild as evidence of competence. The Guild officers also supervised the number of apprentices and the conditions of work and often also materials. Some guilds bought in bulk for members, others allowed only panels stamped with their seal to be used for painting on. The tendency to uniformity of practice and to a 'trade-union' mentality led to painters like Leonardo and Michelangelo insisting on the freedom and originality of the artist and his status as a professional man and a scholar (and gentleman). This new conception of the inspired being, instead of the honest tradesman, led to the decline of the guilds and the rise of the ACADEMIES, which took over the all-important function of teaching. As one might expect, the power of the guilds lasted longer in N. Europe than in Italy. As late as 1655 the Guild at Malines made itself ridiculous by trying to prevent Jan Cossiers from completing a commission, painted in his Antwerp studio, *in situ* in Malines – on the grounds that he was not a resident and was therefore forbidden to work in their town. A similar situation arose in Toronto as recently as 1960, when the Brotherhood of Painters, Decorators and Paper-Hangers of America did their best to prevent the completion of a mural cycle by its designer and his assistants.

GUILLAUMIN, Armand (1841–1927), was one of the lesser lights of IMPRESSIONISM. From the age of 17, he was a poor clerk in the Paris municipality, painting in his spare time, and he met the other Impressionists after he met Cézanne in 1861 at the Académie Suisse. He exhibited at the SALON des Refusés, and in the Impressionist group exhibitions from 1874, except for 1876 and 1879. He was also a friend of Gauguin, van Gogh and Signac, and lived next door to Cézanne in Paris. In 1891 he won a lottery for 100,000 francs, which enabled him to paint at leisure. His understanding of Impressionism was more superficial, his pictures more loosely constructed than those of the major artists in the group despite his having worked alongside Cézanne. In his later years his colour tended towards the stronger effects of the Fauves. There are works in Amsterdam (van Gogh Mus.), Birmingham, Limoges, New York (Met. Mus.), Paris (Mus. d'Orsay), Washington (NG) and other collections where the Impressionists are well represented.

GÜNTHER, Ignaz (1725–75), was a German ROCOCO sculptor, mainly in painted wood. He was the son of a rural woodworker and sculptor and was trained in Munich from 1743, going to Vienna, where he won a prize at the Academy in 1753, before returning to Munich in 1754. His *Empress Kunigunde* (1762, Rott am Inn) and *Guardian Angel* (1763, Munich, Bürgersaal) are like sculptured versions of Tiepolo and Guardi respectively, full of cheerful Rococo gaiety, in pink, blue and gold, but the *Pietà* (1758, Kircheiselfing) and the one of 1774 (his last work) in the Cemetery Chapel at Nenningen show that the style was also capable of rendering deep and genuine religious emotion. Most of his works are in Munich and its neighbourhood, but there is one in Cleveland Ohio, and another in Detroit.

GUTTOSO, Renato (1912–87), was born in Sicily and was the leading Italian (or European) exponent of SOCIAL REALISM. He studied Law and began to paint only in 1931. His works attacked Fascism and the Nazis, especially in his bitter drawings, 'Gott mit uns', which arose from his service with the Communist Partisans 1943–5. He became a Communist Senator in 1974. His style was necessarily realistic, but the influence of Picasso (especially of *Guernica*) is evident. There are works in London (Tate), New York (M of MA), Prague and Sydney NSW. He designed the cover and illustrations for Elizabeth David's 'Italian Food' (Penguin Books, 1954).

GUYS, Constantin (1802–92), was a draughtsman who chronicled the wars and the fashions of Europe in the 19th century. He travelled enormously and took part in the Greek War of Independence and the Crimean War (which he reported as correspondent of the 'Illustrated London News'), but he is best known for his witty drawings of soldiers, horses and courtesans. Baudelaire wrote a long essay on him as *le peintre de la vie moderne*. Paris (Mus. Marmottan) has a series of drawings by him which belonged to Monet.

H

HAARLEM, C. van *see* CORNELISZ. van Haarlem.

HACKERT, Philipp (1737–1807), was a German landscape painter of the early Romantic period, whose chief claim to fame is the Life of him written by Goethe. He was trained in Berlin and travelled in Sweden and France before arriving in Rome in 1768 and Naples in 1770. He spent most of the rest of his life in Italy, becoming Court Painter in Naples in 1786. Goethe visited him in 1787, became his friend, and wrote a posthumous biography (1811). In 1777 he visited Sicily with Payne Knight, the English writer on the PICTURESQUE. There are works by him in the Royal Coll., Berlin, Glasgow and Vienna, and a large group in Attingham Park, Shropshire (National Trust) and other English country houses.

HAGUE SCHOOL, The. A group of Dutch landscape and peasant genre painters, active *c.*1860–90, the principal members of which were BOSBOOM, ISRAELS, the MARIS brothers, and MAUVE. They arose from the BARBIZON SCHOOL and influenced the GLASGOW one, as well as van GOGH in his early period, and SEGANTINI.

HALF-TONES are all those shades of tone between the lightest and the darkest. Thus, there is the illogical situation that a series of distinct tonal values can all be described as 'half-tones'. A half-tone block is used in process-engraving and obtains the tonal varieties by dots, as may be seen in a newspaper photograph.

HALS, Frans (1581/5–1666), was born in Antwerp of Flemish parents, but spent most of his life in Haarlem. He was a pupil of Karel van MANDER (1600–03), and entered the Haarlem Guild in 1610. His earliest dated work (*Jacobus Zaffus*, 1611, Haarlem) was painted in Haarlem, but by 1616 he was probably in Antwerp and may have been in contact with Rubens, who visited him in Haarlem in 1624. His great gift was for portraiture, and especially for catching the fleeting expression, and he is best known for the huge but lively groups of the companies of Archers and Musketeers raised during the wars against Spain, the earliest of which was painted in 1616. These DOELENSTUKKEN solve the difficult problem of composing a picture out of a number of figures all of whom demand the same prominence (since all the sitters subscribed), thus precluding the classical solution of subordinating the minor figures. Hals used a very virtuoso technique to enliven the whole picture surface and each portrait is caught in a fleeting gesture or expression. The whole is perhaps a little like a school photograph, but that is what the sitters wanted, and the very informality caused his work to be a great influence on Manet and the Impressionists. In his single figures his dazzling skill sometimes runs away with him – as in his most famous work, the *Laughing Cavalier* (1624, London, Wallace Coll.) – and he never quite achieved the sympathy and insight of his greater contemporary Rembrandt. During the years 1624–8 he was strongly influenced by the UTRECHT SCHOOL and adopted the type of genre portrait common to Terbrugghen and Honthorst. He used these largely for technical experiments, making his drawing even more simplified and his handling appear almost monochromatic and *alla prima*: he did in fact employ a very limited colour range and used greys a great deal, but all the bravura of the handling is a deal less spontaneous than it appears at first sight. After the Peace of 1648 the Military Companies were disbanded, but their place was taken, for artists, by the great group portraits commissioned by Regents and Governors of Charities. Hals painted several of these, particularly in his last years when he was destitute and dependent on charity for himself and his wife: these have greater feeling for character and greater humanity than many of his earlier groups, and they are also strangely closer to the late Rembrandt in handling.

Both his brothers were painters, but only Dirk (1591–1656) achieved any independence, though his subjects and style were similar to Frans's. All seven of his sons were also painters, though of little significance. His pupils probably included BROUWER, Jan MOLENAER and his wife Judith LEYSTER, A. van OSTADE, and WOUWERMAN, while Jan de BRAY owed much to Hals's development of the Regent groups. Hals had a large workshop, and as many as twenty versions of some works are known. The most important collection, including five Officer groups and three of Governors, is in the Hals Museum at Haarlem. Other works, by him or from his studio, include those in the Royal Coll. and in Amsterdam (Rijksmus.), Antwerp, Baltimore, Berlin, Birmingham (Barber Inst. *Man with a Skull, c.*1611), Boston (Mus.), Brussels, Cambridge (Fitzwm), Cape Town, Cassel, Chicago, Cincinnati, Cleveland Ohio, Cologne (Wallraf-Richartz Mus.), Denver, Detroit, Dresden, Dublin, Edinburgh (NG), Frankfurt (Städel), Glasgow (Burrell), The Hague, Hartford Conn., Houston Texas, Hull, Kansas City, London (NG and Kenwood), Los Angeles, Munich, New York (Met. Mus. and Frick Coll.), Ottawa, Paris (Louvre), Richmond Va, San Diego Cal., St Louis, Sarasota Fla (Ringling), Stockholm, Toledo Ohio, Toronto, Vienna, Washington (NG), Yale and elsewhere.

HAMEN y Leon, Juan van der (1596–1631), was the son of a Flemish painter of still-life, Jan van der Hamen, and a Spanish mother. He was a major painter of BODEGÓN still-life and genre in a style still markedly Flemish. He also painted religious subjects and portraits, but they were less successful. His *Cook* (*c.*1630, Amsterdam, Rijksmus.) is curiously like an AERTSEN or a BUECKELAER, though he presumably never saw one. Other works are in Brussels, Cleveland Ohio, Houston Texas, Madrid (Prado), Washington (NG, a still-life of 1627) and Williamstown Mass.

HAMILTON, Gavin (1723–98), was a Scots laird who graduated at Glasgow and then went to Rome and trained as a painter in the 1740s. After practising as a portrait painter in Britain in 1753/4 he returned to Rome for good and became well-known as a dealer and antiquary and as a member of the NEOCLASSIC school centred round Mengs and Winckelmann. He was painting Poussinesque historical compositions by 1758 and is thus one of the original exponents of the doctrine preached by DAVID some fifteen years later. He employed the engraver Cunego to make his compositions more widely known (as Raphael had employed Marcantonio), and he also obtained many commissions for vast historical compositions as *douceurs* in connection with his activities as an antique dealer. There are pastels by him in Montpellier and paintings in Edinburgh (NG), Glasgow (Univ. and Gall.), London (Tate and Drury Lane Theatre) and Yale (CBA), but his most influential works are in the Villa Borghese and Museo di Roma in Rome.

HAMILTON, Gawen (1698–1737), not to be confused with Gavin Hamilton (no relation), was a painter of small portrait groups. He was a contemporary of Hogarth, and, in some respects, Vertue considered him superior. His *Artists' Club, 1735* (London, NPG) or his conversation pieces in London (Tate) or Enfield Mus., Middx, are typical. Glasgow and Yale (CBA) have works by both Gavin and Gawen, making the difference easier to see.

HAMILTON, Richard (*b.*1922), is a British painter who was one of the founders of POP ART. His *Just what is it that makes Today's Homes so different, so appealing?* (1956), a collage assembling images from popular culture, was one of the key works of its early development.

HANDLING (Fr. *facture*; Ital. *fattura*) is the name given to the most personal part of a work of art, the actual execution. The general features of composition, of subject, of drawing or colour, can be used to assign a picture or other work to a given School or period; the handling of the paint, pencil, clay or other medium is personal to the artist and is what the forger tries hardest to imitate. Just as a man's signature is highly personal and executed without thinking about it, so a painter will handle shapes and planes and even come to see them in terms of his own BRUSHWORK.

HARD-EDGE PAINTING. A form of abstract painting based on geometrical forms planned in advance, with sharply defined edges, and therefore unlike the spontaneity and blurring of forms in TACHISME.

HARNETT, William Michael (1848–92), was the leading American painter of *trompe l'oeil* ILLUSIONISM. He was born in Ireland, but brought up in Philadelphia, where Raphaelle PEALE (*d.*1825) had founded a tradition of realistic still-life painting. In 1871 Harnett went to New York, and from 1875 began painting highly illusionistic still-lifes: in 1876 he returned to Philadelphia and became friendly with another still-life painter, J. F. PETO, whose works have often been confused with Harnett's, not always innocently. He went to Europe in 1880 and stayed, mostly in Paris, until 1886, but on his return ill-health prevented him from working much and he died young. His works typically contain a letter-rack, with letters, newspaper cuttings, pipes and perhaps trophies of the chase. Examples are in Boston, Chicago, Mount Holyoke College Mass., New York (Met. Mus.), San Francisco and Yale, and there is also one (of 1889) in Sheffield.

HARPIGNIES, Henri (1819–1916), was a French landscape painter who was principally influenced by Corot and the BARBIZON painters. In his old age his failing eyesight forced him to generalize in a manner not unlike the late Corot. He was popular in England and America and there are four pictures by him in the NG, London, and in many US museums.

HARTUNG, Hans (1904–89), was born in Leipzig and began as an Expressionist, but became an abstract painter about 1922; in 1925 he saw works by KANDINSKY, which confirmed him in this trend. He settled in Paris in 1935, fought in the Foreign Legion and lost a leg at Belfort (1944), and became a French citizen. His works are a mesh of calligraphic brushstrokes, usually dark on a light ground, which an admirer has described as 'a blend of the exacting discipline that governs French art with what is best and most distinguished in Germanic poetry'. The effect is often similar to the works of KLINE, the American, for whom no such background has been claimed. His paintings have no titles, but are distinguished by numbers, thus: *T54–16* means Toile (i.e. canvas), 1954, number sixteen. There are examples in Basle,

Birmingham, Grenoble, London (Tate), New York (Guggenheim), Paris (Mus. d'Art Moderne) and Philadelphia.

HASSAM, Childe (1859–1935), was an American Impressionist, particularly influenced by MONET. He studied in Paris 1883–6 and was represented in the ARMORY Show of 1913. There are works by him in many American museums.

HATCHING is shading carried out in parallel lines; cross-hatching is shading in two layers of parallel lines, one layer crossing the other at an angle.

HAYDON, Benjamin Robert (1786–1846), British historical painter. Like BARRY, Haydon attempted to be a pure HISTORY painter in the Grand Style adumbrated by Reynolds in his 'Discourses'. His life was a tragi-comedy of high endeavour and High Art which ended in imprisonment for debt, and suicide. His tireless propaganda forced the Government and nobility to accept the novel idea that the patronage of the arts was socially desirable, and he was partly responsible for the Government's purchase of the Elgin Marbles in 1816. There are pictures in Exeter (*Marcus Curtius*, 1842), London (NPG and Tate) and Yale (CBA), but his best memorial is his 'Autobiography and Memoirs' (first published 1853).

HAYEZ, Francesco (1791–1882), was born in Venice of a Venetian mother and a French father. Poverty caused him to be apprenticed to a restorer, but he began to study painting in 1798. In 1809 he won a three-year scholarship to Rome, under the patronage of CANOVA and Count Cicognara, a noted art-lover who for years was his chief patron. In Rome he came in contact with the NAZARENES and was friendly with INGRES, who was the chief influence on his style, although he is regarded as the leading Romantic painter of Italy, mainly on account of his subjects. In 1814, after a visit to Florence following an attack on him by a jealous lover, he won a scholarship to Naples, but the fall of Napoleonic power in 1815 ended it. He returned to Rome and, with Cicognara's help, got commissions for decorative paintings, including his first frescoes (1817) in the Vatican, paid for by Canova. Later, he also painted frescoes in the Royal Palace, Milan, but they were destroyed in 1943. In 1820 and 1821 he visited Milan, the headquarters of Italian literary Romanticism, and settled there in 1822, becoming a professor at the Brera in 1850 and Director in 1860. He was knighted by the Austrian Emperor and visited Vienna in 1835 and again in 1852, when he completed his portrait of Ferdinand I. His knowledge of contemporary French Romantic painting must have been derived from engravings and photographs, as he does not seem ever to have visited France. By far his most famous picture, *The Kiss* (1859, Milan, Brera), is an example of the costume history and biblical subjects which owe much to the influence of DELACROIX and DELAROCHE (e.g. *The Last Moments of Doge Faliero*, 1867, Brera). His semi-classical nudes and 'fancy' heads, curiously like those of Etty, are halfway between Ingres and Delacroix, but his masterly portraits, especially of aristocratic ladies, can hold their own with Ingres himself. He painted almost all the eminent men of his time, including the writers Manzoni and Massimo d'Azeglio, the statesman Cavour (1864, from a death-mask), the composer Rossini and many others. In his old age he exploited in his self-portraits his resemblance to Titian. The largest collection of his works is in the Brera, Milan, and others are in Berlin, Florence (Uffizi), Naples, Rome (Gall. d'Arte Mod.), Turin and Vienna.

HAYMAN, Francis (1708–76), was a scene-painter and illustrator who became one of the Founder-Members of the RA in 1768 and was later its first Librarian. He painted several small portrait groups which influenced Gainsborough (who may have worked under him), but his most famous pictures were the decorations for the fashionable Vauxhall Gardens, begun in the mid-1740s. Some of these survive in the Tate and V&A, London, and show the strong French element in his style, perhaps derived from his friend GRAVELOT: indeed the *Quadrille* (Birmingham) was engraved in 1743 as 'by Hayman, designed by Gravelot'. In 1748 he went to Paris with HOGARTH, and with him was 'clapt into the Bastille' as a spy. Like HIGHMORE he illustrated the novels of Samuel Richardson – Southampton has a scene from 'Clarissa Harlowe' – while *The Painter's Studio* and *Lord Clive . . . Nawab of Bengal*, the *modello* for a Vauxhall piece (London, NPG) and his *Finding of Moses* (1746, London, Coram Fdn, formerly Foundling Hospital) are other aspects of his work. Other pictures are in his native Exeter and Yale (CBA). In 1760 he led the Society of Artists in the negotiations which resulted in the foundation of the Royal Academy.

HECKEL, Erich (1883–1970), studied architecture in Dresden in 1904, where he met KIRCHNER and SCHMIDT-ROTTLUFF, with whom he founded the BRÜCKE in 1905. A trip to Italy in 1909 was a great influence on him, and so were FEININGER, MACKE and MARC, whom he met in 1912 and who introduced him to the DELAUNAY form of Cubism. He served in the German medical corps, 1915–18, and met Ensor and Beckmann in Belgium. From 1918 he lived in Berlin until he fled to Switzerland in 1944, after no fewer than 729 of his works had been removed from German museums. From 1949 to 1956 he taught at Karlsruhe, but finally returned to Switzerland. There are pictures by him in Berlin, Cardiff, Cologne, Detroit, Hagen, Harvard University and New York (M of MA).

HEDA, Willem Claesz. (1594–1680), was a Dutch painter of still-life, of the type known as monochrome BREAKFAST PIECES, which were almost confined to Haarlem. His contemporary Pieter CLAESZ. was the other major exponent of the genre, but Heda's later style is closer to KALF. He is documented in the Hague Guild from 1631. There are examples in Amsterdam (Rijksmus.), Boston, Dresden, Dublin, Madrid, Munich, Paris (Louvre), Vienna and elsewhere. His son, Gerrit Heda (*c.*1620–before 1702) was also a still-life painter in a similar vein. There are works in Amsterdam (Rijksmus.), London (NG), Munich, Oxford, Rotterdam and elsewhere.

HEEM, Jan Davidsz. de (1606–83/4), worked at Utrecht and Leyden before the religious troubles drove him to settle at Antwerp in 1636 (although Sandrart says that he went there to obtain rare fruits in good condition). Usually his pictures contain a profusion of flowers, fruit, oysters etc. with elaborate goblets, but in Leyden he painted some VANITAS subjects (e.g. The Hague) and he also painted occasional 'Melancholia' still-lifes, with a figure surrounded by books, papers and pictures. He was in the Utrecht Guild in 1669, but returned to Antwerp in 1672 and remained there until his death. He was influenced by CLAESZ. and HEDA, but in Antwerp he inclined to the richness of Flemish Baroque (e.g. London, Wallace Coll.). He was the most brilliant still-life painter in a family of them: his father David (1570–1632) worked in Utrecht, and his own son Cornelis (1631–95) worked in Leyden and Antwerp.

There are works by one or other of them in Amsterdam (Rijksmus.), Berlin, Birmingham (Barber Inst.), Brussels, Cambridge (Fitzwm), Cheltenham, Dresden, Dublin, Edinburgh (NG), Glasgow (Gall. and Burrell Coll.), London (NG and Wallace Coll.), Los Angeles, Madrid, Manchester, Melbourne, Munich, New York (Met. Mus.), Oberlin Ohio, Ottawa, Oxford, Paris, Philadelphia (Johnson), Southampton, Stockholm, Toledo Ohio, Utrecht, Vienna (Akad. and K-H Mus.) and Washington (NG).

HEEMSKERCK, Maerten van (1498–1574), worked with SCOREL in Haarlem 1527–9 and learned most of the Italianate manner from him before going to Italy in 1532 himself. Before he left he gave his *St Luke painting the Virgin* to the Haarlem Guild (now in Haarlem, Hals Mus.); this is almost a parody of the Italian manner, as conceived by a Northerner at second hand. In Rome he made a large number of drawings (1532–5) of the antiquities and works of art, and two of his sketchbooks (Berlin) are invaluable evidence for the monuments of antiquity as they existed in the 16th century, as well as for such things as the building of New St Peter's. He settled in Haarlem in 1537 and worked there for the rest of his life except for a flight to Amsterdam (1572–3) while the Spaniards were besieging Haarlem. He painted a number of fine portraits, like those of Scorel, as well as Italianate religious pictures. There are works by him in Amsterdam (Rijksmus.), Barnard Castle (Bowes Mus.), Berlin, Brussels, Cambridge (Fitzwm, *Self-Portrait with the Colosseum in the Background*), Cassel, Ghent, The Hague, Lille, Linköping Cath. Sweden, New York (Met. Mus.), as well as in Haarlem and elsewhere.

HELST, Bartholomeus van der (1613–70), was a fashionable Amsterdam portrait painter and one of the founders of the Guild there (1653). He was probably a pupil of ELIAS and was influenced by both Hals and Rembrandt, some of whose business he may have taken: in turn, he may have influenced BOL and FLINCK. There are works by him in Amsterdam, Berlin, Brussels, Cambridge (Fitzwm), Detroit, Dublin, The Hague, London (NG and Wallace Coll.), New York, Paris, Philadelphia (Johnson), Rotterdam, Vienna and elsewhere.

HENRI, Robert (1865–1929), was the founder of the Group of Eight (*see* ASHCAN SCHOOL) and an important teacher. He was trained in Philadelphia and in Paris, and returned to Philadelphia to teach in 1891. He revisited Paris in 1894–5 and settled in New York in 1899. He was inspired by the Realism of COURBET, and by Hals and Velázquez, whom he studied on frequent visits to Spain and Holland. He is represented in Boston, New York (Whitney) and other American museums.

HEPWORTH, Barbara (1903–75), was one of the first British abstract sculptors. For most of her life she was a direct carver in wood and stone, but in her last years she also used bronze, usually cast from forms at least partly carved in plastic rather than entirely modelled. She was in Italy in 1924–5, but from 1931, under the influence of Ben NICHOLSON (to whom she was married for eighteen years), she became more interested in abstract form and began piercing holes in her sculpture. She was trained in Leeds, like Henry MOORE, whom she also knew in London, and was influenced by French sculptors like BRANCUSI. In 1939 she settled in St Ives, Cornwall, where her studio is now a museum, and began a series of abstract works in which the large masses are set off by string or wire, giving an effect like a musical instrument. She made a *Madonna* for the church in St Ives, as a memorial to her son, killed in 1953 while serving with the Royal Air Force. There is also a very large group on a hillside in Cornwall. Her works can be seen in the open air at Harlow New Town Essex, Hatfield Herts., and the Royal Festival Hall and Dulwich Park in London. Two big works of 1963 are at State House, London, and the United Nations Building, New York. Other works are in Aberdeen, Birmingham, Bolton, Bristol, Cardiff, Coventry, Leeds, London (V&A and Tate), Manchester, Wakefield and several American and European museums.

HERM, Term. A head, or bust-length statue, set on a quadrangular pillar tapering towards the base. They were common in Antiquity and were revived in the Baroque period (e.g. at Versailles).

HERMETIC CUBISM. A phrase sometimes used to describe the 'difficult' (or hermetic) Cubism of Braque and Picasso around 1910.

HERRING, John F. (1795–1865), was a stage-coachman who turned animal painter. After driving local coaches for four years he drove the 'High Flyer' between London and York until he devoted himself entirely to painting racehorses. He worked for many years in the Doncaster district and painted thirty-three successive winners of the St Leger. From 1833 he worked in London. He exhibited at the RA from 1818 to 1846 and worked for George IV and Queen Victoria. His works were very popular in the United States through engravings: there are paintings in London (Tate) and Yale (CBA). His son, John Frederick Herring the Younger, worked in the same style and died as recently as 1907.

HEYDEN, Jan van der (1637–1712), was the first painter in Amsterdam to paint townscapes, although this was being done in Haarlem by the BERCKHEYDES. Van der Heyden began as a still-life painter and at the end of his life he took it up again, but his architectural subjects date mostly from the 1660s. He painted walls and masonry with minute skill, but his topography is often wilful. His pictures are often said to have figures by A. van de VELDE – who died in 1672. From *c.*1670 he designed fire-engines and hoses and street lighting, both of which activities made him very rich: his 'Fire-engine Book', with etchings by him, was published in 1690. There are works in the Royal Coll., in Amsterdam, Barnsley, Berlin, Cambridge (Fitzwm), Dresden, Edinburgh, Florence (Uffizi: *Amsterdam Town Hall*, 1667, which has been in Florence since at least 1672), Glasgow, The Hague, Hamburg, London (NG, Wallace Coll., Wellington Mus. and Dulwich), New York (Met. Mus.), Paris (Louvre), Philadelphia, Rotterdam, Vaduz (Liechtenstein Coll.), Vienna, Waddesdon Bucks. (National Trust), Washington (NG) and elsewhere.

HICKS, Edward (1780–1849), was a famous Quaker preacher, who was also a coach-maker, sign-writer, and the most famous 19th-century American PRIMITIVE. His *Peaceable Kingdom* exists in more than sixty versions, all based on Isaiah xi, 6–9: 'and the leopard shall lie down with the kid . . .', often with William Penn and the Indians in the background: ironically, it arose from a bitter schism among the Quakers themselves. Many American museums – e.g. Brooklyn, Buffalo, Newark, New York (Met. Mus.) – have examples, and the composition has worldwide coverage as a Christmas card. He painted about 122 pictures in all.

HIGHMORE, Joseph (1692–1780), was an English portrait painter, contemporary with HOGARTH, who retired in 1761, when Reynolds had established himself. Apart from portraits Highmore also painted some illustrations to literature, the most famous being a Hogarth-like series from 'Pamela', by his friend

Samuel Richardson (there are twelve in all, completed by 1745 and now divided between Cambridge (Fitzwm), London (Tate and V&A), and Melbourne). In 1732 he travelled in the Low Countries to study Rubens and van Dyck, and in 1734 he visited Paris: the French influence is very clear in the *Pamela* series, but it is important to remember the influence of Richardson on French writers, and especially on the *comédie larmoyante* (*see* GREUZE). In 1746, inspired by Hogarth, he presented a history picture to the Foundling Hospital, where it still hangs. He was originally bred to the law, and in his later years published various writings on art. Other pictures are in the Royal Coll., Barnsley, Cardiff, Hull, Liverpool, London (NPG, Tate and Dulwich), Oxford, Wolverhampton (a very large family group of 1736) and Yale (CBA).

HILDEBRAND, Adolf von (1847–1921), was the leading German sculptor of the classic tradition in the late 19th century. He went to Rome in 1867 and met the writer Konrad Fiedler, as well as the painter MARÉES, who had a decisive effect upon him. In 1872 he returned to Italy for five years, and in 1873 helped Marées on his frescoes in Naples. His most famous work is the Wittelsbach Fountain in Munich, begun in 1891; but he is probably better known as a writer, whose book on aesthetics, 'Problem der Form', first published in 1893, had reached its ninth edition by 1914. This was written under the influence of Fiedler, but became one of the most famous books on aesthetics ever published in Germany. Hildebrand's realist strain is seen in his portrait busts and monuments, which include one to Brahms. There are works in Berlin, Dresden, Frankfurt, Munich and other German galleries.

HILLIARD (Hillyarde), Nicholas (*c.*1547–1619), is the first great British artist about whom we know a few details. He was the son of a goldsmith and was himself trained in, and practised, that art although he was painting miniature portraits by 1560. He may have been in Geneva (aged 10) in 1557, as one of a family of Protestant refugees, at about the same time as a goldsmith from Rouen called OLIVER. He is recorded in the Goldsmiths Company in 1570 and in the same year he painted his first dated portrait of Queen Elizabeth, to whom he had probably already been appointed Limner and Goldsmith: in the latter capacity he designed a Great Seal for her. He was certainly in France between 1576 and 1578 and was probably the Nicholas Belliart who was attached to the Duc d'Alençon, the Queen's suitor. About 1600 he composed a treatise 'The Arte of Limning' (first published in 1912), in the course of which he records conversations with the Queen and, in particular, their agreement that portrait-painting should be done without shadows: '... best in plaine lines without shadowing, for the lyne without shadows showeth all to a good jugment, but the shadowe without lyne showeth nothing'. About this time he was in financial difficulties, perhaps partly caused by his old-fashioned insistence on line without modelling, for his pupil Isaac Oliver was by now a serious rival to him. In 1617 he was actually imprisoned, although it seems to have been as a surety for someone else. His miniatures are always intended to be thought of as jewels, to be held in the hand and in this his goldsmith's training was no doubt decisive. There are no known oil-paintings which can be attributed to him with any certainty, but a small group of portraits shows his style: the so-called 'Pelican' portrait of Queen Elizabeth (Liverpool) and the 'Ermine' portrait at Hatfield House are the best-known. The 'Ermine' is now also attributed to W. Segar, and one in a private collection is thought to be by Hilliard, but derived from the drawing by ZUCCARO. There are works by him in the Royal Coll., and in Birmingham (Barber Inst.), Cambridge (Fitzwm), Cleveland Ohio, The Hague, London (NPG, V&A and Nat. Marit. Mus.), New York (Met. Mus.), Oxford (Bodleian Library) and Yale (CBA). His son, Laurence Hilliard (1582–after 1640), was also a limner and is represented in London (V&A).

HISTORY PAINTING, in fully developed academic theory, is the noblest form of art, and consists of generalized representations of the passions and intellect as symbolized in classical history or mythology or in subjects taken from Christian iconography. The word 'history' was usually meant to refer to ancient history and mythology, but the Christian story was admitted as conformable to the highest flights of imaginative art. Modern history, and particularly subjects which involved modern dress instead of nondescript drapery, was admitted only in the late 18th century in England (WEST's *Death of Wolfe* (1771) is one of the classic examples), and even later elsewhere. The theory of history painting was pushed to extremes by men like BARRY and HAYDON, who died of it, but it was also truly responsible for some of the greatest works of such masters as Raphael, Poussin and David.

HITCHENS, Ivon (1893–1979), was the son of a painter, and studied at the Royal Academy Schools. In 1940 he went to live in Sussex, and his main subject matter was the richly wooded landscapes around his home, expressed in non-naturalistic, almost abstract and *tachiste* terms, usually in long rectangular format. He also painted flowers and figures; these culminated in his enormous (69 × 20 ft) murals for the English Folk Song and Dance Society in London (1954), and for the University of Sussex (1963). There are characteristic works in Aberdeen, Birmingham, Cambridge (Fitzwm), Cardiff, Edinburgh (M of MA), London (Tate and V&A), Nottingham, and also in Adelaide, Buffalo NY, Gothenburg, Melbourne, Montreal, Oslo, Ottawa, Paris (Mus. d'Art Moderne), Seattle, Toledo Ohio, Toronto and Wellington NZ.

HOBBEMA, Meindert (1638–1709), was the friend and pupil of Jacob van RUISDAEL, whom he met in Amsterdam before 1659. His earliest pictures are dated 1658 (Detroit) and 1659 (Frankfurt and Grenoble) and not only are some of his works virtually indistinguishable from Ruisdael's but they also occasionally painted the same views, e.g. the pair in Amsterdam and Washington. In 1668 he married the maid of the Burgomaster of Amsterdam, and through the influence of one of his wife's fellow-servants he obtained a minor post in the Excise, and from then onwards he seems to have painted much less. It used to be thought that his most famous work, the *Avenue at Middelharnis* (London, NG), was dated 1669 and was his swan-song, but the date is now read as 1689, and there are pictures of 1671 (also in the NG) and 1689 (private collection), so he presumably continued to paint but omitted to date his pictures. In any case it is difficult to understand how a man of such gifts could bring himself to stop painting and spend forty years gauging wine in casks. Unlike Ruisdael he painted quiet landscapes, usually with watermills, with none of the romantic quality or the splendid clouds and skies of Ruisdael's pictures. Although his work was little prized in his own time it was very much sought after by English collectors of the 18th and 19th centuries and exerted great influence on English landscape painting: for this reason the best collection of his works is in London (NG). There are others in the Royal Coll. and Amsterdam, Antwerp, Berlin, Brussels, Cambridge (Fitzwm), Cape Town, Chicago, Cincinnati, Detroit, Dublin, Edinburgh (NG), Frankfurt (Städel), Glasgow, The Hague, Indianapolis, London (Wallace Coll. and Dulwich), Malibu Cal. (Getty), Minneapolis, Munich, New York (Frick Coll., Historical Soc. and Met. Mus.), Ottawa, Paris, Philadelphia, Rotterdam, Toledo Ohio, Washington and Vienna.

HOCKNEY, David (*b*.1937), is a British painter, etcher and film-maker who began in the POP ART fold, but has developed into a straightforward representational artist, exploiting, in particular, strong, light colours, often using flat acrylic paint. His subjects include moving and reflecting surfaces – water, glass, tiles – and, above all, portraits: frequently double ones in which the sitters do not seem to have been introduced to each other (London, Tate). He has illustrated Grimm's *Fairy Tales* (1969), designed a setting for Stravinsky's 'Rake's Progress' (1975), and has also produced suites of etchings.

HODGKINS, Frances (1869–1947), was a New Zealand painter who lived, from 1901 onwards, mainly in England and France. In Paris she taught watercolour painting at the Académie Colarossi from 1907, and later in her own school, becoming known as a *plein-air* painter. She probably met Emily CARR about 1910/11. She returned to Australia and New Zealand to exhibit in 1906 (unhappily) and 1912–13 (very successfully). In 1914 she moved from Paris to Cornwall, returning for a time to Paris in 1920, when her style was transformed from a sub-Impressionist one with overtones of Bonnard and Vuillard to one which, particularly after 1930, shows a number of influences, some transitory, from Gauguin, Matisse and Chagall, as well as lesser figures such as Dufy and Laurencin. Her subjects are quietly domestic; figures, occasional portraits, flowers and landscapes, at first in watercolour, but after 1914 in oils, and lyrical in colour. There are works in New Zealand (Auckland, Christchurch and Dunedin) and in Bristol, London (Tate), Temple Newsam nr Leeds and elsewhere.

HODLER, Ferdinand (1853–1918), was, with BÖCKLIN, the leading Swiss painter of the 19th century. He visited Madrid (1878–9) and Paris (1891), where he was influenced by Corot and Courbet, but he ultimately developed a very linear, flat style, much closer to PUVIS de Chavannes. About 1891 he was much influenced by Symbolist ideas, by ART NOUVEAU, and, like many others, by the Rosicrucians. From the mid-1890s he concentrated on large-scale historical and mythological works such as those for Jena Univ. (1907) and Hanover Town Hall (1910). There are works by him in Zurich and other Swiss and German museums.

HOFER, Carl (1878–1955), is usually classed as a German Expressionist, but his art is profoundly French in its adherence to classical ideals. He first went to Paris in 1900, after which he worked for two years under THOMA in Karlsruhe and then spent five years in Rome (1903–8). He returned to Paris, 1908–13, except for two trips to India, and was interned in France 1914–17. He became a professor in Berlin in 1918, was dismissed in 1933, and reinstated in 1945. An air-raid in 1943 destroyed many of his works, and he set himself to paint some again from memory. His sober classicism, influenced by MARÉES, and above all by CÉZANNE, is very similar to that of DERAIN. He wrote an autobiography and also a book, published posthumously, on discipline in art. There are works in Cologne, Detroit and Harvard (Univ.).

HOFMANN, Hans (1880–1966), was born in Bavaria. He studied in Munich, and in Paris in 1904–14, partly in the PURRMANN and MATISSE circle. He taught in Munich from 1915 until he emigrated to America in 1932. In New York he became an influential teacher and exponent first of Expressionist and Fauve ideas, then of abstract painting which changed, during the 1950s, into vigorous ABSTRACT IMPRESSIONISM, in which he used dribbles and splodges of paint to create strongly coloured and free patterns of explosive force. He was a formative influence on POLLOCK, as in *Spring* (1940, New York, M of M A).

HOGARTH, William (1697–1764), was apprenticed to a goldsmith, but began engraving *c.*1720. He studied at the St Martin's Lane Academy in London, but never achieved any real proficiency as a draughtsman: he was, however, well aware of the need for academic training and later promoted another Academy in St Martin's Lane which was the principal forerunner of the Royal Academy. He began painting small groups and conversation pieces and by 1729, when he married THORNHILL's daughter, he had begun to make a name – VERTUE in 1730 records: 'The daily success of Mr Hogarth in painting small family peices & Conversations with so much Air and agreeableness Causes him to be much followed & esteemed whereby he has much imployment & like to be a master of great reputation in that way'. The *Beggar's Opera* (several versions exist, one in the Tate Gall.) was perhaps the most successful of these, and it probably formed the transition from portraiture to his best-known works, the moralities. Hogarth himself said, 'I then married, and commenced painter of small conversation pieces, from twelve to fifteen inches high. This having novelty, succeeded for a few years . . . I therefore turned my thoughts to a still more novel mode, *viz.* painting and engraving modern moral subjects, a field not broken up in any country or any age . . . I therefore wished to compose pictures on canvas, similar to representations on the stage; and farther hope, that they will be tried by the same test, and criticised by the same criterion . . . I have endeavoured to treat my subjects as a dramatic writer; my picture is my stage, and men and women my players, who by means of certain actions and gestures, are to exhibit *a dumb show*.' The first of these moral subjects was the *Harlot's Progress*, showing the downfall of a country girl at the hands of the wicked Londoners (several of whom were recognizable). The comparison with 'Moll Flanders' shows how close Hogarth's links were with contemporary literature. The original paintings were probably executed in 1731/2 (they are now lost) but the popularity of the series depended on the engravings made from them in 1732; this was so great that they were frequently pirated, and Hogarth ultimately got a Copyright Act passed in 1735 which was of great benefit to artists and engravers alike. The next series was the *Rake's Progress* (1735, paintings in the Soane Mus., London) and it was followed by the *Marriage à la Mode* (1743–5, London, N G) and the *Election* (1754, Soane Mus.). He visited Paris in 1743 and again in 1748 and was strongly influenced by French Rococo, but the influence was perhaps strongest early in his career, e.g. in *Before* and *After* (Cambridge, Fitzwm), which is also a *sujet galant*, and other pictures of the 1730s. He was in fact rabidly anti-French (his chief characteristics seem to have been pugnacity and self-assertion) and his xenophobia was not helped by the fact that, in 1748, in company with HAYMAN, he was arrested as a spy for drawing the fortifications at Calais, celebrated in his picture *O the Roast Beef of Old England!* (*'Calais Gate'*) (1748, London, NG). In 1741 he even signed a portrait (London, Dulwich) 'Wm Hogarth Anglus', perhaps as a protest against J. van LOO. His efforts in the Italian Grand Manner had little success, although the *Pool of Bethesda* and *Good Samaritan* (1735–6, London, St Bartholomew's Hospital) were certainly better received than the *Sigismunda* (1759, Tate Gall.) which he painted to show that he could treat a tragic subject in as grand a manner as a Bolognese picture of the same subject which was sold at auction for a price higher than Hogarth thought right. This was painted at the end of his life and was savagely attacked by John Wilkes who had recently been roughly handled by Hogarth in an engraving.

His fame was, and is, most firmly based on the engravings of his moral subjects, which have to be read, detail by telling detail, rather than contemplated as works of art; nevertheless, all through his life he was capable of pieces of superb painting. He continued to paint portraits, the most successful being those of sitters of his own type, e.g. the *Captain Coram* (1740, Coram Fdn, London). This was painted for the Foundling Hospital which Coram founded and of which Hogarth himself became a Governor. Not only is the portrait itself important as an adaptation of the Baroque state portrait to a middle-class sitter, but Hogarth managed to persuade a number of other artists, including HAYMAN and HIGHMORE, to join with him in presenting a history picture each to the Foundling Hospital. These were shown to the public for the benefit of the Hospital, but the Exhibition was so popular that it led ultimately to the establishment of public exhibitions in London and thus to the Royal Academy. Hogarth also wrote a treatise on aesthetics, 'The Analysis of Beauty' (1753), and an Autobiography, the MS of which is in the BM, and which was printed in J. Burke's edition of the 'Analysis' (Oxford, 1955). There are pictures in the Royal Coll. and in Aberdeen, Birmingham, Bristol (St Nicholas Church Mus.), Buffalo, Detroit, Dublin, Edinburgh (NG), Glasgow (Burrell), Liverpool, London (NG, NPG, Tate, Nat. Marit. Mus., Dulwich, Soane Mus. and Coram Fdn, i.e. the Foundling Hospital), Manchester, Minneapolis, Montreal, New York (Met. Mus. and Frick Coll.), Northampton Mass., Oberlin Coll. Ohio, Ottawa, Philadelphia, St Louis, Toledo Ohio, Vancouver, Washington (Corcoran and Nat. Coll.), Worcester Mass., Yale (CBA) and in many English provincial galleries.

HOLBEIN, Hans the Elder (*c.*1465–1524), was a Late Gothic painter with a large workshop in Augsburg in which his sons Hans the Younger and Ambrosius worked. By 1514 the shop had broken up, and Holbein senior moved to Isenheim probably by 1517. His major work was the *St Sebastian Altar* (1515/17, Munich) but there is also a *Death of the Virgin*, signed and dated 149–, in Budapest, and a sketchbook, mostly of portrait drawings, in Berlin, which includes a double portrait of his two sons.

HOLBEIN, Hans the Younger (1497/8–1543), was probably the most accomplished and penetratingly realist portrait painter the North has produced, He began in his father's shop, but by 1515 he and his brother were in Basle, working for a local painter. He was soon working for publishers, notably for Froben, through whom he probably met Erasmus about 1515/16. His early portraits (*Burgomaster Meyer* and his *Wife*, 1516, and *Bonifacius Amerbach*, 1519, Basle) show his gift for characterization, and his religious works (*Dead*

Christ, 1521, Basle; *Solothurn Madonna*, 1522, Solothurn) show him either grimly realist or decorative rather than devotional. In 1517 he left Basle, visited Lucerne, and probably went to Italy; he returned to Basle after the death of his brother in 1519, became a citizen in 1520, and married. He was commissioned to paint the Council Chamber with frescoes of justice scenes, civic virtues, and law-givers in 1521, but the work was interrupted by the disturbances connected with the Reformation and by his absences (he was in France 1523/4) and was not finished until 1530. He illustrated the Luther Bible and designed the *Dance of Death*, 1523/4 and the *Alphabet of Death*, 1524. Both these add the bitterness of the Peasants' War to the medieval theme, and the Dance is dropped in favour of Death depicted as the harvester of every class of man. The *Dance of Death* was published in Lyons (1538), and ran to ten editions in twelve years. In 1526, however, he began a large *Madonna, with Burgomeister Meyer and his Family*, perhaps the closest Northern parallel to the great Italian High Renaissance altarpieces. After his return from England in 1528 the painting was altered to include a posthumous portrait of Meyer's first wife, and, to some extent, became a symbol of Meyer's position as leader of the Catholic party in Basle, where, in 1529, the Town Council ordered the removal of all religious pictures from the cathedral. In the 19th century there was a dispute over the claims of the two versions (Darmstadt and Dresden) of this *Madonna*, but it is now clear that the Darmstadt version is the original.

His international reputation as a portraitist was established by three portraits of Erasmus in 1523 which were strongly influenced by MASSYS. In 1526, possibly because the continued religious troubles were affecting his business, he left Basle and travelled via Antwerp (where he met Massys) to London, bringing introductions from Erasmus to Sir Thomas More and Archbishop Warham. He stayed for 18 months, during which time he painted the large group of the More family (now known only from copies and sketches) and may have been temporarily employed by the Crown on decorations. He returned to Basle until 1532, but the religious strife was now more acute (a document of 1530 shows him anxious about the meaning of the Communion Service), and even an offer by the Town Council of a pension could not retain him. When he arrived back in London in 1532 More was in disfavour, and from 1532 to 1536 he worked mainly for the Merchants of the Steelyard (the wool-staple and the Hanseatic League) on half-length portraits of amazing virtuosity. He probably entered the Royal service after painting *The Ambassadors* (1533, London, NG) – a tour-de-force of representation and iconographical allusion. One of his chief works for Henry VIII was the dynastic group (1537) of Henry with his Queen, Jane Seymour, and Henry VII and Elizabeth of York (burnt in 1698; part of the cartoon is in London, NPG). The figure of Henry served as a model for the many versions of the King, who also employed Holbein as a goldsmith's designer and on painted and architectural decorations, and sent him abroad to paint prospective brides (the *Duchess of Milan*, 1538, London, NG; *Anne of Cleves*, 1539/40, Paris, Louvre). His late practice of painting from drawings instead of from the sitter was reinforced by the exigencies of extensive Court portraiture. His portraits – life-size and in miniature – became more linear in style and more hieratic in treatment than his early works, partly through their emphasis on detail, partly because working only from drawings led him to be less sensitive in handling and perception. None of his decorations or goldsmith's work in England has survived, though drawings and miniature versions exist. A pair of organ shutters in Basle, and many drawings for the now destroyed Council Chamber decorations and house façades in Basle and Lucerne, are the only records of his large decorative works, which were strongly influenced by Italian – particularly Milanese – style.

The largest collections of Holbein's works are in Basle and the Royal Coll. (there are eighty-five of the drawings for portraits at Windsor). Other works, by him or his studio, include those in Berlin, Boston (Mus. and Gardner), Brunswick, Cleveland Ohio, Detroit, Dresden, Edinburgh (NG: an *Allegory of the Old and New Testaments*), Florence (Uffizi), Frankfurt (Städel), Freiburg im Breisgau (Cath.), The Hague, Karlsruhe, Liverpool, London (NG, NPG, V&A, Wallace Coll. and Barber Surgeons' Hall), Los Angeles, Munich, New York (Met. Mus., Frick Coll.), Ottawa, Paris (Louvre), Parma, Philadelphia (Johnson), Rome (Gall. Naz.), St Louis, Stuttgart, Toledo Ohio, Upton House Banbury (National Trust), Vienna, Washington (NG) and Zurich.

HOLLAR, Wenceslaus (1607–77), was born in Prague but was the most important illustrator and topographer working in England in the 17th century. He travelled in Germany after leaving Bohemia in 1627 and was taken into the service of the Earl of Arundel in Cologne in 1636. He was captured by the Parliamentarians at the siege of Basing House in 1645, along with Inigo JONES, and left England for Antwerp in the same year but returned in 1652 and, after the Restoration, was appointed 'H.M. Scenographer and Designer of Prospects'. His work consists of etchings and watercolour drawings dealing with almost everything that could interest the 17th-century Englishman: they are principally illustrations to books but include maps, portraits, the series of Women's Costumes, plates of contemporary events, and, above all, the series of views of London before the Great Fire of 1666 and the plates of buildings like St Paul's, as well as reproductions of works of art, all of which are now invaluable historical material.

HÖLZEL, Adolf (1853–1934), was a German painter who went to Paris in 1882. He began to experiment with what he called 'coloured sounds' in 1917–18, and from 1923 produced many pastels of abstract compositions. His school at Dachau, opened in 1893, numbered NOLDE, SCHLEMMER, and BAUMEISTER among its pupils. There are works by him, including stained-glass windows, at Cologne, Hanover and Stuttgart.

HOMER, Winslow (1836–1910), was, with EAKINS, one of the most influential of late 19th-century American painters. He earned a living as an illustrator – he recorded the Civil War – and this sense of actuality remained in all his works even after 1875, when he devoted himself to painting. He spent ten months in France (1866–7) and twice visited England (1881–2), where the sea at Tynemouth deeply affected his work. In the 1880s and 1890s he revolutionized American painting by his quasi-Impressionist style allied to Courbet-like studies of the sea, and shooting and fishing subjects appealing to the American male. He was also affected by the Japanese craze which arrived in Europe in the 1860s and is visible in his work in the 1870s. He is represented in the NG, Washington, and many other US museums.

HONDECOETER, Melchior (1636–95), was the last and best of a family of Dutch painters. He painted mainly still-life and scenes of birds, many of them exotic, and his speciality was the representation of a farmyard, or a courtyard, with a great number of different birds. He was the pupil of his father Gysbert (1604–53) and of his uncle J. B. WEENIX. He worked at The Hague and Amsterdam and his numerous pictures include examples in the Royal Coll., Amsterdam (Rijksmus.), Boston, Brussels, Cardiff, Cologne, Derby, Glasgow, The Hague, London (NG and Wallace Coll.), Lyons, Munich, New York (Met. Mus.), Nottingham, Paris (Louvre) and Vienna (Akad.).

HONE, Nathaniel (1718–84), was a Dubliner who painted portraits in the English provinces (often in miniature or in enamel), until a fortunate marriage allowed him to spend two years (1750–52) in Italy. After this he settled in London and became a Founder-Member of the RA, exhibiting regularly from 1769 until his death. In 1775, however, he submitted *The Conjuror*, which represents a conjuror who points with a wand to prints after Michelangelo, Maratta, Pietro da Cortona and others, clearly implying plagiary, and this was thought to refer to Reynolds's use of his sources. The picture also contains a figure of a young woman, and Angelica KAUFFMANN (whose exact relationship with Reynolds was a matter of interested speculation) felt herself impugned. She petitioned the Council and the picture was rejected: it was subsequently exhibited elsewhere. The picture (now in Dublin; sketch, *c.*1773, now in London, Tate) was rediscovered in 1944, and it is clear that the imputations were not without foundation. Other pictures by Hone are in London (NPG: *Henry Fielding*, 1762; RA, V&A), Belfast, Birmingham (Barber Inst.), Cardiff, Dublin, Leeds, Manchester, Oxford and Yale (CBA).

HONTHORST, Gerrit (Gerard) van (1590–1656), was one of the leading masters of the UTRECHT SCHOOL. He trained under BLOEMAERT and was in Rome *c.*1610/12–1620, where he was much influenced by Caravaggio (who died in 1610). SANDRART, who was Honthorst's own pupil, said that he was also much influenced by Caravaggio's follower MANFREDI. He worked for the Marchese Giustiniani, who had been Caravaggio's patron, and for him he painted the *Christ before the High Priest* (London, NG). This has the characteristic Northern Caravaggesque device of using one candle as the sole source of light, the direct rays being shielded by the figures. His night scenes were very popular and earned him the nickname in Italy of 'Gherardo delle Notti': he had 'much of ye manor of Caravaggioes colouringe; whch is nowe soe much esteemed in Rome' (letter from Lord Arundel, 1621). He settled in Utrecht until 1628, when he visited England and painted the huge *Charles I and Henrietta Maria with the Liberal Arts* (Hampton Court), which marks the transition from his early Caravaggesque style and genre or mythological subjects to his second, Court, style based on realistic portraiture in a version of the elegant van Dyck manner. He succeeded MIEREVELD as Court Painter at The Hague (1637), and his later works are in a style very like Miereveld's, but the *Lady* of 1639 (London, Dulwich) is still close to van Dyck. His brother Willem (1594–1666) worked with him. There are pictures in the Royal Coll. and in Alkmaar, Amsterdam, Berlin, Cleveland Ohio, Cologne, Dresden, Dublin, Florence (Uffizi), Glasgow, Greenville SC, Haarlem, The Hague (a series of Court portraits), London (NG and NPG), Munich, Ottawa, Paris (Louvre), Rome (Borghese and churches), Utrecht, Vienna, Worcester Mass. (dated 1622) and elsewhere.

HOOCH (Hoogh), Pieter de (1629–84), was the Dutch genre painter who came nearest to VERMEER in his feeling for the play of light. He was born in Rotterdam and is said to have been trained by BERCHEM, along with OCHTERVELT. What are thought to be his earliest works are tavern scenes and KORTGAARDJES in the manner of BROUWER or TENIERS. By 1652 he was in Delft, where he must have known Vermeer. He chose the same kind of subject – an interior with two or three figures engaged in some household task – and he occupied himself with rendering the fall of sunlight on surfaces, his favourite effect being that of a dark foreground with an open door leading through into a second room which is brightly lit. As in the case of Vermeer this interest in light is an ultimate legacy, via the UTRECHT SCHOOL, of Caravaggio, but he seems to have painted such scenes in the 1650s – i.e. possibly before Vermeer. His earliest dated works are of 1658 (e.g. in the Royal Coll., Edinburgh (NG), London (NG) and the Louvre), so there is some doubt about this. De Hooch moved to Amsterdam by 1661. The works of the Amsterdam period are poorer in quality and also different in subject: unlike the simple interiors of the Delft period they are often rather bogus scenes of High Life, such as hardly existed in Holland, based on adaptations of the grand new Town Hall of Amsterdam or of Italian architecture. He is now known to have died in an asylum in 1684, the date of his last painting. There are pictures in the Royal Coll. and in Amsterdam, Berlin, Boston, Brussels, Cape Town, Cincinnati, Cleveland Ohio, Cologne, Copenhagen, Detroit, Dublin, The Hague, London (NG, Wallace Coll. and Wellington Mus.), Los Angeles, Malibu Cal. (Getty), Manchester, Minneapolis, New York (Met. Mus.), Paris (Louvre), Philadelphia, Rome (Borghese), Rotterdam, San Francisco, St Louis, Stockholm, Toledo Ohio, Vienna (K-H Mus. and Akad.), Waddesdon Bucks. (National Trust), Washington (NG and Corcoran), Worcester Mass. and elsewhere.

HOPPER, Edward (1882–1967), was a realist painter of urban America. He exhibited at the ARMORY SHOW (1913) and sold a painting, but was unable to sell another for ten years so he supported himself as a commercial artist and illustrator, which had some effect on his paintings. His scenes of desolate streets and cheap eating-houses express the loneliness of big cities, especially New York, where he lived most of his life. He visited Europe three times 1906/10, but was quite untouched by contemporary European art. He is well represented in the Whitney Mus., New York, and in other US museums.

HOPPNER, John (1758–1810), was one of the principal followers of Reynolds and a formidable rival to LAWRENCE. This rivalry occasionally led him into a stylistic meretriciousness in the endeavour to compete with Lawrence's brilliance. The portrait of Mrs Jordan, a comic actress (London, Kenwood), is one of his best works, since the style is suited to the subject. He was a student at the RA in 1775, became Principal Painter to the Prince of Wales in 1793 and RA in 1795. There are works by him in the Royal Coll. and in London (NG, NPG, Tate, V&A, Wallace Coll., Kenwood and RA), New York (Met. Mus.), Ottawa, Paris (Louvre), Washington (NG), Yale (CBA) and elsewhere.

HORTUS CONCLUSUS (Lat. enclosed garden). The phrase is taken from the Song of Songs (iv, 12: *Hortus conclusus soror mea, sponsa* ... A garden enclosed is my sister, my spouse ...) and is used to describe paintings of the Madonna and Child in a garden with a fence round it, and often with a fountain inside it (*Hortus conclusus, fons signatus* . . . A spring shut up, a fountain sealed). Occasionally there are also several female Saints present, as in one of the finest examples, the *Paradise Garden* by an unknown German master of about 1415 (Frankfurt, Städel). The *Virgo inter Virgines* type has the female Saints, but need not have the fenced garden.

HOSKINS, John (*d.*1665), was, according to his earliest biographer, 'bred a Face-painter in Oil but afterwards taking to *miniature*, he far exeeded what he did before'. His earliest miniatures date from *c.*1620, so he was probably born at the end of the 16th century and some of his early works show some influence from HILLIARD and OLIVER. Nevertheless, he was probably the first 'who gave the strength and freedom of oil to miniature', although this was actually said of his nephews and pupils, Alexander and Samuel COOPER. Hoskins was Limner to Charles I and naturally came under the influence of van DYCK whose style he adapted to miniature. There are examples in the Royal Coll., Cambridge (Fitzwm), The Hague, London (V&A, Ham House and Wallace Coll.) and Oxford.

HOT COLOUR, TONE. Colours which tend to be reddish in hue. The phrase generally has a pejorative sense, implying that the balance of colour or tone is unduly inclined to the red end of the spectrum. This effect is sometimes due to BOLUS grounds. *See* COLD and WARM COLOUR.

HOUDON, Jean-Antoine (1741–1828), was the most celebrated French sculptor of the 18th century. He was a pupil of LEMOYNE and PIGALLE before going to the ÉCOLE royale des Élèves protégés (where his father was for many years the concierge) with a Rome Prize in 1761. He went on to Rome in 1764 and made his name with his simple and classical *S. Bruno* (1766) in S.M. degli Angeli. In 1769 he was back in Paris and an associate of the Academy; he became a full Academician in 1777 with his *Morpheus* (now in the Louvre). He narrowly escaped imprisonment during the Revolution and continued to work under the Empire. He retired in 1814 but continued to teach at the École des Beaux-Arts until 1823, when he became senile. Among his better-known works are the *Girl Shivering* (1783, Montpellier), the *Diana* (1780, Gulbenkian Coll., and 1790, Louvre), and the *Minerva* in the Institut, Paris, which is reproduced on all the Institut's publications. His portraits are, however, his most numerous as well as his finest works and they include many of the greatest men of his time, among them the seated *Voltaire* of 1781 in the Comédie Française (there are several other *Voltaires*, including one in terracotta in Cambridge (Fitzwm) and one in London (V&A) and another in the Comédie, where there is also a *Molière*); his *Franklin* led to a commission from the State Parliament of Virginia for a statue of Washington. Houdon went to the US in 1785 to execute it and spent fourteen days at Mount Vernon. The marble was completed by 1791 (although it is signed and dated 1788) and is in Richmond, Va; perhaps ironically, there is a bronze copy in London, outside the NG. Los Angeles has a bust of Washington. There is a *Franklin* in New York (Met. Mus.) – the original plaster is in St Louis – and a *Diderot* in the Louvre, a *Buffon* in Glasgow, two busts in the Wallace Coll., London, and many others in France and in Gotha and elsewhere. His busts of children are particularly sensitive.

An unusual work is the *Anatomical Man*, a flayed figure done in the French Hospital in Rome, a cast of which was once in every art school.

HOURS of Turin. A manuscript (the 'Très Belles Heures') begun by JACQUEMART de Hesdin *c.*1385/90 but left unfinished at his death and divided *c.*1412/13, so that the unfinished parts went to Count William of Holland (*d.*1417), elder brother of Jan van EYCK's patron. This part, finished by various artists by the middle of the 15th century, was later subdivided between the Prince Trivulzio (Milan) and the Royal Library, Turin: the Turin parts were burnt in 1904 and the Trivulzio portion has now passed to the Mus. Civico, Turin. Hulin de Loo was the only scholar to study both portions in the original and he declared that some twenty-five of the miniatures were by the van Eycks; controversy now rages – and presumably always will – over the exact attributions, since some of those destroyed (and known only from old photographs) had close links with the mature style of Jan van Eyck.

HUBER, Wolf (*c.*1490–1553), was a painter and designer of woodcuts, who, after ALTDORFER, was the most important member of the DANUBE SCHOOL. He was in contact with Altdorfer by *c.*1510 and may have been his assistant; certainly he shares Altdorfer's feeling for the poetry of landscape, as may be seen in his drawings of pure landscape as well as in his pictures. From 1515 he worked in Passau, where he was much disliked by the local painters. There are pictures by him in Dublin, Munich and Vienna, and drawings in London (BM and Univ. Coll.).

HUDSON RIVER SCHOOL. A school of American landscape painting, highly Romantic in feeling and glorifying the wonders of Nature as visible in the American landscape. The type begins soon after 1800 with the landscapes of Washington ALLSTON, but the name is properly applied to the period from 1825, when COLE settled in New York, until the 1870s. DURAND was a typical painter of the school, and his 'Letters on Landscape Painting' (1855) sums up its aims.

HUDSON, Thomas (1701–79), was the son-in-law of Jonathan RICHARDSON I and inherited the same kind of stereotyped face-painting practice, although Hudson's figures are more solid in drawing and usually cooler in colour. Many of his portraits exist as man-and-wife pairs. He is best known as Reynolds's master (1740–43) but he painted a considerable number of portraits 1745–60, after which (like HIGHMORE) he virtually retired, probably because Reynolds was getting the business. He is well represented in London (Tate, Nat. Marit. Mus., Dulwich, NPG and Coram Fdn), in Bristol, Edinburgh (NG and NPG), Exeter, Manchester, New York (Met. Mus.), Waddesdon Bucks. (National Trust), Yale (CBA) and elsewhere.

HUNT, William Holman (1827–1910), was in the RA Schools in 1844, and there met MILLAIS and ROSSETTI with whom, in 1848, he founded the PRE-RAPHAELITE BROTHERHOOD; this term gave rise to much acrimony, from which they were rescued by RUSKIN. Hunt went to Egypt and the Holy Land in 1854, 1869 and 1873 to paint Biblical scenes with accurate local settings and types – e.g. *The Scapegoat* (1854, Port Sunlight): *see* TISSOT. He was the only member of the group to remain faithful to PRB principles, accumulating detail on detail. His best-known works are perhaps *The Light of the World* (versions in Oxford, Keble Coll., 1853–6, and London, St Paul's Cath., 1899–1904), and *The Awakening Conscience* (1853–4, London, Tate), its secular counterpart in which a multitude of details emphasize the sudden repentance of a kept woman. His late works are characterized by excessive detail (probably due to long sight) and by overworked surfaces and hot colour; yet in 1855 Delacroix said 'I am really amazed by Hunt's sheep' (*Strayed Sheep*, 1852, Tate). In 1905 he published 'Pre-Raphaelitism and the Pre-Raphaelite Brotherhood', the best documented memoir of the movement. He was given the O M in the same year. There are works in Birmingham, Liverpool, London (Tate), Manchester, Ottawa, Oxford (Ashmolean and Jesus Coll.), and elsewhere.

HUYSUM, Jan van (1682–1749), was a Dutch flower-painter, son of the flower-painter Justus van Huysum (1659–1716), many of whose works are confused with his more famous son's. Jan's flower pictures are very highly detailed, rich and crowded in composition and sometimes set against a light background (an innovation made by him). He often delayed completion as the right flowers bloomed at different times, and several of his paintings have two dates – e.g. one in London (N G) dated *1736 en 1737*. There are examples in many museums. He also painted a few landscapes (there are three signed ones in Paris, Louvre) and mythologies (a *Rape of Proserpine*, London, Wellington Mus., is ascribed to him) and there is a *Self-portrait*, probably unique in his work, in Oxford.

His younger brother, Jacob (*c.*1687/9–1740?), who often imitated him, worked in England and died in London. Cambridge (Fitzwm) has twelve pictures symbolizing the *Months of the Year*. Other imitators continued down to van Os (*d.*1861).

I

ICON (Ikon, Gk. image) originally meant a picture of Christ or a Saint on a panel, as distinct from a wall-painting. These icons were extremely limited in subject matter and were objects of great veneration. Because of this the actual forms and shapes were prescribed and maintained unchanged for centuries in the Orthodox world: thus, the earliest surviving examples may date from the 6th or 7th centuries but are virtually indistinguishable from those painted in Greece or Russia a thousand or more years later. An *Iconostasis* is a screen dividing the sanctuary of an Orthodox church from the lay part and is covered with icons. *Iconoclasm* is the destruction of images, the most famous outbreak being the Iconoclastic Controversy of the 8th century. The Second Nicene Council (787) decided that the veneration of icons was not idolatrous, since the honour was being paid to the prototype, not to the actual icon, but the controversy dragged on until 843, when it was finally settled in favour of icons. *Iconography* and *Iconology* are the knowledge of the meanings to be attached to pictorial representations: thus, a lamb with a flag is a simple problem in Christian iconography, but many of the more complicated Baroque allegories, in which Christian and pagan mythological figures are used side by side, may now be almost beyond interpretation. Some knowledge of iconography is essential to a full understanding of medieval and Renaissance art; the frescoes of Giotto or Piero della Francesca being only partially intelligible to those who regard them as no more than coloured shapes.

There is also an older meaning of Iconography, namely a collection of portraits, as in van Dyck's *Iconography*.

IDEAL ART. 'Any work of Art which represents not a material object, but the mental conception of a material object, is in the primary sense of the word, ideal; that is to say, it represents an idea, and not a thing. Any work of Art which represents or realizes a material object is, in the primary sense of the term, un-ideal' (Ruskin). According to Plato the only realities are ideas, and everything perceptible to the senses is merely an imperfect realization of the primary idea: thus, the idea of a dog is the true dog and all dogs in the visible gutter merely approximate to the idea of dogness. From this arises a perennial theory that the true function of art is to mirror those Ideal forms that are the sole realities, approaching them by way of the physical phenomena which are their distorted images. The story, told by Pliny, which served for centuries as the basis of this Ideal Art, tells how Zeuxis had to paint a *Venus* and, after inspecting all the most beautiful girls in Crotona, he selected five and painted the mouth of one, the legs of another, and so on: the theory being that the sum of perfect parts must add up to a perfect whole. Later, a similar story was told of Raphael; the point of it is the same but he is made to add, significantly, that not only must he see many beautiful women, but he must also have *a certain idea* (*una certa idea*) in his mind. This theory is obviously not impregnable, but such is the hold of PROPORTION, classic harmony, and geometry on the human mind that for centuries (but most vocally in the NEOCLASSIC period) artists have sought to select, to refine, and to ennoble various details of the human figure into a whole which should express all these ideals and symbolize the highest aspirations of the mind. Naturally, this has meant an exclusive concern with the nude ('The human figure concealed under a frock-coat and trowsers is not a fit subject for sculpture. I would rather avoid contemplating such objects.' John GIBSON). Nevertheless, fallacious or not, the theory has produced many of the greatest works of art in existence and its perennial quality is perhaps best illustrated by the fact that it is still, under a new guise, one of the most fertile theories of aesthetics; for many forms of abstract art depend upon it, and the works of BRANCUSI, MALEVICH or MONDRIAN ultimately spring from Platonic Idealism.

ILLUSIONISM is the virtuoso use of pictorial techniques such as PERSPECTIVE and FORESHORTENING to deceive the eye into taking that which is painted for that which is real. The principal moments when this was practised were the Late Antique period (at Pompeii and elsewhere) and the Italian Baroque, when it was common to use sculptural and architectural means to heighten the impression of actuality, e.g. by using plaster figures in three dimensions attached to a frame so that the painted and carved figures are indistinguishable. One of the first pieces of illusionism is, however, the Camera degli Sposi at Mantua by MANTEGNA, completed in 1474. When such technical skill is lavished on things like a fly painted on a frame or a view through a non-existent window the French term *trompe-l'oeil* is often used, while the Italian word *quadraturista* is sometimes used for the professional painter of illusionist decorations (*quadrature*).

IMAGO PIETATIS (Lat. Image of Pity). A representation, most popular in the late Middle Ages, of the Dead Christ standing upright in the Tomb. He is sometimes surrounded by symbols of the Passion and sometimes supported by the Virgin, Saints, or Angels, but in any case the stress is laid on the suffering involved in the Redemption. The PIETÀ expresses the same basic idea in less symbolic terms.

IMPASTO is a word, Italian by origin, used to describe the thickness of the paint applied to a canvas or panel. When the paint is so heavily applied that it stands up in lumps with the tracks of the brush clearly evident it is said to be 'heavily impasted'.

IMPRESSION. A print from an ENGRAVING. A poor impression is usually caused by wear of the plate or block, or by under-inking. A *maculature* is a blind impression, pulled without re-inking, either to clean the plate or to see the effect produced.

IMPRESSIONISM was the derisive name given to the most important artistic phenomenon of the 19th century and the first of the Modern Movements. The name was derived from a picture by MONET, *Impression, Sunrise* (1872, Paris, Musée Marmottan, stolen in 1985), which represents the play of light on water, with the spectator looking straight into the rising sun. The occasion of the derision was the first Impressionist Exhibition, held in 1874, when Monet, RENOIR, SISLEY, PISSARRO, CÉZANNE, DEGAS, GUILLAUMIN, BOUDIN, Berthe MORISOT and others held an independent exhibition. In fact, the true aim of Impressionism was to achieve ever greater naturalism, by exact analysis of tone and colour and by trying to render the play of light on the surface of objects. This is a form of sensualism in which traditional ideas of composition and drawing – that is, putting a line round a concept – were bound to suffer. Impressionist interest in colour and light was at least partly due to the researches into the physics of colour carried out by scientists like

Chevreul; and the idea that an object of any given colour casts a shadow tinged with its complementary (though known already to Delacroix) suggested one of the principal ways in which they animated the surface of their canvases. The flickering touch, with the paint applied in small, brightly-coloured dabs, and the lack of firm outline, combined with the brightness of the colour, even in the shadows, and the generally high key undoubtedly alienated the public. In the course of time these technical devices became petrified into a quasi-scientific method of applying paint (NEO-IMPRESSIONISM) which was supposed to give the maximum of truth – optical truth – to nature: it also led naturally to POST-IMPRESSIONISM; that is, to a purely artistic and anti-naturalistic movement. The great decade of Impressionism was 1870–80, but most of the major figures, such as Monet, Pissarro and Sisley, continued to produce masterpieces in a more or less Impressionist style for many more years. Degas, Renoir and Cézanne were only dubiously Impressionists even in the 1870s (many of the original group felt that Cézanne was more than they could swallow) and they very soon moved away from it. Cézanne said that he wanted 'to make of Impressionism something solid and durable, like the art of the Museums', thus clearly defining the main weakness of the movement, its lack of intellectual rigour. Nevertheless, most painting of the last 100 years has been profoundly affected by it, and even the RA and the Salon would nowadays be lost without it. There is a large collection in the Musée d'Orsay in Paris and there is now also an important collection in the Mus. Marmottan, Passy, Paris; but the very nature of the movement, with its emphasis on painting landscapes out of doors and catching the fleeting impression, meant an enormous output of pictures so that they are not difficult to find. The eight Impressionist Exhibitions were held in 1874, 1876, 1877, 1879, 1880, 1881, 1882 and 1886.

IMPRIMITURA (Ital.). The priming or GROUND, often tinted, laid on canvas or panel.

INC. (Lat. *incidit*, he cut it) on an engraving refers to the engraver, or more commonly etcher: *see also* SCULP.

INGRES, Jean Auguste Dominique (1780–1867), was born at Montauban. His father, a mediocre artist, recognized his son's abilities and sent him to Toulouse Academy (1791) and on to DAVID in Paris in 1797. He won the Prix de Rome in 1801 with the *Ambassadors of Agamemnon* which was praised by FLAXMAN, who had a great influence on him. He earned a living by portraits until 1806, when he finally went to Italy intending to stay three or four years and remaining eighteen. His Rivière family portraits (1805, Louvre), with their stress on sinuous line forming a silhouette that both contains and explains the form, established a type that he developed and perfected, but hardly modified. Works sent back from Rome were bitterly criticized, and the fall of Napoleon forced him to seek a precarious livelihood making pencil drawings of visitors to Rome. In 1820 he settled in Florence and completed the *Vow of Louis XIII*, commissioned for Montauban Cathedral (still there) and exhibited in the 1824 Salon with enormous success. This work placed him in the front rank and established him as the official opponent of the ideas expressed by DELACROIX, and the main prop of a rigid classicism in opposition to the Romantic Movement. While his main works were portraits – which he professed to dislike, and in which he both influenced and was influenced by the earliest photographs – he also painted subject pictures and poeticized Oriental scenes providing an excuse for voluptuous nudes. His wall-paintings were not happy; the *Golden Age* (1842–9) in the Château de Dampierre, which replaced the decoration by GLEYRE, was abandoned and has deteriorated, leaving only the superb nude studies made for it. In 1834 he returned to Rome as Director of the French Academy, having applied for the position in a fit of pique over the reception accorded his *Martyrdom of St Symphorian* (Autun Cath.). After his return to Paris in 1841, his intransigent opposition to any ideas but his own, backed by his academic standing, gave him an influence which he used blindly not only against Delacroix, but also against younger rebels opposing what had become in the hands of his imitators, entrenched in mediocrity, a stereotyped academicism. His own style hardly changed and to the end he pursued his piercingly exact vision, his sinuous line, and his worship of Raphael; while his deliberately charmless handling stresses his supreme draughtsmanship. He said 'Drawing is the probity of art' and 'Drawing includes everything except the tint': opposed views were those of Théophile Sylvestre '. . . he is a Chinese painter lost . . . amid the ruins of Athens' and Delacroix's 'His art is the complete expression of an incomplete intelligence'. He became a Member of the Institute in 1825, and Grand Officer of the Legion of Honour in 1855, and a Senator in 1862. None of his many pupils except CHASSÉRIAU achieved lasting reputation: his real continuator was DEGAS.

There is a large Musée Ingres at Montauban and other works are in Aix-en-Provence, Algiers, Antwerp, Baltimore, Bayonne, Brussels, Cambridge Mass. (Fogg), Chantilly, Cincinnati, Florence (Uffizi), Hartford Conn., Kansas City, Leningrad, Liège, London (NG and V&A), Lyons, Montpellier, New York (Met. Mus. and Frick Coll.), Northampton Mass., Paris (Mus. d'Orsay, Carnavalet and Invalides), Philadelphia, Rouen, Stockholm, Toulouse, Versailles, Washington (NG) and elsewhere.

INNES, James Dickson (1887–1914), was a Welsh landscape painter with a powerful sense of design and a feeling for strong colour. He first worked in the Wilson STEER brand of Impressionism, and was then strongly influenced by Augustus JOHN. His premature death invites speculation whether he might not have developed into an English *Fauve*. There are works in Aberdeen, Cardiff, Leeds, London (Tate), Manchester, Southampton and Yale (CBA).

INNESS, George (1825–94), was an American landscape painter originally influenced by the HUDSON RIVER SCHOOL. He went to Rome and Florence in 1847, and in 1854–5 he was in Paris, where he was influenced by the BARBIZON SCHOOL. He spent many years in Europe, with four years in France and Italy (1870–4). In his last decade he came under the influence of Swedenborg and as a result his landscapes took on Symbolist overtones. There are many works in Boston and in New York (Met. Mus.) and other US museums, and one in London (NG).

INTAGLIO (from Ital. *intagliare*, to cut into, engrave: also *Cavo-rilievo*) consists of cutting forms out of a surface so as to make a kind of relief in reverse. The commonest example is an engraved seal-ring, hence the opposite term is often Cameo. For Intaglio processes, *see* ENGRAVING.

INTERNATIONAL GOTHIC. Towards the end of the 14th century there arose a new approach to Nature which first found expression in the Court art of France and Burgundy (*see* BROEDERLAM, LIMBOURG), but which rapidly spread to Italy, Germany (LOCHNER), and Bohemia (MASTER of WITTINGAU). As a style it remained fundamentally Gothic, for the new realism was confined to details, particularly to details of landscape, or animals, and of costume. This form of realism has almost nothing in common with the slightly later realism, classical and naturalistic in inspiration, practised by MASACCIO and DONATELLO. Aspects of both may, however, be detected in the work of GHIBERTI. In Italy the principal exponents of International Gothic were GENTILE da Fabriano and PISANELLO: a comparison between the *Madonna* by Gentile in the Royal Coll. and the Masaccio *Madonna* in the NG, London, or the Gentile *Adoration* in the Uffizi, Florence, and Masaccio's Brancacci Chapel, will make clear the difference of intention as well as of style. The influence of International Gothic remained active for many years, and was even revived towards the end of the 15th century.

INTIMISME. A form of Impressionist technique applied to the depiction of everyday life in domestic interiors rather than to landscape. The work of BONNARD and VUILLARD is usually meant.

INTONACO *see* FRESCO.

INV., INVENIT (Lat. he invented it) often appears on an engraving as the credit-title of the original author of the design, which may have been drawn (DEL.), painted (PINX.), engraved (INC. or SCULP.), and published (EXCUDIT) by other people. There is a beautiful small etching by Domenico Tiepolo after a painting by his father, inscribed 'Io Bapta Tiepolo INV. et PIN. / Dom: Filius DEL et IN' (i.e. G. B. Tiepolo invented and painted (this picture); Domenico (his) son drew and etched (this plate).

ISABEY, Eugène-Gabriel (1803–86), was the son of the miniature painter Jean-Baptiste (1767–1855). Eugène made a dramatic debut at the Salon of 1824 with marine and landscape paintings, gaining a medal. He went to Algiers in 1830 with the French navy as a marine-painter, but the Romantic influence on his colour came from Delacroix. He visited England several times and BONINGTON probably inspired him to employ watercolour. He was the painter of many of the events of the reign of Louis-Philippe (pictures in Versailles and the British Royal Coll.). Other works are in the Louvre, and in Bayonne, Boston, Cardiff, Cleveland Ohio, Douai, London (NG and Wallace Coll.), Nancy, New York (Met. Mus.), Orleans and York.

ISENBRANDT (Ysenbrandt), Adriaen (*d.*1551), was a painter active in Bruges from 1510. He is said to have been a pupil of Gerard DAVID and for this reason a diptych of the *Madonna of the Seven Sorrows* (Bruges, Notre Dame, and Brussels Mus.) has been ascribed to him: around this not very certain attribution a large accretion of early 16th-century Bruges School work has accumulated under his name, a good example being the *Adoration of the Magi* in Birmingham. To make matters worse, some of these were once attributed to MOSTAERT by Waagen; hence *Der Waagen'sche Mostaert* or *The Pseudo-Mostaert* = 'Isenbrandt'.

ISRAËLS, Josef (1824–1911), was one of the leaders of the HAGUE SCHOOL, who studied at the Beaux-Arts in Paris under DELAROCHE, and, after his return to Holland in 1847, painted similar costume-history pieces. In 1855 he went to Zandvoort and began to paint realist pictures of the life of the fishermen there. These influenced van GOGH, which is why Israëls is now remembered, but he was also an influence on the GLASGOW SCHOOL. There are works in Amsterdam and many other Dutch museums, as well as Aberdeen, Boston, Chicago, Edinburgh, Glasgow, London (NG) and New York (Met. Mus.).

ITALIANIZERS are Northern artists, generally Dutch or Flemish, who adopt as far as possible a style based on Italian models or who import Italian motives into their repertory. The word is often used of 17th-century Dutch landscape painters like ASSELYN, BOTH and BERCHEM, but is also used of 16th-century Flemings like MABUSE or van ORLEY, although they are usually called ROMANISTS.

ITTEN, Johannes (1888–1967), was a Swiss painter who was trained in Germany, became an abstract painter in 1915, joined the BAUHAUS staff in 1919, and established the foundation course there which has had an enormous – and largely harmful – influence on European and American 20th-century art. He was responsible for KLEE joining the Bauhaus, but after 1938 he returned to Switzerland. His 'Design and Form', based on his course at the Bauhaus, was published in English in 1975, and his 'Art of Colour' in 1986.

IVES, James, *see* CURRIER.

J

JACOBELLO del Fiore (*d.*1439) was a Venetian painter who was active from 1394. He broke away from the Byzantine tradition exemplified by PAOLO Veneziano which dominated Venetian art until the end of the 14th century, but was in turn influenced by the INTERNATIONAL GOTHIC style of the early 15th century. Most of his works are in Venice, but the earliest signed and dated work by him is of 1407 (US private coll. in 1982).

JACQUEMART de Hesdin (*d.c.*1411) was a Painter to the Duke of Berri from 1384 until 1411, when he was succeeded by the LIMBOURG brothers. He made the *Grandes Heures du Duc de Berri* (Paris, Bibliothèque Nationale), as well as the *Très Belles Heures* (Brussels, Bibliothèque Royale), but is principally remembered as having started what became the HOURS of Turin.

JAMESONE, George (*d.*1644), was an Aberdeen painter who was trained in Edinburgh, and not, as a highly improbable tradition would have it, by Rubens. He painted portraits in a style not unlike that of Cornelius JOHNSON – i.e. basically a Flemish manner. He was painting in Aberdeen in 1619/20; in 1633 he painted Charles I in Edinburgh and also visited Italy; and from 1634 he worked mainly in Edinburgh. There are pictures by him in Edinburgh (NG and SNPG) and a number in Aberdeen (Gall. and especially the University Coll.).

JANET *see* CLOUET.

JANSENS (JANSSENS), Cornelius, *see* JOHNSON.

JAPONAISERIE (Fr. Japaneseness). In the 1850s Japanese 19th-century woodcuts began to arrive in Europe, often as wrapping paper round porcelain imports, and in 1856 prints by the great master Hokusai were certainly known in Paris, although the Exhibition of 1867 was the cause of the great interest shown by many artists, especially the Impressionists, in the simplified forms, stressed outlines, flat areas of colour, and unusual perspective in these prints. PISSARRO was interested on account of his own preoccupation with the graphic arts, but DEGAS, WHISTLER, MONET, A. E. STEVENS, and even van GOGH were all influenced in one way or another.

JARDIN, K. du *see* DUJARDIN.

JAWLENSKY, Alexej (1864–1941), was a Russian painter, originally an officer in the Imperial Guard, who spent most of his life in Germany, although the major Western influence on his style was MATISSE. He studied in Munich from 1896, meeting KANDINSKY there, although he did not join the BLAUE REITER group. Later, with Kandinsky, KLEE and FEININGER he formed a group known as the Blue Four. He settled in Wiesbaden in 1921 and his later works became more abstract, more Byzantine, and more expressive: he himself said that 'art is nostalgia for God'. There are many works in Wiesbaden and in Pasadena Cal.

JEAN de Boulogne *see* BOLOGNA.

JOHN, Augustus Edwin, OM (1878–1961), was born in Tenby in Wales. He was trained at the Slade, taught at Liverpool (1901–2), and joined the NEW ENGLISH ART CLUB in 1903, gaining early recognition through his superb draughtsmanship. He was strongly influenced by PUVIS de Chavannes and Post-Impressionism, 1910–14, and made many cartoons for large decorations, only one of which (Johannesburg) was executed. His brilliant portraits derive from the grand manner tradition enlivened by a semi-Impressionist handling, colour high in tone, and a very un-Impressionist solidity of drawing. He travelled much in England and France, often gipsy-fashion, and was always a passionate opponent of academism, in art and life. He became an RA in 1928, later resigned with *éclat*, but was re-elected in 1940. There are works in Aberdeen, Birmingham, Brighton, Buffalo, Cambridge (Fitzwm), Cardiff, Detroit, Dublin, Glasgow, Leeds, Leicester, London (Tate), Manchester, Melbourne, Ottawa, Oxford, Sheffield, Stockholm, Swansea, Sydney, Toronto, Washington (NG), Yale (CBA) and elsewhere.

JOHN, Gwen (1876–1939), was the sister of Augustus. She studied at the Slade and with WHISTLER in Paris (1898), living in poverty with Ida Nettleship, who later married Augustus. She was also a friend of his second wife, Dorelia McNeil. She moved to Meudon to be near Rodin, but her long association with him ended in disappointment in 1906. She was friendly with the poet Rilke, 1906–9, and with her neighbour the Catholic philosopher Jacques Maritain. His influence on her art has been exaggerated, but she became a Catholic in 1913 and many of her paintings depict the nuns in a nearby Dominican convent. Her pictures are the antithesis of her brother's; her timid, reticent nature was expressed in a delicate art, muted in colour, and in tone and handling closer to William NICHOLSON than to her brother, and of an introspective, almost neurotic, quality. Much of her life was spent in poverty verging on squalor, in obsessive retirement and independence. There are examples of her work in Birmingham (Barber Inst.), Buffalo NY, Cambridge (Fitzwm), Cardiff, Dublin, Leeds, London (Tate and NPG: *Self-portrait*), Manchester, Melbourne, New York (Met. Mus. and M of MA), Northampton Mass., Norwich, Sheffield, Southampton, Tenby, Yale (CBA) and elsewhere. Augustus once said that he would be remembered only as her brother, and it is true that her reputation has risen as his has declined.

JOHNS, Jasper (*b.*1930). With RAUSCHENBERG, he was one of the main formative influences on the New York variety of POP ART. He uses painting, collage, assemblages of objects, plastic, metal, bronze, either separately or in combination, as in the bronze *Beer Cans* of 1961, with their painted labels. There is an example in London (Tate).

JOHNSON (Jonson), Cornelius (also called Jansens, Janssen van Ceulen) (1593–1661/2), was born in London of Netherlandish parents and became one of the most notable portrait painters in England before the arrival of van DYCK in 1632. He painted in a straightforward but sensitive Dutch manner sometimes indistinguishable from that of MYTENS, but he tended to confine himself to bust portraits set in an oval, although there is a fine family group in London (NPG). After 1632 he came under van Dyck's influence until, in 1643, the Civil War caused him to retire to Holland, where he adoped a more Dutch manner, closer to that of MIEREVELD. There are works by him in Amsterdam (Rijksmus.), Bath (Holbourne Mus.), Blackheath, Boston, Cardiff, Cleveland Ohio, Dublin, The Hague, Liverpool, London (NPG, Tate, BM, V&A at Ham House and Dulwich), New York (Met. Mus.), Ottawa (NG), Sheffield and Yale (CBA). His son, Cornelius the Younger (after 1622–after 1698), imitated him. Amsterdam (Rijksmus.) has a signed and dated portrait of 1668, certainly by him.

JONES, David (1895–1974), was a Welsh painter, engraver and writer, who illustrated his own books 'In Parenthesis', 1937, the result of his experiences in the trenches during the First World War; 'The Anathemata', 1952; and 'Epoch and Artist', 1959). In the 1920s he was much influenced by Eric GILL. His watercolours, and pencil drawings heightened with splashes of watercolour, develop the important aspects of his art; luminous, visionary, almost hallucinatory in imagery and often containing allusions to Welsh legends, Christian symbolism and Ancient Rome. His mental breakdowns in 1932 and 1947 perhaps contributed to his hermetic imagery. Until about 1964 his subjects were landscapes, gardens and vegetation, animals, portraits and mythologies, but in his last years he made a series of painted inscriptions, partly calligraphic and partly abstract in a sense closer to Islamic inscriptions than to the inscriptions of Gill. He is represented in the Imperial War Mus. and the Tate Gallery, London, Cardiff and other British museums.

JONES, Sir E. Burne-Jones, *see* BURNE-JONES.

JONES, Inigo (1573–1652), is principally important as an architect, but was first recorded (in 1603) as a 'picture-maker', and there are over 450 drawings by him, mostly at Chatsworth, Derbyshire, for stage scenery and costumes. He was responsible for revolutionizing the English stage and designed about twenty-five masques and two plays. He is recorded as saying: 'Being naturally inclined in my younger years to study the Arts of Design I passed into foreign parts to converse with the great masters thereof in Italy.' He seems to have lived in Venice and probably visited Florence, where Buontalenti's career as artist-impresario exactly presages his own. He worked for the court of Denmark and was employed by James I's Queen, Anne of Denmark, on a masque in 1605. He was in Rome 1613–14 and still, apparently, thought of a career as a painter, but most of his life was passed as artistic adviser to the English court and as an architect. One painting, also at Chatsworth, is traditionally ascribed to him.

JONES, Thomas (1742–1803), was a Welsh landscape painter who was a pupil of Richard WILSON, 1763–5, and went to the RA Schools from 1769. He was in Naples and Rome 1776–83 (his Memoirs of this period were published in 1951), and there he painted small landscapes on the spot, very like those to be painted much later by Michallon, Valenciennes or even COROT. He gave up painting professionally on his return to London, but continued to exhibit at the RA, 1784–8, and in 1798. There are six of his Corot-like landscapes in Cardiff.

JONGKIND, Johan Barthold (1819–91), was a Dutch landscape and marine painter, who, along with BOUDIN, was the precursor of Impressionism and a formative influence on MONET (who wrote to Boudin in 1860 that Jongkind (whom he had not then met) 'is quite crazy'). Jongkind met Boudin in 1862 and exhibited at the SALON des Refusés in 1863. He spent most of his later life in France, living in squalor near Grenoble and ending in madness like van Gogh. He never painted in oils out of doors, working from drawings and watercolours made on the spot, but the results are very like those of the early Impressionists. In 1864 he painted two views of Notre Dame in Paris under different atmospheric conditions but from the same spot, thus anticipating the series-type later exploited by Monet. There is a typical work in London (NG).

JOOS van Cleve (Cleef) (*c.*1485–1540/1) became a Master in Antwerp in 1511. He is usually identified with the MASTER OF THE DEATH OF THE VIRGIN, but there are wide discrepancies between the portraits and the religious pictures attributed to him (or them). Joos was a contemporary of MASSYS, and many of the portraits attributed to him are in a cool, realistic style not unlike that of Massys or even Holbein and Mabuse; they are perhaps closest to Barthel BRUYN. Joos seems to have been to Genoa *c.*1515 and is reasonably supposed to have worked at the Court of François I of France *c.*1530; certainly many portraits of François and his Queen exist and are attributed to him, but there are no portraits ascribed to him which are signed or satisfactorily documented; the *Self-Portrait* (*?*) in the Royal Coll. is recorded in the 1639 Inventory of Charles I's collection 'Sotto Cleve done by himself . . .' (see below), but the features are those of Joos as known from 16th–17th-century engravings. Other pictures attributed to Joos van Cleve are in the Royal Coll. and in Antwerp, Berlin, Boston, Brussels, Cambridge (Fitzwm), Cologne (Wallraf-Richartz), Detroit, Dresden, Edinburgh, Florence (Uffizi), Genoa (S. Donato), Liverpool, London (NG, Courtauld Inst.), Madrid, Manchester New Hampshire, Michigan (Univ.), Munich, New York ((Met. Mus.), Paris (Louvre), Philadelphia (Johnson), Toledo Ohio, Vienna, Washington (NG and Corcoran) and Worcester Mass. His son Cornelis (1520–67), known as 'Sotte (i.e. mad) Cleve', was also a painter and visited London *c.*1554, hoping for Royal patronage. He was, however, anticipated by MOR and he went mad in 1556. Cornelis is often identified with the painter of an *Adoration of the Magi* in Antwerp (Mus.) – the so-called Master of the Antwerp Adoration.

JOOS van Gent (van Wassenhove), called Justus of Ghent (active 1460–after 1475), became a Master in Antwerp in 1460 and in Ghent in 1464. There he met Hugo van der GOES (whom he sponsored in the Guild in 1467) and is recorded up to 1469, but by 1475 he had gone to Rome. In 1473–4 'Magistro Giusto da Guanto' was in Urbino, painting the *Institution of the Eucharist* (Urbino), the commission for which was originally given to PIERO della Francesca, while the predella is by UCCELLO, who was paid for it 1465–9. Among the works attributed to him are a *Crucifixion* (Ghent, Cath.) and a series of twenty-eight *Famous Men* (*c.*1476, half in Paris, Louvre, and half in Urbino), the hands (at least) of the Duke of Urbino in Piero della Francesca's *Brera Madonna*, and other works in the Royal Coll., London (NG), New York (Met. Mus.) and Urbino. Two formerly in Berlin were destroyed in 1945. The *Famous Men* and the Duke's hands (and some of the other pictures) have been ascribed to P. BERRUGUETE, in spite of a specific mention in a 15th-century Italian writer of the *Famous Men* as by 'a Netherlander'. Joos is the only Netherlandish painter known to have worked in Urbino.

JORDAENS, Jacob (1593–1678), was born and died in Antwerp where he worked as an assistant to RUBENS. After Rubens's death he finished the incomplete works ordered for Spain, van DYCK's pretensions making it impossible to negotiate with him. He is an example of the pervasive effect of Rubens's style, for he uses a boisterous, restless type of Baroque derived from Rubens, but without his taste and control, or his imagination and versatility in design and colour. Late in life he became a Calvinist and his style accordingly became more sober, but he continued to accept Catholic commissions. He worked for the House of Orange on portraits and decorations during the 1630s, and his late works include large genre scenes of drinking bouts – *Le roi boit* in Brussels is an example – full of overtones of BROUWER and STEEN. There are works in Antwerp, Belfast, Bristol, Brunswick, Brussels, Budapest, Cassel, Cleveland Ohio, Dresden, Karlsruhe, Lille, London (NG and Wallace Coll.), Madrid, New York (Met. Mus.), Paris (Louvre), Southampton, Stockholm and Stonyhurst College, Lancs. (*The Four Doctors of the Church*).

JOURNEYMAN (from Fr. *journée*, a day). An artist who had completed his apprenticeship but was not yet a Master in a GUILD. He earned his living as a day-labourer in the shops of various Masters (often making it difficult to distinguish between the products of shop A and shop B when he crossed the road to work in the other shop for a change). Some painters spent their WANDERJAHRE in this fashion; others never set up for themselves.

JOUVENET, Jean (1644–1717), was born in Rouen, one of a family of artists, and went to Paris in 1661. He soon began to work under LEBRUN, especially at Versailles, and made a series of decorations at Rennes, Rouen and Paris (Invalides), as well as a set of very large paintings for S. Martin-des-Champs before 1706 (now in the Louvre). His style was close to Lebrun's and LE SUEUR's, but with more Baroque emotionalism and also a greater degree of naturalism. There are many works in French museums and others in Florence (Uffizi), Madrid, Munich, Northampton Mass. and Stockholm.

JUAN de JUANES (*c*.1523–79), was a Spanish painter, the son of the painter Vicente Macip (*c*.1475–*c*.1545), who had almost certainly studied in Italy, and probably in Venice. Juanes painted 'ideal' Counter-Reformation images, based on Leonardo's *Last Supper* (engraved by Marcantonio) and Raphael's *Madonnas*, but also with some influence from Flanders, e.g. MASSYS. There are works in Madrid (Prado and Acad.) and elsewhere in Spain.

JUEL, Jens (1745–1802), was a Danish painter who trained in Hamburg *c*.1760–5 and Copenhagen 1765/6. He went to Italy in 1772 and was in Rome 1774–6, and then in Paris and Switzerland 1776–80, when he returned to Denmark and became Court Painter and Director of the Academy (his pupils included FRIEDRICH, 1794–8, and RUNGE, 1799–1801). His portraits were influenced by TOCQUÉ, who twice visited Denmark (cf. the Juel in London, NG). There are many works in Copenhagen, and some in Geneva (Univ.).

JUGENDSTIL *see* ART NOUVEAU.

JUSTUS of Ghent *see* JOOS van Gent.

K

KALF, Willem (1619–93), was a Dutch still-life painter who worked in Paris as well as Rotterdam and Amsterdam, specializing in the elaborate BANCKET PIECES known as Pronkstilleven. Kalf was in Paris 1642–6 and he may have painted his largest picture (over 6 feet high), the *Still-Life with Armour* (Le Mans), in France: it was once said to be signed and dated 1643, but this is not now visible. He was back in Holland by 1651 and settled in Amsterdam in 1653. The depth and brilliance of his colour and the sureness of his touch suggest the influence of Vermeer, as in his still-life in The Hague (Mauritshuis), with orange, acid yellow and amber and the soft colours of an Oriental rug with dots of light like Vermeer's. Usually his Pronkstilleven contain elaborate gold, silver and glass vessels, fruit, and a Turkey carpet against a dark ground, often with a watch in the foreground. A good example is in London (NG). There are works in Amsterdam (Rijksmus.), Berlin, Cleveland Ohio, Dresden, Frankfurt (Städel), Glasgow, The Hague (Bredius), Indianapolis, Malibu Cal., Manchester, Melbourne, Munich, New York (Met. Mus.), Oxford, Paris (Louvre), Philadelphia (Johnson), Rotterdam, Rouen, St Louis, Stockholm, Vienna, Washington (NG) and elsewhere.

KALRAET, Abraham, *see* CALRAET.

KANDINSKY, Wassily (1866–1944), was born in Moscow but trained in Munich, after abandoning a legal career. He painted his first purely abstract work in 1910 (one such is in the Tate Gall., London), and was therefore one of the founders of 'pure' abstract painting. In 1911 he was one of the founders of the BLAUE REITER group and in 1912 he published a book which was translated into English in 1914 as 'The Art of Spiritual Harmony'. He returned to Russia 1914–21 and then went back to Germany and taught at the Bauhaus from 1922, again coming into contact with KLEE. In 1933 he went to France. New York (Guggenheim Mus.) has many works, and so have Munich and Russian museums. His 'Sounds', an English translation of poems with woodcuts, was published in 1981, and his 'Complete Writings on Art' in 1982.

KANE, John (1860–1934), was one of the leading American PRIMITIVE artists of the early 20th century. He was born in Scotland, but emigrated to America in 1879 and lived in Pennsylvania and Ohio, painting industrial scenes, particularly of the railroads, from *c.*1910. He became famous at the Carnegie Exhibition in 1928.

KAUFFMANN, Angelica (1741–1807), was a Swiss decorative painter. She seems to have been an accomplished musician and painted an allegory of herself hesitating between the Arts of Music and Painting (1760; later versions exist). Having chosen painting she went to Rome in 1763, where she painted a portrait of WINCKELMANN (1764, Zurich, Kunsthaus) which helped to make her name. In 1765 she went to Venice and was in London the following year, where she remained until 1781. She became friendly with REYNOLDS (there were rumours of a romantic attachment; *see* HONE) and imitated his style in her portraits. Her first marriage, to a bogus Count, was a disaster, but her second marriage was to the decorative painter Zucchi, with whom she retired to Italy in 1781. She was a Founder-Member of the RA in 1768. Her rather anaemic little decorative history pieces were widely engraved and the engravings used in the manufacture of *objets d'art*; from this has grown the habit of associating all decorative painting in all houses of the Adam period with her, although in fact only four such panels are known (two in the RA). Several of the best (e.g. those in Home House, London) are, in fact, by Zucchi. Later, when she lived in Rome, her portraits became more Neoclassic in feeling. There are pictures in Brighton, Edinburgh (NG), London (NPG and Kenwood), Manchester, New York (Met. Mus.), Plymouth, Yale (CBA) and elsewhere.

KEEPING *see* VALUES.

KENT, William (1685–1748), is celebrated as an architect, landscape gardener, interior decorator and furniture designer. He studied painting in Rome 1709–19, where he painted a ceiling in S. Giuliano dei Fiamminghi (1717), and there met Lord Burlington, his most constant and influential patron. He completed, in 1719, the paintings which RICCI had left unfinished in Burlington House (now the Royal Academy) and the commission to decorate Kensington Palace was given to him in 1723 instead of to THORNHILL. This was virtually his last work in painting and led to the savage satire by HOGARTH (Thornhill's son-in-law) in which Lord Burlington is shown as a builder's labourer and Raphael and Michelangelo gaze, awe-struck, on the figure of Kent *triumphans*.

KETEL, Cornelis (1548–1616), was born in Holland but came to England in 1573. He is known to have painted Queen Elizabeth in 1578, but he returned to Holland in 1581, settling in Amsterdam. There are several signed and dated works by him, including *Sir Martin Frobisher* (Oxford, Bodleian Library) and a group portrait of the Amsterdam Civic Guard, of 1588 (Rijksmus.), which looks forward to the great compositions of the 17th century. The most controversial attribution to him was *Queen Elizabeth as a Vestal Virgin* (Siena), which is now known to be by Q. MASSYS the Younger.

KETTLE, Tilly (1735–86), was an English portrait painter who was the first to seek his fortune in India. He was born in London and was influenced at the beginning of his career by Reynolds, as may be seen in the portraits he painted in Oxford in 1762 and 1763. In 1769 he went to India, where he had a great success, and remained there until 1776. On his return to London he found competition greater than he expected and his extravagant living forced him to return to India in 1786, but he died in the desert near Basra. There are pictures by him in London (Tate, NPG, V&A, Nat. Marit. Mus., Dulwich and Courtauld Inst., which has an important double portrait painted in India), Oxford, Versailles and Yale (CBA). There are also works said to be still in India.

KEY. A painting is said to be high or low in key according to the average of the tone and colour values: thus an Impressionist picture is high in key, all the tones being kept nearer white than black and most of the colours being pale and bright. Very low-keyed pictures, such as those by the followers of Caravaggio, are TENEBRIST.

KEYSER, Thomas de (1596/7–1667). An Amsterdam portrait painter of the ELIAS generation, he first influenced REMBRANDT (e.g. Keyser's *Constantine Huyghens*, 1627, London, NG) and was then influenced by him. Later works include small equestrian portraits with landscape backgrounds, often by other painters. Other works are in Amsterdam, Haarlem, The Hague, Hull, New

York, Oxford, Paris, Philadelphia, Raleigh NC, Rotterdam, Toledo Ohio and elsewhere.

KINETIC (Gk 'moving') ART is based on the idea that light and movement can create a work of art. Objects may be made to gyrate, and make interesting patterns of light and shadow as they do so; elaborate assemblages of moving pieces of metal, glass, or any other material may be combined with changing effects of coloured lights to create shadows and reflections. The mobiles of CALDER or CHADWICK are simple forms of kinetic art; more complicated forms often incorporate an electric motor, like the constructions by Bryan Wynter made of painted cards reflected in a concave mirror, Pol Bury's activated plastic hairs or wooden balls and cubes, or Julio Le Parc's random effects of glinting light made by moving squares of coloured metal hanging on nylon threads. GABO's *Standing Wave* (1920, London, Tate) is an early use of the idea, and links kinetic art with CONSTRUCTIVISM.

KIRCHNER, Ernst Ludwig (1880–1938), was a German Expressionist painter who was an original member of the BRÜCKE. From 1917 Kirchner lived in Switzerland suffering from tuberculosis until his eventual suicide in 1938. Many of his pictures were confiscated by the Nazis, but the best collection is now in Stuttgart. He also made a large number of woodcuts and some sculpture. Kirchner formulated the programme for the Brücke in 1906 and wrote its obituary in 1913, although his close friend HECKEL was the most enterprising member. It is said that Kirchner occasionally deliberately dated some of his pictures too early in order to claim priority. There are works by him in Edinburgh, London (Tate), and New York and other American museums as well as those in Germany.

KITAJ, R. B. (*b.*1932), is an American painter closely connected with the development of the British stream of POP ART. His personal aim was to create a compromise between the abstraction of Cubism, the distortion of Picasso, the colour of Matisse, and the demands of a complex subject matter. He returned to America in 1967. There are works in London (Tate, NPG: *Sir E. Gombrich*, 1986) and New York (M of MA).

KIT CAT (Kitkat). A canvas, size 36 × 28 inches, which is adapted to a portrait showing the head and one hand. *See* KNELLER.

KLEE, Paul (1879–1940), was a Swiss painter and etcher, whose art of free fantasy, perhaps the most poetic of modern times, is best defined in his own words as 'taking a line for a walk'. He was trained in Munich and went to Italy (1901–2), after which he returned to Switzerland and began etching. His early graphic work was influenced by Blake and Beardsley as well as Goya and, later, ENSOR. He worked in Germany from 1906 until 1933, teaching for many years at the celebrated Bauhaus in Weimar and Dessau, and later at Düsseldorf Academy. He was an impassioned teacher and many of his 'Pedagogical Sketchbooks' and theoretical writings have been published. From 1911 he was associated with the BLAUE REITER artists, and was especially close to KANDINSKY, FEININGER and JAWLENSKY (they were known, from 1924, as the 'Blue Four'); all four were German by adoption, not by birth. In 1914 he went to Tunisia with MACKE, an experience which revealed a new world of colour to him. From the 1920s he was famous, and no fewer than 102 works of his were confiscated from German galleries by the Nazis. There are works in most galleries of modern art now, and there is a Klee Foundation in Berne.

KLEINMEISTER, Die (Ger. The Little Masters). A group of 16th-century German engravers who worked on a small scale (hence the name). They were all more or less influenced by Dürer, but otherwise had little in common. By far the greatest was ALTDORFER, but others included ALDEGREVER, BALDUNG, the BEHAM brothers, BURGKMAIR and PENCZ.

KLIMT, Gustav (1862–1918), was the principal Austrian *Jugendstil* (ART NOUVEAU) painter, and one of the founders of the Vienna SEZESSION (1898), although he resigned in 1903. He was essentially a decorator and, from 1883 to 1892, he shared a studio for decorative painting with his brother and another artist: they worked in the Kunsthistorisches Museum, Vienna, in 1891. From *c.*1898, after a barren period of about six years, he was influenced by Japanese art and by contemporary English painters like BURNE-JONES and ALMA-TADEMA. A more realist style characterized his ceilings for Vienna University (1900–3), which were very unpopular. He was perhaps most successful as a designer for the applied arts (e.g. mosaic), but he was also a great influence on SCHIELE and KOKOSCHKA. There are works in Vienna (Oesterreichische Galerie), Paris (Mus. d'Orsay) and a portrait in London (NG).

KLINE, Franz (1910–62), was one of the leading representatives of the post-war American movement which had a great influence in the 1950s and 1960s. He was an exponent of ABSTRACT EXPRESSIONISM who was deeply influenced by oriental calligraphy (*see* TOBEY) and whose colour schemes were normally limited to black, white and grey. He is well represented in American museums and there is a picture in the Tate, London.

KNAPTON, George (1698–1778), was a pupil of Richardson and went to Italy for seven years in 1725. He was a Founder-Member of the Society of Dilettanti in 1736, and painted, between 1741 and 1749, twenty-three portraits of fellow-members (all but one in fancy dress) which brought him into contact with the principal patrons of his day. From about 1737 he used pastel a good deal, a medium which provoked Vertue to remark 'Small pains and great gains in this darling modish study'. He was the master of COTES. There are examples in the Royal Coll. (including the huge group of Prince Frederick Lewis and his family: 1751, London, Marlborough House), Birmingham, Cambridge (Fitzwm), London (Dulwich and Chiswick House), New York (Met. Mus.), Sheffield and Yale (CBA).

KNELLER, Sir Godfrey (1646 or 1649–1723). Born in Lübeck, Kneller was trained in Amsterdam under Rembrandt's pupil BOL, and he may even have come into contact with the aged Rembrandt himself. He then went to Italy (he was in Rome in 1672) and finally arrived in England *c.*1676, rapidly becoming the leading portrait painter. He was made Principal Painter to the King jointly with RILEY in 1688 and succeeded to the whole office when Riley died in 1691; in 1692 he was knighted and in 1715 he became the first painter in England to be made a baronet. There is a gap in his career between 1678 and 1682 and it has been conjectured that he was then abroad again. His first works in England are entirely in the style of Bol, but they later take on some of the softness of MARATTA; by 1683 Kneller had established his mature style and from then on there are hundreds of documented portraits by him, many signed and dated. Of these a great many are careless and mechanical in handling, and some are simply based on LELY's style and poses; yet his best works show a great grasp of character and are painted *alla prima* in a free and vigorous technique which became the normal English style for many years to come – in fact, until the more French manner of Allan RAMSAY superseded it. Part of his influence is due to his large employment of assistants, part due to Kneller's Academy, founded in 1711, which was the first attempt at an ACADEMY in England. His best works are the forty-two portraits, now in the NPG, London, known as the Kit Cat series, because they were painted for Christopher Cat. These all date from 1702 to 1717 and are a standard size (36 × 28 inches, generally known later as Kit Cat), showing the head and one hand. They represent the members of a Whig club of which Cat was the secretary. A direct comparison with Lely may be made in the two series of *Beauties*, at Hampton Court, and the *Admirals*, in the Nat. Marit. Mus. There is a picture at Lübeck dated 1668 and one in the Tate of 1672; others are in the Royal Coll., Cambridge (Trinity Coll.), London (NG, NPG and Tate), Yale (CBA) and many other galleries.

Kneller's conceit was vast. He is said to have swallowed the suggestion that things might have been better managed had the Deity consulted him at the Creation, but the suggestion was made by Pope, who was a hunchback, and Kneller replied unkindly that *some* things would, indeed, have been better made.

KØBKE, Christen (1810–48), was the major painter of the Danish Golden Age, equivalent to FRIEDRICH (who was trained in Copenhagen) in the BIEDERMEIER style. Købke was a pupil of ECKERSBERG (1828–*c*.34) before going to Dresden in 1838, where Friedrich lived, and on to Italy. He was in Rome, Naples, Pompeii – where he copied the wall-paintings – and Capri, before returning to Denmark in 1840. He painted mostly landscapes and portraits of friends and relations – his decorations, e.g. in the Thorwaldsen Museum, are less successful. Almost all his works are in Copenhagen, but there are examples in Edinburgh (NG), London (NG), Paris (Louvre) and Stockholm.

KOCH, Joseph Anton (1768–1839), was an Austrian landscape painter, born in the Tyrol, who was fundamentally a Romantic artist, but, like many others, was influenced by Neoclassic principles. In 1794 an English patron financed a trip to Italy, and in Rome he met CARSTENS and THORWALDSEN (1795). His first known landscape, of a waterfall, is of 1796 (Hamburg) and is of the POUSSIN type, but his fully Romantic style is seen in works like the *Schmadribachfall* (1805/11, Leipzig; version 1821/2 in Munich). He worked in Vienna 1812–15 before returning to Rome, where he took part in the decoration of the Casa Massimo (1825–9) by the NAZARENER. He died in Rome. His landscapes are of the Italianate type deriving from Poussin which were popular in the early 19th century, and he said himself that he wanted to give landscape 'an elemental character such as one may imagine when reading the Bible or Homer' (cf. HUDSON RIVER SCHOOL). There are works by him in Berlin, Cologne, Copenhagen, Düsseldorf, Karlsruhe, Munich, Vienna and other Austrian and German galleries.

KOEKKOEK. A Dutch family of painters of landscapes, seascapes and town views. The first was Johannes (1778–1851), who mostly painted sea-pieces, but the most famous was his son, Barend Cornelis (1803–62), a landscape painter whose style was founded on such 17th-century masters as Hobbema, van Goyen and Wynants. He wrote an autobiography in 1841. His younger brother Hermanus (1815–82) painted sea and coast scenes; Hermanus's son, Willem (1839–95), mostly painted townscapes like the 17th-century ones by Berckheyde or van der Heyden (a good example is in London, NG). He settled in London in 1881 and died there. The family is well represented in Dutch and German museums and there are also works in Glasgow, New York (Met. Mus.) and Sheffield.

KOKOSCHKA, Oskar (1886–1980), was an Austrian painter who developed, between 1908 and 1914, a highly imaginative Expressionist style. In Vienna, he was a pupil of KLIMT (1904–9). He was severely wounded in the head in 1915, but taught at the Dresden Academy from 1919, was influenced by painters who had worked in the BRÜCKE group, and from 1924 to 1931 travelled widely in Europe, North Africa and the Near East. He lived in Vienna from 1931 to 1934, and then went to Prague and afterwards to London, where he lived until 1953, becoming a British citizen in 1947 and being created CBE in 1959. His portraits, landscapes, and, chiefly, town views, often seen almost in bird's-eye view, are vivid in colour and of a restless energy of drawing; he also painted many allegories, inspired by legends or, more commonly, by ideological themes; one of these, in London (Courtauld Inst.), is a large ceiling decoration. There are works in Cardiff, Edinburgh (NG and SNPG), London (Tate), New York (M of MA) and many other museums of modern art. He also wrote plays (1909–11), which are part of the Expressionist theatre, and his autobiography was published in 1974.

KOLLWITZ, Käthe (1867–1945), was one of the most powerfully emotional German artists of this century. She married a doctor in 1891 and settled in Berlin in a slum where she lived until she was bombed out in 1943. She soon began to make etchings, woodcuts and lithographs mainly of the Mother and Child theme and often with left-wing intentions (*Weavers' Rising*, 1893–7, and *Peasants' War*, 1903–8). Most of her best works are tragic and many of them are specifically pacifist – her son was killed in 1914 and her grandson in 1942. In 1927 she made a journey to Russia, but was subsequently disillusioned. In 1933 she was expelled from the Academy and in the following years made eight large lithographs called *Death*. In her later years she also made some bronzes of which the most important is a memorial to her son in Diksmuide, Flanders (1924–32).

KONINCK, Philips de (1619–88), may have been a pupil of Rembrandt before learning landscape painting from his brother Jacob de Koninck. He painted several rather unpleasing genre scenes in the manner of Brouwer, some not very distinguished portraits, and some superb panoramic views of the flat landscape and luminous skies of Holland. The figures in these are sometimes his own and sometimes by Lingelbach or Adriaen van de Velde. His very numerous drawings are in most big museums and have frequently been confused with Rembrandt's – a further possible confusion is between Philips and Salomon Koninck. There are pictures in the Royal Coll. and in Amsterdam (Rijksmus.), Berlin, Cape Town, Edinburgh (NG), Frankfurt (Städel), Glasgow (Univ.), The Hague, London (NG and V&A), Los Angeles, Munich, New York (Met. Mus.), Oxford, Philadelphia (Mus.), Rotterdam and elsewhere.

KONINCK, Salomon (1609–56), was an Amsterdam painter who, from the early 1630s, imitated Rembrandt, especially in his small figures and groups of bearded old men. Like Philips de Koninck – to whom he may have been distantly related – many of his drawings have passed as Rembrandt's. There are works in Amsterdam (Rijksmus.), Berlin, The Hague, Liverpool, Vaduz (Liechtenstein Coll.) and elsewhere.

KONRAD (Conrad) von Soest was the principal Westphalian painter of the early 15th century. His only certain work is the signed polyptych in Niederwildungen Parish Church, obscurely dated, but probably 1404. This shows the influence of the SOFT STYLE, and, more precisely, contemporary Franco-Burgundian work. Other works attributed to him are in churches in Soest and Dortmund.

KOONING, Willem de (1904–89), was born in Rotterdam, but lived in the US from 1926. He was trained under the influence of De STIJL, but became a leading Action Painter. His works have a brutal quasi-realism similar to that of the Dutchman APPEL. He painted a mural for the New York World's Fair of 1939 and there are pictures by him in Buffalo, London (Tate) and New York (M of MA).

KORTEGAARDJE, a Dutch word, from Fr. *corps de garde*, used to describe the guard-room scenes popular in the 17th century, which show soldiers engaged in drinking, gambling, quarrelling and similar military occupations. The genre seems to have been invented by MANFREDI, but was popular in the North. David TENIERS II painted several fine examples, e.g. one in London (Dulwich).

KRAFT (Krafft), Adam (1455/60–1508/9), was a leading Late Gothic sculptor in Nuremberg, the friend of Peter VISCHER I. His works, invariably in stone, are all in Nuremberg and have strongly characterized figures. The most important is the Tabernacle in S. Lorenz, of 1493–6, more than 60 feet high and containing scores of figures.

KRICKE, Norbert (*b.*1922), is a German sculptor fascinated by the movement of water. His *Water Forest*, 9 feet high, in the grounds of the Gelsenkirchen Opera House (1957), is made of plexiglass, through which water circulates. He has also made compositions in wire, e.g. at Münster Theatre (1959).

KRIEGHOFF, Cornelius (1815–72), was born in Amsterdam, but trained mainly in Düsseldorf, and would have been a minor BIEDERMEIER painter had he not gone to N. America in 1837. He wandered about in the US and served in the US Army before going to Canada *c.*1840/1, where he became one of the first Canadian painters, making pictures and chromo-lithographs of Indians and similar frontier subjects. He returned for a short visit to Europe, but his importance is as a recorder of Canada. He is well represented in Ottawa and other Canadian galleries.

KRÜGER, Franz (1797–1857), was the leading painter of the BIEDERMEIER style in Berlin, where he was Professor at the Academy and Court painter. He specialized in horses, portraits and ceremonial pictures very similar to those of his contemporary Horace VERNET, who, like him, worked in St Petersburg for the Czar and whom he met on a visit to Paris in 1846. He also met DELACROIX and was influenced by him (his diary records watching Delacroix making a sketch). Many of his portrait drawings were published as lithographs after his death. Most of his works are in Berlin.

KULMBACH, Hans Süss von (*c.*1480–1522), was a Nuremberg painter who, with SCHÄUFFELEIN, was the best and closest of DÜRER's followers. He formed his style on Dürer's with a leaning towards the Venetians (who had so profoundly influenced Dürer himself), as transmitted to him by Jacopo de' BARBARI. He probably went to Cracow in 1510/11 and was certainly there 1514–16. There are works by him in Berlin, Cracow, Dublin, Florence (Uffizi), The Hague, Hanover, Leipzig, Munich, New York (Met. Mus.), Nuremberg, Turin, Vaduz (Liechtenstein Coll.) and Vienna.

KUNSTVEREIN (Ger. ART UNION). The first German art union was founded in Berlin in 1814 and others quickly followed. The British and American unions had the same aims of educating public taste and offering a chance of acquiring original works of art for a small outlay.

KUPKA, Frantisek (Frank, Franz) (1871–1957), one of the founders of abstract art, was trained in Prague and Vienna before going to Paris *c.*1895. He practised as a spiritualist medium, as well as a Fauve painter, but *c.*1911 he began to evolve an abstract style under the influences of KLIMT, ORPHISME and the SECTION D'OR Cubists led by Jacques VILLON: his *Planes by Colours* (1911, Paris, Mus. d'Art Moderne) is comparable with KANDINSKY's abstract watercolours and antedates the work of MALEVICH and MONDRIAN. Kupka also wrote a book on artistic creation. There is a Kupka Mus. in Prague (some fifty pictures) and other works are in London (Tate), New York (M of MA) and Paris (Mus. d'Art Moderne).

L

LABILLE-GUIARD, Adélaïde (1749–1803), was a French portrait painter in oil and pastel (which she studied under M. Q. de LATOUR). She became an Academician in 1783, on the same day as her great rival Élisabeth VIGÉE-LEBRUN, but Vigée-Lebrun's career in France was ended by the Revolution, whereas Labille-Guiard supported the new regime and painted portraits of the Deputies to the National Assembly. In 1793, however, her hopes of fame as a history painter were shattered when she was ordered to destroy her huge *Reception of a Knight of S. Lazare*, because it contained a portrait of the Grand Master, Louis XVI's brother. She was a dedicated teacher of other women painters. There are works in New York (Met. Mus.), Paris (Louvre) and Versailles.

LADBROKE, Robert *see* NORWICH SCHOOL.

LAER, Pieter van, *see* BAMBOCCIO.

LA FARGE, John (1835–1910), was an American painter who began studying law, but was in Paris by 1856, working under COUTURE. He visited London and was impressed by the PRE-RAPHAELITE BROTHERHOOD. From *c.*1860 he painted Barbizon-type landscapes, still-life and flowers, and in 1876 he was commissioned to paint frescoes for H. H. Richardson's Trinity Church in Boston. He worked for other churches in New York and designed stained glass, involving him in the American Arts and Crafts movement. In 1886 he visited Japan with the writer Henry Adams and went with him to Tahiti in 1890; like Gauguin, he sought to escape from the industrialized world. He also wrote two books on art (1895, 1897). There are pictures by him in Boston, Buffalo, Cambridge Mass (Fogg), Cincinnati, Detroit, New York (Brooklyn), St Louis, Washington (NG, Corcoran) and Williamstown Mass.

LAGUERRE, Louis (1663–1721), was a French painter who, after working for some time under LEBRUN, came to England in 1683/4. He worked for VERRIO at Christ's Hospital in 1684, and, with a French architectural painter called Ricard, decorated the Chapel, the Painted Hall, and several State Rooms at Chatsworth, 1689–94. He worked in many country houses, including Burghley and Blenheim (his best work) and also at Marlborough House in London. In his last decade, he suffered from the competition of THORNHILL, who learned much from him. After 1715 he decorated the church of St Lawrence, Stanmore, near London.

LAM, Wifredo (or Wilfredo) (1902–82), was born in Cuba of Negro and Chinese parents, and studied in Havana, Madrid and Paris. He lived in Spain, 1923–38, and, from 1952, in Paris, where he became a Surrealist influenced by Breton and Picasso. He returned to Cuba in 1942, and then went to the US. His pictures make use of folklore and include totems and jungle scenes. There are examples in London (Tate) and New York (M of MA).

LAMA, Giulia (*c.*1685–after 1753), was a follower of PIAZZETTA, who made a drawing of her *c.*1720 (Lugano, Thyssen Coll.). Her style was very close to his, and is known from two altarpieces in Venice (S. Vitale, Sta Maria Formosa), one in the parish church of Malamocco, and one now in Ca' Rezzonico, Venice.

LAMBERT, George (*c.*1700–65), was an early English landscape painter. He was a pupil of WOOTTON and imitated him as well as Wootton's own model, Gaspar POUSSIN. His first dated work is of 1723 (private coll.). He painted the landscapes in his friend HOGARTH's large religious pictures in St Bartholomew's Hospital, London, and there are other works in Cardiff, Gateshead, London (Tate and V&A), Manchester and Yale (CBA).

LANCRET, Nicolas (1690–1743), was, with PATER, the principal imitator of WATTEAU. After failing as a history painter he was influenced by Gillot's theatrical scenes, as Watteau had been, and he spent the rest of his life painting *fêtes galantes*. He is well represented in the Wallace Coll., London, and in Waddesdon Bucks. (National Trust).

LANDSEER, Sir Edwin (1802–73), the celebrated painter of sentimental animal subjects, was an infant prodigy who first exhibited at the RA at the age of 12. He was the son of an engraver and his eldest brother devoted his life to making engravings of his pictures, examples of which were once to be found in practically every public house in England. At the beginning of his career he was an excellent painter of animals who owned STUBBS's drawings for the 'Anatomy of the Horse', but he very soon discovered that by giving animals, and especially dogs, quasi-human expressions he was able to touch the hearts of a large public. He was entranced by his first visit to Scotland in 1824 and very soon began to move in the highest society, particularly on deer-stalking expeditions; he was Queen Victoria's favourite painter and the lifelong friend of the Duchess of Bedford. Landseer was elected ARA at the earliest possible age (24), and RA in 1831; he refused the Presidency in 1865, as he had already refused a knighthood in 1842 (though he accepted in 1850). His best-known work is the group of lions at the foot of the Nelson monument in Trafalgar Square, London, 1857–67. It has been observed that many of his pictures of animals have an unpleasant substratum of cruelty; *The Cat's-Paw*, exhibited in 1824 and very popular in engravings, shows a monkey using a cat's paws to fish roast chestnuts out of a fire. In 1869 his mind gave way and he died four years later hopelessly insane. There are many pictures in the Royal Coll. and others in Birmingham, Liverpool, London (Tate, NPG, RA, V&A, Kenwood), Yale (CBA) and elsewhere. The *Stag at Bay*, perhaps the best known of his numerous Highland subjects, is now in a private collection in Dublin.

LANFRANCO, Giovanni (1582–1647), was born near Parma, where he was a pupil of Agostino CARRACCI, and was also much influenced by the domes by Correggio. He was in Rome in 1612, and about 1616 decorated the ceiling of the Casino Borghese in a manner derived entirely from the Farnese Gallery. He developed Correggio's SOTTO IN SÙ type of illusionism to an extravagant point, and painted several domes and apses in Roman and Neapolitan churches in this manner. To him DOMENICHINO lost part of the commission for the decoration of S. Andrea della Valle in Rome, a slight he resented so bitterly that – so the story goes – he weakened part of the scaffolding, hoping that Lanfranco would break his neck. Lanfranco completed the dome with an *Assumption*, Correggiesque in inspiration, between 1625–7, and such was its success that he was then employed at St Peter's until 1631. From 1633/4 to 1646 he was in Naples, and in 1641–3 painted the dome of the S. Gennaro chapel in the Cathedral, which by its more up-to-date illusionism and greater showiness appealed far more to local tastes than Domenichino's works there. His dome is based on Correggio's type of illusionism and replaces one actually begun by Domenichino. He died in Rome, where his last work was the apse of S. Carlo ai Catinari. Apart from Rome and Naples, there are works in Amsterdam, Berlin, Dublin, Florence (Pitti), Leningrad, London (Coram Fdn.), Lyons, Madrid (Prado), Marseilles, Oxford (Ashmolean), Paris (Louvre), Parma, Versailles and Vienna.

LAOCOÖN. The famous antique statue, described by Pliny and now in the Vatican, was discovered near Rome in 1506. The 16th-century restorations have been removed, but most reproductions still show it as it was. It represents the death agonies of Laocoön and his two sons, crushed by the serpents. The horrible naturalism of this late Hellenistic work led to erroneous ideas about the nature of Greek art and to a long controversy over whether Laocoön was really suffering in noble silence (WINCKELMANN, 1755) or (as he obviously is) howling with pain; part of this controversy was Lessing's 'Laocoön' published in 1766, and dealing with the relationship between painting and poetry.

LARGILLIERRE (Largillière), Nicolas de (1656–1746), was born in Paris but passed his youth in Antwerp and, from *c.*1674, spent some years in England as LELY's assistant. He was thus almost a Flemish painter when he returned to Paris in 1682. He became a member of the Academy in 1686 and ultimately its Director. His principal rival was RIGAUD, but Largillierre specialized in portraits of the wealthy middle classes, leaving the aristocrats to Rigaud. There are typical examples in London (NG and Wallace Coll.), New York (Met. Mus.), and Paris (Louvre). The *S. Geneviève* (Paris, S. Étienne) is the only survivor of the large *ex-voto* type of picture that he painted for the Corporations. He also painted a few pictures of still-life.

LARIONOV, Mikhail, *see* RAYONISM.

LARKIN, William (active *c.*1605–*d.*1619), was a British portrait painter contemporary with the Flemings van SOMER and JOHNSON, but he may have been a pupil of HILLIARD. His work has only recently been reconstructed, but the Ranger's House, Blackheath, London, now has a series of portraits of the Suffolk family attributed to him. The attributions are based on standard carpet and curtain patterns and have only a slight connection with the two portraits at Charlecote Park nr Stratford-on-Avon (National Trust), which are documented as his. Other portraits are in London (NPG) and Yale (CBA).

LASTMAN, Pieter (1583–1633), was an Amsterdam history painter who went to Italy *c.*1604 and was influenced by Caravaggio – which makes him akin to the UTRECHT SCHOOL – and by ELSHEIMER. His *forte* was small figures in exotic and brightly-coloured costumes. He was back in Amsterdam by 1607. His real importance lies in the fact that LIEVENS was his pupil in 1617 and REMBRANDT in 1624/5. There are good examples in Amsterdam, Dublin, Gateshead, London (NG), Los Angeles and Providence RI. One signed and dated 1620 has been discovered in Trinity Hospital, Retford, nr Lincoln.

LA TOUR, Georges de (1593–1652), worked all his life in Lorraine. He painted religious and genre subjects in a style that stems ultimately from Caravaggio, although it seems more likely that he derived from the UTRECHT SCHOOL than directly from Caravaggio or his Italian followers. In his later works he adopts a form of indirect lighting from a candle or other concealed source of light, which is close to Dutch Caravaggisti like HONTHORST. In his last works he evolved a figure style in which all masses are reduced to the simplest, almost geometrical, shapes, arranged in a static calm which is itself an expression of French classicism. His religious subjects seem to be connected with a contemporary religious revival in Lorraine particularly associated with the Franciscans. Like VERMEER, his output was tiny – about forty paintings, including those in the Royal Coll. and in Bergues nr Dunkirk, Berlin, Cleveland Ohio, Detroit, Épinal, Fort Worth Texas, Grenoble, Hartford Conn., Kansas City, Leicester (discovered in 1984), Le Mans, Malibu Cal. (Getty Mus.), Nancy, Nantes, New York (Met. Mus. and Frick Coll.), Paris (Louvre), Rennes, Rouen, Stockholm and Stockton-on-Tees.

LATOUR, Maurice Quentin de (1704–88), was, with PERRONNEAU, the most celebrated French pastellist of the 18th century. He was born in St Quentin and went to Paris as a young man; after visits to London and other places he settled in Paris 1724–84. He soon found that the vogue for pastel portraits started by Rosalba CARRIERA in 1719/20 was still capable of exploitation and he devoted the rest of his life to it. His portraits are characterized by an extreme vivacity of handling – sometimes rather vulgar – and a firm grasp of character. As a very old man the study of politics drove him crazy, and he retired to St Quentin, where the largest and best collection of his works is to be found: it includes many studies and sketches which are sometimes superior to the finished portraits. There is a good example in London (NG).

LAURANA, Francesco (*c.*1430–1502?), was Dalmatian by birth (at La Vrana, near Zadar) but Venetian by nationality although he worked much in Sicily and France. He is first recorded as working on the Triumphal Arch in Naples (1453–8), but it is difficult to know what he did. He was in France 1461–6 and in Palermo in 1467 – two *Madonnas* dated 1471 are in Palermo, Sta Maria della Neve and Noto, Church of the Crucifixion – returning to France in 1477 for six years. He must have gone back to France (*c.*1498?), since he died there before 12 March 1502. He is best known as the sculptor of a series of busts of enigmatic-looking women, now in several French provincial museums as well as in Berlin, Paris (Louvre), Vienna and Washington (NG). They include *Battista Sforza, Duchess of Urbino* (*d.*1472, Florence, Bargello), probably made *c.*1474 from a death-mask. During his last years in France he made tombs in Tarascon, Le Mans, and a figure of *St Martha* in the old Cathedral at Marseilles. It has been suggested that he went back to Naples *c.*1483/98 and there made a further series of busts, stylistically very different from the earlier ones. His *Madonnas* and female busts are bland and tender, with curious drooping eyelids, rather like AGOSTINO di Duccio. Apart from works in Naples and Sicily, others are in Avignon, New York (Frick Coll.) and Paris (Jacquemart-André).

LAURENS, Henri (1885–1954), was a Cubist sculptor whose works are often of still-life subjects and are coloured, almost approaching COLLAGE: from 1911 he associated with Picasso, Braque, Léger, Gris and other Cubist painters and thus, like LIPCHITZ, evolved a Cubist sculpture. From the late 1920s his work became more realistic, particularly when he treated Greek mythological themes. He also illustrated several books. There are works in Calais, Dieppe, Dijon, Grenoble, Liverpool, London (Tate) and Paris (Mus. d'Art Moderne).

LAUTREC *see* TOULOUSE-LAUTREC.

LAWRENCE, Sir Thomas (1769–1830), was born in Bristol but was so precocious that, at the age of 10, he was in practice as a portrait draughtsman in crayons in Oxford: at 17 he wrote to his mother: 'excepting Sir Joshua, for the painting of a head I would risk my reputation with any painter in London' – and that was in Gainsborough's lifetime. In 1787, however, he was a student at the RA Schools for a short time and exhibited at the Academy of that year. From then on he was enormously successful, being made ARA in 1791, appointed Painter to the King on the death of Reynolds in 1792, and elected RA in 1794; he became President of the RA in 1820, having been knighted five years earlier. He had a European reputation as a portrait painter, partly because of the very real glitter and force of his best works, partly because he was commissioned by the Prince Regent (later George IV) to paint all the great personalities of the struggle against Napoleon, making a kind of triumphal progress through Vienna and Rome to do so. His income was huge, but he was always heavily in debt, which probably explains the empty flashiness of his worst work, produced for immediate cash. It is, however, notable that his style was formed very early and scarcely changed. Two of his masterpieces, *Miss Farren* (New York, Met. Mus.) and *Queen Charlotte* (London, NG) were both in the 1790 RA – i.e. they were painted before he was 21 – yet there is little difference between them and *The Archduke of Austria* and *Pius VII* (both Royal Coll.) of 1819 (the *Pius* was still in his studio at his death). He formed a superb collection of Old Master drawings – probably one of the best ever made – and his will offered it to the nation on very easy terms: by a piece of more than usual governmental imbecility it was refused, and many of the finest drawings dispersed. Fortunately, a part was later bought for Oxford (Ashmolean). The best collection of his works is in the Waterloo Chamber at Windsor Castle, which houses the set of European sovereigns and statesmen painted for George IV. Other works are in museums all over the world, including Brighton, Chicago, London (NG, NPG, BM, Tate, V&A, Wallace Coll., RA, Dulwich, Guildhall, Soane Mus., Kenwood and Wellington Mus.), Ottawa, Paris (Louvre), San Marino Cal., the Vatican, Vienna, Washington (NG, Corcoran, and Phillips) and Yale (CBA).

LAY-FIGURE. A jointed wooden figure, often life-size, which can be used either to arrange drapery on or as a guide to a complicated pose. It is said to have been invented by Fra Bartolommeo, but no doubt small clay figures or manikins were in use much earlier.

LAY-IN. In the traditional method of OIL-PAINTING, as opposed to ALLA PRIMA, the painter began by making an exact drawing on his canvas. This was then 'laid in' in monochrome, so that the whole tonal effect – but not the colour – was worked out in full. This 'dead colour' was usually a brown, grey, or greenish tint, occasionally a dull red. The purpose was to get the whole design and tonality worked out, so that the painter could then concentrate on the colour values. SICKERT was one of the last great exponents of the method.

LEAL, Valdés, *see* VALDÉS.

LEAN *see* FAT.

LEAR, Edward (1812–88), best known as a writer of Nonsense Verses, began as a zoological draughtsman, which brought him into contact with Lord Derby, for whose children Lear wrote the 'Book of Nonsense' (1846). His detailed studies of birds (1828–31) resulted in his 'Psittacide' (1832), but he then turned to topography and began a long series of watercolours, lithographs and illustrated travel books. He lived in Rome 1838–48, in an international community of artists, and began to work in oils as well as producing twenty-five views of Rome in lithographs (1841). He was in England 1849–53, when he studied at the RA and met Holman HUNT, whom, with Turner, he revered all his life. (He was dismissive of Millais.) From 1853 he lived abroad, travelling much of the time – he was in India and Ceylon 1873–5 – in search of new scenery, but he was always more famous for his nonsense. There are examples in the Royal Coll. (he gave Queen Victoria lessons), and in Brighton, Bristol, Cambridge (Fitzwm), Cambridge (Harvard Univ.), Chicago, Glasgow, Liverpool, London (BM, Tate and V&A), New York (Met. Mus.) and Yale (CBA).

LE BRUN, Mme Vigée, *see* VIGÉE.

LEBRUN, Charles (1619–90), was the virtual dictator of the arts in France under Louis XIV, until the death of his protector Colbert. He was the type of artist-politician, and as early as 1641 he gained Richelieu's patronage with an allegorical portrait of King Louis XIII. He was a pupil of VOUET and went to Rome, probably with Poussin, in 1642; he studied partly under Poussin and partly from the works of the Roman Baroque decorators, such as PIETRO da Cortona. He returned, without permission, in 1646, as he was bored with Rome. In 1647 he exhibited an altarpiece for Notre Dame (a MAI), which began his success, and in 1648 he had so far taken over Vouet's position that he was one of the leaders in the foundation of the ACADEMY in 1648. He was to be Rector, Chancellor and Director of it. He began the decorations for Vaux-le-Vicomte, for the minister Fouquet, in 1658. After Fouquet's fall Colbert recognized Lebrun's talent as well as the advantages of a centralized institution as an instrument of policy, and advanced Lebrun, who became director of the huge undertakings at the Gobelins factory as well as *premier peintre* in 1664 (he had received his first Royal commission in 1661). In 1665 Bernini arrived in Paris, where he seems to have been critical of Lebrun's talent. This may have some connection with the sabotaging of Bernini's plans for the Louvre and the general failure of his visit: on the other hand, Lebrun was elected to the Academy of St Luke in Rome in 1675 and made Director in the same year (and in 1676). For the French Academy he laid down a strict system of rules and even wrote a treatise on the expression of the passions ('Méthode pour apprendre à dessiner les Passions', 1698). His most important paintings are at Versailles, where he decorated the *Galerie des Glaces* (1679–84) and the *Salons de la Guerre* and *de la Paix* (completed 1686). After the death of Colbert in 1683 Lebrun, though promoted Director of the Academy in that year, was gradually superseded by MIGNARD. There are paintings by him in Bristol, Cambridge (Fitzwm), Detroit, Dublin, London (V&A and Dulwich), Montreal, Munich, Nottingham, Ottawa, Paris (Louvre), Prague, Venice, Wakefield and many French provincial museums. There are about 2,000 drawings by him in the Louvre.

LEGA, Silvestro (1826–95), like FATTORI, fought for Italian independence in 1848–9 and was a leading member of the MACCHIAIOLI *c.*1860. Unlike Fattori, however, Lega carried his political opposition to the French so far as to dislike French art: nevertheless, his masterpiece *The Pergola* (1868, Milan, Brera) is unthinkable without the example of COROT and the beginnings of Impressionism. He suffered from eye trouble from 1880 and was blind for some years before his death, in great poverty, in Florence. There are works in Florence, Milan and Rome.

LÉGER, Fernand (1881–1955), met BRAQUE and PICASSO in 1910 and eventually from his early block-like figures evolved, by *c.*1917, a form of curvilinear CUBISM, dependent on the dynamic shapes of machinery and their geometrical bases: cones, cylinders, cogged wheels, pistons and brilliant metallic surfaces. These forms also influenced his massive, robot-like figures, and increased the effect of his clear greys and his strong, unbroken colours. He designed for the Swedish Ballet in 1921–2, and in 1924 made the first abstract film, 'Le Ballet Mécanique', from actual objects, not animated abstract drawings as had been used by Eggeling and Richter some seven years earlier. Among his last works were the huge murals for the UN building in New York. He also made a set of stained-glass windows for the Sacré Coeur, Audincourt nr Belfort (Doubs). There are works in Edinburgh, London (Tate), New York (M of MA), Paris (Mus. d'Art Moderne), and there is a Musée Léger at Biot, Côte d'Azur.

LEGROS, Alphonse (1837–1911), was a French painter of peasant genre, influenced by COURBET, but probably drawing more on his own experience of poverty. He had a picture in the Salon des Refusés in 1863, and was a friend of Fantin-Latour, Manet, Degas and Whistler. In 1863 he went to London, where he settled, and became the main link between French and English *avant-garde* painters. He was Slade Professor in London 1876–92, and was largely responsible for the reputation of the Slade School for draughtsmanship. In the 1880s he drifted away from Impressionism, and in 1883 Pissarro warned his son Lucien, who was about to enter the Slade, against Legros, because his style then showed a hardness of outline and his 'open-air' pictures were largely painted in the studio. Monet and Degas shared this distrust. In fact, he was more important as a graphic artist than as a painter. There are works in Cologne, Dijon, London (Tate and V&A), Paris (Mus. d'Orsay) and many drawings in Glasgow.

LEGROS, Pierre II (1666–1719), was a French sculptor, pupil of his father, Pierre I, who worked mainly at Versailles. Pierre II won the Rome Prize in 1686, was in the French Academy there 1690–5, and settled there permanently. He worked extensively for Roman churches, especially for the Jesuits, and at the end of his life at Montecassino (*Gregory the Great*, 1714–19). For the altar of S. Ignatius in the Gesù in Rome he made a large marble relief (1695–9) of *Religion defeating Heresy* (*modello* in Montpellier), and a silver statue of S. Ignatius which was melted down by Pius VI to pay reparations to Napoleon in 1797. The present statue is a replica. Other works include a relief of *S. Luigi Gonzaga*, in collaboration with G. COUSTOU I, in S. Ignazio (1698–9), but his most famous work is the polychrome marble statue of *St Stanislas Kostka on his Deathbed* for the Jesuits of S. Andrea al Quirinale. He wished it to be placed in the church, but the Jesuits maintained that it would interfere with the uniformity of the church, which Bernini had insisted upon. It is in a nearby oratory. Legros's art is still Baroque, but in the more restrained manner practised particularly by French sculptors trained in Rome. There are other works in Rome and a *bozzetto* in Los Angeles.

LEHMBRUCK, Wilhelm (1881–1919), was a German sculptor trained in Düsseldorf, where he was a contemporary of MACKE. He went to Italy in 1905 and lived in Paris 1910–14. He was influenced by both RODIN and MAILLOL, but his own forms are more elongated, and his masterpiece, the *Kneeling*

Woman, of 1911, has a Gothic expressiveness. In Paris he also met MODIGLIANI, Brancusi and Archipenko. He committed suicide in 1919. There are many works in his native Duisburg and others in Auckland NZ, Buffalo, London (Tate), Louisville Kentucky, New York (M of MA), Otterlo and several German museums.

LEIBL, Wilhelm (1844–1900), was a Cologne painter who was the leader of German Realism in the late 19th century. He met COURBET in Munich at the time of Courbet's exhibition in 1869, and later spent six months in Paris before the outbreak of the Franco-Prussian War (1870). His technical experiments included the use of tempera to obtain an enamel-like surface, and the minuteness of his handling can be seen in his masterpiece *Three Women in a Village Church* (1878–82, Hamburg). He lived in Bavarian villages and used peasant models, thus exerting a great influence on THOMA and the School of Munich. Many German museums possess examples, including Berlin, Cologne, Frankfurt, Hamburg, Leipzig and Munich.

LEIGHTON, Frederic (later Lord Leighton of Stretton) (1830–96), was, like ALMA-TADEMA, one of the leading exponents of a rather bloodless Greek classicism in the later 19th century, e.g. the *Bath of Psyche* (1890, Leighton House). He began his studies at 14, in Florence in 1844, and continued in Frankfurt, Brussels and Paris until 1849. He was influenced by the NAZARENES, settled in Rome in 1852, where he was a friend of Nino COSTA, and painted the large *Cimabue's Madonna borne in Procession*, which was exhibited in the RA of 1855 and bought by Queen Victoria (still in the Royal Coll.). He settled in London in 1860 and became ARA in 1864, RA 1868 and PRA ten years later. In London he was friendly with WATTS. Just before his death he was made a peer, the only British artist, so far, to be ennobled. His extraordinary 'Moorish' house in Kensington, London, is a museum with works by him and his contemporaries. There are examples in London (NPG, Tate and V&A) and many British galleries, Boston, New York (Met. Mus.) and Yale (CBA).

LELY, Sir Peter (1618–80), was born in Germany of Dutch parents – his real name was van der Faes – and studied in Haarlem under Pieter de Grebber (*c.*1600–52/3), becoming a Master in the Haarlem Guild in 1637. No works of this Dutch period are known, though there is a *Diana and Nymphs* in Nantes, dated 1640 or 1646: this may have been painted there, though Lely probably arrived in London in the early 1640s and was certainly there in 1647. The earliest works produced in this country are still more or less in the style of de Grebber: they are history and subject pieces, even religious pictures, which he continued to paint throughout the Commonwealth. By 1647, however, he had painted the King as well as the Royal children and the double portrait of Charles I and the Duke of York (1647, Syon House Middx) inspired Lovelace's poem 'See what a clouded majesty . . .'. With the Restoration Lely at once began the production of that huge flood of portraits which made him the most influential of English 17th-century painters; more important even than van Dyck, to whose position he succeeded when he became Principal Painter to Charles II in 1661. From then until his death he maintained a large studio turning out hundreds of portraits painted in an International Baroque style and exactly catching that atmosphere of sensual languor which most of Charles's Court saw themselves as possessing. The two poles of his art are represented by the sleepily voluptuous *Beauties* of Charles II's Court (Royal Coll., Hampton Court) and the splendidly masculine *Admirals* (Nat. Marit. Mus.). These represent the twelve Admirals under the command of the Duke of York (later James II), for whom the set was painted to commemorate the victories in the Second Dutch War. Pepys records (18 April 1666): 'To Mr Lilly's, the painter's; and there saw the heads, some finished, and all begun, of the Flaggmen in the late great fight . . .' and, in the next year he described Lely as 'a mighty proud man, full of state'. He was knighted in 1680. There are other pictures by him in the Royal Coll. and in Birmingham, Edinburgh (SNPG), Kingston Lacy Dorset (National Trust), London (NG, NPG, Tate, Courtauld Inst., Dulwich, Guildhall and Ham House), Manchester, New York (Met. Mus.), Ottawa, Yale (CBA), York and elsewhere.

LE MOYNE (Le Moine), François (1688–1737), continued, in the age of WATTEAU, the Grand Manner of LEBRUN. He did many decorations at Versailles, and his *Time revealing Truth* in the Wallace Coll., London, painted just before he committed suicide, shows the pure 17th-century style unaffected by Watteau, although it does show the triumph of RUBÉNISME. Boucher was his pupil.

LEMOYNE, Jean Baptiste (1704–78), was the son of a sculptor. He won the Rome Prize in 1725 but never made the journey. His *Baptism of Christ* (1731, Paris, St Roch) is his most famous religious work, but he is best known for his splendid portrait busts and as a teacher – his pupils included FALCONET, PIGALLE, PAJOU and HOUDON. There are works in Paris (Louvre, Jacquemart-André, and Comédie Française), Versailles, Stockholm, Toledo Ohio, Vienna and many French provincial museums.

LE NAIN. There were three brothers of this name, all born in Laon. Antoine (*c.*1588–1648) was in Paris from 1629 and his two brothers Louis (*c.*1593–1648) and Mathieu (*c.*1607–77) from 1630. All three were elected members of the Academy on its foundation in 1648. The snag is that there are about fifteen signed and dated pictures – but no signature has any initial and all the dates are in or before 1648; i.e. there is no certain means of telling one from another. However, there is a group of small pictures, mostly on copper with small figures painted in strong colours: these are usually associated with Antoine. Another group is much larger in scale, painted in cool greyish tones, sometimes (like Antoine's) of peasant families, but also sometimes of religious or mythological subjects treated very simply and directly and with no Baroque overtones: these are called 'Louis' and are perhaps the most valuable artistically. Louis is supposed to have been to Italy. Any remaining, including the occasional KORTEGAARDJE, tend to get ascribed to Mathieu. Their subject matter and style link them with the followers of Caravaggio, although the painters of the UTRECHT SCHOOL were often more flamboyant. Pictures by one or other are in Berlin, Birmingham (Barber Inst.), Boston, Bristol, Cardiff, Dublin, Glasgow (Burrell Coll. and Univ.), Hagerstown Md, Hartford Conn., London (NG and V&A), New York (Met. Mus.), Paris (Louvre), San Francisco (Legion of Honor), Scarborough, Springfield Mass. and several French provincial museums.

LENBACH, Franz von (1836–1904), studied at Munich before going to Rome in 1858–9. In 1863 he returned to Rome with BÖCKLIN. He visited Spain in 1867 before settling in Munich in 1868, where he became a successful portrait painter working in a style derived from Rembrandt and Reynolds. He painted some eighty versions of Bismarck (one in Edinburgh, NG). There is a Lenbach Gallery in Munich, and other German galleries have examples; his *Lord Acton* is in London (NPG), and *Gladstone* in Edinburgh (SNPG).

LEON, Juan van der Hamen y, *see* HAMEN.

LEONARDO da Vinci (1452–1519) was one of the greatest of the Universal Men produced by the Renaissance. His intellectual powers were such that he anticipated many later discoveries in anatomy, aeronautics, and several other fields, as well as being one of the greatest of Italian artists. He has always been counted as one of the three great creators of the High Renaissance of the 16th century, yet he was born in 1452 and was thus a contemporary of Perugino and Signorelli and much older than either Michelangelo (*b.*1475) or Raphael (*b.*1483). The intellectual powers which allowed him to overcome the 'dry and hard manner' (as Vasari called it) of the Quattrocento were, however, so diffused over an enormous range of interests that he brought hardly any major enterprise to a conclusion: he almost discovered the circulation of the blood, he invented the first armoured fighting vehicle, projected several aircraft and helicopters and anticipated the submarine, but not one of these discoveries was completed; and in the same way he left thousands of notes and drawings but only a handful of paintings, and still fewer completed ones.

He was born at Vinci, the illegitimate son of a Florentine notary, but was brought up in his father's house and trained as a painter, traditionally under VERROCCHIO. He is said to have painted the left-hand angel in Verrocchio's *Baptism* (Florence, Uffizi), as a result of which Verrocchio gave up painting. On stylistic grounds there is every reason to accept the truth of the story, and Verrocchio may well have felt that he could stick to sculpture if he could have so good a painter in the firm; for it is certainly true that Leonardo was living in Verrocchio's house in 1476, presumably as his assistant, since in that year an anonymous accusation of homosexuality which was made against him says so. He had already become a Master in the Guild in 1472, and his earliest datable work is a drawing of an Arno landscape (1473) which already shows his interest in rock-formation and the structure of the earth. There are also some drapery studies, made in the 1470s, which show him breaking new ground, for earlier painters had been content to invent a formula for the folds in drapery and stick to it all their lives, but it is typical of Leonardo that he should have made a special study of fold-structure. In the 1470s he was also experimenting with the technique of oil-painting, as may be seen in the *Madonna* in Munich, in which the detail of the dewdrops on the crystal vase astounded his contemporaries, and in the *Ginevra de' Benci* (probably 1474, Washington, NG), which may originally have had hands, like the Verrocchio bust of a lady with flowers. This half-length with the hands shown would thus be a new type of portrait, looking forward to the *Mona Lisa*. In 1481 his reputation must have been considerable, for he was commissioned to paint a large *Adoration of the Kings* for the monks of S. Donato a Scopeto, near Florence. The composition of this work is of great importance as summing up all the aims of the later 15th century in creating a surface pattern which should also be a pyramidal form in depth, compact yet dynamic. Many drawings of this period exist, but the picture (now in the Uffizi) was never finished and the payments to Leonardo ceased in 1481. Nothing is known of his activities until he is documented in Milan in 1483, where he may have gone in the previous year. A draft letter exists, in which Leonardo offered his services to Lodovico Sforza, Il Moro, Duke of Milan, and in which he claimed at great length to be a highly skilled military engineer, ending with the words: 'In peace I believe that I can give you as complete satisfaction as anyone in the construction of buildings, both public and private . . . I can further execute sculpture in marble, bronze or clay, and in painting I can do as much as anyone, whoever he may be. Moreover, I would undertake the commission of the bronze horse, which will endow with immortal glory and eternal honour the auspicious memory of your father and of the illustrious house of Sforza . . .'.

Soon after his arrival he probably painted the *Lady with an Ermine* (now in Cracow) which almost certainly represents Cecilia Gallerani, the mistress of Lodovico Il Moro (Gallerani is almost Greek for 'ermine'): this picture shows the same stylistic characteristics as those attributable to his earlier Florentine period, a point which it is important to bear in mind when considering the problems raised by the two versions of the *Virgin of the Rocks* in Paris (Louvre) and London (NG). Briefly, the problem may be stated thus: Leonardo rarely finished one work, so that it is not likely he would have painted two versions, almost, but not quite, identical, of a picture for which only one set of documents is known to exist. These documents run from 1483 to 1506 and they seem to refer to a picture which must be identified with the NG one, the history of which is known in detail. Nevertheless, the Louvre version is indubitably the earlier – i.e. more Florentine – in style, which corresponds with a date *c.*1483 for the commission. Leonardo remained in Milan until 1499, working on a few artistic projects and several scientific ones but principally acting as resident genius at the Court. Originally he had intended to carry out the elaborate bronze equestrian monument to Francesco Sforza, father of Lodovico Il Moro, but the project got no further than a huge clay model of the horse without its rider. It was never cast, and perished early in the 16th century, but there are some superb drawings of horses connected with it. Leonardo was a famous horseman and he seems to have projected a book on the anatomy of the horse while he was working on the Sforza Monument. One other major work was carried out at this time – the *Last Supper* in S.M. delle Grazie, Milan, on which he was working in 1497. Owing to his slow methods and his desire for experiment he worked on the plaster in oil instead of fresco, with the result that the painting was already a wreck in his own lifetime. Nevertheless, this is the first work of the High Renaissance, with its stress on the psychology of the Disciples and the tension of the moment when Christ announces that one of them is about to betray Him, a subtlety of interpretation quite foreign to the 15th century. The stories of Leonardo's slowness in working on this wall-painting and his search for psychological expressiveness justify the claims made by a later generation which regarded Leonardo as the originator of the idea of the artist as a contemplative and creative thinker, the equal of the philosopher, and not a mere artisan who was paid to cover so many square yards of wall a day. Certainly all the 16th-century ideas on the dignity of the artist can be traced back to the example set by him.

In 1499 the French invaded Milan, the dynasty fell, and Leonardo left the city, returning to Florence in 1500 and working in 1502–3, with what seems a cynical detachment, as a military engineer for Cesare Borgia. During his second Florentine period he did a great deal of dissection and made himself into incomparably the finest anatomist of his day, but he also worked on three major artistic projects. The most important was the commission given by the city to its two greatest artists, Leonardo and Michelangelo (who disliked each other intensely). This was for two gigantic wall-paintings, to commemorate Florentine victories, in the Council Chamber of the new Republic. Neither was ever finished. Leonardo's was to represent the Battle of Anghiari, but no more than the central group was ever painted; and this was apparently in some wax medium, in imitation of an antique technique described by Pliny the Elder, which failed miserably. Work was begun in 1503 and stopped in 1505. During these years he was also working on a number of versions of the Madonna and Child with St Anne, seeking a solution to the problem of creating a single compositional form from two adult figures and one or more children. The two survivors are probably the first and last of the series, the one in London (NG) being probably begun in Milan and taken to Florence, and the one in the Louvre dating from *c.*1506. One of his few finished works is the celebrated portrait of the wife of a Florentine official, known as *Mona Lisa* or *La Gioconda*. This was painted between *c.*1500 and *c.*1504, and, apart from its accretions of fame as a *femme fatale*, is important as a type of portrait and as a feat of oil-technique, particularly in its SFUMATO effects.

In 1506 Leonardo returned to French-occupied Milan and was made *Peintre et Ingénieur* to Louis XII of France in 1507: he died in France, at Cloux near Amboise, in a château given him by the King. His last years were spent mainly in scientific pursuits although he also projected another equestrian monument, this time to Trivulzio, the commander of the French troops, but the idea got no further than drawings. Between 1513 and 1516 he spent most of his time in Rome, living in the Vatican, but he was now out of touch with the art of Michelangelo and Raphael. His last painting, probably done before he moved to France in 1517, was the *St John* (*c.*1514/15, Paris, Louvre). In this androgynous object the defects of Leonardo's qualities are painfully apparent: the search for solidity of modelling has led to inky shadows and the total suppression of colour in favour of chiaroscuro; and the search for subtlety of facial expression has led to the smirk with which Leonardo's Milanese followers (e.g. LUINI) have made us all too familiar.

A treatise on painting, for which many notes were made, was never written by Leonardo, but it was published from the notes for the first time in 1651 (and in full in 1956). Incomparably the finest collection of his drawings is in the Royal Library, Windsor Castle. There are also paintings by him in Leningrad, Milan (Ambrosiana) and the Vatican.

LÉPINE, Stanislas (1835–92), was a pupil of Corot and the friend of Boudin, Jongkind, and the Impressionists. He spent his life painting views of Paris in a style derived from Corot and Impressionism. There are good examples in Edinburgh (NG), Glasgow and London (NG).

LE SUEUR, Eustache (1616/17–55), was, from 1632, a pupil of VOUET whom he closely followed. He worked at the Hôtel Lambert in Paris, first on a *History of Cupid* for the Cabinet d'Amour, 1646–7, then in the Cabinet des Muses, 1647–9, where he turned more consciously towards Raphael and Poussin, the great influences on the later part of his career. Poussin, whom he may have known in 1640–2, dominates the *Life of St Bruno* series painted for the Charterhouse of Paris (*c.*1648, Louvre), and in his last works his imitation of Raphael (though he never went to Rome) turns him into a dully derivative artist. There are works in Paris (Louvre) and French provincial museums, as well as Birmingham (Barber Inst.), Hartford Conn., London (NG: sketch for the MAI of 1649 in Notre-Dame, Paris), Malibu Cal. (Getty) and Toledo Ohio.

LE SUEUR, Hubert (active 1610–43), worked first in France, where he was sculptor to the King by 1610, and is mentioned as working in 1624. He was in England by 1629, when he made figures for the catafalque of James I, and soon after was employed to make the monstrous tombs of the Duke of Lennox and Richmond, and the Duke of Buckingham, in Westminster Abbey. His equestrian statue of Charles I at Charing Cross, begun in 1630, is an effective *pastiche* of the Henri IV on the Pont Neuf in Paris, but, like all his works, suffers from his pedestrian style and his emptiness of form. Charles I seems to have been aware that his sculptor was far below his painter, van Dyck, in quality. There are works in the Royal Coll., and in Cardiff, London (V&A), and Oxford (St John's Coll., Schools Quadrangle and Bodleian Library).

LEWIS, John Frederick (1805–76), specialized in Oriental and Mediterranean subjects, often in watercolour, with bright colours and much detail. He began to exhibit at the RA in 1821, but lived in Spain 1832–4, visited Italy and Greece, and settled in Cairo 1841–50, when he did not exhibit at all. He resumed in 1850, with great success, becoming an ARA in 1859 and RA 1865. There are works in Birmingham, Cambridge, Dublin, Edinburgh, London (Tate and V&A), Manchester, Oxford and Yale (CBA).

LEWIS, Wyndham (1884–1957), was an English painter and writer who flourished on controversy. He was the founder of VORTICISM, which derived from Cubism and Futurism, and edited its paper 'Blast'. He is supposed to have painted the first English picture to be influenced by Cubism, in 1912. The Vorticist group amalgamated itself with the LONDON GROUP – but Lewis soon resigned. He wrote a number of novels and satires, and is represented as a painter in Edinburgh, London (Tate), Manchester, Yale (CBA) and elsewhere.

LEYDEN, Lucas van, *see* LUCAS.

LEYDEN, Nicolaus Gerhaert von, *see* GERHAERT.

LEYSTER, Judith (1609–60), and her husband, Jan MOLENAER, whom she married in 1636, were Haarlem painters and were probably pupils of Frans HALS. They painted groups of people laughing and drinking which are strongly influenced by, if not entirely derived from, Hals, against whom Judith brought a lawsuit for the enticement of an apprentice from her workshop into his. Her *Lute-playing Fool* (Amsterdam, Rijksmus.) – a very UTRECHT SCHOOL subject – for many years passed as a Hals. There are works by her in Amsterdam (Rijksmus.), Dublin, The Hague, London (NG), Philadelphia, Stockholm, Washington and elsewhere.

LIBER STUDIORUM *see* LIBER VERITATIS.

LIBER VERITATIS (Lat. book of truth) was the name given by CLAUDE to the collection of 195 drawings after his own paintings which he assembled as a record of authentic works. The number was later made up to 200 by the addition of five drawings not related to paintings: the entire collection, for centuries the property of the Dukes of Devonshire at Chatsworth, is now in the BM. They were engraved in mezzotint by R. Earlom in 1777, with a note based on BALDINUCCI's account of the origin of the drawings. This collection inspired TURNER to compile his own *Liber Studiorum: Illustrative of Landscape Compositions, viz., Historical, Mountainous, Pastoral, Marine, and Architectural* . . . (1807 onwards). These were compositions drawn, and partly engraved, by Turner, intended to form a corpus of landscape types, quite different in intention from Claude's index to his paintings. Turner was particularly demanding on his engravers, and the *Liber* may have raised standards in this respect.

LICHTENSTEIN, Roy (*b.*1923), is a leading American POP artist. His usually large pictures are based on the magnification of details from advertisements of everyday objects – a foot on a pedal-bin, a hand holding a sponge, a cooker with food in the open oven – and strip cartoons – *Blonde waiting* (1964) or *Whaam* (1963, London, Tate). His technique imitates the coarse screen process of cheap newspaper printing, and his stylized forms translate his commonplace sources into simple but powerful patterns, expressed in strong primary colours, or in black and white. Some of his imagery is sub-Picasso in origin, and he has also experimented with curiously dazzling effects of coloured plastics, and brass and enamelled metal sculpture.

LIEBERMANN, Max (1847–1935), was the principal Impressionist painter in Germany. In 1872 he went to France and was much influenced by the BARBIZON painters, especially MILLET. He returned to Germany in 1878 and painted rather sentimental genre scenes until the 1890s when he began to work more and more in the Impressionist manner. When the Berlin SEZESSION was founded in 1899 Liebermann became its President. He visited Holland regularly and was influenced by ISRAËLS. He is well represented in German museums (though out of favour under the Nazis) and in London (Tate), New York (Met. Mus.) and Washington (Corcoran).

LIEVENS, Jan (1607–74), of Leyden was the friend and contemporary of REMBRANDT. He was a pupil of LASTMAN in Amsterdam and then shared a studio with Rembrandt in Leyden in the later 1620s: many works of this period show one influencing the other. Lievens went to England, probably in 1632 after Rembrandt moved to Amsterdam, but he was in Antwerp by 1635, where he was influenced by the courtly style of van Dyck. He returned to Holland in 1639 and became a successful painter of portraits and allegories. There are works in Amsterdam, Berlin, Besançon, Birmingham (Barber Inst.), Brighton, Copenhagen, Dublin, Edinburgh (NG), The Hague (Mauritshuis and Huis ten Bosch), Leyden, Lille, London (NG), Malibu Cal. (Getty), Nancy, Ottawa, Paris (Louvre), Raleigh NC, Rotterdam and Vienna.

LIMBOURG, Paul (Pol, Polekin), Jean (Jacquemin, Hennekin) and Herman de (*d.*1416) were three brothers who were illuminators of MSS. Paul was the eldest, but the first mention of any of them occurs in 1400, when Herman and Jacquemin Maleuel, 'young children' – which means minors, probably teenagers – nephews of MALOUEL, were apprentices of a goldsmith in Paris and had been sent to their native Guelders to escape the plague. They were imprisoned in Brussels because of strife between Guelders and Brabant. Their widowed mother was responsible for them, but the Duke of Burgundy paid their ransom, probably on account of their connection with Malouel. In 1402, Paul and Jean were contracted to illuminate a Bible for the Duke: this is probably the *Bible moralisée* (Paris, Bib. Nat.). The Duke died in 1404, when only part was finished. One of the brothers was working in 1405 for the Duke's brother, Jean, Duc de Berri, whose *Très Belles Heures* (New York, Met. Mus.) appears to have been finished by 1408/9. In 1411 all three seem to have been in the service of the Duc de Berri, and it was about then that the most sumptuous of all his MSS was made – the *Très Riches Heures* (Chantilly, Mus. Condé), one of the greatest achievements of the INTERNATIONAL GOTHIC style. All three brothers, as well as the Duke, were dead by the end of 1416. Copies after Taddeo GADDI and others seem to indicate a visit by Paul to Florence and Siena.

LIMNING. An old-fashioned word, now coming back into use for portrait painting 'in little' – i.e. miniatures. In America, portrait painters of the colonial period are often called limners, even when they painted 'in large', and Raeburn held the title of King's Limner in Scotland.

LINEAR COMPOSITION. A composition which depends for its effect on the pattern made by the outlines of the forms represented (whether naturalistic or not) rather than on the masses of tone and colours, which tell as shapes rather than edges.

LINGELBACH, Johannes (1622–74), was an Amsterdam painter of Italianate landscapes and BAMBOCCIATE (he visited France and Italy 1642–50). He often painted figures in landscapes by others, e.g. Hobbema and Wynants. London (Dulwich) has a good example of him imitating J. B. WEENIX, and the NG has one in the manner of WOUWERMANS.

LINNELL, John (1792–1882), painted miniatures, landscapes and Bible illustrations. He was disliked by many fellow-artists, and Constable is usually blamed for spreading the gossip about sharp practice in dealing which caused his constant rejection at RA elections. His son-in-law PALMER loathed him, and his one saving grace was the help he gave to BLAKE, whom he met in 1818. He commissioned engravings for *Job* (1823–5), and also suggested the idea of illustrating Dante. His major Biblical landscape *Noah* (RA, 1848) is in Cleveland Ohio, and there are other works by him in Brighton, Cambridge, Dublin, Liverpool, London (BM, NPG, Tate, V&A and Guildhall), Manchester, Oxford, Preston and Yale (CBA).

LINOCUT *see* ENGRAVING.

LIOTARD, Jean Étienne (1702–89), was a Swiss pastellist who worked in Paris from 1725, went to Italy in 1738 and there met two English noblemen who took him to Constantinople, where he adopted Turkish dress and a beard which he retained afterwards for the notoriety they brought him. He was in England from 1753 to 1755 painting portraits which Walpole described as 'too like to please', but their liveliness of colour and expression had great success and influenced COTES. He worked in Holland after his English visit, and returned to London 1772–4, but without his earlier success. There are works in Amsterdam (Rijksmus.), Dresden, Geneva (many of his best works), London (V&A), Vienna and elsewhere.

LIPCHITZ, Jacques (1891–1973), was born in Lithuania but went to Paris in 1909. His sculpture shows the influence of CUBISM – he met Rivera and Picasso in 1913 – but by *c.*1925 he had evolved a personal style of openwork sculpture (*sculptures transparentes*). In 1941 he went to America, where he spent most of the rest of his life, but in 1946 he was commissioned to make a *Madonna* for one of the new French churches, at Plateau d'Assy. The Barnes

Foundation, Merion Pa, has many works bought in 1922 by Dr Barnes, and the Tate Gall., London has some fifty maquettes in plaster, terracotta, etc. Other works are in Amsterdam (Stedelijk), Boston, Edinburgh (NG Modern Art), Karlsruhe, New York (M of MA and Columbia Law School), Ottawa, Paris and many US museums.

LIPPI, Filippino (1457/8–1504), was the son of Fra Filippo and completed his father's works (or at least cleared up his estate) in Spoleto, after which – at the age of about 12 – he set off alone for Florence on 1 January 1470. He was with BOTTICELLI in 1472 but the first certainly datable work by him is the *Annunciation* (1483/4, S. Gimignano) on two *tondi*. This long gap, coupled with the existence of a group of pictures which are close to both Filippino and Botticelli, led to the creation of AMICO di Sandro, but the group has now been redivided between the two. His first major commission was to complete the fresco cycle in the Brancacci Chapel in the Carmine, Florence, which had either been left unfinished by Masaccio or had been partially destroyed. This was probably *c.*1484, and in 1486 he completed one of his best known and most typical paintings, the *Vision of St Bernard* (Florence, Badia), which shows his restless, fluttering line and bright colour. Between 1487 and 1502 he painted a fresco cycle in the Strozzi Chapel in S.M. Novella, and another one in Rome. This was the cycle in the Caraffa Chapel, S.M. sopra Minerva (1488–93), and his years in Rome gave him the opportunity to study antique remains: ever afterwards he introduced bits and pieces of antiquity into all his pictures, whether suitable or not. There are many panels datable in the 1490s and the last years of his life, but, like Botticelli, his style went out of date in his lifetime: it is sometimes called 'Quattrocento Mannerism'. There are pictures by him in Berlin, Bologna, Chantilly, Cleveland Ohio, Copenhagen, Edinburgh (NG), Florence (Accad., Uffizi, Pitti, Horne Mus. and S. Spirito), Genoa, Glasgow, London (NG), Munich, New York (Met. Mus.), Ottawa, Oxford (Ch. Ch.), Toledo Ohio, Utrecht, Washington (NG) and elsewhere.

LIPPI, Fra Filippo (*c.*1406–69), was probably the only direct pupil of MASACCIO. He was an orphan and was put into the Carmine in Florence in 1421, presumably to get him out of the way although he was temperamentally unfitted to be a monk. In the 1420s Masaccio was painting the Brancacci Chapel there and in 1430 (after Masaccio's death) Fra Filippo is first recorded as a painter. The hypothesis that he was Masaccio's pupil is much strengthened by the fresco fragments, datable *c.*1432, of the *Relaxation of the Carmelite Rule* which are his earliest works: they reflect the influence of Masaccio to the exclusion of almost everything else. In 1434 Fra Filippo had left the Carmine and was in Padua, but his work there has disappeared. The first picture by him which bears a date is the *Tarquinia Madonna* (1437, Rome, Gall. Naz.), and this shows that Masaccio's influence was being gradually superseded by that of Donatello and of Flemish painting. The *Barbadori Altarpiece* (Paris, Louvre) was also begun in 1437 and shows him using the new SACRA CONVERSAZIONE type of composition, with the old divisions of a triptych modified into a unified composition, the kneeling figures at the sides being used to form a pyramidal shape which stretches across the old divisions. His frescoes at Prato are perhaps his major achievement, and show him developing a progressively more dramatic style, with great interest in the problem of rendering movement, with by now no trace of Masaccio. The Prato cycle was begun in 1452 and was still incomplete in 1464: these years include Lippi's trial for fraud (1450) and his abduction of the nun Lucrezia (and the consequent birth of Filippino). The Medici family, his constant patrons and friends, obtained him a dispensation to marry Lucrezia – but he does not seem to have been suitably grateful. In spite of his secular activities, his late works are infused with religious feeling and are far more lyrical than the early ones. The three *Nativities* (Berlin and Florence) are examples. His last works were the frescoes in Spoleto Cathedral, but from the beginning in 1466 until his death there in 1469 he seems to have been in bad health and most of the work was done by pupils and assistants. The final receipts are signed by his son Filippino, who was then about 12. BOTTICELLI was probably also Fra Filippo's pupil in the 1460s. There are works by him in Baltimore, Berlin, Cleveland Ohio, Empoli, Florence (Uffizi, Pitti, Pal. Medici and S. Lorenzo), London (NG and Courtauld Inst.), Milan (Castello), Munich, New York (Met. Mus.), Oxford, Prato (Mus.), Rome (Pal. Venezia), Washington (NG) and elsewhere.

LISS (Lys), Johann (*c*.1597–1629/30), was a German painter who seems to have trained in the Netherlands, perhaps under GOLTZIUS, and in Paris, before settling in Venice by 1621. He died there of the plague. His Roman BENTNAME 'Pan', given on his visit *c*.1622, sufficiently expresses his robustly Rubensian art, crossed with Venetian colouring, and his preferred subjects. There are examples in Berlin, Bremen (Kunsthalle, Roseliushaus), Budapest, Cambridge (Fitzwm), Cassel, Dresden, Dublin, Florence (Uffizi), The Hague (Bredius Mus.), London (NG), Nuremberg, Pommersfelden (Schloss Schönborn), Venice (Accad. and S. Niccolò dei Tolentini) and Vienna (K-H Mus. and Akad.).

LITHOGRAPHY *see* ENGRAVING.

LLANOS, Fernando de (active 1507–20), was a Spanish painter, trained in Italy, who introduced the style of LEONARDO da Vinci to Spain in the retable which he painted for Valencia Cathedral (1507–10) in collaboration with Fernando Yañez.

LOCAL COLOUR is the actual colour of an object, uninfluenced by reflected light or colour: thus, the local colour of lips is pink although they may appear brown in certain lights.

LOCHNER, Stefan (*d*.1451), was active in Cologne from at least 1442 and is the major master of the Cologne School, an important representative of the SOFT and pretty style associated with INTERNATIONAL GOTHIC. He seems to have been trained in the Netherlands, at least under the influence of the MASTER OF FLÉMALLE (he was a contemporary of Roger van der Weyden) and perhaps also of the LIMBOURG brothers. His masterpiece is the *Patron Saints of Cologne* (*'Das Dombild'*) in Cologne Cath. There are two dated works by him: in the Gulbenkian Fdn, Lisbon (1445) and in Darmstadt (1447). Other works are in Cologne (Wallraf-Richartz Mus. and Archiepiscopal Mus.), Frankfurt (Städel), London (NG), Munich and Nuremberg.

LOMAZZO, Giovanni Paolo (1538–1600), was a Milanese painter, trained under Gaudenzio FERRARI, whose career was cut short at the age of 33, in 1571, by blindness. He devoted his later years to writing, mainly on the theory of art, and his treatise 'L'Arte della Pittura', first published in Milan in 1584, has been described as 'the Bible of Mannerism'. It was translated into English by the Oxford physician and amateur engraver, Richard Haydocke, as early as 1598, and this edition, with thirteen of Haydocke's own engravings, must have been known to Shakespeare. It has the additional interest of mentioning English artists such as HILLIARD and OLIVER, who are not in the original Italian edition. He also wrote the 'Idea del Tempio della Pittura' (Milan, 1590) and some poems. There is a self-portrait in Milan (Brera).

LOMBARDO, Pietro (*c.*1435–1515), and his sons Tullio (*c.*1455–1532) and Antonio (*c.*1458–1516?) were the major Venetian sculptors and architects of their time. Pietro, who came from Lombardy, was first recorded in Padua in 1464 (Roselli tomb in the Santo, 1467), but his style suggests that he had already been in Florence. He settled in Venice probably *c.*1467, and with his sons ran the principal sculpture workshop; they executed many tombs, the Mocenigo tombs in SS. Giovanni e Paolo, finished by 1481, being the most important. He also worked at Treviso, and made Dante's tomb in Ravenna. His style is characterized by rather thick-set figures of markedly Antique derivation, soft modelling, and a certain hesitancy in form and movement. Tullio's career depended upon his father's, but in style he is more emphatic, dramatic, and even more influenced by the Antique. Antonio was also strongly classical in inspiration, reflecting the tastes of his patrons, but he finally dwindled into decorative work for the Este of Ferrara. Tullio and Antonio did most of the decorative sculpture and statues for S. Maria dei Miracoli, which their father built (1481–9), and they also did the strange perspective reliefs on the lower part of the façade of the Scuola di S. Marco. Besides numerous works in churches in Venice and in Treviso Cathedral, there are examples by Tullio in London (Wallace Coll.), New York (Met. Mus.), Northampton Mass. (Smith) and Vienna (K-H Mus.).

LONDON GROUP. Founded in 1913, the London Group arose from a fusion between the CAMDEN TOWN GROUP and the VORTICISTS, together with some other artists. The first president was GILMAN and the members included SICKERT and Wyndham LEWIS. The Group still exists.

LONGHI, Alessandro (1733–1813), was the son of Pietro Longhi, and a well-known portrait painter. His reputation was established as early as 1760, and two years later he published a book on Venetian painters of his own times ('Compendio delle Vite . . .', 1762) which is an important source-book. There are pictures in Venice and in Boston, London (NG), New York (Met. Mus.), Toledo Ohio and elsewhere.

LONGHI, Pietro (1702–85), was a Venetian genre painter whose small scenes of life in Venice are of great value to the social historian. The comparison with Hogarth is often made, but it is not really valid, since Longhi entirely lacks Hogarth's biting satire. His forte was for the scene of quiet domestic intimacy, of everyday life in a patrician or rich merchant household, and the details of manners, setting and costume, which he portrays in a dry and thin technique, give an insight into Venetian daily life. These pictures are very numerous and were often repeated by pupils or imitators and are therefore very common: the largest collection is in the Querini-Stampalia Gall., Venice. Others are in London, New York (Met. Mus.), Oxford and Washington (NG).

LOO, van. A family of painters of Flemish descent working in France, of whom the most important were Jean Baptiste, Carle and Louis Michel. Jean Baptiste (1684–1745) was the eldest, but was the fourth generation of the family to be a painter. He was born in Aix-en-Provence and worked there until he went to North Italy and on to Rome in 1714. From 1720 he was settled in Paris, becoming a Member of the Academy in 1731. He established himself as a portrait painter in the circle of the Regent, and also painted a version of the state portrait of Louis XV. In 1737 he moved to London, for reasons which are not clear; he had an immediate success, and was patronized by the Prime Minister, Sir Robert Walpole. He had great facility in catching a likeness, and by 1738 VERTUE wrote: 'The English painters have had great uneasines it has much blemishd their reputation – and business'. According to van Loo's own account, Walpole said he would have made him Painter to the King, but this was impossible since no foreigner could hold the post (this was clearly an excuse – George II was a foreigner himself, and Holbein was a good precedent for the employment of foreigners). In 1741 Vertue recorded his complaints about the English climate, and in 1742 he retired to his native Aix. His work had considerable influence on his English rivals such as HUDSON and HOGARTH. There are works by him in Aix, Brussels, Glasgow, Leningrad (Hermitage: a portrait of Walpole), London (NPG), New York (Hist. Soc.), Paris (Louvre and churches), Plymouth, Turin, Versailles and Worcester (Town Hall).

Carle (1705–65) was Jean Baptiste's brother and pupil and went with him to Rome in 1714, and back to Paris in 1720. After study in Paris he returned to Rome in 1727, the year BOUCHER arrived there. Rivalry between them continued in Paris, and Boucher did not become Principal Painter to the King and Director of the Academy until 1765, after van Loo's death. Carle van Loo worked in Turin for two years before returning to Paris in 1734. He was elected to the Academy in 1735, and became the most famous member of the family in France, being appointed Principal Painter to the King in 1762, and Director of the Academy in 1763. There are works by him, principally decorations, in many French museums and also in Barnard Castle (Bowes Mus.), Florence (Uffizi), Glasgow, Leningrad (Hermitage), London (Wallace Coll.), Madrid, New York (Met. Mus.), Paris (Louvre, Notre Dame and churches), Potsdam, Quebec, Stockholm and Vienna.

Louis Michel (1707–71) was the son of Jean Baptiste and the brother of three further painters. Like his uncle Carle, who was only two years his elder, he was Jean Baptiste's pupil in Turin and Rome, and he won a prize at the Academy in Paris in 1725. With his uncle he went to Rome in 1727–32, but in 1736 he became Court Painter in Madrid where he painted many portraits. He was a Founder-Member of the Academy in Madrid in 1752, but returned to Paris in 1753, and made many versions of the state portraits of Louis XV for presentation to the Courts of Europe. In 1765 he succeeded his uncle as Director of the special school of the French Academy known as the ÉCOLE Royale des Élèves Protégés. There are works by him in Copenhagen, Leningrad, London (Wallace Coll.), Madrid (Prado and Acad.), Paris (Louvre), Versailles and other French museums.

LORENZETTI, Pietro (active 1306?–45) and Ambrogio (active 1319–47), were brothers, Pietro probably being the elder. They were Sienese painters who extended the side of Duccio's art that was concerned with rendering solidity of form and emotional depth: in this they were opposed to Simone MARTINI and were influenced by the sculpture of Giovanni PISANO (as Duccio himself was) and also by contemporary work in Florence by Giotto and his immediate followers. Like some of their Florentine contemporaries such as DADDI they form a stylistic link between Duccio and Giotto, between the Schools of Siena and Florence. Pietro was perhaps Duccio's pupil, but his earliest known work, the polyptych in the Parish Church, Arezzo, which was commissioned in 1320, shows an independent style already, even though it has Ducciesque characteristics and is comparable with the polyptych by Simone Martini at Pisa, also of 1320. Pietro's beginnings are much complicated by two facts, the interpretation of which is controversial. Firstly, there is a payment from Siena Town Council for a picture in 1306: it was made to 'Petruccio di Lorenzo', whom most scholars would now identify with Pietro. Secondly, the *Sta Umiltà* panels in Florence (Uffizi) were recorded in the 19th century as dated – but the date could be read as 1316 or 1341 (i.e. MCCCXVI or MCCCXLI). Stylistically, the later date is now thought more likely. There are several frescoes and other panel pictures by Pietro, the most notable being the frescoes at Assisi (S. Francesco, Lower Church), the *Carmine Altar* (1329, Siena, Pinacoteca), and the *Birth of the Virgin* (1342, Siena, Opera del Duomo). The Assisi frescoes show the impact of the art of Giotto on him, and they are certainly the most tragically grand and simple works produced by a Sienese in the 14th century. The *Birth of the Virgin* is probably later – the date of the Assisi frescoes is very controversial – and, by comparison with the more complex *Presentation* by his brother (also 1342, Florence, Uffizi), it seems very simple, yet it has great narrative power and it shows Pietro as a colourist. The setting is reminiscent of his brother's *Presentation*, but simpler and less accurate in its perspective, and it is thought that Ambrogio was the more inventive of the two. He may have been in Florence *c.*1318 and the earliest work attributed to him, a *Madonna* of 1319, from Vico L'Abate (now in Florence, Mus. Diocesano), is much more influenced by Florentine ideas than by Sienese. He entered the Guild at Florence in 1327 and was in the city again in 1331–2, so that he was in constant touch with the art of Giotto and his followers. His most important works are the frescoes of *Good* and *Bad Government* in the Town Hall of Siena (1337–9). There is a large allegorical fresco, a sort of political manifesto, which shows the influence of Giotto in the bulky forms of the allegorical females, but the two most interesting are those representing *Good Government in the Town* and in the *Country*, where the streets of Siena are represented in perspective of astonishing mastery at that date, and the great panoramic landscape in the *Country* with its small figures riding through the peaceful countryside (the bandits have been hanged by the Good Government) is perhaps the first landscape in modern art to be used as an essential component of a composition, both reflecting and creating a mood. Ambrogio is last recorded in 1347, and it is probable that both brothers died in the Black Death of 1348 which ravaged Siena with particular severity and killed off most of the artists – hence the rapid decline of the Sienese School in the second half of the 14th century.

There are works by one or both in Baltimore (Walters), Berlin, Borgo San Sepolcro, Budapest, Cambridge Mass. (Fogg), Cleveland Ohio, Cortona, Dijon, Fiesole, Florence (Uffizi, Horne Mus. and Sta Lucia), Frankfurt (Städel), Le Mans, London (NG), Massa Marittima, Milan (Poldi-Pezzoli), New York (Met. Mus.), Paris (Louvre), Philadelphia (Johnson), the Vatican, Washington (NG), Yale and elsewhere.

The so-called 'UGOLINO-LORENZETTI' is an invention and was not another member of the family.

LORENZO DI CREDI *see* CREDI.

LORENZO Monaco (i.e. Lorenzo the Monk) (*c.*1370/2–1422/5, probably 1425) was a Sienese who settled in Florence and took vows in the Camaldolensian monastery of S. Maria degli Angeli, which was famous as a school of manuscript illuminators: Don Lorenzo is also known to have painted illuminations. He was a follower of Agnolo GADDI and the Sienese strain in late Trecento art, but he was also influenced by GHIBERTI, and, like him, by INTERNATIONAL GOTHIC. His principal works are the *Coronation of the Virgin* (1413 Florentine Style, i.e. 1414, Florence, Uffizi), painted for his own monastery, and a similar *Coronation* (London, NG), probably also for a Camaldolensian house. Both these are traditional Trecento altarpieces, with gold backgrounds and flat figures, bright in colour and occupying no space in the picture. What is probably his last picture is the *Adoration of the Magi* (Florence, Uffizi) and this shows a complete change to the International Gothic style – dark colour, realistic detail and landscape background, and an attempt at depth, though with very elongated figures. He is thus important as one of the introducers of the style into Florence before the arrival of GENTILE da Fabriano in 1422. There are other works in Florence (Accad., Uffizi, Bargello, Mus. di S. Marco and churches) and in Amsterdam, Assisi (S. Francesco), Baltimore (Walters), Berlin, Cambridge (Fitzwm), Edinburgh (NG), Leicester, London (NG and Courtauld Inst.), New York (Met. Mus.), Paris (Louvre), Philadelphia (Johnson), Siena, Toledo Ohio, the Vatican, Washington (NG), Worcester Mass., Yale (Univ.) and elsewhere.

LORRAIN(E), Claude, *see* CLAUDE.

LOST WAX *see* BRONZE.

LOTH, Johann Carl ('Carlotto') (1632–98), was born in Munich, the son of Johann Ulrich Loth, the Court Painter there. Ulrich had been in Rome 1619–23 and in Venice, and knew SARACENI. Carl also went to Rome for two or three years and settled in Venice *c.*1656, where he died. He painted altarpieces for Venetian and South German churches, and also trained a number of German Baroque painters (cf. ROTTMAYR). His early style derived from the Tenebrism of Ribera, but later became lighter and closer to PIETRO da Cortona. There are works in Amsterdam, Gateshead, London (NG), Prague and Vienna as well as Venice.

LOTTO, Lorenzo (1480–1556/7), was probably born in Venice. He worked in Treviso, Bergamo, Venice and Ancona, and in 1509 was painting in the Vatican, though what he did there and how long he stayed is unknown; certainly he was influenced by Raphael, then working in the Stanze. He arrived in Venice and stayed until 1531/2; later he settled in the monastery of the Santa Casa at Loreto (1552), becoming a lay brother in 1554.

His early works were strongly influenced by Giovanni BELLINI, but after his removals to Bergamo and Venice he developed a chameleon-like quality, reflecting Botticelli, Fra Bartolommeo, Raphael, Correggio, Giorgione, Titian, and even something of Dürer and Holbein, though always with an intensely personal quality and with a steady development from the detailed, episodic vision of the 15th century to the broader handling of the 16th century. He used strong colours and intense reflected light in his mostly religious works, although his portraits have great psychological depth. He painted a few mythologies (e.g. the *Venus and Cupid* now in New York, Met. Mus.). His account book (a rare survival), kept from 1538 onwards, suggests a troubled and difficult character and little material success. His principal frescoes are in and near Bergamo, and there are works by him in the Royal Coll., Ancona and the surrounding district, Bergamo (Accad. Carrara and churches), Berlin, Boston, Brescia, Budapest, Cambridge Mass. (Fogg), Cleveland Ohio, Dresden, Edinburgh (NG), Florence (Uffizi), Jesi, Leningrad, London (NG and Courtauld Inst.), Loreto, Madrid (Prado), Milan (Brera, Castello and Poldi-Pezzoli), Munich, Naples, New Orleans, Oxford (Ch. Ch.), Paris (Louvre), Philadelphia (Johnson), Princeton, Recanati (Mus. and churches), Rome (Borghese, Barberini, Capitoline, Castel S. Angelo and Doria Gall.), Sarasota Fla, Treviso, Upton House Banbury (National Trust), Venice (Accad., Correr and churches), Vienna, Washington (NG) and elsewhere.

LOUIS, Morris (1912–62). American painter, who worked mostly in Washington. His speciality was the large canvas of fine material, on to which bright, pure colours were floated like patches of stain, without visible brushstrokes.

LOUTHERBOURG, Philipp de (1740–1812), was trained in Paris under C. van LOO and Casanova, the brother of the amorist. He exhibited landscapes based on Dutch examples and became a member of the Académie in 1767. He went to London in 1771 and soon began to work as a stage-designer for David Garrick, revolutionizing the art within a few years. He also began to exhibit at the RA from 1772 and was made RA in 1781, the year he invented the *Eidophusikon*, a kind of peep-show with changing scenes which fascinated Gainsborough: Loutherbourg and Gainsborough had already painted each other in 1778 (his portrait of Gainsborough is in Yale, and Gainsborough's of him in London, Dulwich). In the 1780s he was involved with the quack Count Cagliostro and gave up painting: in 1788, however, he challenged Cagliostro to a duel in Switzerland, but this was averted and he returned to painting, his later works being in a highly Romantic style. In 1801 and 1805 he published books of 'Picturesque Scenery'. There are works in the Royal Coll. and in Birmingham (two religious pictures of 1797 and 1798), London (Nat. Marit. Mus., Science Mus. – *Coalbrookedale by Night* – and Dulwich), Ottawa, Stratford (Shakespeare Inst.), Vienna, Yale (CBA) and York.

LOWRY, L. S. (1887–1976), was born and spent his life in the Manchester area, painting industrial and slum landscapes, usually peopled by matchstick figures, which soon degenerated into a tedious formula. He lived as a recluse and had his first London exhibition in 1939, becoming an RA in 1962. He is well represented in Manchester and Salford and in other British galleries, including Edinburgh and London (Tate).

LUCAS van Leyden (1494 or perhaps 1489–1533) is said to have been precociously capable in 1508: the evidence for this is a supremely competent line-engraving, *The Drunkenness of Mohammed*, which is signed 'L 1508'. He was the pupil of his father, by whom no works are known, and Cornelis ENGELBRECHTSZ., with whose paintings his are sometimes confused: almost nothing is known about the Leyden school. He married in Leyden in 1515, met Dürer in Antwerp in 1521, and may have entered the Guild there in 1522. He visited Mabuse in Middelburg, and travelled in Flanders with him in 1527, when Lucas gave banquets for local painters. His paintings are characterized by fluid, calligraphic brushwork and surprising colour. His numerous woodcuts and engravings lean heavily on Dürer; they display sensitive, brilliant draughtsmanship and the inventiveness in subject matter common in the North. The volume of his *oeuvre* belies van Mander's stories of his dilettante travelling, working in bed, and wining and dining in yellow silk clothes. There are works in Amsterdam, Boston (Mus.), Bremen, Brunswick, Brussels, Cambridge Mass., Leningrad, Leyden, London (NG and Courtauld Inst.), Munich, Nuremberg, Paris (Louvre), Philadelphia (Johnson) and elsewhere.

LUINI, Bernardino (*c.*1481/2–1532) was one of the most popular Milanese painters in the early 16th century, principally because he succeeded in vulgarizing the style of Leonardo (as indeed all his Milanese followers tried to do). He was certainly active by 1512, but there is a picture in the Musée Jacquemart-André, Paris, which is dated 1507 and is the work of a Bernardino: partisans for and against the attribution to Luini may be found. Before his domination by the style of Leonardo he seems to have been influenced by BRAMANTINO and other Milanese and to have painted gay and enjoyable works like the fresco fragments in Milan (Brera), Pavia, Paris (Louvre) and London (Wallace Coll.), all from a villa at Monza. His very numerous works are mostly in Milan (Brera, Castello, Poldi-Pezzoli, Ambrosiana and churches), but there are others in the Royal Coll. and in Berlin, Boston, Cambridge Mass. (Fogg), Chiaravalle nr Milan (the fresco *Madonna* dated 1512), Cleveland Ohio, Como (Cath.), Detroit, Florence (Uffizi), London (NG, Wallace Coll., Wellington Mus. and Courtauld Inst.: dated 1526), Lugano (S.M. degli Angeli), Minneapolis, Ottawa, Paris (Louvre), Pavia (Mus. and Certosa), Philadelphia (Johnson), Sarasota Fla, Saronno nr Milan (S.M. dei Miracoli), Vienna, Washington (NG) and elsewhere.

LUKASBRÜDER *see* NAZARENER.

LUKE, Academy of Saint. S. Luke is traditionally the patron of painters, since he is supposed to have painted a portrait of the Virgin and Child. Hence ACADEMIES were often named after him, the most famous being those of Rome and Paris.

LUMINISM. A word coined recently to describe a certain sensibility to light found among American painters of the mid-19th century, the greatest of whom was BINGHAM. It does not imply a school or movement.

LURÇAT, Jean (1892–1966), was the only great tapestry designer for generations. He began as a painter and was influenced by Cézanne and by Cubist ideas, but after being wounded in 1914 he began to work on tapestries in 1917. He lived for years in Spain and eventually abandoned Cubism. From 1937 he worked as designer at Aubusson, and from 1939 for the Gobelins; in the post-war period he did much to revive this art, many of his tapestries being woven for the French Government to use in Embassies abroad. He also made a 'rationalist' tapestry for Angers, to oppose the famous medieval one of the Apocalypse. Other examples are in Beaune (a very large tapestry of *Wine, Source of Life, triumphing over Death*: there seems to be no equivalent in Bordeaux), Cambridge (Churchill Coll.), St Céré (Lot), London (the BBC) and Strasbourg. There are paintings by him in Paris (Mus. d'Art Moderne), Melbourne, Toledo Ohio and Washington (NG). He also wrote a book on tapestry design (published in London in 1950).

LYON, Corneille de, *see* CORNEILLE.

M

MABUSE, Jan Gossaert called Mabuse (*d.c.*1533), probably came from Maubeuge in Hainault, and is first documented in the Antwerp Guild in 1503. His early style derives from Gerard David, Hugo van der Goes and Dürer, well seen in his large *Adoration of the Magi* (London, NG), but he introduces flamboyant, overabundant detail, amounting almost to a *horror vacui*. About 1508/9 he went to Italy, and after this his works display florid Italianized detail, particularly in the architectural settings, and borrowed poses, with no understanding of the essentials of the Italian Renaissance. He became an important ROMANIST, and, according to Vasari, was the first to introduce into Flanders classical subjects with nude figures. This new style is evident in his earliest dated work, *Neptune and Amphitrite* of 1516 (Berlin) and in *Hercules and Deianeira* (1517, Birmingham, Barber Inst.) or *Danäe* (Munich). He was an excellent portrait painter in a much more realist style. He travelled in Flanders with LUCAS van Leyden in 1527. There are works in the Royal Coll., and in Antwerp, Barnard Castle (Bowes Mus.), Brussels, Chicago, Cleveland Ohio, Kansas City, Lisbon, London (NG and Courtauld Inst.), Ottawa, Palermo, Paris (Louvre), Prague, Toledo Ohio, Vienna, Washington (NG) and elsewhere.

MACCHIAIOLI, I (Ital. *macchia*, a stain or blot). A group of Italian painters working mainly in Florence *c.*1855/65, who, in revolt against academism, exploited the individual blob or touch of paint (cf. TACHISME). Influenced by COROT and by COURBET's Realism, some produced landscapes and genre subjects (the best among these were COSTA, LEGA, FATTORI and SIGNORINI), while others turned out pseudo-Romantic costume-history pieces. The only ones much influenced by Impressionism were Degas's friends DE NITTIS and ZANDOMENEGHI, and BOLDINI who became a glossily fashionable portraitist in Paris. Diego Martelli, who was painted by Degas (Edinburgh, NG), was their chief critic and apologist.

MACKE, August (1887–1914), was a German painter deeply influenced by contemporary French painting, particularly by DELAUNAY's very bright colour used in conjunction with near-Cubist ideas. Associated with MARC and KANDINSKY in the BLAUE REITER, and influenced by Futurist ideas, he remained a more visual and representational artist than these associations suggest. In 1914 he went to Tunisia with Klee. He was killed in France at the beginning of World War I. There is a good collection of his work in Munich (Städtische Gall.).

MACLISE, Daniel (1806–70), was born in Cork and was one of the first pupils at the Academy there (founded 1822). He lived by making portrait drawings (examples in London (BM and V&A) and Oxford) before moving to London in 1827, where he entered the RA Schools, exhibited at the RA from 1829 and became an RA in 1840 (in 1866 he refused to stand for the Presidency). During the 1830s he was a successful caricaturist and he became a close friend of Dickens, whose intemperate attack on the PRE-RAPHAELITE BROTHERHOOD and on MILLAIS he may have inspired. He painted portraits and Irish genre scenes, similar to the works of WILKIE, but gradually became the most successful history painter of his day, under the influence of

DELAROCHE and the NAZARENER. From 1841 he was connected with the project for historical frescoes in the new Houses of Parliament and he executed two of the best-known – the *Death of Nelson* and *Wellington and Blücher on the Field of Waterloo* (1845–65, House of Lords). There are other works in Cardiff, Dublin, Edinburgh, Glasgow, Hamburg, Liverpool, London (NPG and Tate), Manchester, Oxford, Toledo Ohio and elsewhere.

MACULATURE *see* IMPRESSION.

MADONNIERI. A Venetian word, applied to anonymous producers of devotional Madonna images, often of little artistic value, but the greatest of them was Giovanni BELLINI.

MAELWEL *see* MALOUEL.

MAES, Nicolaes (1634–93), was a Dordrecht painter who became a pupil of Rembrandt *c.*1648. From then until about 1665 he painted genre and portraits in a Rembrandtesque manner and some genre subjects rather like those of P. de HOOCH. About 1665/6 he went to Antwerp and was much impressed by the modishness of Flemish portraiture in the French taste: this elegance he took back with him and applied to his Dutch sitters. There are examples in Amsterdam (Rijksmus.), Antwerp, Barnard Castle (Bowes Mus.), Birmingham (Barber Inst.), Boston, Brighton, Brussels, Dordrecht, Glasgow (Burrell), The Hague, Leamington, London (NG, Wallace Coll. and Wellington Mus.), Manchester, New York (Met. Mus.), Ottawa, Oxford (a *Still-life*), Toledo Ohio, Washington (NG) and elsewhere.

MAESTÀ (Ital. majesty) is an abbreviation for the Madonna and Child enthroned in Majesty and surrounded by Saints and/or Angels. The subject is most common in the Dugento and Trecento and the best-known example is the *Maestà* by Duccio, painted for the High Altar of Siena Cathedral 1308–11. It is not the same as the *Majestas Domini*, a subject popular in the early Middle Ages, but uncommon after *c.*1300 and very rare in Italy. This shows Christ Enthroned as Ruler of the Universe, usually in a MANDORLA, blessing with one hand and holding a book in the other. Sometimes the symbols of the four Evangelists are also present. The sources are the Vision of Ezekiel and the Apocalypse.

MAGISCHER REALISMUS (Ger. Magic Realism) was a Munich movement deriving from NEUE SACHLICHKEIT, but with strong links with the Italian PITTURA METAFISICA and NOVECENTO. Objects were represented realistically, but lit or juxtaposed to give 'magic' overtones. It has been succinctly described as 'poor man's Surrealism'.

MAGNASCO, Alessandro (1677–1749), painted extremely melodramatic landscapes, usually with storm-tossed trees and frenetic monks, in an 18th-century version of Salvator ROSA's 'savagery'. Some of Marco RICCI's works are almost indistinguishable from his, e.g. one in London (Courtauld Inst.) which was long regarded as a Ricci. Amsterdam (Rijksmus.) has several works.

MAGNELLI, Alberto (1888–1971), was an abstract painter of the type of LÉGER and MONDRIAN, practising what is sometimes called CONCRETE ART. He was born in Florence, but went to Paris *c.*1910, and came in contact with the Cubists and Futurists. Later he met Picasso and Léger. He began painting abstract pictures in Florence in 1915, but reverted to figurative forms until he returned to France, settling in Paris in 1933. In 1958 he was awarded the Guggenheim Prize. There are works in Paris (Mus. d'Art Moderne) and several other museums in Europe, and in the US.

MAGRITTE, René (1898–1967), was a Belgian Surrealist painter who was trained in Brussels and travelled in France, Britain, Germany and Holland. He lived near Paris, 1927–30, and came into contact with the French Surrealist movement, although he painted some Impressionist-style pictures during the Second World War. He later lived in Brussels and painted murals for Belgian public buildings. His pale and dryly painted works have a dream-like clarity, with, frequently, an unexpected wittiness. They often have nude women, sometimes accompanied by men in bowler hats. There are examples in Brussels, Cardiff, Charleroi, Chicago, Edinburgh, London (Tate), Los Angeles, New York (M of M A) and Paris (Mus. d'Art Moderne).

MAHLSTICK (Maulstick). A short stick with a padded knob used as a rest for the hand when painting detailed passages. The word probably derives from Dutch *maalstok*, painting stick, and they are often shown in 17th-century Dutch pictures of artists at work.

MAI (Fr. May). A large altarpiece, commissioned by one of the Paris Guilds from a leading painter of the day, and presented to the Cathedral of Notre-Dame, Paris, in honour of Mary, in May (which is specifically associated with her). There are still fourteen, presented by the Goldsmiths' Guild 1634–51, including works by LEBRUN, BOURDON and LE SUEUR. The last surviving one is of 1702, and the custom seems to have died out about then.

MAIANO, Benedetto da, *see* BENEDETTO.

MAILLOL, Aristide (1861–1944), was a French sculptor whose works are devoted almost exclusively to the female nude. He returned to the ideals of Greek art of the 5th century BC in a reaction against RODIN's fluid forms, changing silhouettes, and dramatic content, although it was Rodin who helped to make his name. By contrast, Maillol stressed the static and monumental qualities of the human figure. He sometimes made use of the 'fragment' device, but never sought the dramatic contrasts of the NONFINITO. From 1889 he was friendly with BOURDELLE, although he did not begin sculpture until 1895; from 1900 he had links with the NABIS and became a life-long friend of Matisse. In 1908 he went to Greece. One of his most famous works, the Cézanne Monument, commissioned in 1912 for Aix, was formally rejected by the city in 1925 and was finally placed in the Tuileries in Paris. He is represented in the museums of modern art in London, Paris and New York. Oxford (Ashmolean) has one of his rare paintings.

MAINO (Mayno), Fray Juan Bautista (1578–1649), was a Spanish painter whose father was Italian. He was in Rome in Caravaggio's lifetime (*c.*1600/10), but was back in Toledo by 1611, in El Greco's lifetime. In Rome he was influenced by the followers of Caravaggio – Gentileschi, Saraceni – and also by the Carracci, Domenichino and even Elsheimer in his landscapes. He became a Dominican friar in 1613 and moved to Madrid *c.*1620, becoming drawing-master to the future Philip IV and thus knowing VELÁZQUEZ, whose portraits influenced his own. He painted a *Recovery of Bahia* in 1635 for the scheme in Buen Retiro which contained histories by Velázquez and Zurbarán. There are works in Madrid (Prado) and in Leningrad, Oxford (Ashmolean), Toledo and Villanueva y Geltrú nr Barcelona (parts of a huge altarpiece).

MAJESTAS DOMINI *see* MAESTÀ.

MAKART, Hans (1840–84), was an Austrian painter, very famous in his own lifetime, whose lush style is based on Rubens, as in his most famous work, the *Death of Cleopatra* (1874–5, Cassel). He visited Italy in 1862. Other works are in Berlin, Dresden, Graz, Hamburg, Munich, New York (Met. Mus.), Paris (Mus. d'Orsay), Vienna and elsewhere.

MALERISCH. This German word, meaning painterly, pertaining to a painter, was given a special sense by the great Swiss art historian Heinrich Wölfflin. In this technical sense it is used to denote the opposite of linear; that is, a feeling for form which does not see in terms of outline or drawing, but in patches of coloured light and shade; or painting in which the edges of the forms merge into one another or into the tone of the background. Titian and Rembrandt are among the most *malerisch* of painters, Botticelli or Michelangelo among the least.

MALEVICH, Kasimir (1878–1935), was a Russian artist who, not content with Cubism, invented SUPREMATISM and painted the picture which should have ended all abstract pictures – a white square on a white ground (*c.*1918, New York, M of MA). From *c.*1904 in Moscow he was aware of modern French painting, mainly from the splendid Shchukin collection; about 1912 he went to Paris for a month, and came back a Cubist. He claimed to have invented Suprematism as a purer form of Cubism in 1913, but it was more probably in 1915. Later in Germany 1928/32, he seems to have dated works 1910/20. After the Revolution he had a violent disagreement with CHAGALL over aesthetics: part of his 'Decree A in art, Vitebsk, 15 November 1920' reads '1. The fifth dimension is established ... 18. To summon an economic council (of the fifth dimension) for the liquidation of all the arts of the old world ...'. Amsterdam (Stedelijk) has the most important collection outside Russia: there is one of 1916(?) in London (Tate).

MALOUEL (Maelwel, Maleuel, i.e. paints well), Jean (*d.*1419), was a Dutch painter working in Gelderland in 1386, but who had gone to Paris by 1396. He became Court Painter to the Dukes of Burgundy in 1397 and was succeeded by Bellechose in 1415. He was the uncle of the LIMBOURGS. Malouel is known to have painted five works for Dijon in 1398 but no work certainly by him can now be identified. On the other hand, the large round *Pietà* (Paris, Louvre) which dates from 1400/10 is probably either by him or by Bellechose. Another picture in the Louvre, the *Martyrdom of St Denis*, has been identified with one of the five Dijon altarpieces of 1398, but it seems more likely that it is a picture completed in 1416 by Bellechose. It has been suggested that the *St Denis* was begun by Malouel and completed by Bellechose, but this is pure guesswork.

Henri Bellechose was born in Brabant but worked mostly in Dijon. He is known to have worked for the Dukes of Burgundy at Dijon 1415–25 and he died at Dijon 1440/4.

MANDER, Karel van (1548–1606), was a Flemish painter who was in Rome in 1575 and in Vienna in 1577. He settled in Haarlem where he opened an academy with GOLTZIUS and CORNELISZ. van Haarlem which propagated Italianizing tendencies in the North. He is most celebrated for his 'Schilderboek', published in 1604 – a poor imitation of Vasari's 'Lives'. Despite its gossipy inaccuracies, is the best early source on Northern painters.

MANDORLA (Ital. almond). An almond-shaped glory of light which is shown as enclosing the whole figure of the Resurrected Christ or of the Virgin at the Assumption.

MANESSIER, Alfred (*b*.1911), is a French abstract painter who differs from many others in that some, at least, of his pictures have a specifically religious intent. He made a retreat at the Trappist monastery at Soligny and has designed stained-glass windows for churches in Bresseux (Jura), Arles and Basle (1953). His picture of the Crown of Thorns (Paris, Mus. d'Art Moderne) is clearly based on a meditation on the Passion, but the connection between his *Salve Regina* and the great 11th-century Latin antiphon is less evident (though probably susceptible of exegesis by the Dominicans of S. Germain-des-Prés). There are pictures by him in Basle, Brussels, London (Tate), New York (Guggenheim), Oslo, Paris, Pittsburgh, Stockholm and Turin.

MANET, Édouard (1832–83). His well-to-do bourgeois father reluctantly allowed him to study under COUTURE 1850–6. He then reacted very strongly against the academic history painting of his teacher and began his career as an artistic rebel with the *Absinthe Drinker* (1859, Ny Carlsberg Mus., Copenhagen), a scene from the seamier side of life. His brilliant technique, founded on the opposition of light and shadow with as little half-tone as possible, on painting directly from the model with intense immediacy, and on a restricted palette in which black was extremely important, helped him to create a new style; yet one founded on Velázquez, Goya and Hals, all of whom could be studied in Paris. His early works include many Spanish subjects inspired by troupes of dancers visiting Paris and he did not actually visit Spain until 1865. These Spanish pieces include numerous bull-fighting scenes, *Lola de Valence* (1862, Mus. d'Orsay) and the *Guitarist* (1860, private coll.), his only successful Salon exhibit before *Le bon Bock* (1873, Philadelphia). He had previously travelled in Italy, Holland, Flanders and Germany.

His work was frequently rejected by the SALON jury (he played an important part in the 1863 Salon des Refusés) and, if hung, was ill-received by critics, his friend Zola being almost alone in defending him. The *Déjeuner sur l'herbe* and *Olympia* were particularly ill-received (both 1863, both Mus. d'Orsay), but both were objected to more on moral grounds than aesthetic ones – the *Déjeuner* represents two fully-clothed men and two naked women having a picnic in a park, and the *Olympia*, ostensibly an *odalisque* in the Ingres manner, was generally thought to be a portrait of a prostitute attended by her negro maid. After 1870, due partly to the influence of Berthe MORISOT, he adopted the Impressionist technique and palette, abandoning the use of black and his genius for analysis and synthesis for a lighter, sweeter colour and a freer handling. He also tended more to sentimental subjects, such as *Washing Day* (1875, private coll.), *Chez le Père Lathuile* (1880, Tournai), and his last masterpiece, the *Bar at the Folies-Bergère* (1881, London, Courtauld Institute). He always longed for official recognition and refused to take part in the Impressionist exhibitions organized by Degas. Although he was friendly with Monet, Renoir, Sisley and Pissarro he bitterly resented being coupled with them in newspaper criticisms as the leader of 'Manet's gang'. At the end of his life he was given the Legion of Honour and the vilification of his works abated, chiefly because Impressionist handling and colour were beginning to affect academic painting. The tragedy of his life was that he was the perfect academic painter, unrecognized and rejected by the body whose dying traditions he alone could have revivified.

Other works are in Baltimore, Berlin, Berne, Boston, Bremen, Budapest,

Buenos Aires, Cardiff, Chicago, Copenhagen, Dijon, Dresden, Essen, Frankfurt (Städel), Glasgow (Burrell Coll.), Hamburg, London (NG, Tate, Courtauld Inst., including a sketch for the *Déjeuner*), Lyons, Mannheim, Melbourne, Merion Pa (Barnes Fdn), Moscow, Munich, Nancy, New York (Met. Mus. and Frick Coll.), Northampton Mass., Oslo, Philadelphia (Johnson), Providence RI, St Louis, São Paulo, Stockholm, Toledo Ohio and Washington (NG and Phillips).

MANFREDI, Bartolommeo (*c*.1587–1620/1), was a Mantuan follower of Caravaggio, who seems not to have been above a little Caravaggio-faking immediately after the latter's death in 1610. His greatest claim to fame lies in the fact that it seems to have been he – and not Caravaggio – who popularized subjects such as cardsharpers and soldiers in guard-rooms (KORTEGAARDJES), with half-length figures on a largish scale. These were the works which influenced the Northerners in Rome (Honthorst and other UTRECHT painters, as well as French and Germans) and there are cases where the early writers mention such painters as being followers of Manfredi rather than of Caravaggio. It is also recorded that his works were exported to Holland. There are no signed or fully documented works by him, and most of what are now regarded as characteristic examples of his style were, at one time or another, called Caravaggios. There are examples in Brunswick, Brussels, Chicago, Dayton Ohio, Dresden, Florence (Uffizi and Pitti), Moscow, Munich, Rome (Gall. Naz., Capitoline) and Vienna.

MANIÈRE CRIBLÉE *see* DOTTED PRINT.

MANNER. Usually now used as a pejorative alternative for 'style': my friends have style, yours merely manner (cf. MANNERISM). The original Italian term *maniera* meant personal style, 'handwriting', and the word manner is usually used in this sense in 18th-century criticism – 'a fine, free manner'.

MANNERISM is a term developed in the present century to describe the artistic manifestations, principally Italian, of the period *c*.1520–1600. During these years many major works were produced which cannot be called RENAISSANCE or BAROQUE without rendering these terms meaningless. The word *maniera*, from which Mannerism is derived, was used by Vasari (himself a notorious practitioner) to describe the schematic quality of much of the work produced, based on intellectual preconceptions rather than direct visual perceptions. Much of Mannerism consists of deliberately flouting the 'Rules' deduced from classical art and established during the Renaissance. This presupposes an educated spectator; otherwise there is no point in breaking the rules. The effect is more obvious in architecture, since the Rules are both more simple and more rigid, and the works of GIULIO Romano show him to have been a major Mannerist architect although less important as a painter.

The principal characteristics of a Mannerist work of art include an insistence on the primacy of the human figure, which, however, is set in strained poses, wilfully distorted and elongated, while the muscles are sometimes also grossly overemphasized. The composition is usually forced and unclear, with the principal subject set in a corner or in the background, with great discrepancies of scale between the figures and with the perspective treated more often as a piece of virtuosity than as a contribution to the lucidity of the narrative. The colour of a Mannerist picture is always vivid and often harsh, since it is intended to heighten the emotional effect rather than describe the forms;

many Mannerists also have a preference for 'shot' colours, red blending into orange, yellow into green, and so on. It is essentially an unquiet style, subjective and emotional, and was therefore well fitted to be rediscovered and defined during the 1920s, but it is certainly wrong – as Marxist critics do – to equate it wholly with the disturbed political and social conditions prevailing in Central Italy after the Sack of Rome in 1527. These conditions, however influential, were more or less permanent; but it is fair to say that these disturbances, and particularly the unsettling effect of the Reformation (with its doctrine of private judgement) and the Counter-Reformation (with its repressive and didactic aspects), led to the abandonment of the serenity and calm classicism of the High Renaissance, of the art of Bramante and Raphael. Much of Mannerism is a conscious artistic revolution against the qualities summarized in Raphael: it is even possible to see Michelangelo's *Last Judgement* as a renunciation of the ideas underlying his own Sistine Ceiling. By about 1520 it was clear that the very perfection of Raphael was an impasse for his successors, leading only to pointless emulation; and his gifted pupil, Giulio Romano, therefore turned to an exaggeration of facial expression, gesture and lighting, derived partly from Raphael himself (the *Transfiguration*) but even more from Michelangelo, in an attempt to conquer entirely new fields of emotional expressiveness. The overwhelming greatness of Michelangelo is another major factor. His single-minded and sculptural devotion to the male nude led to many minor painters eschewing the painting of landscapes and accessories in a desire to storm the artistic heights of DISEGNO, with all its difficulties of anatomy, composition and CONTRAPPOSTO. This was particularly important to sculptors like Giovanni da BOLOGNA or AMMANATI.

On the whole, Mannerism is a style best suited to neurotic artists such as Pontormo, Rosso and Parmigianino, all of whom produced major works, as well as such great masters as Michelangelo, Tintoretto and El Greco. There were also many very dull painters who strained every nerve to be neurotically interesting, but produced only frenziedly gesticulating and twisted figures in insipidly repetitive *contrapposto*, derived from Michelangelo. It should be observed, however, that Mannerism had relatively little effect in Venice, where the political conditions which favoured the style in Central Italy did not obtain. From Vasari and Pellegrino TIBALDI elegant petrifaction set in – as in the splendidly null Court portraits of Bronzino – and the style eventually died of inanition at the hands of the Cavaliere D'ARPINO. It was succeeded by a wave of returning confidence and vitality coupled with a return to Nature in the BAROQUE. (For Antwerp Mannerism *see* ANTWERP.)

MANTEGNA, Andrea (*c*.1431–1506), was a pupil and adopted son of the archaeologist-painter SQUARCIONE, and is first recorded in the contract for the decoration of the Ovetari Chapel in the Eremitani Church (destroyed 1944) in Padua, where he completed a fresco cycle in 1459 with four scenes from the Life of St James, an *Assumption* and a *Martyrdom of St Christopher* (of which only the *Assumption* and *St Christopher* survive). In these, as in his *Madonna and Saints* (*c*.1456/9, Verona, S. Zeno) and in all his other works, his forms appear to be made of tinted stone or bronze, a result of the powerful influence of DONATELLO. The *S. Zeno Madonna* is extremely important as an early example of a SACRA CONVERSAZIONE treated as a group of figures in a single, comprehensible space instead of as a triptych or other form of subdivided space. The *St Sebastian* (*c.*1460, Vienna) is referred to by Vasari as in his 'stony manner' and it also shows the painter's interest in the details of classical antiquity, an interest that made him a leading expert on archaeology and tended to swamp his paintings. In 1460 he left Padua and settled as Court Painter in Mantua, remaining there for the rest of his life except for a stay in Rome (1488–90). He painted the frescoes of the *Camera degli Sposi* (finished in 1474) in the Castello as a memorial to the Gonzaga family, whose portraits on the walls appear to the spectator to be in an extension of the room-space; while on the ceiling is a view of a balcony with figures looking down, beneath an open sky, into the room. This is the first completely illusionistic SOTTO IN SÙ decoration of the Renaissance, but the idea was not exploited again until RAPHAEL and CORREGGIO and not fully developed before the Baroque. Other works executed for the Gonzaga include the very large canvases of the *Triumph of Caesar* (before 1486–94, Hampton Court, the Royal Coll.) and the *Madonna della Vittoria* (1495–6, Louvre), a large votive picture commemorating the Gonzaga part in the battle of Fornovo (1495). He painted the *Parnassus* (Louvre) for Isabella d'Este, and a chapel in the Vatican (*c.*1490, destroyed). The BELLINI were his brothers-in-law. There are other works by him in Berlin, Cleveland Ohio, Copenhagen, Dresden, Dublin, Florence, Fort Worth Texas, London, Madrid, Malibu Cal. (Getty), Milan (Brera, Castello and Poldi-Pezzoli), Naples, New York, Tours, Venice, Vienna, Washington and elsewhere.

MANZÙ, Giacomo (*b.*1908), the leading Italian sculptor, was born of poor parents in Bergamo and apprenticed to a wood-carver in 1919: after military service he went to Paris, *c.*1927, and settled in Milan in 1930, where the Archbishop gave him his first large commission, for the Catholic University chapel. Among modern sculptors he has been influenced by Medardo ROSSO, RODIN and MAILLOL, but it is probable that DONATELLO has been the greatest factor, both in his exploitation of very low relief and in the feeling for drama in religious imagery. In 1939 and during the war years he made many religious works, including eight reliefs of Christ, and these culminated in the great bronze doors for St Peter's, Rome, and for Salzburg Cathedral. The commission for St Peter's was the subject of an international competiton in 1949 and was given to Manzù in 1950: they were consecrated in 1964. The subject of the panels is Death in various forms. The doors of Salzburg Cathedral were completed in 1958. He has also made more than fifty sculptures of cardinals, including one portrait (of Cardinal Lercaro, in Bologna, S. Petronio). Manzù is also a painter and has illustrated several books. There are works by him in Antwerp (Middelheim Park), Bristol, Cleveland Ohio, London (Tate, Westminster Cath.), Milan (S.M. in Chiesa Rossa), New York (M of MA), Rome (Gall. Moderna and S. Eugenio), Turin and the Vatican (a portrait of Pope John XXIII).

MAQUETTE (Fr. small model). Used only of sketches in clay, wax, etc., for sculpture. A BOZZETTO.

MARATTA (Maratti), Carlo (1625–1713), was the last representative of one aspect of Baroque art and the first Neoclassic: his ideal was a return to the calm and noble style of Raphael and the Carracci and he was opposed to the more dramatic style of PIETRO da Cortona or BACICCIO. Not surprisingly, he was a pupil of Andrea SACCHI and, like him, a fine portrait painter although most of his works are altarpieces. His enormously long career began in 1645 and he made his name in 1650 with a *Nativity* for S. Giuseppe dei Falegnami, Rome; he was still painting in 1706 and continued to teach for some years after that. Much of his work looks forward to the 18th century, as for example the *Robert, 2nd Earl of Sunderland in Antique Costume*, which was painted in 1661 (Althorp, Earl Spencer). There are pictures by him in many of the churches and galleries of Rome, in the Royal Coll., and in Ancona, Berlin, Brussels, Cambridge (Fitzwm), Cassel, Chatsworth, Dresden, Dublin, Florence (Pitti), Greenville SC (Bob Jones Univ.), Hanover, Leeds, Leningrad, Lille, London, Madrid, Munich, Naples, Paris, Stockholm, Toledo Ohio, Vaduz (Liechtenstein Coll.), Versailles, Vienna and elsewhere.

MARC, Franz (1880–1916), was a German Expressionist painter, associated with MACKE and KANDINSKY in the BLAUE REITER. His chief subjects were animals, and his variants on the theme of the Blue Horse are perhaps his best known works. He met DELAUNAY in Paris in 1912 and his last works (1914) are more abstract. He was killed in the battle of Verdun. There is a good collection of his work in Munich (Städtische Gall.); others are in Leicester, Minneapolis, New York (Guggenheim) and several German galleries.

MARE, John (1739–after 1795), was a New York portrait painter whose few known works are of little interest, except for the *Unknown Man* of 1767 (New York, Met. Mus.) which has a nervous elegance comparable with European Neoclassic portraits.

MARÉES, Hans von (1837–87), was a German painter, mainly of mythologies, who went to Italy in 1864. In 1869 he visited Spain, France and Holland with the writer on art, Konrad Fiedler, his future biographer. He served in the Franco-Prussian War of 1870–1, but was able to return to Italy in 1873 and began his most famous work, the frescoes in the Aquarium at Naples, on which he was assisted by HILDEBRAND. He spent the rest of his life in Italy, and, like BÖCKLIN and FEUERBACH, he was essentially a German Romantic who longed for Italy: unlike LEIBL, he was untouched by the Realist movement and all that it implied. In spite of his interest in wall-painting and the success of his Naples frescoes he never succeeded in obtaining another monumental commission. The style of the frescoes is similar to that of his great French contemporary PUVIS de Chavannes. There are oil paintings by Marées in Berlin, Hamburg and Munich.

MARGARITO(NE) of Arezzo, active *c*.1260–90 (*d*.1293?), was one of the few Italian painters of the mid-13th century known to us from signed works, such as those in Arezzo, Siena, London (NG) and Washington. The London example was acquired in 1857 'to show the barbarous state into which art had sunk even in Italy previously to its revival' (under CIMABUE and GIOTTO).

MARIESCHI, Michele (1710 not 1696–1743), was a Venetian painter whose works have often been confused with those by other members of the same family. He was working in Saxony before 1735, and on his return to Venice was much influenced by CANALETTO; the vivacious quality of his own handling probably made him an influence on GUARDI. His early works seem mostly to be architectural CAPRICCI, but after his return from Germany the VEDUTE are much more accurate representations of Venice. He made a series of twenty-one etchings of views of Venice, published in 1741 as *Magnificentiores ... Urbis Venetiarum Prospectus* ... Paintings by him are in Bristol (the only signed one), Cambridge (Fitzwm), Dublin, London (NG and Guildhall), Philadelphia, Stockholm, Venice and Vienna (Akad.).

MARIN, John (1870–1953), was an American painter, best-known for his semi-abstract watercolours, often of the sea. He began as an architect, but in 1905 he went to Paris, where he was influenced by WHISTLER. He returned to the US from Europe in 1911, and in 1913 he took part in the ARMORY SHOW. New York (Met. Mus.), Washington (Phillips) and many other American museums have works.

MARINETTI, Filippo (1876–1944), was an Italian poet and publicist closely associated with the FUTURIST movement, which he is said to have named. His career reached its apogee in friendship with Mussolini.

MARINI, Marino (1901–80), was originally a painter, but became one of the leading Italian sculptors of the 20th century. He was trained in Florence and Paris, but worked mainly in Milan. His first major work was the *Pomona* (1941), which already shows the influences of Etruscan and Archaic Greek art which were to be decisive for him, together with those of Medardo ROSSO, RODIN and MAILLOL, who also influenced his contemporary, MANZÙ. About 1935 he began to explore the theme of the horse and rider – also an Archaic Greek idea – and produced many sculptures in bronze and wood (a good one, of 1947, is in London, Tate). He gave a Marini Museum to Milan in 1974, with several of his portrait busts, including those of Moore and Chagall.

MARINUS van Reymerswaele (active 1509?–after 1567?), was a painter of three themes, all more or less caricatural. He painted a number of straightforward *S. Jeromes*, all derived from Dürer's picture of 1521 (Lisbon) but stressing the crabbedness of scholarship. The other two themes are interdependent: two exceedingly ugly and covetous *Tax Gatherers* and a *Banker and his Wife* (the banker counting his profits). The *Banker* is closely related to MASSYS's picture of the same subject, and it may be that the *Tax Gatherers* derive from Massys's borrowings from the caricatures of Leonardo da Vinci. There are about thirty versions of the *Tax Gatherers* (the best is in London, NG; another has the date 1552), and what nobody has so far explained is why so many people should want to own a picture of tax collectors (and excessively ugly ones at that) gloating over their imposts. There are also examples in the Royal Coll. and in Antwerp, Berlin, Ghent, Madrid, Munich and Vienna.

MARIS. There were three members of this family of Dutch painters: Jacob (1837–99), Matthijs (1838–1917) and Willem (1844–1910). With ISRAËLS, MAUVE and BOSBOOM they were leading members of the HAGUE SCHOOL. Jacob was mainly a landscape painter, although he also painted some genre scenes in the manner of P. de Hooch. He went to Paris and was influenced by the BARBIZON painters, as well as by COROT and JONGKIND. Matthijs was influenced at first by German Romanticism. He settled in London in 1877 and was then influenced by the PRE-RAPHAELITE BROTHERHOOD and BURNE-JONES. Willem was mainly a landscape painter. There are works by one or other of the brothers in Amsterdam, Boston, Edinburgh, Glasgow, The Hague, London (NG), New York (Met. Mus.), Philadelphia and Rotterdam.

MARLOW, William (1740–1813), was trained as a topographical artist by SCOTT, 1754–9, after which he travelled in France and Italy, 1765–6, where he made many drawings for use on his return (London, BM and V&A): it is possible that he produced imitations of BELLOTTO's Italian views, and a *Verona*

(London, Courtauld Inst.) may be a Marlow imitation of a Bellotto now in Powis Castle (Nat. Trust), if 18th-century gossip is to be believed. He also produced many views of London and of British scenes, as well as *capricci* such as *St Paul's and the Grand Canal* (London, Tate). From about 1785 he painted only for his own pleasure, but he exhibited at the RA from 1788, and in 1795 he published a series of six etchings of Italian landscapes.

MARMION, Simon (active 1449–*d.*1489), was a painter and illuminator who worked in Amiens and Valenciennes. The most important painting attributed to him is the *St Bertin Altarpiece* (*c.*1459, Berlin and London, NG) which is light in colour and not unlike LOCHNER; other paintings attributed to him are in London (NG), New York (Met. Mus.), Paris (Louvre), Philadelphia (Johnson), Rome (Gall. Naz.) and Strasbourg.

MAROUFLAGE. To marouflay (Fr. *maroufle*, strong glue) is to stick canvas or linen on to a wooden panel (or, occasionally, on to plastered wall) in order to strengthen it while retaining the texture of canvas.

MARQUET, Albert (1875–1947), exhibited at the original FAUVE show in 1905, but never shared either the ideas or the style of the other participants. He developed into a good latterday Impressionist, specializing in simple landscapes and town views, executed with an undemanding technique, but with a nice perception of tonal values. He was a great friend of MATISSE.

MARSHALL, Benjamin (1768–1835), was a British sporting painter who was a pupil of ABBOT and travelled in Italy, but who was principally influenced by STUBBS, and, in his brushwork, Raeburn. In 1819 he was crippled in a coach smash. He also wrote on horse racing, which was almost exclusively the subject of his pictures, but he found 'many a man who will pay me fifty guineas for painting his horse, who thinks ten guineas too much for painting his wife'. There are examples in the Royal Coll. and in Baltimore, Canterbury, Leicester, London (Tate), San Marino Cal., Toronto, Upton Park nr Banbury (National Trust) and Yale (CBA).

MARTIN, John ('Mad') (1789–1854), was the most spectacularly melodramatic history painter of the early 19th century. He exhibited at the RA from 1811 and soon attained fame with his *Joshua Commanding the Sun to Stand Still* (1816) and others in the next few years. He developed a type of enormous canvas, crowded with tiny figures set in fantastic architecture and beneath lowering skies that now seems merely Hollywood, but which seems to have influenced the French Romantics. He chose subjects like *The Bard: 'Ruin seize thee, ruthless King!'* (1817, Newcastle), and the *Destruction of Herculaneum* (1822, Manchester); but the public taste soon faded, to be revived by the *Coronation of Queen Victoria* (1839, Tate), although he returned to the melodramatic with *The Great Day of His Wrath* (*c.*1853, London, Tate). He also illustrated Milton's 'Paradise Lost' with very fine mezzotints in 1827. The Balston Coll., now in London (V&A), is very large. Other works are in the Royal Coll. and in Beckenham Kent (Bethlem Royal Hospital), Cambridge (Fitzwm), Glasgow, Liverpool, Scarborough and Stratford-upon-Avon (Shakespeare Memorial Theatre).

MARTINI, Simone (*c.*1284–1344), was a Sienese painter, the pupil of DUCCIO, who developed the use of outline for the sake of linear rhythm as well as the sophisticated colour harmonies implicit in Duccio. He was also deeply influenced by the sculpture of Giovanni PISANO, and even more by French Gothic art. His first work was a large fresco of the *Maestà* (1315, reworked 1321) painted for the Town Hall of Siena as a counterpart to the huge *pala* by Duccio in the Cathedral. This shows the formative influence of Duccio on him, but there is already a perceptible Gothic influence in it which is much strengthened in his next work, the *St Louis of Toulouse* (1317, Naples). At this date Naples was a French kingdom, ruled by Robert of Anjou, who sent for Simone and commissioned him to paint a new kind of picture: Robert's claim to the throne of Naples was not impeccable, and he therefore caused Simone to paint a large votive image of the newly canonized St Louis of Toulouse (a member of the French Royal house) shown in the act of resigning his crown to Robert. From this time on, Simone's is essentially a Court art, refined and elegant, and much influenced by France. The type of *Madonna* evolved by Simone was of great importance in Sienese painting and may be seen in his Pisa polyptych (1320) and in several others. In 1328 Simone painted another fresco for the Town Hall, Siena, this time a commemorative equestrian portrait of the mercenary soldier Guidoriccio da Fogliano. It is one of the earliest of such commemorative images, and contains a vast panoramic landscape with the tents of the soldiers in the background. (Since the 1970s there has been an unresolved controversy raging over this picture, since a fresco, probably of 1331, seems to be painted below it – i.e. antedates it. The painted date 1328 is therefore almost certainly wrong, and should very probably be 1333, but the total rejection of the attribution to Simone by no means follows.) At some date not yet established Simone went to Assisi and painted a fresco cycle in S. Francesco, of scenes from the life of S. Martin, which again show both the interest in French Gothic art and the sense of chivalric pomp that distinguish Simone. His best-known, and perhaps his finest, work is the *Annunciation* (1333, Florence, Uffizi) which was painted in collaboration with his brother-in-law Lippo Memmi (*d.*1357). Lippo often worked with him, but in this case they both signed the picture. It is perhaps the most splendid example of pure craftsmanship produced in Siena in the 14th century, with its elaborate tooling of the burnished and matt gold, but it is also an almost abstract essay in pure line and two-dimensional pattern, at the furthest possible remove from either Giotto or even their Sienese contemporary Ambrogio LORENZETTI. In 1340/1 Simone went to France. It seems that he went on official business, and not as a painter, to the Curia at Avignon, where the Papacy was then established, and in this Franco-Italian enclave he spent the rest of his life. There he painted the jewel-like *Christ Returning to His Parents after disputing with the Doctors* (1342, Liverpool), a most unusual subject that perhaps once formed half of a diptych. In Avignon he met Petrarch and became friendly with him, illustrating a Virgil codex for him (Milan, Ambrosiana); he also painted frescoes in Notre Dame des Doms, of which the SINOPIE remain (now in the Palais des Papes). They are probably datable in 1341. His influence on French 14th-century painting is hard to assess, but a century later the Sienese (so Ghiberti informs us) regarded him as their greatest painter. There are works in Antwerp, Berlin, Birmingham (Gall. and Barber Inst.), Boston (Gardner Mus.), Cambridge (Fitzwm), Cambridge Mass. (Fogg), Leningrad, London (Courtauld Inst.), Malibu Cal. (Getty), Naples, New York (Met. Mus.), Orvieto (Cath.), Ottawa, Paris (Louvre), Siena (S. Agostino), the Vatican, Washington (NG), Yale and elsewhere.

MASACCIO (1401–probably 1428) was born Tommaso di Ser Giovanni di Mone and nicknamed 'Masaccio' (Hulking Tom). He was the first and arguably the greatest of the succession of great masters in 15th-century Florence; certainly the greatest in that he achieved so much in a lifetime of 27 years. He is first recorded as a painter in 1422, when he entered the Guild in Florence, which disproves the tradition that he was MASOLINO's pupil, since Masolino did not register with the Guild (and therefore could not take pupils) until 1423. An altarpiece of 1422 may prove important in this connection, but the attribution to Masaccio is still under discussion. (It comes from S. Giovenale, near Florence, and is now in the Uffizi.) The first major work by Masaccio for which documentary evidence exists is the Pisa Polyptych, painted for the Carmelite Church in Pisa in 1426, but now dismembered and largely lost. According to a recent conjectural reconstruction it may have been the first SACRA CONVERSAZIONE of a unified type. The central panel, of the *Madonna and Child*, is now in the NG, London, and shows that, at the age of 25, Masaccio had already developed his austere and heroic style in opposition to the INTERNATIONAL GOTHIC then being so successfully practised in Florence by GENTILE da Fabriano. This new style, in its realism, sobriety of gesture, narrative power, and the economy with which it creates its effects of space, light and solidity of form, is akin to Giotto's, and is comparable among contemporaries only with the humanist and intellectual art then being developed by the much older DONATELLO in sculpture and BRUNELLESCHI in architecture. For this reason Masaccio has always been regarded as one of the founders of modern painting. Between the end of 1425 and his death, probably at the end of 1428, Masaccio certainly painted a fresco of the *Trinity* in S.M. Novella, Florence, and his major surviving work, the frescoes in the Brancacci Chapel of the Carmelite Church in Florence (S.M. del Carmine). The Chapel was decorated with scenes from the Acts of the Apostles, and may have been begun by Masolino in 1425, but a large part of the frescoes, including the earlier ones, perished in the 18th century. Those that survive are by three hands – a 15th-century source says that the Chapel was 'painted by three masters, all good but he (Masaccio) was marvellous' – and the puzzle is to sort out the shares. The parts by Filippino LIPPI are half a century later and fairly easily distinguishable; approximate agreement has now been reached over the remainder, it being generally accepted that the *Expulsion* on the entrance arch, the *Tribute Money*, parts of the *Raising of the Praetor's Son* and all of *St Peter enthroned, St Peter's Shadow Healing the Sick, St Peter Giving Alms*, are by Masaccio, while the *Baptism of the Neophytes* is probably by him, but is sometimes contested. The remainder of the original commission is by Masolino. Again, Masaccio's style is fully realistic and uncompromisingly grand, which probably explains why these frescoes long served as an art school without enjoying general popularity. Indeed, much of later 15th-century painting flatly contradicts the principles enunciated in the Brancacci Chapel. Parts of the frescoes may still have been incomplete when Masaccio went to Rome and died there. The remaining parts of the Pisa Polyptych are in Malibu Cal. (Getty), Naples, Pisa and Berlin. Other works by or attributed to him are in Berlin, Boston (Gardner Mus.), Florence (Uffizi and Horne Mus.), London (NG) and Washington (NG).

MASO di Banco, active in the second quarter of the 14th century, was perhaps the greatest of Giotto's followers, and the only one to retain something of Giotto's amplitude of form; indeed, some of his figures are even more massive than Giotto's. The only work that can be attributed to him with certainty is the fresco cycle of *St Sylvester and the Emperor Constantine* in Sta Croce, Florence, conveniently placed for comparison with Giotto. Other works are attributed to him – in Assisi, Berlin, Budapest, Edinburgh, Florence and elsewhere – but it is now agreed that he is not identical with GIOTTINO, and a good many revisions may be necessary.

MASOLINO (*c*.1383/4–1447?) was not the master of MASACCIO, as Vasari thought, but rather his pupil for a short time, in spite of the great difference in age. Masolino may have worked under Ghiberti on the First Baptistry Doors (1403/7), and this would explain his normal INTERNATIONAL GOTHIC style. He entered the Guild of Painters in Florence in 1423 – there is nothing to explain what he was doing 1407–23 – and in the same year painted a *Madonna* (Bremen) which shows the influence of late Trecento art, and Lorenzo Monaco in particular. In 1427 he went to Hungary, but it is probable that he worked in the Brancacci Chapel in S.M. del Carmine in Florence in the interval; there he came under the influence of Masaccio to such an extent that it is not easy to distinguish them. He may also have worked in the Brancacci Chapel after Masaccio's death (1428) and before he went to Rome *c*.1430 to decorate a chapel in S. Clemente for Cardinal Branda Castiglione, for whom he later worked in Castiglione Olona, near Como, one of the frescoes being dated 1435: the frescoes in the Collegiata and the Baptistry there are very markedly less Masacciesque than those in the Brancacci Chapel and it would seem therefore that Masolino reverted in his later years to the style he had practised as a young man. The two wings of *Saints* (London, NG), belonging to an altarpiece of which the most important panels are in Naples, are now generally thought to be one by Masolino and the other by Masaccio. There are other works in Detroit, Empoli, Munich, Naples, New York (Met. Mus.), Philadelphia (Johnson), Todi, the Vatican and Washington (NG).

MASSES. In art criticism, the masses are the largest, simplest and most fundamental shapes to which the component parts of a painting, a piece of sculpture or a building can be reduced. To think (or see) in masses means the ability not to be distracted by unimportant detail and to concentrate on the forms which must be completely realized for a satisfactory aesthetic effect. Such an effect may be totally different from a naturalistic representation.

MASSYS (Matsys, Metsys), Quentin (1464/5–1530), was born at Louvain but became a Master in the Antwerp Guild in 1491. His earliest certain work is the *St Anne Triptych* (1509, centre in Brussels, wings in the Liechtenstein Coll., Vaduz), a large work painted in clear, pale, cool colour, with a subject – the Kinship of the Holy Family – traditional in the North. Many of his works introduce landscape backgrounds of fantastic wooded and rocky mountains, some of which may have been painted by PATENIER, and the type became common among Antwerp painters. His use of *contrapposto* and of florid architectural detail of a debased classical type suggests some knowledge of Italian art (cf. MABUSE), and he also knew a version of Leonardo's *Madonna and Child with St Anne* (Louvre). He may have visited Italy between 1514 and 1519. In the latter year he built himself a house in Antwerp with a frescoed façade and polychromed statue, which was visited by Dürer in 1520, although he failed to find Massys at home. He painted genre subjects such as the *Banker and His Wife* (1514, Louvre), which may have a recondite religious or moral significance, and is connected with other contemporary paintings of bankers, usurers or tax-gatherers (cf. MARINUS), and the *Ill-matched Pair* i.e. an old man lusting after a pretty girl, with caricature types and an equivocal moral lesson. This is probably connected with Prodigal Son subjects and is the ancestor of the Flemish tavern scene picture. Besides his portraits of sitters seen against a landscape, Massys introduced a new type, derived from paintings of St Jerome, of the scholar in his setting of desk, books and papers, and he used this form appropriately for his *Erasmus* (1517, Royal Coll. and a version in Rome, Gall. Naz.) and his *Egidius* (private coll., Longford Castle), both of which look forward to portraits by van Orley and HOLBEIN. There are works in many European and US museums.

His son, Quentin II (*c.*1543–89), is now known to have signed and dated (1583) the controversial *Queen Elizabeth as a Vestal Virgin* (Siena), previously attributed to KETEL, ZUCCARO and others.

MASTER E. S. *see* E. S., Master.

MASTER OF 1456 *see* FOUQUET.

MASTER OF THE AIX ANNUNCIATION. A triptych of the *Annunciation* and two *Prophets* was completed in 1445 and placed in the Église des Prêcheurs in Aix-en-Provence. The *Annunciation* is still there, but one of the wings is now in Brussels and the other is divided into two parts, one in Amsterdam (Rijksmus.) and the other in Rotterdam. The style of the altarpiece shows many points of contact with Flemish art, and others with the art of Naples; various identifications of the artist have been suggested, but it is likely that the painter was a Frenchman, and Jean Chapus, who lived in Aix and was working for King René of Anjou and Naples in 1437 and 1448, seems to fit the bill.

MASTER OF THE ANTWERP ADORATION *see* JOOS van Cleve.

MASTER OF ST BARTHOLOMEW (active in the late 15th and early 16th centuries). A German painter whose name derives from an altarpiece formerly in S. Columba, Cologne, and now in Munich. Two other altarpieces by him are still in Cologne and probably date from *c.*1500, although the S. Bartholomew Altar itself is perhaps as late as 1510. The painter was probably a Cologne man, but his earliest works show the influence of the Netherlands, especially Roger van der WEYDEN and the school of Utrecht, so that it is sometimes suggested that he may have worked in Utrecht *c.*1470. This influence is seen in a *Virgin and Child With St Anne*, now in Munich. His work is characterized by bright enamel-like colour; there are examples in Berlin, Brussels, London (NG and Courtauld Inst.) and Paris (Petit Pal. and Louvre: based on Roger van der Weyden's Escorial *Deposition*).

MASTER OF ST CECILIA. An anonymous Italian painter active before 1304, influenced by GIOTTO, who painted the *St Cecilia Altarpiece* (Florence, Uffizi). The most important attribution to him is the beginning and end of the fresco cycle of St Francis of Assisi. In recent years attempts have been made to attribute the whole cycle to him, an honour for which he seems totally unfitted.

MASTER OF THE DEATH OF THE VIRGIN. A painter, active 1507–37, who is named from two altarpieces of the *Death of the Virgin* in Cologne and Munich. He is often identified with JOOS van Cleve, and certainly he influenced BRUYN.

MASTER OF FLÉMALLE. A name given to the painter of some pictures in Frankfurt (Städel) which are (wrongly) supposed to have come from the Abbey of Flémalle. He is also supposed to have painted another fragment in Frankfurt; the *Merode Altar* now in New York (Met. Mus.); the *Werl Altar* dated 1438 in the Prado, Madrid; pictures in the NG, London, and some other works. His style is slightly earlier than that of Jan van EYCK, but almost as revolutionary in its naturalism. An *Entombment* (London, Courtauld Inst.), thought to be his earliest work, is probably earlier (perhaps 1410/20) than any surviving painting by Jan and seems to show a style not compatible with that of any other painter. Various attempts have been made to identify him, the most satisfactory being that which equates him with CAMPIN and the least satisfactory that which identifies him with Roger van der WEYDEN, whose style is certainly similar but more subtle – and there is evidence that Roger was Campin's pupil.

MASTER OF THE FOGG NATIVITY *see* 'UGOLINO-LORENZETTI'.

MASTER OF ST GILES (active *c.*1500) was a Flemish painter (or Flemish-trained painter) who worked in France. He is named after the two *Scenes from the Legend of St Giles* in London (NG): two other panels, now in Washington (NG), have been connected with them, but they seem to come from another altarpiece by the same hand. Other pictures attributed to him are in Berlin, Boston, Brussels, Chantilly (Mus. Condé) and Paris (Louvre).

MASTER OF THE HOUSEBOOK (Meister des Hausbuchs) was a Rhenish or Dutch painter, draughtsman, and engraver active in the last quarter of the 15th century. He is named from a series of drawings in the so-called *Hausbuch* in Schloss Wolfegg in south-west Germany; many of the drawings show scenes of everyday life and so do the engravings (about ninety are known) attributed to him. By far the best collection of the engravings is in Amsterdam Print Room, and he was therefore once known as the Master of the Amsterdam Cabinet. Because of this, and because he seems to fit into the Bosch–Bruegel tradition, he is often thought to have been Dutch and various identifications have been suggested: the latest is Erhard REUWICH, who worked on the Middle Rhine *c.*1480. A few paintings are also ascribed to the Housebook Master, including the *Pair of Lovers* (Gotha) and one in Mainz, dated 1505, but perhaps finished by another hand. Other paintings are in Berlin and Frankfurt (Städel), but his work as an engraver was historically far more important.

MASTER OF THE LIFE OF MARY, Master of the Life of the Virgin, Meister des Marienlebens (active *c.*1463/5–*c.*1480/90) was a Cologne painter whose name derives from a series of eight panels of *Scenes from the Life of the Virgin*, formerly in S. Ursula, Cologne, and now divided between Munich (seven) and the NG, London (one). The altarpiece is known to have been the gift of a Councillor who was active *c.*1460, while a *Crucifixion with Nicholas of Cusa as Donor* (Cues, Hospital Church) seems to date from *c.*1465. The Master may have been trained in the Netherlands, since his style is based on Roger van der WEYDEN, and, especially, BOUTS, with skinny figures, rather small in scale and lost among their surroundings. The Master of the Lyversberg Passion may be identical with the Master of the Life of Mary, while the Master of Werden is probably only an aspect of his studio.

MASTER OF THE LIFE OF THE VIRGIN *see* MASTER OF THE LIFE OF MARY.

MASTER OF THE LYVERSBERG PASSION. A German painter responsible for a

Passion series (now in Cologne), which was at one time thought to be the work of the MASTER OF THE LIFE OF MARY. The relationship between the two masters is very close indeed, but is not necessarily that of identity.

MASTER OF MERODE *see* MASTER OF FLÉMALLE.

MASTER OF MOULINS (active *c.*1480–*c.*1499) has been identified with PERRÉAL, Jean Prévost (a collaborator of Perréal) and Jean Hey. The Master, one of the great French 15th-century painters, much influenced by Hugo van der Goes, takes his name from a triptych of the *Madonna and Child with Angels and Donors* in Moulins Cathedral datable *c.*1498/9. Other works attributed to him are in Autun (Mus.), Brussels, Chicago, Glasgow, London (NG and Wallace Coll.), Munich, New York (Met. Mus.) and Paris (Louvre).

MASTER OF THE OSSERVANZA *see* SASSETTA.

MASTER OF OULTREMONT *see* MOSTAERT.

MASTER OF TŘEBOŇ *see* MASTER OF WITTINGAU.

MASTER OF THE VIRGO INTER VIRGINES. The Virgo Master was a Dutch painter active *c.*1470–*c.*1500 who was influenced by BOSCH and GEERTGEN and who ranks with them as an artist, although almost nothing is known about him. He was perhaps working in Delft 1490/5, where he seems to have influenced woodcut book-illustrations for which he may have made the designs. His name is derived from the *Madonna and Child with Four Female Saints* (*Virgo inter Virgines*) in Amsterdam (Rijksmus.). There are important pictures by him in Barnard Castle (Bowes Mus.), and Liverpool, and others in Aachen, Berlin, Brussels, Chicago, Florence (Uffizi), Glasgow (Burrell Coll.), St Louis, Madrid, Milan (Brera), New York (Met. Mus.), Philadelphia, Princeton N.J., Rotterdam, Salzburg and Vienna. *See* HORTUS CONCLUSUS.

MASTER OF WERDEN. The painter of a series of panels, in the NG, London, which have now been reattributed to the Studio of the MASTER OF THE LIFE OF MARY.

MASTER OF WITTINGAU (Master of the Třeboň Altarpiece). In the NG of Prague there are three double-sided panels representing three Passion scenes and three sets of Saints, from an altarpiece in a church at Třeboň (Wittingau) in Czechoslovakia. They date from about 1390 and represent the next stage in Bohemian painting after Master THEODORIC, being related to the SOFT STYLE. The Master may have gone on working until *c.*1420.

MASTERS, The Little *see* KLEINMEISTER, Die.

MATHIEU, Georges (*b.*1921). A French ABSTRACT IMPRESSIONIST painter who began exhibiting in Paris in the late 1940s, in association with HARTUNG, DE KOONING, GORKY, POLLOCK and others.

MATIÈRE (Fr. material). The *matière* of a picture is simply paint.

MATISSE, Henri (1869–1954), was the principal artist of the FAUVE group. He was a pupil of the academician BOUGUEREAU for a few months in 1892, and from 1892 to 1897 was a pupil of Gustave MOREAU, in whose studio he met ROUAULT, MARQUET, Manguin, Camoin and Piot. He copied in the Louvre, and was strongly influenced by Impressionism, and his *Dinner Table* (*La Desserte*) of 1897 shows him working close to Bonnard and Vuillard. In 1901 he first met Vlaminck in the company of Derain, whom he already knew. He tried the Divisionist technique about 1899, but turned to Cézanne by 1901/3, painting in strongly modelled form and dark tones to offset the rather superficial quality of Signac's bright colour. The influence of Signac was renewed in 1904 when Matisse stayed with him in the South of France, and this renewed contact inspired the *Luxe, Calme et Volupté* (1904, Paris, Mus. d'Orsay), which started the train that led to the explosion of colour of the Fauve movement. This came in 1905, but in the midst of the general abuse Matisse acquired patrons in the Stein family who encouraged him, bought pictures and encouraged other Americans to buy, and later the Russians Shchukin and Morosov became his chief patrons. He began collecting African sculpture (in which Derain and Vlaminck also were interested), although it affected him less than it did the Cubists, and less also than the native artefacts he brought back from a visit to Algeria in 1906. In that year he exhibited the *Joie de Vivre* (Philadelphia, Barnes Fdn), which marked a radical change of direction in that it turned away from Signac's form of pointillism towards Cézanne, though still with Fauve colour. Exhibitions in Germany followed and in 1908–10 Matisse (or, rather, PURRMANN) ran a school which was thronged by American, German and, above all, Scandinavian pupils. By this time Picasso had appeared on the scene, and after all the years of preparation for the leadership of modern painting, Matisse found that the artistic centre of gravity had shifted to CUBISM. In 1910 Matisse saw the exhibition of Near Eastern art at Munich, and it is clear that this highly decorative and brilliantly coloured art had a deep and lasting influence on him, reinforcing his Algerian experience, particularly in his development of flat patterns with arabesques, flowered backgrounds, and in his use of brilliant and pure colours either juxtaposed or separated only by thin white lines or contours (*anti-cernes*). He travelled widely in Europe and North Africa (and also visited America and the South Sea Islands), and in 1914 went to Nice for the winter, to remain for most of the rest of his life on the Riviera, where he painted the long series of Odalisque and still-life subjects which are his main *oeuvre*. He had done a certain amount of sculpture from the start of his career, but it never assumed an importance equal to that of his painting; he also made several illustrated books, notably editions of Ronsard and Baudelaire, done at the end of the Second World War. His last major work was the decoration of the interior of the Chapel of the Dominican nuns at Vence, and in his last years he used a mixture of cut-outs in coloured paper with gouache and crayons to overcome the handicaps of age and illness.

Matisse's works are to be found in nearly every museum of modern art throughout the world. The two largest collections are the Moscow collection, made up of paintings bought by Shchukin and Morosov, and that at the Barnes Foundation at Merion Pa, which contains, among other important works, the huge murals of the *Dance* done in 1932–3. There is now a Musée Matisse in his native Le Cateau (Nord).

MATSYS *see* MASSYS.

MATTA (i.e. Roberto Sebastiano Matta Echaurren) (*b*.1911) is a Chilean painter, living in Paris, who began as an architect (1934) under Le Corbusier. From 1938 to 1947 he was a Surrealist, and is still a Freudian. He went to the US in 1939, where he met DUCHAMP. There are works by him in London (Tate), New York (M of MA), and a huge mural in Paris (1956, UNESCO).

MATTEO di Giovanni (*c*.1435–95), a Sienese painter, was a pupil of VECCHI-

ETTA. In Borgo San Sepolcro he completed in 1465 the polyptych of which the central panel (*Baptism of Christ*, London, NG) was by PIERO della Francesca. His linear and decorative style also shows the influence of POLLAIUOLO. There are works in Birmingham (Barber Inst.), Edinburgh, London (NG) and Siena (Mus. and Cath.).

MATTOIR *see* ENGRAVING 2(d).

MAULBERTSCH (Maulpertsch), Franz Anton (1724–96), was the major Viennese painter of the 18th century, becoming a member of the Academy in 1759 and Professor in 1770. There is no record of his having been to Italy, although it seems highly likely that he did go. Almost all his works are frescoes and altarpieces in Austrian, Hungarian and Czech churches, which combine a certain Rembrandt influence with a very marked similarity to contemporary Venetian decorative painters such as PITTONI. There are sketches by him in Vienna (Barockmus.) but most of his works are still in the churches for which they were painted.

MAUVE, Anton (1838–88), was a Dutch painter of peasant genre and landscapes and a leading member of the HAGUE SCHOOL. He worked with W. MARIS, but was principally influenced by MILLET and the BARBIZON painters. He was related to van GOGH, who worked under him for a brief period before they quarrelled. There are works by him in Amsterdam (Rijksmus. and Stedelijk), Baltimore, Boston, Edinburgh, Glasgow, The Hague (Mesdag Mus.), New York (Met. Mus. and Brooklyn), Rotterdam and elsewhere.

MAYER, Constance (1775/8–1821), was the pupil and mistress of PRUD'HON, whom she first met in 1802 in the studio of GREUZE, then her teacher. Under Prud'hon's influence she turned from genre and pastoral portraits to allegorical subjects in the strong chiaroscuro which he affected, collaborating with him in the soft, languishing compositions characteristic of his style, so that the authorship was disputed between them. Her life was saddened by bereavements and by the hostility of Prud'hon's children by his estranged and mentally afflicted wife. When, after his wife's death, she overheard him say that he would never remarry, she cut her throat with his razor, and he never recovered from the shock of her suicide. There are works in Dijon, London (Wallace Coll.), Nancy, Paris (Louvre) and elsewhere.

MAYNO *see* MAINO.

MAZO, Juan Bautista del (*c.*1612/16–67), was the pupil of VELÁZQUEZ, whose daughter he married in 1634. He had an appointment in the Royal Household by 1646, visited Italy in 1657, and succeeded to his father-in-law's position as Court Painter in 1661. His close relationship to Velázquez has led to the attribution to him of several pictures not considered good enough for Velázquez: his own style is not sufficiently distinguished to prevent this. There are very few certain works by him, but one is the *Queen Mariana* of 1666 (London, NG). The *Artist's Family* (Vienna) is almost certainly his (there is a related picture in London, Dulwich), and there are other pictures in Madrid (Prado). A good example of the Velázquez-type portrait is the *Admiral Pulido Pareja* (London, NG) which is now attributed to Mazo, as is the version of the *Fraga Philip* in London (Dulwich), the original being the Velázquez in New York (Frick Coll.).

MAZZUOLI, Giuseppe (1644–1725), was a Sienese Late Baroque sculptor. He was a pupil of FERRATA and CAFFÀ and worked for BERNINI, especially on the Tomb of Alexander VII. He kept the Berninesque tradition alive and untouched by French classicism. He worked in Rome, Gesù e Maria, after 1686, and completed Caffà's *Baptism of Christ* in Valletta Cathedral, Malta, after Caffà's early death. His twelve *Apostles*, originally in Siena Cathedral, are now in the Oratory, London; *bozzetti* are in Birmingham and Oxford (Ashmolean). Originally, the Siena Cathedral series had statues of Christ and the Virgin; these are lost, but *bozzetti* for them are in Edinburgh (Royal Mus. of Scotland).

MEDICI E SPEZIALI. The Florentine GUILD of Doctors and Apothecaries to which the painters belonged. This seems to have been on account of their using rare minerals like lapis lazuli, which were part of the druggist's stock in trade.

MEDINA, Sir John Baptist (*c.*1655/60–1710), was a portrait painter of Spanish descent, born in Brussels, who worked in London – in the style of KNELLER – from 1686 until *c.*1693 when he went to Edinburgh and introduced the Kneller style there with a stock of ready-painted figures requiring only the faces. He was knighted in 1706 and left a prosperous portrait business to his son. AIKMAN was his pupil. There are thirty-one portraits by him in the Royal Coll. of Surgeons, Edinburgh, and others in Edinburgh (SNPG), Glasgow, Florence (Pitti) and Providence RI. The first illustrations (1688) to Milton's 'Paradise Lost' were by him.

MEDIUM. The liquid used to bind powdered colour to make paint. By extension, the various techniques of painting; thus, the oil medium is oil-painting, powdered colour mixed to a thick consistency with oil, usually linseed. Other media are size (for distemper), egg yolk (for tempera), and gum arabic (for watercolour or pastel). In a more general sense it is possible to talk of pen-and-ink or pencil as media.

MEISSONIER, Jean-Louis-Ernest (1815–91), belonged to the circle of Mme Sabatier which included Baudelaire and Sir Richard Wallace (hence the sixteen Meissoniers in the Wallace Coll.). He was a painter of historical genre subjects, treated with Hollywood 'historical correctness', and most of his small pictures closely resemble 17th-century Dutch works, not only in the minuteness of handling. His larger canvases are less microscopic and now have a Wardour Street appearance. He was the first artist to receive the Grand Cross of the Legion of Honour, but this may have had something to do with his choice of Napoleonic subjects. The Musée d'Orsay has many of his pictures, including the *Campagne de France 1814* and the *Siege of Paris, 1870*. Others are in Bordeaux, Boston, Brussels, Chantilly, London (NG), New York (Met. Mus.) and Versailles.

MELANCHOLIA Still-life *see* HEEM.

MELENDEZ (Menendez), Luis (1716–80), was a Spanish painter, born in Naples, and trained by his father and L. M. van LOO in Spain. He was van Loo's assistant *c.*1742–8. He worked in Madrid and revisited Italy before 1775. He was the finest Spanish painter of still-life in the 18th century, continuing the austere traditions of the BODEGÓN established by SANCHEZ COTÁN, as well as Velázquez and Zurbarán. Most of his works are in Madrid (Prado), but there are others in Antwerp (Smidt van Gelder Mus.), Barcelona, Bilbao, Boston, Cleveland Ohio, Fort Worth Texas, Hartford Conn., London (NG), Munich, Raleigh NC and York. A *Self-portrait* in Paris (Louvre), signed and dated 1746, is his earliest known work, in which he looks younger than thirty.

MELOZZO da Forlì (1438–94) was famous in the 16th century as the inventor of extreme foreshortening – SOTTO IN SÙ. Most of his works exist in such fragmentary condition that it is impossible to be sure if this is correct, but it is clear that he was connected with PIERO della Francesca. His *Platina appointed Vatican Librarian* (1477, Vatican) shows his knowledge of perspective and a certain link wih Piero. Some fragments of an important fresco are in the Vatican, but his dome (1493/4) in S. Biagio, Forlì, was destroyed 1939/45. There are frescoes at Loreto.

MEMLINC (Memling), Hans (*c.*1430/40–94), was born in Seligenstadt, near Frankfurt-am-Main, but was traditionally – and very probably – a pupil of Roger van der WEYDEN. His art is purely Netherlandish, and he seems to have spent his life in Bruges, where he became a citizen in 1465 and was one of the largest taxpayers by 1480. He painted calm and devotional pictures, full of the gentle piety which is one aspect of the later Middle Ages, and also some fine portraits, such as the *Diptych of Martin van Nieuwenhove* (1487, Bruges, Hospital Mus.), which show a type of half-length that may have been known to Italians such as Perugino or even Giovanni Bellini. (A portrait in Venice was long attributed to ANTONELLO da Messina.) His religious pictures add nothing to what he took from the styles of Roger van der Weyden and Dieric BOUTS. The *Donne Triptych* (London, NG) was for long believed to date from 1469, but is more probably of 1477: his earliest dated work is of 1472 (Ottawa), but a picture in Turin, painted for the Portinari, Hugo van der GOES's patrons, may date from *c.*1470, and a *Last Judgement*, also painted for an Italian in Bruges, was captured at sea in 1473. It is now in Gdansk (formerly Danzig). The *Passion Altar* in Lübeck was formerly dated 1491 on the frame. There are several dated works in Bruges (Hospital Mus., including the *Shrine of St Ursula*, consecrated 1489, and Mus.); other works are in the Royal Coll., and Antwerp, Berlin, Birmingham, Boston, Brussels, Chicago, Cincinnati, Cleveland Ohio, Cologne, Copenhagen, Florence (Uffizi), Frankfurt (Städel), Glasgow (Burrell), Granada (Capilla Real), The Hague, Lisbon, London (NG and Wallace Coll.), Madrid (Prado), Melbourne, Montreal, Munich, New York (Met. Mus.), Paris (Louvre and Jacquemart-André), Philadelphia (Johnson), Turin, Upton House nr Banbury (National Trust), Vicenza, Vienna (K-H Mus. and Akad.) and Washington (NG).

MENENDEZ *see* MELENDEZ.

MENGS, Anton Raffael (1728–79), one of the earliest exponents of NEO-CLASSICISM, was the son of the Dresden Court Painter who named him Anton (after Correggio) and Raffael (= Raphael) and brought him up with excessive severity to be a great painter. The boy was taken to Rome in 1741 and soon developed into something of a prodigy, specializing in pastel portraits. He was made Court Painter at Dresden in 1745, but his real career began in 1755, when he met WINCKELMANN, who praised him highly and whose theories Mengs adopted in return. He wrote a treatise on 'Beauty in Painting' (published in 1762), which was apparently borrowed by an Englishman named Daniel Webb who published it as his own in 1760, when it had a considerable success. Mengs was employed by the Duke of Northumberland 1752–5 to make a full-size copy of Raphael's *School of Athens* (now London, V&A), but his first major work in Rome was the ceiling of S. Eusebio (1757–8, sketch in Manchester), which cannot be called Neoclassical. After this he went to see the antiquities then being excavated at Herculaneum, drew them, and returned to Rome to paint his best-known work, the *Parnassus* (1761, Rome, Villa Albani), which breaks completely with the Baroque tradition of illusionism and treats a ceiling as if it were a relief, composed from drawings after the Antique, and seen orthogonally – i.e. as if it were at the spectator's eye-level, and not SOTTO IN SÙ. In 1761 he went to Spain as Court Painter and began decorating the Royal Palaces; when TIEPOLO arrived he found Mengs formidably entrenched, but Mengs's ceilings are markedly less Neoclassical in face of the competition from Tiepolo. In 1771 he returned to Italy, becoming Principe of the Accademia di S. Luca, and worked in the Vatican 1772–3. He went back to Spain 1773–7 and died in Rome. He had met VIEN in Rome and, like him, he was really no more than a precursor for the full Neoclassicism of DAVID, who arrived in Rome in 1775. Mengs was a fine portrait painter, and in this he was close in style to his principal rival, BATONI. Portraits of English Grand Tourists, similar to Batoni's, are in Stourhead (National Trust) and Yale (CBA). There are other works by him in Dresden and in Cambridge (St John's College), Cardiff, Chicago, Ipswich, Liverpool, London (NPG and Wellington Mus.), Madrid (Prado), Milan, Naples, New York (Met. Mus.: *Winckelmann*), Oxford (Ashmolean and All Souls College), Paris (Louvre), Vienna and Washington (Corcoran).

MENZEL, Adolf (1815–1905), was one of the leading German painters of the 19th century. He was trained in Berlin and took over his father's business as a lithographer in 1832, thus beginning a long career as an illustrator. Perhaps his most important graphic works are the drawings for the Life of Frederick the Great (1840–2), which were admired by Degas. In 1839 he saw some pictures by Constable in Berlin, and in the 1840s and 1850s he made a series of paintings which are very free in handling and seem to anticipate Impressionism, although later he rejected the theory (he was a friend and admirer of MEISSONIER). There are pictures by him in many German museums (especially Berlin) and in Cambridge Mass. and London (Tate).

MERCIER, Philip (1689/91–1760), was born in Berlin of French descent and worked mostly in England, where he introduced a French taste, based on Watteau and Chardin. He began by engraving (and perhaps faking) Watteaus before coming to England *c.*1716. By 1725/6 – i.e. before HOGARTH – he was painting CONVERSATION PIECES. Later, he introduced 'fancy pictures', more or less derived from Chardin, which were well received. He lived in York 1739–51, painting the local gentry in a semi-French style akin to RAMSAY's. There are works in the Royal Coll. and in Barnsley, Cracow, Detroit, Edinburgh, London (NG, NPG, Tate and V&A at Ham House), Paris (Louvre), Yale (CBA), York and several other British provincial museums.

MERYON, Charles (1821–68), ranks with Piranesi as the greatest of architectural etchers. He was the illegitimate son of an English doctor and a dancer at the Opéra and began his career in the French Navy, spending 1842–6 in the South Pacific. There are some drawings of exotic scenes and ships, but his reputation rests on the great series of views of Paris, described by Victor Hugo as 'visions', which he began *c.*1850. The series ranges from straightforward *vedute* through Romantic horror (the *Gargoyle of Notre-Dame*, the *Morgue*) to uncomfortable fantasies like the *Ministry of Marine With Flying Devils*. The series was not popular, and Meryon was very difficult in his personal character: he spent

1858–9 in an asylum and also the last two years of his life, believing himself to be Christ. All his etchings date from 1849 to 1866. He also drew Dr Gachet, later to befriend van Gogh in his madness.

MERZ *see* SCHWITTERS.

MEŠTROVIČ, Ivan (1883–1962), was the greatest Yugoslav sculptor. He was the son of Dalmatian peasants and began as a woodcarver, later serving an apprenticeship to a mason. He studied in Vienna until 1904 and his early works, reflecting the Yugoslav patriotic movement, soon brought him fame. The freedom of his handling gave his works a certain kinship to that of RODIN. He went to America in 1947 and died there. There are examples of his religious works and also of his portraiture in London (Tate), and others in American museums, Belgrade and Zagreb.

METAPHYSICAL ART *see* PITTURA METAFISICA.

METSU, Gabriel (1629–67), was a Dutch painter, born in Leyden but mainly active in Amsterdam, of interiors and genre subjects, representing nice, clean and well-behaved people. He also painted a few portraits, religious subjects and perhaps some still-life. He was probably a pupil of DOU and was slightly influenced by Rembrandt, but on the whole he closely resembles Ter BORCH and de HOOCH and his works can be confused with theirs. In his best works, such as the *Sick Child* (Amsterdam, Rijksmus.), he approaches Vermeer. There are works by him in the Royal Coll. and in Aix, Amsterdam, Barnsley, Berlin, Boston, Brussels, Cape Town, Cheltenham, Dresden, Florence (Uffizi), The Hague, Leningrad, London (NG and Wallace Coll.), Montpellier, Munich, New York (Met. Mus.), Oxford, Paris (Louvre), Rotterdam, Stockholm, Venice, Vienna (Akad. and K-H Mus.) and Washington (NG).

METZINGER, Jean (1883–1956), became a Cubist painter and, with GLEIZES, published in 1912 'Du Cubisme', the first book on the movement (English edition, 1913). He used the flat-pattern type of Cubism in rather bright colour. There is an example in London (Tate) and several in Paris (Mus. d'Art Moderne).

MEZZO-RILIEVO *see* RELIEF.

MEZZOTINT *see* ENGRAVING.

MICHEL, Georges (1763–1843), was employed by the Louvre on the cleaning and restoration of, principally, Dutch pictures, and the influence of Dutch 17th-century landscapes is clearly visible in his own works. He rarely moved away from his native Paris, and declared that no painter needs more than four square miles in which to find all the subjects he desires. Michel's simple pictures of muddy lanes, stormy skies, and unprettified fields and heaths are probably late works; they presage the landscape based on the observation of nature alone, exploited by the BARBIZON SCHOOL, and his concentration on tone rather than colour links him with COROT. There are works in Besançon, Berwick-on-Tweed, Cambridge (Fitzwm), Edinburgh, Glasgow, Hanover, Leningrad, London (NG and V&A), New York (Met. Mus.), Paris (Louvre), Strasbourg and elsewhere.

MICHELANGELO Buonarroti (1475–1564), was born at Caprese, a village in Florentine territory, where his father was the resident magistrate. A few weeks after Michelangelo's birth the family returned to Florence, and, in 1488, after overcoming parental opposition he was formally apprenticed to Domenico GHIRLANDAIO for a term of three years. Later in life Michelangelo tried to suppress this fact, probably to make it seem that he had never had an ordinary workshop training; for it was he more than anyone else who introduced the idea of the 'Fine Arts', having no connection with the craft that painting had always previously been. His stay in the Ghirlandaio shop must also have coincided with his beginning to work as a sculptor in the Medici Garden, where antiques from their collection were looked after by BERTOLDO. Although this connection drew him into the Medici circle as a familiar, the account by Vasari of an established 'school' is now discredited. It must, however, have been Ghirlandaio who taught him the elements of fresco technique, and it was probably also in that shop that he made his drawings after the great Florentine masters of the past (copies after Giotto and Masaccio; now in the Louvre, in Munich, and in Vienna). In 1492, Lorenzo de' Medici died. Michelangelo then studied anatomy with the help of the Prior of the Hospital of Sto Spirito, for whom he appears to have carved a wooden crucifix for the high altar. A wooden crucifix found there (now in the Casa Buonarroti) has been attributed to him by some scholars. The next few years were marked by the expulsion of the Medici and the gloomy Theocracy set up under Savonarola, but Michelangelo avoided the worst of the crisis by going to Bologna and, in 1496, to Rome. There he carved the first of his major works, the *Bacchus* (Florence, Bargello) and the St Peter's *Pietà*, which was completed by the turn of the century. It is highly finished and shows that he had already mastered anatomy and the disposition of drapery, but above all it shows that he had solved the problem of the representation of a full-grown man stretched out nearly horizontally on the lap of a woman, the whole being contained in a pyramidal shape. The *Pietà* made his name and he returned to Florence in 1501 as a famous sculptor, remaining there until 1505. During these years he was extremely active, carving the gigantic *David* (1501–4, now in the Accad.), the *Bruges Madonna* (Bruges, Notre Dame), and beginning the series of the *Twelve Apostles* for the Cathedral which was commissioned in 1503 but never completed (the *St Matthew* now in the Accad. is the only one which was even blocked in). At about this time he painted the *Doni Tondo* of the Holy Family with St John the Baptist (Florence, Uffizi) and made the two unfinished marble *tondi* of the Madonna and Child (Florence, Pitti; London, RA). After the completion of the *David* in 1504 he began to work on the cartoon of a huge fresco in the Council Hall of the new Florentine Republic, as a pendant to the one already commissioned from Leonardo da Vinci. Both remained unfinished and the grandiose project of employing the two greatest living artists on the decoration of the Town Hall of their native city came to nothing. Of Michelangelo's fresco, which was to represent an incident in the Pisan War, we now have a few studies by him and copies of a fragment of the whole full-scale cartoon which once existed (the best copy is the painting in Lord Leicester's Coll., Holkham, Norfolk). The cartoon, which is known as the *Bathers*, was for many years the resort of every young artist in Florence and, by its exclusive stress on the nude human body as a sufficient vehicle for the expression of all emotions which the painter can depict, had an enormous influence on the subsequent development of Italian art – especially MANNERISM – and therefore on European art as a whole. This influence is more readily detectable in his next major work, the ceiling of the Sistine Chapel. In fact, however, the *Battle of Cascina* was left incomplete because the Signoria of Florence found it expedient to comply with a request from the masterful Pope Julius II, who was anxious to have a fitting tomb made in his lifetime. The Julius Monument was, in Michelangelo's own view, the Tragedy of the Tomb. This was partly because Michelangelo and Julius had the same ardent temperament – they admired each other greatly – and very soon quarrelled, and partly because after the death of Julius in 1513, Michelangelo was under constant pressure from successive Popes to abandon his contractual obligations and work for them while equally under pressure from the heirs of Julius, who even went so far as to accuse him of embezzlement. The original project for a vast free-standing tomb with forty figures was substantially reduced by a second contract (1513), drawn up after Julius's death; under this contract the *Moses*, which is the major figure on the extant tomb, was prepared as a subsidiary figure. Two others, the *Slaves* in the Louvre, were made under this contract but were subsequently abandoned. The third contract (1516) was followed by a fourth (1532), and a fifth and final one in 1542, under the terms of which the present miserably mutilated version of the original conception was carried out by assistants, under Michelangelo's supervision, in S. Pietro in Vincoli (Julius's titular church) in 1545. Michelangelo was then 70 and had spent nearly forty years on the tomb.

Meanwhile, the original quarrel of 1506 with Julius was made up and Michelangelo executed a colossal bronze statue of the Pope as an admonition to the recently conquered Bolognese (who destroyed it as soon as they could, in 1511). In 1508, back in Rome, he began his most important work, the ceiling of the Sistine Chapel in the Vatican for Julius, who, as usual, was impatient to see it finished. Dissatisfied with the normal working methods and with the abilities of the assistants he had engaged, Michelangelo determined to execute the whole of this vast work virtually alone. Working under appalling difficulties (amusingly described in one of his own poems), most of the time leaning backwards and never able to get far enough away from the ceiling to be able to see what he was doing, he completed the first half (the part nearer to the door) in 1510. The whole enormous undertaking was completed in 1512, Michelangelo being by then so practised that he was able to execute the second half more rapidly and freely. It was at once recognized as a supreme work of art, even at the moment when Raphael was also at work in the Vatican Stanze. From then on Michelangelo was universally regarded as the greatest living artist, although he was then only 37 and this was in the lifetimes of Leonardo and Raphael (who was even younger). From this moment, too, dates the idea of the artist as in some sense a superhuman being, set apart from ordinary men, and for the first time it was possible to use the phrase *il divino Michelangelo* without seeming merely blasphemous.

The Sistine Ceiling is a shallow barrel vault divided up by painted architecture into a series of alternating large and small panels which appear to be open to the sky. These are the Histories. Each of the smaller panels is surrounded by four figures of nude youths – the Slaves, or *Ignudi* – who are represented as seated on the architectural frame and who are not of the same order of reality as the figures in the Histories, since their system of perspective is different. Below them are the Prophets and Sibyls, and still lower, the figures of the Ancestors of Christ. The whole ceiling completes the chapel decoration by representing life on earth before the Law: on the walls is an earlier cycle of frescoes, painted in 1481–82, representing the Life of Moses (i.e. the Old Dispensation) and the Life of Christ (the New Dispensation). The Histories begin over the altar and work away from it (though they were painted in the reverse direction): the first scene represents God alone, in the Primal Act of Creation, and the story continues through the rest of the Creation to the Fall, the Flood, and the Drunkenness of Noah, representing the human soul at its furthest from God. The whole conception owes much to the Neoplatonic philosophy current in Michelangelo's youth in Florence, perhaps most in the idea of the *Ignudi*, perfect human beauty, on the level below the Divine story. Below them come the Old Testament Prophets and the Seers of the ancient world who foretold the coming of Christ; while the four corners have scenes from the Old Testament representing Salvation. The Prophet Jonah is above the altar, since his three days in the whale were held to prefigure the Resurrection. On the lowest parts – and very freely painted – are the human families who were the Ancestors of Christ. There can be no doubt that the splendour of the conception and the size of the task distracted Michelangelo from the Tomb, but he at once returned to it as soon as the ceiling was finished, from 1513 to 1516, when he returned to Florence to work for the Medici.

His new master was Pope Leo X, the younger son of Lorenzo de' Medici, who had known Michelangelo from boyhood; he now commissioned him to complete the façade of S. Lorenzo, the family church in Florence. Michelangelo wasted four years on this and it came to nothing. In 1520 he began planning the Medici Chapel, a funerary chapel in honour of four of the Medici – two of them by no means the most glorious of their family. The chapel is attached to S. Lorenzo. Leo X died in 1521 and it was not until after the accession of another Medici Pope, Clement VII, in 1523 that the project was resumed. Work began in earnest in 1524 and at the same time he was commissioned to design the Laurenziana Library in the cloister of the same church. Both these buildings are turning-points in architectural history, but the sculptural decoration of the chapel (an integral part of the architecture) was never completed, although the figures of Giuliano and Lorenzo de' Medici set over their tombs, eternally symbolizing the Active and the Contemplative Life, above the symbols of Time and Mortality – *Day* and *Night*, *Dawn* and *Evening* – are among his finest creations. The unfinished *Madonna* was meant to be the focal point of the chapel. In 1527, the Medici were again expelled from Florence, and Michelangelo, who was politically a Republican in spite of his close ties with the Medici, took an active part in the defence of Florence up to the capitulation in 1530, although in a moment of panic he had fled in 1529. During the months of confusion and disorder in Florence, when he was proscribed for his participation in the struggle, it would appear that he was hidden by the Prior of S. Lorenzo. A number of drawings on the walls of a concealed crypt under the Medici Chapel have been attributed to him, and ascribed to this period. After the reinstatement of the Medici he was pardoned, and set to work once more on the Chapel which was to glorify them until, in 1534, he left Florence and settled in Rome for the thirty years remaining to him.

He was at once commissioned to paint his next great work, the *Last Judgement* on the altar wall of the Sistine Chapel, which affords the strongest possible contrast with his own Ceiling. He began work on it in 1536. In the interval there had been the Sack of Rome and the Reformation, and the confident humanism and Christian Neoplatonism of the Ceiling had curdled into the personal pessimism and despondency of the *Judgement*. The very choice of subject is indicative of the new mood, as is the curious fact that the mouth of Hell gapes over the altar itself where, during services, stands a crucifix symbolizing Christ standing between Man and Doom. It was unveiled in 1541 and caused a sensation equalled only by his own work of thirty years earlier, and was the only work by him to be as much reviled as praised, and only narrowly to escape destruction, though it did not escape the mutilation of having many of the nude figures 'clothed' after his death. Most of the ideas of Mannerism are traceable implicitly or explicitly in the *Judgement* and, more than ever, it served to imprint the idea that the scope of painting is strictly limited to the exploitation of the nude, preferably in foreshortened – and therefore difficult – poses. Paul III, who had commissioned the *Judgement*, immediately commissioned two more frescoes for his own chapel, the Cappella Paolina; these were begun in 1542 and completed in 1550. They represent the *Conversion of St Paul* and the *Crucifixion of St Peter*.

Michelangelo was now 75 years old, but since 1546 he had been increasingly active as an architect; in particular, he was Chief Architect to St Peter's and was doing more there than had been done for thirty years. This was the greatest architectural undertaking in Christendom, and Michelangelo did it, as he did all his late works, solely for the glory of God. In his last years he made a number of drawings of the Crucifixion, wrote much of his finest poetry, and carved the *Pietà* (now in Florence Cath. Mus.) which was originally intended for his own tomb, as well as the nearly abstract *Rondanini Pietà* (Milan, Castello). This last work, in which the very forms of the Dead Christ actually merge with those of His Mother, is charged with an emotional intensity which contemporaries recognized as Michelangelo's *terribilità*. He was working on it to within a few days of his death, in his 89th year, on 18 February 1564. There is a whole world of difference between it and the 'beautiful' *Pietà* in St Peter's, carved some sixty-five years earlier.

Unlike any previous artist, Michelangelo was the subject of two biographies in his own lifetime. The first of these was by VASARI, who concluded the first (1550) edition of his 'Vite' with the Life of one living artist, Michelangelo. In 1553 there appeared a 'Life of Michelangelo' by his pupil Ascanio Condivi (English translations 1903, 1976 and 1987); this is really almost an autobiography, promoted by Michelangelo to correct some errors of Vasari and to shift the emphasis in what Michelangelo regarded as a more desirable direction. Vasari, however, became more and more friendly with Michelangelo and was also his most devoted and articulate admirer, so that the very long Life which appears in Vasari's second edition (1568), after Michelangelo's death, gives us the most complete biography of any artist up to that time and is a trustworthy guide to the feelings of contemporaries about the man who can lay claim to be the greatest sculptor, painter and draughtsman that has ever lived, as well as one of the greatest architects and poets. He is the archetype of genius.

Pure FRESCO was his preferred painting technique; he despised oil-painting, though the now authenticated unfinished *Entombment* (London, NG) is in oil over a TEMPERA underpainting. The *Doni Tondo* is in tempera. In sculpture, his usual method was to outline his figure on the front of the block and, as he himself wrote, to 'liberate the figure imprisoned in the marble', by working steadily inwards, with perhaps a few more finished details. Occasionally he made drawings for parts of a figure, and a few small wax models survive as well as one large one, made for the guidance of assistants working on the Medici Chapel figures. The four abandoned *Slaves* intended for a later version of the Julius Tomb (Florence, Accad.) and the two marble *tondi* left unfinished in 1505 provide fine examples of his direct carving technique and his consistent use of various sizes of claw chisel. No *modelli* exist for any paintings or frescoes, and only one cartoon (London, BM), made to help Condivi, has survived.

Apart from the works mentioned above, there are others in Florence (Accad., Bargello, Casa Buonarroti – the house of his family, which contains relics of him – and Pal. della Signoria) and in Bologna (S. Domenico), London (NG and RA), and Rome (S.M. sopra Minerva). There are also some 500 drawings by him, the majority of which are in the Royal Coll., Florence (Uffizi and Casa Buonarroti), London (BM), Oxford and Paris.

MICHELOZZO Michelozzi (1396–1472), though more famous as an architect, was the collaborator of Ghiberti and DONATELLO. He worked with Ghiberti from *c.*1417 on his bronze Doors, and again in 1437, and was in partnership with Donatello from *c.*1425 until 1433/8, during which time he was mainly responsible for the architecture and the decorative sculpture in their joint works. In 1427 the partners were engaged on three major commissions, the Monuments for Antipope John XXIII (Florence, Baptistry), Cardinal Brancacci (Naples, S. Angelo a Nilo) and Bartolommeo Aragazzi. Most of the sculpture on the Aragazzi Monument was Michelozzo's, and pieces of it survive in Montepulciano and in the V&A, London. He also made the *Baptist* for the Silver Altar (1452, Florence, Cath. Mus.).

MIEL, Jan (1599–1663), was born in Antwerp, but was in Rome by 1636. There he became friendly with BAMBOCCIO, and most of his pictures are scenes of low life – *Bambocciate.* He did, however, paint frescoes in Roman churches and palaces, such as the *Crossing of the Red Sea* (1656, Quirinal) and *S. Lambert* (S.M. dell' Anima; sketch in Cambridge, Fitzwm), as well as briefly collaborating with SACCHI 1641/3. He also painted figures for CLAUDE's landscapes. In 1658 he was made Court Painter at Turin, where he died. There are works in the Royal Coll. and in Birmingham (Barber Inst.), Bologna, Edinburgh (NG), Grenoble, London (Dulwich), Northampton and elsewhere.

MIEREVELD, Michiel Jansz. (1567–1641), was a prolific portrait painter, who was born and died in Delft, but was in The Hague in 1625 and became Painter to the Princes of Orange. His portraits are mostly small in size, often busts only, and always sober in handling, like those of his English contemporary, JOHNSON. There are examples in Amsterdam (Rijksmus.), Boston, Delft, The Hague, London (NG, NPG and Wallace Coll.), Manchester, New York (Met. Mus.), Rotterdam and elsewhere.

MIGNARD, Pierre (1612–95), was the rival of LEBRUN but an exponent of the same Academic theories. Like Lebrun he was a pupil of VOUET, but he went to Rome in 1636 and remained there until 1657, forming his style on the approved models of the Carracci, Domenichino and Poussin. He returned to

Paris on the orders of Louis XIV and decorated the dome of the Val-de-Grâce (1663), but his principal importance was as portrait painter to the Court. He revived the earlier Italian type of allegorical portrait, and a good example is the *Marquise de Seignelay as Thetis* (1691, London, NG). He was strongly opposed to the Académie royale, and, in spite of his own stylistic origins, championed the Venetian or 'colourist' school (*see* RUBÉNISME); this, however, was probably only to oppose Lebrun. When Lebrun died in 1690 Mignard was at once made *premier peintre*, and, on the King's orders, the Academy had, in a single sitting, to appoint Mignard Associate, Member, Rector, Director and Chancellor of the body he had so long opposed. There are pictures by him in the Royal Coll., Honolulu, London (NPG), Raleigh NC and many French museums.

MILANO, Giovanni da, *see* GIOVANNI.

MILLAIS, Sir John Everett (1829–96), was in the RA Schools in 1840 – an infant prodigy. In 1848, he, HUNT and ROSSETTI founded the PRE-RAPHAELITE BROTHERHOOD (PRB); his *Christ in the House of His Parents* (RA 1850, now Tate) was savagely attacked by Charles Dickens, but Ruskin defended him and the PRB generally. In 1853 he was elected an ARA. In 1855 he married Ruskin's former wife, and his friendship with Ruskin was broken off. Millais developed into a fashionable and technically brilliant academic painter of portraits, costume history and genre pieces, forsaking his original PRB theories, and went on to become RA (1863), and President in 1896, just before his death. He was made a baronet in 1885. There are works in Birmingham, Cambridge (Fitzwm), Detroit, Liverpool, London (Tate, NPG and Guildhall), Manchester, New York (Met. Mus.), Oxford and Yale (CBA).

MILLES, Carl (1875–1955). With SERGEL the greatest of Swedish sculptors, Milles was one of the most famous sculptors since Rodin, by whom he was much influenced at the beginning of his career. He started to emigrate to Chile in 1897, but got no further than Paris, where he stayed for eight years. His strong feeling for architecture distinguishes him from Rodin, and most of his best works are fountains, in which the figures must be seen against the water and sky as part of an architectural whole. Much of his best work is in the US, where he soon became famous. There is a fountain by him in Kansas City, his last work, and another forms part of the Metropolitan Mus., New York.

MILLET, Jean François, called Francisque (1642–79), worked in Paris from 1659, painting landscapes in the style of Gaspar POUSSIN. He had relatives of the same name, and it is not clear what is by him: examples of what is associated with his name are in Birmingham, London (NG), Toledo Ohio and York. Three etchings are also now attributed to him.

MILLET, Jean François (1814–75), was the son of a peasant. He was trained under a local painter at Cherbourg and then in Paris (1837) under DELAROCHE. His earliest works are pastiches of the pastorals of the 18th century and rather erotic nudes, but he also painted portraits for a time. The influence of DAUMIER seems to have been decisive, and in 1848 he exhibited at the Salon a peasant subject, *The Winnower* (London, NG; versions are in Paris, Louvre). From *c.*1850 his choice of subject matter led to accusations of Socialism (e.g. *The Sower*, Salon of 1850). In 1849 he moved to BARBIZON and remained there for the rest of his life, living in the most gruelling poverty, painting scenes of peasants and their labours as well as ordinary landscapes and marines. *The Angelus* (1857–9: Paris, Mus. d'Orsay), though his best-known work, shows him with an unusually sentimental approach. His works are particularly well represented in Boston, and in America generally. There are works in many French museums, and in Birmingham (Barber Inst.), Cardiff, Edinburgh, Glasgow (Mus. and Burrell), London (NG and V&A), Ottawa (NG) and Vienna.

MINIATURE. A painting 'in little', usually a portrait, executed in gouache or watercolour. The 16th-century type of miniature, exemplified in the work of HILLIARD or OLIVER, was normally executed in body colour on playing cards or on vellum, the material used by the medieval illuminator. This type of portrait, with its allegories and symbolism, is a direct descendant of manuscript illumination. In the hands of men like COOPER, in the 17th century the portrait miniature became more closely allied to contemporary oil-painting (some miniatures were actually executed in oil, usually on metal). In the 18th century the whole character of miniature painting was changed by the introduction of ivory as a ground and support; this could be left as a white ground and was most effective in conjunction with transparent watercolour. COSWAY used this technique.

MINO da Fiesole (1429–84), was a Florentine sculptor who was traditionally a pupil of his contemporary DESIDERIO da Settignano, but was in Rome by 1454, where he did several works for churches. His principal tombs are those in Fiesole and Florence, particularly the Tomb of Count Ugo in the Badia, Florence, of 1469–81: this shows the delicacy and virtuosity of his marble carving, as well as the influence of the Antique. He also made a number of strongly characterized busts; the earliest dated portrait bust of the Renaissance being his *Piero de' Medici* (Florence, Bargello) of 1453, and one of the best being that of Niccolò Strozzi (1454, Berlin). There are works by him in Florence (Bargello), London (V&A and Courtauld Inst.), Paris (Louvre) and Washington (NG).

MIRANDA, Carreño de, *see* CARREÑO.

MIRÓ, Joan (1893–1983), was a Spanish Surrealist painter, who lived for some time in the US. He went to Paris in 1919, but before then he had already met PICASSO – a fellow-Catalan – in Barcelona. In 1925 he took part in the First Surrealist Exhibition, and, with DALI, was recognized as the leading Spanish Surrealist. His work tended to become abstract, although he said: 'For me a form is never something abstract; it is always a sign of something. It is always a man, a bird, or something else. For me painting is never form for form's sake.' During the Second World War he returned to Spain and in 1944 he began making ceramics, which resulted in huge wall-decorations for the UNESCO building in Paris and Harvard University. He designed the ballet 'Jeux d'Enfants' in 1932. There are works in several US museums and London (Tate), Paris (Mus. d'Art Moderne) and Washington (NG: a large tapestry), and there are Miró Foundations in Barcelona and Palma (Majorca), where he lived. A selection of his writings on art was published in English in 1987.

MISERICORDIA, MADONNA DELLA (Ital. Madonna of Pity). A representation of the Madonna standing erect and sheltering under her outspread mantle a number of people, usually members of a *Confraternità della Misericordia* or other charitable organization.

MIXED METHOD. Oil glazes over TEMPERA underpainting, or any other combination of media, e.g. pure water-colour and body colour.

MOBILE. A form of sculpture invented in 1931/2 by CALDER, and named by DUCHAMP. Essentially a mobile consists of a series of shapes cut from wood, plastic or sheet metal and connected by wires or rods of metal so that a gentle touch will cause the whole to revolve like a planetarium, giving an ever-changing sequence of planes, solids and colours in three-dimensional movement. The interior decoration of the 1950s and 1960s was much affected by coloured shapes linked with wire.

MOCHI, Francesco (1580–1654), was an Italian sculptor whose *Annunciation* group in Orvieto Cathedral, finished in 1609, has been called the first piece of Baroque sculpture. He made two equestrian statues in Piacenza, of Ranuccio and Alessandro Farnese, completed in 1629, but his best-known work is the *S. Veronica* in St Peter's, Rome (1629–40: *see* BOLGI).

MODELBOOK *see* PATTERN-BOOKS.

MODELLING. (i) The three-dimensional representation of forms, by means of some plastic material, usually modelling clay. The opposite of carving. *See* SCULPTURE. (ii) The representation of three-dimensional forms on a two-dimensional surface, in such a way that they appear solid. Thus it is usual to speak of the modelling of a hand or figure, meaning the apparent solidity of it, or the painter's comprehension of the form.

MODELLO, MODELLETTO. Italian words used to describe a small version of a large picture, not strictly speaking a preliminary sketch, which was shown to the person or body commissioning the large work for approval before the final design was put in hand. Many such small versions, often quite highly finished, still exist, e.g. by TIEPOLO and RUBENS. Most *modelli* are in oil paint or a combination of chalk, ink and paint such as BAROCCI's *Madonna of the Rosary* (Oxford, Ashmolean). A very beautiful chalk drawing by Camillo Procaccini (New York, Met. Mus.) shows a cut-out figure pasted over another and obviously introduced as a modification of the original design. A *modello* some 18 inches high, in blue-grey wash heightened with white, for Veronese's huge altarpiece in Sta Giustina, Padua, was formerly at Chatsworth: it is about one-eleventh scale with fully realized figures and has been squared-up for transfer. *See also* BOZZETTO.

'MODERNO'. An anonymous Italian sculptor and maker of plaquettes who signed his works *Opus Moderni* (cf. ANTICO). He was active at the turn of the 15th/16th centuries and a document of *c.*1549 mentions him as having worked in Rome. There is a signed stone-carving in Vienna (K-H Mus.), but the largest collection of his plaquettes is in the Kress Coll., Washington (NG). There are others in Berlin, Brescia, London (BM, V&A, and six in the Wallace Coll.), Oxford (Ashmolean) and Paris (Louvre).

MODERSOHN-BECKER, Paula (1876–1907), was the most important German woman artist of her day and one of the main precursors of EXPRESSIONISM. She was born in Dresden and trained in Berlin (1896–8) before settling in the artists' colony of Worpswede, near Bremen. She went to Paris in 1900 and again in 1903, 1905 and 1906: these visits brought her under the influence of Gauguin and the Fauves (who exhibited in 1905). The simplification of form and colour and the stress on line were introduced by her into Germany, making her a link with the development of the

BLAUE REITER and BRÜCKE groups. There are several works in Bremen and in other German museums. She was a friend of the poet Rainer Maria Rilke, who wrote a biography of her, and her portrait of him is in a private collection.

MODIGLIANI, Amedeo (1884–1920), was known as 'Modi' for short, from which by natural corruption the French referred to him as *un peintre maudit* – and those who were like him were equally accursed. He was born in Leghorn of a distinguished Italian Jewish family and had his first training in Italy before going to Paris in 1906. He spent the rest of his life there, working at first in a manner influenced by Toulouse-Lautrec, but his *Cellist* of 1910 won him recognition and shows that his real style was based on African sculpture, Cézanne, Picasso and, above all, his Italian heritage. He was a superb draughtsman, and all his work contains echoes of Botticelli, of Sienese Trecento painters, and of some of the Mannerists, so that he is truly the greatest Italian artist of the 20th century, and not a French painter at all. He was handsome, amorous and addicted to drink and drugs. He said, 'I am going to drink myself dead', and he did. There are paintings or sculpture by him in Buffalo, Chicago, London (Tate, V&A and Courtauld Inst.), Los Angeles, New York (M of M A), Norwich (Univ.), Paris (Mus. d'Art Moderne), Philadelphia, São Paulo, Washington (Phillips) and elsewhere.

MOHOLY-NAGY, László (1895–1946), was a Hungarian law student who, after the First World War, studied art in Berlin and by 1923 was teaching at the BAUHAUS. In 1928 he went to Berlin. He emigrated to Amsterdam in 1934, lived in London 1935–7, and then settled in Chicago, where he was head of the New Bauhaus (later called the Institute of Design) 1937–9. His greatest importance was as a teacher, writer and experimenter, especially with new materials, such as plexiglass, and he also used semi-industrial techniques. His constructions, called Space Modulators, have interchangeable elements. As early as 1919 he came under the influence of MALEVICH, and in the early 1920s he was associated with SUPREMATISM, CONSTRUCTIVISM, DE STIJL and DADA. At the Bauhaus he edited the Bauhausbücher and he also did much film and stage design, including the sets for H. G. Wells's 'Shape of Things to Come' in London; the last book he published in his lifetime was called 'The New Vision'. There are works by him in Cologne, Edinburgh, Harvard University, Manchester, New York (Guggenheim) and Northampton Mass.

MOILLON, Louise (1609/10–96), was, like STOSKOPFF, a French painter of still-life. Her works bear dates between 1629 and 1674, but are rather in the manner of early 17th-century Flemish works. Like the mysterious BAUGIN, as well as Stoskopff, her works have a gravity and classic austerity not usual in Flemish or Dutch work, and closer to Spanish. She came of a Huguenot family, and in 1640 married a Calvinist, but persecution forced two of her three children to emigrate to England, and the third, like herself, became Catholic under pressure. For many years after her marriage she was inactive, but later resumed painting, possibly for financial reasons; her pictures appealed more to bourgeois than to aristocratic patrons. There are works in Grand Rapids Michigan, Paris (Louvre), Strasbourg and Toulouse.

MOLA, Pier Francesco (1612–66), was trained in Rome under ARPINO and then in Bologna under ALBANI and was influenced by Guercino and the Venetians.

He painted frescoes in Rome (Gesù and Quirinal) and there are oil-paintings by him in Birmingham, Brunswick, Chicago, Leningrad, London (NG and V&A), Milan, Oxford (Ashmolean and Ch. Ch.), Paris (Louvre), Parma, Rome and the Vatican.

MOLENAER, Jan Miensz. (*c*.1609/10–68), was a Haarlem genre painter, active from 1629, who married Judith LEYSTER in 1636. He spent his time in Haarlem and Amsterdam and his earlier works, like those of his wife, are strongly influenced by HALS. The later pictures are more like the genre scenes of A. van OSTADE. There are works by him in Amsterdam, Berlin, Boston, Brussels, Frankfurt (Städel), Haarlem, The Hague, London (NG), Stockholm and Vienna.

MOMPER, Joos de (1564–1634/5), was the leading member of an Antwerp family of landscape painters. He was trained by his father, but he probably went to Italy in the 1580s, in which case he would have seen the Alps: he lived in Antwerp, but his works are invariably of great mountains, sometimes influenced by BRUEGEL, and they form a transition between Mannerist landscape and the realistic type developed in the Netherlands in the 17th century, e.g. by van GOYEN. His pictures usually have blue mountains in the background, with a yellowish-green middle distance and a darker foreground peopled by small figures, often painted by Momper himself. Attribution is difficult because of the other members of the family who worked in a similar style. There are several works in Vaduz (Liechtenstein Coll.) and four *Seasons* in Brunswick; others are in Amsterdam, Antwerp, Berlin, Manchester (Whitworth) and Oxford.

MONACO, Lorenzo, *see* LORENZO.

MONDRIAN, Piet (1872–1944), was a Dutch painter who went to Paris in 1911 and abandoned his realistic landscapes for Cubist ones. In 1914 he returned to Holland and had six essays published in the first number of De STIJL (1917–18), but he lived in Paris 1919–38, then in London. He went to New York in 1940, where he exerted great influence on the development of the New York School. His form of Abstraction was a peculiarly rigorous one known as Neo-Plasticism, which consists principally of restricting forms to purely geometrical shapes, set at right angles to the horizontal or vertical axes and coloured in the three primary colours, and white, black or grey. He came from a Calvinist background (although, like KANDINSKY, he was influenced by Theosophy). The only enlivening touch he permitted himself was in his titles – *Boogie-Woogie*, for example (he was a jazz enthusiast). As might be expected, he was a prolific writer (often in De STIJL) and his 'Plastic Art and Pure Plastic Art' (1937) summarizes his theories: his collected writings were published in London in 1987. There are early works in The Hague and most museums of modern art have examples of his geometrical abstractions.

MONET, Claude (1840–1926), was the leading member of the IMPRESSIONIST group, and the one who longest practised the principles of absolute fidelity to the visual sensation and painting directly from the object, if necessary out of doors. Cézanne is said to have described him as 'only an eye, but my God what an eye!' and this description is certainly true in that his constant search for optical verisimilitude led at times to a neglect of form. He was born in Paris but went as a child to Le Havre. There he met BOUDIN – whose work he did not then like – and was persuaded by him to become a landscape painter (1856/8); at this time he also bought his first Japanese prints, then newly coming into Europe. In 1859 he went to Paris to study, meeting PISSARRO in the ATELIER Suisse. From 1860 to 1862 he was in Algeria as a conscript, but in 1862 he met JONGKIND – who influenced him considerably – and returned to Paris, where he met most of the major artists of his own time: in 1862 Bazille, Sisley and Renoir, in 1864 Courbet, in 1865 Cézanne and Whistler, and 1866 Manet, whose work he had earlier admired. Then and for many years to come he was extremely poor. In 1870 to escape the Franco-Prussian War he came to London, where he painted some views, and, in 1871, with Pissarro he visited the National Gallery and the V&A, where they studied Turner and Constable, but, according to Monet himself, were not tremendously impressed. He returned to Paris via Holland and in 1872 visited Le Havre, where he painted *An Impression, Sunrise*, which, when exhibited in 1874 at what is known as the First Impressionist Exhibition, was used derisively to name the whole movement IMPRESSIONISM. (This picture was stolen, with other Impressionist works, from the Musée Marmottan, Paris, in 1985.) During the 1870s and 1880s he gradually became known and for the last thirty years of his very long life he was generally regarded as the greatest of the Impressionists. From about 1890 he began to paint series of pictures of one subject, the first being the *Haystacks* (from 1888) and the *Poplars* (from 1891), representing them under various conditions and at different times of day; other series are those of *Rouen Cathedral* (1892–5), of the *Thames* (1899–1904: these were certainly finished in France, as he had by now given up the original practice of painting exclusively from nature), the second *London* series (1905) and the *Venice* series (1908), and, most famous of all, the *Water-lilies* painted in the elaborate garden he had made for himself at Giverny from 1883. He painted these over and over again, but the most important are the large ones begun in 1916 and retained by him until his death. They were painted for the State and are in a special museum (Paris, Orangerie). It has recently been claimed that these shimmering pools of colour, almost totally devoid of form, are the true starting-point of abstract art, or at least certain forms of it, particularly that now called ABSTRACT IMPRESSIONISM. They were, however, painted after CUBISM had been invented and can be seen equally as the logical outcome of Monet's lifelong devotion to the ultimate form of naturalism, truth of retinal sensation. He was enormously prolific, and many museums possess works: two very rich collections are Paris (Mus. d'Orsay) and Boston.

MONNOYER, Jean Baptiste (1636–99), called 'Baptiste', was a Franco-Flemish flower-painter who was trained in Antwerp, but became a member of the Academy in Paris in 1665 and worked for Louis XIV. It is said that he was annoyed because his son Antoine, an inferior flower-painter, was allowed to alter some of his works, and in a fit of pique he went to London *c.*1685. There he worked for the Duke of Montagu's new (and very French) town house (many of these pictures have passed by inheritance to the Duke of Buccleuch), and he remained in London until his death. His flowerpieces are rich and splendid, yet painted with the greatest regard for botanical accuracy: they frequently appear in English sale-rooms under his nickname 'Baptiste'. He also published books of engravings of flowers. Apart from those in British private collections and French provincial museums there are paintings by him in Dublin, Munich and New York (Met. Mus.).

MONOCHROME. A painting or drawing executed in any one colour. *See* GRISAILLE.

MONOTYPE. A single print, not strictly an engraving at all, made by painting, with oil-paint or printer's ink, on an untouched copper plate, and printing on paper in the normal way. The only reason for doing this instead of painting directly on the paper is the quality of texture given by the pressure of printing. It is also possible to follow some of the indications left on the plate and repeat the process with slight variations. The technique was practised by CASTIGLIONE, who invented it, and DEGAS, among others.

MONRO, Dr Thomas (1759–1833), was a London physician and amateur draughtsman who befriended or patronized many artists, including Turner and Girtin, De Wint, J. R. COZENS and Cotman. According to FARINGTON ('Diary', 1794 and 1798) Turner and Girtin were employed by Dr Monro to draw at his house in the evenings, and in the winter evenings his house was like an Academy, being full of young painters whom he encouraged to use it as a studio. Some of his own drawings are in London (V&A and Courtauld Inst.).

MONTAGE is the sticking of one layer over another, especially as in photomontage when photographs of objects are applied to a photograph of an unusual or incongruous background. The technique was used by the Cubists, who frequently stuck newspaper cuttings on to their canvases: it is now much exploited by advertising agents. *See* COLLAGE.

MONTAGNA, Bartolommeo (*d.*1523), was the principal painter of Vicenza in the late 15th century. He is first documented in 1459 and is recorded as living in Venice in 1469. He was then presumably training as a painter, since he is first mentioned as such in Vicenza in 1474. His works are markedly influenced by Giovanni BELLINI, the VIVARINI and ANTONELLO, especially his SACRA CONVERSAZIONE of 1499 (Milan, Brera). There are examples in Vicenza, and in Amsterdam (Rijksmus.), Baltimore (Walters Gall.), Bergamo, Berlin, Budapest, Columbus Ohio, Dublin, Glasgow, Liverpool, London (NG and Courtauld Inst.), Milan (Brera, Poldi-Pezzoli and Castello), Naples, New York (Met. Mus.), Ottawa, Oxford, Paris (Louvre), Philadelphia (Johnson), Rome (Borghese), San Francisco, Springfield Mass., Venice, Verona, Washington (NG), Williamstown Mass and Worcester Mass.

MONTAÑÉS, Juan Martínez (1568–1649), was the greatest Spanish exponent of polychrome wood sculpture. The painting of his statues was often the work of PACHECO, whose iconographic theories influenced Montañés deeply. He entered the Seville Guild in 1588 and worked there all his life: most of his works are still in the region. He made the transition from Mannerism to a contained Baroque that influenced Velázquez and Zurbarán, especially in his masterpiece, the crucifix known as *Christ of Clemency* (1603–6, Seville Cath.), where the contract specified that Christ should be 'alive before His death . . . looking at any person who might be praying at His feet . . . the eyes should be completely open . . .' This is also one of the first Spanish crucifixes with four (instead of three) nails, as recommended by Pacheco. The sculptures for Santiponce, near Seville, were made 1609–13 and in 1635 Montañés went to Madrid to model the head of Philip IV (now lost) for TACCA's equestrian monument, now in Madrid, Plaza de Oriente. CANO was his chief follower.

MONUMENTAL. The most overworked word in recent art history and criticism. It is intended to convey the idea that a particular work of art, or part of such a work, is grand, noble, elevated in idea, simple in conception and execution, without any excess of virtuosity, and having something of the enduring, stable and timeless nature of great architecture. The word may properly be applied to the Pyramids, the paintings of Poussin or Piero della Francesca, and some few other works of art. It is not a synonym for 'large'.

MOORE, Henry, OM (1898–1986), was trained in Leeds, where he met Barbara HEPWORTH, and in London, where he won a travelling scholarship to Paris and Italy in 1925. He was one of the advocates of direct carving and expressed natural forms in terms of stone or wood, although he also used bronze extensively, especially for MAQUETTES. His first big commission was the *North Wind* (1928), for the London Underground headquarters. It was followed by several commissions for architectural sculpture, e.g. the Time–Life Building in London (1952–3), and works in the open air in Arnhem, London, Paris, Rotterdam and Stevenage New Town. From 1940 he made many drawings of the underground air raid shelters and of coal miners, while his *Madonna* for St Matthew's, Northampton, completed 1944, was followed by others in Claydon, Suffolk, and Much Hadham, where he lived. His international reputation began in 1948, when he won the sculpture prize at the Venice Biennale. He is well represented in museums, especially Leeds, London (Tate) and Ontario, Canada.

MOR, Anthonis (Antonio Moro) (*c*.1517/21–76/7), was an Utrecht portrait painter, the pupil of SCOREL, who became the Court Painter of the Spanish Netherlands and superimposed the grand air of Titian's portraits on to his own acute Dutch sense of character and polished technique. He was working for Cardinal Granvella in 1549 and visited Rome soon afterwards. In 1554 he painted Queen Mary Tudor (Madrid, Prado), presumably in London and to celebrate her marriage with Philip of Spain. His portraits had enormous influence on the development of a Court style of portraiture in both Spain and the Netherlands, but the presence of the HOLBEIN tradition in England meant that he had no influence here, and in any case he could have had little opportunity in what must have been a very short visit. He was Court Painter to Philip II of Spain by 1560 and the Spaniard SÁNCHEZ COELLO was his pupil. There are pictures by him in Amsterdam (Rijksmus.), Barnard Castle (Bowes Mus.), Berlin, Brussels, Cambridge (Fitzwm), Dresden, Florence (Uffizi), Glasgow (Univ.), The Hague, London (NG and NPG), Madrid (Prado), Munich, New York (Met. Mus.), Ottawa, Paris (Louvre), Sheffield, Vaduz (Liechtenstein), Vienna (K-H Mus.) and Washington (NG).

MORALES, Louis, 'El Divino' (active 1547–86). Morales is the most typical Spanish Mannerist, whose style was formed by a combination of the Flemish-Italianate painters such as MASSYS, and the Italian artists who influenced them, principally LEONARDO and his Milanese followers. Morales seems to have studied under a Dutch painter called Sturmio who worked in Spain, but the final result is a highly personal style of exalted religiosity. He is first documented in 1547, but there is a *Madonna* attributed to him which is dated 1546. He spent most of his life in Badajoz where there are still works by him, although he may have worked in Madrid for Philip II in 1564. He thus precedes El GRECO as an exponent of extreme Mannerism in Spain. Outside Spain and Portugal there are works by him in Berlin, Cardiff, Castres, Catania, Dresden, Dublin, Florence (Uffizi), Leeds, Leningrad (Hermitage), London

(NG), Mexico City, Minneapolis, New York (Hispanic Soc.), Oxford, Paris (Louvre) and Rome (Gall. Naz).

MORANDI, Giorgio (1890–1964), was an Italian still-life painter. He never left his native country (except for a fleeting visit to Switzerland at the end of his life), but (apart from such Italian masters of the 15th century as Piero della Francesca) Cézanne and Chardin were the painters most akin to his withdrawn and meditative spirit. He lived in Bologna and painted some landscapes and flowerpieces, but most of his works are simple arrangements of bottles, treated in austere brownish tones approximating to monochrome. The PITTURA METAFISICA of CHIRICO, purged of its bombast, influenced him. He was also a celebrated etcher – again mainly of bottles – and made some ninety plates, mostly dating from 1921 to 1924, and 1927–33. There are pictures by him in Birmingham, Edinburgh (NG of Modern Art), Hamburg, London (Tate), Northampton Mass. and Toledo Ohio.

MORAZZONE, Pier Francesco Mazzuchelli, called Morazzone (1571 or 1573–1626), was, with G. B. CRESPI and G. C. PROCACCINI, the leading Milanese painter of the early 17th century. Like Crespi, he was in Rome in the 1590s, where frescoes by him survive in S. Silvestro in Capite. Even more than Crespi and Procaccini, however, he based his art on Gaudenzio FERRARI, and his principal works are also for chapels on the Sacri Monti at Varallo, Varese and Novara. At the time of his death he was painting frescoes in Piacenza Cathedral, completed by Guercino. There are many works by him in Milan (museums and churches) and one in Los Angeles.

MORBIDEZZA (Ital. softness). A term much used in 18th-century criticism to indicate a softness of edges and a fusion of tones which is characteristic of CORREGGIO: hence the 18th-century mockery 'the Correggiosity of Correggio' as a cant phrase suitable for the would-be connoisseur. Its use is not now recommended.

MOREAU, Gustave (1826–98), painted elaborate Biblical and mythological fantasies in a detailed, almost encrusted, technique. With PUVIS and REDON he was a leading SYMBOLIST painter. His importance – except for his slight influence on Surrealism – lies in his tolerant and intelligent teaching at the École des Beaux-Arts in Paris from 1892 to 1898, when ROUAULT, MATISSE and MARQUET were his pupils. He left his collections to the State as a Museum, of which Rouault was to be the Curator. There is a *St George* in London (NG), an *Oedipus* (1864) in New York (Met. Mus.) and an *Orpheus* in Paris (Mus. d'Orsay).

MORETTO, da Brescia (*c.*1498–1554) worked mainly in the Brescia and Bergamo districts until he visited Milan and Verona in the 1540s. His religious works are of a warm, late Bellini and Giorgionesque type, but influenced by the ideals of the Counter-Reformation (he was associated with S. Angela Merici, the founder of the Ursulines, the first teaching order dedicated exclusively to the education of girls). His portraits are outstanding, showing the influence of LOTTO and Titian, and developing types that Titian did not use until much later. He was probably the first to introduce the full-length portrait into Italy as an independent subject, not part of a religious work (cf. the *Nobleman* dated 1526 in the NG, London) – an idea developed from German examples, notably from CRANACH, although CARPACCIO may have been one of the first to use it. MORONI was his pupil. There are works in Bergamo, Brescia

(Mus., churches), Budapest, Cambridge Mass. (Fogg), Detroit, Frankfurt (Städel), Glasgow (Pollok House), London (NG), Milan (Ambrosiana, Brera and Castello), New York (Met. Mus.), Oxford (Ashmolean), Paris (Louvre), Philadelphia (Johnson), the Vatican, Venice (Accad.), Verona, Vienna and elsewhere.

MORISOT, Berthe (1841–95), was the first woman to join the IMPRESSIONISTS – the other was Mary CASSATT. She met Fantin-Latour in 1859, and in 1860 was encouraged by Corot, who influenced her early work. In 1868 she met MANET and in 1874 married his younger brother Eugène. She exhibited in all but one (1879) of the Impressionist Exhibitions. Her great importance lies in her influence on Manet, for it was partly through her that he came to adopt the Impressionist palette and to abandon black of which he was so great a master. She could never persuade him into joining the group, but their close family tie made it even more difficult for him to dissociate himself from them. After about 1885 she was very strongly influenced by Renoir. There are works in Boston (Mus.), London (NG, Tate and Courtauld Inst.), New York (Met. Mus.), Paris (Mus. d'Orsay) and Washington (NG).

MORLAITER, Gianmaria (1699–1781), was born in Austria, but became the leading Venetian sculptor of the 18th century. His reliefs are similar in pictorial quality to the paintings of Tiepolo and their expressive quality is best seen in the *bozzetti*, of which there are more than a hundred in the Donà dalle Rose collection in Venice (Ca' Rezzonico). Most of his works are in Venetian churches.

MORLAND, George (1762/3–1804), was an exponent of picturesque rustic genre painting who based himself on Dutch and Flemish 17th-century models such as BROUWER or TENIERS. Like them, he refused to work for individual patrons and preferred to sell through an agent, thus altering the whole basis of patronage in 18th-century England. His very numerous works were popularized through engravings, many of which were executed by William Ward, brother of James WARD, Morland's own brother-in-law, and imitator. The son of a painter, Henry Morland (*c.*1730–97), he exhibited drawings at the RA at the age of 10 (1773), and his first oil-painting was shown there in 1781. From then on he lived wildly, and in 1799 was arrested (as a French spy) while actually on the run from his creditors; after which he was in the King's Bench Prison until 1802. He died in prison after producing an enormous amount of scamped work to pay his debts. His reputation immediately declined and his place was taken by WILKIE. Among his most purely Dutch works are the *Industry* and *Idleness* (Edinburgh, NG), while the *Stable* (1791, London, NG) is one of his best rustic subjects. Other works are in London (Tate, V&A and Kenwood) and Birmingham, Bristol, Glasgow, Leeds, Leicester, Manchester, New York (Met. Mus.), Nottingham, Ottawa, Port Sunlight (Lever Gall.), Rouen, Wellington NZ, Wolverhampton, Yale (CBA) and York.

MORO *see* MOR.

MORONI, Giovanni Battista (1520/4–78), was a pupil of MORETTO and was his assistant during the 1540s. He was also much influenced by LOTTO. He attended the sessions of the Council of Trent in 1548 and 1551/3, which affected his religious works (although some are dull and derivative, like Moretto's they were influenced by Counter-Reformation austerity). He also produced Spanish-influenced portraits for his patrons, in which, like his master, he blended the realism of Holbein with Venetian style to produce the placid and intimate portrait-style of the Lombards. His portraits have a grey tonality, unlike any contemporary Italian work, and curiously anticipatory of Whistler's delicacy. Towards the end of his life he painted altarpieces exclusively. The best collection of his works is in London (NG), but there are others in Baltimore, Bergamo (Mus., Almenno S. Bartolommeo and other local churches), Berlin, Boston, Brescia, Budapest, Chicago, Cleveland Ohio, Detroit, Dublin, Edinburgh (NG), Florence (Uffizi and Pitti), Milan (Brera, Ambrosiana and Castello), Minneapolis, New York (Met. Mus.), Ottawa, Oxford, Paris (Louvre), Philadelphia (Johnson, Widener and Wilstach), Princeton, Sarasota Fla, Vienna, Washington (NG), Worcester Mass. and elsewhere.

MORRIS, William (1834–96), met BURNE-JONES when at Exeter College, Oxford. He then studied architecture under Street, but abandoned it to become a painter under the influence of ROSSETTI. In 1861 he founded the firm of Morris and Co., to produce wallpapers, furniture, tapestries and stained-glass windows (many designed by Burne-Jones), carpets and furnishing materials in a style entirely different from that of contemporary Victorian decoration, but one which, nevertheless, tended towards a different kind of *horror vacui* and the use of equally dark and heavy colours. He is particularly important for the development of the private press, and did much with his Kelmscott Press, founded in 1890, to raise the standards of book design and printing, although he favoured a revival of medieval black-letter where Lucien Pissarro's Eragny Press (1896) concentrated on modern type faces. His poems and other writings are anti-industrialist and support a socialist theory for the regeneration of man by handicraft. There are drawings and a painting in the Tate and the V&A, London, the latter also having a room entirely decorated with Morris products, and there is a Morris Museum at Walthamstow, London.

MORSE, Samuel (1791–1872), was an American painter and first President of the National Academy (1826), but is better known as the inventor of the electric telegraph (hence Morse code). After leaving Yale in 1810 he went to London and trained under ALLSTON and WEST: his ambitions as a history painter led him to exhibit a successful *Dying Hercules* at the RA (1815, now at Yale), but on his return to America in 1815 he had to live by portrait painting. He was in France and Italy 1829–33, but after his return to New York he invented the telegraph and painted relatively little. He gave money from his invention to the Met. Mus. in New York, which has a good collection of his works. His best-known portraits are the *House of Representatives* (1822, Washington, Corcoran) and *Lafayette* (1825, Brooklyn Mus.).

MORTIMER, John Hamilton (1740–79), was a contemporary and friend of WRIGHT of Derby. He was trained in London as a portrait painter under HUDSON (*c.*1757) and, in 1764, won the prize offered by the Society of Arts with his (somewhat uncanonical) *St Paul Preaching to the Britons* (now in High Wycombe Town Hall). His portraits are close to Wright, but about 1770 he began to draw, engrave and paint banditti and similar savage subjects under the influence of Salvator ROSA. Like BARRY and FUSELI he was a Neoclassic Romantic. He was elected ARA in 1778, but died the following year. There are works in his native Eastbourne and in Detroit, London (Tate and RA), Norwich, Paris (Louvre) and Yale (CBA).

MOSAIC. One of the oldest and most durable forms of mural decoration, mosaic was in constant use from the earliest times up to about the 13th century, when it was largely superseded by fresco and other forms of painting which are both much cheaper and much more adaptable to a realistic style. Recently, however, the very stylization inherent in mosaic has led to its revival as a decorative art. The technique is simple but laborious. A cartoon is drawn on the wall to be decorated and a small area covered with cement. Previously, small cubes (called *tesserae*) have been chipped from slabs of coloured stone, marble and coloured or gilt glass; the *tesserae* are then stuck into the cement. Great care was taken in the best early mosaics to ensure that all the *tesserae* were not perfectly flat and level, since an uneven surface catches the light and reflects it in different ways according to the angle of incidence and the material used for the *tesserae*. Mosaic was much used for the decoration of Early Christian and Byzantine churches and there are splendid cycles in Rome, Ravenna, Venice, Constantinople and Sicily, as well as in Greece. The great 13th-century revival in Rome preceded the realistic movement in painting (CAVALLINI, GIOTTO) and the art was still practised in Venice in the 15th century (e.g. by UCCELLO in St Mark's).

MOSER, Lucas, is known only from the Magdalen Altar in the church at Tiefenbronn, near Pforzheim, which is signed and dated 1431 and has an inscription roughly translatable as: 'Cry, Art, cry and lament loudly, nobody nowadays wants you. So alas, 1431.' In fact, the style of the picture is markedly modern and forms a German counterpart to the realism of WITZ or van EYCK and CAMPIN.

MOSTAERT, Jan (*c*.1475–1555/6), was a Haarlem painter who is recorded, on fair evidence, as having painted a *West Indian Landscape* as well as having worked for the Regent of the Netherlands. A picture at Haarlem (Hals Mus.) is presumably the landscape, and a group of pictures showing stylistic affinities with GEERTGEN – i.e. 'Dutch', rather than Flemish – can be considered as his. He must be distinguished from the 'Waagen'sche Mostaert', who is now identified with ISENBRANDT: on the other hand, the Master of Oultremont is probably identical with Mostaert. There are pictures ascribed to him in Amsterdam (Rijksmus.), Brussels, Cologne, Liverpool, London (NG), Paris (Louvre and Petit Pal.), Philadelphia (Johnson), St Louis, Sarasota Fla, Worcester Mass. and elsewhere.

MOTHERWELL, Robert (*b*.1915), is an American Abstract Expressionist painter who began by studying philosophy at Harvard. He has said: 'Without ethical consciousness, a painter is only a decorator.' After a visit to Europe in 1938 he exhibited with the Surrealists in New York (1939) and later associated with POLLOCK, De KOONING and ROTHKO (with whom he founded an art school). He was editor (1944–57) of the important 'Documents of Modern Art' series.

MOTIVE (Fr. *motif*). A visual theme. Cézanne's phrase 'sur le motif' means the visual facts before his eyes, as in a landscape; not an imaginary theme. Phrases like 'the motive of the upraised hand' show how it has become adapted into English terminology. A few (generally elderly) writers in English still insist on spelling it *motif*.

MUCHA, Alphonse (1860–1939), was a Czech artist who worked in Paris from 1889 onwards and achieved great fame as one of the chief exponents of ART

NOUVEAU. He designed many posters from 1894 for Sarah Bernhardt, and also did magazine covers, book-illustrations, stained glass, furniture, bindings, jewellery and the interior of a jeweller's shop in Paris, in curvilinear flourishes, almost always framing a dreamlike female figure. After 1900 over-production affected the quality of his work, and after 1903 he concentrated on large decorative paintings, many in America. He returned to his native country in 1910, but retained close contacts with Paris. New York (Met. Mus.) has *Maude Adams as Joan of Arc*.

MÜLLER, Otto (1874–1930), was a member of the BRÜCKE who experimented with techniques involving the use of distemper and beeswax rather than oil paint. The flatness inherent in this medium, and his passion for Egyptian art, led to striking simplifications of form which influenced the other members of the group. He studied lithography in Breslau (now called Wroclaw) from 1890 to 1895 and was trained at the Dresden Academy before going to Berlin in 1908, where he met HECKEL and subsequently joined the Brücke. He was much influenced by the sculptor LEHMBRUCK as well as by Gauguin, and his decorative paintings of gipsies and skinny nudes are less brutal than the works of most of his contemporaries. There are examples in Berlin, Cologne and Harvard (Univ.).

MÜLLER, William James (1812–45), was a landscape painter, born at Bristol of German extraction, who was much influenced by Constable and Cox. He visited Egypt in 1838–9, and was one of the first English artists to paint Arabian subjects. In 1842–3 he was a member of an expedition to Asia Minor in search of antique marbles. The largest collection of his work is in Bristol, but there are examples in London (BM, Tate and V&A) and Yale (CBA).

MULREADY, William (1786–1863), was born in Ireland, came to England as a child and entered the RA Schools at 14. He became a highly successful Victorian genre painter, influenced – as was WILKIE – by Dutch 17th-century genre. His technique of painting in thin layers on a white ground links him tenuously with the PRE-RAPHAELITE BROTHERHOOD, but his pretty and undemandingly trivial subject matter, his use of a middle tone, and traditional 18th-century systems of composition, later incurred their particular displeasure and rejection. He became an ARA in 1815, and, following the success of his *The Fight Interrupted* in 1816, an RA. He designed the first penny post envelope issued by Rowland Hill in 1840. There are works in Dublin, Edinburgh, Leeds, London (Tate, V&A and NPG), Manchester, Paris (Louvre) and Yale (CBA).

MULTIPLES. Not exactly reproductions, but works of art produced by such processes as SERIGRAPHY or lithography which yield limitless numbers, in contrast to, e.g., etching, where the edition is necessarily limited. Multiples are said not to be 'collectors' pieces', but rather consumer goods; the prices asked, however, do not confirm this view.

MULTSCHER, Hans (*c.*1400–before 1467), was active in Ulm for some forty years, principally as a sculptor. His sharp sense of realism, noticeable in his sculpture, is even more marked in the first documented picture by him, the eight panels of the *Wurzach Altar* (1437, Berlin), of which the central part is lost. These panels belong to the same slightly crude realist school as MOSER's *Tiefenbronn Altar*, or even the work of WITZ. A second altarpiece, including eight paintings, was commissioned in 1456 and completed in 1459; it was for Sterzing (now Vipiteno, S. Tyrol) and is in the Museum there.

MUNCH, Edvard (1863–1944), a Norwegian painter, was one of the forerunners of EXPRESSIONISM, whose most formative years were spent in Paris and Berlin, where a large exhibition of his work, as early as 1892, was a formative influence on much German painting, since the repercussions led to the foundation of the Berlin SEZESSION in 1899. Formally, he was much influenced by van GOGH and GAUGUIN but his subjects (especially his *Frieze of Life* project) deal with basic themes of love and death, for which he sought pictorial equivalents. He was friendly with Strindberg, and his art, though sometimes powerful, is always neurotic and frequently hysterical. His graphic works were perhaps even more influential than his paintings. About 1,000 of his pictures are in the Munch Mus., Oslo, but there are others in most museums of modern art. Oslo University has a large mural (1909–16).

MUNNINGS, Sir Alfred (1878–1959), was the last representative of the sporting painters such as STUBBS and MARSHALL, whose style he crossed with Impressionism. He was President of the RA 1944–9, but not a successful one. There is a Munnings Museum in Dedham, where he lived.

MÜNTER, Gabriele (1877–1962), was a German painter who studied in Düsseldorf and Munich 1897–1902. In 1902 she met KANDINSKY, and from 1903 to 1915 she lived and worked with him in France, Africa, Italy, Austria and Switzerland. Her own work was influenced by Fauvism. In 1957 she gave 120 early works by Kandinsky and about 30 of her own to Munich (Städtische Galerie).

MURAL *see* WALL-PAINTING.

MURILLO, Bartolomé Estebán (1617/18–82), was the leading painter in Seville after VELAZQUEZ left for Madrid in 1623. His earliest works are controversial and may have been influenced by Velázquez's realism, but his name was made by a series of eleven paintings for the Franciscans (1645–6: some still in Seville, others in Dresden, Madrid (Acad.), Ottawa, Paris, Raleigh NC and Toulouse), in which ZURBARÁN and RIBERA were plainly influential. Soon Murillo's fame eclipsed Zurbarán's (he was actually later to receive ten times Zurbarán's prices): as a result Zurbarán tried to compete by softening and sweetening his own style. The main problem in Murillo's stylistic development concerns his knowledge of van Dyck, Rubens, Titian and Barocci, which could hardly have been acquired in Seville, although he certainly used engravings as source material. He is now known to have been in Madrid in 1658, but it is likely that he was there 1648/50 or 1655 (or on both occasions) when he could have studied all these masters in the Royal collections. In 1660 he was one of the founders, and the first President, of the Seville Academy. His *estilo vaporoso* dates from the 1660s, succeeding the *estilo frio*, cool and detached, of his early works, and the *estilo cálido* of such devotional works as the *Madonna del Rosario* (Madrid, Prado). He does not seem to have employed many assistants, but his very large output of Madonnas, versions of the Immaculate Conception (cf. PACHECO), and genre scenes was very widely copied and imitated well into the 19th century, often as a style rather than as deliberate forgeries. His later *Beggar Boys* (the best are in London (Dulwich), Munich and Paris) exploit the sentimental side of his art, and he found a ready market for these glamorized, picturesque urchins in fancy-dress rags, exuding the charms of Bohemianism and serving to exorcise poverty by robbing it of its power to inspire pity and horror. He was, however, an excellent portrait painter. Among the most important series of works are twenty-odd for the Capuchins (1665–6 and 1668 onwards: mostly still in Seville, one in Cologne), a series of six for the Hospital de la Cáridad (completed 1670), a charitable foundation, where Murillo had been a member since 1665 (some still there, others in Leningrad, London (NG), Ottawa and Washington (NG)). In 1679 he painted two pictures for the Hospital de los Venerables Sacerdotes (Madrid, (Prado) and Budapest). In 1681 he went to Cadiz, but fell from the scaffolding while working on his *Mystic Marriage of St Catherine*. He returned to Seville and died in the following year. Apart from the galleries mentioned, there are works in Amsterdam, Baltimore, Barcelona, Berlin, Birmingham (City and Barber Inst.), Bordeaux, Boston, Brussels, Cambridge (Fitzwm) and Cambridge Mass. (Fogg), Castres, Chicago, Cincinnati, Cleveland Ohio, Dallas Texas, Detroit, Dresden, Dublin, Florence, Genoa, Hartford Conn., Indianapolis, Kansas City, Liverpool, London (Wallace Coll. and Wellington Mus.), Minneapolis, New York (Met. Mus. and Hispanic Soc.), Notre Dame Indiana, Philadelphia, Rome (Corsini), San Diego Cal., St Louis, Sarasota Fla, Sheffield, Stockholm (*The Two Trinities*, *c.*1640, a very early version of the picture in London, NG), the Vatican, Vienna, Williamstown and Worcester Mass.

MYTENS, Daniel (*c.*1590–before 1648), was trained in The Hague, probably under MIEREVELD, but was in England by 1618 and was working for the Crown soon after that. He was appointed Painter to Charles I in 1625 and painted a number of portraits, including several full-lengths, which had a great success before the arrival of van DYCK in 1632. In 1626 and 1630 he revisited the Low Countries, perhaps to refresh his knowledge of Rubens and van Dyck. Some of his works are difficult to distinguish from JOHNSON's, but his masterpiece is the full-length *Duke of Hamilton* (Edinburgh NPG) which was painted in 1629 and therefore shows most of the elegance associated with van Dyck, before he arrived in England. From *c.*1635 Mytens seems to have lived in Holland. There are works by him in the Royal Coll. (including portraits of Charles I and his Queen which show why van Dyck's success was immediate) and in Leeds, London (NPG, Tate and Nat. Marit. Mus.), New York (Met. Mus.), Ottawa and St Louis.

N

NABIS, Les (from Hebrew, prophet), was the name taken by a small group of French artists, including BONNARD, VUILLARD and MAILLOL, between *c.*1889 and 1899. They were attracted by GAUGUIN's advice to paint in flat, pure colours; and one of them, Maurice DENIS, 'uttered one of the great battle-cries of modern art' when he said: 'Remember that a picture, before being a horse, a nude, or some kind of anecdote, is essentially a flat surface covered with colours assembled in a certain order.'

They reacted sharply away from the naturalism implicit in Impressionism, but their links with the SYMBOLISTS meant that they attached considerable importance to subject matter. The best painters of the group, Bonnard and Vuillard, eventually reverted to a modified Impressionist style known as INTIMISME.

NAIN, Le, *see* LE NAIN.

NAÏVE ART differs from PRIMITIVE art in that it is not produced by unsophisticated societies, but by untrained artists in a sophisticated society, e.g. 'Grandma' Moses, Alfred Wallis, the Douanier ROUSSEAU, KANE or SÉRAPHINE.

NANNI di Banco (*c.*1384–1421), was a Florentine sculptor who was working with his father on the Cathedral in 1406/7 and received the commission for a *Prophet* on the Porta della Mandorla (1407/8), the companion figure being by DONATELLO. In 1408 he and Donatello again shared a commission for the Cathedral (Donatello: *David*; Nanni: *Isaiah*). His best-known works are the four *Saints* (*Quattro Santi Coronati*) in a niche on Orsanmichele, where there are others by him, and the *Assumption* over the Porta della Mandorla of the Cathedral. His early death cut short a career which promised to rival Donatello's and in some respects, such as the use of classical exemplars, Nanni may have been in advance.

NARRATIVE painting is not quite conterminous with GENRE, since it implies a literary element by no means always found in genre painting. A narrative picture implies the choice of a moment in the story so that the spectator will know (or can guess) what has happened and what is about to happen – *When did you last see your father?*

NASH, Paul (1889–1946), was trained at the Slade School and served in the 1914–18 War at the front before being appointed an Official War Artist in 1917. He was again appointed in the Second World War. His poetic imagination was stimulated by Surrealism and he exhibited with them in their Paris Exhibition, 1938. He did much work as a designer and book-illustrator. There are paintings by him in Belfast, Blackpool, Durban, Leeds, Leicester, Liverpool, London (Tate and Imperial War Mus.), Manchester, Ottawa, Sheffield, Toronto and Yale (CBA).

His brother John (1893–1977), RA, worked in Suffolk, growing and painting his own flowers. There are works in London (Tate, V&A and Imperial War Mus.) and he also illustrated Gilbert White's *Natural History of Selbourne* (1951).

NASMYTH, Alexander and Patrick, were the principal members of a large Scottish family of portrait and landscape painters. Alexander (1758–1840), was the founder of Scottish landscape painting, influenced by Claude and the Dutch

Italianate painters. He was a pupil and assistant of Allan RAMSAY from 1774, working with him in London until he returned to Edinburgh in 1778 to paint portraits and conversation pieces on his own. He was in Italy 1782–5 and became interested in landscape painting in Rome, turning to it more and more after his return to Edinburgh, using the drawings he made in Italy for the rest of his life. In the later 1780s he was a friend of the poet Burns and painted his portrait (London, NPG).

Patrick (1787–1831), his eldest son, was more influenced by Romantic ideas of landscape (and influenced his father) but, after settling in London in 1810, he turned to Dutch sources such as Hobbema and Ruisdael, as in his *New Forest* (1815, London, Tate) or *Leigh Wood* (1830, Cambridge, Fitzwm). There are works by one or both in Aberdeen, Birmingham, Edinburgh (NG), Glasgow, Liverpool, Manchester (City Gall. and Whitworth), New York (Met. Mus.), Sheffield and Stirling.

NATTIER, Jean Marc (1685–1766), began his career as an engraver of the Rubens *Marie de' Medici* cycle in Paris, but later became established as the painter of the ladies of Louis XV's Court. In 1717 he was in Amsterdam, painting Peter the Great and Catherine I of Russia (both portraits in Leningrad, Hermitage). In 1718 he became a member of the Academy with *Perseus turning Phineas to Stone* (Tours), but his first success as a portrait painter of fashionable ladies was *Mlle de Lambresc as Minerva* (1737, Louvre), which shows his predilection for mythological dressing-up and his occasionally ludicrous idealization of his sitters into gods and goddesses (he was better with women, perhaps for that reason). TOCQUÉ was his son-in-law. There are works in Versailles and Paris (Louvre and Jacquemart-André), French provincial museums and London (NG and Wallace Coll.), New York (Met. Mus. and Frick Coll.), Stockholm, Toledo Ohio and elsewhere.

NATURALISM *see* REALISM.

NATURE MORTE (Fr. STILL-LIFE).

NAVEZ, François-Joseph (1787–1869), was a pupil of DAVID, and the leading Belgian neoclassical painter. He won a prize in Brussels and was sent to Paris in 1813, where he entered the studio of David. On the fall of Napoleon his pension ceased, but he went with David to Berlin and then to Brussels (1816), where he painted his best-known work, the *Hemptinne Family* (1816, Brussels), which shows how he developed a portrait style from David in exactly the same way as INGRES. In 1817 Navez went to Rome, where he knew Ingres and Granet and, like them, admired Raphael. In 1821 he returned to Belgium and settled in Brussels, where he became a *chef d'école* and a famous teacher at the Academy. He painted many histories and allegories, but was always a fine portraitist, insisting on the veracity which he saw in the Early Flemish painters, such as Memlinc. There are works in Brussels and other Belgian museums, and in Amsterdam, Berlin, Munich and Paris (Louvre).

NAY, Ernst Wilhelm (1902–68), was trained under HOFER at the Berlin Academy (1925–8), and then went to Paris, where he was influenced by Picasso. He was in Rome, 1930–1, and with MUNCH in Norway, 1936–7. He was fortunate in being able to continue painting during World War II when he was stationed at Le Mans in northern France, 1942–4; and, beginning from Nolde and the Expressionists, he moved towards abstraction although he later developed an interest in Zen. There are works in Cologne.

NAZARENER. In 1809 two young painters, OVERBECK and PFORR, founded a quasi-religious order, the *Lukasbrüder* (i.e. the Brotherhood of St Luke, the patron saint of artists), in Vienna with the intention of regenerating German religious art in imitation of the works of Dürer, Perugino and the young Raphael. Both went to Rome in 1810 and began working in the deserted monastery of Sant' Isidoro, where they were soon joined by others, the most important of whom was CORNELIUS. Several, including Overbeck, became Catholics and the group became known mockingly as 'Nazarenes'. As an experiment in medieval workshop practice they painted jointly some frescoes (1816–17, now in Berlin) and decorated the Casino Massimo in Rome (1817 and later), partly by KOCH. Their ideas were known and admired in England, e.g. by DYCE, and influenced the Pre-Raphaelites; they also influenced INGRES.

NEAC (New English Art Club). The New English was founded in 1886 as a challenge to the complacent conventionalism of the Royal Academy (*see* SEZESSION), by a group of artists who were either French-trained or admirers of the French elective jury system. WHISTLER was admired by most of them, and he actually sat on the jury for a while before his inevitable resignation. STEER was an original member and SICKERT joined in 1886, and within a few years the Club tended to become an apanage of the Slade School, reflecting its tradition of draughtsmanship in the work of members like JOHN. The CAMDEN TOWN GROUP was founded in 1911, by GILMAN, GORE and SICKERT, but in the winter of 1910/11 the Post-Impressionist Exhibition in London led to schism in both groups and the foundation of a new group, influenced by Cézanne, Gauguin and van Gogh rather than the Impressionists. This was the LONDON GROUP, presided over by Gilman, and consisting of most of the Camden Towners, the VORTICISTS and a few others. A century later the NEAC still exists.

NEEFFS, Peeter I (active 1605–56/61), was an Antwerp painter of church interiors in the manner of Steenwyck, many of whose subjects he repeated: his interiors, mostly of Gothic churches based on Antwerp Cathedral, are more pedestrian than those of the great architectural painter SAENREDAM. His earliest known work (Dresden) is signed and dated 1605, but it is very difficult to distinguish his works from those of his son, Peeter II (1620–after 1675). There are works by Peeter I in Barnard Castle (Bowes Mus.), The Hague, London (NG, V&A, Wallace Coll. and Dulwich), Oxford and Vienna, and by Peeter II in Cambridge (Fitzwm) and Leeds.

NEER, Aert van der (1603/4–77), was a Dutch landscape painter who specialized in moonlight effects, usually showing the canals around Amsterdam, where he lived. He seems to have had difficulty in making a living and took to keeping a wineshop during 1658–62, but he was no more successful at this and returned to painting. He also painted some winter scenes, rather in the manner of Hendrick AVERCAMP; but his moonlights are unique. There are typical examples in Amsterdam (Rijksmus.), Cambridge (Fitzwm), Leicester, London (NG, V&A and Wallace Coll.) and New York (Met. Mus.).

His son Eglon Hendrik (1634–1703) painted a few landscapes but is best known as a genre painter in the manner of Metsu. He is represented in Boston, Glasgow, London (NG and Wallace Coll.), New York (Met. Mus.) and elsewhere.

NEOCLASSICISM is the name given to the movement which originated in Rome in the middle of the 18th century and spread rapidly over the civilized world. It arose partly in reaction against the 'excesses' of BAROQUE and ROCOCO – the former of which was also largely a Roman movement – and partly from a genuine desire to recreate the art of Greece and Rome, a desire much stimulated by the chief prophet of the movement, WINCKELMANN. From 1748 the discoveries at Herculaneum and Pompeii gave impetus to the movement – it has been argued that they created it – but, even more important, they provided some evidence of what ancient art actually looked like. This knowledge was disseminated by publications like 'Le antichità di Ercolano' (1757 and later), plates from which were much used as models by MENGS and many others. Even Winckelmann knew practically nothing of Greek originals; and one main reason for the tendency of the Neoclassic movement in the 18th century to equate the Antique with Roman art, where the 19th century equated it with the purer style of the Greeks (as they would have expressed it), lies in the great discoveries of the archaeologists in the late 18th century and early 19th century.

Neoclassicism differs from all the earlier Classic revivals in that for the first time, artists consciously imitated antique art and knew what they were imitating, both in style and in subject matter. This is particularly true of sculpture, which survives in much greater quantity and in better preservation than either painting or architecture. This is one reason for the adaptation of bas-reliefs as pictures, in sharp reaction against the composition in depth of Baroque artists. The imitation of ancient subject matter was carried very far – as by DAVID, whose *Horatii* drew an ancient moral for modern circumstances – and is a different matter from the earlier type of History painting, where a subject such as the *Death of Caesar* was an excuse for dramatic grouping, not an incitement to tyrannicide.

Some of the principal exponents of various forms of Neoclassicism were BARRY, CANOVA, FLAXMAN, MENGS, PIRANESI, THORWALDSEN, VIEN and WEST.

NEO-IMPRESSIONISM has, properly speaking, little to do with Impressionism. In its purest form, as it is found in SEURAT, it involves the use of Divisionism (*see* OPTICAL MIXTURES) and a strict, formal composition; both were too cerebral and too consciously applied by the artist to have much relation to the fleeting colour effects and the accidental, 'snapshot' composition of Impressionism. Neo-Impressionism was first seen in an exhibition held in 1884 in Paris by the Salon des Artistes Indépendants, where Seurat exhibited the *Bathers at Asnières* (London, NG), and in 1886 Seurat, SIGNAC and PISSARRO all showed works at the last Impressionist exhibition based on Seurat's theories, hence the tendency to regard the movement as an offshoot of Impressionism. According to Signac it 'guaranteed all the benefits of luminosity, colour, and harmony by the optical mixture of pure pigments (all the colours of the prism and all their tones); by the separation of different elements (local colour, the colour of the light, and their interactions); by the balancing of these elements and their proportions (according to the laws of contrasts, of gradation, and irradiation), by the selection of a size of touch proportionate to the size of the picture'.

The theory had a strong but passing effect on van Gogh during his years in

Paris (1886–8), on Gauguin *c.*1886, on Toulouse-Lautrec *c.*1887, and on Segantini *c.*1891; other adherents include Maximilien Luce (1858–1941), Henri-Edmond Cross (1856–1910), Charles Angrand (1854–1926), Albert Dubois-Pillet (1846–90), and Théo van Rysselberghe (1862–1926).

NEUE SACHLICHKEIT, Die (Ger. new objectivity). About 1918 a reaction against EXPRESSIONISM took place in Germany and the phrase *die neue Sachlichkeit* was coined in 1923 to distinguish a new attention to realistic representation of actual objects in a detailed way – thus also reacting against the muzziness of Impressionism. An exhibition was held at Mannheim in 1925 under the Neue Sachlichkeit label. The movement petered out, but the new feeling for the subject is distantly related to SURREALISM. *See also* DIX and MAGISCHER REALISMUS.

NEW ENGLISH ART CLUB *see* NEAC.

NEWLYN SCHOOL. Like the GLASGOW SCHOOL, this was a colony of like-minded artists rather than a regional school such as the NORWICH SCHOOL. They were based on Newlyn in Cornwall in the 1880s and most of the members were French-trained and influenced by BARBIZON ideals. The influence of BASTIEN-LEPAGE is noticeable in the work of Bramley and Stanhope Forbes, the two leading members of the group, both represented in London (Tate).

NEWMAN, Barnett (1905–70). American painter, born in New York. He was best known for his very large canvases, many from 6 to 9 feet high, painted from the 1940s onwards. These often consist of a single strong colour, modified only by changes of direction in the brushstrokes, or bisection by one or more horizontal or vertical streaks. He is represented in New York (M of MA) and London (Tate).

NICHOLSON, Ben and William. Sir William (1872–1949) was an English painter, especially of still-life, who is best known for his woodcuts of Victorian types and characters and for having contributed much, with his brother-in-law James Pryde (1866–1941), to the development of the poster. The two were known as the Beggarstaff Brothers. Nicholson's paintings are well represented in London (Tate) and Cambridge (Fitzwm).

His son, Ben (1894–1982), OM, was a British abstract painter and the first winner of the Guggenheim Award. His paintings and reliefs (plain and coloured) are geometrically inspired and derive from the austerer forms of Cubism and from MONDRIAN and De STIJL. Of his own *Au Chat Botté* (Manchester) he wrote: 'About space-construction: I can explain one aspect of this by an early painting I made of a shop window in Dieppe . . . The name of the shop was "Au Chat Botté" . . . the words themselves had also an abstract quality – but what was important was that this name was printed in very lovely red lettering on the glass window – *giving one plane* – and in this window were reflections of what was behind me as I looked in – *giving a second plane* – while through the window objects on a table were performing a kind of ballet and forming the "eye" or life-point of the painting – *giving a third plane.*' In the 1930s he was associated with ABSTRACTION-CRÉATION. His first wife was the painter Winifred Nicholson and he was also married to Barbara HEPWORTH. Between 1958 and 1971 he lived in Switzerland. He is represented in Aberdeen, Bristol, Cambridge, Cardiff, Edinburgh (NG of Modern Art), Hull (Univ.), London (Tate), Manchester, New York (M of MA), Oxford, Stromness Orkney, Toronto, Yale (CBA), York and elsewhere.

NIELLO is a branch of goldsmiths' work which was of great importance in the early development of line engraving. A *niello* is a small plate of silver or gold which has a pattern engraved on it, the pattern being then filled with *niello*, a mixture of lead, silver, copper and sulphur. This composition is fused into the lines of the pattern and the plate is then polished, so that the pattern shows up as black on a burnished ground. Sometimes the goldsmith would test his work by making a sulphur cast from the *niello* or by printing from it on to paper: from this it is a short step to making engravings for the sole purpose of being printed on paper. A few such impressions and sulphur casts still exist.

NITTIS, Giuseppe De (1846–84), was trained in Naples, but was expelled in 1863 and went to Florence, where he came in contact with the MACCHIAIOLI. From Florence he went to Paris (1867), where he settled in 1872 and spent the rest of his life except for a visit to London in 1875. He was much influenced by the Impressionists, particularly by DEGAS, like his contemporary ZANDOMENEGHI. He exhibited in the First (1874) Impressionist Exhibition, to help give it respectability. His *vedute* are similar to those of SIGNORINI, who was his friend and companion on the trip to Britain. The largest collection of his works is in his native Barletta (190 pictures bequeathed by his widow), but there are others in Florence, Paris, Philadelphia (Wilstach) and Rome.

NOCTURNE. A night-piece. The term was first used by WHISTLER, who borrowed it from Chopin. He frequently gave his paintings musical titles, but the idea of painting landscapes as night scenes goes much further back, and most of A. van der NEER's works are of this kind.

NOLAN, Sir Sidney (*b.*1917), is recognized as the leader of the modern Australian School. He was born in Melbourne and trained there. His grandfather was a policeman who told stories of the 'Kelly Era', and Nolan painted a series of works (1946 onwards) on the theme of the semi-mythical outlaw in his home-made armour, which express the violence of his deeds and death and the hallucinatory quality of the Outback with a visionary intensity. Another Australian folk-hero, Mrs Fraser, has also figured in his private mythology, as has the better-known Leda, more accessible in symbolism but equally the vehicle for his multi-layered exploration of the significance of form, colour and emotional content. The series of the carcasses of sheep in the Outback has an almost Surrealist quality. Nolan first saw modern European painting in 1939, and in 1940 had his first one-man show, of abstract works. In 1951 he visited Europe, and in 1958–60 he worked in the USA. With DOBELL and DRYSDALE he represented Australia at the Venice Biennale of 1954. He was knighted in 1981. There are works in Australian museums and in Bedford, Liverpool, London (Tate) and New York (M of MA).

NOLDE, Emil (1867–1956), was a German Expressionist painter of landscapes, Biblical scenes, and figure subjects based on a private mythology. He shared in the BRÜCKE movement in 1906–7, and in 1913–14 travelled through Russia, China, Japan and Polynesia, where he was impressed by the demonic quality of primitive art and religion. He was persecuted by the Nazis, although many of his ideas were close to theirs. His pictures have a particularly ferocious quality, distorted drawing, violent colour and a tormented technique. He also worked in etching, lithography and wood-cut. There is a Nolde Foundation at Seebüll, on the German–Danish border, and many museums of modern art have works.

NOLLEKENS, Joseph (1737–1823), was an English sculptor who, from 1760 (or perhaps 1762) to 1770, worked in Rome where he also dealt in antiques and fragments which he restored and sold to English tourists. In Rome he also made busts of Garrick (1763) and Sterne (versions in London, NPG and Shandy Hall, Coxwold, N. Yorkshire). He became an ARA in 1771, and RA in 1772, and enjoyed a very considerable reputation. His able and life-like busts ensured him a position in sculpture almost equal to that of Reynolds in painting; his character, mercilessly delineated by his pupil J. T. Smith in the first 'debunking' biography 'Nollekens and His Times' (1828), is that of a grasping man only outdone in miserliness by his wife. He made the bust of Dr Johnson in Westminster Abbey, where there are also several tombs by him, and there are works in the Royal Coll., Cambridge (Fitzwm), Edinburgh (NPG), London (V&A, Wellington Mus. and Kenwood), Malibu Cal. (Getty), Oxford and Yale (CBA). There are said to be over seventy replicas of his bust of *Pitt*, which contributed handsomely to his fortune of £200,000.

NONFINITO (Ital. unfinished). The quality of suggestion implied in an unfinished work of art. It is usually applied to sculpture, and the two leading exponents are Michelangelo and Rodin: the difference being that Michelangelo leaves the forms implicit in the stone, so far unrevealed by the sculptor's awakening chisel, whereas Rodin (who was essentially a modeller, in spite of his training as a mason) imagines an 'unfinished' form which is then patiently carved by a mason, or else he employs the TORSO as an emotive fragment, not wishing to realize the figure as a whole.

NON-OBJECTIVE ART is a purer form of ABSTRACT ART: an abstract painting might have barely recognizable elements of the real world – a pipe, say, or a mandolin – but a non-objective one will consist of no more than stripes or patches of colour.

NORTHCOTE, James (1746–1831), was pupil and assistant of Reynolds (1771–5), and studied in Rome (1777–80). He was a tame follower of Reynolds's portrait style, and his history pictures – mostly for Boydell's Shakespeare Gallery – are full of figures from the Antique and the Italian grand manner, roughly transplanted into an alien land and made to toil humbly at unsuitable tasks. He wrote a biography of Reynolds and some gossipy reminiscences ('Conversations of James Northcote', edited by William Hazlitt, 1830). London (V&A) and Glasgow (Univ.) have large-scale pictures. Cambridge (Fitzwm) has a portrait of the sculptor NOLLEKENS. Exeter, London (Dulwich) and Yale (CBA) also have works.

NORWICH SCHOOL. This was the only regional School of painting in England which had an internal cohesion comparable to the Italian local Schools – the NEWLYN SCHOOL, and, in Scotland, the GLASGOW SCHOOL had less of a regional quality. Its two great masters were COTMAN and CROME, and it began at a meeting at Crome's house in Norwich on 19 February 1803, when his friends, patrons and pupils formed the Norwich Society 'for the purpose of an Enquiry into the Rise, Progress and present state of Painting, Architecture, and Sculpture, with a view to point out the Best Methods of study to attain to Greater Perfection . . .' From 1805 it became an Exhibiting Society and was joined by Cotman in 1807. Because of the strong links between East Anglia and Holland the chief characteristic of the Norwich School is a dependence on 17th-century Dutch realistic landscape (HOBBEMA, RUISDAEL), the artists who had inspired GAINSBOROUGH in his East Anglian years. The School came to an end *c.*1833. Among the many minor artists the sons of Crome and Cotman, Joseph Stannard (1797–1830), James Stark (1794–1859) a pupil of Crome in 1811, John Thirtle (1777–1839) the brother-in-law of Cotman, and George Vincent (1796–1831?) are the best known. All are well represented in Norwich Museum, and examples of one or more of the artists are in Cambridge (Fitzwm), Edinburgh (NG), London (BM, Tate and V&A), Manchester (City Gall. and Whitworth), New York (Met. Mus.) and Yale (CBA).

NOTKE, Bernt (*c.*1440–1509), was the most important painter and woodcarver active in the late 15th century in the Baltic area. He was recorded at Lübeck in 1467 and was specifically exempted from the regulations of the Guild, so he may have been of higher social status than most German artists of his time. His main work, the High Altar for Aarhus Cathedral in Denmark, was being worked on in 1478/9 and was completed by 1482. The paintings are probably his, but the sculpture may be by his assistants. In 1477 he had carved the great cross for Lübeck Cathedral in polychromed wood with a combination of Late Gothic pathos and light-hearted elegance. The spiky elegance, coupled with an extreme realism of detail, is best seen in his most famous work, the huge statue of St George killing the Dragon, completed in 1489 (Stockholm, S. Nicholas). This was an important commission given by a leading Swedish statesman and was intended as a national memorial to a victory over the Danes. Notke appears to have spent several years in Stockholm and he also made the High Altar for S. Nikolai, Reval (now called Tallin) in Estonia in 1482/3.

NOVECENTO (Ital. nine hundred). The 20th century, i.e. the nineteen-hundreds. It was also the name given to a movement, founded in 1926, which became associated with Fascism on account of its 'back-to-the-great-Italian-past' character.

O

OBJET TROUVÉ *see* FOUND OBJECT.

'OCCHIALI' *see* WITTEL.

OCHTERVELT, Jacob (1634–82), was a Dutch genre painter, often of high life, who was much influenced by Pieter de HOOCH, and, through him, by Vermeer. He was particularly celebrated for his rendering of silk and satin. There are works in Amsterdam, Berlin, Birmingham, Brussels, Chicago, Dublin, Glasgow, London (NG), Manchester, Pittsburgh, Raleigh NC, Rotterdam, St Louis, Stockholm, Vienna and York.

O'CONOR, Roderic (1860–1940), was an Irish painter who lived and worked in France. He was trained in Antwerp (1884) and Paris, and lived in BARBIZON, Paris and later in PONT-AVEN. He knew, and was greatly influenced by, van GOGH and GAUGUIN: he may have met van Gogh in Paris, and he certainly knew Gauguin by 1894, and probably much earlier. He exhibited in Paris and in Brussels with Les XX. There are works in Dublin (NG and Municipal Gall.) and in London (Tate).

ODALISQUE is a French word corrupted from the Turkish for a female slave. In art it is a name for a type of voluptuous nude (sometimes wearing harem trousers), such as Ingres or Matisse delighted in.

OEUVRE (Fr. work). The *oeuvre* of an artist is the total of his output, and an *Oeuvre Catalogue* is, therefore, an attempt to record every single painting, or drawing, or statue, by a given artist. A *catalogue raisonné* (Fr. methodical catalogue) is slightly different, in that it attempts a complete description of works, with details of provenance, autograph quality, condition and similar facts.

OFFSET *see* COUNTERPROOF.

OIL-PAINTING is the most usual technique for painting pictures of some size and importance. Basically, it consists of covering a slightly absorbent surface (usually primed canvas) with one or more layers of pigment, ground in just enough oil to make the mixture pleasantly sticky. The oil used is normally linseed, but poppy or nut oils have also been used, since they remain workable for long periods. On the other hand, 'dryers' (siccatives) are sometimes mixed with linseed oil to speed up the drying processes. The use of oil mixtures for house and decorative painting probably goes back to antiquity, but the 'invention of oil-painting' – i.e. the technique adapted to the painting of pictures – is traditionally credited to the EYCKS. This is not true, but it does seem certain that a much improved technique, probably based on better-quality oil, was practised in Flanders early in the 15th century. Italian painters were slow in catching up, and a picture like the *S. Sebastian* by the POLLAIUOLO brothers (1475, London, NG) shows that they were still far from proficient towards the end of the century.

There are two principal ways of painting pictures in oil. One, known as ALLA PRIMA or 'direct' painting, consists of just putting the paint on and hoping it comes out right. If this fails, the proper cure is to take another canvas and start again. The second, more elaborate, technique is the one favoured by the Old Masters. This involves a good deal of planning ahead, since the canvas is first drawn on, then covered with one or more layers of monochrome so that the whole picture is virtually complete except for the colour; this is then applied in layers, so that the underlying layers show through to a predetermined extent, while the colours themselves are modified by their application as transparent films (GLAZES) or as opaque paste (SCUMBLES), much extra effect being gained from IMPASTO and BRUSHWORK. This technique, in the hands of a master-craftsman such as Rembrandt, Rubens or Titian, is capable of almost unlimited subtlety and variety; which is why oil-painting has practically superseded all its rivals, although ACRYLIC paints may provide formidable competition in the future.

O'KEEFFE, Georgia (1887–1986), was born in Wisconsin and trained in Chicago and New York, and taught in Texas and Virginia until 1918. About 1916 she began to make abstract drawings, influenced by Mexican children's art and by the desolate landscape of the Texas Panhandle, when the dealer Stieglitz (whom she married in 1924) recognized her talents. Her abstractions, often in watercolour, are based on landscapes and natural forms in the American South-West; buildings, plants and bones found in the deserts of New Mexico. She is well represented in US museums, including New York (Met. Mus., M of MA and Brooklyn), Washington (NG) and Chicago, which has a large mural of 1966. Her autobiography was published in 1983.

OLDENBURG, Claes (*b.*1929), was born in Sweden, but went to the US as a child, becoming one of the leaders of POP Art there. In 1962 he began a series of painted plaster replicas of food, e.g. *Dual Hamburger* (New York, M of MA), *Floor Burger* (Toronto), some of which are 7 feet wide. He also invented 'soft' sculpture, usually vinyl stuffed with kapok. In 1967 he dug a hole in Central Park, New York, and then filled it in again.

OLEOGRAPH. A reproduction made by printing from blocks inked with oil-paint rather than printer's ink: *see* BAXTER Prints and BOYS.

OLIVER, Isaac (*d.*1617), was brought to England from France as a child in 1568 to escape the persecution of the Huguenots. He learned the art of miniature painting from HILLIARD and became his chief rival by about 1595. He may have gone abroad in 1588, and he was certainly in Venice in 1596 – when he described himself as a Frenchman – and he must have seen a good deal of Italian art, principally that of Parmigianino, for he had ambitions, unlike Hilliard who painted only portraits, towards history painting in miniature. One of his three wives was a GHEERAERTS and he was popular at the Court of James I. He is well represented in the Royal Coll. and in the V&A, London. His son Peter (1594?–1647) completed some of his works, and there is a signed miniature by Peter in the V&A. Portraits of Peter Oliver and his wife are in London (NPG), and there are miniatures by both in Amsterdam (Rijksmus.).

OMEGA WORKSHOPS *see* FRY.

ONTBIJT *see* BREAKFAST PIECE.

OP or OPTICAL ART is based on the idea that the painter or sculptor can create optical effects that persuade the spectator to see visual illusions. The patterns made by VASARELY and Bridget RILEY are themselves static, but the spectator is so dazzled by them that they appear to move. The complex layers of clear and coloured perspex arranged by Eric Olsen or Francisco Sobrino create illusions of space and depth. The fields of inclined and painted nails by Günther Uecker, or Sue Fuller's string compositions, derive more obviously from GABO's CONSTRUCTIVIST objects, which early exploited the optical effects created by light and shadow within complex surfaces. Most op, kinetic and constructivist art is technically very accomplished, since much of the effect depends on the contrast of simple shapes and the weird optical effects generated by them.

OPIE, John (1761–1807), was launched in London in 1781 as the 'Cornish Wonder', an untutored natural genius, by John Wolcot, doctor, sometime pupil of Wilson, satirist ('Peter Pindar') and skilful impresario. The young Opie's talent lay in painting peasant types in strong chiaroscuro, and he is best with old people and children, whom he treats with Rembrandtesque effects of light: 'Ah!' said Reynolds to Northcote, newly back from Italy, 'there is *such* a young man come out of Cornwall . . . like Caravaggio, but finer!' His large compositions for Boydell's Shakespeare Gallery, popular in engravings, were influential in establishing the costume-history piece, but once his Tenebrist vision was smothered by elegant face-painting, he declined into insipidity. His second marriage, in 1798, to the novelist Amelia Alderson led to his painting more 'literary' subjects. From 1799 he had a studio in Norwich and knew CROME. He became an RA in 1787, was made a Professor at the RA in 1805, and gave a series of lectures, published posthumously in 1809. There are works in London (Guildhall, Tate and NPG: portraits of himself and his second wife), Aberdeen, Birmingham, Brighton, Bristol, Canterbury (*Murder of Becket*), Cardiff, Exeter, Glasgow, Leeds, Norwich, Plymouth, Southampton, Truro, Yale (CBA) and elsewhere.

OPTICAL MIXTURES. According to the colour-theory of NEO-IMPRESSIONISM, it is possible to obtain brighter secondary colours, such as green, by making a series of blobs of both primaries (which in the case of green would be blue and yellow) so that the blue and yellow blobs are very closely intermingled but not actually mixed. In this way, the colours mix in the spectator's eye at a certain distance from the picture, giving a much brighter and cleaner green than is obtainable by actual mixing of the pigments on the palette. For this reason, the Neo-Impressionists painted their pictures entirely in small dots or commas of colour, either the colours of the spectrum used pure, or blended only with white, and they varied the size of the blob according to the size of the picture and the distance at which it was to be seen, relying always on distance to make the mixture in the spectator's eye. The Neo-Impressionists disliked the term Pointillism, preferring Divisionism as a description of their technique: a full description is given in SIGNAC's book 'De Delacroix au Néo-Impressionnisme' (Chap. I). The Impressionists had already used a known variant of the technique, by juxtaposing different shades and tones of one or more colours, so as to enhance the brilliance and shimmering quality of their colour. Optical greys are also obtained in this way, and are claimed to be superior to mixtures with black pigment in them; they were essential to Impressionism, the theory of which does not recognize the existence of black in Nature. Many of Degas's pastels show the use of optical mixtures – not in the rigid manner of the Neo-Impressionist theory, but in a much more elaborate form than that employed by the Impressionists, and he frequently used superimposed scumbles to achieve depth of colour.

ORCAGNA, Andrea (*c.*1308–68), was a painter, sculptor and architect active in Florence in the mid-14th century, one of the first major figures to arise after Giotto, whose ideals he did not entirely share. The first document to mention him (1343) speaks of his 'many defects and faults'. He was admitted to the Guild of Painters in 1343/4 and Stonemasons in 1352. His only certain painting is the large altarpiece in the Strozzi Chapel of S.M. Novella, Florence (1354–7). This shows a wiry sense of form and a rejection of the sense of spatial depth that had been one of Giotto's greatest achievements: in its place Orcagna creates a much more hieratic art, in which gold backgrounds play an important part, probably directly related to a change in religious feeling after the Black Death of 1348. His main work in sculpture is the Tabernacle, with a relief of the *Death and Assumption of the Virgin* (signed and dated 1359), in Orsanmichele, Florence. In 1368 an altarpiece of *St Matthew* (Florence, Uffizi) was completed by his brother Jacopo di Cione on account of Orcagna's illness and almost certainly he died in that year. His brothers Nardo (active 1343/6–*d.*1365/6) and Jacopo (active 1365–98) di Cione were the most influential painters in Florence at the end of the 14th century. The fresco of the *Inferno* in the Strozzi Chapel does not seem to be by the same hand as the altarpiece (i.e. it is not by Orcagna), and Ghiberti ascribes it to Nardo. All attributions to Nardo are based on this slender evidence, but there is no doubt that the two brothers were the dominant influence on late Trecento painting in Florence. There are many works which are vaguely Orcagnesque and seem to date from the end of the 14th century: these are usually attributed to Jacopo. Pictures by one or another are in the Royal Coll. and in Berlin, Budapest, Florence (Accad., Uffizi, S.M. Novella and other churches), Liverpool, London (NG, V&A and Courtauld Inst.), New York (Met. Mus. and Hist. Soc.), Oxford, Philadelphia (Johnson), St Louis, Utrecht (dated 1350), the Vatican, Washington (NG) and Yale (Univ.).

ORLEY, Bernard (Barent) van (*c.*1491/2–1541), was a Brussels painter, head of a large workshop. He was called in his own day the Raphael of the Netherlands, from his garbled imitation of Italian Renaissance ideas and forms, derived from his knowledge of the Raphael tapestry cartoons, which were woven in Brussels *c.*1516/19, and from two highly conjectural visits to Italy. He was Court Painter to the Spanish Governors of the Netherlands; was, with MABUSE, one of the principal ROMANISTS; was a prolific designer of tapestries and stained glass, and executed occasional portraits in the Massys and Holbein style. In 1520, when Dürer visited the Netherlands, Orley gave a banquet for him, and Dürer drew his portrait. There are examples in the Royal Coll. (tapestries), Antwerp, Brussels, Detroit, Edinburgh, Glasgow, Munich, Toronto, Turin, Vienna, Waddesdon Bucks. (National Trust) and elsewhere.

OROVIDA *see* PISSARRO.

OROZCO, José (1883–1949), was a Mexican painter who used an Expressionist style for his decorations, frequently huge, often in fresco or in imitations of fresco achieved with modern building materials. Most of his works have strong political overtones, and, like RIVERA, he executed many commissions for revolutionary governments.

ORPHIC CUBISM, ORPHISME. A term invented in 1913 by Apollinaire to describe 'the art of painting new structures out of elements that have not been borrowed from the visual sphere but have been created entirely by the artist himself, and have been endowed by him with the fullness of reality. It is pure art.' This art was attributed to DELAUNAY, who was mainly concerned with the primacy of colour over form. He thus achieved a fusion of CUBISM, Futurism, and the independent colour of Fauvism to produce a precursor of pure Abstract painting. Through KANDINSKY and KLEE his ideas exerted great influence in Germany. He also used the spectrum to produce what he called the Law of Simultaneous Contrasts. Orphic Cubism is so called because it was regarded as more oracular and esoteric (and therefore 'purer') than ordinary Cubism.

OS, Jan van (1744–1808) and his son Georgius (1782–1861), continued the van HUYSUM tradition of flower- and fruit-painting well into the 19th century: works by both men are in London (NG), which also has an early marine by Jan in the manner of W. van de VELDE the Younger.

OSTADE, Adriaen van (1610–85), was a Haarlem genre painter said to have been a pupil of Frans Hals, though it is difficult to see any influence of Hals in his interiors with drunken peasants or conversations between hags. In the 1640s he was influenced by Rembrandt (the *Slaughtered Pig*, 1643, Frankfurt, Städel, is a case in point), but the principal influence seems to be that of BROUWER, in the sense that both painted the same kind of peasant scenes: Brouwer and Ostade are supposed to have been fellow-pupils of Hals *c.*1626/7. He painted about 1,000 pictures, so that he is well represented in museums. Jan STEEN was his pupil, and so was his own brother Isack. Another pupil, Cornelius Dusart (1660–1704), often worked with him, and at a sale after Dusart's death several paintings were described as their joint work.

OSTADE, Isack van (1621–49), was the younger brother and pupil of Adriaen. In his short life he painted a large number of pictures, some of genre subjects like his brother's, but the best are of landscape: there are good winter scenes by him in London (NG, Wallace Coll. and Kenwood).

OTTOCENTO (Ital. eight hundred). The 19th century, i.e. the eighteen-hundreds.

OUDRY, Jean Baptiste (1686–1755), was one of the greatest French painters of hunting, animal, and still-life subjects, particularly those with game and dead beasts in the open air. He was a pupil of his father and of Largillierre, and was influenced by DESPORTES, his only equal in his chosen genre. After painting portraits, still-life and flower subjects, he concentrated from *c.*1720 on animals, hunts and landscapes, with occasional portraits. He was appointed Court Painter to Louis XV, and painted the royal hounds, and from 1726 onwards he worked for the Beauvais tapestry factory. After he became manager (in 1734) he designed the illustrations to the Fables of La Fontaine that brought the factory world fame. He also worked for the Gobelins from 1736, and designed for it the *Hunts of Louis XV*. His works show a careful attention to detail, but also have a largeness of handling in light and shade and feeling for colour. There are works in Barnard Castle (Bowes Mus.), Caen, Cambridge Mass. (Fogg), Compiègne, Copenhagen, Fontainebleau, Leningrad (Hermitage), London (Wallace Coll.), Marseilles, Moscow, New York (Met. Mus.), Paris (Louvre, Carnavalet, Mus. des Arts Décoratifs and Petit Pal.), Schwerin (the largest collection: forty-three), Stockholm, Toledo Ohio and elsewhere.

OUWATER, Albert van (mid-15th century). All that is known about this painter is that he was a Haarlemer who was the master of GEERTGEN tot Sint Jans, and that he made a painting of the *Raising of Lazarus* which is unmistakably the one in Berlin under his name (or perhaps the Berlin picture is a copy of a lost original). This information comes from van MANDER, writing *c.*1604, and it is possible that Ouwater was working at the same time as the major Haarlem painter, BOUTS the Elder. It used to be thought that he was documented in Haarlem in 1467, but this is now known to be a misreading. He may have designed for the new craft of woodcut book-illustration. A fragmentary *Head of a Donor* (New York, Met. Mus.) and two wings in Granada (Capilla Real) are attributed to him, and recently an attempt has been made to add the Eyckian *Man with a Pink* (Berlin).

OVERBECK, Johann Friedrich (1789–1869), was the most important of the NAZARENER group, which he founded originally as the Lukasbrüderschaft, with Franz PFORR in Vienna in 1809. From 1810 he lived almost entirely in Rome and painted in a purely 'Quattrocento' style; like INGRES, he idolized Raphael. He became a Catholic in 1813. He exerted considerable influence on the PRE-RAPHAELITES through BROWN and DYCE, and on European religious art in general. There are works in Assisi (S.M. degli Angeli), Basle, Berlin, Cologne (Cath.), Munich and elsewhere.

OVILE MASTER *see* 'UGOLINO-LORENZETTI'.

OZENFANT, Amédée (1886–1966), was a French painter who, with the architect Le Corbusier, invented PURISM. From about 1924, the human figure began to creep back into his works, culminating in two huge paintings entitled *Life*. In 1937 he founded a school in London, but moved the following year to New York, where he spent some ten years. He is represented in the museums of modern art in London, New York and Paris. His book *Art* (English edition 1931, published as *Foundations of Modern Art*) had considerable influence.

P

P., Pinx., Pinxit (Lat. he painted), following a name on a painting or, more commonly, an engraving after a painting, refers to the authorship of the original picture.

Pacheco, Francisco (1564–1654), was a Spanish painter and writer on art. He was the master of Cano and Velázquez, who was also his son-in-law. Pacheco worked mostly in Seville and is not known to have visited Italy, although he had a large collection of engravings including some after Michelangelo, Veronese, Dürer and Lucas van Leyden. In 1611 Velázquez became his pupil, and in the same year Pacheco made a trip to Madrid and Toledo where he visited El Greco. In 1618 he was appointed Censor of Paintings to the Inquisition and in 1619 was made a Painter to the King. His book *El Arte de la Pintura* took thirty years to write and was completed in 1637/8. It was published in 1649, but a recent and fuller edition appeared in 1956. It is perhaps the most important Spanish treatise on painting, in that it contains detailed treatment of such Counter-Reformation subjects as the Immaculate Conception, described in the minutest detail (*see* Antolínez), and also exemplified in his own picture in Seville Cath. His friend and collaborator Montañes may also have been influenced in his representation of the Crucifixion with four nails. Pacheco was also a notable portraitist – he claimed to have painted 150 by 1647 – and there are drawings by him in Madrid (Mus. Galdiano). Most of his paintings are still in Seville, but there is one in Barnard Castle (Bowes Mus.) and another in Williamstown Mass.

Pacher, Michael (*c.*1435–98), was the principal Tyrolean painter and was active also as a wood-carver, but his sculpture is more Gothic in style than his paintings. As his geographical position would imply, Pacher is a sort of half-way house between the Gothic qualities of German 15th-century painting and the more intellectual interests of the Italians – in his case, Mantegna seems to have been the principal influence. There is an altarpiece by him in Munich and other works in Cologne (Schnütgen Mus.) and Vienna (Belvedere), and a panel of his school in London (NG), but the majority of his works remain in the parish churches for which they were painted or carved, his masterpiece being the S. Wolfgang (Salzkammergut) altarpiece, completed by 1481.

Painterly *see* Malerisch.

Painting Techniques *see* Acrylic, Encaustic Wax, Fresco, Gouache, Oil-painting, Pastel, Secco, Size Colour, Tempera, Watercolour.

Pajou, Augustin (1730–1809), was a French sculptor who was a pupil of J. B. Lemoyne and studied in Rome 1752–6. He is best known for his decorative sculpture in the Opera House at Versailles (1768–70) and for his numerous portraits – *Lemoyne* (1758) and *Buffon* in the Louvre, *Descartes* and *Bossuet* in the Institut. He worked much for Mme du Barry. In 1777 he was appointed Keeper of the King's Antiquities and in 1792 he served on a Revolutionary Committee on the Conservation of Works of Art. His *Psyche abandoned* (1791, Louvre) is a piece of Neoclassic sentiment.

Pala. An Italian word for a large altarpiece: unlike an Ancona a pala may consist of one picture only. A 'Pala of a unified type' is one in which all the action (if any), and all the figures, are represented as inhabiting one single space, which is treated as a consistent pictorial continuum. In most POLYPTYCHS each scene, or even each Saint, has its own space.

PALIOTTO is Italian for an *antependium* or altar frontal, i.e. the hanging which covers the front of an altar. These are normally of cloth, the colour agreeing with the liturgical colour of the day, but there are examples of carved, painted or enamelled frontals. They are often very ancient, and the most famous is perhaps the golden one (the Pala d'Oro) in St Mark's, Venice, which is 13th-century, or that in Sant' Ambrogio, Milan, of the 9th century.

PALMA, Jacopo, called Palma Giovane (*c*.1548–1628), was the grand-nephew of Palma Vecchio. He may have entered TITIAN's studio and he completed, *c*.1576, the *Entombment* intended for Titian's own tomb. He began in a style related to Roman Mannerism, having spent some years there in the 1560s and 1570s, but developed towards the style of TINTORETTO. There are works by him in most Venetian churches and galleries, in the Royal Coll. and in Birmingham, Cambridge (Fitzwm), Florence (Uffizi), London (NG), Madrid, Milan (Brera), Munich, Naples, New York (Met. Mus.), Oxford, Rouen and Vienna.

PALMA, Jacopo, called Palma Vecchio (*c*.1480–1528), was a Venetian painter who was a pupil of Giovanni Bellini and was much influenced by Titian, as well as by GIORGIONE and Lotto. The *Man in a Fur Cloak* (Munich), sometimes attributed to him, following Vasari, is very Giorgionesque. He is chiefly remembered as the painter of a particularly splendid type of blonde, said to be characteristically Venetian in her ample charms. For this reason, many of his works are *Sacre Conversazioni* with several female Saints. His masterpiece is perhaps the *St Barbara and other Saints* (1522–4) in S.M. Formosa, Venice, but there are other works in Venice and in the Royal Coll. and Berlin, Budapest, Cambridge (Fitzwm), Chicago, Detroit, Dresden, Dublin, Florence (Uffizi), Glasgow, London (NG, Courtauld Inst. and RA), Milan (Brera), Oxford, Paris (Louvre), Philadelphia, Prague, Rome (Gall. Naz., Borghese, Capitoline), San Marino Cal. (Huntington), Sarasota Fla, Vienna, Worcester Mass., York and elsewhere. Pictures in Berlin, Chantilly and Ottawa have signatures, but all have been doubted.

PALMER, Samuel (1805–81), was a painter of pastoral landscape and the most important follower of BLAKE, whom he met in 1824. He was very precocious and exhibited at the RA from 1819. His 'Shoreham Period' (1826–*c*.34) was the moment of perfect balance between inner and outer vision – a landscape charged with fecundity and Christian symbolism, expressed in terms of observed detail. Others influenced by Blake – they called themselves 'The Ancients' – included Palmer's life-long friend CALVERT, the VARLEY brothers, and George Richmond. This 'primitive and infantine feeling' (his own words) for landscape began to fade *c*.1832. In 1837 he married the daughter of John LINNELL and visited Italy, and his son later wrote of these events: 'After the Shoreham and Italian periods, the whole of my father's life became a dreadful tragedy'; but this view is now regarded as a melodramatic overstatement. His early work has influenced modern Romantic painters, e.g. SUTHERLAND: examples are in London (BM, V&A, Tate and Courtauld Inst.), Cambridge (Fitzwm), Manchester, Oxford (Ashmolean), Philadelphia, Yale (CBA) and elsewhere. In 1976 T. Keating claimed to have forged several Palmer drawings.

PANINI (or Pannini), Giovanni Paolo (*c.*1692–1765/8), was the first painter to specialize in ruins, treating them as Roman VEDUTE of a special kind. He was working in Rome by *c.*1717, but the earliest surviving dated picture is of 1727 (London, Wellington Mus.); in 1729 he was concerned in a Fête given by Cardinal de Polignac in honour of the birth of the Dauphin and this began a long connection with France and the French Academy in Rome. Paintings of the Fête are in the Louvre (1729) and Dublin (1731). His views of modern Rome, as well as his *capricci* based on the better-known ruins, had an enormous vogue among Grand Tourists and examples are to be found in most older galleries. PIRANESI, though far more of an archaeologist, was influenced by him, and so was CANALETTO.

PANORAMA. The word and the thing seem to have been invented by Robert Barker in Edinburgh, and patented by him in 1787. It was a landscape painted on the inside of a cylinder, so that a spectator standing inside the cylinder would have the impression of an actual landscape all round him: later, it was sometimes based on rollers moving the landscape in relation to the viewer. The first example, painted in 1789, was a view of Edinburgh, exhibited in London by Barker and based on CAMERA OBSCURA views. It was a great success and led to GIRTIN's *Eidometropolis* of 1802, which was perhaps the most successful artistically of all panoramas. The idea reached New York in 1795 and was popular in the US up to the mid-19th century, COLE, DUNLAP and TRUMBULL all being influenced by it. One of Rome in 1824, by Carracciolo, is one of the very few survivors (London, V&A). *See also* LOUTHERBOURG.

PANTOJA de la Cruz, Juan (*c.*1553–1608), was the pupil and successor of SANCHEZ Coello, becoming Court Painter to Philip III in 1596. His official portraits are flat and hieratic, but his religious works show the influence of Italian Caravaggismo. There are works in the Escorial and Madrid (Prado) and in the Royal Coll. and Cambridge Mass. (Fogg), Chicago, Munich, New York (Met. Mus. and Hispanic Soc.) and Vienna.

PAOLO Veneziano (*d.c.*1362), was the principal painter working in the Byzantine style in 14th-century Venice. In 1358 he and his son Giovanni jointly signed a *Coronation of the Virgin* (New York, Frick Coll.) which is the last known work by him, but another *Coronation* (Washington, NG) attributed to him is dated 1324. His son Luca was also a painter and the father and both sons jointly signed the cover which they made for the PALIOTTO, the *Pala d'Oro*, in St Mark's in 1345.

PAOLOZZI, Eduardo (*b.*1924), was born in Edinburgh of Italian parents. He worked in Paris 1947–50, where he was influenced by Klee and knew GIACOMETTI. He was one of the main impulses behind the development of POP ART in London in the mid-1950s and now specializes in large, abstract, metal sculptures. There are works in London (Tate).

PAPIER COLLÉ (Fr. glued paper) is a form of COLLAGE built up from layers of paper stuck on a ground such as canvas. It was invented *c.*1911 by Picasso and Braque, but Matisse, in his last works, used it for the intensity of colour it could give, in quite a different sense from collage.

PARIS, THE SCHOOL OF (*L'École de Paris*). Since about 1900 Paris has been the Mecca of young painters of every nationality, Picasso being perhaps the most obvious example. The term now means little more than contemporary painting, predominantly non-figurative, without regard to national schools: Eastern European and German refugees, Spanish and American painters can all be included in the term, and De STAËL, HARTUNG and RIOPELLE equally with SOULAGES, MANESSIER or DUBUFFET are covered by it. The phrase tends to mean something different to French writers, who imply hegemony.

PARMIGIANINO, Francesco (1503–40), was one of the most sensitive and elegant of the early Mannerists. He was born in Parma and was commissioned to decorate the S. transept of Parma Cathedral as early as 1522 and was painting frescoes in S. Giovanni Evangelista there in 1522/3: as this church contains frescoes by CORREGGIO the principal influence on his style was Correggio, soon followed by Pordenone and Raphael. He was in Rome by late 1523 and was captured in the Sack of Rome (1527) while working on the *St Jerome* (now London, NG). He was able to escape to Bologna and travelled to Verona and Venice before returning to Parma in 1530. The last ten years of his life were spent in painting frescoes in S.M. della Steccata, Parma, and quarrelling with the overseers of the works; although he was supposed to start in 1531 he did so little that, finally, in 1539 the authorities sacked him and had him imprisoned for breach of contract. They then approached GIULIO Romano, who, at first, attempted to evade the commission, since Parmigianino had written begging him not to act against the interests of a fellow artist. In the event, the overseers were dissatisfied with Giulio as well. The next year Parmigianino died, and it is a sufficient description of his neurotic temperament to quote Vasari: 'having his thoughts filled with alchemy . . . [he] changed from the delicate, amiable, and elegant person that he was, to a bearded, long-haired, neglected, and almost savage or wild man . . . he was there interred naked, as he had wished, and with a cross of cypress placed upright on his breast in the grave'. His work, both in painting and perhaps even more through his etchings, which had wide currency, was very influential in Italy and also in N. Europe. His figures have long necks and hands and seem almost swooning in their ecstasy, much of which is truly Counter-Reformation in taste. The so-called *Madonna with the Long Neck* (*c.*1535, Florence, Uffizi) is one of the best examples. His portraits, when he had a congenial sitter, have deep spiritual insight (especially, perhaps, the very early *Self-portrait* in Vienna, in which he saw himself distorted in a convex mirror). There are paintings by him in the Royal Coll. and in Berlin, Bologna (Pinacoteca, S. Petronio), Copenhagen, Detroit, Dresden, Florence (Uffizi, Pitti), Frankfurt, Glasgow, London (NG, Courtauld Inst.), Madrid (Prado), Milan (Ambrosiana), Naples, Parma (Gall., S. Giovanni Evang., Madonna della Steccata, Canonica di Bardi), Rocca di Fontanellato nr Parma, Rome (Borghese, Doria Pal.), Vienna and York.

Parmigianino was, after Dürer, one of the earliest painter–etchers – i.e. he used the medium for making works of art of his own. His compositions were also very widely reproduced as engravings and as CHIAROSCURO WOODCUTS, for which he was probably among the first to make designs.

Girolamo Mazzola-Bedoli (1500–69) married Parmigianino's cousin and imitated him. There are paintings by him in Parma and elsewhere.

PASCIN, Jules (1885–1930), was born Julius Pincas in Bulgaria, but settled in Paris and called himself Pascin. He was trained in Vienna and Munich and worked for the famous satirical paper 'Simplizissimus' before going to Paris in

1905, where he settled soon afterwards. He spent the 1914–18 War in the US and became an American citizen, but returned to Paris in 1922 and lived there until he hanged himself on the opening day of his one-man show in 1930. His pictures are all of equivocally young girls in sprawling poses, a sort of Lolita *avant la lettre*, and have much in common with certain French 18th-century *peintres galants* and engravers; perhaps for this reason he is not well represented in public galleries, although there are examples in Paris (Mus. d'Art Moderne), Minneapolis, Southampton and Toledo Ohio.

PASMORE, Victor (*b.*1908), was one of the members of the EUSTON ROAD group in the late 1930s. He was unable to paint full-time until 1938, but from then until 1947 he painted the most subtle landscapes and interiors seen in England since Steer or Whistler. The later scenes of the Thames were almost Oriental in their tonal subtlety and hinted at the abstraction which he embraced in 1947: since the 1950s he has made constructions in the manner of GABO, usually of simply coloured wood and Perspex. He has been a most influential teacher, first in Newcastle and then in London, of a course based on abstract principles of design. There are works by him in many British and Commonwealth galleries; he was concerned also with the design of the New Town at Peterlee, Durham.

PASTEL is a medium consisting of dry powdered colour mixed with just enough gum (usually gum arabic) to bind it. The mixture is allowed to set in moulds, forming very fragile sticks about the size of a finger. These sticks, when rubbed on paper, disintegrate so that the powder adheres to the paper; but one of the great drawbacks of the medium is the ease with which the powder falls off again or smudges. The softest pastels give an effect which is virtually that of painting, the whole surface of the paper being covered by the pigment layer, but it is also possible to use much harder, grittier pastels (like the chalk used in schools) to get an effect more closely related to drawing. The first method was used by such French masters as Quentin LATOUR or CHARDIN; the second is more usual for making studies instead of finished works. DEGAS, perhaps the greatest of pastellists, tended to use the medium as a form of drawing rather than painting, but he also had various technical tricks (such as soaking the paper in turpentine) which have helped to preserve his pastels, although they incur the wrath of the purists.

PASTICHE, PASTICCIO. Sometimes an imitation or forgery which consists of a number of motives taken from several genuine works by any one artist and recombined in such a way as to give the impression of being an independent original creation by that artist. More often, however, it is not intended as a forgery, but a deliberate, often witty, exercise in an earlier style – e.g. Rex Whistler's murals and book-illustrations in an 18th-century manner.

PATENIER (Patinier or Patinir), Joachim (*d.c.*1524), is documented in the Antwerp Guild in 1515. Dürer, who owned a picture by him, mentions him as a landscape painter, attended the festivities at his second marriage in 1521 and drew his portrait. His small landscapes have something in common with Antwerp Mannerism in that they are cool in colour and very blue in the distances, and they represent fantastic scenery with jagged mountains, farmlands dotted with villages and ruins, rocky shores, and little figures of saints, hermits and country people. They offer a wonderful mixture of fantasy and naturalistic detail that presages the more naturalistic landscapes of BRUEGEL.

Sometimes the figures are by others; in one case at least by MASSYS, who became the guardian of Patenier's children in 1524. There are only four signed works to serve as a basis for attributions to him: in Antwerp, Karlsruhe, Vienna, and, recently discovered, in a Belgian private coll. Other works are in Basle, Berlin, Birmingham (Barber Inst.), Cambridge (Fitzwm), London (NG), Madrid (Prado), Minneapolis, New York (Met. Mus.), Oxford, Paris (Louvre), Philadelphia (Mus. and Johnson), Rome (Borghese), York and elsewhere.

PATER, Jean Baptiste Joseph (1696–1736), was an imitator of WATTEAU, whose only pupil he was. Apparently they separated on account of Watteau's extreme irritability, due to his illness, but in his last days Watteau repented of this, sent for Pater, and gave him his final lessons. Pater soon wore out his own talent in repetitions of *Fêtes galantes*, typical examples of which are in London (Wallace Coll., Kenwood) and Waddesdon Bucks. (National Trust).

PATINA is the greenish incrustation on the surface of old BRONZE. It is esteemed for its own sake, and the word has had its meaning extended to cover all forms of mellowing with age. When a picture has had the dirt cleaned off its surface it is often described as having 'lost its patina'.

PATINIR *see* PATENIER.

PATROON (Dutch, patron). An American term for the anonymous portrait painters active in the New York area in the late 17th and early 18th centuries, painting the mainly Dutch merchants and settlers. Some were stylistically Dutch, others English, but mezzotints imported from England were often used as the basis for their works.

PATTERN-BOOK. Usually a collection of architectural models, but also a SKETCHBOOK, with copies after the Antique or drawings of figures used in studios to provide models for compositions, by painters like PISANELLO or BELLINI.

PEAKE, Robert (active 1576–*d.*1626?), was an English portrait painter in the reigns of Elizabeth I and James I. His only signed work is a *Military Commander*, dated 1593 (Yale, CBA), but there is portrait of Charles I as Prince of Wales painted for Cambridge University in 1613, and a fine group of Henry, Prince of Wales, and Lord Harington, dated 1603 (New York, Met. Mus.), is almost certainly by him.

PEALE. A family of American painters and naturalists. The two earliest members were Charles Willson Peale (1741–1827) and his brother James (1749–1831). Charles was a saddler and woodcarver who had lessons from COPLEY, went to London 1767–9 and worked under WEST, returning to settle in Philadelphia. He painted a number of portraits of the leading figures in the Revolutionary War including the earliest (1772) of Washington. In 1786 he founded the Peale Museum and from then on was principally concerned with the scientific aspect of his museum – e.g. in 1806 he exhibited the skeleton of the first American mastodon. He began to paint again at the age of 74 and died at 86, his death being brought on by carrying a trunk for a mile on his way to court his fourth wife. He wrote an autobiography, and his three wives gave him seventeen children who were ambitiously christened, the boys including Raphaelle, Rembrandt, Titian, Rubens, and the girls being christened Angelica Kauffmann, Rosalba Carriera, and Sophonisba (after ANGUISSOLA). Raphaelle (1774–1825) painted some very fine and austere still-lifes, not at all

Dutch in feeling, but far closer to Spanish 17th-century work; and, indeed a SÁNCHEZ-COTÁN (now in San Diego Cal.) was in Philadelphia in 1820. He was the best painter of the family, but his attempt with Rembrandt Peale to run the family museum was a failure; he was unhappily married and eventually took to drink. Rembrandt (1778–1860) also painted still-life and some very fine, detailed portraits (*Rubens Peale with a Geranium Plant*, Washington, NG). He visited England in 1802–3 and worked under West and painted a number of French statesmen in Paris 1808–10 for his father's museum. He settled in New York in 1822 and was one of the founders of the National Academy (1826), but revisited Europe in 1829/30, and finally returned to Philadelphia in 1831, although he signed and dated a portrait in London in 1833. He was one of the first American artists to practise lithography and he also painted one of the best-known portraits of Washington, the so-called *Porthole Portrait* painted in 1823, twenty-four years after Washington's death. The original is now in the Capitol, Washington, in the Vice-President's room, but about eighty replicas are known. Rubens (1784–1865) and Titian the Elder (1799–1881) were also painters, but less important.

Charles Willson's brother James was a miniaturist in Philadelphia and may have been one of the first painters of still-life in America. He had seven children, five of whom were painters, but they were less eccentrically named than their cousins. There are works by one or other of the Peales in many American museums including Baltimore, Boston (thirteen in all), Detroit, New York (Met. Mus. and Hist. Soc.), Philadelphia, Richmond Va, Washington (NG and Corcoran), and Worcester Mass., and one in London (NPG).

PEARCE (Pierce), Edward (*d.*1695), was a prolific and able wood and stone carver, who worked on decorative sculpture for country houses and churches, for Wren's City churches (he made the wooden model of the copper dragon for the vane of St Mary-le-Bow), the Guildhall, St Paul's Cathedral, Hampton Court, several City Companies, and Clare Coll., Cambridge. His bust of Wren (1673, Oxford, Ashmolean) shows him with a gift for the restrained Baroque current in England, and a ready eye for liveliness of character. There are works in the Royal Coll., London (NPG and London Mus.) and Yale (CBA).

PECHSTEIN, Max (1881–1955), was one of the leading German Expressionists. He was trained in Dresden and in 1906 became a member of the BRÜCKE group, founded in the previous year by KIRCHNER, SCHMIDT-ROTTLUFF and others. In 1907–8 he went to Italy and Paris and in 1914 was able to go to the South Seas, to the island of Palau, where his works were very obviously influenced by GAUGUIN's example. In 1915 he was arrested by the Japanese and sent to Nagasaki, returning to Germany via New York. He served in the German Army until 1918. In 1934 he was expelled from the Prussian Academy and forbidden to exhibit: after 1945, like Schmidt-Rottluff, he became a Professor in Berlin. There are works in several German museums as well as Baltimore, Los Angeles and Toledo Ohio. His autobiography was published posthumously.

PEDIGREE *see* PROVENANCE.

PEETERS, Clara (1594–after 1657?), was an important Flemish woman painter, who introduced the Dutch type of BREAKFAST PIECE into Antwerp at a very early date. She must have been precocious, as she signed and dated a painting in 1608 (private coll.); others dated 1611 and 1612 are in Madrid (Prado) and Karlsruhe. The Prado picture and one in Oxford (Ashmolean) have self-portraits as reflections on pewter vessels. She visited Amsterdam in 1612 and perhaps Haarlem *c.*1612/17. She is said to have dated a painting (now lost) 1657, and this is the last record of her.

PEINTURE À L'ESSENCE *see* DEGAS.

PELLEGRINI, Giovanni Antonio (1675–1741), was a Venetian decorative painter who was a pupil of Sebastiano RICCI and one of the most important of TIEPOLO's predecessors. Like PITTONI, he worked for many foreign patrons and travelled widely. He was first recorded as a painter in 1703 and soon after this he married the sister of Rosalba CARRIERA, who mentions him in her diary on several occasions. In 1707 Lord Manchester went on an embassy to Venice; he commissioned a picture to celebrate the event from CARLEVARIS and brought Pellegrini and Marco RICCI back to London with him in 1708. Pellegrini soon had considerable success and became a Director of Kneller's Academy in 1711. VERTUE says that Pellegrini 'painted prodigious quick, had a very noble and fruitfull invention' which may be seen in the decorations at Kimbolton Castle (now a school), done for Lord Manchester, or in the decorations at Castle Howard (1709, mostly destroyed in 1941). In these decorative series Pellegrini shows that he was a true precursor of Tiepolo in the lightness and gaiety of his touch which contrasts with the duller history painting of Pittoni. In 1713 he went to Germany and Flanders, returning to England in 1719 when, according to Vertue, he was less successful because Marco Ricci had sent for his uncle Sebastiano, who was generally agreed to be a better painter. (Vertue: 'Richi . . . Excelling of Pelegrini in every respect . . .') Pellegrini also painted a splendid ceiling for the Bank of France (since destroyed) in Paris, decorated the Great Hall in the Mauritshuis in The Hague (1718), and worked in Prague, Dresden and Vienna. There is a sketch of 1710 in London (V&A) which may represent his design for the cupola of St Paul's for which, according to Vertue, 'he made several designs and a moddle for painting the Cupolo at St Paul's for which he was paid tho' he had not the cupolo to paint': *see* THORNHILL. There are works by him in Barnard Castle (Bowes Mus.), Berlin, Birmingham (Gall. and Barber Inst.), Boston, Cleveland Ohio, Dresden, Dublin, The Hague, Leeds (*Hector* from Kimbolton), London (NG), Oxford (Ashmolean), Paris (Louvre), Toledo Ohio, Vienna and elsewhere.

PEÑA, *see* DIAZ de la Peña.

PENCIL in 18th-century usage means 'brush' and *Pencilling* means BRUSHWORK. The modern lead pencil, which is a compressed mixture of clay and graphite in a wooden casing, contains no lead. It was invented by N. J. CONTÉ in 1790.

PENCZ, Georg (*c.*1500–50), was a German painter first recorded in the Nuremberg Guild in 1523. About two years later, along with the engravers B. and H. S. BEHAM, he was banished from the city for expressing anarchistic and atheistic ideas. He may have been a pupil of DÜRER and, like him, was profoundly influenced by Venetian art. His best works are his portraits, which are very like those of AMBERGER; that is, a combination of Dürer and Venice. Pencz almost certainly visited Italy, and may have studied in Rome, since his mythological pictures show the influence of Raphael, while a ceiling painting in Nuremberg seems to derive from GIULIO Romano's work at Mantua. In the 1540s his portraits are less obviously Italianate and probably owe something to Holbein and Massys, both of whom he is known to have copied. He was also active as an engraver, and some copper-engravings signed G. P. are dated between 1534 and 1547 (*see* KLEINMEISTER). There are pictures by him in Berlin, Brunswick, Cologne, Copenhagen, Darmstadt, Dresden, Dublin, Florence and Munich, as well as Nuremberg.

PENSIERO (Ital. a thought). A sketch, BOZZETTO, MAQUETTE.

'PENSIONANTE DEL SARACENI' *see* SARACENI.

PENTIMENTO (Ital. *pentirsi*, to repent). When a painter changes his mind in the course of a picture and alters, say, the position of a leg, it sometimes happens that as the paint ages the old form will begin to show through in a ghostly way; this ghost is a *pentimento*. It is sometimes inferred that, because there are *pentimenti* visible, a painting must be an original – since it shows the artist changing his mind – and not a copy. The validity of this argument is open to doubt. The word may also be used to denote several attempts to fix a contour with precision in a drawing, as is clearly visible in Cézanne's drawings.

PERMEKE, Constant (1886–1952), was a Belgian Expressionist painter. He was the son of a painter, and was trained in Bruges before settling in the village of Laethem St Martin, an artists' colony, where he met several other Expressionists. He lived there 1902–12 and was called up in 1914, but was wounded in the same year and spent the rest of World War I in England. About 1920 he was slightly influenced by Cubism, but on the whole he was a latter-day MILLET whose deep sympathy for farmers and fishermen is evident in his best work. In 1929 he settled at Jabbeke, near Ostend, where his house is now a museum. Other works by him are in Antwerp, Brussels, Edinburgh, London (Tate), Rotterdam and São Paulo.

PERMOSER, Balthasar (1651–1732), was the leading Late Baroque sculptor in Dresden, where he helped to create the Zwinger. He was trained in Salzburg *c*.1663 before going to Italy for fourteen years. He arrived there *c*.1675 and went to Venice, Rome, Florence and other cities; in Florence he carved the façade of S. Gaetano (*c*.1684) and worked for the Grand Duke Cosimo III, who tried to secure him as Court Sculptor. Permoser, however, went to Dresden as Court Sculptor in 1689. He spent the rest of his life there, except for several trips to Berlin, a visit to Italy in 1697/8 and another in 1725, when, at the age of 74, he walked to Rome. He returned in 1728. As might be expected from his strong Italian leanings, he was much influenced by Bernini, but, like the other Northerners PUGET, DONNER and SCHLÜTER, he introduced an element of restrained classicism – though this is not very obvious in his most famous work, the *Apotheosis of Prince Eugene* (1718–21, Vienna, Lower Belvedere). Most of his Dresden works were damaged in 1945, but have been restored. There are others in Bautzen, Freiberg (Saxony), and a small *Deposition* is in London (V&A).

PERRÉAL, Jean (*c*.1455–1530), used to be identified with the MASTER OF MOULINS. He was Court Painter to the Bourbons and later worked for Charles VIII of France and his successors, Louis XII and François I. He was in Italy several times 1499/1505 and in London in 1514, to paint Princess Mary Tudor and supervise her new dresses. He also designed tombs, notably those (unexecuted) at Brou (1509–12). The most important attributions to him are the *Louis XII* in the Royal Coll. and a miniature in London (BM).

PERRONNEAU, Jean Baptiste (1715?–83), was a French portrait painter in oil and pastel. From *c.*1755 he journeyed all over Europe, dying in Amsterdam. He was the only rival to LATOUR as a pastellist in the later 18th century, and the popular *Girl with a Kitten* (1745, London, NG) shows his charm.

PERSPECTIVE. A quasi-mathematical system for the representation of three-dimensional objects in spatial recession on a two-dimensional surface, i.e. for the creation of an independent pictorial space as a microcosm of nature. As normally practised now, perspective is a sophisticated version of the COSTRUZIONE LEGITTIMA invented in the early 15th century, perhaps by Brunelleschi, and improved by ALBERTI, UCCELLO and PIERO della Francesca. The basic assumption of all perspective systems is that parallel lines never meet, but that they appear to do so; and that, further, all parallel lines going in any one direction meet at a single point on the horizon known as a Vanishing Point (VP). The early systems were based on a single, central Vanishing Point; all other parallels were automatically assumed to be parallel to the picture plane and therefore exempt from the assumption that they must meet at some point in the distance. This system is perfectly satisfactory as an aesthetic system, i.e. for the creation of an independent order of reality, a picture-world distinct from the real world; but it is inadequate for an exact representation of physical reality. In order to obtain this greater naturalism – with all the possibilities of illusionism it implies – a system was evolved which uses two VPs on the horizon, and more if necessary to obtain up-hill and down-dale effects. A further refinement is the use of Measuring Points, which allow of the exact representation of objects to scale. All this can be learnt by any moderately mathematically-minded art student in a few hours; for this very reason, many artists are no longer interested in verisimilitude of space and prefer either to renounce the representation of the third dimension altogether (as most abstract artists do), or else to create a spatial illusion of their own, stressing the independence of the world created by the artist from the laws which govern appearance in the physical world.

Aerial Perspective deals with the changes in tone and colour values which are observable in objects receding from the spectator. Because of the density of the atmosphere all tone contrasts are muted and all colours tend towards blue in proportion to their distance from the observer. Thus, mountains in the background are always bluish. The difference between the atmospheres of Northern Europe and the Mediterranean accounts for the greater interest in aerial perspective to be found in the North, particularly among the Impressionists.

PERUGINO (*c.*1445/50–1523), may have been a pupil of PIERO della Francesca late in the 1460s, after which he went to Florence and probably worked in the shop of VERROCCHIO, where in the early 1470s LEONARDO was also active. He was in Rome in 1479 and is recorded in the 1481 contract for the frescoes in the Sistine Chapel (along with BOTTICELLI, GHIRLANDAIO and Cosimo ROSSELLI), where his *Charge to St Peter* demonstrates his qualities of simplicity, order and clearly articulated composition. He seems to have been the leader of the team. The influence of his friend SIGNORELLI strengthened his draughtsmanship, that of Flemings like MEMLINC suggested the landscape background for his portraits as well as their general composition, and to the persistence of Piero's influence is due the use of architectural and landscape settings for his figure compositions. The *Pietà* (Florence, Accad.) set centrally in a receding arcade, and above all the *Cruxifixion with Saints* (Florence, S.M. Maddalena de' Pazzi), a fresco of 1496 with an extensive landscape linking the three apparent divisions of the wall, are perfect examples of his quiet, pietistic art, with gentle, rather sentimental figures with drooping postures, tip-tilted heads, and mild rounded faces – a type he repeated all his life with, in his later years, dull and routine repetitiveness.

From *c.*1500 to *c.*1504 RAPHAEL was a pupil in his shop and may have helped with the fresco cycle in the Sala del Cambio at Perugia, Perugino's largest (but not best) work in fresco. Raphael's own early work in S. Severo at Perugia was later – after his death in 1520 – completed by his master. In 1506 Perugino retired to Perugia, since his style was now hopelessly outmoded in Florence, where, however, it had served to counter-balance the confusion of late Quattrocento style. It was to be the herald of the High Renaissance.

Apart from Rome, Florence and Perugia there are works by him in Baltimore, Brussels, Cambridge (Fitzwm), Cerqueto nr Perugia (the earliest work, of 1478), Chicago, Detroit, Edinburgh, Frankfurt, Liverpool, London (NG), Lyons, Munich, Nancy, New York (Met. Mus.), Paris (Louvre), Philadelphia, Vienna and elsewhere.

PESELLINO (*c.*1422–57), is confused in the old sources with his own grandfather, Giuliano Pesello, who was a painter and probably taught Pesellino; he was certainly influenced by Fra Filippo Lippi and the only documented work by Pesellino, the *Trinity with Saints* (1455–7, London, NG, part on loan from the Royal Coll.), was in fact completed after his death by Fra Filippo's workshop. There are works attributed to him in Berlin, Boston (Gardner), Cambridge Mass. (Fogg), Dresden, Florence (Uffizi and Sta Margherita), London (Courtauld Inst.), Milan (Poldi-Pezzoli), New York (Met. Mus. and Hist. Soc.), Paris (Louvre), Philadelphia (Johnson), Toledo Ohio, Washington (NG), Worcester Mass, Yale (Univ.) and elsewhere.

PETERS, The Revd Matthew William (1741/2–1814), was a pupil of HUDSON and went to Rome, where he studied under BATONI, in 1762. He returned to Dublin *c.*1765 and went on to London, where he painted portraits influenced by Reynolds. He was back in France and Italy, 1772–6, and must have seen works by GREUZE, whose simpering *demi-vierges* were imitated by him. He became an RA in 1777, the year in which he exhibited *A Lady in Bed*, which was widely attacked as indecent and was held against him when he entered the church in 1781. In 1782 (as the Revd W. Peters) he exhibited the sentimental and immensely popular *Angel Bearing the Spirit of a Dead Child*. He resigned from the RA in 1788, but continued as its chaplain, painting for his own pleasure and working for Boydell's Shakespeare Gallery 1786–90, e.g. *Juliet* (Washington, Folger Library). A scheme for an institute of Fine Arts at Oxford University under his direction came to nothing. Belfast and Nottingham have works.

PETO, John Frederick (1854–1907), was an American painter of *trompe l'oeil* still-life. He was born in Philadelphia, where there was a still-life tradition established by the PEALE family, and was influenced by HARNETT, six years his senior, and by the realism of EAKINS. In fact, many of Peto's pictures were given false Harnett signatures, but it seems that Peto's still-life was less elegant and glossy than Harnett's, and he specialized in the letter-rack picture, with a board, criss-crossed by tapes, holding newspaper cuttings, letters and other odds and ends. He sold many of these to shops and offices as *trompe l'oeil* decorations. Boston has several characteristic examples.

PEVSNER, Antoine (1886–1962), was GABO's elder brother. He was born in Russia and trained in Kiev, where the Byzantine works had a profound effect on him. In 1911 he went to Paris and was influenced by Cubist ideas, but in 1914 he joined his brother in Norway and in 1917 they returned to Revolutionary Russia, hoping for a revolution in the arts. He was made a professor and worked with TATLIN and MALEVICH, going on to CONSTRUCTIVISM. The growing dissatisfaction of the Soviet authorities with abstract art drove him back to Paris in 1923. There are works by him there (Mus. d'Art Moderne) and also in London (Tate) and New York (M of MA).

PFORR, Franz (1788–1812), was the friend of OVERBECK, with whom he founded the *Lukasbrüderschaft* in Vienna in 1809. This was later to become the NAZARENE group of German artists in Rome, where both Pforr and Overbeck went in 1810. Pforr died at 24, but there are works by him in Berlin, Frankfurt and Vienna (Akad.).

PHOTOGRAPHIC ETCHING *see* ENGRAVING 2(c).

PIAZZETTA, Giovanni Battista (1683–1754), was a Venetian painter, son of a woodcarver, who studied under G. M. CRESPI in Bologna and was probably influenced by him to take up genre subjects. He settled in Venice by 1711, and after his death his family petitioned the State for a pension, claiming that his 'constant studies and his pursuit of glory rather than gain had reduced him to poverty and hastened his death'. His works are comparatively few, and though appearing to be executed with speed and facility were the product of careful deliberation and infinite pains. He made many drawings for collectors and as book-illustrations in order to support his family; his work was much influenced by Rembrandt's etchings and his paintings evolve from Baroque contrasts of chiaroscuro towards a freer and more fluid Rococo handling. Piazzetta's influence on the young TIEPOLO was very great and it was Tiepolo who completed the transition to the Rococo. Most of his paintings are in Venice, including his only ceiling decoration, the *Glory of S. Dominic*, painted before 1727 (SS. Giovanni e Paolo). Other works are in Birmingham, Boston, Cambridge (Fitzwm), Cologne, Cortona (S. Filippo), Chicago, Cleveland Ohio, Detroit, Dresden, Dublin, Florence (Uffizi), Hartford Conn., London (NG), Los Angeles, Milan (Brera), New York (Met. Mus.), Padua, Paris (Louvre), Parma, Prague, Rome (Gall. Naz., Accad. di S. Luca), Springfield Mass., Stockholm, Vicenza, Washington (NG) and elsewhere. His drawings are well represented in the Royal Coll. at Windsor Castle.

PICABIA, Francis (1879–1953), was born in Paris. He has some claim to have painted the first abstract picture – a watercolour of 1908/9, now in Paris (Mus. d'Art Moderne) – which would antedate KANDINSKY. In 1912 he joined the SECTION D'OR Cubists, subsequently running through DADAISM and, from 1924, SURREALISM: he also painted anatomically precise nudes for sale in Algiers. He visited America on several occasions and exhibited at the ARMORY SHOW; with DUCHAMP he was a founder of American DADA. There are works in Chicago and Leeds as well as Paris (Mus. d'Art Moderne).

PICASSO, Pablo Ruiz y (1881–1973), was born in Malaga, the son of an art teacher. The boy showed exceptional talent at an early age, and the artistic current flowing into Barcelona (where the family had settled) from France and Northern Europe stimulated him into trying out the personal languages of Munch, Toulouse-Lautrec, Renoir and other northerners. In 1900 he visited Paris for a short time, and returned in 1901 to join the cohort of young Bohemians attracted to the capital by the stimulating and exciting atmosphere then prevailing in the arts. Lautrec, Gauguin, van Gogh, Steinlen, late Impressionism flit across his canvases in a bewildering medley and leave behind a passion for blue, which became the dominant colour for his portrayal of the squalid tragedy of the Paris streets – the beggar, the harlot, the sick child, the hungry. Through this welter of contemporary influences ran the steady current of the things he had grown up with: the elongated forms of Catalan Gothic sculpture and Italian Mannerism, the simplified colour and straightforward approach of Velázquez, Zurbarán and Goya. These also inform his pictures of actors, mountebanks and harlequins, where tender fawns and pinks replace the earlier drab and sad colours. Until then nothing unusual had transpired: even his interest in Iberian sculpture in 1906, and the radical simplification of form and colour it led to, gave little hint of the position when the FAUVE outbreak was at its height. Picasso took no part in this. He was questioning the whole basis of painting and was therefore unable to follow still further the road from Impressionism to the dissolution of form and its translation into colour and imaginative feeling. Picasso's reply to Matisse's 'Composition is the art of arranging in a decorative manner the various elements at the painter's disposal for the expression of his feelings' was to turn to Cézanne, whose *petite sensation* never had any truck with pure decoration and whose composition was based on the rigorous discipline of the relations of form and space on a two-dimensional surface. Picasso's *Demoiselles d'Avignon* (New York, M of MA) of 1907 was begun in the vein of his harlequin series, but ended as a semi-abstract composition, in which the forms of the nudes and their accessories are broken up into planes compressed into a shallow space. The influence of Negro sculptures, which first appears in the *Demoiselles*, also fitted in with his quest for the expression of form and helped, by the bizarre nature of their forms, to release him from the tyranny of the representational tradition in art. In 1907 he met BRAQUE, who had drifted into the Fauve circle and out of it again, and by 1909 they found that they faced the same problems and were striving to solve them in the same way. Both rejected decorative arabesques and bright, sensuous colour and were striving to devise a pictorial language which would define volumes and their relationships without destroying the flat surface of the picture, and without descending to the imitation of accidental and superficial appearances. Together they evolved what is now called Analytical Cubism.

By 1912, colour had begun to creep back among the greys, olive greens and drab browns, and actual objects – a piece of cane seating, a newspaper heading – were imported so as to stress by their complaisant acquiescence in becoming an element in a design the modest role of Nature in the Ideal, and also to serve as an example of the way in which nature may be recreated. COLLAGE was a natural extension of this. Objects could be literally reconstituted with bits of wood, wire, paper and string, their forms distorted by the artist into a flat composition whose inherent third dimension is alluded to at the same time as it is suppressed – although Picasso, having started this hare, did not course it, any more than he did that of SURREALISM, born from the juxtaposition of recognizable objects and reconstituted forms.

At the moment when the War broke out in 1914, Braque and Picasso were separated by a quarrel (the breach was never healed) and both had consistently held aloof from the host of minor artists who had by now realized that Cubism was the coming thing and had climbed aboard the bandwagon – Gleizes, Metzinger, Delaunay, Marcoussis, Duchamp-Villon, Picabia, La Fresnaye and Derain. From 1915 he had shown his interest in Ingres's drawings by precise and restrainedly stylized pencil drawings, and his connection with the Diaghileff Russian Ballet in Rome in 1917 led to works showing a return to traditional vision, with parallel works in a glitteringly sophisticated Cubist idiom. Finally, contact with the Antique and with Roman classicism ushers in a series of paintings and drawings of monumental female nudes, at first almost motionless and then, by 1923, galvanized into terrifying movement which distorts them into frightening caricatures before dissolving them, via calligraphic curves and lines, into the convulsive and repellent distortions of the *Three Dancers* of 1925 (London, Tate). For the next ten years Picasso developed these distorted and disquieting figures through what is generally called the Metamorphic phase, in which he was perhaps somewhat influenced by Miró and Tanguy. By the early 1930s he was rather taking the wind out of Matisse's sails with a series of nudes – odalisques almost – which combine brilliance of colour with flat pattern of a violent intensity; soon afterwards, he began the series of bull-fighting subjects which culminated in the imagery present in *Guernica* (1937, Madrid, Prado). This huge composition, inspired by the Spanish Civil War, expresses in complicated iconography and personal symbolical language, comprehensible after careful study, the artist's abhorrence of the violence and beastliness of war. This dark mood persisted in the dislocated forms and frightening imagery of his work during the Second World War. He remained in Paris during the occupation and gradually acquired by his aloofness the stature of a symbol of resistance, but from 1946 to his death he lived mainly in the South of France. During these years he experimented with ceramics and also painted a large mural for UNESCO in Paris.

No man has changed more radically the nature of art. Like Giotto, Michelangelo and Bernini he stands at the beginning of a new epoch. Most museums of modern art throughout the world have examples of his paintings, prints, sculpture or ceramics. His own large private collection, of his own work and that of his friends, has been given to the French state as the Musée Picasso in Paris (Hôtel Salé). The collection documents his protean changes of style throughout his life, and his very varied use of materials, ranging from the traditional oil-paint on canvas, graphic work, sculptures, collages, constructions, to his amusing pieces of 'sculpture' made from bits of bicycles and children's toys, or assemblages of metal oddments, some of which have been deprived of all spontaneity by being magniloquently cast in bronze. One quality which this lifetime hoard displays is the tendency to *horror vacui*, and also, in the very late work, a self-indulgent repetitiveness as well as a less than attractive surface.

PICKENOY (Picquenoy) *see* ELIAS.

PICTURE PLANE. The extreme front edge of the imaginary space in the picture. It lies immediately behind the glass of the frame and is the vertical plane at which the world of the spectator and of the picture make contact.

PICTURESQUE (Ital. *pittoresco*, pertaining to a painter). Originally (in the 18th century) this meant that a landscape looked as though it came straight out of a picture (by CLAUDE or Gaspar POUSSIN), but the original meaning has been reversed so that it now means that a scene is pictorially worthy to be transferred straight to canvas (it is used in this sense by the sophisticated only with a derogatory implication). In the 18th century, particularly in connection with landscape gardening, there arose a long, complicated and dreary controversy over The Picturesque (satirized by Jane Austen in 'Sense and Sensibility' and 'Northanger Abbey'), but it served some purpose in that it established a new kind of Beauty, midway between Burke's Sublime and Beautiful (this latter we would call Pretty), which was dependent for its effect on roughness, irregularity and a certain amount of deformity. The different types are contrasted in Thomson's 'Castle of Indolence':

> Whate'er Lorraine light-touched with softening hue,
> Or savage Rosa dashed, or learned Poussin drew.

The idea was greatly extended by the Romantics of the 19th century.

PIERCE *see* PEARCE.

PIERO della Francesca (de' Franceschi) (1410/20–92), long neglected, is now probably the most popular painter of the Quattrocento. This is due to the mathematical perfection of his forms and to his superb sense of interval, the whole giving a timeless and serene air to his works, increased by his pale and soft colours. A generation brought up on Cubism and the intellectual rigour of Cézanne has the right to appreciate Piero. He is first recorded in 1439, when he was in Florence with DOMENICO Veneziano, painting frescoes in Sant' Egidio which are now lost. He came from the small town of Borgo San Sepolcro (now called Sansepolcro) in Umbria, and the experience of Florentine art, in the works of Domenico Veneziano, Andrea del Castagno, Uccello and Masaccio, must have been decisive in his artistic education. In 1442 he was back in Borgo – he had a deep affection for his native place and spent as much time as possible there – and was then serving as a Town Councillor, which would indicate a certain maturity. The Compagnia della Misericordia, a charitable foundation in Borgo, commissioned a polyptych of the *Madonna della Misericordia*, showing the Madonna protecting humanity (and in particular the members of the Compagnia) under her mantle, from him in 1445 for delivery in three years: it was not finally paid for until 1462 and the execution may therefore have dragged on for years. Piero always seems to have worked with the greatest deliberation, and other cases are known of his taking several years over a work: he even seems to have developed, at Arezzo, a technique which allowed him to work slowly in fresco.

The length of time taken over the Borgo *Madonna* makes it difficult to know what his early style was like, but the *Baptism* in London (NG) is accepted as an early work, showing traces of Florentine (and Sienese) influence, yet standing for a calm and classic stillness totally opposed to all that the Florentines then sought. A *St Jerome* at Berlin, signed and dated 1450, is unfortunately too damaged for use in stylistic comparisons, but a damaged fresco of 1451 in S. Francesco at Rimini, *Sigismondo Malatesta and his Patron Saint*, shows Piero's love of symmetry and of counterchanged patterns in the two dogs. By this time he had probably painted some frescoes, now lost, in Ferrara, the influence of which is discernible in the local School. About 1452 Piero began the work on which his fame chiefly rests, the fresco cycle in the choir of S. Francesco at Arezzo depicting the story of the True Cross. The narrative is highly complicated, being based on several different accounts in the Golden Legend, and it is not made easier to follow by the fact that Piero, presumably for artistic reasons, has treated the story in a cavalier way and arranged, for example, the two battle scenes out of order in the story but facing each other at the bottom of each of the side walls, thus forming one of the symmetries he loved. The frescoes were almost unknown for centuries and suffered from neglect, but at least they were not repainted much and therefore give a good idea of Piero's mature style, and of what he owed to Domenico Veneziano and to Florence. In 1459 Piero was in Rome, by which time the Arezzo frescoes were presumably finished. The work in the Vatican which Piero is known to have done has vanished, but a *St Luke* in S.M. Maggiore is, perhaps optimistically, ascribed to him. The ascription is not made any more plausible by the fact that two of his masterpieces are likely to date from this time – the fresco of *The Resurrection* in Borgo and the diptych with the portraits of his friends and patrons the Duke and Duchess of Urbino (Florence, Uffizi). The portraits have been associated with a poem of 1465, but look stylistically rather later (*c.*1472?). They show strong influence from Flemish painting in the use of the oil technique, perhaps due to the presence of Flemish pictures in Italy. Later on, JOOS van Gent worked at Urbino. The curious *Flagellation of Christ*, which again shows Flemish influence, was also painted for Urbino. Various explanations of the subject and date have been advanced. All this time Piero was working on a large altarpiece, parts of which survive. It was commissioned for Borgo San Sepolcro in 1454 and completed fifteen years later: the centre panel was probably a *Madonna* but is now lost; on either side were *SS. Augustine, Michael, John* (?), and *Nicholas of Tolentino*, now in Lisbon, London (NG), New York (Frick Coll.), and Milan (Poldi-Pezzoli). The last two pictures Piero painted are the *Madonna with the Duke of Urbino as Donor* (Milan, Brera), known as the *Brera Madonna*, which is datable between *c.*1472 and *c.*1475, and the unfinished *Nativity* (London, NG). It is sometimes said, on exiguous evidence, that the hand (or even the head) of the Duke in the *Brera Madonna* is by BERRUGUETE. In any case, it seems clear that Piero stopped painting in the 1470s – the last document to record him as a painter is of 1478, concerning a lost fresco – although he lived on until 1492. One explanation for this is that he became increasingly interested in perspective and mathematics, for he wrote two treatises, *De prospectiva pingendi* and *De quinque corporibus regularibus*, and it is also likely that his sight failed, for he seems to have been blind in his last years. His chief pupils were PERUGINO and SIGNORELLI, both of whom reacted against his style. There are other works by him in Arezzo, Boston (Gardner), Monterchi nr Sansepolcro, Oxford (Ch. Ch.), Perugia, Sansepolcro, Urbino, Vaduz (Liechtenstein Coll.), Venice (Accad.) and Williamstown Mass.

PIERO di Cosimo (*c.*1462–1521?), was a pupil of Cosimo Rosselli and probably assisted him on his frescoes in the Sistine Chapel of the Vatican, *c.*1481. He was much influenced by Signorelli and Leonardo da Vinci and his mature works differ entirely from Rosselli's in that they are mostly rather obscure, but very poetically felt, mythologies. He was famous in his own day as a designer of the *Trionfi* processions, especially for his gruesome *Triumph of Death* of 1511. In his later years he became a recluse, living (according to Vasari) on hard-boiled eggs. There are pictures by him in Amsterdam, Berlin, Chantilly, Florence (Uffizi, Pitti, Horne Mus. and Innocenti), Hartford Conn., London (NG, Wallace Coll. and Dulwich), Munich, New York (Met. Mus.), Ottawa, Oxford, Paris (Louvre), Philadelphia (Johnson), Rome (Borghese and Gall. Naz.), Sarasota Fla, Toledo Ohio, Washington (NG), Worcester Mass., Yale and elsewhere.

PIETÀ (Ital. pity). A representation of the Dead Christ supported on His Mother's lap, with or without other mourning figures. The idea originated in 14th-century Germany (Ger. *Vesperbild*) and is an expression of Northern piety which stressed the human relationship between Christ and the Virgin, and which here drew a parallel with the Madonna holding the infant Christ on her lap. The earliest example (*c.*1320?) is at Veste Coburg. These early German works emphasize the sufferings of Christ by distortion and exaggeration: in Michelangelo's *St Peter's Pietà* (*c.*1500), for the first time, Northern expressiveness is combined with the Hellenistic qualities of form and beauty. *See* IMAGO PIETATIS.

PIETRO Berrettini da Cortona (1596–1669), painter and architect, was one of the founders of the Roman High Baroque, comparable with BERNINI in sculpture. His first works were painted for the Sacchetti family and are now in the Capitoline Gallery, Rome, along with other works of his, but he was soon taken up by the powerful Barberini family – the family of Urban VIII – for whom he painted frescoes in Sta Bibiana, Rome (1624–6), followed by his greatest work, the ceiling in the Barberini Palace (now the Galleria Nazionale, Rome). This is a huge fresco representing an *Allegory of Divine Providence and Barberini Power*, begun in 1633 and completed in 1639: a sketch for it is now exhibited with it, but its authenticity is open to doubt. The fresco is a huge illusion, like the ceilings of LANFRANCO or GUERCINO, with the central field apparently open to the sky and scores of figures seen *al di* SOTTO IN SÙ apparently coming into the room itself or floating above it. While working on this Pietro also went to Florence and began a series of similar frescoes in the Pitti Palace; he also began a series of frescoes in the Chiesa Nuova, Rome, which was not finished until 1665 (the *modello* for the cupola is now in Hartford, Conn., Wadsworth Atheneum). Towards the end of his life he devoted much of his time to architecture, but he published a treatise on painting in 1652 under a pseudonym and in collaboration. He refused invitations to both France and Spain. With the help of numerous pupils, of whom Ciro FERRI was the most important, he painted many other frescoes and easel pictures in Rome and Florence. Outside Italy there are works by him in the Royal Coll., and in Berlin, Birmingham, Bristol, Chatsworth, Edinburgh (NG), London (Dulwich), Madrid, Munich, Paris, Sarasota Fla, Toledo Ohio and Vienna.

PIGALLE, Jean Baptiste (1714–85), was a French sculptor, a pupil of LEMOYNE, who failed to win a scholarship to Rome, went at his own expense in 1736, nearly starved, and was rescued by G. Coustou II. He returned to France in

1739 and worked for churches and for Mme de Pompadour, for whom he made the *Love and Friendship* (1758) now in the Louvre (the plaster is in Baltimore). His major works include the Tomb of Maréchal de Saxe in S. Thomas, Strasbourg (1753–76), and his *Nude Voltaire* (1776) in the Institut, Paris. He also made the base of BOUCHARDON's equestrian *Louis XV*. There is a characteristic portrait bust in Cambridge (Fitzwm).

PILON, Germain (*c*.1531–90), was a French sculptor who worked in marble and bronze. His early style (e.g. in the three *Graces* of the Monument for the Heart of Henri II, 1560, Louvre) is based on the elongated, Mannerist elegance of Primaticcio's plaster decorations at Fontainebleau. Later, his work becomes more fluid and more realist at the same time; his softly flowing forms invest with poignancy the relaxed recumbent marble figures of the dead Henri II and his Queen, Catherine de' Medici, in their tomb, while above on the canopy the living figures of the monarchs are sharply characterized in bronze (1563–70, S. Denis). His marble relief of Valentine Balbiani has a strange rippling quality which stresses the dead woman's angular, skeletal forms beneath the taut skin and the loose curling hair. Pilon seeks to create emotion through the marriage of virtuosity of handling and dramatic intensity. His use of Michelangelo and Pontormo is apparent, but never obvious or derivative. He also made portrait medals and busts, chiefly of the French Royal family, during the 1570s. Most of his works are in Paris (Louvre and S. Denis), but there is a bronze bust of Charles IX in London (Wallace Coll.).

PINTORICCHIO (Pinturicchio), Bernardino (*c*.1454–1513), was active in Perugia in 1481, but before that he was probably in Rome assisting Perugino with the frescoes in the Sistine Chapel (1481/2). The influence of Perugino remained dominant for the rest of his life. His principal works are the fresco cycles in the Borgia Apartments in the Vatican (1492–*c*.1495) and in the Piccolomini Library of the Cathedral of Siena (1503–8). These are scenes from the life of Pius II Piccolomini, and include some fanciful landscapes said to be in Scotland. His numerous works include those in Baltimore (Walters), Berlin, Boston (Mus., Gardner), Cambridge (Fitzwm), Cambridge Mass. (Fogg), Cleveland Ohio, Dresden, London (NG), New York (Met. Mus.), Oxford, Paris (Louvre), Perugia, Philadelphia (Johnson), Rome (churches), San Marino Cal. (Huntington), Siena (Mus. and Cath.), Spello (Mus. and churches), Spoleto (Cath.) and Washington (NG).

PIOMBO, Sebastiano del, *see* SEBASTIANO.

PIPER, John (*b*.1903), began as an abstract painter, but turned to Romantic realism under the influence of PALMER and the earlier English topographical painters. He has always had a strong feeling for architecture, which explains his success as a topographer and stage-designer, though his feeling for devastation in his war pictures was less tragic than SUTHERLAND's. He made several stained glass windows including those at Eton and Coventry Cath. There are works in London (Tate) and New York (Met. Mus.).

PIRANESI, Giovanni Battista (1720–78), was a Venetian architect who went to Rome in 1740 and became the recorder of Roman antiquities in hundreds of etchings. His feeling for the poetry of ruins, his romantic archaeology, and his intensely dramatic exploitation of the contrasts of light and shade possible in etching exerted great influence on 18th-century architecture, and even more on the whole visual approach to Antiquity and the Decline and Fall. His most original works are the *Carceri d'Invenzione* (1749/50, reworked 1761) of imaginary and megalomaniac prisons, but he was far more famous for his *Vedute*, 135 etchings of ancient and modern Rome, published from 1745 onwards, and for his violent archaeological polemics (pro-Roman and anti-Greek). The *Vedute* continued to be printed long after his death and formed the basis of the mental image of Rome possessed by thousands who never went there, and, with PANINI, he created a lasting picture of Rome, as Canaletto and Guardi created one of Venice. In his lifetime (1771) Horace Walpole spoke of '... the sublime dreams of Piranesi, who seems to have conceived visions of Rome beyond what it boasted even in the meridian of its splendour. Savage as Salvator Rosa, fierce as Michael Angelo, and exuberant as Rubens, he has imagined scenes that would startle geometry, and exhaust the Indies to realise.'

PISANELLO, Antonio (probably 1395–1455/6), was the major Italian exponent of INTERNATIONAL GOTHIC in succession to GENTILE da Fabriano, who was very probably his master. He was trained in Verona, probably under STEFANO da Verona, and then went to Venice where he seems to have succeeded Gentile in painting a series of frescoes in the Doge's Palace (1415/22, all destroyed); he also succeeded Gentile in Rome, at the Lateran Basilica (1431/2, also destroyed). These were probably works in the International style, and the fact that he succeeded Gentile makes it seem likely that he was regarded as his heir. The earliest extant major work by Pisanello is the *Annunciation* (1423/4, Verona, S. Fermo) and in it, as in the later *St George and the Princess* (1437/8, Verona, S. Anastasia), his courtly interests and narrative gifts are clearly shown. In 1438 he made his first datable portrait medal, and it is as a medallist and draughtsman that he is best known. In 1448/9 he made a set of medals of Alfonso of Aragon, King of Naples, and he is known to have been there. The Vallardi Codex (Paris, Louvre) is one of the most important surviving collections of 15th-century drawings, and contains not only Pisanello's own drawings – studies of animals, costume, antiques, sketches for pictures and copies of other drawings – but also what seem to be drawings by pupils and by other artists kept in case they came in handy one day. His wonderful studies of animals reveal how sharp his observation was in this typical International Gothic interest, and his portraits confirm this (Bergamo and Paris). The closeness of his ties with Burgundy is demonstrated by the *Profile of a Girl* (Washington, NG) which is still undetermined between him and the Franco-Flemish School *c.*1420. The only other paintings by him are in London (NG) and some fragments of frescoes and *sinopie* rediscovered in Mantua in 1968; good sets of his medals are in London (V&A), and Washington (NG).

PISANO, Andrea (*c.*1290–1348/9), appears for the first time in 1330, when he began work on the bronze doors of the Baptistry of Florence. This implies that he was already a sculptor of some renown, and his name perhaps indicates that he was trained in Pisa. He finished the bronze doors in 1336, and the type of Gothic relief and the general disposition of the relief fields conditioned the form of GHIBERTI's first Baptistry Doors some seventy years later. The only other work associated with him is a series of reliefs, and possibly some statues, on the Campanile of Florence Cathedral, where Andrea succeeded Giotto (*d.*1337). Giotto may have designed some of the reliefs, and Andrea's bronze door certainly contains reminiscences of Giotto's work in the Peruzzi Chapel. In 1347 Andrea became head of the works at Orvieto Cath., where he was succeeded by his son Nino Pisano (*c.*1315–68?), also a sculptor, and influenced by French Gothic, by whom there is a signed *Madonna* in Florence (S. M. Novella), and a *Madonna del Latte*, perhaps the first in Italy, is attributed to him (Pisa, S. M. della Spina).

PISANO, Nicola (*c.*1220/5 or earlier–1284?) and his son, Giovanni (*c.*1245/50–after 1314), were the creators of modern sculpture, preceding such painters as GIOTTO in the 'rebirth of the arts'. They are jointly documented between 1258 and 1314 and there is a considerable body of work certainly attributable to them, either individually or in collaboration, including the four great Pulpits which are their main claim to fame. The first of these is the work of Nicola alone and is signed and dated 1260 (1259 modern style). It stands in the Baptistry at Pisa, and, by its affinity to antique sarcophagi such as the one in the Campo Santo nearby, clearly proclaims that its creator was using antique art as a model, and was attempting to create a Christian art with the realism and dignity of Late Roman sculpture, thus distinguishing it from the art of the Gothic North of Europe. The place of Nicola's birth is unknown, but there is some evidence for the view that he must have imbibed this feeling for Roman art in South Italy, where the emperor Frederick II (*d.*1250) was promoting a deliberate revival of Roman grandeur. Between 1265 and 1268 Nicola was engaged on the Pulpit in Siena Cathedral, but he had several assistants including ARNOLFO and his own young son Giovanni, who was employed on the understanding that he would come to Siena and would stay there and be patient in his work. Opinion is divided on the relative shares of these masters, since there is a noticeable increase in French Gothic influence in the relief panels with New Testament scenes and in the rest of the work. Much the same is true of the Fountain in the Piazza at Perugia, which is signed by both and dated 1278. (It was rebuilt in 1948/9.) This was Nicola's last major work, the last two pulpits being certainly by Giovanni alone. The French influence in them, as in much of his other work, has led to the hypothesis – for which there is no evidence – that he paid a visit to France at some point in his career. The pulpit in S. Andrea, Pistoia, was completed in 1301 and traditionally took four years to make. It shows what is perhaps the highest point of the French influence on Giovanni's style; for the last and greatest of the Pulpits, that in Pisa Cathedral, is considerably closer in spirit to his father and seems to show that Giovanni was working towards a new and personal synthesis of Gothic and classical elements. This pulpit was commissioned in 1302 and completed in 1310, although it is signed and dated 1311 (1310 modern style). There is also a curious and cryptic inscription alluding to the difficulties and tribulations experienced by Giovanni in the course of the work.

Giovanni was also active as an architect and worked much at Siena Cathedral, where many of the figures on the façade were carved by him (a fragment is in London, V&A). As early as 1284 he was exempted from all taxes on account of his work at the Cathedral. Other works by him include an ivory *Madonna* (*c.*1299) in Pisa Cathedral, and *Madonnas* in Padua (Arena Chapel: *c.*1305) and Prato Cathedral. Fragments of the Tomb of Margaret of Luxembourg (*d.*1311) are in Genoa (Pal. Bianco).

PISIS, Filippo de (1896–1956), was an Italian painter who worked in Ferrara and Paris. He was influenced by CHIRICO and PITTURA METAFISICA in 1918–19, but he lived in Paris 1920–40 and then based his style on the fluent, quasi-

Impressionist brushwork of Manet and GUARDI, whom he especially imitated in his views of Venice and other towns. There are works in the Modern Museums of Florence, Milan, Rome, Turin and Venice.

PISSARRO, Camille (1830–1903), was born in St Thomas in the West Indies, the son of a Creole mother and a father of Portuguese-Jewish descent. He worked as a clerk in his father's general store until in 1852 he ran away to Venezuela with a Danish painter, after which his reluctant parents resigned themselves to his becoming an artist. He arrived in Paris in 1855, in time to see the great exhibition at the World Fair (when COURBET exhibited his rejected pictures independently). Soon afterwards he met COROT, by whom he was deeply influenced, although by 1866 Corot disapproved of the way that the younger landscape painters were going, and was particularly severe about Pissarro's connection with Courbet and Manet. He met MONET in 1859, and in 1863 several of his pictures were in the SALON des Refusés. From 1866 to 1869 he worked at Pontoise on landscapes painted entirely in the open, but he could sell almost nothing and he and his family lived in the most cruel poverty. In 1870 he fled before the German invasion, first to Brittany and then to London, where eventually news reached him that his house in Louveciennes had been used as a butchery by the invaders, and his store of 200 to 300 pictures used as duckboards in the muddy garden. In 1872 Cézanne joined him in Pontoise and worked with him, with a radical effect on his own style. In 1874 he took part in the first IMPRESSIONIST Exhibition: he was the only one who exhibited in all eight, and it was he who introduced first Gauguin, then Seurat and Signac into the Impressionist exhibitions, with consequent disruption among the group. He was much influenced from 1884 by Seurat's theories of OPTICAL MIXTURE, which he used until 1888, when he declared that the method 'inhibits me and hinders the development of spontaneity of sensation'. In 1890 he exhibited in Brussels with Les XX. From 1895 the worsening of his eye trouble forced him to give up working out of doors, and he painted many town views from windows in Paris; he died blind.

His production was enormous and in all techniques – chiefly oil-painting, but he also used pastel, gouache, drawing in all media, etching and lithography. Of all the Impressionists he was the most consistent: he never compromised, he did his best to compose the bitter quarrels which broke out around him, he never blamed any for their defections, intolerance, impatience and occasional spites. In return, they gave him respect and admiration for his principles as much as for his art. There are paintings by him all over the world, in almost every museum of modern art. The largest collection of his drawings is in Oxford (Ashmolean).

His son Lucien (1863–1944) followed in his father's stylistic footsteps. He settled in England in 1890, where he founded the Eragny Press (named after his father's final home) in 1896 and exerted great influence on book-illustration and printing in this country. He was a member of the NEAC and the CAMDEN TOWN GROUP. His daughter, known as Orovida (1893–1968), was also a painter.

PITATI, Bonifazio de', *see* BONIFAZIO.

PITLOO, Antonio (1790–1837), was a Dutch landscape painter whose real name was Anton Sminck Pitlo. He studied in Paris under COROT's teacher, Victor Bertin, 1808–11, and as a prize-winner in Rome until the fall of Napoleon in

1815, when he settled in Naples. He was influenced by Turner and Bonington and his freely-handled open-air paintings of the scenery round Naples were the foundation of the School of Posillipo and the inspiration of GIGANTE. There are works in Naples (Capodimonte, Mus. di S. Martino) and Sorrento, as well as Amsterdam (Rijksmus.) and Nantes.

PITTONI, Giovanni Battista (1687–1767), was, with PELLEGRINI, one of the principal Venetian Rococo painters on a lower level than TIEPOLO. He was influenced by Tiepolo and by Sebastiano RICCI and was highly regarded by his contemporaries. He entered the Guild in Venice in 1716, and in 1758 succeeded Tiepolo as President of the newly-established Venetian Academy. Much of his work was done for German, Polish and Russian patrons and it is likely that his basic sentimentality and the brightness of his colour appealed to them. There are many works by him in Venice and others in Berlin, Cambridge (Fitzwm), Dresden, Edinburgh, Florence (Uffizi), Leicester, Liverpool, London (NG and Courtauld Inst.), Paris (Louvre), Southampton, Turin and Vicenza.

PITTURA METAFISICA (Ital. metaphysical painting) was the result of CHIRICO's dissatisfaction with the mechanical aspect of Cubism, which he experienced in Paris. In 1917, in Ferrara, he was in the Italian army and met CARRÀ, with whom he founded Pittura Metafisica. The movement did not last long, but it influenced de PISIS and MORANDI, and, more remotely, SURREALISM and MAGISCHER REALISMUS.

PLASTER CASTING is an intermediate stage in the production of a piece of sculpture which is often the last process actually to be carried out by the sculptor himself. Once his model has been cast in plaster it can be regarded as a finished work, rather fragile in nature, or it can be executed in bronze, lead, or any other metal, or, with a POINTING MACHINE, it can be mechanically reproduced in marble or stone.

Any work of sculpture which is not a piece of direct carving in some hard substance is normally carried out in clay or wax. If, say, a head has been modelled in wax it can be left at that; if in clay it will dry up and crumble to pieces unless it is either kept permanently damp or transformed into terracotta or plaster. Terracotta is really no more than baking the clay, in the same way as a common flower-pot is produced. The result is the same in texture and usually varies in colour from grey-brown to brick red. A plaster cast is rather more complicated, but the basic process is simple enough. First, a mould has to be made. The clay head is first divided into two or three parts by strips of zinc, usually stuck like a fringe round the sides of the head at ear level (figures and more complex shapes may require multi-part moulds), the purpose being to ensure that the two halves of the mould lift off easily. Some plaster of Paris is now mixed up and tinted with dye, and as soon as it is firm and creamy it is thrown at the head, so that it sticks to the whole surface and forms a coating about $\frac{1}{8}$–$\frac{1}{4}$ in. thick. This is then thickly coated with untinted plaster and left to harden, the two halves being pulled apart when the plaster has set (the head in clay often gets damaged in this process). The mould is now cleaned out and the inside brushed over with oil and soft soap to prevent the cast from sticking to it. Next, the halves of the mould are re-united and tied together and fresh plaster is poured into it from the open base, swirled around to drive it into all the crevices, and then allowed to harden. The outer waste-mould is now destroyed by chipping it away with mallet and chisel, the purpose of the thin layer of tinted plaster being to warn the sculptor when he is nearing the surface of the cast. When all the plaster mould has been removed the finished cast is revealed and it can then be left white, painted or bronzed over, or handed to the bronze-founder or mason for reproduction in bronze or marble. *See* BRONZE and POINTING MACHINE.

PLASTICITY. The quality of appearing three-dimensional. A painting is said to have great plasticity (or plastic values) if it gives the impression that the figures are fully modelled and are capable of moving freely in the pictorial space. Plasticity is often obtained by emphasizing the tonal contrasts and by keeping the greater part of the picture in shadow. Confusingly, the *plastic arts* are the various forms of sculpture. *See also* VALORI PLASTICI.

PLATE MARK. The indentation made by printing an intaglio plate on paper (*see* ENGRAVING 2, *Intaglio*).

PLEIN AIR (Fr. open air). The feeling that a picture really conveys the sensation of the open air, a quality much sought by the Impressionists. In a more restricted sense it applies to landscapes actually painted out of doors, with the intention of catching this quality. This practice is relatively recent, at least as far as finished pictures are concerned (but *see* CLAUDE), and it was this concern for a non-aesthetic quality which underlies the remark said to have been made by Degas, that Monet's pictures always made him turn up his coat collar.

PLEYDENWURFF, Hans (*c.*1420–72), was the major Nuremberg painter immediately before WOLGEMUT and DÜRER. He became a citizen there in 1457, and introduced the realism of the Netherlands, especially that of BOUTS. In 1462 he completed the altarpiece for the high altar of S. Elizabeth in Breslau (now called Wroclaw), where fragments still remain. He may also have worked in Cracow. His son Wilhelm (*d.*1494) was also a painter and woodcut maker, and worked in the shop of Wolgemut, who married Pleydenwurff's widow.

POCHADE (Fr.). A sketch, usually a small one in oils, made in front of some actual scene with the intention of working up a large picture from it.

POINTILLISM *see* OPTICAL MIXTURES.

POINTING MACHINE. A mechanical device for reproducting a PLASTER cast in stone or marble without the exercise of any artistic skill on the part of the carver. It was originally developed by the ancient Greeks, but was perfected in the 18th and 19th centuries and became very popular among academic sculptors of the later 19th century, since it allows the sculptor to work in clay or wax and leave all the dirty work to professional masons. The whole idea is repugnant to most modern sculptors, who feel that the form taken by the finished work should be conditioned by the material from which it is carved (e.g. a carving in wood ought to take account of the grain); for this reason most modern sculptors prefer to carve direct, working only from a sketch and not even using a model made of clay, which would be unglyptic.

A pointing machine works by triangulation from three points selected on the surface of a full-size model – e.g. top of the head, tip of the nose, cheekbone – and these are measured against a given frame, usually of wood, and repeated on the marble block, so that the carver can cut to the depth measured on the machine. Further points can then be measured against the original three. Normally, a skin of stone is left, so that the sculptor himself can give the final touches. Several plaster models, with the metal 'points' still in them, are preserved in the CANOVA museum at Possagno near Treviso. Any number of marbles can be carved from such a cast.

POLIAKOFF, Serge (1906–69), was born in Moscow, of a well-off family. He emigrated in 1919 and for many years earned a living as a guitarist, settling in Paris and beginning to paint in 1930. He worked in London at Chelsea and the Slade School 1935–7 and then returned to Paris, meeting KANDINSKY in 1937 and DELAUNAY in 1938. From then on he painted abstract pictures, and, later, was influenced by the more mathematical art of MALEVICH. He also made colour lithographs.

POLLAIUOLO (Pollaiolo, Pollajuolo), Antonio (*c*.1432–98) and Piero (*c*.1441–96), were brothers who ran one of the most advanced and successful workshops in Florence in the second half of the 15th century. They worked as painters, sculptors, engravers, goldsmiths and designers of embroidery, and their knowledge of anatomy and the new technique of oil-painting, together with the study they made of the problems of representing violent action, placed them at the head of the scientific painters immediately preceding Leonardo. It is now customary to assume that all the best work was done by Antonio, and all the bad by Piero. This view receives considerable support from the fact that documented work by Piero – a set of *Virtues* in Florence, Uffizi (one other was by BOTTICELLI), and an altar-piece (1483) in San Gimignano – is very poor. On the other hand, a signed engraving by Antonio of a *Battle of the Nude Gods* is of very high quality indeed, and fully justifies the praise early lavished on him as a draughtsman and anatomist; yet no painting can be certainly ascribed to him. The influence of DONATELLO and of Andrea del CASTAGNO is paramount in their work, and Piero (not Antonio) is said to have been Castagno's pupil for a short time. Their most ambitious works are the *S. Sebastian* (1475, London, NG) and the Tombs of Popes Sixtus IV (1493) and Innocent VIII (1492–8), both in St Peter's. Other works are in Berlin, Florence (Uffizi, Bargello, Cathedral Mus., S. Miniato and Villa Gallina), London (NG and BM), Milan (Poldi-Pezzoli), Naples, Staggia nr Siena, Turin and Yale.

POLLOCK, Jackson (1912–56), the chief American exponent of ACTION PAINTING, made studies for his apparently unpremeditated works, done on continuous lengths of canvas tacked to the floor, and later cut up with selective care. He abandoned the use of brushes in 1947, pouring the paint straight on to the canvas, but in 1953 he began to employ brushes again. He said of his paintings (1951): 'I don't work from drawings or colour sketches. My painting is direct . . . I want to express my feelings rather than illustrate them. I have a general notion as to what I am about. I *can* control the flow of paint: there is no accident, just as there is no beginning and no end.' He used metallic paints and ordinary commercial synthetic enamel and plastic paint, with results that are already unfortunate. There are examples in London (Tate), Rio de Janeiro and many US museums.

POLYCHROMATIC SCULPTURE is sculpture which, like most sculpture before the 16th century, has been painted in naturalistic colours to heighten its lifelike effect.

POLYMER *see* ACRYLIC.

POLYPTYCH. A picture or relief, usually an altarpiece, which is made up of two or more separate panels. Two panels form a diptych, three a triptych, five a pentaptych; more than three are usually called simply a polyptych. A typical Italian 14th/15th-century polyptych consists of a large central panel of the *Madonna*, with perhaps two *Saints* on either side and an *Annunciation* on top. The PREDELLA would then consist of narrative scenes from the Lives of Saints 1 and 2, with a scene from the Life of Christ – perhaps the *Adoration of the Magi* – in the middle and then scenes from the Lives of Saints 3 and 4.

POMPIER (Fr. Fireman, pompous). *L'art pompier* is a peculiarly frigid and pompous form of NEOCLASSICISM, deriving mainly from the works of CANOVA and DAVID. The word is not defined by Larousse, though it is mentioned as in use in a literary sense by 1888. Probably, however, the nickname dates back to the Romantic period, and is said to be derived from the custom, prevalent in the academy and in the studios of painters like David, of posing the nude male model wearing a fireman's helmet, as an approximation to classical Greek heroes (cf. David's *Sabines*, 1799). By extension, and because of its connection with 'pompous', it became a term of generalized abuse.

PONTATA. An Italian word, meaning the amount of wall that can be plastered or painted from a scaffolding (*ponte*) at one time – i.e. a band about 6–8 feet high and stretching across a wall. In FRESCO painting these horizontal joints, not to be confused with *giornate*, clearly indicate the different levels of scaffolding used in a cycle.

PONT-AVEN is a small town in Brittany where GAUGUIN lived, on and off, between 1886 and 1890. There he met BERNARD and SÉRUSIER and the ideas behind SYNTHETISM and the NABIS were promulgated.

PONTORMO, Jacopo (1494–1556), was born at Pontormo, near Empoli. He went to Florence and was influenced by Leonardo, Piero di Cosimo and Albertinelli, before working under Andrea del Sarto *c.*1512, when he met ROSSO, with whom he was to be one of the creators of MANNERISM. He was working on his own by about 1513, in S. M. Novella and SS. Annunziata in Florence, and in 1518 he painted the *Madonna*, still in S. Michele Visdomini, Florence, which is one of the first Mannerist pictures: profoundly influenced still by Andrea del Sarto, but with a new unease, an agitation which sharply distinguishes it from the complacency of Andrea's Madonnas. Pontormo was a profoundly religious painter and this probably underlies the forms he chose. He came to the notice of the Medici family and was commissioned by them to decorate their villa at Poggio a Caiano (1521) which he did with a gay and light fresco. His next frescoes were the Passion cycle in the Certosa near Florence (1522–5), disturbing, thoroughly Mannerist, and containing such un-Florentine features as borrowings from Dürer, whose angularities of form expressed deeply-felt religious ideas. While working on these frescoes Pontormo was assisted by BRONZINO, who was more or less his adopted son, though a totally different kind of artist. What is perhaps his supreme masterpiece, and one of the central pictures in the development of early Mannerism, is the *Deposition* painted about 1525 as the altarpiece for a chapel in Sta Felicita, Florence, where there are other frescoes by Pontormo and Bronzino. Here the darkness of the chapel probably dictated the very light tone and bright colours, but the crowding and agitation of the figures powerfully reinforce the direct emotional effect of the sharp, pale colours. In the drawing the influence of Michelangelo is patent, and this was to become more marked after 1530 when

Pontormo was in contact with Michelangelo; indeed, the composition itself is based on Michelangelo's St Peter's *Pietà*. Little is known about his later years, principally because the frescoes in S. Lorenzo, on which he worked 1546–56, have all gone and are known only through the drawings. He was a great draughtsman even in an age of great draughtsmen, and there is a huge collection of his drawings in Florence (Uffizi). His character was strange, sensitive, withdrawn and highly neurotic: his Diary (1555–6) shows him obsessed with his work, his solitariness (often shunning even Bronzino), and above all the state of his bowels. There are works in Amsterdam (Rijksmus.), Baltimore, Carmignano nr Florence, Chicago, Dijon, Dublin, Empoli nr Florence, Florence (Uffizi, Pitti, Accad., Pal. Vecchio, Medici Mus. and Innocenti Mus.), Frankfurt, Hanover, Leningrad, London (NG), Lucca, Malibu Cal. (Getty Mus.), Milan (Castello), Munich, Naples, Oxford (Ch. Ch.), Paris (Louvre and Jacquemart-André), Philadelphia (Johnson), Rome (Borghese and Gall. Naz.), San Francisco, Sansepolcro, Vienna, Washington (NG) and Yale.

Pop Art is based on the acceptance and use of artefacts, mass advertising and press media, and products of modern life (i.e. Pop Culture) as valid art forms in themselves, and, subjected to various transformations which increase their impact without destroying their character, as material for further artistic creation. Photographs, posters, advertisements, strip-cartoons, packaging; objects of everyday life such as furniture, machinery, cars, washbasins, quilts, stuffed animals; the transmogrification in three dimensions by means of coloured plastics of sausages, tomatoes, sandwiches, typewriters; the representation in bronze – either left as itself, or painted realistically – of such things as beer cans or apples; the painted imitations of tins of soup: all is grist to the Pop artists' mill, since no aspect of modern life is excluded as an art form.

Its origins are complex. Cubist COLLAGES with real newspapers or cane seats; PICABIA's 'object portraits'; brand-name wafers used by PICASSO in 1914, and biscuits and matchboxes used by CHIRICO in 1916–17; Stuart DAVIS; the Surrealists' FOUND OBJECTS of the 1930s; the ready-mades of DADA, in particular of DUCHAMP; Léger's flat, impersonal handling, extolling machines, and his enthusiasm for window dressing, or the plastic quality of manufactured objects, as materials for artists; BACON's use of photographs; Cinerama, television and the wide-screen close-up as prototypes for environmental art and the huge-scale detail; the composer John Cage's distinction between accidental and chosen sounds transferred to art, since the artist may be inspired by casual combination of forms or by the deliberate selection of commonplace and cliché aspects of life, and actions may themselves become works of art, as in 'Happenings', although these tend to be more destructive than constructive.

Two independent streams are discernible. The English stream came first, during the 1950s (Lawrence Alloway appears to have coined the term Pop Art in about 1955/6), the main originating artists being PAOLOZZI, Richard HAMILTON, and Magda Cordell, later joined by a second wave including R. Smith, Wm Green, Roger Coleman, Wm Denny and Peter Blake; a third wave includes Barrie Bates ('Billy Apple'), Derek Boshier, David HOCKNEY, the American R. B. KITAJ, P. Caulfield, N. Toynton, Allen Jones and Peter Phillips, although this wave also contains artists notably more subjective in approach, with overtones of the erotic, the romantic, and the optical illusion (leading to OP ART).

American Pop Art appeared mainly in the 1960s and is more dependent on Duchamp. It uses hard-edge techniques and colours of commercial-art origin (but never of the glossy-magazine type, only of bill-board and cheap journalism), collage and assembly of objects. It is rarely romantic, often humorous, sometimes macabre or scabrous, always close to its source in artefacts and unsophisticated mass-media. Its chief protagonists are Andy WARHOL, LICHTENSTEIN, James Rosenquist, WESSELMANN and OLDENBURG, and its originators (who are less strictly Pop than their successors) are Jasper JOHNS and RAUSCHENBERG. In California, its other main centre, it could have developed independently of East Coast forms, as a reaction against ABSTRACT IMPRESSIONISM, which was East Coast in origin, but had swept all before it across the Bay. The formative influence was Kienholz, whose assemblages of detritus, arranged anecdotally, seem to point a bitter allegory on the nastiness beneath the glossy surface of modern urban life. In such artists as Bengston, Mel Ramos, Wayne Thiebaud and Ruscha it developed rapidly and quite differently from the East Coast branch. One of the characteristics of much of Pop Art is that it is suitable only, and appears to have been designed only, for museums and the like. Few private collectors could expect to house rooms of bizarre furniture, or giant plastic pouffes such as Oldenburg makes, or Marjorie Strider's 10-ft striped styrofoam clouds hanging three deep from the ceiling. In this it resembles much of Abstract Impressionism, which also tended to produce pictures from 6 to 14 feet in size, as if scale were the only measure of content.

PORDENONE, Giovanni Antonio (1483/4–1539), was a North Italian painter who was influenced by the Venetians – especially Titian and Giorgione – and also by German art, particularly in its more violent aspects. This fusion leads to a kind of Mannerism in his style as early as the 1520s. He may have gone to Rome *c.*1515–16, as there is a Raphaelesque phase in his art just then. In 1519/20 he was painting a dome in Treviso in the illusionistic manner introduced by Mantegna, but his dome precedes the one by Correggio, whose influence is, however, discernible in the dome at Piacenza (*c.*1530). For a brief moment in the 1530s Pordenone presented a serious challenge to the supremacy of Titian himself, and he eventually settled in Venice, but his frescoes in Treviso Cath. (1520) do not compare very well with the *Annunciation* by Titian, painted as the altarpiece for the chapel. His principal works are in Cremona, Piacenza, Treviso and Venice; others are in the Royal Coll. and in Budapest, London (NG), Milan (Brera), Philadelphia, Prague, Sarasota Fla and Vienna.

PORTE-CRAYON (Fr. crayon-carrier). A short tube of metal, split at each end and fitted with rings, so that pieces of chalk or charcoal can be inserted and held tightly by sliding the rings forward.

PORTINARI, Cándido (1903–62), the leading Brazilian painter, studied in Europe 1928–30. From the mid-1930s he was influenced by the Mexican muralists (RIVERA, OROZCO) and painted Brazilian peasants, often on large walls. He also decorated the Library of Congress in Washington (1941–2) and the UN building in New York (1950–6) in a style more influenced by Picasso.

POSILLIPO, School of, *see* GIGANTE.

POST, Frans (*c.*1612–80), was a Dutch landscape painter not unlike Philips de Koninck, who went to Brazil, 1637–44. On his return to Haarlem he continued to paint Brazilian landscapes (no other works by him are known), with exotic animals and plants in Dutch-looking landscapes. There are examples in the Royal Coll. and in Amsterdam (Rijksmus.), Dublin, The Hague, London (V&A at Ham House), Paris (Louvre) and several U S museums.

POST-IMPRESSIONISM is a rather vague term applied to the movement which developed in reaction against both Impressionism and Neo-Impressionism and had as its chief aim either a return to a more formal conception of art or a new stress on the importance of the subject. The most important figures covered by the term are van Gogh, Gauguin and Cézanne. It was given currency in England by the Exhibition arranged by Roger FRY in the winter of 1910–11, called 'Manet and the Post-Impressionists', which caused much heart-burning in London art circles and led to the formation of the LONDON GROUP.

Le post-impressionnisme has now come into use in French as the equivalent term.

POTTER, Paulus (1625–54), one of the most famous Dutch animal painters, was the son of a painter and very precocious – his first works are of 1640, and his most famous picture, the life-size *Bull* (The Hague), is signed and dated 1647. On the whole, however, his smaller pictures are better. There are works by him in the Royal Coll. and in Amsterdam, Berlin, Brussels, Copenhagen, Dresden, Dublin, London (NG and Wallace Coll.), Munich, Paris (Louvre), Philadelphia, Washington and elsewhere.

POURBUS, Pieter (1523–84), worked mainly in Bruges where he followed, in his religious works, the florid Italianizing style of Lancelot Blondeel, whose daughter he married. His portraits are stiff and formal affairs, but equal to those of his contemporaries MOR or JOOS van Cleve. There are works in Antwerp, Bruges (Mus. and churches), Brussels, London (Wallace Coll.), New York (Met. Mus.) and elsewhere.

Frans I (1545–81), his son and pupil, painted religious pictures and portraits. He worked mainly in Antwerp, where he was also the pupil of Frans FLORIS, whose niece he married. His religious works are usually in the Italianizing style of Floris, but markedly Reformed Church in content; his portraits (like his father's) are close to the sober style of Mor. There are works in Berlin, Brussels, Dresden, Edinburgh (NPG), Ghent (Mus. and S. Bavon), London (Wallace Coll.), Rotterdam, Vienna and elsewhere.

Frans II (1569–1622), son of Frans I, worked for the Court of the Spanish Regents of the Netherlands in Brussels, and in 1600 became Court Painter to the Duke of Mantua, being there at the same time as Rubens. He also worked in Innsbruck, Naples and Turin, and in 1609 became painter to Marie de' Medici at the French Court. His is the most international style of any member of the family. There are works in the Royal Coll. and in Amsterdam (Rijksmus.), Berlin, Leeds, Madrid (Prado), Munich, New York (Met. Mus.), Paris (Louvre), Vienna and elsewhere.

POUSSIN, Gaspard (1615–75). His name was Dughet but he adopted the name of his illustrious brother-in-law Nicolas, whose pupil he was *c.*1631–*c.*1635. He lived and worked in Rome and its surroundings and attempted, not entirely unsuccessfully, the difficult feat of combining the landscape style and principles of POUSSIN and CLAUDE. The Land Storm landscape was invented by him. He was immensely popular during the 18th century so that most of the older galleries and collections have examples, although these are always attributions, for apart from some frescoes in S. Martino ai Monti in Rome (probably 1648–51) nothing can positively be assigned to him, although frescoes in Rome (Quirinal (1657), Borghese (1671–2), and Colonna palaces) are accepted as his. Birmingham, Cambridge (Fitzwm), Edinburgh (NG), London (NG, Dulwich and Kenwood), Manchester (Whitworth) and Oxford have examples of what the 18th century understood by 'Gaspar'.

POUSSIN, Nicolas (1594–1665), was born in Normandy and after some training went to Paris about 1612. At some time between 1612 and 1624 he worked with the Flemish portrait painter ELLE. Little is known about him before 1621 when he was employed with Philippe de CHAMPAIGNE on decorations in the Luxembourg Palace. His style was probably based on the second School of FONTAINEBLEAU, modified by the Antique and Italian Renaissance works in the French Royal Coll. In 1624 he went to Rome and in his early struggling years there worked in the studio of Domenichino, whose lucid composition and cool colour affected him strongly. In 1628 he obtained a commission for an altarpiece for St Peter's, the *Martyrdom of St Erasmus* (now in the Vatican), a work painted in competition with Le VALENTIN and not wholly successful since it involved a compromise between Baroque eloquence and Poussin's less dramatic style. About 1629–30 he had a serious illness. This marks a change in his style, for he now stopped trying to compete with the increasingly popular opulent Baroque and turned to smaller works and to patrons from the upper middle class. He made many experiments in these early Roman years, one being his short interest in Venetian art which led, for instance, in the Louvre *Inspiration of the Poet*, to a combination of classical form and Venetian colour of supreme beauty. He turned from religious to classical subjects, to mythologies, and to Tasso. But this elegiac phase was short-lived, and by 1633 he was working on compositions filled with figures grouped in dramatic poses chosen to make the narrative plain; the influence of Venetian colour gave place to a more rigid use of local colour, and Raphael and the Antique are paramount. Poussin used the device of a miniature stage with small draped wax models to try out effects of gesture, grouping and lighting.

In 1640 he was persuaded to return to Paris to work for the King and Cardinal Richelieu. This brought him into uneasy competition with most of the artists working for the Crown, of whose work he was outspokenly critical, and in particular with VOUET, but the artistic climate of Paris and the conditions of his employment were highly uncongenial and in 1642, after just over eighteen months, he made an excuse to return to Rome which he never again left. In 1642 he finished the first set of the *Seven Sacraments*, of which the *Baptism* is now in Washington (NG) and the remainder in Belvoir Castle (Duke of Rutland's Coll.) except for *Confession* (destroyed). His trip to France enabled him to make new contacts among bourgeois patrons, such as Chantelou, for whom he had worked in Rome and who was his host in Paris (as he later was to Bernini) and for whom the second set of the *Seven Sacraments* (Edinburgh NG, on loan from the Duke of Sutherland) was painted between about 1644 and 1648. These patrons were highly educated, intellectual men of strict piety, and the classical themes he now chose were the heroic and stoical ones of Roman moral victory and sacrifice paralleling the dramas of Corneille, or dramatic Biblical themes where the action turns on the psychological impact of the moment. The late works are essays in solid geometry, with facial expressions eliminated and immobile figures. By comparison with his early works they are frigid and cerebral, but they are the logical exposition of his theories: a picture must contain the maximum of moral content expressed in a composition which shall convey its intellectual content; the pattern must be pleasing in itself and not conflict with the two-dimensional quality of the picture plane; the colour must offer no sensuous charm to lessen the unity of vision. Nowhere is this severe attitude expressed with more finality than in his landscapes which exemplify his utter dissimilarity to CLAUDE. This doctrine of the subordination of colour led to the quarrel between the Poussinists and the RUBENISTS. There are works in Berlin, Birmingham, Boston (Mus. and Fogg), Brighton, Cambridge (Fitzwm), Cardiff (Nat. Mus.), Chantilly, Chicago, Cleveland Ohio, Copenhagen, Detroit, Dresden, Dublin, Edinburgh (NG), Fort Worth Texas, Glasgow, Hartford Conn. (Wadsworth), Kansas City, Leningrad, Liverpool, London (NG, Dulwich and Wallace Coll.), Madrid, Minneapolis, Montreal, Munich, New York (Met. Mus.), Ottawa, Paris (Louvre), Philadelphia, Providence R.I., Rouen, Sarasota Fla (Ringling), Stockholm, Toledo Ohio, Toronto, Vaduz (Liechtenstein Coll.), the Vatican, Vienna and Washington (NG).

POUSSINISME *see* RUBÉNISME.

POWERS, Hiram (1805–73), was an American sculptor, born in Vermont, whose first attempt at going to Italy ended in New York in 1829 when the money ran out. By 1835 his bust of Andrew Jackson brought him fame and he received many commissions for busts for the rest of his life; he finally went to Italy in 1837 and never returned to the US. His status as an American Neoclassic sculptor was first established with his *Fisher Boy* (1841, New York, Met. Mus.) and great fame came with the *Greek Slave* (1843, Washington, Corcoran, and several replicas). This nude girl represents a Greek Christian sold to lustful Turks, and coming at the time of the Greek War of Independence its sentimental eroticism was extremely popular. The statue toured America in 1847 and was a great success at the Crystal Palace Exhibition of 1851.

POYNTER, Sir Edward (1836–1919), was trained in Paris under GLEYRE, 1856–9, where he met Whistler, returning to London in 1860. He painted scenes from Ancient Greece and Rome, like LEIGHTON, often with a genre content as in *Faithful unto Death* (Liverpool), a Roman sentry staying at his post during the destruction of Pompeii. He was made an RA in 1876 and PRA in 1896, but he was also influential in the teaching of art and as Director of the National Gallery. He was knighted in 1896 and made a Baronet in 1902. There are works in Liverpool, London (Tate and V&A), Manchester, Montreal and Sydney.

POZZO, Andrea (1642–1709), was the most skilful of all perspective experts and *quadraturisti*. He was born and trained in the north of Italy and became a Jesuit lay brother in 1665 (he is often given the courtesy title 'Padre') and wanted to abandon painting but was made to continue by his superiors. From 1681 to 1702 he was in Rome and his masterpiece of illusionism and SOTTO IN SÙ (which only works from one point in the nave) is the ceiling of the Jesuit church of S. Ignazio (1691–4). This is an allegory of the missionary activity of the Society of Jesus, and Pozzo himself explained it in a letter to Prince Liechtenstein (1694, published as a pamphlet in 1828). In 1702 he went to Vienna, where he died, and he introduced similar ideas there, which were of great importance in the development of Austrian Rococo. His influence was spread by his treatise 'Perspectiva pictorum . . .' (1693–8), which was translated into English in 1700 and is said to have led Reynolds to decide to become a painter; the book was even translated into Chinese, by Portuguese Jesuits in 1737.

PRADIER, James (1790–1852), French sculptor, was born in Geneva of a French Huguenot family. He went to Paris by 1809, won the Prix de Rome in 1813, was in Italy until 1819 and again 1821–3. His first exhibited works established his coldly classicizing manner, derived from the CANOVA of the Empire period. Some of his legion of Bacchantes, Nymphs or Psyches evoke a gentle sensuality and something of Ingres's cool silhouette, but they are as predictable as they were successful, without any feeling in the execution, because of the extensive use of the POINTING MACHINE. He was the most highly-considered and fashionable sculptor of his day, wielding an enormous influence as a teacher and member of the Institut, and a Salon judge, rigorously excluding any deviation from his narrow classicism in the cause of safeguarding the purity of art. He made the nude figures of Fame in the spandrels of the Arc de l'Étoile, the two statues of Lille and Strasbourg in the Place de la Concorde, Paris, and the twelve sentinels surrounding Napoleon's tomb in the Invalides – compared favourably, in his own day, with the caryatides of the Erechtheon. There are many works in French provincial museums, churches, and public squares, as well as in the Louvre and Versailles. There is a large collection, mainly of original plasters, in the museum of Geneva.

PRB, PRE-RAPHAELITE BROTHERHOOD. The mysterious initials first appeared following ROSSETTI's signature on his *Girlhood of Mary Virgin* exhibited in 1849. They were the outcome of talks between HUNT and MILLAIS in 1848, although the choice of the expression 'Pre-Raphaelite' was largely fortuitous. It had already been said of the NAZARENER that they sought to emulate the painters earlier than Raphael, and this was more or less the idea of the original Brotherhood (Hunt, Millais, Rossetti and his brother William, Collinson, Woolner the sculptor and Stephens) – they knew very little about Italian painting earlier than Raphael, but they did know that they thought Raphael himself over-praised and they did not like Bolognese and Roman 17th-century painting, which they thought insincere. From the first the movement was very literary (a periodical called 'The Germ' ran for four numbers) and the painters insisted on the importance of a serious subject and on a highly elaborated symbolism and freshly thought-out iconography. The technical means – such as bright colour, extreme detail, study of outdoor motives on the spot, and the famous method of working into a wet white ground – all these were no more than means, although they had great influence on later painters who had no connection with the movement, such as Ford Madox BROWN. In 1850 Rossetti revealed the meaning of the initials and at once a great storm broke; the principal accusations being that they set themselves up as better than Raphael, that they were secret Romanists (i.e. linked with the Oxford Movement), and that they were blasphemers. This last point was made – in an exceptionally savage and unperceptive attack – by Dickens, the victim being Millais's *Christ in the House of His Parents*, better known as *The Carpenter's Shop* (RA 1850, London, Tate). He described the picture as showing 'the interior of a carpenter's shop. In the foreground . . . is a hideous, wry-necked, blubbering, red-haired boy in a nightgown, who appears to have received a poke in the hand playing in an adjacent gutter, and to be holding it up for the contemplation of a kneeling woman, so horrible in her ugliness that (supposing it were possible for any human creature to exist for a moment with that dislocated throat) she would stand out . . . as a monster in the vilest cabaret in France or the lowest gin-shop in England'. After further attacks in 1851, RUSKIN came to their defence, commending them for copying nature, not the Quattrocento, and saying that they were 'laying in our England the foundations of a school of art nobler than the world has seen for three hundred years'. Such was Ruskin's reputation that their success was assured: Millais' *Ophelia* (1851–2, Tate) in the next Academy exhibition was a great success, but shortly after this the group, which had never had any avowed theoretical basis, dissolved: Millais to become the typical successful RA and PRA, Rossetti to found a sort of second Brotherhood at Oxford with MORRIS and BURNE-JONES, and Hunt alone, working in Palestine on religious pictures, to maintain the original ideas. Collinson soon drifted away, leaving as his best memorial *The Empty Purse* (1857, Tate, also called *For Sale*), Woolner emigrated to Australia, providing the inspiration for Brown's *The Last of England*, and various other artists – e.g. Hughes and Martineau – adopted their ideas. From the mid-1850s they were well supported by the new middle-class patrons. There are good collections of their works in Birmingham, Manchester, Oxford and London (Tate).

PREDELLA. An Italian word for the small strip of paintings which forms the lower edge or socle of a large altarpiece (*pala*). Such a POLYPTYCH consists of a principal, central panel with subsidiary side and/or top panels, and a *predella*: the *predella* usually has narrative scenes from the lives of the Saints who are represented in the panels above. Because of the small size of *predelle* – they are not usually more than 10–12 inches high, though often relatively very wide – they were frequently used for pictorial experiments that the painter did not wish to risk making in the larger panels. The first datable example seems to be that in Simone Martini's *S. Louis of Toulouse* (1317, Naples).

PRE-RAPHAELITE BROTHERHOOD *see* PRB.

PRETI, Mattia (Il Cavaliere Calabrese) (1613–99), was in Rome by 1633 but had presumably already absorbed the influence of Caravaggio in Naples, since he came from Calabria. He also visited Venice and Emilia, where he was influenced by GUERCINO and LANFRANCO. His easel pictures are more Caravaggesque than his frescoes in Rome (1650–1, S. Andrea della Valle and S. Carlo ai Catinari) and Modena, which show the influence of Guercino and Lanfranco. He was in Naples 1656–60 and spent most of the rest of his life in Malta, where he went in 1661 to decorate St John's in Valletta, being made a Knight of Malta in the same year. Other works are in Aix-en-Provence, Birmingham (Barber Inst.), Dublin, Greenville SC, Liverpool, London (NG), Los Angeles, Mdina Malta, Naples, New York (Met. Mus.), Oxford, Sarasota Fla, Toledo Ohio, Toronto and Valletta (Mus.).

PRÉVOST *see* MASTER OF MOULINS.

PRIMARY COLOURS are the three colours, red, blue and yellow, from which, in theory, all others can be obtained. A secondary colour, such as green or orange, is obtained by the mixture of two primaries, and a tertiary colour (and in theory black as well) from three. White and black are not primary colours.

PRIMATICCIO, Francesco (1504/5–70), was the head of the First School of FONTAINEBLEAU, and a universal impresario – painter, sculptor, architect, interior decorator. He learned these arts under GIULIO Romano in the Palazzo del Tè at Mantua, from 1525/6 until 1532, when he was summoned to France by François I and began to work at Fontainebleau, where he met ROSSO. From 1540 until 1542 he was in Rome buying for François, and on his return he found that Rosso was dead and Cellini had arrived (Cellini later threatened to kill him 'like a dog'). With Niccolò dell'ABBATE he worked on the (lost) decorations of the Galérie d'Ulysse at Fontainebleau, and in 1546 he was again in Rome to get casts made, including Michelangelo's *Pietà* in St Peter's, while in 1563 he revisited Bologna, his native town, and met Vasari there. There are works by him in Barnard Castle (Bowes Mus.), Bologna, Chantilly, Florence (Uffizi), Glasgow, Montpellier, Paris (Louvre and Cluny Mus.), Pittsburgh, and Toledo Ohio, but his main contribution is the combination of painted and high relief stucco decoration evolved at Fontainebleau and still partially preserved there.

PRIMING. The first coat on which all subsequent paint layers (including the GROUND) are applied. For oil-painting on canvas, the sized canvas is usually primed with white lead, either plain or slightly tinted.

PRIMITIVE. A word which is now almost meaningless, being applied to (i) painters, particularly of the Netherlandish and Italian Schools, working before *c.*1500 – i.e. Netherlandish painters of the late 14th and all the 15th centuries, and all Italian painters between Giotto and Raphael, but mainly of the Trecento. They have no obvious connection with (ii) the naïve, unsophisticated, unspoilt vision consistent with amateur, or 'Sunday' painter, status, admired for its connotations of genuineness and purity of artistic impulse, and freedom from the trammels of professionalism, tradition, technique and formal training. This type of Primitive varies from the genuine American Primitives of the 19th century such as Edward HICKS or John KANE, to charwomen (SÉRAPHINE), peasants and fishermen in modern Europe. The Douanier ROUSSEAU is their *chef d'école*, but the American 'Grandma' Moses may provide greater thrills for the sophisticated pursuit of the innocent eye.

PRIX DE ROME *see* ROME PRIZE.

PROCACCINI, Giulio Cesare (1574–1625), was one of the painters of the *Martyrdom of SS. Rufina and Seconda* (Milan, Brera), which is one of the key pictures of Lombard Mannerism. The other painters who worked on it were G. B. CRESPI ('Il Cerano') and MORAZZONE. Giulio was born in Bologna, the younger brother of the painter Camillo (*c.*1560–1629), but the family settled in Milan *c.*1590, where Giulio began his career as a sculptor. He later worked as a painter in Modena (1613–16), where he was influenced by Correggio and Parmigianino, and in Genoa (1618), where he came in contact with Rubens. Most of his works are in Milan, but examples are in Berlin, Dublin, Edinburgh, Liverpool, New York (Met. Mus.), Oxford (Ch. Ch.), Paris, Sheffield, Turin, Vienna and Worcester Mass.

PROFIL PERDU (Fr. lost profile) is that view of a head in which the profile is lost because the whole head is turned so far away that only the outline of the cheek is visible. By extension the *profil perdu* of any object is what is seen of it when it is more than half turned away from the spectator.

PRONKSTILLEVEN (Dutch, ostentatious still-life). An extremely elaborate form of BANCKET PIECE; there is a splendid example by KALF in London (NG).

PROOF. Usually this means a print of any kind of engraving, made either by the artist himself or under his supervision and for his own satisfaction or information, before he hands the plate over to a professional printer. Some proofs – e.g. some of Turner's *Liber Studiorum* – were extensively worked on by the artist before he was finally satisfied.

A Proof Before All Letters is one made before an engraving was handed over to the lettering engraver for the title, dedication, etc. to be added: they are naturally rare, and, as they are also supposed to be made while the plate is still very new, they command higher prices than ordinary prints. This has led to the Artist's Proofs racket – i.e. the first ten or twenty prints of a run, signed or marked in some special way (REMARQUE PROOFS), and sold at inflated prices.

PROPORTION. The relation of one part to a whole or to other parts. In the arts it usually means a will-o'-the-wisp search for significant mathematical relationships between the parts of the human body. Such a search certainly began in classical times – the evidence is in much Greek sculpture – and the codified rules given in Vitruvius's 'Treatise on Architecture' (early in the 1st century AD) led to much theorizing in the Renaissance. Leonardo da Vinci and Dürer were the two artists who devoted the most energy to these studies ('There is no excellent beauty that hath not some strangeness in the proportion. A man cannot tell whether Apelles or Albert Durer were the more trifler; whereof the one would make a personage by geometrical proportions: the other, by taking the best parts out of divers faces to make one excellent': Bacon, 'Of Beauty'). In practice, the normal human body is about 7 or 7½ times as tall as the height of its own head, and the total height is also roughly equal to the width of the outstretched arms. In IDEAL ART, therefore, it is usual to make the height equal to the full width of the arms; and further to gain mathematical harmony by elongating the body so that the total height becomes eight heads. This gives a body which can be inscribed in squares and circles and also the convenient divisions so beloved of classically-minded artists – e.g. the groin becomes the exact half, the legs can be again halved at the knees, and so on. *See also* GOLDEN SECTION.

PROUT, Samuel (1783–1852), was an architectural and topographical draughtsman in watercolour, soft-ground etching, and lithography, whose illustrated travel-books precede those of BOYS. He went to school with HAYDON, but did not have historical ambitions. In 1803 he met WEST in London and began his picturesque tours, his first visit to France being in 1819, and to Italy in 1824. As an architectural draughtsman he was comparable to Cotman, or even Turner, and it brought him the admiration and friendship of RUSKIN. In 1829 he was made Painter in Watercolour in Ordinary to George IV. His long series of illustrations for travel-books began in 1812. There is a large collection of his works in London (V&A), and others are in Manchester (Whitworth).

PROVENANCE (Fr. source, origin). The provenance of a work of art is its pedigree. A complete record of its ownership is its provenance, and it is the duty of a cataloguer to establish, as far as humanly possible, the provenance of a work of art. In some cases – e.g. the Sistine ceiling – no doubt is possible, but the exact pedigree of a picture by Vermeer or van Gogh or Samuel Palmer is a matter of great importance, especially to the dealer trying to sell it. The English form 'provenience' is occasionally advocated, but it has a stilted sound and is not usual.

PRUD'HON, Pierre Paul (1758–1823), was born at Cluny. The Bishop of Mâcon sent him to Dijon Academy in 1774 and in 1780 he went to Paris, where he worked for engravers. In 1784 he won the Rome Prize offered by the States of Burgundy; in Italy he became a friend of Canova and did almost no work, but his pictures show the influence of Raphael, Correggio and Leonardo. In 1787 he returned to Paris and earned a precarious living drawing for engravers and painting portraits in the provinces. He was almost unaffected by the current Neoclassicism in painting – DAVID called him the Boucher of his day – and he became almost the only competitor to David and his pupils, through the warm patronage of both of Napoleon's Empresses to whom he was drawing master and Court Painter. He gave his, mostly female, sitters an indefinably romantic and mysterious air, but his faulty technique and free use of bitumen have caused the deterioration of much of his work, particularly his large decorations. He designed all the furniture and decorations for the Empress Marie Louise's bridal suite, and cradles for the King of Rome, and his considerable influence on interior decoration was, unlike his painting, strongly classicist and Greek revival. From 1803 he found relief from his disastrous marriage, made in haste at 19, in a liaison with his favourite pupil, Constance MAYER, many of whose pictures he designed or worked on, but the shock of her suicide in 1821 eventually killed him. There are works in Amsterdam (Rijksmus.), Chantilly, Chartres, Dijon, Lille, London (Wallace Coll.), Lyons, Montpellier, New York (Met. Mus. and Hist. Soc.), Paris (Louvre, Carnavalet and Jacquemart-André), St Louis and Versailles.

PRYDE *see* NICHOLSON.

PUGET, Pierre (1620–94), was a French sculptor whose controlled Baroque (derived from Michelangelo and Bernini) made no appeal to the classicizing taste of Louis XIV, and whose intransigent character was unacceptable to Colbert. He worked much in Italy and the South of France and was a pupil of PIETRO da Cortona (1640–*c.*1644), with whom he worked on the Pal. Barberini in Rome and the Pal. Pitti in Florence. In 1656 he was in Toulon, but was in Genoa in the 1660s. A recently discovered bust proves that he was in Rome again in 1662. Despite his successful *Milo of Crotona* of 1683, made for Versailles (now in the Louvre), his hopes of Court patronage were frustrated, and other works for the King were refused. There are examples in Toulon (caryatids, Hôtel de Ville, 1656–7), Cleveland Ohio, Genoa (S.M. in Carignano, S. Filippo and Albergo dei Poveri), Marseilles, New York (Met. Mus.), Paris (Louvre) and Quebec (Laval Univ.).

PUNCH *see* STONE CARVING.

PURISM. In 1918 OZENFANT and Édouard Jeanneret (better known as the architect Le Corbusier) published *Après le Cubisme*, in which they accused the Cubists of turning to mere decoration. Purism, which they therefore invented, was to be an art unsullied by decoration, fantasy or individuality, and inspired by the machine as a form of creation from which all unnecessary detail has been eliminated. Such is the waywardness of man that this arid doctrine produced almost no art; only to the architecture of le Corbusier has it proved of any consequence.

PURRMANN, Hans (1880–1966), studied in Germany before going to Paris in 1906, where he met and greatly admired MATISSE. In 1908 Purrmann organized a school to which Matisse gave his name: it petered out in 1910/11, as Matisse gave less and less time to it. Purrmann also organized several Matisse exhibitions in Germany which greatly influenced the Expressionists. In 1943 he was forced to leave Germany and go to Switzerland, where he died. There are works in Basle, Berlin, Cologne, Karlsruhe and Munich.

PUTTO (Ital. boy). A chubby naked boy: an AMORINO.

PUVIS de Chavannes, Pierre (1824–98), attempted to recreate something of the monumental Italian fresco style in his huge decorative canvases painted in oil, but kept flat and pale in colour and simplified in the drawing to give something of the effect of fresco. He decorated many Town Halls and other official buildings in France, the most famous being the Panthéon, Paris (1874–8, 1898, *Life of St Geneviève*), and the Hôtel de Ville, Paris (1889–93). He was particularly admired by the artists grouped under POST-IMPRESSIONISM and NEO-IMPRESSIONISM as a painter of symbolical and allegorical decorations who respected the plane of the wall and composed his murals in simple areas of colour and with a rhythmic linear pattern: with MOREAU and REDON he was a leading SYMBOLIST. He decorated the Library at Boston in 1893–5, and there are other works by him in Birmingham (Barber Inst.), Budapest, Chicago, Dresden, Edinburgh (NG), Frankfurt (Städel), London (NG), Melbourne, New York (Met. Mus.), Northampton Mass., Paris (Louvre, Mus. des Arts Décoratifs, Mus. d'Orsay and Cluny Mus.), St Louis, Washington (NG) and many French provincial museums.

PYNACKER, Adam (1622–73), was a landscape painter from Delft who spent three years in Italy, but was back in Delft by 1649. He moved to Amsterdam *c.*1658. His landscapes are very like those of BOTH but are often hard and bluish, with silver tree-trunks and blue foliage. There is a particularly fine one in London (Dulwich) which has a curious blue where one would expect green in the foliage; this is due to the use of fugitive yellow pigments which have faded out of the greens. There are examples in Amsterdam, Barnsley, Boston, Cambridge (Fitzwm), Copenhagen, Florence (Uffizi), Hamburg, Hartford Conn., London (Wallace Coll.), Munich, Nottingham, Paris (Louvre), St Louis and Vienna (K-H Mus. and Akad.).

PYNAS, Jan (1583/4–1631) and Jacob (*c.*1585–1656 or later), were brothers who were both in Rome *c.*1605 and returned to Holland with a new kind of history painting, much influenced by Italian ideas and also by ELSHEIMER: their principal importance is that they passed these ideas on to Rembrandt, who may have been Jacob's pupil for a few months. There are works by them in Amsterdam (Rijksmus, Rembrandt House), Hartford Conn. (Jacob's earliest work, of 1617), London (NG), New York (Met. Mus.), Paris and Philadelphia (Johnson).

Q

QUADRATURISTA. A painter of *quadrature*. *See* ILLUSIONISM.

QUADRO RIPORTATO (Ital. carried picture). A term applied to easel paintings seen in normal perspective which have been inserted into a ceiling decoration so that the effect is not the same as the ILLUSIONISM of *quadrature*.

QUARTON, Enguerrand (*c.*1410–66 or later), sometimes wrongly called Charonton, was a French painter working in Avignon. There are two documented works by him, in Chantilly (Musée Condé) and in Villeneuve-lès-Avignon (Hospice): the latter is a large *Coronation of the Virgin*, completed in 1454, which is one of the most important surviving 15th-century French paintings. It is unique in that the contract for it survives and contains the joint theological views of the priest who commissioned it and the painter himself, who reserved the right – which he exercised – to treat the picture as seemed best to him: 'Contract of 24 April 1453 between Dominus Jean de Montagnac and Master Enguerrand Quarton, of the diocese of Laon, painter. (1) There should be the form of Paradise, and in that Paradise should be the Holy Trinity, and there should not be any difference between the Father and the Son; and the Holy Ghost in the form of a dove; and Our Lady in front as it will seem best to master Enguerrand; the Holy Trinity will place the crown on the head of Our Lady. (2) . . . Item: in paradise below should be all the estates of the world . . . After the heavens, the world in which should be shown a part of the city of Rome . . . the church of S. Peter at Rome . . . On the other side of the sea, will be a part of Jerusalem . . . the cross of Our Lord, and at the foot . . . a praying Carthusian. On the left side will be Hell . . .'

The greatest of all 15th-century French pictures – the *Pietà* from Villeneuve-lès-Avignon now in the Louvre – is generally accepted as his.

QUATTROCENTO (Ital. four hundred). The 15th century, i.e. the fourteen-hundreds. *Quattrocento Mannerism* is a phrase sometimes used to describe the agitated and nervous style of a Botticelli or a Filippino Lippi, the assumption being that it is a 15th-century precursor of MANNERISM.

QUELLIN, Arnold (Arnout) (1653–86), was the son of Artus I (*see below*). He was born in Antwerp but settled in London in 1680, where he died at the age of 33. He worked with Grinling GIBBONS (1682–6) and probably did much of the work for which Gibbons was paid – e.g. the *James II*, outside the NG, London. Their major joint work was the Catholic chapel in Whitehall Palace, designed by Wren in 1685–6 for James II, which Evelyn visited on 29 December 1686: 'Nothing can be finer than the magnificent marble work and Architecture at the End, where are four statues representing st. Joh: st. Petre, st. Paule, and the Church, statues in white marble, the worke of Mr Gibbons . . .' The Chapel was demolished in 1695, but some fragments survive at Westminster Abbey and in Burnham Church, Somerset. The Thynne Monument (1682/4), in Westminster Abbey, is Quellin's and there are other works in London (Guildhall and Soane Mus.).

QUELLIN, Artus I (1609–68), was one of the leading sculptors in the Netherlands in the 17th century. He was the son of the sculptor Erasmus Quellin and the father of the sculptors Artus II and Arnold. He studied in Rome, where he was much influenced by the classical Baroque of DUQUESNOY and ALGARDI, and on his return to Antwerp in 1639 he combined these influences with that of Rubens. In this he resembled Philippe de CHAMPAIGNE, his contemporary and fellow-Netherlander. In 1650 he moved to Amsterdam and spent fourteen years working on the Town Hall (now Royal Palace), employing many assistants; this was his major work and many sketches for the decorations there are now in Amsterdam (Rijksmus.). Other works are in Antwerp (S. Andreas), and Brussels (Cath.).

QUERCIA, Jacopo della (1374/5–1438), was the greatest Sienese sculptor and a contemporary of Ghiberti and Donatello. He took part in the 1401 Competition for the First Baptistry Doors (won by Ghiberti) in Florence, but his entry is lost and the earliest work attributed to him is the Tomb of Ilaria del Carretto (*c.*1406) in Lucca Cathedral. This is now fragmentary, but it seems to show a knowledge of Northern motives, and it is often said that Jacopo must have had some knowledge of the Burgundian School around SLUTER. The sarcophagus is also decorated with *putti* carrying garlands, perhaps the earliest Renaissance use of an ancient Roman motive. In 1409 he was commissioned to make a public fountain, the Fonte Gaia, for his native Siena, and he executed it 1414–19 (he seems always to have been dilatory): it is now dismembered in the Palazzo Pubblico, Siena. Between 1417 and 1431 he was working on reliefs for the Baptistry of Siena on which both Ghiberti and Donatello also worked. Indeed, the *Salome* relief by Donatello was originally commissioned from Quercia; in 1425 all three sculptors had to return money advanced to them, on account of their unsatisfactory progress. From 1425 Quercia was also working on another commission, the stone reliefs outside S. Petronio, Bologna, which occupied him until his death. These reliefs in particular show an almost Donatellesque vigour of handling and were much admired by Michelangelo. Other works are in Bologna (S. Giacomo), Ferrara (Cath.), Lucca (S. Frediano) and S. Gimignano.

R

RAEBURN, Sir Henry (1756–1823), was the portrait painter who recorded the personalities of the 'Athens of the North', the lawyers and scholars of the great age of Edinburgh, and also some of the more picturesque representatives of the Highland lairds before the depopulations and emigrations. Raeburn was left an orphan at an early age and was apprenticed to a jeweller *c.*1772, when he probably began to paint miniatures. Very little is known of his early career, but in 1776, at the age of 20, he was commissioned to paint a full-length portrait in oil of George Chalmers, for Dunfermline Town Council (to whom it still belongs). This clearly betrays his lack of professional training; equally, it is an astonishing performance under the circumstances. In 1780 he married a well-off widow and was able to devote himself to painting, but there are few datable works of this period. Traditionally, the *Rev. Robert Walker Skating* (Edinburgh, NG) was painted in 1784. In this year Raeburn went to London, where he met Reynolds, and on to Italy. He was back in Edinburgh by 1787, totally unaffected by his Italian experience, but much influenced by Reynolds, becoming the leading Scots painter. In the course of the 1790s he developed a virtuoso handling of paint, generally drawing straight on to the canvas with his brush (no drawings are known by him). This executive skill often over-reaches itself, and the celebrated 'square touch' which he developed in the first years of the 19th century can render the beefy common sense of one of the great Law Lords (*Lord Newton*, 1806/11), while at other times it is merely insensitive. Perhaps his best-known work is *The Macnab* (1803/13, private coll.), where the sitter himself was enough to startle any painter out of a rut – particularly in the age of Scott. Hoppner died in 1810 and Raeburn went to London, apparently with the intention of taking over Hoppner's house and practice, but he decided against this, probably because of LAWRENCE's position, and returned to Edinburgh, where he reigned alone. Nevertheless, from 1810 he exhibited regularly at the RA and visited London again in 1815 when he was elected RA. In 1822 George IV made his celebrated State Visit to Edinburgh and Raeburn was knighted and appointed King's Limner for Scotland.

Many of Raeburn's portraits are still in the families for whom they were painted – Fyvie Castle, Aberdeenshire (National Trust) has a dozen good ones – but there are several in Edinburgh (NG and SNPG, Univ. and RSA) and in Aberdeen, Baltimore, Berwick, Boston, Cambridge (Fitzwm), Cardiff, Chicago, Cincinnati, Cleveland Ohio, Detroit, Dublin, Glasgow, Kansas City, London (NG, Tate, NPG, RA, Osterley Park (V&A), Courtauld Inst. and Kenwood), Melbourne, Montreal, Newcastle, New York (Met. Mus., Frick Coll. and Brooklyn), Ottawa, Paris (Louvre), San Marino Cal. (Huntington), Toronto, Washington (NG, Nat. Coll. and Corcoran), Yale (CBA) and elsewhere.

RAGGI, Antonio (1624–86), was an Italian sculptor, born near Como, who was one of BERNINI's chief collaborators for about thirty years; he worked first for ALGARDI, but by 1647 he was working for Bernini, like FERRATA. He made the *Danube* for the fountain in Piazza Navona (1650–1) and worked on many other of Bernini's great undertakings. On his own he made the *S.*

Cecilia in S. Agnese (1660–7), the *Baptism* in S. Giovanni dei Fiorentini (*c.*1665) and the huge stucco decoration accompanying BACICCIO's painting in the Gesù.

RAMSAY, Allan (1713–84), was the Scottish counterpart to Reynolds and Gainsborough, with something of the learning of Reynolds and some of Gainsborough's grace. He was the son of the author of 'The Gentle Shepherd' and received his first training in Edinburgh and London; unlike his English contemporaries, however, he underwent a full Italian training as a pupil of Imperiali and SOLIMENA (1736–8): Solimena's work was known in Scotland by 1731, which may explain Ramsay's choice of master. He settled in London and was 'much cried up by the Scotch Gentry': worse, his style was far more elegant and Frenchified than the face-painting practised by Kneller's successors. VERTUE noted in 1739 that: 'Ramsay still accustomes him self to draw the faces in red lines shades &c. finishing the likeness in one red colour or mask before he puts on the flesh Colour, which he proposes as a method to make the flesh clear & transparent – and such a method was used in Italy, by Cavaliere Luti & others. & so did Titian he says. (but is doubted this last) however when the faces are painted four, five, or six times over little or nothing of that first red is to be seen – certain it is that hitherto, the manner he paints in, neither like the valuable Manner of Dahl Kneller. Lilly [i.e. Lely], Riley, Dobson Vandyke. Rubens or Titian – however it is rather lick't than pencilld, neither broad, grand, nor Free, has more of the finishd labourd uncertain – or modish French, German & dutch way – his good fortune has been much improved in this years worke.' This was the time when J. B. van LOO was in London, and the French influence was very strong (and disapproved of by HOGARTH). His Italian Grand Manner portraits precede Reynolds's by several years but he lacked Reynolds's ambition and spent much time in travel – he visited Italy four times, in 1755/7, 1775–7, and 1782–4 – and in conversation, in which Dr Johnson himself admitted his prowess. In 1755 he published anonymously 'The Investigator, a Dialogue on Taste', which championed Greek and Gothic and was sharply attacked by PIRANESI. In 1759 Horace Walpole acutely observed: 'Mr. Reynolds . . . is bold and has a kind of tempestuous colouring, yet with dignity and grace; the latter [Ramsay] is all delicacy. Mr Reynolds seldom succeeds in women, Mr. Ramsay is formed to paint them.' During the 1760s he was appointed Painter to George III, to Reynolds's chagrin, but produced only a series of Royal images, executed by assistants, for public buildings. His best works are in Edinburgh (NG and SNPG), including hundreds of the drawings which were the foundation of his pictures, in contrast with English practice. Other works are in London (NPG, Tate, Courtauld Inst., V&A and Coram Fdn), Aberdeen, Berwick, Birmingham, Glasgow, Liverpool, Newcastle, Ottawa, Warwick, Yale (CBA) and elsewhere.

RAPHAEL (1483–1520), was the youngest of the three great creators of the High Renaissance and was the most eclectic of great artists. He was the son of the painter Giovanni SANTI, and his real name was Raffaello Sanzio. His father died in 1494 and Raphael's earliest years are obscure, but by 1500 he was working in the shop of PERUGINO, probably on the frescoes at Perugia; and in this year he received his first recorded commission, fragments of which are in Naples and Brescia. Probably at this time he painted the *Knight's Dream* (London, NG). He was thus a prodigy, but, what is more extraordinary, in

1500 he was 17 while Leonardo da Vinci was 48 and Michelangelo 25 and yet in less than ten years the provincial youth, who had not had their advantage in being born and brought up in Florence, was generally admitted to be their equal. The decade 1500–10 not only saw the emergence of Raphael as a great master, it also saw the creation of the High Renaissance, in which Raphael played a leading part and which hardly survived him.

His early works show the influence of Perugino and not much else, as in the *Mond Crucifixion* of *c.*1502/3 (London, NG), of which Vasari observed that if Raphael had not signed it, everyone would take it for a Perugino; but the *Betrothal of the Virgin* (*Lo Sposalizio*) (1504, Milan, Brera), although derived from a Perugino, already shows powers of composition and draughtsmanship far in advance of him. At this point in his career Raphael went to Florence, where he must have found that all he knew was old-fashioned and provincial. He began at once to learn all he could from the Florentines, and a whole series of drawings and paintings demonstrates how rapidly he assimilated all they could teach him. From Leonardo's cartoons of the *Virgin and Child with St Anne* he developed a series of small *Madonnas* (e.g. those in Florence, Paris and Vienna); from the *Mona Lisa* he learned a new portrait type which he used for his *Maddalena Doni* (Florence, Pitti), while Leonardo's experiments in chiaroscuro are the reason for the dark background in the *Madonna del Granduca* (Florence, Pitti). Michelangelo's influence is principally to be found in a new severity and power in drawing, but the *Deposition* (1507, Rome, Borghese) contains several Michelangelesque motives, not all of them digested. Raphael seems also to have come into close contact with Fra BARTOLOMMEO at this time.

Probably towards the end of 1508 Raphael went to Rome, perhaps because he had heard that the Pope, Julius II, was having new apartments decorated. By 1509 he was certainly employed in the first of these rooms, the Stanza della Segnatura, and he rapidly became the principal master employed in the Vatican, with the sole exception of Michelangelo who was then painting the Sistine Ceiling. At 26 Raphael was in the front rank, and there he remained for the rest of his short life. The Stanza della Segnatura is the first of the series of relatively small rooms, known collectively as the Stanze, which Raphael and his pupils and assistants decorated for Julius II and Leo X. It was painted between 1509 and 1511, the theme of the room being the human intellect. The two principal frescoes represent Philosophy and Theology and are known respectively as the *School of Athens* and the *Disputa*, or *Disputation Concerning the Blessed Sacrament*. These two frescoes, balanced and serene, calm and classically poised, are perhaps the best examples of the High Renaissance at its apogee. The second Stanza, that of Heliodorus (the Stanza d'Eliodoro), has a different theme – Divine intervention on behalf of the Church – and in keeping with this more dramatic theme, the style is more dramatic and colourful. This may also be due to the fact that the Stanza was painted between 1511 and 1514 and Michelangelo's Sistine Ceiling was unveiled in 1512. The principal subjects are the *Expulsion of Heliodorus from the Temple*, the *Liberation of St Peter* and the *Miracle of the Mass at Bolsena*. The remainder of the decorative scheme – the Stanza dell'Incendio and the Sala di Costantino – was almost entirely executed by Raphael's numerous and well-trained assistants, and the exact amount of Raphael's responsibility is a matter of controversy.

The principal reason for this is that Raphael was increasingly overwhelmed with work, not only in commissions for pictures from the Pope and from Kings and Princes, but also in that he succeeded Bramante (*d.*1514) as architect of the new St Peter's, and he was also engaged on innumerable other tasks. The most important of these were the frescoes in the Farnesina, Rome, and the tapestry cartoons designed in 1515–16 and intended to be used for tapestries to hang below the 15th-century frescoes on the walls of the Sistine Chapel. The surviving tapestries are still in the Vatican, and the original cartoons for seven of them are in the V&A, London (loaned from the Royal Coll.). At this time he also supervised the execution of the series of Old Testament scenes in the Logge of the Vatican: these were completed in 1519, but no more than the general design can be attributed to Raphael. The *Sistine Madonna* (Dresden) dates from 1512–13 and is unusual in that it is all by Raphael himself, although it was for a small religious community in Piacenza. It was commissioned by Julius II and may have been carried at his funeral. It shows, by comparison with any of his Florentine *Madonnas*, how his style had become larger and simpler and also how the very conception of the Madonna had changed, from the simple naturalism of the 15th century to the superhuman being which the 16th century thought more appropriate to the Mother of God – hence the figure floating in the clouds.

The last major work on which Raphael was engaged was the *Transfiguration* (Vatican), commissioned in 1517 but still unfinished when he died in 1520. It was completed after his death, partly at least by his heir and most important pupil, GIULIO Romano, and it is controversial to what extent the MANNERISM discernible in the picture is due to Giulio. The basic design (including the twisted figure of the woman) and all the drawings, however, are certainly by Raphael and it seems likely that his art was on the point of taking a new direction. When he died at the age of 37, Raphael occupied a unique social position, on terms of friendship with Cardinals and Princes, a position never before attained by an artist. The (baseless) rumour current at his death that the Pope had intended to make him a Cardinal is the most eloquent proof of the change that had come over the status of the artist, a change wrought principally by Leonardo, Michelangelo and Raphael.

There are pictures by him, in addition to those already mentioned, in Baltimore, Bergamo, Berlin, Bologna, Boston (Gardner Mus.), Budapest, Chantilly, Città di Castello, Cracow, Detroit, Dresden, Florence (Pitti and Uffizi), Leningrad, Lisbon, London (NG and Dulwich), Madrid, Milan (Ambrosiana and Brera), Munich, Naples, New York (Met. Mus.), Paris, Perugia, Princeton NJ (Univ. Gall.), Rome (Borghese, Doria Gall., Accad. di S. Luca, S. Agostino, S.M. della Pace and S.M. del Popolo), Vaduz (Liechtenstein Coll.), the Vatican and Washington.

RAUSCHENBERG, Robert (*b.*1925), was associated with his friend Jasper JOHNS in New York in the early 1960s in the creation of POP ART. His works include paintings, collages and combinations of disparate objects – *Monogram* (1959, Stockholm, Moderna Mus.) consists of a stuffed goat girdled by a tyre on a painted base.

RAY, Man (1890–1977), was an American DADAIST who was impressed by the ARMORY Show and became the lifelong friend of DUCHAMP, whom he met in 1915. He worked in New York until 1921 when he went to Paris, exhibiting at the first SURREALIST Exhibition of 1925. He returned to America in 1940 and worked in Hollywood – he was celebrated as a photographer – until his final return to Paris in 1951. There are works in New York (M of MA).

RAYONISM (Rayonnism, Rayonnisme) was a short-lived Russian offshoot of CUBISM. 'Rayonism is concerned with the special forms which may arise from the intersection of reflected rays from different objects, forms selected by the artist at will', according to its inventor, the painter Mikhail Larionov (1881–1964), in 1912/13. He also claimed that it was a synthesis of Cubism, Futurism and Orphism. Few works have survived, but there are examples in London (Tate) and New York (Guggenheim). The only other important figure was GONCHAROVA.

RAYSKI, Ferdinand von (1806–90), was trained in Dresden before joining the army in 1825; he served as an officer for four years. He then began to paint portraits of the Saxon nobility, and in 1835 he visited Paris. From 1839 he was settled in Dresden, with a strong connection both for portraits and animals among the local gentry. His style was based on Dutch 17th-century portraits brought up to date by reference to contemporary Frenchmen such as DELACROIX. He visited England in 1862. Most of his works are in Dresden.

READY-MADE *see* DUCHAMP, Marcel.

REALISM as an aesthetic watchword does not go any further back than COURBET, and in the visual arts, as in literature, it generally signifies the search for the squalid and depressing as a means of life-enhancement. It is in fact the total repudiation of IDEAL ART (which in the mid-19th century was necessary). It should not be confused with Naturalism, which is no more than the ingenuous pleasure in being able to make an accurate transcript of nature – 'a speaking likeness' – nor should it be confused with its cousin-german SOCIAL REALISM. Some English painters – notably Bratby, Greaves and Middleditch – practise a style which some critics have seen fit to call Neo-Realism. The crucial distinction is between the realism of van Kessel's insects or even Madame Tussaud's waxworks, and the Zola-type realism of Degas's washerwomen and Toulouse-Lautrec's prostitutes, a form of art which goes back at least to BROUWER's drunken peasants or Murillo's beggars.

REALTÀ, Pittori della *see* CERUTI.

RECCO. A Neapolitan family of painters of flowers, still-life and BODEGÓNES. Three of them – Giacomo, Giovanni Battista and Giuseppe – used the monogram GR, which causes problems of attribution. Giacomo (1603–before 1653), was the eldest, and was the father of Giuseppe (1634–95), the most famous of the family. Giuseppe may have visited Lombardy and may have been influenced by BASCHENIS, but his works are all in the Spanish realist tradition of Bodegón painting – some have been attributed to Velázquez – which goes back to Caravaggio. They are very similar to the works of his contemporary RUOPPOLO. He died in Spain. Giovanni Battista (1615?–1660?), may have been his brother, but was more likely his uncle. There are works by one or more of the family in Amsterdam (Rijksmus.), Florence (Uffizi), Rotterdam, Stockholm, Vienna (K-H Mus), Warsaw and especially in Naples (Capodimonte and elsewhere).

RECESSION is the name given to the ability to make the objects in a picture appear to recede into the depth of the imaginary picture space. It is most readily obtained by the use of linear and aerial PERSPECTIVE.

REDON, Odilon (1840–1916), created two entirely different types of picture: colourful, semi-Impressionist vases of flowers, animals or landscapes, and highly imaginative drawings, lithographs and paintings of fantastic subjects such as plants with human heads, phantoms and figments from dreams, visions and nightmares. He maintained stoutly that the fantasy pictures were only possible because of his contact with reality. His work became known in Paris between 1879 and 1882, and he was hailed as one of the principal SYMBOLIST painters, particularly by the literary Symbolists. He was a great friend of Mallarmé, and, like him, seems to have experienced a spiritual crisis (*c.*1894/5). His journal 'À Soi-Même', from 1867 to 1915, was published in 1922. There are works in Bordeaux, Bristol, London (NG and V&A), New York (Met. Mus., M of MA), Otterlo (Kröller-Müller), Paris (Mus. d'Orsay) and many other European and US museums.

REFUSÉS *see* SALON.

RELIEF sculpture is that which is not free-standing, and, in having a background, approximates to the condition of painting. There are several names to indicate the varying depth of projection, ranging from *alto-rilievo*, or high relief – which is almost detached from the ground – through *mezzo-rilievo* to bas-relief (*basso-rilievo*) and further still to *rilievo stiacciato* (or *schiacciato*) which is scarcely more than scratched. *Cavo-rilievo* is the same as intaglio, that is, relief in inverse, sunk into the surface instead of embossed upon it.

REMARQUE PROOFS are PROOFS with a scribbled drawing or other mark in the margin to indicate a supposed superiority to ordinary proofs.

REMBRANDT van Ryn (1606–69), was born in Leyden, the son of a miller, at the time when Holland became an independent nation. After about a year at Leyden University he was apprenticed for three years to an obscure painter named Swanenburgh, but this was followed by a much more important six months in Amsterdam (1624/5) with Pieter LASTMAN, who was the means of his introduction to the rhetoric of early Baroque and perhaps also the channel by which the influences of CARAVAGGIO and ELSHEIMER reached him. He may also have spent some time with the PYNAS brothers. In 1625 he returned to Leyden where he set up in company with Jan LIEVENS, an association that lasted until Rembrandt's move to Amsterdam in 1631/2. By 1628 he was sufficiently well-known to have DOU as his pupil. The earliest works known to us are dated 1626, and in them – e.g. the *Clemency of Titus* (Utrecht) – the influence of Lastman is still dominant. Many paintings of the Leyden period show great interest in light and represent scholars in lofty rooms, or are studies of old age; examples are the Melbourne *Scholars Disputing* (1628), the *Scholar in a Lofty Room* (London, NG), and *Rembrandt's Mother as the Prophetess Hannah* (1631, Amsterdam, Rijksmus.). At the end of 1631 or early in 1632 he moved to Amsterdam and set up as a portrait painter, attracting attention in 1632 with the *Anatomy Lesson of Dr Tulp*, a group portrait of the Amsterdam Guild of Surgeons (The Hague, Mauritshuis). This made his name and for the next ten years he prospered, producing highly finished likenesses, often in pairs, such as *Maerten Soolman* and his *Wife* (1634, private coll., Paris), *Jan Pellicorne and his Son* and his *Wife and Daughter* (*c.*1635/7, both in London, Wallace Coll.), or the *Unknown Man* of 1641 in Brussels and its pendant, the *Woman with a Fan* in the Royal Coll. In 1634 he married Saskia van Uylenborch, who brought him a considerable dowry as well as good connections, and Rembrandt promptly began to live well beyond his means; the *Portrait of Himself with Saskia* (*c.*1634, Dresden) shows them in a mood of blatant opulence. There are many portraits of Saskia, painted, drawn and etched (e.g. *Saskia as Flora*, 1635, London, NG), but in 1642 she died, leaving him with a son, Titus. In the same year his great group portrait, the *Company of Captain Frans Banning Cocq* (Amsterdam, Rijksmus.), better-known as the *Night Watch*, was painted. It was one of several such commemorative groups of the volunteer militia enlisted to defend Amsterdam. Each man paid according to the prominence given to his portrait, some finding themselves subordinated to the exigencies of Rembrandt's art in a way which HELST or KEYSER, or even HALS, would never have attempted.

After 1642 Rembrandt's business declined and the inevitable bankruptcy followed in 1656. It used to be thought that this was because of the revolutionary character of the *Night Watch*, but it now seems certain that Captain Cocq and his men were perfectly content with their picture. Meanwhile he was living with Hendrickje Stoffels, who, with his son Titus, 'employed' him from 1660 onwards, thus affording some relief from creditors. During these years he turned to Biblical subjects, creating a Protestant iconography, to landscape, and to studies of the Jews among whom he lived. He had been painting religious subjects from the start of his career, and had painted a series of Passion scenes for Prince Frederick Henry, 1633–9 (now in Munich), and such dramatically Baroque works as the *Blinding of Samson* of 1636 (Frankfurt), but the later works are deeper in emotional content and far less superficially dramatic. The same contrasts can be seen in his etchings – compare the *Annunciation to the Shepherds* of 1634 with the 'Hundred Guilder Print' (*Christ Healing*) of *c.*1649 – and the landscapes which he drew and etched in the 1640s compared with the romantic ones of the period from *c.*1635 when he was much influenced by SEGHERS. His portraits of the 1650s and 1660s include such masterpieces of psychological penetration painted to please himself as the *Jewish Merchant* of *c.*1650 (London, NG), the *Old Jew in an Armchair* (1652, London, NG) and the portrait of *Jan Six* (1654, still in the family coll., Amsterdam), as well as portraits like the *Man* (1663, Washington) the *Man with a Magnifying Glass* (New York, Met. Mus.), and the *Woman with a Plume* (Washington), the last two painted in the 1660s and clearly commissioned works.

The long series of self-portraits, datable between 1629 and 1669, records every stage of his career, every moment of disillusion, with ever-deepening self-analysis. In his last years he continued to receive some important commissions, such as the *Anatomy Lesson of Dr Deyman* (1656, Amsterdam, Rijksmus.), or the *Conspiracy of the Batavians*, commissioned in 1661 for the Amsterdam Town Hall but removed at once for alterations (and now in Stockholm National Mus.); both these now exist only as fragments. In 1662 he completed the group of the *Staal Meesters*, the Syndics of the Guild of Drapers, and this, the greatest of all Dutch group portraits, is now in the Rijksmuseum, Amsterdam. Later still he painted the *Family Group* now in Brunswick, and these very late works impressed the aged Hals so much that Rembrandt's influence is perceptible in his last works. It is an influence which has never died out. Rembrandt's output was prodigious, and there are about 650 paintings by him (of which some sixty are self-portraits) as well as about 300 etchings and 1,500–2,000 drawings. He maintained for many years a large teaching studio, and among his numerous pupils were BOL, FLINCK, EECKHOUT, KONINCK and Aert de GELDER. There are paintings by Rembrandt in the Royal Coll., and in Aix-en-Provence, Amsterdam, Antwerp, Baltimore, Bayonne, Berlin, Boston, Brunswick, Brussels, Cambridge (Fitzwm), Cambridge Mass. (Fogg), Cape Town, Cassel, Chicago, Cincinnati, Cleveland Ohio, Cologne, Copenhagen, Detroit, Dublin, Edinburgh, Florence, Frankfurt, Glasgow (Mus., Burrell and Univ.), The Hague, Kansas City, Leningrad, Leyden, Liverpool, London (NG, Dulwich, Kenwood, V&A and Wallace Coll.), Los Angeles, Madrid, Melbourne, Milan, Minneapolis, Munich, New York (Met. Mus., Frick Coll. and Hist. Soc.), Ottawa, Paris (Louvre and Jacquemart-André), Philadelphia (Johnson), Raleigh NC, Rotterdam, San Francisco, Sarasota Fla (Ringling Mus.), Stockholm, Toledo Ohio, Toronto, Utrecht, Vienna, Washington and Worcester Mass.

RENAISSANCE (Fr., or Ital. *Rinascimento*, rebirth). Usually defined as the 'revival of art and letters under the influence of classical models in the 14th–16th century' (*OED*). As early as 1550 Vasari used the word *rinascita* to describe this rebirth, which he believed to have culminated in his own days, but it probably received the wide currency it now has from Jacob Burckhardt's 'Civilization of the Renaissance in Italy', first published in 1860. In the visual arts the term is now used with some care, if any degree of precision is desired. It is obvious that the influence of classical models is not easy to distinguish in Italy, where the classical tradition is virtually unbroken, and a term which can be made to cover Giotto at one end and Tintoretto at the other is too vague to be useful in any discussion of style (the case was once even worse in English architectural history, where 'Renaissance' used to be made to cover Elizabethan buildings, Wren and the Adam brothers). It is generally agreed that Giotto may be said to have begun the Renaissance in the other sense, that of according a new dignity to man and his works, but that the classical ideals hardly came into play before the first years of the 15th century, when the humanist ideals of ALBERTI were indistinguishable from those of MASACCIO, BRUNELLESCHI and DONATELLO, and, to a lesser extent, GHIBERTI. The period from *c.*1420 to 1500 is therefore now generally called the Early Renaissance and the term High Renaissance is reserved for the tiny span of time when a pure, classical, balanced harmony was attained, and when artists of the first rank were in absolute control of their techniques, able to render anything they wanted with the maximum of fidelity to nature. It is this mastery of technique which, with the elimination of superfluous detail, is one of the distinguishing marks between Early and High Renaissance. The High Renaissance lasted from *c.*1500 to about 1527, the date of the Sack of Rome, and it includes the earlier works of MICHELANGELO, all the Roman works of RAPHAEL, and most of LEONARDO's work. The later work of Michelangelo is dedicated to different ideals, and the style of the period 1530/1600 is now generally known as MANNERISM, while the style of the 17th century, in accordance with yet other ideals, is BAROQUE. All these have a passion for classical models as a distinguishing mark, so that the Renaissance style must also have the classical qualities of serenity and harmony – qualities which were lost sight of in the period of the Counter-Reformation, or the Thirty Years War.

RENI, Guido (1575–1642), was a Bolognese painter who enjoyed the highest reputation in the 17th and 18th centuries until it was blasted by Ruskin, following the revulsion of the NAZARENER and the PRB. In spite of Reni's sentimental religiosity his pictures are now returning to favour, on account of their combination of CARAVAGGIO and the CARRACCI. To the surprise of his fellow-countrymen he remained a life-long virgin; this, however, he is said to have compensated for by an addiction to gambling. He was a pupil, with ALBANI and DOMENICHINO, of the Fleming CALVAERT (*c.*1584–93) until his conversion to the manner of the Carracci *c.*1594. About 1600/1 he went to Rome for the first time, where he was influenced to some extent by the naturalism of Caravaggio (who, typically, is said to have threatened to kill him); his own style, however, depends much more on the Raphaelesque classicism of the Carracci Academy and is best seen in the *Aurora* (1613–14, Rome, Casino Rospigliosi). This is a ceiling fresco that makes no attempt at SOTTO IN SÙ illusionism (cf. GUERCINO's *Aurora* of 1621–3), but is treated exactly as an easel picture seen in the normal way; it also contains some conscious quotations from the antique. Apart from a trip to Naples in 1622 he worked in Rome, and, mainly, in Bologna. The plague of 1630 in Bologna was the cause of his great votive *Madonna* (1631–2, Bologna, Pinacoteca). There are many works by him in Bologna and Rome (Capitoline, Borghese, Quirinal Palace, S. Gregorio Magno and other Roman churches) and others in Auckland NZ, Baltimore (Walters), Birmingham, Bradford, Cambridge (Fitzwm), Chicago, Cleveland Ohio, Detroit, Dresden, Dublin, Edinburgh (NG), Florence (Uffizi and Pitti), Genoa (Gall. Naz., Pal. Rosso and S. Ambrogio), Glasgow, Greenville SC, Kingston Lacy Dorset (National Trust), Leeds, London (NG and Dulwich: a splendid *Baptist*, 1640–2), Los Angeles, Madrid (Prado), Malibu (Getty), Manchester, Munich, Naples, New York (Met. Mus.), Paris (*Deeds of Hercules* set, 1617/21, in the Louvre, and *Job*, 1622–36, recently rediscovered in Notre Dame), Prague, Sarasota Fla, Toledo Ohio, the Vatican and Vienna (K-H Mus. and Akad.).

RENOIR, Pierre Auguste (1841–1919), was one of the greatest of the painters affected by IMPRESSIONISM. He worked from the age of 13 in a china factory and his early training as a painter on porcelain predisposed him towards the light palette of Impressionism. In 1861 he spent some time in the teaching studio of GLEYRE, where he met MONET, BAZILLE and SISLEY. He also frequented the Louvre, and was particularly interested in Watteau, Boucher and Fragonard: all his life he was conscious of the need to study art in museums, and dissatisfied with the purely visual aspects of Impressionism. The main influence on his early career was COURBET, until about 1868, and during this time he used heavy impasto and rather dark colour. In 1868 he and Monet worked together on the Seine, and as a result of painting continually out of doors – and of Monet's influence – his colour became lighter and lighter in key, and his handling freer, the whole canvas being managed in patches of coloured light and shadow without any definite drawing. He exhibited in the first three Impressionist exhibitions, and then in the seventh; after 1877 he was successful in getting some of his portraits into the Salon (e.g. *Mme Charpentier and her Children*, 1878, New York, Met. Mus.), and was unwilling to risk the market that this offered for the sake of the often disadvantageous advertisement provided by the group shows. In 1881 (and again in 1882) he visited North Africa, was in Guernsey in 1883, and made the first of several trips to Italy in the winter of 1881–2; he later travelled widely, visiting

London, Holland, Spain and Germany, studying in museums. He deeply admired Raphael and Velázquez – more even than Rubens, to whose art his own was so much indebted. After his first Italian journey his drawing became much firmer, his Impressionism much less the spontaneous result of purely visual stimuli than the conscious use of colour to recreate Nature and form, and this in turn involved departure from Monet's form of Impressionism – direct painting before the object – by the adoption of a more elaborate technique, with preparatory drawings and successive sessions on the canvas while the figure and its setting were worked up: '*Il faut meubler la toile*', was his way of putting it. Where his early works include portraits, landscapes, flowers and groups of figures in settings of café, dance-hall, boats or riverside landscapes, his late works are mostly nudes, or near nudes. The warmth and tenderness of pink and pearly flesh entranced him and gave him full scope for his favourite colour schemes of pinks and reds, and the exploitation of a chosen colour scheme is in itself an un-Impressionist idea: '*Il faut avoir*,' he said, '*le sentiment des fesses et des tétons*.'

In 1906 he settled in Cagnes in the south of France, but he was already crippled with arthritis, which finally rendered him completely helpless, so that his last pictures were painted with brushes stuck between his twisted fingers. He also 'made' a certain amount of sculpture – 'dictated' rather, since the clay was worked by an assistant who added or removed on his instructions, to create rather Maillol-like figures of impressive simplicity and solidity. In his last years he saw a good deal of Matisse, who lived nearby, and he was interested in and sympathetic to the ideas behind Fauvism. He painted about 6,000 pictures: there is a large collection in Paris (Mus. d'Orsay), and there are works in Berlin, Birmingham, Boston (Mus.), Budapest, Cambridge (Fitzwm), Cambridge Mass. (Fogg), Cardiff, Chicago, Cologne (Wallraf-Richartz), Essen, Glasgow, London (NG, Tate and Courtauld Inst.), Manchester, New York (Met. Mus.), Ottawa, Rouen, São Paulo, Stockholm, Toronto and Washington (NG, Phillips). America is particularly rich in Renoirs, since they were bought there when the artist was still unappreciated in Europe: Williamstown Mass. has a particularly instructive contrast between nudes by Renoir and BOUGUEREAU.

REPIN, Ilya (1844–1930), was a Russian painter of genre, history and portraits, who is sometimes seen as a forerunner of SOCIAL REALISM, partly on account of the occasional political content of his pictures. He was in Vienna, Rome and Paris in 1871 and revisited Paris in 1883, when he was influenced by Impressionism. After 1917 he lived in Finland. Outside Russia there are works in New York (Met. Mus.).

REPLICA. An exact copy of a picture, made by the painter of the original or at least under his supervision. It is often used to describe two or more paintings, exactly alike, when one is in doubt which (if any) is the prime original.

REPOUSSOIR (Fr. *repousser*, to push back) is used to describe a figure or other object placed in the extreme foreground of a picture, usually at the right or left edge, with the object of deflecting the spectator's eye into the centre of the picture. A *repoussoir* figure often aids in this by gesticulating in the required direction.

REREDOS, RETABLE. A fixed altarpiece. There is no clear distinction between the various forms taken by large-scale altarpieces, which differ considerably between Italy, Germany and Spain at various periods. The earliest retables are of the 12th century, and were built on the back of the altar-table itself, or against the wall behind it, and soon became complexes of painting and sculpture, in relief or in the round, painted and gilded. In Germany the *Schnitzaltar*, or carved altar, could be extremely elaborate, moveable, with additional painting and carving: examples can be found in the work of PACHER and STOSS, but GRÜNEWALD's Isenheim Altar, of *c*. 1515, is perhaps the most elaborate form of such a POLYPTYCH, with no fewer than three central layers – the innermost being carved, and the two sets of outer panels painted; with six painted scenes on the wings, as well as a PREDELLA. The 17th-century Spanish *retablo* was equally elaborate, but usually consisted of a very large fixed framework containing multiple panels and, occasionally, sculpture as well. El Greco's High Altar, formerly in Santo Domingo el Antiguo, Toledo, of 1577–9, is an early example, and there are others by Zurbarán and Murillo. The Italian ANCONA is generally simpler in form and gradually came to replace the others as the basic form of altar decoration – i.e. a single PALA, often very large, in a simple architectural setting, with any sculpture confined to statuary on the altar itself or perhaps a relief as a predella.

RETABLE *see* REREDOS.

RETHEL, Alfred (1816–59), was, with CORNELIUS, the major early 19th-century German painter on a monumental scale. He was influenced by the NAZARENER, but worked on a much larger scale. He visited Italy in 1844–5 and again in 1852–3, but his career was cut short by madness in 1853. His major works were the frescoes for the Town Hall, Aachen, projected from 1840, begun in 1847, and left incomplete. He also made a woodcut series *Another Dance of Death* (1849), in imitation of Holbein, but satirizing the 1849 Dresden Revolution.

RETROUSSAGE, is a term used in etching to describe the action of passing a pad of muslin lightly over an inked plate with the intention of dragging some of the ink out of the lines and smearing it across the plate.

REUWICH, Erhard, active in Mainz *c*.1475–*c*.1500, is often identified with the MASTER OF THE HOUSEBOOK. B. von Breydenbach's *Peregrinationes in Terram Sanctam* (Mainz, 1486) mentions him as a Utrecht painter who accompanied Breydenbach on his travels, making a drawing of Venice on the spot in 1483. The woodcuts in the book (as well as a view of Venice, of 1486) are attributed to him, and, by stylistic comparison, the Housebook Master's engravings and paintings have been added to his *oeuvre*.

REYMERSWAELE (Roymerswaele) *see* MARINUS.

REYNOLDS, Sir Joshua (1723–92), is, historically, the most important figure in British painting. He was born at Plympton St Maurice in Devon, where his father was a clergyman, headmaster of the Grammar School, and a former Fellow of Balliol: this is worth mentioning because it shows that Reynolds was born and brought up in an educated family at a time when most English painters were hardly more than ill-educated tradesmen. Reynolds himself became the close friend of Dr Johnson, Goldsmith, Burke and Garrick, and it is probably true that he did more to raise the status of the artist in England through his learning and personal example than by his actual quality as an artist. He was apprenticed to HUDSON in 1740, in London, but in 1743 he left his master and returned to Devonshire; from 1743 to 1749 he was in practice on his own in London and Devonshire, before leaving for Italy in 1749. As early as 1746 he painted the *Eliot Family Group*, based on a famous van Dyck at Wilton House, and this already shows the fundamental basis of his art – the deliberate use of allusion to the Old Masters or Antique sculpture, as a classical literary allusion might have been used by an 18th-century speaker or writer. This appeal to the educated eye, above and beyond the needs of mere likeness, is the essence of his own style and the reason for the rise in public esteem for the visual arts which is so marked a feature of his age. In 1749 he had the chance to go to Italy with Commodore (later Admiral Viscount) Keppel, who was also to become one of his best friends. Up to this time the main influences on his style had been Hogarth, Ramsay and, to a moderate extent only, Hudson; he now spent two years (1750–2) in Rome, where he made a really prolonged study of the Antique, of Raphael and, above all, of Michelangelo. Here he learned the intellectual basis of Italian art (just as WILSON was doing), and this was something that scarcely any other British painter, with the possible exception of Ramsay, had done up to then, even in Rome itself. In fact, Reynolds's own practice as a portrait painter was more profoundly influenced by the few weeks he spent in Venice on his way home in 1752. He never ceased to exhort his students to master the principles of the Grand Style, and indeed he genuinely regarded Venetian art, and portrait painting, as of less importance. In 1753 he set up in London, met Dr Johnson, and began rapidly to make a name. He sought consciously to marry the Grand Style with the demands of face-painting (and earning a living), and he succeeded so well that he was soon employing assistants, although the Kneller school was not converted ('Shakespeare in poetry, and Kneller in painting, damme!' as one of them observed). Only Ramsay and Cotes were rivals of any significance, but by 1768, when the Royal Academy was founded, it was obvious that Reynolds was the only possible choice for the President. He was knighted in 1769, given an Honorary Doctorate at Oxford (an honour previously given only to Kneller among painters), and elected Mayor of his native Plympton in 1772. The works of the years following 1768 show him at his most classical and most learned, determined to use the Academy as an instrument to forge a British School of History painters to stand beside those of Rome or Bologna. To this end he composed and delivered at intervals (1769–90) the fifteen 'Discourses' which are the most lucid and sensible exposition of the Academic position that, by well-directed labour, it is possible to learn the Rules of Art and to use the inventions and ideas of one's predecessors to create a new style of one's own. During these years Reynolds exhibited regularly at the Academy and usually showed a skilful blend of large portraits treated in an historical manner, history pictures proper, and some curious combinations of the two, such as *Dr Beattie* (*The Triumph of Truth*) (Aberdeen Univ.), or *Three Ladies Adorning a Term of Hymen* (London, NG), both in the RA of 1774. This idea had been exploited by him as early as 1760/1 in his *Garrick between Tragedy and Comedy*, a thoroughly 'learned' picture which he exhibited in 1762 at the Society of Artists, the Academy's precursor. He won the victory in general terms, although many ladies still preferred to be painted by Gainsborough in a fashionable gown rather than the 'nightgowns' which Sir Joshua insisted on, as less subject to the vagaries of fashion and more nearly classical in type; although pictures like *Lady Sarah Bunbury sacrificing to the Graces* (Chicago) come close to the ridiculous. In 1781 he made a journey to Flanders and Holland and was profoundly influenced by the force and freedom of Rubens's handling, and from then until his sight failed in 1789 his works are less consciously classical and painted with greater warmth and feeling. The overwhelming majority of his vast output consists of portraits, which include almost every man and woman of note in England in the second half of the 18th century. Unlike GAINSBOROUGH, he employed many pupils and assistants and his work also differs from Gainsborough's in being frequently poorly preserved on account of his bad technical procedures. The faces of his sitters are often deathly pale because the carmine (a fugitive red) has faded out completely. There is a fine double portrait of Burke and Rockingham in Cambridge (Fitzwm), which is unfinished and shows his methods. Most of his sitter-books (diaries of appointments) and ledgers still exist and thus nearly all his works are documented: practically every major museum in Britain and America contains one or more, and others are as far afield as Leningrad and São Paulo, Dresden and Adelaide, Budapest and Ottawa.

RIBALTA, Francisco (1565–1628), was a Catalan painter whose first known work is the *Christ Nailed to the Cross* of 1582 (Leningrad, Hermitage). This is a crude work in the Mannerist tradition, but after Ribalta settled in Valencia in 1599 his style seems to have undergone a considerable change. He was one of the first of the 17th-century Spanish Realists, and his mature works have an austere, almost grim, sobriety, combined with dramatic lighting which seems to show CARAVAGGIO's influence. It seems that he had actually studied in Italy, as he copied the Caravaggio *St Peter* in Rome (S.M. del Popolo); but his earliest Caravaggesque paintings are not earlier than 1615, by which date other Spaniards had been influenced by Italian TENEBRISM. In his last works there is an affinity with the style of RIBERA. The *Vision of Fr Simon* (1612, London, NG) is a good example of his devotional style, although it does not yet show Caravaggio's influence. His son Juan – who died in the same year as his father, 1628 – was also a painter. There are works in Dublin, Madrid (Prado) and Valencia.

RIBERA, Jusepe or José (1591–1652), called 'Spagnoletto' was born near Valencia and may possibly have studied under RIBALTA before going to Italy, where he travelled, became a member of the Accademia di S. Luca in Rome, and settled in Naples by 1616. He was in Rome in 1615, where he came in contact with the Northern Caravaggisti (Caravaggio himself had died in 1610). The style of his early works (the first dated ones are of 1626: *St Jerome* and *Silenus*, both in Naples, Capodimonte) shows a blending of Spanish realism with a degree of idealization derived from the Carracci, expressed in the strong chiaroscuro of Caravaggio. This invests his often brutal subjects with a powerful but unsubtle forcefulness, e.g. the *Martyrdom of St Bartholomew*, *c.*1630 (Florence, Pitti), now accentuated by the darkening of his colours through the use of bitumen and bolus grounds. His etchings are frequently better composed than his paintings of related subjects in that they are free of these excessive contrasts of light and shadow. By the mid-1630s his style had changed to a greater softness and the blocks of light in a sea of dark gave place to suaver colour and more even handling, reflecting the influence of Velázquez, who was in Naples in 1630, and, from *c.*1634, that of van Dyck and the Venetians, especially in his portraits. The tales of his bloodthirsty opposition to the competition in Naples of Guido RENI and DOMENICHINO are probably apocryphal. He enjoyed the patronage of successive Viceroys and his works were very popular in Spain, since they exploited the essentially Spanish subjects of Counter-Reformation painting – half- or, less frequently, full-length figures of strongly characterized male saints or rapt female ones, occasional mythologies in which even Venus is fully clothed, tender Nativities, scenes from the Passion or the lives of the saints, full of emotion and devotion. In his later years his reputation was diminished by his reduced output and slowness of execution, due to ill-health, which was probably affected by the *éclat* of the seduction of his daughter by Don Juan of Austria, a natural son of Philip IV of Spain, who was sent to Naples to quell the Masaniello rising in 1647. The large school of Neapolitan Tenebrist painting probably owes more to Ribera than to Caravaggio, since it develops along his lines, to the point that when it is impossible to decide whether a work is Spanish or Italian, the answer is usually to call it Neapolitan, as in the case of the *Locksmith* (London, Dulwich).

There are many works by him in Madrid (Prado and Academia), and in Naples (Pinacoteca, Palazzo Reale, Cath., Mus. di S. Martino and Mus. Civico), and also in Bilbao, Berlin, Boston (Mus.), Brussels, Budapest, Cambridge Mass. (Fogg), Cardiff, Castres, Cleveland Ohio, Dallas Texas, Dresden, Dublin, the Escorial, Hartford Conn. (Wadsworth), Hull, Leeds, London (NG and Wellington Mus.), Milan (Poldi-Pezzoli), Montreal, New York (Hispanic Soc. and Met. Mus.), Paris (Louvre), Pasadena Cal., Philadelphia, Rome (Doria, Corsini and Gall. Naz.), Rouen, Salamanca (Immaculate Conception), Toledo Ohio, Vitoria, Worcester Mass. and Yale.

RICCI. There were two, Sebastiano and his nephew Marco, both Venetians. Sebastiano (1659–1734) was the first of the itinerant Venetian painters (cf. CANALETTO, BELLOTTO, TIEPOLO), working in Bologna, Rome, Modena, Florence and Parma, before going to Vienna, where he worked in the Schönbrunn Palace. In 1712 he went to England with his nephew. They left in 1716, after Sebastiano failed to get the commissions to decorate the dome of St Paul's and Hampton Court Palace, both of which went to THORNHILL. Nevertheless, they collaborated on an imaginary *Tomb of the Duke of Devonshire* (Birmingham, Barber Inst.) as part of a Whig propaganda series. Sebastiano's major English work is the *Resurrection* painted in the apse of Chelsea Hospital Chapel (sketches in London (Dulwich) and Columbia SC); it has a light, quick rhythm and a decorative feeling quite new after the ponderous and tasteless works of VERRIO. He left the decoration of Burlington House incomplete (it was finished by KENT) when he returned to Venice, and on the way home he stopped in Paris and visited Watteau, some of whose drawings he copied. There are twenty-one paintings by Sebastiano in the Royal Coll., including a *Finding of Moses* originally attributed to Veronese. This stresses the fact that Sebastiano had been so well trained in the Veronese tradition that his works could pass as by the 16th-century artist: his stay in London was enlivened by several rows over his abilities as a *pasticheur*. His translations of Veronese into 18th-century style were an important influence on the young Tiepolo. Marco (1676–1730) was a pupil of Sebastiano's, and probably worked with him in Florence, 1706–7. He may also have visited Rome and Milan, where he perhaps knew MAGNASCO, who influenced him. He went to England in 1708 with PELLEGRINI, with whom he worked on stage scenery, and in 1710 he seems to have gone back to Venice to fetch his uncle. They returned together in 1712, travelling via the Netherlands, and remained for about four years, arriving back in Venice *c.*1717. The remainder of his life is ill-documented: he appears to have worked for Sebastiano on landscape backgrounds for large religious works and to have executed small landscapes in tempera on leather (several are in the Royal Coll.). His landscapes are often *capricci*; they are usually lively and free in handling. He was one of the first of the Venetian etchers of the 18th century, and his *Experimenta* were published posthumously in 1730.

There is a large number of drawings by both Riccis in the Royal Coll., and many of the older galleries have paintings by them, as well as Brighton, Gateshead, Leeds and London (Chiswick House).

RICCIO, Andrea (1470–1532), was a Paduan sculptor who is supposed to have been a pupil of Bellano, who was himself an assistant of DONATELLO. Riccio was trained as a goldsmith, which may account for the very delicate handling of his small bronzes. He was working in Padua by 1496/7 and his most famous work is the Paschal candlestick in the Santo at Padua of 1507/15. His *Shouting Horseman* seems to reflect Leonardo's lost cartoon for the *Battle of Anghiari*, which he must have known in Florence. His bronze statuettes are in most major museums, and reflect the humanist tastes of Padua in the 15th and 16th centuries. Fine examples are in Birmingham (Barber Inst.), Écouen, Florence (Bargello), London (V&A and Wallace Coll.), New York (Frick Coll.), Oxford, Paris (Louvre) and Yale.

RICHARDS, Ceri (1903–71), was a Welsh painter whose abstract pictures are often based on themes taken from poetry (Dylan Thomas: 'Do not go gentle into that good night . . .') or music (Debussy, *La Cathédrale engloutie*), or based on earlier paintings, such as the *Lion Hunt*, after Delacroix. He was a friend of David JONES and ARP in the 1930s, but Picasso and Miró were dominant influences. In 1958 he painted the altarpiece for St Edmund Hall, Oxford, and in 1964 made two stained-glass windows for Derby Cathedral, as well as a huge decoration for the Shakespeare Festival. He decorated the Chapel of the Blessed Sacrament in the new Catholic Cathedral in Liverpool in 1968 (thirty-five sketches in Liverpool Gallery) and there are other works by him in Aberdeen, Cardiff, Edinburgh (M of MA), London (Tate), Manchester (City Gall. and Whitworth), Ottawa, Swansea (Gallery and Parish Church) and Toledo Ohio.

RICHARDSON, Jonathan (1665–1745), a pupil of Riley, *c.*1688–91, and inheritor of his teacher's stiff and solemn manner, was the principal portrait painter of the period between Kneller and Hudson. In 1711 he and Kneller founded the St Martin's Lane Academy, from which eventually sprang the RA Schools. He had a considerable influence through his books, 'The Theory of Painting', 1715, and the guidebook widely used by Grand Tourists, 'An Account of the Statues . . . and Pictures in Italy', which he wrote with his son, Jonathan the Younger (1694–1771), in 1722. His son also painted, but is better known for his writings on connoisseurship. There are works in Oxford and Cambridge Colleges, Edinburgh (SNPG), Leeds, London (NPG), Yale (CBA) and elsewhere.

RICHIER, Germaine (1904–59), was a French sculptress, who also made engravings, book-illustrations, and ceramics. She worked with BOURDELLE 1925–9 and then, under the influence of Surrealism, she began to make spindly figures similar to those by GIACOMETTI (who had also been a pupil of Bourdelle). She lived in Switzerland 1939–45, but in 1950 was commissioned to make a crucifix for the new and controversial church at Assy (Haute-Savoie), which has works by Braque, Matisse, Lipchitz and other leading artists. There are works in Amsterdam, Basle, Brussels, Edinburgh (NG of Modern Art), London (Tate), Minneapolis, Paris, Rome, Stockholm and Zurich.

RIEMENSCHNEIDER, Tilman (*c.*1460–1531), was, with STOSS, the leading German sculptor of the Late Gothic style. His life was dramatic – he became Bürgermeister of Würzburg, took part in the peasants' wars and was tortured *c.*1525, after which he probably never worked again. From 1483 he worked in Würzburg, where he kept a very large shop which produced scores of carvings, mostly in wood, of emotional subjects such as the Lamentation. He also worked in stone and his *Adam* and *Eve* are curiously reminiscent of RIZZO. There is a splendid collection in Würzburg and other works in Bamberg Cath. (Tombs of the Emperor Henry II and his wife), Berlin, Cleveland Ohio, London (V&A), Munich, Providence RI, and many German churches.

RIGAUD, Hyacinthe (1659–1743), was born in Perpignan and went to Paris in 1681. He won the second Prix de Rome in 1682, but, on the advice of LEBRUN, did not go to Italy. He was the principal official painter to the court of Louis XIV and also worked under Louis XV in a style derived from van Dyck and Philippe de Champaigne. Like his friend and rival LARGILLIERRE, he expressed the pomp of *le roi soleil* in his great state portraits, and occasionally the character of his sitters. His non-official portraits show the influence of Rembrandt, seven of whose works he owned. He had a very active studio and few of his pictures – on the evidence of his account books – can be wholly his own work. He painted an average of thirty-five portraits a year for sixty-two years. There are examples in Paris (Louvre), Versailles, and many French provincial museums, and also in Dresden, Florence (Uffizi), London (NG, NPG, Wallace Coll., Dulwich and Kenwood), Melbourne, Munich, Naples, New York (Met. Mus.), Ottawa, Stockholm, Toledo Ohio, Vienna and elsewhere.

RILEY, Bridget (*b.*1931), is a British painter who specializes in OP ART. Her works – most of them until *c.*1964 in black and white, and large in scale – concentrate on provoking sensations of dazzle and visual disturbance in the spectator, being entirely dependent on pattern and an effect of movement. She now uses assistants to execute her carefully plotted designs of curving and swirling lines, strongly influenced by the ideas of VASARELY. There are examples in Edinburgh, London (Tate) and elsewhere.

RILEY, John (1646–91), was the leading English portrait painter in the short interval between the dominations of Lely and Kneller. Nothing is known of Riley's work before 1680, but by 1688 his fame was so well grounded that he was appointed Principal Painter to William and Mary jointly with Kneller; nevertheless, his best works may well be the portraits of humble people, such as the *Bridget Holmes, a Nonagenarian Housemaid*, in the Royal Coll., or the *Scullion* at Ch. Ch., Oxford. The *William Chiffinch* (London, Dulwich) is probably of about 1680 (or earlier). There are other pictures by him in the Royal Coll., London (NPG and Tate), Oxford (Ashmolean and Bodleian Library), Waddesdon Bucks. (National Trust) and Yale (CBA).

RILIEVO *see* RELIEF.

RIOPELLE, Jean Paul (*b*.1923), is the leading Canadian abstract painter, although he has lived in Paris since 1947. His work shows the influence of Kandinsky, Miró and Pollock. In 1949 he exhibited at the Surrealist Exhibition in Paris, but later moved away from them. London (Tate), New York (M of MA), Ottawa and Paris (Mus. d'Art Mod.) have examples.

RIVERA, Diego (1886–1957), was a Mexican painter who worked in Paris during the years that brought Cubism to birth, and he knew most of the principal artists in that movement. He held aloof from it, however, and eventually returned to Mexico (in 1921), where, like OROZCO, he was powerfully affected by politics. His first teacher, in Mexico City, had been a pupil of Ingres and Rivera's art was always more revolutionary in content than in style. His 'Mexican' art is largely dependent on a vocabulary evolved from a mixture of Gauguin with Aztec and Mayan sculpture. In his large commissions for the decoration of public buildings Rivera used *buon fresco*, a technique that he revived, as he also revived the use of ancient encaustic methods. His mural in the Rockefeller Centre, New York, was replaced by one by BRANGWYN on account of the introduction of a portrait of Lenin rather than for any objection to the style. Detroit has two very large murals of 1933.

RIZZO, Antonio (*c*.1430–1499/1500), made the earliest Venetian Renaissance free-standing tomb, of Orsato Giustiniani (*d*.1464), dismembered but known from a drawing of the whole, and fragments in New York (Met. Mus.), El Paso Texas and Pavia (Cassa di Risparmio). He may have worked with Antonio BREGNO on the Arco Foscari. Rizzo also made tombs for Doge Tron (S.M. dei Frari, 1476–82) and Giovanni Emo (Servi, after 1483, now also dismembered but known from a drawing). He became architect to the Doge's Palace in 1483 and at about the same time made the *Adam* and *Eve* now in the Palace. He fled Venice in 1498 after being accused of peculation, and died in Foligno.

ROBBIA, Luca della (1399/1400–82), was ranked by contemporaries as one of the great innovators at the beginning of the 15th century, along with Ghiberti and Donatello, who were much older, and Masaccio, who was his contemporary but had a very short life compared to Luca's very long one. His first major work was the *Cantoria* or *Singing Gallery* for the Cathedral in Florence (1431–8, now in the Cath. Mus.), which was commissioned from him before its companion was ordered from Donatello. This shows his use of antique examples, but it has also his warm and cheerful humanity, quite unlike the drama and grandeur of Donatello. Much later, between 1464 and 1469, he made the bronze doors of the Cathedral Sacristy, and again the comparison with Donatello's Sacristy in S. Lorenzo can hardly be avoided. Early in his career – perhaps even before 1430 – Luca discovered a means of applying the vitrified lead glazes used by potters to sculpture in terracotta, and he exploited this discovery in a number of smallish works with figures in white against a clear blue background. He was also able to use a large number of colours in this way, but he restricted them to architectural and decorative works (e.g. the entrance of the Pazzi Chapel, Florence). To some extent this discovery was the ruin of his art (but not so much as is commonly supposed), for he was able to found a flourishing family business which later undertook some very large and highly coloured commissions. His nephew, Andrea della Robbia (1435–

1525), carried on the business and is best known for the *Foundling Children* on the façade of the Spedale degli Innocenti, Florence (1463–6). Andrea's sons, Giovanni (1469–after 1529) and Girolamo (1488–1566), and other sons for a short time as well, all carried on the tradition well into the 16th century. There are works by Luca in Berlin, Florence (Bargello, Cath., Campanile, Sta Trinita, Sta Croce (Pazzi Chapel) and other churches and palaces), Impruneta, London (V&A), New York (Met. Mus.), Nynehead church Somerset, Paris (Louvre, Cluny Mus. and Jacquemart-André), Peretola nr Florence, Pescia, Toledo Ohio, Urbino (S. Domenico), Vienna and Washington (NG).

ROBERT, Hubert (1733–1808), went to Rome in 1754 and spent eleven years in Italy, where he became a friend of PIRANESI and PANINI, whose type of Romantic ruin-painting he introduced to France. In 1761 he went to South Italy and Sicily with FRAGONARD and the Abbé de Saint-Non, and he and Fragonard influenced each other profoundly in style, though not in subject matter. He returned to Paris in 1765, became a member of the Academy and painted decorative compositions for a number of great houses; later, his range widened and he painted views and street-scenes in Paris. He became Keeper of Louis XVI's pictures and was later one of the first Curators of the Louvre. He is represented in the Louvre and many French provincial museums and also in Baltimore, Barnard Castle (Bowes Mus.), Birmingham (Barber Inst.), Boston, Bristol, Cambridge (Fitzwm), Chicago, Detroit, Leningrad (a large collection in the Hermitage), New York (Met. Mus.), Washington (NG), Worcester Mass., York and elsewhere.

ROBERTI, Ercole d'Antonio de' (*c*.1448/55–96), was active in Ferrara from 1479 and from 1486 was Court Painter to the Este family there. He may have been a pupil of COSSA and worked with him in Bologna before settling in Ferrara, but he was also influenced by the Ferrarese TURA and above all by Giovanni BELLINI, although he is not known to have had any contacts with Venice. The only work reasonably certainly his is a large altarpiece of 1480/1 (Milan, Brera) by 'Ercole', but his highly personal style, with its nervous sensibility and deep pathos in such works as the Liverpool *Pietà*, is easily recognizable: nevertheless, much confusion has been caused by the introduction of Ercole di Giulio Cesare de' Grandi, who is said to have died in 1531. This man may well have existed and may even have been a Bolognese painter, and was conceivably influenced by Ercole Roberti – only there is no evidence at all for any work by him. Other works by Roberti are in Berlin, Bologna (Pinacoteca, Univ.), Chicago, Dresden, Ferrara, Fort Worth Texas, London (NG), Paris (Louvre), Philadelphia (Johnson), the Vatican and Washington (NG).

ROBERTS, David (1796–1864), called 'the Scottish Canaletto', was a topographical and architectural painter who was born in Edinburgh, but went to London in 1822, where he worked with STANFIELD. He travelled widely in Italy, Spain and the Middle East. There are works in Edinburgh, Glasgow and London (Tate, V&A and Wallace Coll.). His *St Paul's with the Lord Mayor's Procession* (Liverpool) is a good example.

ROBERTS, William (1895–1980), was influenced by CUBISM as early as 1913, when he travelled in France and Italy, and in 1914 he signed the Vorticist Manifesto with Wyndham LEWIS. He was a war artist from 1917 and there are several works in London (Imperial War Mus.), where his rather mechanical style suited the subject. For the rest of his life he painted puppet-like figures of tubular form, but often with a sardonic humour. He was made ARA in 1958 and RA in 1966. There are works in the Tate Gallery.

ROCKER. A wide chisel with a rounded blade cut into saw-like teeth, used to roughen the surface of a mezzotint plate. *See* ENGRAVING, 2(e).

ROCOCO. Immediately after the death of Louis XIV of France in 1715 there was a reaction of relief against the excessive splendours and pomps of Versailles and the whole ceremonious *Roi Soleil* way of life. One of the results was to transfer the centre of French life back to Paris and to build new town houses which were both smaller and much more comfortable than the Baroque palaces. Rococo – which comes from a French word *rocaille*, meaning rock-work – is basically a style of interior decoration, and consists principally in the use of C scrolls and counter-curves, and, in its fullest form around 1730, asymmetrical arrangements of curves in panelling and elsewhere. Porcelain, and gold- and silversmiths' work of the first half of the 18th century exemplify the tendencies admirably. The characteristics of small curves, prettiness and gaiety can also be found in painting and sculpture of the period – Watteau and Boucher, and even, in a very modified form, in Hogarth. Nevertheless, England did not take to Rococo and in France it fell out of fashion in the 1740s to be decisively superseded by the earnest ideals and Republican Roman virtue of NEOCLASSICISM, which was largely propagated by Germans. Yet the one country in which the Rococo produced numerous great works of art (and not merely amusing interiors) was Germany, or rather, Germany and Austria. There, in the Catholic South, the style produced scores of absurdly beautiful churches and statues, by artists like Ignaz GÜNTHER, which are elegant, modish and deeply moving. Guardi, Tiepolo and Goya all produced masterpieces, but Rococo had relatively little currency in Italy and Spain.

RODIN, Auguste (1840–1917), was the most celebrated sculptor of the late 19th century, achieving during his lifetime a fame which has done much to obscure his real qualities. He worked as a mason from about 1864, and in 1871 was sent to Brussels to do the decorative figures on the new Stock Exchange building, on which he eventually worked as a freelance. He supplemented his technical training by studying in museums and became interested in Michelangelo, to whom he was probably led by his admiration for PUGET. In 1875 he visited Italy, and soon afterwards began working on his first independent freestanding figure, *Bronze Age* (1877). Its lifelike quality, accuracy of proportion and anatomy, and rendering of movement gave rise to the tale that it had been made from a cast taken from a live model. Though the absurd accusation was later dropped, the figure received no real recognition until it was shown in London in 1884. This put Rodin into much the same position of anti-Academism as the Impressionists and their successors, although he never had to face opposition as vehement and entrenched as they did. Most of his public commissions were unlucky: the base of the *Claude Lorraine* monument in Nancy was altered to suit the town council; the town council of Calais refused to erect his *Burghers* (1884–6, replica outside the Houses of Parliament, London) according to his design; his only equestrian statue, *General Lynch*, was destroyed before erection in Santiago by a Chilean revolution (a small bronze of the model is now in Santiago), his *Thinker* was not erected as he wished and was savaged by a vandal with a chopper; his *Victor Hugo* was produced in several versions to meet endless objections and was finally not put up as planned; his *Balzac* monument was refused by the commissioning committee in 1893 and only erected much later; his *Gate of Hell*, commissioned in 1880 as a door for the École des Arts Décoratifs, was still unfinished at his death, and is now in the Mus. d'Orsay.

This door, inspired by Ghiberti's so-called *Gates of Paradise* for the Baptistry in Florence, contained a large number of figures which provided him with a fount of ideas which he used over and over again in larger independent statues and groups in bronze and marble (e.g. *The Thinker*, *The Prodigal Son*). He also employed many marble-cutters and cast-makers to make replicas, which he often completed himself: BOURDELLE and DESPIAU both worked for him. He was the creator of a new form in sculpture – the fragment as a finished work, usually a head and trunk, but sometimes a pair of hands only – and he also employed a variant of Michelangelo's unfinished figures, giving to some parts a waxy delicacy of finish, while leaving other parts buried in the hardly touched block. It is important, however, that his NONFINITO quality is contrived from the standpoint of a modeller in clay, and not as a mason would actually leave unfinished forms roughed-out in a block of stone, contrary to his own early training. This problem was discussed by HILDEBRANDT. His great influence was through the possibilities opened up by his use of fragments, through his expression of emotion and movement, his use of symbolism and distortion, and the amazing sensitiveness of his modelling. This is seen particularly in his male portraits which combine vivid characterization with a deliberately free handling. Rodin himself described his methods in 1913, saying: 'I place the model in such a way that it stands out against the background and so that the light falls on this profile. I execute it, and turn both my turn-table and that of the model so that I can see another profile. Then I turn them again and gradually work my way round the figure', an essentially pictorial approach to sculpture.

There is little point in listing museums containing works, since there are, for instance, 150 or more replicas of the *Bronze Age*, but the Musée Rodin in Paris and the V&A in London have perhaps the most examples. There is also a Rodin Mus. in Philadelphia, and forty-four works in Los Angeles (County Mus.).

ROHLFS, Christian (1849–1938), was the son of a farmer, but a leg injury enabled him to study art at Weimar, where he lived until *c.*1900, painting in an Impressionist manner. An exhibition of works by van Gogh (his younger contemporary) at Hagen in Westphalia in 1902 was a major influence on him, as was his friendship with NOLDE from *c.*1905. He then began to practise a gentle form of Expressionism, and, like MÜLLER, he abandoned oil-paint in favour of tempera and watercolour (from 1911). He painted several series of buildings – the church at Soest and Erfurt Cathedral – but his finest works are the delicate flowerpieces, mostly painted when he was nearing 80. Many of these were painted at Ascona, on Lake Maggiore, where he spent most of the years 1927–37. There are works by him in Cologne, Dresden, Essen, Hagen, Harvard University, Karlsruhe, Mannheim and Paris (Mus. d'Art Moderne).

ROMANISTS were the Northern artists who went to Italy and returned fired with the idea of rivalling Raphael and/or Michelangelo. The name is principally given to painters of the first half of the 16th century, such as MABUSE, van

ORLEY or Maerten van HEEMSKERCK, all of whom imported a quasi-Renaissance style into Northern Europe.

ROMANO, Giulio, *see* GIULIO.

ROMANTIC *see* CLASSIC.

ROMBOUTS, Theodor (1579–1637), was an Antwerp painter who became a Master in the Guild there in 1601, but he went to Rome *c.*1616 and stayed until *c.*1625, where he immediately became strongly influenced by Caravaggio. Like the members of the UTRECHT SCHOOL he took his Caravaggism home to the Netherlands, but on settling in Antwerp again he changed his style under the fresh influence of Rubens and van Dyck. There are pictures in Antwerp, Ghent, Karlsruhe, Lawrence (Kansas Univ. Mus.), Lille, Madrid, Munich, Paris and Vaduz (Liechtenstein).

ROME PRIZE (Prix de Rome). The French Academy in Rome was founded in 1666 for the reception and further training of the twelve best young painters, sculptors and architects, who often spent years in Rome before returning to France – the usual term was about six, but one spent eighteen. After the foundation of the École des Élèves Protégés, the six yearly prizemen had the right to a place in Rome. In 1793 the Convention abolished the Academy in Paris, but the Roman Academy continued, with a period of residence fixed at five years. In the same year, the Royal arms were replaced by those of the new Republic and the mob sacked the Palazzo Mancini, the Academy's premises in Rome. The students dispersed to Florence and Naples, until the Academy was re-established in Rome in 1803 in the Villa Medici, where it still is. The idea was copied by other nations, e.g. Britain and Spain, who established Academies in Rome for similar purposes. DAVID and INGRES were among the great artists who won the *Prix de Rome*.

ROMNEY, George (1734–1802), was, with Gainsborough and Reynolds, the most famous English portrait painter of the later 18th century, before the rise of Lawrence. He was, however, artistically inferior to all of them, even as a portrait painter. He was born in Lancashire and practised in the North until 1762, when he moved to London. His earliest portrait, of his brother James (1750), is now in Kendal. He visited Paris in 1764 and in 1773 he took the serious step of abandoning his London practice (Reynolds was then at the height of his powers, and Gainsborough arrived in London in 1774) to go to Italy, where he stayed till 1775. In Rome he was infected with a longing for the Grand Style, and much of the rest of his life was spent in making sketches for vast historical pictures, some of which were begun on canvas, and painting prosaic portraits, which he did with skill if without passion: John Wesley noted in his Journal (5 January 1789) that he 'struck off an exact likeness at once, and did more in one hour than Sir Joshua did in ten'. He is best known for his Lady Hamilton pictures. He met her in 1781 and seems to have had some kind of liaison with her (his wife having been left in the North), and he could paint portraits of her in more or less *déshabille*, imagining them to be history pieces if called *Lady Hamilton as Circe* or some such title. Many hundreds of his execrable drawings exist, mostly scribbles for historical compositions or illustrations to the poems of Hayley, with whom he was in close contact: in this way he had some importance as a Neoclassic and as a link with FLAXMAN, FUSELI and BLAKE. He rarely exhibited his works, and never at the RA: an exception is the fine group in Melbourne (NG), exhibited at the

Free Society, 1768. In his last years he became senile and returned to his wife to die. At one time his pictures were popular in America and many are in museums there: representative works are in Birmingham, Boston, Brighton, Cardiff, Edinburgh (NG), Kendal, London (NG, Tate, NPG, Wallace Coll., Courtauld Inst., Dulwich and Kenwood), Manchester, New York (Met. Mus.), Ottawa, Paris (Louvre), Rotherham, San Marino Cal., Waddesdon Bucks. (National Trust), Washington (NG) and Yale (CBA).

ROSA, Salvator (1615–73), painter, etcher, poet, actor and musician, was the 19th century's ideal Romantic artist. Traditionally, he was a bandit for a time; unfortunately, this story seems to have been invented in the 19th century. He was very precocious as a painter of landscapes near his native Naples and of battle-pieces, and is said to have attracted the notice of LANFRANCO. He went to Rome in 1635, but contracted malaria, and had to return to Naples in 1636; in 1639 he returned to Rome and settled there, painting battles, marines and landscapes: in the same year, however, he was rash enough to compose and recite a lampoon on Bernini. He arrived safely in Florence in 1640 and did not venture back to Rome until 1649, when he set up as a religious and historical painter, but met with less success. He was one of the first artists to sell his works from exhibitions instead of waiting for commissions (from about 1651), which gave him much greater freedom of choice in subject matter. His landscapes are infused with the Pathetic Fallacy, thus having a 'poetic' quality quite different from that of POUSSIN or CLAUDE – in fact, a PICTURESQUE quality – that appealed greatly to the Age of Reason, so that he was immensely popular in England in the 18th and early 19th centuries; indeed, the celebrated lines from Thomson's 'Castle of Indolence':

> Whate'er Lorraine light-touched with softening hue,
> Or savage Rosa dashed, or learned Poussin drew

more or less sum up the 18th-century connoisseur's equipment. He began etching in the 1650s and completed fifty-six plates, as well as many more unfinished ones, mainly done as experiments. His very numerous works are in all the older galleries, but there are good examples in Berlin, Cambridge (Fitzwm), Chantilly, Chicago, Detroit, Florence (Pitti), Glasgow, Hartford Conn., Kansas City, London (NG, Wallace Coll. and Dulwich), Malibu Cal., Modena, Newcastle (Hatton), New York (Met. Mus.), Oxford (Ashmolean and Ch. Ch.), Paris (Louvre), Richmond Va, Rome (Gall. Naz.), Sarasota Fla, Vienna and Yale.

ROSALBA *see* CARRIERA.

ROSE + CROIX, Salon de la, *see* SYMBOLISM.

ROSLIN, Alexandre (1718–93), was a Swedish portrait painter in oil and pastel, who studied in Italy, worked much in Paris, and is stylistically indistinguishable from a French painter. He arrived in Paris in 1752, revisited Stockholm in 1774, going in 1775 to St Petersburg and returning to Paris, via Warsaw and Vienna, in 1779. His best work is the portrait of his wife (herself an accomplished portraitist in pastel, and a pupil of LATOUR) in a black mantilla (1762, Stockholm, Nat. Mus.). Other works are in Dublin, Glasgow (Univ.), London (NG) and Paris (Louvre).

ROSSELLI, Cosimo (1439–1507), was a Florentine painter who ran an important workshop despite his being one of the most uninspired and pedestrian of the better-known painters of his day, and gifted particularly in irrelevant and trivial details. Part of the contract for the 1481 fresco cycle in the Sistine Chapel in the Vatican was with him, and he appears to have been given a large share of the work. Among his pupils were PIERO di Cosimo and Fra BARTOLOMMEO. There are works by him in Baltimore (Walters), Berlin, Birmingham (Barber Inst.), Boston (Mus.), Cambridge (Fitzwm), Florence (Accad., Uffizi, Mus. di S. Marco and churches), Liverpool (Walker), Lucca (Cath.), New York (Met. Mus.), Oxford (Ashmolean), Paris (Louvre), Philadelphia (Johnson), San Marino Cal. (Huntington) and elsewhere.

ROSSELLINO, Bernardo (1409–64) and Antonio (1427–*c.*1479), were brothers. Bernardo was active as an architect as well as a sculptor, and both seem to have done a certain amount of decorative work. Bernardo's principal work is the Tomb of the Florentine Chancellor Leonardo Bruni (1444/50, Florence, Sta Croce), which derives directly from the Tomb of John XXIII by DONATELLO and in its turn sets the type of Tomb in a niche which was normal for the rest of the century. There are other works by him in Florence and in Empoli and Forlì. Antonio was his pupil and was also much influenced by Donatello, although, like MINO, DESIDERIO and BENEDETTO da Maiano, he rejected the rugged side of Donatello and concentrated on grace and beauty of line. He is best known for his Madonna reliefs, but he also made portrait busts and a Tomb which derives from his brother's but is a grander affair: it is that of the Cardinal-Prince of Portugal (1461–6, Florence, S. Miniato al Monte). There are works by him in Berlin, Empoli, Faenza, Florence (Bargello, Sto Spirito), London (V&A), Naples, New York (Met. Mus.), Pistoia (Cath.), Prato (Cath.), Toledo Ohio, Vienna, Washington (NG) and elsewhere.

ROSSETTI, Dante Gabriel (1828–82), poet and painter, was the son of an Italian political refugee in London. He was taught drawing by Cotman and after a few unsuccessful months with Ford Madox BROWN he went to Holman HUNT in 1848. Under Hunt's guidance he painted his first major work, *The Girlhood of Mary Virgin*, the first picture exhibited (in March 1849) with the initials of the PRB. His adherence to the tenets of the Brotherhood was, however, very shortlived. His subjects were drawn mostly from Dante and from a medieval dream-world also reflected in his verse, e.g. *The Wedding of St George*, or *Arthur's Tomb*. Many of these were highly-elaborated water-colours. In 1850 he met Elizabeth Siddal, who also posed for Hunt and MILLAIS, and from 1852 onwards she developed under his inspiration into an artist of poetic and neurotic intensity. His best work was produced during the years of their uneasy association. They married in 1860; in 1862 she died of narcotics and he became virtually a recluse and eventually a chloral addict. In 1857 he was concerned (with MORRIS, BURNE-JONES and others) in the decoration of the Oxford Union and he did one painting directly on a white-washed wall. It perished immediately. His poor technique and his use of studio assistants are obvious in many of his later works. From the 1860s Elizabeth Siddal's place was taken by Morris's wife Jane, and he painted many versions of the full-lipped sultry beauty which came to be associated with his name. There are works in Aberdeen, Birmingham, Boston, Bournemouth, Cambridge (Fitzwm), Cambridge Mass. (Fogg), Dublin, Edinburgh, Hamburg, Liverpool, London (NPG, Tate and V&A), Manchester, New York (Met. Mus.), Ottawa, Wilmington Delaware and Yale (CBA).

ROSSINI, Luigi (1790–1857), was born in Ravenna and trained as an architect and decorator. He decided to follow in the footsteps of PIRANESI and produced a series of etchings of Roman antiquities from 1817 (some of the early plates have charming figures by B. Pinelli). He was fortunate in the early-19th-century excavations in Rome, which gave him new subjects as well as a new market among the tourists who came to see them. He etched about 1,000 plates.

ROSSO, Giovanni Battista ('Rosso Fiorentino') (1495–1540), was a friend and contemporary of PONTORMO and, like him, worked under Andrea del Sarto, and was one of the founders of MANNERISM. He worked in Florence from 1513 to 1521, executing during these years a *Madonna and Saints* (Uffizi) which was refused by the commissioner, who complained that the saints looked like devils; a tormented *Deposition* (1521, Volterra); and, on his return to Florence in 1522, the *Dei Madonna* (Pitti), and the *Moses defending the Daughters of Jethro* (*c.*1523, Uffizi). In it the figures in violent action, strained poses and exaggerated foreshortening are the epitome of the tension inherent in early Mannerism. He then went to Rome and stayed there until the Sack (1527), after which he wandered around Italy until 1530 when he went to Venice and then, in the same year, to France for François I. In Rome (?*c.*1526) he painted the *Deposition*, now in Boston, which was rediscovered in this century. He worked at Fontainebleau with PRIMATICCIO and was thus one of the founders of the Fontainebleau style and had a great influence on French painting. According to Vasari he committed suicide, which would have been in keeping with his neurotic temperament, but he seems in fact to have died a natural death. His *Deposition* (Paris, Louvre) was painted in France and its dead Christ with His livid body and reddish hair is typical of his later emotional style. There are works by him in Arezzo, Berlin, Bradford, Città di Castello, Florence (Uffizi, Pitti, SS. Annunziata and S. Lorenzo), Frankfurt, Liverpool, London (NG), Los Angeles, Naples, Pisa, Rome (Borghese), Siena and Washington (NG).

ROSSO, Medardo (1858–1928), was one of the leading Italian sculptors of the late 19th century, although he was a painter until 1883 and only turned to sculpture as a result of reading Baudelaire's *Curiosités esthétiques*. He was fascinated by the play of light on surfaces – an essentially Impressionist preoccupation – and, like RODIN, he translated this into sculpture, although he differed from Rodin in preferring the single viewpoint. His favourite medium was wax, since this has a colouristic effect as well as allowing very slight modulations of the surface. He did, in fact, exert some influence on Rodin, with whom he later quarrelled, as well as on later Italian sculptors (e.g. MANZÙ), but his fame has been largely confined to Italy, since his stay in Paris (1884–6) was disastrous. There are works by him in Cardiff, Edinburgh, London (Tate), Paris (Mus. d'Orsay and Mus. Rodin) as well as in Italian museums, particularly Rome (Gall. Naz. d'Arte Moderna) and the Rosso Museum in Barzio (Como).

ROTHKO, Mark (1903–70), was born in Russia but went to America in 1913. He began painting in 1926 and was originally influenced by the European Surrealists who settled in the US after 1940. His characteristic works, however, are large abstract pictures which consist of horizontal bands of colour with muzzy edges. He committed suicide in 1970. There are examples in London

(Tate: ten very large paintings, as well as works of all periods), New York (M of M A and Rothko Fdn: about 1,000 works) and other American museums.

ROTTENHAMMER, Johann (1564–1625), was born in Munich, but went to Venice in 1596 and was deeply influenced by TINTORETTO. He settled in Augsburg in 1606 and painted mainly small, highly-finished, works on copper. His *Coronation of the Virgin*, *c.*1598 (London, NG) is an exceptionally large example. Other works are in Augsburg, Cambridge (Fitzwm), Dresden, Munich, Paris (Louvre) and Vienna.

ROTTLUFF, Karl Schmidt, *see* SCHMIDT.

ROTTMAYR, Johann Michael (1654–1730), was the leading Austrian Baroque painter. According to his own account, he went to Venice in 1675 and worked there for thirteen years in the studio of Johann Carl LOTH (known in Italy as Carlo Lotti): no works of his are known from this period, but his style is certainly Italianate (Correggio and *cf.* Pittoni) with a trace of French influence. He returned to Salzburg *c.*1688 and lived in Vienna from 1696, but was often away painting ceilings all over Austria. His large ceiling in the Karlskirche, Vienna (1726–30), is very close to Correggio, but other late works show some influence from Rubens. There are many ceilings still in existence in Vienna, Melk and elsewhere, and paintings in Munich, Nuremberg, Passau Cathedral, Sarasota Fla and Vienna (Oesterreichische Gall.).

ROUAULT, Georges (1871–1958), had already completed his apprenticeship to a stained-glass window maker when he entered, in 1891, the École des Beaux-Arts, where he was a pupil of MOREAU from 1892 to 1895. He became the first Curator of the Musée Moreau in 1898. His early works show Moreau's influence, but by 1903 he had abandoned his dark and overworked oil-paintings of Biblical subjects for the series of *Prostitutes, Clowns* (from 1904, 1907 and again during the 1930s) and *Judges* (from 1908). These usually have heavy dark contours enclosing areas of violent colour, and express the painter's loathing of vice, hypocrisy, cruelty and complacency. Although he exhibited at the famous FAUVE show in 1905, he remained aloof from all groups and systems of aesthetics, and developed one of the purest forms of Expressionism. Before 1908 he worked mostly in watercolour and gouache, only returning to oil-painting after about 1918; he also executed a large amount of graphic work. His series of etchings, originally made for two books *Guerre* and *Miserere* from 1916 to 1927, were eventually published in 1948 under the title *Miserere*, and he also made lithographs and coloured etchings. His themes remained within the limits of his three series, religious subjects – chiefly of the Passion (Rouault was a devout Catholic) – landscapes of bleak and hostile country, and an occasional bouquet of flowers. He worked for the Diaghileff Ballet in 1929, executed tapestry cartoons in 1933, and in 1945 designed stained-glass windows for the church of Plateau d'Assy (Haute Savoie). There are works in most museums of modern art.

ROUBILIAC, Louis François (?1705–62), was born in Lyons. He came to England *c.*1732, and in 1737 carved the statue of Handel for Vauxhall Gardens (now London, V&A; terracotta in Cambridge, Fitzwm) which made his name. From 1745 he taught sculpture at the St Martin's Lane Academy, precursor of the Royal Academy schools, and he worked for a short time as a modeller at the Chelsea china factory *c.*1750. His was probably the finest sculpture done during the 18th century in England: his busts have a vivid look of life, allied to a great style in presentation and a superb technique. His nearest rival, RYSBRACK, was more restrained and classical. His monument to Lady Elizabeth Nightingale (1761, Westminster Abbey) has been decried as theatrical, despite its allusion to the circumstances of her death (she was struck by lightning). The skeletal figure of Death issuing from the tomb to strike at the living owes much to Bernini's monument to Alexander VII in St Peter's in Rome. Roubiliac had visited Italy in 1752. He executed a number of other tombs in Westminster Abbey (including the very fine and influential one of the Duke of Argyll, 1748), a statue of Newton, and a large series of fine busts for Trinity Coll., Cambridge. There are other works in the Royal Coll., Birmingham (Barber Inst.), Castres, Detroit, Leeds, London (NPG, Nat. Marit. Mus., RA and V&A), Yale (CBA) and elsewhere.

ROUSSEAU, Henri, called 'le Douanier' (1844–1910), was an amateur or 'Sunday' painter with a direct, simple and hauntingly naive vision who painted some unusually large and complicated pictures of elaborately fanciful and picturesquely exotic subjects in a matter-of-factly pedestrian technique and strong colour. He served as a regimental bandsman – according to his own account, in Mexico in 1861–7, which provided him with his fantastic settings – and as a Sergeant in the Franco-Prussian War of 1870–1. It is now thought, however, that he was never in Mexico and got his exotic animals and scenery from books. He entered the Paris municipal Customs service (hence 'le Douanier'), and began painting about 1880, exhibiting at the Indépendants from 1886. A dinner in his honour was given in Picasso's studio in 1908, and this gesture has played its part in the transmogrification of 'le Douanier' into a symbol of sophisticated interest in the pseudo-Primitive and in the opening of the floodgates of both the psychological and the sentimental school of writers on art. He seems to have combined a certain peasant shrewdness and bland self-esteem with gullible simple-mindedness; he kept a school where he taught elocution, music and painting, wrote two plays, got himself involved, though guiltlessly, in a trial for fraud, and finally died, it is said, as a result of a disappointment in love in pursuit (like C. W. PEALE) of a third wife. There are works in London (NG, Tate and Courtauld Inst.), New York (Met. Mus., M of MA), Paris (Mus. d'Orsay), Zurich and elsewhere.

ROUSSEAU, Théodore (1812–67), was a French landscape painter, the friend of MILLET and DIAZ, who settled at BARBIZON in 1844. His aims, style and development are characteristic of the Barbizon School, of which he was one of the principal members. Like others in the group he suffered great hardship as a result of his attempts to introduce a non-academic landscape style, although this did not make him any more understanding or friendly to the Impressionists in later years. From 1863 he was deeply interested in Japanese art, at the time when it was just becoming known in Europe. There are pictures by him in Boston, Glasgow, London (NG, V&A and Wallace Coll.), New York (Met. Mus.), Ottawa and many French and US museums.

ROWLANDSON, Thomas (1756–1827), was the finest of the draughtsmen and caricaturists who portrayed life and manners in 18th- and early-19th-century England. He was born in London, went to Paris for two years at 16 and studied there, and was at the RA Schools before and after his stay abroad. He started as a painter of serious subjects and portraits, but was an inveterate gambler, and after dissipating the fortune inherited from his French aunt, earned a living and paid his debts with a flood of drawings of popular and low-life subjects, full of rollicking humour and an outsize sense of the ridiculous. He also made many book-illustrations, e.g. for the 'Tours of Dr Syntax'. His gift for exuberant and flowing line is more French – and Rococo – than English, but his handling of tone is typically English in the delicacy of its effects, which often enhance by contrast the robustness of his subjects. Much of his work was produced for the print-publisher Ackermann. Most English museums, as well as Yale (C B A), have examples of his drawings, watercolours or coloured engravings.

ROYAL ACADEMY *see* ACADEMY.

ROYMERSWAELE *see* MARINUS.

RUBÉNISME was the most important artistic movement in France at the end of the 17th century, reaching a climax in the work of WATTEAU. In 1671–2 there was a violent argument in the Academy of Painting (known as the Quarrel of Colour and Design), concerning the relative importance of colour in painting. The Poussinistes regarded it as a mere decorative adjunct to the formal essentials of drawing and design, as typified in the works of Raphael, the Carracci and the Frenchman Poussin (thus cunningly introducing a patriotic note). The strong suit of the Colourists was naturalism: painting is an imitation of appearances, and, they said, colour was the most convincing means of imitation. This theory depends on Titian as much as Rubens, but the fact of the existence in Paris of the great Rubens cycle of the *Life of Marie de' Medici* coupled with the undoubted naturalism of most Flemish painting led to the Party of Colour becoming transformed into Rubénistes. In 1672 LEBRUN himself had officially settled the matter once and for all: 'The function of colour is to satisfy the eyes, whereas drawing satisfies the mind' – that is, he merely repeated the classic theory of DISEGNO. The critic Roger de Piles published a *Life* of Rubens in 1677; in 1699 he was elected an Honorary Member of the Academy, thus marking the final victory of Rubénisme, and he then republished his earlier 'Dialogue sur le Coloris' (1st edn 1673). Thus, by the beginning of the 18th century the way was prepared for Watteau and also for the new ideas in ROCOCO.

RUBENS, Sir Peter Paul (1577–1640), was born at Siegen in Westphalia. His family came from Antwerp and they returned there by 1589. For six months in 1591 he became the pupil of a landscape and decorative painter, Verhaecht, who had been to Italy, and was then, for four or five years, in the studio of Adam van Noort before becoming a pupil of Otto van Veen, a travelled and scholarly painter, until 1599. He entered the Antwerp Guild in 1598, and in 1600 went to Italy and became Court Painter to Vincenzo Gonzaga, Duke of Mantua. In 1603 he accompanied an embassy taking horses and pictures from Mantua to Philip III in Madrid, where he admired the Titians and Raphaels in the Spanish Royal Coll. From 1604 to 1608 he was in Mantua, Rome, Genoa and Milan: in 1606 he was in Rome, where he met ELSHEIMER and Paul BRIL and bought Caravaggio's *Death of the Virgin* for Mantua. In the same year he got the commission for the altarpiece for the Chiesa Nuova (S.M. in Vallicella). The first version was not a success and was replaced by one painted on slate, to reduce reflections, which is still in the church. In 1608 he received news of his mother's illness and returned – too late – to Antwerp. The first version of the altarpiece was placed by him over his mother's tomb (it is now in Grenoble; a sketch is in London, Courtauld Inst.). After his mother's death he intended to return to Italy, but accepted an offer to become Court Painter to the Spanish Governors of the Netherlands, an appointment he held until his death. He settled in Antwerp, where he built himself an Italianate palace, married Isabella Brandt in 1609 (*Wedding Portrait*, Munich), and started on what was perhaps the most energetic and fruitful career in the history of art, and one which made him the most important artist in Northern Europe and the greatest Northern exponent of the Baroque.

In Italy he had studied the artists of the High Renaissance, particularly Titian and Michelangelo, and after his return to Flanders his first works show how deeply indebted he was to the Roman works of CARAVAGGIO. After the success of the *Raising of the Cross* (1610, Antwerp Cath.), he evolved, in the *Descent from the Cross* (1611–14, also Antwerp Cath.), a less passionately dramatic style, so that numerous assistants could work under him to fulfil the multitude of commissions that poured in. His letters prove how carefully he controlled the execution of his designs, and in most cases he did the final work on a picture himself to ensure something of the unity of the first sketch; the amount of personal execution was a question of price. His chief assistants were of the first ability: the young van DYCK entered his studio about 1617, and JORDAENS and SNYDERS were employed by him for many years. Without the methods he devised for the division of labour his vast output over so many years could never have been achieved, much less maintained at so high a standard. His practice was to make small sketches, very free in handling, usually on panels with a light, streaky, buff or grey ground, the loose drawing touched in with indications of the local colours. Many of these *modelli* are preserved (e.g. London, Courtauld Inst. and Dulwich), and it is interesting that the contract for the Jesuit Church in Antwerp (1620) specifically allows Rubens to retain the *modelli* – which means that we know what the lost ceilings looked like. Some of his designs for tapestries were larger, more worked-out, and more fully coloured, as may be seen in the *Constantine* series (1621–2, Paris, Mobilier National and Philadelphia), the *Eucharist* series (1625–8, mostly Madrid, Prado) and the recently discovered, controversial, *Aeneas* series (Cardiff). The first of his major commissions was the decoration, already mentioned, of the Jesuit Church in Antwerp, begun in 1620 with the assistance of van Dyck. This called for thirty-nine ceiling paintings and three altarpieces, which alone survive, the ceilings having been destroyed in the fire of 1718. After this he painted the Medici cycle for the Luxembourg Palace in Paris (1622–5, Paris, Louvre); the ceiling of the Banqueting Hall in Whitehall, London, for Charles I, completed in 1634 (his only surviving ceiling-painting); the huge scheme of decoration (1636–40) for the Torre de la Parada, commissioned by Philip IV of Spain, on which he was still working at his death. Besides these there were countless altarpieces, portraits, hunting scenes, landscapes, religious and mythological pictures, scenes from classical history, tapestry designs, book-illustrations and designs for triumphal processions, such as the *Pompa Introitus Ferdinandi* for the State Entry of the Cardinal Infante Ferdinand of Spain into Antwerp (1634).

He entered politics in 1623 and was employed on various diplomatic missions by the Governors of the Netherlands – to Holland in 1627 (when he visited Utrecht and met HONTHORST); to Spain in 1628 (when he made copies of the Titians he had admired in 1603, and became friendly with VELÁZQUEZ); to England in 1629–30, when he was knighted by Charles I. These missions served as distractions after the death of Isabella Brandt in 1626. In 1630 he married again. The 16-year-old Hélène Fourment became the theme and inspiration of his late mythologies and the subject of many portraits. Since gout was now limiting his activity he could devote more time to the personal side of his art in which his domestic life, hitherto kept in the background, played a dominant part. After his death, his widow wanted to destroy some of his more intimate portraits of her, such as the one in a fur cloak (*Het Pelske*), now in Vienna. His output was huge and his influence almost equally so, especially in France (*see* RUBÉNISME), and most galleries have one or more examples, some entirely autograph, some more or less workshop productions based on his *modelli*. London is particularly rich, especially in *modelli* (NG, Wallace Coll., Dulwich and Courtauld Inst.), as well as having the ceiling of the Banqueting House (sketch in Yale, CBA), a major building by Inigo Jones, decorated by Rubens for Charles I, the greatest patron of the time. In addition, like RAPHAEL, he employed engravers to disseminate his ideas all over Europe.

RUDE, François (1784–1855), was the major French sculptor of the early 19th century, whose principal work is the relief of the *Volunteers of 1792* (better known as *La Marseillaise*), on the Arc de Triomphe in Paris (1833–6). The romanticism of Delacroix is coupled in his work with the classical outlook as well as the Napoleonic enthusiasm of DAVID, whom he accompanied to Brussels 1814–27. His bust of David (1831) is in the Louvre, and his wife Sophie (1797–1867) was a painter and pupil of David. Rude went to Italy in 1842. His works are in Brussels and Paris, and in a Rude museum in his native Dijon. Fixin, near Dijon, has *Napoleon awakening to Immortality*, the plaster model being in Paris (Mus. d'Orsay).

RUISDAEL, Jacob van (1628/9–82), was the greatest of the Dutch realist landscape painters and exerted a huge influence on the development of European landscape painting in the 19th century, although in his own day he was less popular than Italianate painters such as his great friend BERCHEM (who may occasionally have painted figures in Ruisdael's landscapes). He was born in Haarlem, where the realist landscape was first developed in the early 17th century, and may have been a pupil of his father, Isack, about whom little is known. Later he probably worked with his uncle Salomon van RUYSDAEL (whose son, also a landscape painter, was also named Jacob). His early works represent views in the neighbourhood of Haarlem with great fidelity, so that many are still recognizable. In 1648 he entered the Haarlem Guild. About 1650 he travelled with Berchem in East Holland and probably in Western Germany as well, where he saw mountains for the first time. He and Berchem both painted Bentheim Castle in Germany in 1650/1. He settled in Amsterdam *c.*1655 and lived there until his death, although he was buried in Haarlem. In 1676 his name occurs in a list of doctors and he is said to have taken a medical degree at Caen in France. His name, however, is crossed out, and although he is known to have had medical interests it may not be significant. He may have practised as a surgeon in Amsterdam while continuing to paint, but the latest date on any of his pictures is 1678. It is now known that the story of his poverty and death in the Haarlem Poorhouse refers to his cousin Jacob Salomonsz. RUYSDAEL.

His later works have a much more Romantic approach and are more dramatic in handling; some even imitate the kind of mountain landscape popularized by A. van EVERDINGEN. His finest works, however, are generally agreed to be the typical Dutch panoramas with the sun breaking fitfully through the clouds and lighting up patches of the duneland. It has been said that 'he never painted a hot day', and his temper was indeed melancholic and grave; yet unlike his uncle or Jan van GOYEN who sought breadth and used monochromatic effects to get it, he employs strong local colours and gains his atmospheric effects by means of the luminosity of his skies and the vast sweep of his clouds. HOBBEMA was the most important of his many pupils and imitators. He is thought to have painted well over a thousand pictures, so that practically every major gallery has one, but the best collection is in London (NG).

RUNGE, Philipp Otto (1777–1810), was a German painter who studied under JUEL in Copenhagen 1799–1801. After this he went to Dresden where he became the most important German early Romantic painter. In Dresden he met FRIEDRICH and Goethe, who was interested in Runge's theory of colour. He began a series of *The Times of Day* (*c.*1796) which reflect his highly subjective and emotional approach to landscape as a revelation of Nature. He was a naive, almost primitive painter (cf. *The Hülsenbeck Children*: 1806, Hamburg) and his rather austere Romanticism was influenced by English artists, principally FLAXMAN and BLAKE. It is therefore sharply distinguished from the (by comparison) voluptuousness of the later French Romantics. There is a biography of him by his elder brother (1840–1), which gives an account of his ideas. Most of his works are in Hamburg, but there are others in Berlin, Hartford Conn. and Vienna.

RUOPPOLO (Ruoppoli), Giovanni Battista (1629–93), was a Neapolitan, deeply influenced by Caravaggio, who painted still-life, especially fruit, in a manner reminiscent of the great Spanish still-life painters of the 17th century. There is an important early (1659) signed work in Oxford (Ashmolean) and others in Hamburg, Naples, Rome (Corsini) and Vassar Coll. New York State. His nephew and pupil Giuseppe (*c.*1631–1710) painted in the same manner. The monogram GBR, common to Giovanni Battista and to the RECCO family has caused confusion.

RUSKIN, John (1819–1900), was the most influential art critic in 19th-century England. He was the son of well-off parents, who encouraged his precocious artistic and literary gifts, and he was able to travel all over Europe between 1833 and 1888. He met TURNER in 1840, and in 1843 published the first volume of *Modern Painters*, a work designed to establish Turner's supremacy over all other landscape painters. The remaining four volumes, published at intervals up to 1860, were less single-minded and contain a highly personal aesthetic. His many other books deal with architecture, politics, social reform, mineralogy and other subjects, but his advocacy of Gothic – particularly Venetian Gothic – architecture had results so horrible that he himself bitterly repented it: 'there is scarcely a public-house near the Crystal Palace but sells its gin and bitters under pseudo-Venetian capitals copied from the church of the Madonna of Health or of Miracles . . . my present house . . . is surrounded everywhere by the accursed Frankenstein monsters of, indirectly, my own making.' His view of art as an expression of morality, his identification of good art with medieval art, his violent diatribes against Palladian architecture, his powerful and timely support of the Pre-Raphaelites, his sensational attack on Whistler leading to the libel suit, his disastrous marriage to Effie Gray in 1848 and its annulment in 1854 (after which she married MILLAIS), as well as his Utopian agricultural schemes and his hatred of industrialism – all illustrate his complex and many-sided character. He became very famous, and his involved, contradictory and highly emotional prose gave his art criticism an impact so enduring that not only is he still a folk-memory in the English attitude to the arts, but there has lately been a revival of interest in his theories. He died insane.

He was a meticulous draughtsman, particularly of architecture and plant forms, and there are large collections of his drawings in Oxford (where he was the first Slade Professor) and at Bembridge School. Many British and American museums possess examples.

RUYSCH, Rachel (1664–1750), was a Dutch painter of flowers and still-life, who continued the HEEM tradition into the 18th century. She was born in Amsterdam, where her father was Professor of Botany and an amateur painter. Her first works date from 1682. Like HUYSUM, she often painted flowers in unseasonable mixtures, enlivening them with insects, birds and reptiles. There are works in Amsterdam, Brussels, Cambridge (Fitzwm), Cheltenham, Dresden, Florence (Uffizi and Pitti), Glasgow, The Hague, Karlsruhe, London (NG and V&A), Melbourne, Munich, New York (Met. Mus.), Oxford, Preston, Rotterdam, Toledo Ohio and Vienna (Akad.).

RUYSDAEL, Salomon van (*c.*1600/2–70), was one of the leading Dutch realist landscape painters of the first half of the 17th century. He was the brother of Isack and uncle of Jacob van RUISDAEL (the fully signed pictures always have this difference in spelling). He is first recorded in the Haarlem Guild in 1623 but the earliest dated picture is of 1627 (Vienna), and the early works are all of the simplest landscape themes, many of them approaching very closely to the work of Jan van GOYEN, especially those with ferry boats, an expanse of water and a few trees on the bank in an even grey light. He lived in Haarlem, and was a Mennonite, prosperous and esteemed. There are representative pictures by Salomon in the Royal Coll. and in Amsterdam, Antwerp, Baltimore, Barnard Castle (Bowes Mus.), Basle, Berlin, Brussels, Cambridge (Fitzwm), Cambridge Mass. (Fogg), Cleveland Ohio, Cologne, Copenhagen, Detroit, Dresden, Dublin, Frankfurt, Grenoble, The Hague (Mauritshuis and Bredius Mus., which has a *Still-life* of 1662), Hamburg, Leicester, Leipzig, Leningrad, Liverpool, London (NG), Malibu Cal., Melbourne, Merion Pa (Barnes Foundation), Minneapolis, Munich, New York (Met. Mus.), Oslo, Ottawa, Oxford, Paris (Louvre and Mus. des Arts Décoratifs), Philadelphia, Providence RI, Rotterdam, Sarasota Fla (Ringling), Stockholm, Strasbourg, Vienna, Worcester Mass. and York.

His son, Jacob Salomonsz. (1629/30–81) was also a landscape painter who is known to have worked up to at least 1668 and who died, insane, in the Haarlem Poorhouse. There is a picture by Jacob Salomonsz. in London (NG), but the few signed works bear only the monogram JvR which can lead to confusion with his cousin Jacob's pictures.

RYDER, Albert Pinkham (1847–1917), was the most original and poetic late-

19th-century American Romantic painter, and the counterpart to Edgar Allan Poe, whom he admired. He was born in New Bedford, Mass., a whaling port from the world of Moby Dick, and all his life he was haunted by the sea, although he actually lived in squalor in New York. His marine and landscape paintings have a visionary and brooding quality and were very fine in colour, but his deficient technique and the loading of layers of rich, enamel-like pigment have caused them to deteriorate badly. He travelled to Europe, but seems to have been unaffected by it. There are works by him in many American museums, including Boston, Chicago, Cleveland Ohio, Detroit, New York (Met. Mus.), Northampton Mass. (Smith Coll.), St Louis, Toledo Ohio and Washington (NG, Corcoran and Phillips). It is said that many forgeries also exist.

RYSBRACK, John Michael (1694–1770), was the son of an Antwerp landscape painter, Peter, who worked for a time in England. Rysbrack worked at first for Gibbs the architect, but from about 1730 he shared with ROUBILIAC the position of most eminent sculptor in England, until the advent of SCHEEMAKERS in 1741 somewhat affected his business. He was more severely classical than Roubiliac, e.g. in his bust of Sir Robert Walpole as a Roman senator in a toga (in Walpole's house, Houghton Hall, Norfolk). In 1747 he began his celebrated *Hercules* (now at Stourhead, Wilts.) which embodied a variant of the theory of ideal beauty, in that the artist composed it by using as models boxers and wrestlers, from whom he selected the best parts. He executed a number of tombs in Westminster Abbey (including Sir Isaac Newton's), and there are works by him in the Royal Coll., Cambridge (Fitzwm and Senate House), London (NPG, Wallace Coll., BM, V&A and Nat. Marit. Mus.), Oxford (Radcliffe Camera, Ch. Ch. and Ashmolean) and Yale (CBA).

RYSSELBERGHE, Théo van (1862–1926), was a Belgian painter who was one of the founders of Les VINGT (1883). He was deeply affected by the POINTILLISM of SIGNAC, and especially of SEURAT, whose *Grande Jatte* he saw in the last Impressionist Exhibition (1886). He moved to Paris in 1898 and later lived in Provence, where he worked in a looser, less rigidly Pointillist style. There are works in Amsterdam, Brussels, Indianapolis, Paris (Mus. d'Orsay), Rotterdam and elsewhere.

S

SACCHI, Andrea (1599–1661), was the chief representative of the classic strain of ALGARDI and POUSSIN in Roman Baroque painting. He was a native Roman, trained first under ALBANI and then, while still in his teens, in Bologna he came under the influence of Lodovico CARRACCI. Back in Rome he was patronized by the great Barberini family, for whom he painted the *Divine Wisdom* in the Barberini Palace (*c.*1629–33) in a much less Baroque style than PIETRO da Cortona's ceiling in the same Palace. In the mid-1630s there was much argument between the supporters of Sacchi and those of Pietro over the number of figures necessary in a composition. There are two pictures of *Saints* in London (NG), one by Sacchi and the other by Bernini, which may have formed part of a series for the Barberini family. Sacchi's *Vision of S. Romuald* (*c.*1638, Vatican) is still more classic in feeling and this classicism was handed down to the 18th century through his chief pupil, MARATTA. Apart from Rome there are works by him in Berlin, Cardiff (*Hagar*, 1631), Dresden, Madrid, Minneapolis, Ottawa, Philadelphia and Vienna.

SACHLICHKEIT, Die Neue, *see* NEUE SACHLICHKEIT.

SACRA CONVERSAZIONE (Ital. holy conversation) is the name given to a representation of the Madonna and Child with Saints, in which the sacred personages are aware of each other or are united by some common action. This type of representation replaced the earlier form of altarpiece in which each figure occupied one panel of a POLYPTYCH: in a *Sacra Conversazione* the barriers have been broken down and all the figures have moved into a single, unified space. The earliest examples occur in the work of FRA ANGELICO and his contemporaries, Fra Filippo LIPPI and DOMENICO Veneziano, but it has been suggested that the dismembered Pisa Polyptych by MASACCIO may have been the first. Donatello's altar in the Santo at Padua seems to have introduced the idea, in three-dimensional form, to the North and MANTEGNA's S. Zeno altarpiece (1459) forms the link between the Florentine examples and the important altarpieces, all of *c.*1475, by PIERO della Francesca, ANTONELLO and Giovanni BELLINI, which create a single, unified space for the figures and for the spectator.

SAENREDAM, Pieter (1597–1665), was a Haarlem painter who specialized in church interiors, rendered in cool silvery tones with an occasional gleam of sunlight. He never went to Italy, but a few of his pictures were painted from the drawings made in Rome in 1532/5 by Maerten van HEEMSKERCK, which then belonged to the architect Van Campen, a friend of Saenredam. He seems to have made elaborate preparatory drawings, including fully worked-out perspective projections and diagrams. An insight into his working methods is afforded by a drawing (Amsterdam, City Archives), dated '15, 16, 17, 18, 19, 20 Julij 1641' – i.e. a small drawing took six days' work; but it represents the Town Hall which was burnt down in 1651, and in 1657 Saenredam painted a picture from it which he sold to the City Council for 400 guilders. It is now in the Rijksmuseum, and is signed and dated 1657 and inscribed as having been drawn in 1641. There are several other cases of drawings dated ten or more years before the paintings, e.g. the picture in Edinburgh (NG), which is probably his masterpiece, and certainly his largest, being some 6 feet high. It is dated 1648, but the drawing in Haarlem is dated 1635. There are other examples in Amsterdam (Rijksmus.), Copenhagen (the earliest dated work, 1626), Fort Worth Texas, Glasgow, Haarlem (Hals Mus. and Bisschoppelijk Mus.), Hamburg, London (NG), Munich, Orleans, Philadelphia (Johnson), Rotterdam, Utrecht, Washington (NG), Worcester Mass. and elsewhere. Detailed drawings are in London (BM and Courtauld Inst.).

SAINT-GAUDENS, Augustus (1848–1907), was one of the leading American sculptors of the late 19th century. He studied in Paris and Rome 1867–72 and later, but made his name with his Farragut Monument (1881, Central Park, New York). His finest works were the bronze relief on Boston Common, a memorial (1884–97) to Col. Shaw who commanded a black regiment in the Civil War, and the Adams Monument (1891, Washington). His *Lincoln* (1887) is in Chicago, and a replica is in Parliament Square, London. His studio in Cornish, New Hampshire, has casts and works.

SALON. During the 17th century exhibitions of works by members of the French Royal Academy were held in the Salon d'Apollon in the Louvre, hence the name. Originally occasional, it was biennial from 1737 to the Revolution, and then annual, being thrown open to all artists and the jury abolished, although it was soon re-established to limit the huge entry. Since there was no other public exhibition of any standing, the jury (composed almost exclusively of members of the Institut) obtained a stranglehold, using its enormous power to exclude any painter of whom it did not approve. In 1863 the scandal and the protests over the number of works refused were so great that Napoleon III ordered a special exhibition of them, known as the *Salon des Refusés*. So bitter was the official opposition and so uncomprehending was the mass of the public, incapable of independent judgement, that no such exhibition was held again, nor was the rigour of the jury modified. Among the principal exhibitors were MANET, BOUDIN, FANTIN-LATOUR, JONGKIND, PISSARRO and WHISTLER, while CÉZANNE also exhibited at, and COURBET had the distinction of being rejected from, both exhibitions. The present huge yearly Salon is organized by the Société des Artistes Français and has been since 1881, but there are now several other 'Salons' – e.g. d'Automne, des Indépendants (founded 1884) – which cater for different types of art. Between 1882 and 1892 the Exposition des Arts Incohérents was organized in Paris as a mockery of the 'official' Salon. Exhibits included such works as Alphonse Allais's *First Communion of Anaemic Young Girls in the Snow* in 1883 – a sheet of plain white Bristol board with drawing pins at the corners. Illustrated catalogues parodying the official 'Salon Illustré' accompanied the fantastic exhibits, which preceded DADA and SURREALISM by many years.

SALVIATI, Francesco (1510–63), was a Florentine Mannerist and a close friend of Vasari: together they salvaged the arm of Michelangelo's *David*, broken in the riots of 1527. Salviati worked on various decorative schemes in Rome, Venice and Florence and went to France in 1554. He was in Venice *c.*1539, back in Rome in 1541, and in 1543 was in Florence working for the Grand Duke. He was a pupil of Andrea del Sarto and was influenced by Michelangelo, Pontormo and the Venetians: out of this mixture he was able to produce some fine portraits as well as allegories. There are works in Cambridge (Fitzwm), Florence (Uffizi and Pitti), Glasgow, London (NG), New York (Met. Mus.),

Paris (Louvre), Rome (Pal. Sacchetti), Springfield Mass., Turin, Vienna, Washington (NG), Worcester Mass. and elsewhere.

SÁNCHEZ COELLO, Alonso (1531/2–88), was the pupil and successor of MOR as Court portrait painter to Philip II of Spain. He received his education in Flanders and Portugal, and his style is based upon the withdrawn dignity with which Mor invested his sitters; but he was also much influenced by TITIAN (who was Philip II's favourite painter). He began his career in Portugal and painted a few altarpieces, but he is principally known for his portraits, and he worked for the Court at Valladolid from 1557. His portraits, especially the full-lengths, became models for imitation since they perfectly express the rigidity of Spanish Court etiquette, or at least the more pleasing side of it. The dignity and gravity of his style was admirably adapted to those royal icons which were sent as presents to the numerous connections of the Hapsburgs. He is said to have painted S. Ignatius Loyola (*d.*1556) in 1585, but this, which would have been a fascinating document, is unfortunately lost. There are four pictures by him in the Royal Coll., and others in Bamberg, Berlin, Boston (Gardner Mus.), Brussels, Dublin, the Escorial, Glasgow (Pollok House), Madrid (Prado), Munich, New York (Met. Mus. and Hispanic Soc.), San Diego Cal., Vienna (K-H Mus.) and Wisconsin (Univ.).

SÁNCHEZ COTÁN, Juan (1560/1–1627), was one of the first, and finest, of painters of BODEGONES influenced by Caravaggio. He was born in Toledo and became a Carthusian in 1603, after which he painted several not very notable religious works, many in Granada, but his still-life pieces are very early examples – thirty years before e.g. ZURBARÁN – of simple arrangements of fruit and vegetables, seen against a dark ground and parallel to the picture plane. They are simpler, more austere and more geometrical than Caravaggio's and form a special, Spanish, category. His 1602 still-life, now in San Diego Cal., is known to have influenced Raphaelle PEALE. Other works are in Chicago, Granada and Seville (Cath.).

SANDBY, Paul (1730/31–1809) and his brother Thomas (1723–98), were topographical draughtsmen employed by the Crown, and Paul was sent to the Highlands of Scotland in 1747 to work on the Ordnance Survey made after the 1745 Rising. He portrayed landscape not only with accuracy and feeling, but also with a sensitive eye for atmosphere. He studied figure-drawing, etched, and introduced aquatint into England (1775). From about 1752 he lived in London, and he worked a good deal at Windsor, where Thomas was Deputy Ranger of Windsor Forest. He was a founder-member of the RA. From 1770, he visited Wales several times, and was one of the first watercolour painters to appreciate Welsh scenery. He usually painted in transparent washes, and often drew in watercolour as distinct from tinting a pencil drawing; he also painted in gouache, and many of his large series of Windsor (in the Royal Library) use this medium, which in his hands almost rivals oil paint. Gainsborough referred to him as 'the only man of genius' who had painted 'real views from nature in this country'; that is, who did not rearrange the material into picturesque compositions *à la* Gaspar or Claude, or work up his topography (for instance, at Windsor) according to the example of Canaletto's views. Besides the unrivalled series in the Royal Coll., there are examples in Cardiff, Cambridge (Fitzwm), Edinburgh (mainly Scottish scenes), London (BM, Tate, Courtauld Inst. and V&A – a 22-ft high wall-painting of a landscape, 1793), Oxford and Yale (CBA).

Thomas was also a founder-member of the RA, and its first Professor of Architecture. He painted many watercolours, very similar to Paul's, and also designed the landscape of Virginia Water, near Windsor.

SANDRART, Joachim von (1606–88), was a German painter who studied in Utrecht under HONTHORST, accompanied him to London in 1627 (where he met GENTILESCHI), and then went on to Italy 1628–35, where he met many famous artists and went sketching with CLAUDE, POUSSIN and BAMBOCCIO. His paintings are forgotten but his book, 'Teutsche Akademie' (1675–9, Latin edn 1683), was the first of a long line of German art-historical books and is a source of great importance for many 17th-century painters. He was a founder of the ACADEMY in Nuremberg in 1674/5 – the oldest German art school – and was also probably the first German artist to be ennobled (1653). There is a *Self-portrait* in Frankfurt (Historisches Mus.) and other works in Amsterdam (Rijksmus.), Leningrad, Milan (Brera), Munich and Vienna (K-H Mus.).

SANGUINE. A reddish-brown chalk used for drawing.

SANSOVINO, Andrea (*c.*1467/71–1529), was a Florentine sculptor who, according to Vasari, spent nine years in Portugal, although nothing now there supports this, and his entry into the guild in 1491, coupled with a series of works in Italy documented from *c.*1490, makes it unlikely. The *Baptism of Christ*, for the Baptistry in Florence, was begun in 1500 but left unfinished when he went to Rome in 1505; the group was eventually completed by DANTI in 1569 (since altered). In Rome Sansovino made the WALL-TOMBS of Cardinals Sforza and della Rovere, commissioned by Julius II, by 1509; a group for S.M. dell' Anima, *c.*1507; and a *Madonna and Child with St Anne* for S.Agostino in 1512. In 1513 he was appointed to direct the building and decoration of the Holy House at Loreto, but after many difficulties he was demoted to supervising the sculpture only. Carving did not begin until 1517/18, with many sculptors employed, including BANDINELLI, who made himself hated by disparaging everyone else's work. Sansovino's figures show the influence of Fra Bartolommeo and Raphael, and even Leonardo. His wall-tombs became the norm for the whole of the 16th century. Jacopo SANSOVINO was his pupil. Other works by him are in Berlin, Florence (Bargello), Genoa (Cath.) and London (V&A).

SANSOVINO, Jacopo (1486–1570), was the pupil of Andrea Sansovino and took his name. He worked as a sculptor and architect in Florence and Rome before going to Venice in 1527, where he became City Architect and is principally famous as the designer of the Library of St Mark and other buildings. His most famous works in sculpture are the gigantic statues of *Mars* and *Neptune* (1554–67) at the top of the Scala de' Giganti in the Doge's Palace and some figures on the Loggetta (which he designed). Other figures on the Loggetta are by CATTANEO. VITTORIA was also his pupil. Sansovino was friendly with Titian, Tintoretto and the writer Pietro Aretino, and his architecture influenced VERONESE. There are other works in Venice, Cleveland Ohio, Florence (Bargello, Cath.), London (V&A), Oxford (Ashmolean) and Padua (Santo).

SANTI, Giovanni (*c.*1430/40–94), is important for two reasons, neither connected with his pictures. First, he was the father of Raphael; second, he wrote a rhymed Chronicle which mentions a number of 15th-century artists. There are pictures by him in Urbino, where he worked, and in Berlin, London, Milan, the Vatican and elsewhere.

SARACENI, Carlo (1579–1620), was a Venetian painter who went to Rome *c.*1598, where he later came under the influence of CARAVAGGIO and ELSHEIMER; in particular, he imitated Elsheimer's effects of light in small-scale pictures (often on copper) so that they have been confused. Elsheimer and Caravaggio both died in 1610, and Saraceni seems to have succeeded to their market; indeed his *Death of the Virgin* was commissioned to replace Caravaggio's (a version in Rome, S.M. della Scala). By 1613 he was working for the Mantuan Court, and, *c.*1619, he returned to Venice, where he began a painting for the Doge's Palace, completed after his death by a pupil. There are works by him in Berlin, Bologna, Detroit, Dijon, Dresden, Hartford Conn., London (NG), Munich, Naples, New York (Met. Mus.), Padua, Prague, Rome (Capitoline and churches, especially his masterpiece, *The Miracle of S. Benno*, 1618, in S.M. dell' Anima), Toledo (Cath.), Venice (Accad. and Redentore) and Vienna. An anonymous follower, called 'Pensionante del Saraceni', may have been French and was active *c.*1610/20. There are works attributed to him in Detroit, Dublin and the Vatican.

SARGENT, John Singer (1856–1925), was an American virtuoso portrait painter who settled in London and painted High Society in Edwardian and Georgian times. He was born in Italy of American expatriate parents and was trained in Florence and Paris, settling in London in 1884/5 and continuing the *bravura* tradition of LAWRENCE, crossed with Velázquez. He visited the US frequently and painted some large-scale decorations in Boston Public Library (1890–1916), the Museum of Fine Arts (1916–21) and Harvard Univ. (1922), but is best known for his portraits, and for his brilliant watercolours, which may reflect his friendship with MONET, whom he first met in 1870 and whose paintings he bought. In 1880 he visited Spain and the technical skill and simple colour schemes of most of his portraits reflect Velázquez, seen through the eyes of MANET and Courbet: Sargent's *Mme Gautreau*, exhibited in Paris in 1884, shows all this, but was a *succès de scandale* and was one of the causes of his leaving Paris for London. His huge output means that his portraits are almost everywhere in Britain and America. His superficial brilliance is very like that of BOLDINI.

SARTO, Andrea del, *see* ANDREA.

SARTORIUS, John N. (*c.*1755–1828), was a British painter of fox hunts and horse races. Examples are in London (Tate), San Marino Cal. and Yale (CBA).

SASSETTA, Stefano di Giovanni (*c.*1400, perhaps 1392–1450), was, with GIOVANNI di Paolo, the major Sienese 15th-century painter. Like all his Sienese contemporaries, he was quite happy to continue the style of the 14th-century masters, but he was also aware of new trends coming from the North, and the INTERNATIONAL GOTHIC style makes itself felt in his work and is perceptible in the influence on him of painters like MASOLINO or GENTILE da Fabriano. He is first recorded as painting an altarpiece in 1423–6 (parts of it survive, in Siena, Barnard Castle (Bowes Mus.), Budapest, Melbourne and the Vatican): it has a sense of space that is not improperly associable with the work then being painted in Florence, even with MASACCIO's Brancacci Chapel. Sassetta did not develop into a realistic painter, as that would have been understood in Florence, but his essentially mystic character uses the new forms to give a blend of tradition and modern actuality. The best example of this is the altarpiece painted in 1437–44 for S. Francesco, Sansepolcro (where

PIERO della Francesca would have seen it). The altarpiece is now dismembered, the central panel of *St Francis in Glory* belonging to Harvard Univ. in Florence, but the greater part of it is in London (NG) and Paris (Louvre). An altarpiece dated 1436 in the Chiesa dell'Osservanza, Siena, is now thought to be the work of an imitator, known as the Osservanza Master (there are other works by him in Pienza Cath., London (NG) and several US museums). Other pictures by Sassetta are in Assisi (S. Francesco), Berlin, Boston, Chantilly (part of the *St Francis* altar), Cleveland Ohio, Cortona (S. Domenico), Detroit, Florence, London (NG), New York (Met. Mus. and Frick Coll.), Siena, Washington (NG), Yale (Univ.) and elsewhere.

SASSOFERRATO. Giovanni Battista Salvi, called Sassoferrato (1609–85), worked mainly in Rome as a follower of DOMENICHINO. His most famous work is the *Virgin in Prayer*, a half-length devotional image known from innumerable versions and copies, e.g. London (NG, Courtauld Inst.). His *Madonna and Child* (London, NG) is based on a Reni. Other works are in Cambridge (Fitzwm), Cleveland Ohio, Glasgow, Liverpool and Oxford.

SAVOLDO, Giovanni Girolamo (active 1508–after 1548). He was a Brescian who worked mainly in Venice, where he was deeply influenced by GIORGIONE and TITIAN, yet he is first recorded in the Guild at Florence, in 1508. His large altarpiece of 1521 (Treviso, S. Niccolo) is entirely in the Bellini–Giorgione tradition; he may also have worked in Milan *c.*1532/35. His works have a wonderful sense of light effect, and his night scenes are half a century earlier than CARAVAGGIO. The writer Pino was his pupil and records that he painted but few works. In 1548 Aretino referred to him as 'decrepit', and he probably died soon afterwards. There are pictures by him in the Royal Coll. and in Amsterdam, Berlin, Brescia, Cleveland Ohio, Dublin, Florence (Uffizi), London (NG and Courtauld Inst.), Milan (Brera), New York (Met. Mus.), Paris (Louvre), Rome (Borghese and Capitoline), Turin, Venice, Vienna and Washington.

SCHADOW, Gottfried (1764–1850), was one of the leading German Neoclassic sculptors. He was in Rome 1785–7 and was much influenced by his friend CANOVA before returning to Berlin, to become Court Sculptor in 1788. He spent the rest of his life there. His works include many monuments in Berlin churches, the first major one being to the boy Graf von der Marck (1790). He also made the Quadriga on the Brandenburg Gate and numerous busts, including one of Goethe (who had earlier criticized Schadow for his excessive realism), and others for the Bavarian Valhalla. Two very lively small terracotta portraits close to HOUDON are in Harvard Univ. (Busch-Reisinger Mus.). His monuments to Frederick the Great (1793) and Blücher (1819) are at Szczecin and Rostock, but his projected equestrian Frederick the Great was never realized. His son Rudolf (1786–1822) was also a sculptor – there is a work at Chatsworth, Derbyshire – and another son, Wilhelm (1788–1862), was a painter and a member of the NAZARENER.

SCHAFFNER, Martin (1477/8–1546/9), was a painter and sculptor in Ulm. He was influenced by HOLBEIN the Elder (who was in Ulm in 1499), but later tried to adapt the Renaissance ideals of DÜRER, whose work he often used. His sculpture remained more Late Gothic in style. There are works in several German museums, including a curious table-top with allegorical figures in Cassel.

SCHÄUFFELEIN, Hans Leonhard (*c.*1483–1539/40), was a painter and designer of woodcuts. As a painter he was much influenced by DÜRER, his master, but his woodcuts are both more original and more important than his pictures. He often signed his works HS with a little shovel (*Schäuffelein*). There are paintings by him in Basle, Berlin, Chatsworth, Dresden, Gateshead, Hamburg, Munich, Nuremberg, Vienna and Nördlingen, where he lived from 1515.

SCHEEMAKERS, Peter (1691–1781), was the son of an Antwerp sculptor, and first worked in Cologne, but was so determined to get to Rome that he walked there. After a short stay he went to London, where he worked for BIRD, and he was then in partnership with DELVAUX, with whom in 1728 he went again to Rome. His first success was in 1740 with his Shakespeare monument in Westminster Abbey, and the reputation he gained somewhat obscured RYSBRACK's. Scheemakers gave his works a very detailed finish and a high polish which, aided by his habit of undercutting his rivals' prices, brought him much business. He began to retire in 1753, but worked here until 1771, when he returned to Antwerp. There are many tombs by him in Westminster Abbey, in parish churches all over England, and one in Boston Mass. There are also works in many of the greater houses and gardens in England, and some busts in the Trinity Colleges of Cambridge and Dublin.

SCHEFFER, Ary (1795–1858), was born in Holland, but spent almost all his life in France. He was trained under PRUD'HON and Guérin (1811), where he was influenced by his fellow-students GÉRICAULT and DELACROIX. He first exhibited at the Salon in 1812 and was closely associated with the Romantic Movement of the 1830s, although his style was frigidly classical. Nevertheless, like Delacroix his subjects were often taken from literature – Dante, Byron, Goethe. After 1848, because of his links with the Orleans family, he was out of favour and he turned to religious themes at the end of his life, his most famous being the cloyingly sentimental *St Monica and her Son, St Augustine* (1855, Paris, Louvre). He was a fine portrait painter, whose subjects included Chopin and Liszt. His brother Henry (1798–1862) was also a painter.

There is a Scheffer Mus. in his native Dordrecht, and other works are in Baltimore, Boston, Cambridge Mass. (Fogg), London (Tate and Wallace Coll.), Melbourne, Paris (Mus. d'Orsay), Toledo Ohio, Versailles and Washington (Corcoran).

SCHIELE, Egon (1890–1918), was an Austrian Expressionist painter, the contemporary of KOKOSCHKA, and, like him, influenced by KLIMT, as well as by HODLER. He began to exhibit early and was profoundly affected by Freudian psychology, which he endeavoured to apply to portrait painting. It is perhaps more evident in his distasteful erotic drawings. He died in the influenza epidemic of 1918. There are works in Vienna (Oesterreichische Gal.), The Hague and Minneapolis.

SCHILDERSBENT *see* BENTNAME.

SCHLEMMER, Oskar (1888–1943), was a pupil of HÖLZEL. He taught at the BAUHAUS, 1920–9, where he had a great influence, and in Breslau and Berlin until 1933, after which he had to live in retirement until his death. He did a great deal of theatrical design, and his paintings have the slightly desiccated air of those Bauhaus products that were emphatically machine-made. There are many works in Stuttgart, and others in Basle, Cologne, Hartford Conn., Harvard (Univ.) and New York (M of MA).

SCHLÜTER, Andreas (1660/4–1714), was the leading North German Baroque architect and sculptor, whose position in Berlin was in its way analogous to that of Bernini in Rome. He arrived in Berlin from Poland in 1694 and, after short trips to France (1695) and Italy (1696), he began the decorative sculpture for the Zeughaus (largely executed by others) and also his masterpiece, the equestrian statue of the Great Elector. This was begun in 1696, cast in bronze in 1700, set up in 1703, and completed by the *Slaves* made by others from his designs, in 1708/9. It is strongly influenced by similar Italian works, such as the Farnese monuments in Piacenza by MOCHI, and the TACCA *Four Moors* in Leghorn. The monument is now in Berlin-Charlottenburg. His statue of Friedrich III was begun in 1697, and cast in 1698, but was not set up (in Königsberg) until 1802. Early in the 18th century Schlüter was engaged in several architectural undertakings, but they were attended by misfortune and he was sacked in 1706. He accepted an invitation to St Petersburg in 1714, but died there soon after his arrival. There are several pieces of his sculpture in Berlin (churches and public buildings) and also in Homburg-Hessen.

SCHMIDT-ROTTLUFF, Karl (1884–1976), was born Karl Schmidt in the village of Rottluff in Saxony. He became one of the leaders of German Expressionism, especially in the graphic arts (there are some 700 engravings and lithographs by him). He studied architecture in Dresden, where he met KIRCHNER, and in 1906 he met NOLDE. In 1905 he was one of the founders of the BRÜCKE with Nolde and HECKEL. He went to Norway in 1911 and settled in Berlin in that year, where he met FEININGER. During the 1920s his art became rather more naturalistic, although still much influenced by Negro art and by Cubism and with great stress on the outline. He was particularly persecuted by the Nazis, being expelled from the Prussian Academy in 1933 and, in 1941, forbidden to paint at all and supervised by the Nazi police. Over 600 of his pictures were removed from German galleries. After 1945 he was reinstated and lived in East Germany. There are pictures by him in London (Tate) and New York (M of M A), and once again in German galleries (Berlin – where he founded a Brücke Mus. in 1967 – and Hamburg).

SCHNITZALTAR (Ger. carved altar) *see* REREDOS.

SCHNORR von Carolsfeld, Julius (1794–1872), was a German painter and illustrator who was in Italy 1817–25 and joined the NAZARENER in their decoration of the Casa Massimo in Rome (1820–6). His contribution consisted of a combination of 15th-century Italian frescoes and Raphael, but it was successful enough to get him a commission in Munich from the King in 1825. This, and later commissions, occupied him until 1867. He became a professor in Dresden in 1846 and was also Director of the Dresden Gallery. His Bible illustrations were also published in an English edition in 1860. Many German galleries have examples.

SCHONGAUER, Martin (first recorded 1465–*d.*1491), was a Colmar painter and engraver who was much influenced by Roger van der WEYDEN and other Netherlandish painters. His only reasonably certain painting is the *Madonna of the Rosehedge* (1473, Colmar, St Martin), an over-life-size figure which shows the influence of his Flemish models. There are 115 engravings by him, all signed MS, and these were ot great importance in the development of engraving in Germany: it is well-known that Dürer went to visit him, only to find that he had died. Some fragments of a wall-painting of the *Last Judgement* have been discovered in S. Stephan, Breisach, where Schongauer lived from 1488/9. There are pictures ascribed to him in Basle, Berlin, Boston (Gardner), Colmar (Mus.), Frankfurt (Städel), London (NG), Munich and Vienna.

SCHOOL. This word is susceptible of a variety of meanings and no precise demarcation between them is commonly accepted. In its widest sense – Italian School, British School – it means no more than that an experienced eye can detect the country of origin of a particular picture without being able to identify the painter, or indeed to give more than a vague explanation of the processes by which the conclusion was reached. A more limited sense attaches to the term when it is applied to a smaller territorial area, usually in Italy: in this sense an experienced eye can again distinguish with considerable accuracy and speed between a work painted in Florence, say in the 15th century, and one of the same approximate date painted in Venice. The characteristics of such Schools – whether of Florence, Siena, Naples, or of Bruges and Antwerp – are recognizable and could perhaps be imprecisely formulated in words. There seems no point in trying to do so here, as the essential marks of such stylistic varieties are purely visual. Anyone who wishes to distinguish Florentine from Sienese pictures can do so in one way and one way only – looking at them as often and as closely as possible.

A more easily defined use of the word occurs in connection with a painter instead of a place, e.g. School of Raphael. This can be sub-divided into two meanings, according to the intention of the person using it; a good and useful meaning being that a picture has all the characteristics of one by Raphael except genius. In this case, it is licit to assume that it was painted by assistants in Raphael's studio, more or less under his supervision (and probably according to the amount the buyer was offering). A less valid use of the word is as a euphemism for 'copy after' or 'imitation of'. It has been suggested (e.g. in the National Gallery Catalogues) that *School* is best reserved for a geographical designation, while *Style of* . . . or perhaps *Circle of* . . . should be used to indicate relationship to a particular painter, with *Follower of* for remoter connections. This distinction would help to clarify the term.

SCHUTTERSTUK *see* DOELENSTUK.

SCHWIND, Moritz von (1804–71), was an Austrian Romantic painter, influenced by CORNELIUS and Nazarene ideas. He painted the German Middle Ages, with Teutonic Knights in armour, and also designed for the crafts. His frescoes in Karlsruhe Gallery date from 1840. In 1857 he visited London and Manchester (for the great Old Master exhibition) and later designed stained glass for Glasgow Cathedral and for St Michael, Paddington, London (1864, now demolished). There are pictures by him in many German galleries.

SCHWITTERS, Kurt (1887–1948), was a poet and abstract painter, best known as the inventor of *Merz*, a form of DADA. He was influenced by KANDINSKY and the Dadaists, and, after studying in Dresden, he began to experiment with abstract pictures in 1918, using COLLAGES with pieces of torn-up paper attached to them. One such piece had the letters MERZ in red capitals torn from the advertisement of a Bank (*Commerz und Privatbank*). From this circumstance he described his assemblages as *Merz*, and *c.*1920 he began his first Merzbau, a huge construction which expanded so that it nearly filled a house (it was destroyed in 1943). He was particularly fond of rubbish – bits of lino, bus tickets, worn-out shoe soles – as a typical Dadaist gesture in creating art from non-art: in a rather Wagnerian way he said: 'my ultimate object is to combine art and non-art in a *Merzgesamtweltbild*'. In 1929 he first visited Norway, and in 1937 he emigrated there and made his second Merzbau (destroyed 1951). In 1940 he escaped from Norway to Britain, where he died leaving a third Merzbau unfinished at Ambleside, Westmorland (moved to Newcastle University, 1965). There are works by him in London (Tate), Los Angeles (a pre-Merz work of 1919), and New York (M of M A), and there is to be a Schwitters Museum in Oslo. Three of his works are in Kendal, near his English home.

SCOREL, Jan van (1495–1562), was trained in Amsterdam but had gone to Utrecht by 1517. In 1519 he set off on a journey to Germany and went to Nuremberg and visited Dürer, but, it seems, Dürer was so preoccupied with Lutheranism that Scorel found him useless as a teacher. By 1520 he was in Carinthia, where he painted a triptych still in Obervellach Parish Church. He went on to Venice, where he was influenced by Giorgione and Palma Vecchio, and then on to Jerusalem with a pilgrimage (the only surviving record is a a drawing in London (BM) of Bethlehem), returning to Venice in 1521 and going down to Rome where he had the good fortune to arrive in the Pontificate of Hadrian VI, the Utrecht Pope. He was appointed inspector of the Belvedere, painted the Pope, was made Canon of Utrecht, and was deeply influenced by Michelangelo and Raphael. After Hadrian died Scorel went back to Utrecht (1524), and Haarlem, where M. van HEEMSKERCK was his pupil in 1527. In 1540 he went to France and in 1550 restored the Ghent Altar. Many of his large religious works were destroyed by the Iconoclasts in the 16th century, but there are works in Haarlem and Utrecht (including group portraits of *Pilgrims to Jerusalem*), and in Amsterdam (Rijksmus.), Basle, Berlin, Birmingham, Bloomfield Hills Mich., Bonn, Breda, Brussels, Cassel, Detroit, Douai, Florence (Pitti), Lisbon, Oxford (Ch. Ch.), Padua, Palermo, Rome, (Gall. Naz. and Spada), Rotterdam, Stuttgart, Venice (Cà d'Oro), Vienna, Washington (NG), and York. His portrait by his pupil MOR hung over his tomb; it now belongs to the Society of Antiquaries in London.

SCORZO, ISCORZO. An Italian word for a figure in sharp FORESHORTENING.

SCOTT, Samuel (*c*.1702–72), was one of the earliest English marine and topographical painters. He worked in the manner of the van de VELDES, painting naval battles, colonial forts and Thames shipping until CANALETTO's success in London (he arrived in 1746) caused Scott to work in his manner on similar views. There are several scenes by the two men which are nearly identical and it seems that, at least once, Canaletto worked from Scott's drawings. There are pictures in Bath, London (Guildhall, Tate and Nat. Marit. Mus.), New York (Met. Mus.) and Yale (CBA). MARLOW was his pupil.

SCOTT, William (1913–89) was born in Scotland but trained in Belfast and then at the Royal Academy. He visited Italy and lived in France before the Second World War, when he served in the Royal Engineers and learned lithography. In 1953 he went to America, where he met POLLOCK, KLINE and ROTHKO; as a result his work, described before 1951 as hermetically sexually symbolic, became more abstract and greyer in colour. In 1958–61 he painted a mural for Londonderry Hospital and many galleries have pictures, including Belfast, Edinburgh, London (Tate and V&A), Paris (Mus. d'Art Moderne) and Rome.

SCREENPRINT *see* SERIGRAPHY.

SCROTS (or Stretes), Guillim, a Netherlander, was appointed painter to Mary of Hungary, Regent of the Netherlands, in 1537, and was employed in England by Henry VIII from 1545/6 to 1553. His portraits, which are Italianate and Mannerist in type, are important in the development of the full-length portrait – a form which became commoner in England than it was on the Continent at the same period. *Henry Howard, Earl of Surrey* (the best version belongs to the Duke of Norfolk), dated 1546 but probably painted after his execution in 1547, is reasonably attributed to Scrots. Other attributed portraits are in the Royal Coll. and in London (NPG).

SCULP. (Lat. *sculpsit*, he engraved it) on an engraving refers to the name of the engraver. In 17th-century English 'sculptures' means engravings: cf. Evelyn's 'Sculptura, or the History and Art of Chalcography and Engraving in Copper' (1662). *Incidit* also refers to the engraver.

SCULPTURE is the art of creating forms in three dimensions, either in the round or in RELIEF. Basically, there are two opposed conceptions of sculptural form: glyptic, which means carved, and consists essentially in removing waste material until the form is freed from the matter in which it was imprisoned (this Neo-Platonic conception was Michelangelo's) and its opposite, in which form is created from nothing, by building up in some plastic material. Carving and modelling are thus two separate and complementary aspects of sculpture, the present tendency being to exalt direct carving and the feel of the material at the expense of modelling, which involves using clay or wax as a preliminary material for translation into plaster, bronze, lead or even stone (*see* BRONZE, PLASTER, POINTING MACHINE and STONE CARVING). The difference between painting and sculpture has always been that the third dimension is fundamental to sculpture; but a painting with heavy IMPASTO may possess more relief than a *rilievo stiacciato*, and the last fifty years have seen much blurring of the distinctions, with painted sculpture, constructions of wire and plastic in bright colours and so on. KINETIC art may also be considered a form of sculpture.

SCUMBLING is the opposite of GLAZING. It consists of working an opaque layer of oil-paint over another layer of a different colour or tone so that the lower layer is not entirely obliterated, giving an uneven, broken effect. The two processes of glazing and scumbling together demonstrate the range of effects, from transparency to opacity, possible in the oil medium; effects which ensured its universal adoption. ACRYLIC paints now give the same effects.

SEBASTIANO del Piombo (*c.*1485–1547), was a Venetian painter who was perhaps trained under Giovanni BELLINI but was certainly deeply influenced by GIORGIONE. When Giorgione died (1510) Sebastiano may have completed some of his unfinished works: his style at this date can be seen in his *Salome* (1510, London, NG). Probably he painted the *Judgement of Solomon* (Kingston Lacy, Dorset, National Trust) before leaving Venice: this unfinished and very damaged picture, once attributed to Giorgione, is now generally agreed to be by Sebastiano. In 1511 he went to Rome and began working in the Villa Farnesina, in contact with the Raphael circle. He seems to have quarrelled with Raphael and soon became a partisan of Michelangelo, who influenced him deeply and even provided him with drawings to work from (e.g. the *Pietà* in Viterbo and the *Flagellation* in S. Pietro in Montorio, Rome). His gigantic *Raising of Lazarus* (1517–19, London, NG) shows the Michelangelo influence at its height and was painted in more or less open competition with Raphael's *Transfiguration*. In 1531 he received a Papal sinecure (known as 'il Piombo', hence his name) and he painted rather less, but continued to produce admirable portraits which combine the virtues of his Venetian training with the Roman discipline in form: an example is *Cardinal Pole* (*c.*1537, Leningrad). There are other works by him in Arezzo, Basle, Berlin, Budapest, Cambridge (Fitzwm), Dublin, Florence (Uffizi and Pitti), Fort Worth Texas, Glasgow (Pollok House), London (NG), Madrid, Naples, New York (Met. Mus.), Paris (Louvre), Parma, Philadelphia (Johnson), Rome (Doria Gall. and S.M. del Popolo), Sarasota Fla, Venice (Accad. and churches), Vienna and Washington (NG).

SECCO (Ital. dry). A method of wall-painting sometimes used as a substitute for FRESCO and sometimes to retouch parts of a fresco. The wall is soaked with lime-water, but the plaster has already set, so the pigments are applied with some binding medium. It is easier than true fresco, since there is no need to work fast, but it is far less permanent. Occasionally one sees a wall-painting in which the heads and hands are well-preserved but the draperies have virtually disappeared. This is because the heads and hands are in true fresco and the ornamented draperies were painted *a secco*.

SECESSION, Vienna, *see* SEZESSION.

SECTION D'OR (Fr. GOLDEN SECTION) was an offshoot of CUBISM and the title of an exhibition in Paris in 1912 as well as a magazine to accompany it. It was mainly promoted by the brothers DUCHAMP, DUCHAMP-VILLON and VILLON, but others included Archipenko, Gleizes, Gris, La Fresnaye, Laurencin, Léger, Lhote, Marcoussis, Metzinger and Picabia.

SEGANTINI, Giovanni (1858–99), was an Italian painter of Alpine landscapes and subject pictures. He used a method not unlike that of NEO-IMPRESSIONISM to get the maximum effect of the bright mountain light: 'I went out only at sunset, to see and feel its impressions, which I then transferred to canvas during the day.' There is a Segantini Museum in St Moritz.

SEGHERS, Daniel, SJ (1590–1661), was the best exponent of a special form of flower-painting – the painting of garlands around small devotional images, or, occasionally, portraits. He became a Master in Antwerp in 1611 and in 1614 became a Jesuit (although brought up a Protestant) and went to Rome for a short time. On his return to Antwerp he was associated with Rubens. The figures in his pictures are usually by others – e.g. Rubens – but he grew his own flowers. There are examples in Birmingham, Cambridge (Fitzwm) and London (V&A and Dulwich).

SEGHERS, Hercules (1589/90–1638 or earlier), a Dutch landscape painter and etcher, was a pupil of G. van CONINXLOO in Amsterdam and continued the fantastic mountain landscapes of Momper and Savery, but in a far more realistic and at the same time romantic way. Some of his landscapes represent actual places and it has been argued that he must have been to Italy and in the Alps. He was much influenced by ELSHEIMER and was himself probably the most important influence on Rembrandt's landscapes. Rembrandt owned eight of his paintings and actually reworked an etching of his. Seghers was a virtuoso etcher and frequently used coloured paper or tinted the proofs to increase the romantic light effects. There are fifty-four etchings known; his rare paintings include those in Amsterdam, Berlin, Detroit, Edinburgh (Univ.),

Florence, Philadelphia (Johnson) and Rotterdam. Two others, in The Hague (Bredius Mus.) and London (NG), are doubtfully his.

SEGONZAC, André Dunoyer de (1884–1974), though influenced by Cézanne and Cubism was basically a late Impressionist. From 1919 he made etchings (*c*.1,500), often as book-illustrations, and these are probably his best works.

SEICENTO (Ital. six hundred). The 17th century, i.e. the sixteen-hundreds.

SEISENEGGER, Jakob (1505–67), painted portraits of the Emperor Charles V in 1530 and again in 1532 in Bologna, where the copy made by Titian so excelled the original full-length that Titian henceforth painted the Emperor's state portraits. There are pictures by Seisenegger in Vienna and one in London (NG).

SENEFELDER, Alois *see* ENGRAVING (3).

SEPIA. A brown pigment, like BISTRE, made from cuttlefish.

SEQUEIROS *see* SIQUEIROS.

SÉRAPHINE (i.e. Séraphine Louis) (1864–1934) was a domestic servant at Senlis, near Paris, whose talent was discovered in 1912 by the German critic Wilhelm Uhde, who had a special interest in modern primitives. Unlike most of them, however, she was not a naïve realist (like VIVIN, whom Uhde also discovered), but painted only plants and flowers of the greatest complexity and richness of colour, reminiscent of Indian Numdah rugs and Persian miniatures, as well as the stained-glass windows that were certainly familiar to her. She became insane in 1930 and died in an asylum. There is a characteristic example in Paris (Mus. d'Art Moderne).

SERGEL, Johan Tobias von (1740–1814), was the great Swedish sculptor of the 18th century. He was trained in a French Rococo style and won the Gold Medal of the Swedish Academy in 1760, but did not go to Rome until 1767, where he stayed for eleven years. Like his younger contemporaries SCHADOW and CANOVA he turned decisively to Neoclassicism: indeed, on his arrival in Rome he was so struck by what he saw that he was unable to work for four months. His masterpiece, *The Drunken Faun* (1770–4), is in Stockholm (Nat. Mus.) and a replica is in Helsinki. Like Canova he made a version of the *Venus Kallipygos*; but his, commissioned by Gustav III of Sweden in 1780, has a portrait head, of the King's mistress. He also made a bronze statue of Gustav III in the pose of the *Apollo Belvedere* (1790–1808, Stockholm). Most of his work, including many portraits, is in Stockholm. His drawings are very reminiscent of FUSELI, who was also in Rome in the 1770s. In 1785 he wrote an autobiography.

SERIGRAPHY, or silk-screen printing, is not, strictly speaking, a technique of ENGRAVING. The basic principles are those of a stencil, in that it is a method by which paint is brushed over a screen so that the colour penetrates those parts of the screen that have not previously been masked. By using successive masks on the same screen it is possible to produce prints in several colours, and also to obtain colour mixtures by printing one colour over another – for instance, printing blue over yellow to make a green. The screen itself is made of fairly fine silk, and the masks are usually either of paper, or made by painting an impervious lacquer on the screen itself; paint is brushed on and soaks through the silk in the parts which have not been masked. The process was originally developed for commercial purposes, since it is possible to use unskilled labour to make prints once the masks have been prepared. In recent years, however, first in America and later in Europe, the technique has been greatly developed as a method of making large numbers of artist-produced prints which can be sold at fairly low prices, although each print is, like a lithograph, an original work of art. One of the advantages to the artist is that, by very slight, but easily – even accidentally – made changes in mask or paint density, variations are achieved in the prints which can remove serigraphy from the more mechanical processes of printing such as those employed in lithography.

SERODINE, Giovanni (1600–30), was born at Ascona in the Ticino, but was in Rome *c.*1615, where he was deeply influenced by CARAVAGGIO and especially by Caravaggio's Dutch follower TERBRUGGHEN, with whose works Serodine's were often confused; it is, however, difficult to see how this happened, since Terbrugghen was certainly back in Utrecht by 1616. Since Serodine died so young all his works date from the 1620s and there are only about fifteen known (four in Ascona); after his death he was completely forgotten and was only rediscovered in the 1950s. Other works are in Beauvais, Edinburgh (NG), Madrid (Prado), Milan (Ambrosiana), Rome (Gall. Naz. and Pal. Venezia) and Vassar Coll. NY.

SERPOTTA, Giacomo (1656–1732), was a Sicilian sculptor in stucco who came from a family of carvers and stucco-workers and spent most of his life in Palermo. He may have been in Rome when young, and thus acquainted with Late Baroque forms, though his decorations are closer to Rococo, while achieving, occasionally, an almost neoclassical purity. His technical virtuosity was outstanding, both in his figures in the round and in his reliefs, which exploit a pictorial quality in the delicacy of the recession. He is particularly famous for his *putti*, who gambol playfully over the walls of the Oratory at S. Lorenzo in Palermo. He was extremely prolific, and was assisted by his elder brother Giuseppe and his natural son Procopio, though their relations were not easy. In Palermo, from 1697 onwards, he worked in many churches and also at Agrigento and Alcamo. The *bozzetto* for his bronze equestrian *Carlo II* (destroyed 1848) is in Trapani.

SÉRUSIER, Paul (1864–1927), met GAUGUIN at PONT-AVEN in Brittany in 1888, and was deeply influenced by the ideas of SYNTHETISM: Gauguin gave him one lesson – 'How do you see those trees? They are yellow? Well, paint them yellow. The shadow is bluish? Make it pure ultramarine. . . . Red leaves? Use vermilion.' In Paris, Sérusier was, with DENIS, BONNARD and VUILLARD, one of the founders of the NABIS. He visited Italy and Germany, and, in 1897, went to the Benedictine monastery at Beuron in Germany, where he was much influenced by their theories of religious art. His own 'ABC de la Peinture' was first published in 1921. There are works in London (Tate), Ottawa, Paris (Mus. d'Orsay), Stuttgart and Warsaw.

SETTECENTO (Ital. seven hundred). The 18th century, i.e. the seventeen-hundreds.

SETTIGNANO, Desiderio da, *see* DESIDERIO.

SEURAT, Georges (1859–91), studied at the École des Beaux-Arts, when he read Chevreul's book on the theory of colour (first published in 1839, and re-published in 1889). Later he studied the paintings of Delacroix at S. Sulpice in Paris, and Delacroix's theory as it is ascertainable from his Diaries, for precedents for the theories he was himself elaborating. He was also much influenced by the aesthetic theories based on the observations of a scientist, Charles

Henry, and the conclusions of David Sutter's writings on the phenomena of vision, published in 1880. These led him to evolve first the theory of Divisionism (*see* OPTICAL MIXTURES) and then a method of painting by the use of colour contrasts in which the areas of shadow are broken down into the complementaries of adjacent areas of light, the light itself being broken down into local colour, the colour of the light and of reflections, so that for instance bright yellow-green grass will contain reflections from the sky and from the other nearby objects, and shadows in it will tend towards reddish-purple; or the shadows in a reddish-orange dress will be preponderantly greenish-blue. He also evolved a formal type of composition, based on the GOLDEN SECTION, on the proportion and relation of objects within the picture space to one another and to the size and shape of the picture, on the balance of verticals and horizontals, and on figures placed across the picture plane or at right angles to it. Where the Impressionists stressed the flickering quality of light and figures caught in movement, Seurat aimed at a static quality. His *Bathers at Asnières* (*La Baignade*, London, NG), exhibited in 1884 at the Salon des Artistes Indépendants in Paris, was not so thorough-going an exposition of his theories as the *Sunday on the Island of La Grande Jatte* (Chicago) exhibited in 1886 at the last Impressionist exhibition, and the term NEO-IMPRESSIONISM was established for Seurat and the group round him by 1886. He was for long opposed to any popularization of his theories, since he believed that by robbing them of novelty it would also rob them of their effect, but in 1890 he consented to the publication of a *résumé* of his theory. His early death, however, meant that his ideas were developed by SIGNAC, RYSSELBERGHE and others. There are works in Baltimore, Bristol, Brussels, Chicago, Detroit, Edinburgh, Glasgow, Grenoble, Indianapolis, Liverpool, London (NG, Tate and Courtauld Inst.), Merion Pa (Barnes Fdn), Munich, New York (M of MA), Northampton Mass. (Smith Coll.), Otterlo (Kröller-Müller), Paris (Mus. d'Orsay), San Francisco and elsewhere.

SEVEN, The Group of, was actually a group of nine Canadian landscape painters active from 1920, when the original seven – Carmichael, Harris, Jackson, Johnston, Lismer, MacDonald and Varley – formed the group. Johnston resigned and was succeeded by Casson, and the ninth was Tom Thomson, who had died in 1917, but was the inspiration of the group. Their bold colour and brushwork made them akin to the FAUVES.

SEVERINI, Gino (1883–1966), was living in Paris when the original Manifesto of FUTURIST Painting appeared in 1910. He signed it, but thought that it showed his fellow-countrymen in a provincial light, and he induced them to pay more attention to Cubism. He himself was much influenced by SEURAT and Neo-Impressionist theories. In his last years he decorated several churches in Switzerland with frescoes and mosaics in a more Neoclassical manner, and his book 'Du Cubisme au Classicisme' (1921) shows the trend of his thought. His *Suburban Train Arriving in Paris* (1915, London, Tate) is one of a group of Futurist works painted in Paris 1914/18. Others are in Amsterdam (Stedelijk) and New York (Guggenheim).

SEZESSION (Ger. secession). The *Sezessionen* were groups of artists in Germany and Austria who resigned from established academic bodies and exhibiting societies in order to forward the aims of various modern (usually Impressionist) movements. The most important were those of Munich (1892),

Berlin (1899), headed by LIEBERMANN and partly due to the scandal over the MUNCH Exhibition of 1892, Vienna (1897) and Darmstadt. In due course the Expressionists seceded in their turn.

SFUMATO (Ital. evaporated, cleared like smoke) is a word used to describe the transitions of colour or, especially, tone from light to dark by stages so gradual as to be imperceptible. LEONARDO attached great importance to this as a means of obtaining that effect of relief which he regarded as essential to the art of painting, and in some of his works the softness of contour and the darkening of the shadows have now combined to spoil much of the effect intended. In his notes on painting he says that light and shade should blend 'without lines or borders, in the manner of smoke'.

SGRAFFITO (Ital. scratched). A decorative technique in which tinted plaster is covered with a thin layer of white plaster (or vice-versa), the top layer then being scratched with a design, revealing the lower layer. The technique was employed for arabesques and similar decorations in 16th-century Italy, but it can usually be seen in a rudimentary form on any whitewashed wall, and has been exploited in this sense by modern painters such as DUBUFFET. A much earlier form of the technique, found in Italian panel paintings, consists of a gold ground with opaque colour over it, so that scratching the surface provides gold lights. The modern, incorrect, usage of the plural *graffiti* covers anything scribbled or sprayed on any surface.

SHAHN, Ben (1898–1969), was born in Lithuania, but went to the US in 1906 and became a characteristically American exponent of SOCIAL REALISM. His use of photographic realism of detail and some of the technical devices of advertising set him apart from most modern American painters, but his art was always a vehicle for his ideas. The Sacco and Vanzetti case (when two immigrant anarchists were judicially murdered) led to the production of a series (1931–2) of biting comments, mostly drawings. Naturally, he was much influenced by ROUAULT and RIVERA, collaborating with the latter on the Radio City murals in 1933. Other murals are in the Bronx Post Office, New York (1938–9), and the Social Security Building, Washington (1940–2). He also wrote on art.

SHOP WORK *see* WORKSHOP PRODUCTION.

SICKERT, Walter Richard (1860–1942), was, with Wilson STEER, the most important of the British Impressionists – and it is highly characteristic of him that he can hardly be included in any definition of Impressionism, since he worked at the bottom of the tone scale, and his light effects gleam out from sombre colours and tones. Towards the end of his life his palette lightened considerably, when he painted scenes (never on the spot) in Bath and Brighton and also made a series of pictures based either on newspaper and other photographs or on Victorian magazine illustrations. He was profoundly influenced by Whistler and Degas, both of whom he knew, sharing something of their dispassionate wit, and was equally far from being a typical Impressionist. He was at various times connected with the stage and most of his best works are scenes of London music-halls and their audiences, although he also had great feeling for the shabbier parts of London, Dieppe and Venice. The open air and the countryside had no appeal for him. In 1911 he founded the CAMDEN TOWN GROUP (with Islington it was one of his favourite boroughs) and he later belonged to the LONDON GROUP (which absorbed the Camden

Town one), the NEAC and the RA, from which he resigned resoundingly. He was one of the few modern painters to make extensive use of studio assistants and his technical procedures are very like those of the Old Masters. He also etched and wrote a great deal (not all of it sense). He is well represented in London (Tate, Courtauld Inst., Mus. of London and Islington Public Library) as well as Rouen, many British galleries (especially Liverpool), and Dieppe, Melbourne, New York (M of MA), Ottawa, Paris (Louvre), Sydney, Toledo Ohio and Yale. Like the picture in Cambridge Mass., one of the Yale paintings clearly shows his affinity to VUILLARD; another, *The Camden Town Murder, or, What Shall We Do for the Rent?* shows his propensity for perverse titles.

SIGNAC, Paul (1863–1935), was a follower of SEURAT, whose ideas he enthusiastically advocated, and whose style he imitated with more energy than perception. He was the most articulate theorist among the NEO-IMPRESSIONISTS, and his book 'De Delacroix au Néo-Impressionisme' (1899), is the textbook of the movement. In 1898 he visited London on – in his own words – a 'pilgrimage to Turner'. There are works in Paris (Mus. d'Orsay).

SIGNIFICANT FORM. A phrase invented by Clive Bell *c.*1914 to define the specifically aesthetic element in a work of art. That is aesthetically valid ('significant') which is an expression of form: that is formally effective which is significant. A neat example of arguing in a circle.

SIGNORELLI, Luca (*c.*1441/50–1523), was traditionally a pupil, with PERUGINO, of PIERO della Francesca. He is first documented in 1470 and some fragments in Città di Castello, of 1474, are his earliest datable works. Although his earliest works (including two sides of a processional banner in the Brera, Milan) show some influence from Piero they already show the very marked influence of the POLLAIUOLO in the use of figures with exaggerated muscular development in violent action. This Florentine stress on outline as a means of conveying drama, and the use of characteristic gesture, link him with Donatello on the one hand and Verrocchio on the other, as may be seen in his frescoes in the Santa Casa at Loreto. He was in Rome in the early 1480s and probably worked on the Sistine Chapel frescoes with Perugino, Botticelli, Rosselli and others. His masterpiece is the fresco cycle in Orvieto Cathedral, begun by Fra Angelico in 1447, which he was commissioned to complete in 1499. The frescoes depict with vivid realism the End of the World, the Coming and Fall of Anti-Christ and the Last Judgement. His gifts as a draughtsman are fully revealed in the sharp foreshortenings of the figures, their strained poses, the perspective, the hardness of outline, and the imaginative power with which, for example, he peoples Hell, not with pathetically grotesque creatures half-beast, half-fantasy, but with vigorous, muscular devils, passionately engaged in fiendish cruelties and entirely human in form, though with the hideous colour of rotting flesh. His use of the nude figure for dramatic ends, his interest in classical antiquity and his *terribilità* presage, and influenced, Michelangelo. His later works never again reach this pitch of intensity, probably because the Orvieto frescoes were painted at the time of the French invasions and while Savonarola's threats of doom and the coming of Anti-Christ were in all men's minds. He was in Rome again *c.*1508, and again in 1513, but he stood no chance against Raphael and Michelangelo and he settled in Cortona as a good, provincial, master with a large shop, producing hard, repetitive and old-fashioned altarpieces. Vasari claimed to be his great-nephew. There are works in Altenburg, Arezzo, Baltimore (Walters), Bergamo, Berlin, Birmingham (Barber Inst.), Boston (Mus.), Cortona (Mus. and churches), Detroit, Florence (Uffizi, Horne Mus.), Liverpool, London (NG), Milan (Brera, Poldi-Pezzoli), Monte Oliveto Maggiore, Munich, Naples, New York (Met. Mus.), Orvieto (Cath., S. Rocco), Paris (Louvre and Jacquemart-André), Perugia (Mus. and Cath.), Philadelphia (Johnson), Sansepolcro, Toledo Ohio, Umbertide (Sta Croce), Urbino, Venice (Cà d'Oro), Washington, Yale and elsewhere.

SIGNORINI, Telemaco (1835–1901), was an Italian painter and etcher who was a representative of *Verismo*, the Italian form of the Realist movement of the 19th century. He joined the MACCHIAIOLI and was also much influenced by the French Impressionists. He met COROT in Paris in 1861, and travelled to London and Edinburgh with De NITTIS – like his friend he was much influenced by DEGAS and Toulouse-Lautrec. His 'Memoirs' (1893) are the chief source of information about the Macchiaioli. There are works by him in Florence, Milan, Rome, Turin and Venice.

SILK-SCREEN *see* SERIGRAPHY.

SILVA, Vieira da, *see* VIEIRA da Silva.

SILVER POINT. A technique of drawing much favoured in the 15th and 16th centuries but now almost entirely disused. The drawing is made on a sheet of paper which has been prepared by coating it with opaque white (to which a slight tint of colour is usually added), with a piece of silver wire held in wood like the lead in a modern pencil. The silver point produces a silver-grey indelible mark which will not smudge, and the drawing can be heightened, if desired, with Chinese white. Gold or lead may be used in place of silver, all giving a similar effect to a modern pencil, but rather more subtle, and with the advantage of indelibility: which makes the draughtsman think before he puts down a line.

SIMONE Martini *see* MARTINI.

SINOPIA. A reddish-brown earth colour often used for the underdrawing of a FRESCO, and frequently used to mean the drawing itself. Recent advances in the technique of restoration have led to the recovery of many *sinopie*, which are left on the wall when the top layer of fresco is removed. Since the *sinopia* is necessarily covered by the application of the *intonaco* it is common to find that the finished fresco differs considerably from the preparatory *sinopia*, perhaps because the artist changed his mind as he worked. The technique is therefore much less mechanical than the CARTOON, which could be executed in the absence of the master, whereas the *sinopia* method required his constant attention.

SIQUEIROS, David Alfaro (1896–1974), was a Mexican painter imprisoned and exiled many times during his violent career as a political revolutionary in Mexico and Spain. His art stems from RIVERA, whom he met in Paris in 1919, and OROZCO, with whom he worked on projects for huge mural paintings expressing political ideas in a strained yet realist style, and he was also affected by the darker aspects of Surrealism, Mexican folk art and ethnography. In 1935 he had a public controversy with Rivera over the nature of revolutionary art. His best work is in Mexico: his *Human Life* is said to be the largest mural in the world.

SIRANI, Elisabetta (1638–65), was the daughter and pupil of a Bolognese imitator of Guido RENI. Her talents were encouraged by the writer Malvasia, who later wrote an adulatory biography of her in his 'Felsina Pittrice' (1678). She was active by 1655, and by 1662 she had recorded about ninety works, executing at least another eighty before she died at the age of 27. None of her portraits has survived, but religious, mythological and allegorical subjects were painted in full view of a crowd of admirers. She was buried in Reni's tomb, and her style is close to his – idealized, affecting, sentimental, but with strong chiaroscuro and fine colour. There are many works in Bologna (Mus. and churches), and one in Edinburgh (NG), and drawings in the Royal Coll. and New York (Met. Mus.). Her sisters Anna Maria (1645–1715), and Barbara (alive in 1678), were also painters. Barbara's portrait of Elisabetta is in Bologna.

SISLEY, Alfred (1839–99), was an Impressionist painter born in Paris of British parentage. With MONET he was one of the purest of the IMPRESSIONISTS and was practically exclusively a landscape painter; unlike Monet, however, he did not dissolve the forms of the landscape into a sort of coloured mist in his search for light and colour. In 1857 he was sent to London to improve his English and prepare for a commercial career, but he spent much time in museums and studied Constable and Turner especially. Back in Paris in 1862 he was allowed to enter the École des Beaux-Arts under GLEYRE, where he at once met Monet, RENOIR and BAZILLE. An early landscape of St Cloud (1867, Southampton) still shows marked BARBIZON influence, but he exhibited at the First Impressionist Exhibition (1874) and at some of the later ones. During the Franco-Prussian War he went to England (1871) and returned in 1874, when he painted at Hampton Court and in the suburbs of South London. He made further visits, including a final one to Wales in 1897, and almost his last paintings are Welsh seascapes. There are pictures by him in most modern museums, including Aberdeen, Birmingham, Boston, Bristol, Leicester, London (Tate and Courtauld Inst.), Ottawa, Paris (Mus. d'Orsay) and Washington (NG).

SIZE colour. A method of painting in which the powdered pigment is mixed with hot glue-size. It is quick and simple but easily damaged and is now used almost exclusively for scene-painting. Ordinary distemper is a form of size colour.

SKETCH. A sketch is the rough draught of a composition or part of a composition, made in order to satisfy the artist himself on certain points of scale, composition, lighting, etc. It is the trial run – or one of many – for the full-scale work but it must be carefully distinguished from a STUDY. A sketch by a landscape painter is usually a small and rapid note of the effect of light on a given scene, and is intended for future reference and reworking if necessary. The quality of some artists' sketches is, however, so high that what they would have considered their important works are now often undervalued: Rubens and Constable are examples. Constable's sketches, in particular, have been responsible for many subsequent artists painting such rapid notations – and then exhibiting them as works of art. Rubens's sketches were made as guides to his assistants in the layout and first stages of a grand composition. These compositions were often executed almost entirely by the assistants, hence the preference now accorded to the original sketches.

A sketch-book is an album of about twenty to fifty pages of drawing-paper, usually not more than 15 × 10 inches and often much less, so that it can be carried comfortably in the pocket, ready for instant notation of an effect of light or a striking pose. Scores of such pocket-books, filled with Turner's sketches, are in the Tate. Such impressions or first ideas are sometimes called *croquis* (Fr.) or *pensieri* (Ital.). *See also* PATTERN-BOOK.

SLEVOGT, Max (1868–1932), was, with CORINTH and LIEBERMANN, one of the leading German Impressionists. He was trained in Munich before going to Paris in 1889 and then to Italy; later he travelled widely in Denmark, Holland and Egypt (1913–14, where he painted landscapes filled with blazing light). His Impressionist style began *c.*1900, at the same time as he made a name as an illustrator. He worked for 'Simplizissimus' and the Art Nouveau periodical 'Jugend', as well as illustrating many books. His most famous paintings are the series of the singer *D'Andrade as Don Giovanni* (*c.*1902–3), but his last work, a fresco of Golgotha in the Friedenskirche at Ludwigshafen (1932), may be his masterpiece. He painted other frescoes and there are pictures by him in many German museums.

SLUTER, Claus (active *c.*1380–*d.*1405/6), was the greatest realist sculptor of Northern Europe at the turn of the 15th century and preceded both van Eyck and Donatello, the two 15th-century artists most akin to him in spirit. He worked principally for the Dijon Court of Philip the Bold, Duke of Burgundy, but he was himself of Dutch origin and probably worked in Brussels before arriving in Dijon, where he was assistant to the Duke's sculptor, Jean de Marville, 1385–9, when he became Court Sculptor himself. He worked on the sculptural decoration of the Duke's foundation, the Chartreuse de Champmol, 1391–6/7 and from 1395 to 1403 was engaged on his masterpiece, the *Well of Moses*, a well-head with six full-length Prophets around it. This survives, but the upper part, a *Calvary*, is known only from a fragment of the *Crucified Christ* (Dijon, Musée Archéologique). The grandeur of style of the *Moses* and its sharply characterized pose and features mark it as something quite new and totally different from the INTERNATIONAL GOTHIC or SOFT STYLE then current. Sluter also worked on the Tomb of Philip the Bold, but this had been begun under his predecessor in 1384 and was continued by his own successor, his nephew Claus de Werve (*d.*1439), who completed it in 1411. The most famous part of it is the series of Pleurants or Weepers, small mourning figures round the sides, of the greatest realism. One of these is in Cleveland Ohio (Mus.); the surviving parts of the Tomb are in Dijon (Mus.).

SMET, Gustave De (1877–1943), was, with PERMEKE, one of the leading Belgian Expressionists. He was trained in Ghent and settled at the artists' colony of Laethem-Saint-Martin in 1901. Up to 1914 he painted in an Impressionist manner, but became an Expressionist while a refugee in Holland. There are works in Amsterdam (Stedelijk), Antwerp, Basle, Brussels, Ghent, Grenoble, The Hague, Liège and Rotterdam.

SMIBERT, John (1688–1751), was an Edinburgh painter who worked in Italy 1717–20 and went to America with Berkeley (later Bishop Berkeley) in 1728 in an attempt to settle the Bermudas. His portrait of Berkeley is in London (NPG) and the large group-portrait *Berkeley and His Friends*, including Smibert himself, of 1728/9 is in Yale (another version is in Dublin). In 1730 he settled in Boston and painted portraits which recall those of Jervas – i.e. they are not very good imitations of the KNELLER style. He was one of the first landscape painters in America, but none has survived. He also organized the first art exhibition held in America. There are works in Edinburgh (NPG), London (NPG) and many American museums, including Boston.

SMITH, David (1906–65), American sculptor. In 1925, he worked in a car factory, where he learned techniques later useful in his sculpture. In New York, he associated with GORKY, DE KOONING and DAVIES, producing paintings to which he attached 'found objects'. In 1933, influenced by Picasso's sculpture, he began working in welded steel, his chief and preferred medium, making large abstract constructions. In Italy in 1962, he made the *Voltri* series for the 4th Festival at Spoleto.

SMITH, Sir Matthew (1879–1959), first went to Paris in 1910 and was in contact with MATISSE for a month or two, at Matisse's school, which closed in 1911. The influence of the FAUVE movement was decisive and he spent much time in France up to 1939; the richness of his colour and the opulence of his forms always made him seem more of a French than an English painter, and his luscious nudes and flower-pieces evidently owe much to Matisse: Smith was, like Etty, one of the few English painters of nudes. There are pictures by him in Cardiff, Coventry, Leeds (Temple Newsam), London (Tate), Manchester, Scarborough, Ottawa, Yale (CBA) and other museums, but by far the largest collection is in the Guildhall Gall., London.

SNYDERS, Frans (1579–1657), was a pupil of Pieter Bruegel the Younger. He travelled in Italy in 1608–9 and on his return settled in Antwerp, where he was much employed by RUBENS on the still-life and animal parts of his hunting and other pictures. He also worked with JORDAENS, and on his own account produced many vigorous hunting scenes and large still-life subjects of great complexity. He married a sister of the de VOS brothers. There are examples in the Royal Coll., and in Antwerp, Berlin, Boston (Mus.), Brussels, Cape Town, Dresden, Edinburgh (NG), The Hague, London (NG and Kenwood), Madrid, Munich, Ottawa, Paris (Louvre), Toronto and elsewhere.

SOCIAL REALISM is the painting of the contemporary scene, usually from a Leftish viewpoint. The movement probably goes back to DAUMIER and COURBET (and owes much to literary example, e.g. Zola): it was fairly current in the US (SHAHN, the ASHCAN SCHOOL) and in Britain (Bratby, Jack Smith and the New, or 'Kitchen Sink', Realists). GUTTOSO was the leading Italian exponent. It must be distinguished from *Socialist Realism*, which is the official Party Art of the USSR and the Communist Party generally. This is the dreariest kind of academic art, glorifying the party or the Peasant and other stock figures. A victim has said of it: 'Impressionism is painting what you see, Expressionism is painting what you feel, and Socialist Realism is painting what you hear.'

SODOMA. Giovanni Antonio Bazzi, called 'Il Sodoma' (1477–1549), was one of the best-known Sienese painters of the early 16th century. He was born at Vercelli and trained under the minor Lombard G. M. Spanzotti, 1490–7, and was probably in Milan between 1497 and 1501, when he arrived in Siena. He must have seen the work of Leonardo da Vinci in Milan and again in Florence *c.*1504. Between 1505 and 1508 he completed a series of thirty-one frescoes in the Benedictine monastery of Monte Oliveto, near Siena, where Signorelli had begun the scenes from the life of S. Benedict. Sodoma became the leading artist of Siena, but Vasari – who is very severe on Sodoma's general beastliness

– points out that this was not really deserved and much of his work is very uninspired. The obvious interpretation of his nickname seems to be belied by the tax-return (perhaps not wholly serious) that he filled in *c*.1531: 'I have an ape and a talking raven, which I keep in a cage so that he can teach a theological ass to talk. . . . I possess three beastly she-animals, which are women, and I have also thirty grown-up children, which is a real encumbrance . . . and as twelve children exempt a man from taxation I recommend myself to you. Farewell.' In recent years it has come to be realized that the great Sienese artist of the period is not Sodoma but BECCAFUMI. Sodoma painted in the Vatican in 1508 (part of the ceiling of the Stanza della Segnatura, subsequently given to Raphael to complete) and some fine frescoes in the Villa Farnesina in Rome in 1512. He is well represented in Siena and Florence and in London, Paris, New York and many other galleries.

SOEST, Konrad von, *see* KONRAD.

SOFT-GROUND ETCHING *see* ENGRAVING.

SOFT STYLE is a name given to the style found principally in Germany (where it is called *Weiche Stil*), at the end of the 14th and beginning of the 15th centuries. It is very closely related to INTERNATIONAL GOTHIC, and, as the name implies, is characterized by soft and gentle rhythms, especially in the flow of drapery, and by a sweet and playful sentiment. The principal subject is the Madonna playing with the Christ Child and these are sometimes called *Schöne Madonnen* – 'Beautiful Madonnas'. Sculpture and the earliest woodcuts show the style even more clearly than painting.

SOLIMENA, Francesco (called L'Abate Ciccio) (1657–1747), was the major late Baroque painter in Naples and was extremely famous in the 18th century, being described in 1733 as 'by universal consent the greatest painter in the world'. He acquired great wealth, lived in a Palace, became a Baron, and was in constant demand by Kings and Princes. He was a celebrated teacher, and his pupils included such diverse artists as CONCA and Allan RAMSAY, although his style was most faithfully continued by Francesco de Mura (1696–1784). He formed his style on that of Luca GIORDANO but modified it profoundly by the classical tendencies of MARATTA and Pietro da Cortona, as well as Lanfranco and Mattia Preti. He settled in Naples in 1674 and his principal works there are in the churches (all damaged in 1939/45) of S. Paolo Maggiore (1689–90), the Gesù Nuovo (1725) and S. Domenico Maggiore. Many of his best works are the sketches for large compositions in Naples (Mus.) and there are many others in Neapolitan churches as well as Abingdon Berks., Barnard Castle (Bowes Mus.), Berlin, Birmingham (Gall. and Barber Inst.), Bristol, Cambridge (Fitzwm), Cleveland Ohio, Dresden, Dublin, Florence (Uffizi), Glasgow, The Hague, Leeds, Liverpool, London (NG, Courtauld Inst. and St Martin-in-the-Fields), Madrid, Malibu Cal. (Getty), Milan (Brera), New York (Met. Mus.), Northampton, Oxford (Ashmolean), Paris (Louvre), Rome (Gall. Naz.), the Vatican, Venice (Accad.), Vienna and York.

SOMER, Paul van (*c*.1577/8–1622), was an Antwerp painter who settled in London in 1616. He was, with MYTENS and JOHNSON, one of the best portrait painters in England before the arrival of van DYCK. He soon began to work for the Court, and his earliest datable work, *Queen Anne of Denmark with her Horse and Dogs* (1617, Royal Coll.), is perhaps the best. There are others in Liverpool, London (NPG and Tate) and Yale (CBA).

SOPRA PORTE, Superporte. Grand words for overdoors: i.e. paintings, usually landscapes, specially composed to fit the space above a doorway.

SOTTO IN SÙ (Ital. from below upwards). A term applied to the extreme of illusionistic perspective which shows figures painted on a ceiling so foreshortened as to appear actually floating in the space above the spectator. It is first found in a developed form in MANTEGNA (1474) and was taken up by CORREGGIO and Roman Baroque painters, such as LANFRANCO and PIETRO da Cortona and, later, POZZO and TIEPOLO.

SOULAGES, Pierre (*b.*1919), is, with HARTUNG, one of the leading abstract painters of the School of PARIS. He has travelled in the US and Japan and is well represented in American museums. His paintings have no titles, but are referred to by the date of completion – e.g. *23 mai 1953* (London, Tate).

SOUTINE, Chaïm (1893–1943), was born near Minsk but managed to get to Paris in 1913, where he met MODIGLIANI, CHAGALL and other *peintres maudits*. He was much influenced by EXPRESSIONISM and developed a style depending greatly on impasto; this is most noticeable in his slaughter-house pieces. There are many works in America – Dr Barnes bought 100 in 1923 – for instance, the M of MA, New York and Washington (NG and Phillips). The Barnes pictures are now in Merion, Pa.

SPAGNOLETTO, LO *see* RIBERA.

SPENCER, Gilbert (1892–1979), brother of Stanley, painted in a similar style. Hove has his *Air Raid Warning, 1940*.

SPENCER, Sir Stanley (1891–1959), was one of the most original of modern painters; original in iconography rather than formally, with a kind of naive religious feeling that is probably closer to Blake than to anyone else. He was trained at the Slade School 1908–12 and served in Macedonia in the First World War from 1915 to 1918: his experiences in the army medical corps were to be transformed in the next decade into the series of mural decorations in Burghclere Chapel, Hants. He made designs for such a series of pictures, culminating in a *Resurrection of the Soldiers* as an altarpiece, in 1922–3, and in 1926–7 the chapel was built as a memorial to a man killed in the War, and the paintings carried out between 1926 and 1932. At this time he was also painting his huge *Resurrection, Cookham* (1922–7, London, Tate), Cookham being his native village, where he spent most of his life. During the War of 1939–45 he painted a series of *Shipyards*, officially commissioned, in Port Glasgow. After 1945 he returned to the Resurrection theme in a series of large-scale religious works. He was elected ARA in 1932, but resigned in 1935 after a controversy over two of his more imaginative pictures. In 1950 he returned as RA and in 1959, just before his death, he was knighted. There is a Spencer Gallery at Cookham and pictures by him in Aberdeen, Belfast, Birmingham, Cambridge (Fitzwm), Dundee, Hull, Leeds, London (Tate and Imperial War Mus.), Manchester, New York (M of MA), Ottawa, Oxford, Sheffield, Southampton, Toronto, Yale (CBA) and elsewhere.

SPINELLO Aretino (active 1373–*d.*1410/11) came, as his name implies, from Arezzo but was probably trained in Florence, perhaps under Agnolo GADDI. So far from being the last flicker of the Giotto tradition Spinello seems to have returned, about the end of the Trecento, to the massive style of Giotto and was thus a precursor of Masaccio. There are works by him in Amsterdam, Arezzo (Mus. and churches), Budapest, Cambridge Mass. (Fogg), Chicago,

Cleveland Ohio, Copenhagen, Florence (Uffizi, Accad. and churches), Liverpool, London (NG), New York (Met. Mus.), Oxford (Ch. Ch.), Paris (Louvre and École des Beaux-Arts), Pisa (Mus. and churches), Providence RI, St Louis, Siena, the Vatican, Washington (NG) and elsewhere. His son, Parri Spinelli (*d.*1452), worked with him, and later began the *True Cross* cycle in Arezzo which Piero della Francesca took over after Parri's death.

SPITZWEG, Carl (1808–85), was perhaps the most characteristic BIEDERMEIER painter. He was self-taught and worked as a newspaper illustrator before becoming a painter: it was probably this training which prevented him from falling into the pretentiousness which afflicted his friend SCHWIND. He travelled extensively – Italy, Paris, London, Antwerp – and was deeply impressed by both DELACROIX and the BARBIZON painters, but was not tempted into the Grand Style. His *Poor Poet*, of which three versions exist, is a good example of his homely, anecdotal style. There are pictures in Berlin, Berne, Hamburg, Hanover and Munich.

SPOLVERO. A kind of auxiliary CARTOON (from Ital. *spolvero*, fine dust). The purpose of the *spolvero* was to preserve the cartoon itself for the guidance of the assistants working on the final painting, since the *spolvero* was pricked through and pounced with charcoal dust. For this reason it is doubtful whether any have survived, although a drawing of Mantegna's *Madonna della Vittoria* (Mantua, Pal. Ducale) may be one. It has been claimed that Orcagna's fresco in S. M. Novella, Florence, was painted from one.

SPRANGER, Bartholomeus (1546–1611), was an Antwerp painter who worked in Paris (*c.*1565) at the same time as PRIMATICCIO and N. dell' ABBATE, and in Rome (*c.*1567–75) as an assistant to Taddeo ZUCCARO, and in Vienna, for the Emperor Maximilian II, in 1575. He later worked for Rudolf II in Prague, where he died. He was a typical representative of late Mannerism, using numerous nude figures in unlikely attitudes to fill his compositions, which derive ultimately from Correggio and Parmigianino. The engravings of GOLTZIUS made his works very widely known. In Haarlem, besides Goltzius, he influenced CORNELISZ. and van MANDER, and in Utrecht WTEWAEL. He is well represented in the Vienna Gallery, but there are other examples in Antwerp, Brussels, Chicago, Cleveland Ohio, London (NG), Munich, Paris and elsewhere.

SQUARCIONE, Francesco (1397–1468), was a Paduan, first recorded as a painter in 1429. Although he seems to have been active as a painter all his life, he is principally famous on account of his pupils. It is said that he had 137, some of whom he seems to have adopted. The most famous was MANTEGNA who quarrelled violently with him and left his house in 1448. ZOPPO was also a pupil. Squarcione is said to have had a house full of casts of antique sculpture and to have made journeys to Rome and even to Greece in pursuit of antiquities. Only two works are known by him, a polyptych of 1449–52 in Padua (Mus.) and a signed *Madonna* in Berlin. Both demonstrate the extreme dryness of his style and his archaeological interests, and these, coupled with Donatello's influence, go far to explain Mantegna's early style.

SQUARED (for transfer). A drawing is said to be squared (up) when it has been covered with a network of squares. These squares can be numbered, and the same number of squares of a larger size can then be drawn on a wall or canvas: the contents of each small square can then be rapidly transferred to the corresponding large one, thus giving an enlarged version of the original drawing, more or less mechanically.

STABILE. Sculpture that keeps still. The opposite of MOBILE.

STAËL, Nicholas de (1914–55), was born in St Petersburg but was brought up in Brussels. He went to Paris in 1934 and became one of the leading abstract painters, coming under the influence of BRAQUE, whom he met during the war. His later works, after 1952, mark a return to a kind of representation in which the forms, though mostly abstract, were recognizably landscapes, still-life, or other real objects. He always insisted that he was not an abstract painter, but a non-figurative one. He committed suicide in 1955. There are works by him in Berne, Boston, Düsseldorf, Edinburgh, London (Tate), Minneapolis, New York (M of MA), Ottawa, Paris (Mus. d'Art Mod.), Toronto, Zurich and elsewhere.

STAFFAGE. This word, pronounced as French, is used in both English and German to describe the figures and animals which animate a picture intended essentially as a landscape or *veduta*; in other words, figures which are not really essential and could be added by another painter. In the highly specialized world of the Dutch painters of the 17th century this was very often the case, so that a landscape painter like WYNANTS rarely did his own *staffage*; whereas CANALETTO or GUARDI always did.

STANFIELD, Clarkson (1793–1867), was a marine and landscape painter influenced and overshadowed by Turner. He went to sea as a boy and was encouraged by Captain Marryat, the novelist, to devote himself to painting. He was press-ganged into the Navy in 1812, but left it in 1818 and became a scene-painter. He exhibited landscapes and marines at the RA from 1820 (he became an RA in 1835). He travelled a great deal and was in Italy 1838–9; he also illustrated travel books. He was a close friend of Dickens (cf. MACLISE), as well as Marryat. There are works in Bath, Birmingham, Bristol, Cambridge, Dublin, Hamburg, London (RA, Tate, V&A and Wallace Coll.), Manchester, Melbourne, Sunderland as well as other British provincial museums.

STANNARD, Joseph (1797–1830) *see* NORWICH SCHOOL.

STANZE (Ital. rooms). The suite of rooms in the Vatican decorated by RAPHAEL.

STANZIONE, Massimo (1585/6–1656), was one of the leading Neapolitan painters of the Caravaggio School. He was working in Rome by 1617 where he would have seen the Farnese Gallery by Annibale CARRACCI. His style is similar to that of SARACENI in that it is a more graceful and elegant form of Caravaggism than that practised by his fellow Neapolitan RIBERA, although Ribera exerted some influence on him. Stanzione has been called the Neapolitan Guido RENI which aptly summarizes his semi-Bolognese classicism (e.g. his signed picture in San Francisco Cal.). He may have died in the great plague of 1656 in Naples. Most of his pictures are in Naples, but there are others in Dresden, Florence (Uffizi), Frankfurt (Städel), Kansas City, London (NG), Manchester, New York (Met. Mus.) and Sarasota Fla.

STARK, James (1794–1859), was a member of the NORWICH SCHOOL and a pupil of CROME. He often imitated Hobbema, as in his picture in Port Sunlight (Lever Gall.). There are works in Norwich.

STATE is the name given to the stages in the development of an engraving or etching. When the artist has finished his work and pulls the first proofs these constitute the first state; if he decides to add a line here or burnish one out there then each successive printing containing alterations will constitute a fresh state. Many of Rembrandt's etchings run to seven or eight, each marking some definite artistic change, but it is an unfortunate temptation for cataloguers to invent new states, and for artists to meet the demand by introducing meaningless alterations. It should be noted that the twentieth state is not necessarily a poor impression, if only two or three prints have been pulled of each state; equally, a plate can be worn out in its first state. DEGAS's etchings run to twenty-odd states, but this is unusual. *See* PROOF, REMARQUE.

STEEL ENGRAVING, STEEL-FACED. The comparative softness of copper limits the number of prints that can be taken from an engraving, and, in the second quarter of the 19th century, steel plates came into use. These, however, are difficult to engrave and a satisfactory solution was soon found by steel-facing the completed copper plates. This is done by electrolysis, depositing a microscopic film of steel on the surface of the plate, which hardens it sufficiently to allow the printing of large editions, without interfering with the finest work on the plate.

STEELL, Sir John (1804–91), was a Scottish sculptor who studied in Rome. Chantrey urged him to settle in London, but he preferred to stay in Scotland, where he soon became the foremost sculptor, received a Court appointment in 1838, and was knighted in 1876. His *Scott* in the Scott Monument was probably the first marble statue commissioned in Scotland from a Scot. He also introduced bronze-founding into Scotland and his large equestrian *Wellington* in Edinburgh was aptly described as 'The Iron Duke in bronze by Steell'. There are many other works in Edinburgh, and in London (Nat. Marit. Mus.).

STEEN, Jan (1625/6–79), was a Dutch painter of humorous subjects from the life of the peasantry and middle classes in a variety of styles, like those of BROUWER, OSTADE (whose pupil he was) and DOU: he was born in Leiden and was greatly influenced by Dou and the *Fijnschilders*, although his colour is bolder and he was less finicky in detail. Even his rare Biblical subjects are treated as incidents in 17th-century Holland, but his pictures mostly represent tavern scenes or visits to respectable households. He worked in The Hague and Delft, where he leased a brewery, Haarlem and Leyden, where he kept a tavern. He was the son-in-law of van GOYEN, in whose manner he may have painted a few landscapes. He also painted some portraits. His genre scenes, and especially his paintings of Dutch proverbs, are said to carry esoteric meanings. About 700 paintings by him are known, and most galleries have one: London (NG, Wallace Coll. and Wellington Mus.) is especially rich, and there are religious subjects in Birmingham (Barber Inst.), Dublin and Glasgow (Pollok House).

STEER, Wilson (1860–1942), was the son of a portrait painter. He studied in Paris, 1882–3, and in the late 1880s discovered Degas and the Impressionists, particularly Monet. From then on his work reflects these influences, which are very strong in his landscapes, these being Constable revivified by Impressionist technique, although he made occasional excursions into Gainsborough. There are works in Aberdeen, Birkenhead, Bradford, Cambridge (Fitzwm), Cardiff, Edinburgh, Leeds, Liverpool, London (Tate, V&A and Courtauld Inst.), Manchester (City and Whitworth), Ottawa, Oxford, Southampton and elsewhere.

STEFANO da Zevio (or da Verona) (*c.*1375–1451), was the principal Veronese painter in the INTERNATIONAL GOTHIC style. He was much influenced by GENTILE da Fabriano and was probably the master of PISANELLO, continuing a sort of proto-Pisanello style as late as 1435 in his signed and dated *Adoration of the Magi* (Milan, Brera); on the other hand, the *Madonna of the Quail* (Verona) may be by him or by Pisanello. Most of his works are in Verona (Mus. and churches), but there are others in Rome (Pal. Venezia), Mount Holyoke Mass. and Worcester Mass.

STELLA, Frank (*b.*1936), is an American abstract painter. His geometrical abstracts, often on irregularly shaped supports, are opposed to the gestural art of the New York School. There are works in London (Tate) and New York (M of MA).

STEVENS, Alfred (1817–75), was born in Blandford Forum, Dorset, the son of a decorator. He was encouraged by a clergyman who lent him things to copy, so that at 15 he was a competent portraitist in the Reynolds tradition. His patron collected £60 and approached Landseer, but Landseer's premium for an apprenticeship was £500, so in 1833 the boy was put on a ship for Naples. No arrangements had been made for him and no further funds were provided; he knew no Italian, got involved in political intrigues, and fell among thieves. He spent eighteen months in and around Naples, and in 1835 walked to Rome, keeping himself by painting and drawing portraits. He found Rome in an uncongenial political uproar, so went on to Florence, where he remained four years, copying in the Uffizi for a living and producing for dealers what were virtually forgeries. In 1839 he was in Milan and Venice, studying Titian, and in 1840 was in Rome, where he met THORWALDSEN and worked in his studio until he returned to England in 1842. He failed even to get a mention in the 1842 Houses of Parliament competition, worked for industrialists on products exhibited in the 1851 Great Exhibition, and in 1856 had his first success with the Wellington monument in St Paul's Cathedral, although the equestrian statue of the Duke was not erected until forty-five years after the artist's death. He did decorative works in houses now destroyed and on mosaics in St Paul's Cathedral (finished 1864). He painted occasional portraits, but his principal surviving works are drawings, chiefly in sanguine, the main inspiration for which was Raphael. There are large collections of his work in Liverpool and London (Tate) with most of his surviving paintings and sculpture, and Cambridge (Fitzwm), Oxford and Sheffield have many drawings.

STEVENS, Alfred E. L. (1823–1906), was a Belgian painter who was a pupil of NAVEZ in Brussels before moving to Paris in 1844, where he painted chic Parisian ladies in a realist style deriving from his close friend MANET. Like WHISTLER, he was an early enthusiast for *Japonaiserie*. There are works by him in Baltimore (Mus., Walters), Boston, Brussels, Cambridge (Fitzwm), Cardiff, Chicago, London (N G), New York (Met. Mus.), Paris (Mus. d'Orsay) and Washington (N G).

STIACCIATO *see* RELIEF.

STIJL, De, was a Dutch magazine (1917–32) edited by van DOESBURG, devoted to boosting MONDRIAN and Neo-Plasticism in general; it subsequently sank into the hands of DADAISTS. The ideas advocated by it are also sometimes called De Stijl, and these have had a marked influence on the architecture of Gropius and others of the BAUHAUS movement, and on commercial art –

poster designing, packaging, printing – particularly in Germany at first, but later spreading all over the world.

STILL, Clyfford (1904–80). American painter best known for his ABSTRACT EXPRESSIONIST canvases, often in heavy oil impasto, which consist of jagged-shaped islands of contrasting colour, like rock formations. He is particularly well represented in Buffalo NY and San Francisco.

STILL-LIFE was much practised in the ancient world, e.g. at Pompeii, often in the form of ILLUSIONIST mosaics, but the tradition died out and did not re-emerge as a subject in its own right until the 16th century; before that it appeared in religious pictures and portraits as part of the setting. The word itself is a direct translation of the Dutch *Stilleven*, used only from 1656 to describe paintings which were earlier called simply fruit- or flower-pieces, *Ontbijt* (*see* BREAKFAST PIECE), BANCKET or *Pronkstilleven* (from Dutch *Pronk*, ostentation), or, if with religious overtones, *Vanitas*. From the names it is clear that the form was particularly favoured in the north of Europe, especially Holland and Flanders, but there were significant schools of still-life painting in Italy (especially Naples) and Spain and, to a lesser extent, France, although CHARDIN was arguably the greatest still-life painter of the 18th century and CÉZANNE of the 19th. After the Reformation, when religious painting virtually disappeared from the Protestant North, it became popular and was developed along various lines, some with a quasi-religious intention, the chief being the *Vanitas* type, a collection of objects chosen and arranged to remind the spectator of the transience and uncertainty of mortal life. Another was the symbolic type, where the objects portrayed have a significance beyond their individual appearance, and one heightened by their association; into this latter category come many still-life subjects which at first sight appear no more than members of the third type – collections of objects, usually luxurious, arranged to show off the painter's virtuosity. *Vanitas* is named from Ecclesiastes (i.2), 'Vanitas Vanitatum . . .' and is easily recognized – hour-glasses with the sand running out, skulls, mirrors, butterflies, flowers, guttering candles speak an immediate and universal language. The type was probably derived from the closely-related Memento Mori representations of St Jerome, popular in Utrecht, whereas in the theological university city of Leyden the still-life alone could be made to carry the moral. The *Melancholia* type (*see* HEEM) is a variant of the *Vanitas*. The symbolic type is more difficult, but usually contains bread in some form, wine, water and other recondite references to the Eucharist, the Passion, the Holy Trinity or the iconography of the Virgin and the Saints. The last category is self-evident but often difficult to distinguish from the symbolic type. This applies equally to flower-pieces. Many are merely luxuriant bouquets; many are also composite works containing flowers blooming at different times of the year, thus suggesting Time or the Seasons; many of the flowers may have religious or even erotic meanings. There are also large still-life pieces of the 'furniture-picture' type – kitchen interiors, with heaps of raw and cooked food, flowers, guns, dogs and cookmaids. Some of these, particularly those kitchen-pieces called BODEGONES in Spanish, may be based on such religious subjects as Christ in the house of Martha and Mary, or the Feast in the house of Levi. AERTSEN, BUECKELAER and, in Italy, BASSANO painted such pictures in the 16th century. The earliest flower-piece seems to be the vase of flowers on the back of a portrait by Memlinc (Thyssen Coll.,

Lugano), but this probably has a devotional, emblematic meaning; the earliest dated pure flower-piece is of 1562, by the German Ludger tom Ring. This type may have developed from MS Herbals, where accurate representation of medicinal herbs and plants was essential. The earliest known still-life is by the Venetian-trained Jacopo de' BARBARI (1504, Munich), but there is a *Madonna* of *c.*1470, by a follower of Roger van der Weyden, which has a niche containing still-life objects painted on the back (Rotterdam); this, however, must be symbolic in intent, since the objects are those often associated with the Annunciation. The towel, basin, and ewer all figure in the *Annunciation* on the wings of the Ghent Altar. Even earlier is a similar still-life by Taddeo Gaddi (1332–8), but this is a representation of a credence table – i.e. it is a liturgical fitment. Still-life hardly appears in Italian painting independently of a subject, except for the small baskets of fruit by Caravaggio, done early in his career, although notable exceptions are the fruit-, flower- and fish-pieces of the Neapolitan school in the 17th and 18th centuries (*see* RECCO, RUOPPOLO) and the musical instruments painted by BASCHENIS. It is, however, an essential feature of the pictures in wood veneers known as *intarsie* and marble panels inlaid with *pietre dure* – onyx, lapis lazuli, etc. – and also bulks large in Bassano's genre subjects, being, in fact, usually allied to such pictures. The Spanish followers of Caravaggio invested the simplest still-life with drama, as in those by ZURBARÁN, SÁNCHEZ COTÁN and even MELENDEZ. The dramatic element culminates in Goya's *Calf's Head* (Copenhagen) or *Plucked Turkey* (Munich), which has been described as a picture of a murder, rather than a still-life. In France the 17th and 18th centuries saw, with MOILLON and STOSKOPFF, Oudry and Chardin, highly developed forms of the Northern furniture-pictures and the virtuoso still-life, though Oudry verges on animal painting and Chardin eschews *objects de luxe* in favour of kitchen utensils and simple arrangements of food and drink. With the decline in popularity of religious or historical subjects still-life was practised on occasion by many painters, if only as a technical exercise. The Impressionists exploited the colouristic effects possible in flower-pieces, while Cézanne gave the form an unprecedented monumentality, from which Cubism is largely derived. MORANDI was one of the leading recent exponents.

STIPPLED DRAWING is one modelled in light and shade by hundreds of tiny dots and flecks, sometimes also STUMPED, an elaborate technique giving a result not unlike a photograph and consequently very popular in 19th-century art schools. Stipple engraving: *see* ENGRAVING (2*d*).

STOMER (Stom), Matthias (*c.*1600–after 1650), was a Dutch Caravaggesque, whose style has much in common with the UTRECHT SCHOOL. He was born in Amersfoort and was a pupil of HONTHORST, presumably soon after 1620. He entered the Guild in Rome in 1630, but was in Naples *c.*1632, and seems to have spent the rest of his life in Sicily and South Italy, and, perhaps, Malta (where several pictures remain), never returning to Holland. There are works by him in Amsterdam, Baltimore, Berlin, Birmingham, Brussels (Mus. de S. Jean), Budapest, Caccamo nr Palermo (S. Agostino, 1641, the only signed and dated work), Catania, Copenhagen, Darmstadt, Dublin, Greenville SC, The Hague (Bredius Mus.), Houston Texas, Leeds, Madrid, Messina, Montreal, Munich, Naples, Ottawa, Padua, Paris (Louvre), Providence RI, Quebec, Raleigh NC, Rome (Gall. Naz.), Stockholm, Sydney, Turin, Vaduz (Liechtenstein Coll.), Valletta Malta, Vienna (K-H Mus.) and Worcester Mass. The Caccamo picture was stolen in 1971, but recovered in 1985.

STONE CARVING is of incalculable antiquity, and the basic tools employed by the modern sculptor are fundamentally the same as those used by the Greeks of the 6th century BC. It is possible to reproduce a wax or plaster model mechanically by means of the POINTING MACHINE, but many sculptors have always preferred direct carving, since the material conditions the final form. A block of stone is usually more or less rectilinear, and the outlines are first drawn on all the faces of it as a rough guide. The first blocking-out of the form is done with a stonemason's hammer, or *boucharde*, which has a heavy steel head covered with pyramidal points (*see* BOAST). Next, a punch, which is simply a pointed bar of steel, is used with a mallet to knock off large chips of stone. The forms are then defined with more precision by means of a claw chisel, which has three, four, or more teeth, giving a furrow-like effect to the surface of the stone. When the statue is virtually complete, but still furrowed all over by the claw marks, the sculptor takes an ordinary flat chisel and begins to define the forms as closely as possible. If a polished surface is desired it can be obtained by using files and abrasive powders. A drill is often used, and was particularly popular with Baroque sculptors to produce small points of shadow, in the hair or in an eyeball, to give vivacity to the expression.

STOPPING OUT *see* ENGRAVING.

STOSKOPFF, Sébastien (1596–1657), was a Strasbourg painter of still-life, who, like Louise MOILLON, combined a Netherlandish tradition and technique with French classicism. He worked in Paris for twenty years from 1621, painting very simple subjects, such as a wicker basket with a few wineglasses in it. He returned to Strasbourg in 1641, but had been in Venice in 1629 and met SANDRART, whom he already knew. There are works by him in Munich, Paris (Louvre), Rotterdam and Strasbourg.

STOSS, Veit (1440/50–1533), was, with RIEMENSCHNEIDER, the leading German Late Gothic sculptor. He went to Cracow in Poland (where he is known as Wit Stwosz) in 1477, where he carved his masterpiece, the High Altar for the Church of St Mary (1477–89), an enormously complicated shrine, full of figures, and some 40 feet high. He also worked in stone, and other works by him are in the Cathedral and Museum at Cracow. In 1496 he returned to Nuremberg, and in 1503 attempted to exculpate himself from a criminal charge by forging a document, as a result of which he was sentenced to be branded on both cheeks and forbidden to leave Nuremberg. He also made some engravings and was active as a painter. Other works are in Cleveland Ohio, Nuremberg and Florence (SS. Annunziata).

STREETER (Streater), Robert (1624–80), appointed Sergeant-Painter to Charles II in 1663, is best known for his ceiling (1669) of the Sheldonian Theatre, Oxford, painted with an elaborate allegory of the Triumph of Truth and the Arts. It is the most high-flown Baroque composition painted by an Englishman before Thornhill, and it inspired the immortal lines:

> Future Ages must confess they owe
> To Streeter more than Michael Angelo.

(R. Whitehall, 'Urania', 1669). Pepys went to Streeter's studio in London to see these paintings being worked on (1 February 1669), where he met Wren, who thought them superior to Rubens. Pepys disagreed. London (Dulwich) has a landscape.

STRETES *see* SCROTS.

STRIGEL, Bernhardin (*c.*1460/1–1528), was a German painter mainly of portraits who became Court Painter to the Emperor Maximilian I. He was an early exponent of the group portrait – e.g. *The Rehlinger Family* (1517, Munich). All attributions to him are based on the *Cuspinian Family* (private coll.) which has an inscription dated 1520 and giving Strigel's name. There are, however, two pictures (Vienna, K-H Mus.) of *Maximilian and his Family* and the *Virgin and Child with St Anne and other Saints* which are apparently of about 1515 but came from the same complex as the *Cuspinian Family*. Other pictures are in Baltimore, Berlin, Boston, Denver Col., Munich, New York (Met. Mus.), Nuremberg, Stuttgart, Vienna (K-H Mus.), Washington (NG) and York.

STROZZI, Bernardo (1581–1644), was a Genoese painter who became a Capuchin friar at the age of 17 (hence his nicknames 'Il Cappucino' and 'Il Prete Genovese'). From 1607 his art was powerfully affected by Rubens, who was in Genoa then. He was allowed to leave his religious house by 1610 to support his widowed mother and he had a very successful career as a painter, but when she died in 1630 he had a prolonged battle with his rigorous Order and with the Papacy to avoid returning to the cloister, involving him in kidnappings, disguises and escapes. However, in 1631 he removed to the comparative safety of Venice, and all must have been forgiven by 1635, when he was made a Monsignore. He was much influenced by the rich colour and handling of Venetian art, which probably induced him to settle there. He painted mostly tender religious subjects and genre. There are works in the Royal Coll., and in Baltimore, Berlin, Birmingham, Cardiff, Chicago, Cincinnati, Cleveland Ohio, Dayton Ohio, Dresden, Dublin, Florence (Uffizi), Genoa, Greenville SC, Hartford (Wadsworth), Kansas City, London (NG), Milan (Brera), New York (Met. Mus.), Ottawa, Oxford (Ashmolean and Ch. Ch.), Paris (Louvre), Rome (Gall. Naz.), St Louis, Seattle, Venice, Vienna, Washington, Worcester Mass. and elsewhere.

STUART, Gilbert (1755–1828), was born in America but went to Scotland *c.*1770. After returning to America he came back to London in 1775 and studied under his fellow-countryman WEST (1777–82). As a portrait painter, however, he was more influenced by ROMNEY and even Raeburn. After escaping from his creditors by working in Dublin 1787–93 he returned to America and became famous as a portrait painter (twenty-two of his portraits are in the Met. Mus., New York). His *Washington* exists in three main types, versions being in every major American collection. There are also pictures in Dublin and London (NPG, Nat. Marit. Mus. and Tate).

STUBBS, George (1724–1806), painted portraits for a living while studying anatomy in York, where he lectured to medical students. His earliest works are of 1746, followed by his illustrations to a textbook of midwifery (1751). In 1754 he went to Rome, not to study Italian art, but to prove to himself that this was unnecessary, since 'Nature is superior to art'. Returning via Ceuta he saw a lion devouring a horse, a sight which haunted him for the rest of his life and which became one of his most admired subjects. He then lived in a desolate Lincolnshire farmhouse, dissecting horses and drawing them, but during the

1760s he lived in London and worked as an animal painter while preparing his 'Anatomy of the Horse', published in 1766. In 1780 he became an ARA, and was elected RA in 1781, but never confirmed as he failed to provide a Diploma work. From 1795 until his death he worked on a book on the comparative anatomy of Man, Tiger, and Fowl. The text and 125 drawings were discovered in 1957 in the Public Library, Worcester Mass., and are now in Yale (CBA).

Most of his paintings are in oil on canvas, but from 1769 he experimented with enamel, fired on copper plates, or on Wedgwood china plaques (a *Self-portrait* on a Wedgwood plaque is now in London, NPG). Stubbs is far more than an animal painter or a horse portraitist: all nature was his field, and his amazing accuracy of representation is the servant of a highly developed pictorial imagination. There are examples in the Royal Coll., including the strange *Hollyhock* – the horse by Stubbs, and the landscape and figures by VERNET and BOUCHER – and in Bath (Holburne Mus.), Cambridge (Fitzwm), Cape Town, Glasgow (Hunterian), Leeds, Liverpool, London (NG, BM, Tate and RA), Manchester, Melbourne, Mount Stewart (Nat. Trust, *Hambletonian*, 1800, a life-size racehorse), Port Sunlight, Yale and elsewhere.

STUDY. A drawing or painting of a detail, such as a figure, a hand or a piece of drapery, made for the purpose of study or for use in a larger composition. A study should never be confused with a SKETCH, which is a rough draught of the whole, whereas a study may be very highly wrought but does not usually embrace more than a part of the composition.

STUMP. A cigar-shaped roll of paper or soft leather, sharply pointed at each end, which was used to rub charcoal or chalk drawings so as to obtain very delicate transitions of tone. A stumped drawing looks very like a photograph, hence both its popularity in the 19th century and present disfavour.

STYLE CRITICISM requires an exact knowledge of the characteristics of any given School as well as the personal style of any particular artist. With such a knowledge, it is possible to analyse the style of a work of art so that a convincing attribution may be made to a specific artist and even to a particular moment in his career. Further, given a precise knowledge of many works by many masters of any one country or period, it is possible to make general deductions about the style of that country or period as reflected in its practitioners. The proper practice of stylistic analysis is more difficult than it is sometimes made to seem.

SUBLEYRAS, Pierre (1699–1749), was a leading French painter of religious subjects in Rome. He was born in the south of France and trained in Toulouse before going to Paris (1724–8), after which he went to Rome and spent the rest of his life there, working for several Italian religious Orders as well as Pope Benedict XIV, whose portrait he painted, and who commissioned the *Mass of St Basil* (1748) for St Peter's (now in S.M. degli Angeli, Rome). His *Blessed John of Avila* (Birmingham) is a good example; others are in the Louvre, Toulouse and Italian churches and museums.

SULLY, Thomas (1783–1872), was born in England but went to America as a child. He studied under STUART in Boston before working with WEST in London in 1809, but was more influenced as a portrait painter by LAWRENCE, whose poses he copied and whom he often resembles. He returned to America and settled in Philadelphia in 1810, but revisited England in 1837–8 to paint Queen Victoria at the request of the St George's Society of Philadelphia. Sully painted her at Buckingham Palace and said that 'she was very affable, like a well-bred lady of Philadelphia or Boston'. This finished picture is still in Philadelphia, but the original study is in New York (Met. Mus.) and another version is in London (Wallace Coll.). Sully kept an index of his works from 1801 which runs to 2,631 items, most of which are in America, and include portraits of almost all famous Americans of his day. His 'Hints to Young Painters' was published posthumously.

SUPER-REALISM *see* SURREALISM.

SUPPORT. The bottom layer of a painting, e.g. a canvas, wall, sheet of copper, wooden panel. The paint-layer is applied to the GROUND (lead white, gesso etc), which in turn is applied to the support. It is essential to have an intermediate layer in the case of oil-painting on canvas, since the oil will rot the threads of the canvas unless there is a protective ground.

SUPREMATISM was a hyper-orthodox form of CUBISM, invented in 1913/15 by MALEVICH (who later wrote a book about it) as an absolutely pure geometrical abstract art. To the uninitiated it is scarcely distinguishable from analytical Cubism: to the really initiated it must be distinguished from CONSTRUCTIVISM and from the abstract paintings of MONDRIAN.

SURMOULAGE. A French word, now mostly used for re-treaded tyres, which means an after-cast – i.e. a mould made by using the original work of art to cast from, so as to make copies not produced from the original mould but from the original cast.

SURREALISM, which was born of a union between the COLLAGE and CONSTRUCTIVIST aspects of CUBISM, and the nihilism of DADA, claims a long artistic ancestry in the art of Bosch, Arcimboldi, Fuseli, Goya, REDON and any other artist interested in the weird and fantastic. After the demise of Dada in 1922, André BRETON gathered up the remnants of the group, took over the word *surréaliste* from Apollinaire (who had used it in 1917), and defined it as 'Pure psychic AUTOMATISM, by which it is intended to express verbally, in writing or in any other way, the true process of thought. It is the dictation of thought, free from the exercise of reason, and every aesthetic or moral preoccupation.' The object was to free artists from the normal association of pictorial ideas and from all accepted means of expression, so that they might create according to the irrational dictates of their subconscious mind and vision. Surrealism developed in two directions: pure fantasy, and the elaborate reconstruction of a dream-world. The first produced FOUND OBJECTS, either alone or composed – a bottle dryer, a bicycle wheel, or a birdcage filled with sugar-cubes and a thermometer, a random assortment of bric-à-brac – automatic drawing, Ernst's FROTTAGES and abstract works charged with meaning by a strange title – Klee's *Twittering Machine* or Picabia's *Catch as Catch Can*. The second took the form of highly detailed likenesses of objects, straight or distorted, or three-dimensional abstractions, in a fantastic and unexpected juxtaposition, or in a setting of a hallucinatory kind: CHIRICO, TANGUY, DALI, MAGRITTE, DELVAUX, Man RAY's photographs and much of Picasso's painting and sculpture from the late 1920s develop this type, the feverish search for the unexpected being well rendered by Lautréamont's simile: 'Beautiful as the chance encounter of a sewing machine and an umbrella on an operating table.' The First Surrealist Manifesto was published in 1924; the first Surrealist Exhibition held in Paris in 1925; and also in 1925 the fifth number of 'La Révolution Surréaliste', edited by Breton, associated the movement with Communism, but the Communists, as a political party, would have none of it. The movement has had as much currency in literature and drama as in the visual arts, and despite its own particular strait-jacket, has had a liberating influence. Its ideas of strange juxtapositions have been widely commercialized – particularly in sophisticated television advertising and window-dressing – and, its initial force now spent and its edge dulled by surfeit, it survives as a respectable ghost of hauntingly incoherent incantations, and even threatens to become academic.

SUSTERMANS (Suttermans), Justus (1597–1681) was born in Antwerp, but spent some sixty years in Florence in the service of the Medici Grand Dukes. He was in Paris in 1616/17 and worked under Frans POURBUS II (who was painter to Marie de' Medici), before going to Florence *c.*1620, where he became Court Painter almost at once. He travelled widely in Italy and executed Court commissions in Vienna, 1623–4, and Innsbruck, 1653–4, and he may have been in Spain in 1649. Rubens and van Dyck, his contemporaries and fellow-Flemings, knew him and influenced his work. Most of his best works are in Florence, but there are others in Baltimore, Boston, Brussels, Leeds (Temple Newsam), London (N G and Ranger's House Blackheath), New York (Met. Mus.), Oxford (Ashmolean: a sketch for a huge painting in Florence), Paris (Louvre) and Vienna (K-H Mus.).

SUTHERLAND, Graham OM (1903–80), was the leading British Romantic painter of the 20th century. His early works were almost all etchings and engravings, strongly influenced by the Blakean vision of PALMER, CALVERT and other Blake followers. His earliest paintings date from the mid-1930s and were of landscapes, often Welsh, in which the thorns and thistles have been seen as symbols of the Crown of Thorns leading directly to his specifically religious paintings of the post-war years (he became a Catholic in 1926). During the Second World War he was an official artist (from 1941), and his semi-abstract scenes of desolation after bombing exactly express the atmosphere of such awesome sights. In 1946 he was commissioned to paint a *Crucifixion* (in which the influence of Grünewald is evident) by Canon Hussey, who also commissioned Moore's *Madonna*, for St Matthew's, Northampton; in 1963 he painted a second *Crucifixion* for St Aidan's, East Acton, London. His largest religious work – perhaps the largest tapestry ever woven – is the *Christ in Glory* (1962) for the new Cathedral in Coventry (most of the numerous studies are in Coventry Mus.). In his later years he became a successful portrait-painter of the famous – *Somerset Maugham*, 1949; *Beaverbrook*, 1951; *Helena Rubinstein*, 1957, but the most famous was the *Churchill* of 1954, commissioned by Parliament, presented to the sitter and destroyed by Lady Churchill. There is a Sutherland Gallery at Picton Castle, Dyfed, Wales, and other paintings are in Birmingham, Darlington, Hull, London (NPG, Tate and Imperial War Mus.), Manchester, Melbourne, Nebraska Univ., New Brunswick, New York (M of MA), Ottawa, Paris (Mus. d'Art Moderne), Southampton, Toronto and elsewhere.

SUTTERMANS *see* SUSTERMANS.

SUVÉE, Joseph-Benoît (1743–1807), was a Belgian painter from Bruges always referred to by DAVID as 'l'ignare Suvée', who was, like David, a pupil of VIEN, and David's lifelong rival for the leadership of Neoclassicism in France.

He came from Bruges to Paris and won the Prix de ROME against David in 1771, spending a year at the ÉCOLE des Élèves protégés, and then going to Rome 1772–8, after which he returned to Paris and became Agréé (1779) and Member of the Academy (1780) and Painter to the King. He returned to Rome, as Director of the French Academy there, in 1792, but lost his job when David became dictator of the arts. He was imprisoned (like David) under the Terror, 1794–5, but was reappointed to Rome by Napoleon in 1801 and remained there until his death. His works are now largely forgotten, but there are several in Bruges and others in French provincial museums, including Besançon and Lille.

SWANEVELT, Herman van (*c.*1600–*c.*55), was born near Utrecht, but spent most of his life in Rome and Paris. He was in Paris by 1623, and in Rome 1629–41, living in the same house as CLAUDE (1629), and associating with the BENTVUEGHELS, such as BAMBOCCIO, and also with SANDRART. His own Bentname was Eremita, from his solitary character. From 1641 he was alternately in Holland and Paris, but his works are very close to Claude and BOTH, and it is clear that he influenced Claude as well as *vice-versa*. London (Dulwich) has three signed paintings by him (two dated 1645), as well as a *Campo Vaccino, Rome*, which is connected both with him and with Claude, but is probably by neither. He was a link between the first and second generations of Dutch ITALIANIZERS, between BREENBERGH and BERCHEM, BOTH, ASSELYN and WEENIX. He made 116 engravings, mostly of fantasy landscapes with religious or mythological *staffage*. Other paintings are in the Royal Coll. and in Bath, Bradford, Brighton, Cambridge (Fitzwm), Dresden, Florence (Pitti), Glasgow, Madrid, Rome (Borghese), Venice (Accad.) and Vienna (K-H Mus.).

SWEERTS, Michael (1624–64), was a Brussels painter who went to Rome in or before 1646, when he was a member of the Academy, charged with the difficult task of collecting the dues owed to the Roman Guild by the Netherlandish immigrant painters (BENTVUEGHELS). He remained in Rome until 1652 at least, and in 1656 opened a school in Brussels. In 1661, as a lay brother, he began a journey to the East with an unsuccessful religious mission. He died in Goa, in India. His Roman works are good examples of BAMBOCCIATE, but after his return north his works approximated more closely to Dutch genre painting as practised by Pieter de HOOCH, or portraits similar to those by VERMEER. There are works by him in Amsterdam, Detroit, Glasgow (Univ.), Haarlem, The Hague, Hartford Conn., Leicester, Leningrad, London (Wallace Coll.), Milan (Castello), Minneapolis, Munich, Oberlin Ohio, Oxford (Ashmolean), Paris (Louvre), Rome (Capitoline and Accad.), Rotterdam and Worcester Mass.

SYMBOLISM and SYNTHETISM. (i) Symbolism, in its general sense, is the representation of something, usually sacred and immaterial, by a material object – e.g. a lamb as a symbol of Christ, the Paschal Sacrifice being the connecting link. (ii) In a more restricted sense Symbolism was a French literary movement that spilled over into the visual arts in the late 19th century. The literary movement goes back at least to Baudelaire's 'Fleurs du Mal' of 1857, and was continued by Rimbaud's 'Saison en Enfer' (1873) and 'Illuminations' (1886), in which year a Manifesto of literary Symbolism was published in Paris. The principal painters associated with Symbolism are PUVIS de Chavannes (whose first Salon success was as early as 1861), MOREAU and REDON, but GAUGUIN, and RODIN in sculpture, were also associated with the movement. In 1888 Gauguin and BERNARD formulated Synthetism (also sometimes called *Cloissonisme*) at PONT-AVEN, and the NABIS group was also formed (it broke up some twelve years later). Gauguin's first Symbolist/Synthetist work was *The Vision after the Sermon* (1888, Edinburgh, NG), but his most important – perhaps the most important Symbolist picture – is the huge *D'où venons-nous . . .?* (Boston). The 1889 Synthetist Exhibition showed their rejection of Impressionism as too naturalistic and their belief in the expression of ideas, moods and emotions. Their pictures were painted in brilliant colours, separated by heavy black lines, and sought to be decorative as well as the abstractions, or syntheses, of the ideas which inspired them. The Salon de la Rose + Croix, held between 1892 and 1897, was similar in character. Probably the most important works ever exhibited at any of their Salons was the group of thirteen sent to the last one by ROUAULT, encouraged by his teacher, Moreau. Outside France they had some influence on artists such as KLIMT, BURNE-JONES and BEARDSLEY.

SYNCHROMISM (Synchromy) was an American abstract movement, closely based on CÉZANNE and MATISSE, and very similar to ORPHISM in its dependence on pure colour. It originated in Paris in 1912, and the American painters in it – Stanton Macdonald-Wright and Morgan Russell were the founders – exhibited at the ARMORY SHOW in 1913.

T

TACCA, Pietro (1557–1640), was a pupil of Giovanni da BOLOGNA and succeeded him as Sculptor to the Tuscan Grand Dukes. He also finished his master's equestrian statues in Florence (1608), Madrid (1606–13) and Paris (*Henri IV*, 1613, destroyed 1792). His masterpiece is *The Four Moors* (1615–24) on the base of the monument to the Grand Duke Ferdinand I in Leghorn. He also made an equestrian monument to Philip IV in Madrid (1634–40), for which MONTANÉS provided a model (now lost) of the head. There are also monuments in Florence (S. Lorenzo). His works show the influence of Michelangelo, but look forward to the violence of Baroque movement. There are works in Cambridge (Fitzwm), Liverpool and London (V&A).

TACHISME (Fr. *tache*, blot, stain) is very similar to ACTION PAINTING. The most notable exponent was POLLOCK, who now has a host of followers on both sides of the Atlantic, but KANDINSKY painted remarkably similar pictures before the First World War; indeed, Adeline's 'Art Dictionary' (1891) defines *Tachiste* as 'A term used in French art criticism to denote those impressionists who see no charm in a picture beyond *taches* or strong touches of varying colour and intensity, which are not blended with the ground.'

TACTILE VALUES. An illusion of tangibility. The inventor of the phrase, Bernard Berenson, claimed that the representation of three-dimensional objects on a two-dimensional surface in such a way that one receives a strong impression of physical tangibility is 'life-enhancing'. It is not clear why.

TADEMA, ALMA, *see* ALMA-TADEMA.

TAEUBER-ARP, Sophie, *see* ARP.

TAILLE-DOUCE (Fr.). Line ENGRAVING.

TAMAYO, Rufino (*b*.1899). A Mexican painter who, like RIVERA, founded his style on a mixture of his native prehistoric art and modern European art, chiefly Expressionism and Surrealism. He worked a good deal in America, and in 1943 executed frescoes for Smith College Library, Northampton Mass. In 1958 he decorated the UNESCO building in Paris (*cf.* MATTA). His use of sophisticated foreign elements made him something of a prophet in his own land.

TANGUY, Yves (1900–55), was a French Surrealist, who began life as a merchant seaman and took up painting in 1923 after seeing a Chirico. Unlike Chirico, however, Tanguy's pictures rarely contain recognizable forms or buildings, but are lunar landscapes populated by amorphous beings, not unlike those of Ernst. In 1925 he met BRETON and painted his first surrealist pictures in 1926. From 1939 he lived in the US. There are works by him in Basle, Buffalo, Chicago, Hartford Conn. (Wadsworth), New York (Met. Mus., M of MA and Whitney), Paris (Mus. d'Art Moderne) and Philadelphia.

TANZIO da Varallo (*c*.1575/80–*c*.1635), was in Varallo in 1611, but was probably in Rome just before or just after that date, and in Naples before 1616. He was working on the Sacro Monte at Varallo in 1616–17. His style was formed by CARAVAGGIO's followers, and combined Caravaggism with Lombard Mannerism to give a kind of Northern Caravaggism, different from that of the Dutch and Flemish Caravaggisti. His *St Sebastian* (Washington, NG) was formerly attributed to Rubens. Los Angeles has a *Madonna and Saints*.

TÀPIES, Antonio (*b.*1923), studied law before becoming the leading Spanish abstract painter. He began to paint in 1946 and went to Paris in 1950. His works mostly consist of puddled sand and paint, often with incised dashes, giving an effect not unlike the sea-shore after the tide has ebbed. There are examples in Birmingham, London (Tate) and New York (M of MA). A Tàpies Foundation was established in Barcelona in 1990.

TASSI, Agostino (*c.*1580–1644), was a ruffianly Roman landscape painter who may have been a pupil of Paul BRIL. In 1612 he was accused of raping Artemisia GENTILESCHI 'many times', and, although her father forgave him, he was imprisoned. He was the master of CLAUDE, who worked as his assistant in the early 1620s.

TATLIN, Vladimir (1885–1953), was a Russian painter who, in 1913, switched to sculpture and founded CONSTRUCTIVISM. In the same year he met Picasso in Paris. Unlike many other Russian artists – GABO, PEVSNER, CHAGALL – he remained in Russia after the Soviet authorities abandoned their brief flirtation with 'advanced' art. Tatlin worked as a designer, especially for film and stage sets, up to the 1930s, but it is significant that the date of his death is difficult to ascertain. It was certainly 1953, but 1956 is also given in reference books, and some writers speak of him as still alive in the 1970s.

TECTONIC *see* ARCHITECTONIC.

TEMPERA. This word really means any kind of binder which will serve to 'temper' powder colour and make it workable: in practice, however, it is confined to egg tempera, which was the commonest technique of painting until the late 15th century for the production of easel pictures. If a panel is well-prepared with GESSO and then painted on with powder colour which is mixed with fresh egg-yolk thinned with water the result will be a paint film which dries almost instantaneously (making reworking difficult) and is also tough and permanent. It dries several tones lighter than the wet paint. There are many modifications of this basic recipe, and some painters used the whole egg; illuminators of MSS often used only the white. From very early times it was noticed that powder colour could be mixed with some form of drying oil and would then form a rich and transparent film which could be used to modify the semi-opaque tempera layer. Probably the earliest use of this oil GLAZE was to shade off burnished gold or silver leaf, but from this the whole technique of OIL-PAINTING developed. For many years it was usual to paint most of a picture in tempera – which dries in minutes – and then to apply only the final touches in oil. One good reason for this is the fact that tempera, because of the speed with which it dries, has to be hatched and cross-hatched to obtain modelling: a final glaze of oil-colour will spread a unifying film, or, as painters say, 'pull it together'. No one really knows how long this 'mixed method' continued – it was certainly still practised by Rubens – but it is plain that the oil medium has such attractive qualities of its own, notably in IMPASTO, that it became the dominant partner. Rembrandt, whose lifetime overlapped with Rubens, seems always to have used oil alone. In the present century a small number of painters have returned to the pure tempera medium (the paints can now be bought ready mixed), but a judicious use of the mixed method offers great scope for technical virtuosity and could well be revived. *See also* ACRYLIC.

TENEBRISM (from Ital. *tenebroso*, murky) is the name given to painting in a very low KEY, specifically to the works of those early-17th-century painters, mostly Neapolitan and Spanish, who were much influenced by CARAVAGGIO. They did not form any kind of organized group and the *Tenebristi* did not call themselves by that name. SICKERT was a latter-day example.

TENIERS, David I (1582–1649), David II (1610–90) and David III (1638–85). David I was a Flemish Late Mannerist painter, mainly of religious subjects, who worked in Antwerp. He may have been associated with RUBENS before going to Rome, where he worked in the ELSHEIMER circle, *c.*1600–5. He became a Master in Antwerp in 1606, but was constantly in debt and was active mainly as a dealer in his last years. The working lives of David I and his son David II – by far the most famous of the family – overlapped in the 1630s, and it is not clear who painted certain pictures in that period; what is clear is that many of the paintings ascribed to David I in the 19th century are by David II. London (Dulwich) has a pair of *St Peter* and *St Mary Magdalen*, signed, respectively, *Tinier* and *D. Tenier Iv 1634*, which may conceivably be by father and son, the *Iv* standing for Junior. David II became a Master in Antwerp in 1632/3, and worked there until 1651, when he settled in Brussels. He was Court Painter to the Archduke Leopold Wilhelm, Regent of the Netherlands, who was a great collector (many of his pictures are now in Vienna, K-H Mus.). Teniers became Keeper of his pictures, and made many copies of them, 244 of which were engraved in 1660 under the title 'Theatrum Pictorium'. Many of the Teniers copies still exist – there are fourteen in London (Courtauld Inst.) and thirty-nine on long loan to Kenwood. Teniers visited London 1650/5 to buy pictures from Charles I's collection, sold off by the Protectorate. He was the main founder of the Antwerp Academy (1662), which finally opened in 1664. Teniers painted almost every kind of picture – about 2,000 in all – but his best works were done 1640/50, before his move to Brussels. His earliest works were peasant genre scenes in the manner of BROUWER, but he also painted KORTEGAARDJES and religious subjects, landscapes, portraits and genre scenes such as Witches' Sabbaths, or apes and cats dressed up as humans. In 1637 he married Anne, daughter of Jan BRUEGEL, and their son David III was also a painter and imitated his father's works. There are pictures by David II in the Royal Coll. and in Amsterdam, Antwerp, Berlin, Brussels, Dresden, Edinburgh, Glasgow, The Hague, Leningrad, London (NG, Wallace Coll. – examples of almost every kind of picture he painted – Wellington Mus.), Madrid, Munich, New York (Met. Mus.), Paris (Louvre), Vienna (K-H Mus., which also has works attributed to David I) and many other galleries.

TER BORCH (Terburg, Terborch), Gerard (1617–81), was the son of a minor painter and was very precocious. He was in Amsterdam and Haarlem 1632/4, when Rembrandt was making his name and Hals was working in Haarlem; in 1635 he visited England; in 1640 he was in Italy; he returned to Holland probably via France, and in 1646 he went to Münster in Westphalia (presumably to paint portraits of the dignitaries at the Congress of the Peace of Westphalia), and in 1648 he accompanied the Spanish Envoy to Madrid, returning to Holland in 1650. On account of these travels Ter Borch must have had first-hand knowledge of almost all the great 17th-century artists – Rembrandt, Hals, Velázquez, Bernini – and yet his style betrays no hint of this, for he is content to paint small portraits and genteel genre scenes, diligent in style, paying particular attention to the rendering of silk and satin. His most famous work is the *Peace of Münster, May 15, 1648* (London, NG), a group portrait of all the dignitaries at full length, on copper, 17½ × 22½ inches: all his other pictures are small portraits and portrait groups, usually full length, and scenes of well-to-do Dutch family life or else KORTEGAARDJES. Most of his figures have a curious doll-like charm and the costumes and accessories recur so often in his portraits even down to identical folds, that it is possible he painted the pictures in advance and simply added heads and hands as necessary. His works are often similar to those of his junior, METSU, but his subtle treatment of colour and light were far exceeded by VERMEER. There are works by him in the Royal Coll. and in Aix, Amsterdam, Antwerp, Berlin, Boston (Gardner), Bremen, Budapest, Cape Town, Chicago, Cincinnati, Cleveland Ohio, Cologne, Copenhagen, Detroit, Deventer (Town Hall), Dresden, Dublin, Florence (Uffizi), Frankfurt (Städel), Glasgow (Burrell), Haarlem, The Hague, Hamburg, Indianapolis, London (NG, V&A and Wallace Coll.), Malibu Cal. (Getty), Munich, New York (Met. Mus., Frick Coll. and Hist. Soc.), Paris (Louvre and Petit Pal.), Philadelphia, Richmond Va, Rotterdam, Rouen, Toledo Ohio, Vaduz (Liechtenstein Coll.: *Portrait of van Goyen*), Vienna, Washington (NG) and Wellesley College Mass.

TERBRUGGHEN (properly, ter Brugghen), Hendrick (1588–1629), was born in Utrecht and became a pupil of BLOEMAERT before going to Italy at an unknown date. He spent 'several years' in Rome, before leaving in 1615/16 and settling in Utrecht to become one of the leading members of the UTRECHT SCHOOL, together with HONTHORST and BABUREN. His style shows almost no influence of his master Bloemaert and, strictly speaking, little of that of Caravaggio except in the predilection for strong contrasts of light and shadow – and even that disappeaars in his later works, for the *Jacob and Laban* (1628, London, NG) is painted in much lighter and clearer colours and looks forward to VERMEER, who also turned *Caravaggismo* upside down. Some of Terbrugghen's religious subjects are taken from Caravaggio – the *Incredulity of St Thomas* and the *Calling of St Matthew* are reworkings of Caravaggio themes – but the iconography of others goes back to such Northern artists as e.g. Dürer. More typical works are nearer to MANFREDI, e.g. the *Lute Players* and the harlot and the clown of the *Duet* and similar pictures. There are pictures by him in the Royal Coll. and in Amsterdam (Rijksmus.), Augsburg, Basle, Berlin, Bordeaux, Cambridge Mass. (Fogg), Cassel, Cologne, Copenhagen, Deventer (Town Hall), Edinburgh (NG), Gateshead, Gotha, Gothenburg, Greenville SC, Le Havre, London (NG), Malibu Cal., New York (Met. Mus.), Northampton Mass., Oberlin Ohio, Oxford (Ashmolean), Paris (Louvre), Rome (Gall. Naz.), Sacramento Cal., Schwerin, Stockholm, Toledo Ohio, Utrecht and Vienna (K-H Mus.).

TERM *see* HERM.

TERRACOTTA (Ital. baked earth) *see* PLASTER CASTING.

TERRIBILITÀ (Ital. terribleness). A word usually applied to Michelangelo and, by extension, to any art of austere and tragic grandeur.

TESSERAE. The cubes used in MOSAIC.

THEODORIC of Prague (active 1343?–68) was recorded in the Prague Painters' Guild in 1348. He was Painter to the Emperor Charles IV by 1359 and executed over 100 paintings for his Castle at Karlstein in Bohemia by 1365. He was the greatest of the Bohemian painters of the 14th century and began a severe and realistic style that influenced much later German and Bohemian painting.

THIRTLE, John (1777–1839) *see* NORWICH SCHOOL.

THOMA, Hans (1839–1924), spent a few weeks in Paris in 1868 and was profoundly impressed by the Realist ideas of COURBET and the BARBIZON painters. In the 1870s he met LEIBL and BÖCKLIN and in 1874 he went to Italy, where he met MARÉES, and the Romanticism of these latter influenced his work in the direction of what now seems a deplorable sentimentality. He is very well represented in German museums, especially Karlsruhe (where he was Director), and there are other pictures in Cambridge Mass., New York (Met. Mus.), Stockholm, Vienna and Zürich.

THORNHILL, Sir James (1675/6–1734), was the only English decorator in the grand Baroque tradition. In the dome of St Paul's (1715–17) incidents from the saint's life appear in eight grisaille panels picked out in gold, and the decoration does not obtrude on the painted architectural setting. His work at Greenwich Hospital, lasting from 1708 to 1727, includes the immense Painted Hall, the lower Hall and Vestibule, and set him the problem of treating modern history subjects in a grand allegorical setting, which he solved with a display of the most Italianate illusionism. An interesting memorandum of 1717 shows Thornhill asking £5 a yard for the painting of the ceiling, but he accepted £3. He does not appear to have had any direct contact with Verrio or Laguerre, yet both influenced him, though his ceiling of Queen Anne's Bedroom at Hampton Court (1715) is finer than anything of theirs, and he won the commission against PELLEGRINI. He travelled in the Netherlands in 1711, and in France in 1717; was knighted and made Sergeant Painter in 1720, Member of Parliament for his native town of Melcombe Regis in Dorset in 1722, Fellow of the Royal Society in 1723, and Master of the Painter-Stainers' Company. These offices and honours gave him a very different position from that usually accorded to British artists and not reached again until the advent of Reynolds. He appeared at a time when grand decoration was required, and reaped the advantage of being the only English painter able to compete with the many foreigners then seeking work in England (Pellegrini, the Riccis, and Amigoni, besides Verrio and Laguerre) at a moment when anti-foreign feeling prevailed. His son-in-law, Hogarth, is an excellent example of this xenophobia. His only big failure was when Kent was given the job of decorating Kensington Palace, through the influence of his patron, Lord Burlington. There are also works at Blenheim Palace, Chatsworth, Easton Neston, London (Tate and NPG), Yale (CBA) and elsewhere.

THORWALDSEN (properly, Thorvaldsen), Bertel (1768, or, according to his own account, 1770–1844), is the only Danish artist to have attained international fame. He won a scholarship to Italy and went in 1796, living in Rome from 1797 until his triumphal return to Denmark in 1819; in 1820 he returned to Rome for another eighteen years. He was one of the great NEOCLASSIC sculptors, ranking above GIBSON, about level with FLAXMAN and SERGEL, but rather below CANOVA. It was generally felt that he was less influenced by the Italian tradition than was Canova, but he is also rather more matter-of-fact: his works are calm and noble, or insipid copies of the Antique, according to taste. There is a complete collection – originals, casts and copies – in the Thorwaldsen Mus. in Copenhagen (in this, he was imitating Canova and was followed by Gibson): other works are in Naples, Rome (especially St Peter's: Tomb of Pius VII), Liverpool, Manchester and Minneapolis. His full-length *Byron* (1816) is now in Trinity Coll., Cambridge, and was intended for Westminster Abbey, but was rejected on the grounds of Byron's immorality. There are also five reliefs in Stoke Poges Golf Club.

TIBALDI, Pellegrino (1527–96), was a painter, sculptor and architect who was one of the leading Italian Mannerists of the late 16th century and whose work in Spain helped to spread the style there. His earliest painting is the large *Adoration of the Shepherds* (1548 not 1549, Rome, Borghese) painted when he was 21. This shows the influence of Michelangelo and his followers, but Tibaldi was also influenced by PARMIGIANINO and Niccolò dell' ABBATE. He was in Rome by 1549/50, but returned to Bologna in 1553 when he began a series of frescoes of the story of Odysseus (Pal. Poggi, now the University) and the decorations in S. Giacomo Maggiore. From 1560 Tibaldi was connected with S. Charles Borromeo, Archbishop of Milan, for whom he also worked as an architect. In 1585 he was invited to Spain by Philip II, but he did not go until 1587. There he supervised the building and decoration of the Escorial, painting forty-six frescoes in the cloister alone. In 1596, rich and ennobled, he returned to Milan where he died. There are other works by him in Amsterdam, Ancona, Bologna, Leningrad, Milan (Brera) and Vaduz (Liechtenstein Coll.: replica of the Borghese *Adoration*).

TIEPOLO, Giovanni Battista (Giambattista) (1696–1770), was the last of the great Venetian decorators, the purest exponent of the Italian ROCOCO, and arguably the greatest painter of the 18th century. He was trained under an obscure painter named Lazzarini but was really formed by the study of Sebastiano RICCI and PIAZZETTA among living painters and VERONESE among the older masters. He was received into the Fraglia (Guild) in 1717 but had already painted the *Sacrifice of Abraham* (1715/16, Venice, Ospedaletto), a dark picture very much in the manner of Piazzetta and the 17th century generally. In 1719 he married the sister of GUARDI and at about this time his own lighter and looser style began to form. His first great commission for fresco decorations came in 1725, when he began the work in the Archbishop's Palace at Udine (completed 1728). These already show the virtuosity of his handling, the light tone and pale colours necessitated by fresco obviously helping him to break free from the dark Piazzettesque models he had previously followed. The Udine frescoes also show him developing as the creator of a world in steep perspective beyond the picture plane, with the architecture receding into dizzy distances. The highly specialized work of painting these architectural perspectives was done by Mengozzi-Colonna, who did this work for Tiepolo for most of his life. Following the Udine frescoes Tiepolo travelled widely in N. Italy, painting many more frescoes in palaces and churches, as well as altarpieces in oil which culminate in the gigantic *Gathering of the Manna* and *Sacrifice of Melchizedek* (*c.*1735–40, Verolanuova, Parish Church), each of which is about 30 feet high. The frescoes of this period culminate in the *Antony and Cleopatra* series in the Palazzo Labia, Venice, which were probably finished just before 1750, when he left Venice for Würzburg. He was invited to decorate the ceiling of the Kaisersaal in the Residenz at Würzburg by the Prince-Bishop, Karl Phillip von Greiffenklau, and Tiepolo and his sons Giandomenico and Lorenzo arrived in Würzburg at the end of 1750 and remained there until 1753, replacing Johann Zick, a German pupil of Piazzetta. He painted the staircase with frescoes, some overdoors, and some altarpieces as well as the Kaisersaal, helped in the gigantic task by both his sons as well as several other assistants. The Palace itself is a superb example of German Rococo architecture and the combination of architecture and painting into one vast and airy allegory – apparently referring to the Prince-Bishop as a patron, but including Barbarossa and German history – is perhaps the most successful even in Tiepolo's career. In 1755, after his return to Venice, he was elected first President of the Venetian Academy and in 1761 he was invited to Spain to decorate the Royal Palace in Madrid by Charles III. He arrived in 1762, with his sons and assistants, and painted the huge ceilings in the Palace in four years. In 1767 Charles commissioned seven altarpieces for Aranjuez, but Tiepolo's last years in Spain were embittered by intrigues on behalf of MENGS, the representative of that Neoclassicism which was soon to condemn his kind of splendid and carefree painting as frivolous. He died suddenly in Madrid. His enormous output of frescoes and altarpieces was partly due to his practice (like RUBENS before him) of painting small *modelli* which, when approved by the client, could be carried out by his skilled assistants under his own supervision. Scores of these *modelli* and sketches survive, together with hundreds of drawings. He painted very few portraits – the best-known is the so-called *Querini* in the Querini Gall., Venice, but this may, in fact, be by his son Domenico. He also etched many plates, and, with Marco RICCI, was one of the founders of the great school of 18th-century Venetian etchers. There are works in many churches, palaces and galleries in Venice and in Amsterdam, Barnard Castle (Bowes Mus.), Bergamo (Cath., Accad.), Berlin, Boston (Mus. and Gardner), Budapest, Cambridge Mass. (Fogg), Chicago, Cleveland Ohio, Detroit, Dresden, Edinburgh (NG), Este, Fort Worth Texas, London (NG, Dulwich and Courtauld Inst.), Melbourne (NG), Milan (Brera and Poldi-Pezzoli), Montreal, Munich, New York (Met. Mus.), Ottawa, Paris (Louvre), Philadelphia (Johnson), Rovigo, St Louis, Stockholm (Nat. Mus. and Univ. Mus.), Strà (Villa Pisani), Stuttgart, Toledo Ohio, Verona, Vicenza (Villa Valmarana), Vienna (K-H Mus. and Akad.), Washington (NG) and many other places.

His son Giovanni Domenico (1727–1804) was also a considerable painter in his own right, as well as his father's assistant and imitator. His frescoes in the Villa Valmarana (one is now known to be dated 1757) show that he had a different approach from his father's, less allegorical and more sardonic and matter-of-fact, with a delight in the activities of clowns and mountebanks. There are some pictures by him in London (NG), and one in Dulwich which may be by him or his father, but there is a tendency to ascribe works to him which are not quite good enough for his father; if they are not really good enough for Domenico they get ascribed to Lorenzo (1736–76), about whose style little is known. Domenico made some etchings after his father's pictures, and two series, of the *Flight into Egypt* and the *Via Crucis*, which reveal his talents as a religious artist. There are also a few etchings by Lorenzo.

TINO di Camaino (*c.*1285–1337), was a Sienese sculptor, perhaps the pupil of Giovanni PISANO. He was working in Pisa by 1311, and became head of the works at the Cathedral in 1315, when he was commissioned to make a Tomb for the Emperor Henry VII, parts of which survive in the Cathedral. In 1319–20 Tino was head of the works at Siena Cathedral and later worked in Florence before going to Naples in 1323/4 to make monuments for the Angevin rulers. He stayed in Naples until his death, and he seems to have been in close touch with Giotto, who was Court Painter in Naples 1329–33, and also with the Sienese painter Pietro Lorenzetti, who became guardian of Tino's child: Tino's grave, but rather clumsy, figures have much in common with Lorenzetti's. There are works in Florence, Naples, Pisa, Siena, and in Berlin, Detroit, Frankfurt, London (V&A), Paris (Louvre), Turin and Yale.

TINTORETTO, Jacopo (1518–94), was born in Venice. Little is known of his early years; he claimed to have been a pupil of Titian, and was probably associated with Schiavone and Paris BORDONE. He was a master in 1539, but no work can certainly be ascribed to him before about 1545. Titian was his model, and he aimed at the Mannerist conception of the ideal through a synthesis of Michelangelo's drawing with Titian's colour which in his case succeeded, chiefly because his drawing is nothing like Michelangelo's and his colour is nothing like Titian's.

In his early works he composes his figures across the picture in a frieze, with elegant elongated forms and all the devices of placing the principal incident deep into the picture, dispersing the interest over the whole canvas, or using *repoussoir* figures in front and at the sides, opposing diagonals and contrasts of light on dark and dark on light. The earliest datable work is the *Last Supper* (Venice, S. Marcuola) of 1547, but a recently discovered huge *Washing of the Feet* (now in Newcastle Gall.) is probably of the same date, and shows the same characteristic composition. He made his reputation in 1548 with *St Mark rescuing a Slave* (Venice, Accad.), a large and crowded composition with daring foreshortening, brilliant colour and a concentration on one moment and incident. Later he evolved compositions based on an exploding centre or on rapidly receding diagonals, full of figures in violent movement. After the fires in the Doge's Palace in 1574 and 1577, Tintoretto and Veronese were the principal artists commissioned to renew the interior, and for this Tintoretto painted the gigantic *Paradise* (1588–92) for the main hall (*modelli* in Lugano (Thyssen Coll.) and Paris, Louvre).

Like Titian, Tintoretto kept a huge workshop, his chief assistants being his sons Domenico and Marco, and his daughter Marietta. The system in the Tintoretto workshop differed from that in use in the Titian and Veronese workshops in that instead of limiting his assistants to close versions, copies or preparatory work on a commission, he employed them mainly on enlargements and extensively altered variants of his original compositions. Besides his work for the state, he worked for most of the larger Confraternities and began his long association with the Scuola di S. Rocco in 1564, becoming a member in 1565. In 1576 he contracted with the Confraternity for a regular stipend (which was paid regularly: his state pension was often in arrears), in return for which he undertook to complete the decoration of the entire building. This was finished in 1588. The Scuola di S. Rocco consists of a huge lower hall with paintings over 12 feet high illustrating the Life of the Virgin, an upper hall of the same size with paintings over 16 feet high of the Life of

Christ, with a further large room adjoining it with scenes from the Passion. They display to the full his extraordinary use of the unexpected viewpoint, contrasts of scale, unusual movement and visionary effects of colour and flickering light. Vasari disapproved of him, and tempered his admiration by saying that Tintoretto treated art as a joke, 'working at random and without design' – which is a measure of the difference between Central Italian Mannerism and the Venetian kind.

There are few mythologies in his *oeuvre*, for he had none of Titian's classical interests, neither does he match Titian's range and inventiveness in portraits, although his portraits of old men (*Morosini*, London, NG, and especially the very late *Self-portrait* in Paris, Louvre) have great power and depth of characterization. After his death, painting in Venice dwindled in significance, not to revive until Piazzetta or to see similar glories until Tiepolo. Most of the major galleries of the world possess an example, but it is impossible to see him properly except in Venice, and in particular in the Scuola di S. Rocco.

TISCHBEIN, Johann Heinrich Wilhelm (1751–1829), was one of a family of painters and was the pupil of his uncles in Hamburg. He went to Holland in 1771 and began to work as a portrait painter, having a great success at the Court in Berlin after 1777. He became dissatisfied with portraiture and went to Munich, where he studied Dürer and the early German painters, going on to Italy in 1779. In 1783 he was in Rome for the second time and began to paint history pictures, but in 1786 he met Goethe, and in 1786/88 he painted the *Goethe in the Roman Campagna* (Frankfurt, Städel) on which his reputation chiefly rests. In 1789 he became Director of the Naples Academy, and from 1791 supervised the engraving of the Greek vases belonging to Sir William Hamilton which were so important in the spread of NEOCLASSICISM. In Naples he painted the famous beauty Lady Charlotte Campbell as Erato (*c.*1790, Edinburgh, SNPG). He returned to Germany in 1799. There are works by him in Berlin, Hamburg, Weimar and other German museums.

TISSOT, James (1836–1902), was born in Nantes but settled in England after the Franco-Prussian War of 1870–1. From 1876 until her death in 1882 he lived with the beautiful Mrs Newton, who figures in most of the paintings of Victorian high life by which he is now remembered. After her death he spent ten years in the Holy Land, working on his huge series of pictures of the Life of Christ before he returned to France. He was a friend of Whistler, Degas and the Goncourts, and was truly a *peintre de la vie moderne*. There are works in Baltimore, Buffalo NY, Cardiff, Dublin, Leeds, Liverpool, London (NPG, Tate and Guildhall), New York (Brooklyn), Oxford and Paris (Mus. d'Orsay).

TITIAN (Tiziano Vecelli) (*c.*1487/90–1576), was the greatest of Venetian painters, and, in some senses, the founder of modern painting. Traditionally he lived to be 99; but this is highly improbable, since it makes him born in 1477 and therefore older than GIORGIONE, who seems to have been the decisive innovator in the early years of the 16th century. Certainly Giorgione is the only painter mentioned in the documents concerning the frescoes on the Fondaco dei Tedeschi (1508), although Titian traditionally painted those on the less important façade. All these frescoes have now perished, but Titian's earliest style is certainly involved with Giorgione's. Titian seems to have been a pupil first of Gentile BELLINI and then of his brother Giovanni; but long before Giovanni's death in 1516 Titian had been decisively influenced by Giorgione, who, though not his master in any strict sense, was his real teacher. Giorgione's early death, in 1510, led to the completion of some of his works by Titian and SEBASTIANO del Piombo, and to consequent critical confusion: the Dresden *Venus* and the *Noli Me Tangere* (London, NG) may be two such Giorgione/Titians. In 1511 Titian was painting frescoes in Padua, but the unexpected death of Giorgione and the removal of Sebastiano to Rome in 1511 left Titian without a rival in Venice except the very aged Giovanni Bellini: on his death in 1516 Titian succeeded him as Painter to the Republic, and in the same year he began his *Assumption* for the Frari Church in Venice. This was completed in 1518 and laid the foundations of his fame. It is an enormous picture, in the 'modern' style, and marks the beginning of the High Renaissance in Venice. The *Pesaro Altar* (1519–26), in the same church, and *St Peter Martyr* (1528–30: burnt in 1867, but known from copies) contain further innovations and show Titian now firmly established and in possession of a fully developed personal style. In 1532 he met the Emperor Charles V at Bologna, where he painted a copy (1532–3, Madrid, Prado) of a full-length portrait of Charles by his Austrian Court Painter SEISENEGGER, as a result of which Titian was ennobled and made Court Painter in 1533. Subsequently he became a personal friend of the Emperor – an unheard-of honour for a painter in the 16th century, comparable only with Michelangelo's relationship with the Popes. About 1515 he had painted his first mythologies for the Este at Ferrara, to complete the Duke's *studiolo*, for which Bellini's *Feast of the Gods* had been painted. Titian's three paintings of the *Feast of Venus* and *The Andrians* (1517–18, both Madrid, Prado), and the *Bacchus and Ariadne* (1523/4, London, NG) finally resulted in his repainting the background of the Bellini to harmonize with his own pictures. In the mid-1530s he was also working for the Court at Urbino, and some fine portraits, as well as *La Bella* (*c.*1536, Florence, Pitti) and the *Venus of Urbino* (*c.*1538, Florence, Uffizi), in which he takes up the theme of the female nude pioneered by Giorgione, date from this time. His official commissions for the Venetian State (history pictures and portraits of Doges), which he was committed to in return for his broker's patent, were almost all destroyed in the 1577 fire in the Doge's Palace. During the 1540s Michelangelo's influence on Titian can be noted and some Mannerist elements infiltrate into his style, as in the *Crowning with Thorns* (*c.*1542, Paris, Louvre) – these, and also a new interest in classical antiquity, are partly attributable to his visit to Rome in 1545–6, which resulted in subjects such as the *Danaë* (1545–6, Naples) and various *Venuses* (Florence, Madrid, Berlin). During this Roman visit he painted a shatteringly revealing portrait of Paul III and his nasty Farnese grandsons apparently engaged in a family quarrel (Naples). He visited the Imperial Court at Augsburg in 1548–9 and again in 1550–1 and his portraits of these years established the type of official portrait which was later to be exploited by Rubens, van Dyck and many others. He met CRANACH at Augsburg in 1550, when Cranach is said to have painted Titian's portrait (now lost). After the abdication of Charles V in 1555, Titian continued to work for his successor, Philip II of Spain, who, however, employed him less as a portraitist than as a painter of *poesie* (Titian's own word); that is, more or less erotic mythologies which, at first sight, accord ill with the Counter-Reformation ideals of Philip II; examples are the *Diana* *and Actaeon* and *Diana and Callisto* (both Edinburgh), the *Rape of Europa* (Boston, Gardner) and the *Punishment of Actaeon* (London, NG), all of the late 1550s and early 1560s. During these years the old painter developed a very free handling, almost anticipating Impressionism in its disregard for contours and its concentration on the rendering of form as patches of colour and effects of light, as in the *Martyrdom of St Lawrence* (*c.*1550–5, Venice, Gesuiti) and a later version (*c.*1564–7, Escorial), and the second version of the *Crowning With Thorns* (*c.*1570, Munich), or the *Tarquin and Lucretia* (*c.*1570, Cambridge, Fitzwm). In the 1560s there were many criticisms of his failing powers, but in fact he was developing a sublime late style, best seen in the *modelli* he produced and from which his numerous assistants (who included his son Orazio) fabricated 'finished pictures'. The *Entombment* (Venice, Accad.) was left unfinished at his death and was completed by PALMA Giovane, who has left the following description of Titian's technique: 'He laid in his pictures with a mass of colour which served as a groundwork for what he wanted to express. I myself have seen such vigorous underpainting in plain red earth [*terra rossa*, probably Venetian red] for the half-tones, or in white lead. With the same brush dipped in red, black or yellow he worked up the light parts and in four strokes he could create a remarkably fine figure. . . . Then he turned the picture to the wall and left it for months without looking at it, until he returned to it and stared critically at it, as if it were a mortal enemy. . . . If he found something which displeased him he went to work like a surgeon. . . . Thus, by repeated revisions he brought his pictures to a high state of perfection and while one was drying he worked on another. This quintessence of a composition he then covered with many layers of living flesh. . . . He never painted a figure *alla prima*, and used to say that he who improvises can never make a perfect line of poetry. The final touches he softened, occasionally modulating the highest lights into the half-tones and local colours with his fingers; sometimes he used his finger to dab a dark patch in a corner as an accent, or to heighten the surface with a bit of red like a drop of blood. He finished his figures like this and in the last stages he used his fingers more than his brush.'

There are works in most major museums, but the following are particularly rich: Berlin, Dresden, Edinburgh (NG, loan from the Duke of Sutherland), the Escorial, Florence, London (NG and Wallace Coll.), Madrid, Munich, New York (Met. Mus. and Frick Coll.), Paris, Rome, Venice, Vienna and Washington.

TOBEY, Mark (1890–1976), was born in Centreville Wis., and originally worked as a commercial artist. He taught at Dartington Hall School, in England, 1931–8, but visited Japan and China in 1934 with the potter, Bernard Leach. He was much influenced by Chinese calligraphy (taking lessons from a Chinese artist) and was also one of the first American intellectuals to become interested in Zen. From 1935 he painted abstract pictures in what is called 'white writing', based on Chinese calligraphy: the effect is reminiscent of, but more fastidious than, the calligraphy of POLLOCK. These white squiggles have been described by an admirer as: 'looping over layers of interpenetrating space . . . holding icons in a shifting web'. There are works in London (Tate), New York (M of MA) and other museums of modern art.

TOCQUÉ, Louis (1696–1772), was a French portrait painter who was the pupil and son-in-law of NATTIER (who was good at painting pretty women, while Tocqué was happier with plain ones). He admired Rigaud and Largillierre and adapted their styles, and Nattier's, to the requirements of his own time. He worked in Paris except for a trip to St Petersburg and Copenhagen (1756–9), and a second trip to Copenhagen in 1769. There are examples in Boston, Copenhagen, London (NG), Paris (Louvre) and Versailles.

TODESCHINI *see* CIPPER.

TONDO (Ital. round). A circular picture or relief. *Tondi* became fashionable in Italy in the mid-15th century, although earlier examples are known.

TONE VALUES *see* VALUES.

TOOROP, Jan (1858–1928), was the leading Dutch SYMBOLIST painter. He was influenced by BEARDSLEY and was a friend of ENSOR, exhibiting with Les VINGT. There are works in Dutch and Flemish museums.

TORRIGIANO, Pietro (1472–1528), was a Florentine sculptor who, in youth, broke the nose of Michelangelo and for this has been hated by all Florentines ever since. He was in the Netherlands 1509–10. CELLINI tells how Torrigiano, who worked in England 1511–18 on the Tombs of Lady Margaret Beaufort, Elizabeth of York and Henry VII in Westminster Abbey, returned to Florence *c.*1519 and offered him a job in England. 'He had stories every day of his brave deeds among those brutes of Englishmen', but in spite of the prospects Cellini, after hearing how Torrigiano broke Michelangelo's nose, 'felt such a hatred for him that far from wanting to go to England with him I could not bear to look at him'. Torrigiano did return to England – his masterpiece is the Tomb of Henry VII – and then went to Seville, *c.*1522. There, according to Vasari (who also hated him for breaking Michelangelo's nose), he fell into the hands of the Inquisition and starved himself to death from sheer spleen. There is a bust of Henry VII in London (V&A), and other works in the Escorial (a crucifix), London (Westminster Abbey and Wallace Coll.), New York (Met. Mus.) and Seville.

TORSO. The trunk of the human body. Usually applied to a statue which lacks head, arms and legs; the *Belvedere Torso* (often called 'The Torso' in the 18th century) is a celebrated antique statue in the Vatican.

TOTENTANZ *see* DANCE OF DEATH.

TOULOUSE-LAUTREC, Henri Marie Raymond de (1864–1901), had the misfortune to break both his legs in childhood, as a result of which he was stunted in his growth. In 1882 he began to study art seriously in Paris, and by 1885 had a studio in Montmartre. He exhibited at the Salon des Indépendants from 1889 and with Les VINGT in Brussels, and in 1891 his first posters brought him immediate recognition. He made his first colour prints in 1892, and held a one-man show in Paris in the following year. In 1894 he went to Brussels, and in 1895 made the first of several visits to London, where he met Oscar Wilde and BEARDSLEY. He held a second exhibition in 1896, and visited Holland, Portugal and Spain, but in 1898 his health began to suffer from drink. In 1899 he spent three months in a clinic recovering from alcoholism, and during his convalescence he worked on a series of drawings of the circus. After his recovery, he resumed his old life, but in 1901 he broke down completely and was taken to his mother's country house, where he died.

His first teacher had encouraged him to paint animals, particularly horses; after he began studying in Paris he met Émile BERNARD and van Gogh, and he was deeply influenced by the technique and subject matter of Degas, and by Japanese prints, the influence of which was all-pervasive in Impressionist circles. His subject matter was centred narrowly round the life he led: some portraits, many painted out-of-doors, scenes from dancehalls and cafés in Montmartre, such as the Moulin Rouge, or from Aristide Bruant's cabaret 'Le Mirliton', figures of actresses, female clowns, circus artists seen backstage, and a great number of nudes, either *à la* Degas – washing, dressing – or seen sitting around in brothels, waiting for customers. He loathed posed models; these naked women just walking or lounging about provided him with models in movement and under no restraint either in pose or behaviour, and to study them he lived for some time in *maisons closes*.

His technical range was very wide. He was a superb draughtsman with a gift for conveying rapid movement and the whole atmosphere of a scene with a few strokes. Most of his paintings are in spirit-thinned oil-paint on unprimed cardboard, using the neutral buff tone of the board as an element in the design. He executed a large number of posters in lithography, with masterly handling of highly simplified line, large areas of flat colour, and a unique concentration on the eye-catching quality of the design. He also made small lithographs, either for menu-heads, programmes, book-covers or the like, or as single prints or series from his usual subject-matter. Occasionally he used watercolour and pastel, and towards the end of his life his use of oil-paint tended to become heavier, more impasted, with more solidly painted backgrounds. He was not interested in light as were the Impressionists, but only in form and movement, and most of his works are devoid of chiaroscuro; for him, light illuminated, never enveloped. He subscribed to no theories, was a member of no artistic or aesthetic movement, and the works in which he records what he saw and understood contain no hint of comment – no pity, no sentiment, no blame, no innuendo.

There are works in most museums of modern art; Albi (his birthplace) has a notable collection, and the following may be particularly mentioned: London (Tate and Courtauld Inst.), Paris (Mus d'Orsay) and Washington (NG).

TOUR *see* LA TOUR, G. de, and LATOUR, M. Q. de.

TOURNIER, Nicolas (1590–*c*.1639), was a French Caravaggesque, born in the south of France, who was in Rome by 1619, where he was influenced by MANFREDI and VALENTIN (cf. the UTRECHT School). He was back in France by 1627 and settled in Toulouse. There are works in Paris (Louvre), as well as Narbonne and Toulouse.

TOWNSCAPE. A VEDUTA, on the analogy of landscape, where the buildings, rather than trees and fields, are the dominant features. The earliest examples can be found in the ancient world (Pompeii), but the first modern examples are Sienese, especially Ambrogio LORENZETTI's frescoes of the port of Talamone and his *Good Government in the City* (of Siena). There are many examples in MSS of the 15th century, especially those illuminated by the LIMBOURGS and FOUQUET. In the 16th century views of Rome were popular, especially those showing antiquities (cf. HEEMSKERCK), and in the 16th and 17th centuries Dutch artists began to paint pictures of architecture, sometimes fantastic, as well as e.g. church interiors, such as those by SAENREDAM. The great age of Dutch townscape – van der HEYDEN, the BERCKHEYDES and, above all, VERMEER – lasted from *c*.1650–*c*.1712, after which Venice became a centre with CARLEVARIS, CANALETTO and GUARDI, and Naples and Rome with van WITTEL and, later, PANINI and PIRANESI, who introduced a more archaeological note. Canaletto's visit to England influenced SCOTT and MARLOW, and BELLOTTO worked in Central Europe. The genre was revived in Holland in the 19th century, e.g. by W. KOEKKOEK, but the Impressionists, as *peintres de la vie moderne*, exploited it to the full, as in Monet's *Gare St-Lazare*, as well as his views of London and Venice. Pissarro's views of Paris and Sisley's of the Crystal Palace, London, rank with their landscape paintings. UTRILLO was perhaps the last great painter of urban landscape.

TRAINI, Francesco, was first recorded in 1321. He was a Pisan painter much influenced by the Sienese LORENZETTI and by Giovanni PISANO's pulpit in Pisa Cathedral. He signed an altarpiece (Pisa Mus.) in 1345, and a *Glory of St Thomas Aquinas* in Sta Caterina, Pisa, may be the picture referred to in a document of 1363. Much the most important work attributed to him is the *Triumph of Death*, a series of frescoes in the Campo Santo in Pisa. These were almost entirely destroyed by a bomb in 1944, but the destruction of the top layer exposed the SINOPIE which have a strength of draughtsmanship reminiscent of Giotto. Some have now been reconstituted.

TRECENTO (Ital. three hundred). The 14th century, i.e. the thirteen-hundreds.

TRIPTYCH. A tripartite POLYPTYCH. Usually the central panel is twice the width of the wings, so that they can be folded over it to protect it. A common form of triptych, as an object of private devotion, is to have a *Madonna* in the centre and one's patron Saints on the wings: the backs of the wings, which become visible when the triptych is shut, often bear the owner's coat of arms.

TRISTÁN, Luis (1585/6–1624), was a Spanish painter active in Toledo, who was influenced by El GRECO, and was probably his pupil 1603–6, before going to Italy *c.*1606–13. His *Holy Trinity*, signed and dated 1624, in Seville Cath. is still very close to Greco, although Tristán was also influenced by RIBERA and RIBALTA. There are other works by him in Toledo, as well as Cambridge (Fitzwm), Madrid (Prado) and Paris (Louvre).

TROIS CRAYONS (Fr. three crayons). A drawing *à trois crayons* is one executed in three different colours of chalk, usually black, white and sanguine, on a tinted paper, usually buff or slate-grey, to give a pictorial effect. WATTEAU is the greatest exponent of the technique.

TROMPE L'ŒIL (Fr. deceive the eye) *see* ILLUSIONISM.

TROOST, Cornelis (1696–1750), was the contemporary of Hogarth and has been called 'the Dutch Hogarth', but his work lacks the biting satire of the Englishman. Troost was born in Amsterdam and made his name with traditional group portraits, but soon evolved small conversation pieces very like Hogarth's. He also painted scenes from theatrical performances and vaguely moral genre scenes (the *Drinking Scenes* in The Hague), and worked in pastel. His early portrait groups are in the 17th-century Dutch tradition – *The Collegium Medicum of Amsterdam*, 1724, *The Anatomy Lecture of Professor Roëll*, 1728, and the *Governors of the Orphanage*, 1729 (all in Amsterdam, Rijksmus.) – but the *Governors* has a faintly French Rococo air, reminiscent of Hogarth. His early style was founded on Steen and Netscher. Again like Hogarth, his works were popular in engravings. There are examples in the Royal Coll. and in Berlin and Dublin as well as in Holland (Amsterdam has twenty-eight).

TROY, Jean François de (1679–1752), was a French painter, first of classical subjects like LE MOYNE, then of *fêtes galantes* and hunting scenes, and of the elaborate breakfasts and picnics that accompanied them. He also designed two large series of Gobelins tapestries – the *History of Queen Esther* and *Jason and Medea* – and painted some religious subjects, such as Susanna, that afforded opportunities for the nude. He was the son of François de Troy (1645–1730), a Toulouse portrait painter who sent him to Italy at the age of 14. The influence of Venice was permanent. From 1738 to 1751 he was Director of the French Academy in Rome, and, when he was replaced, died of grief at the thought of leaving a young Roman woman with whom he had just fallen in love. His style incorporates the colour and realism of Rubens's hunts, Snyders' animals and still-life, with the pastoral quality of the best Watteau followers – i.e. he is a particularly good example of RUBÉNISME. There are pictures in Paris (Louvre, Carnavalet and S. Étienne du Mont), Toulouse, Versailles and other French provincial museums, Florence (Uffizi), Leningrad, London (NG, V&A and Wallace Coll.), Malibu Cal. (Getty), New York (Met. Mus.) and Rotterdam.

TRUMBULL, John (1756–1843), was an American artist who fought in the War of Independence, after which (1780) he travelled to London and Paris and worked with WEST. He painted principally portraits and historical pictures of the War of Independence, well represented in American museums. His *Battle of Bunker's Hill, 1775*, was painted in London in the studio of the loyalist West; rather to his surprise no English engraver would reproduce it. He was also imprisoned for several months as a spy, but returned to West and made several trips back to London. Unlike West, he was dictatorial and did not get on with younger painters. There is a large collection of his works in Yale, which he gave to the University, *c.*1830, in exchange for an annuity. His 'Autobiography' was published in 1841 (and again in 1953).

TURA, Cosmè (Cosimo) (before 1431–1495), was the first great Ferrarese painter. He worked there from 1451 for the Este Court, but much of his production has been lost. The main influence on his style was MANTEGNA, and perhaps also Mantegna's own inspirer Donatello, and the wiry quality of the forms and the austerity of feeling persist in all the Ferrarese painters of the 15th century – COSSA, COSTA and above all Ercole ROBERTI. Curiously, the very different world of PIERO della Francesca also plays a strong part in Tura's stylistic evolution, most probably through the frescoes, now lost, which Piero painted in Ferrara some time before 1450. Tura's brittle and metallic sense of form hardly changed during his lifetime, but he was succeeded as Court Painter by Roberti in 1486 and died poor. There are works in Ajaccio, Bergamo, Berlin, Boston (Gardner), Caen, Cambridge (Fitzwm), Cambridge Mass. (Fogg), Ferrara (Pinacoteca and Cath.), Florence (Uffizi), London (NG), Milan (Brera and Poldi-Pezzoli), Modena, Nantes, New York (Met. Mus.), Paris (Louvre), Philadelphia (Johnson), San Diego Cal., Venice (Accad. and Correr), Vienna and Washington (NG).

TURNER, Joseph Mallord William (1775–1851), was the son of a barber and born in Maiden Lane, Covent Garden. His talent was precocious. He was admitted to the Royal Academy Schools in 1789 and first exhibited at the RA in 1790; throughout his life he was much indebted to the Academy, which recognized his genius and supported him against many of the arbiters of taste. He became an ARA in 1799, RA in 1802 – at the age of 27 – Professor of

Perspective in 1807, and Deputy President in 1845. His extremely good head for business caused him to be appointed to audit the finances for many years. In 1792 Turner made the first of the sketching tours that were to take up so much of his time for the next half-century. Soon after this, for three years in the mid-1790s he worked with GIRTIN at Dr MONRO's house, Girtin drawing the outlines and Turner washing in the effects. After Girtin's premature death Turner is said to have remarked 'If Tom Girtin had lived I should have starved': apart from the element of exaggeration in this, it is probably true that, at this stage, Girtin was the leader and Turner imitated him so closely that it is not always possible to distinguish the watercolours of the one from those of the other. Up to *c.*1796 Turner was exclusively a watercolourist, working in the topographical tradition, but in 1796 he exhibited his first oil-painting at the RA; the two which he showed in 1797 being markedly influenced by Dutch 17th-century marine painting (the *Millbank, Moonlight*, now in the Tate Gall., is close to the moonlight scenes of A. van der NEER). This influence was almost immediately succeeded by that of WILSON and CLAUDE, and, early in the 1800s, he was composing in a grand manner learned ultimately from Claude; Italian rather than Dutch. In 1802, with scores of other artists, he went to see the pictures looted by Napoleon which were then exhibited in the Louvre, and there he particularly admired Poussin. His next major work, however, was the *Calais Pier* of 1803 (London, NG), which is very unlike Poussin, is thoroughly Romantic, and was generally condemned as unfinished. For many years after this Turner was bitterly attacked, principally by Sir George Beaumont, the artistic dictator of the day, and warmly defended, by Sir Thomas LAWRENCE among others. These attacks led to a decline in the sales of his larger oil-paintings (*Crossing the Brook*, 1815, London, NG, is a case in point) and in 1816 his landscapes were actually called 'pictures of nothing, and very like'. Turner himself, in one of his few recorded epigrams, is said to have remarked of painting in general that it was 'a rum thing', but between 1806 and 1819 he did take steps to defend himself by publishing a series of engravings of different kinds of landscape under the title *Liber Studiorum* (*see* LIBER VERITATIS). The series was not successful, principally because Turner was always very close with his money and underpaid the engravers; he was also extremely exigent in his demands on their skill. In 1819, encouraged by Lawrence, he made his first visit to Italy and from then on his oil-paintings tend more and more to the pale brilliance of colour which he had already achieved in watercolour and he begins to think in terms of coloured light, or, in Constable's phrase, 'tinted steam'. He returned to Italy in 1829 and to Venice (it is now thought) in 1833, and again in 1840, the late Venetian watercolours and gouaches being among the most magical effects of light even in his work. By this time he was rather out of favour and public interest was turning to the detailed approach that culminated in the Pre-Raphaelites, when, rather to his surprise, Ruskin came to his defence with the first volume of 'Modern Painters' in 1843 (the full title is: 'Modern Painters: their superiority in the art of landscape painting to all the ancient masters proved by examples of the True, the Beautiful, and the Intellectual, from the works of modern artists, especially from those of J.M.W. Turner, Esq., RA'). By his will Turner left nearly 300 paintings and nearly 20,000 watercolours and drawings to the nation: his conditions were scandalously disregarded for over a century, but in 1987 a special Turner Gallery was opened at the Tate, containing all the watercolours and drawings formerly in the BM and the vast majority of his oil-paintings. Other works in London are in the NG, Courtauld Inst., V&A, Nat. Marit. Mus. and Kenwood, as well as in Auckland NZ, Boston (Mus.), Cambridge (Fitzwm), Cambridge Mass. (Fogg), Cardiff, Chicago, Cleveland Ohio, Dublin, Dunedin, Edinburgh (NG), Hartford Conn. (Wadsworth Atheneum), Indianapolis (Herron), Manchester (City Art Gall., and fifty in the Whitworth), Melbourne, New York (Met. Mus. and Frick Coll.), Oberlin Coll. Ohio, Ottawa (NG), Oxford, Petworth Sussex (National Trust), Philadelphia, Sheffield, Washington (NG and Corcoran), Yale (CBA) and elsewhere.

U

UCCELLO, Paolo (1396/7–1475), is celebrated in the early sources as a master of perspective; indeed, the invention of it is sometimes wrongly credited to him (but see BRUNELLESCHI). What is clear is that he became absorbed in the study of perspective (and, still more, FORESHORTENING) and that it modified his style in his middle years, but he never used it for the naturalistic purposes envisaged by MASACCIO and others. Uccello is first recorded as a *garzone* in 1407, in the shop where GHIBERTI's First Baptistry Doors were being made, and this semi-Gothic style was to remain the foundation of his own. In 1415 he entered the Painters' Guild, but nothing is known of any paintings by him for about another fifteen years. In 1425 he went to Venice and worked on mosaics in St Mark's for about five years. He was certainly in Florence again in 1431, but he had been out of the city during the years when Masaccio created the new, naturalistic style which was later to influence him in a rather superficial way. In 1436 he was commissioned by the city to paint a fresco in imitation of an equestrian statue to the English mercenary soldier Sir John Hawkwood, known in Italy as Giovanni Acuto. This fresco is still in the Cathedral of Florence, but it was repainted by Uccello himself, since the first version failed to please. In it we see for the first time his intensive study of the new science of foreshortening, since the intention is to deceive the eye into thinking that the painted statue is a real one: in fact, Uccello never really carried out the full implications of a perspective setting, since the plinth and the effigy are seen from two disparate viewpoints, and this inconsistency is usual in all his works. He was able to make another experiment in foreshortening in the *Four Prophets* (1443) round the clockface in the Cathedral, and between 1443 and 1445 he designed stained-glass windows for it. About 1445 he went to Padua, and the *Giants* he painted there are supposed to have influenced MANTEGNA, but they are now lost. On his return, *c.*1445, he painted his most famous work, the *Deluge* in the Chiostro Verde of S.M. Novella, Florence, where he had already painted some Creation scenes (from *c.*1431). The *Deluge* (recently restored, previously almost lost) shows the impact of the new ideas on perspective at their most powerful, and it is often related to the treatise on painting by ALBERTI ('Della Pittura', 1435), where a system of perspective construction is explained and several subjects are suggested which are to be found in the *Deluge*. Similar ideas on foreshortening may be found in the three *Battles* of 1454/7 in Florence (Uffizi), London (NG) and Paris (Louvre), which he painted for the Medici, but here the decorative aspect is far more important and in all his later works the decorative side of his early training comes back strongly. His last documented work is the *predella* for an altarpiece, commissioned by an Urbino Confraternity of the Holy Sacrament (1465–9, Urbino), *see* JOOS van Gent; a *Hunt by Moonlight* (Oxford, Ashmolean), which is equally decorative in character and fairy-tale in atmosphere, is probably of the same date. In 1469, in filling in his tax return he said: 'I am old, infirm, and unemployed, and my wife is ill.' Other works are in Chambéry, Dublin, Florence (S. Martino alla Scala), Paris (Louvre and Jacquemart-André) and Washington (NG).

UGO da Carpi (*c.*1480–*c.*1525) was influenced by Parmigianino and Salviati. He may have invented the CHIAROSCURO Woodcut, since the Venetian state granted him a patent in 1516.

UGOLINO da Siena (active 1317–27), was a close follower of DUCCIO. He painted the High Altar of Sta Croce, Florence, now dispersed: parts of it are in London (NG), Berlin, New York (Met. Mus) and Philadelphia (Johnson). Other pictures attributed to him are in Assisi (S. Francesco), Birmingham (Barber Inst.), Cleveland Ohio, Dublin, London (Courtauld Inst.), St Louis, Siena, Washington and Williamstown Mass.

'UGOLINO-LORENZETTI'. An invented name for an unknown artist midway between the styles of UGOLINO da Siena and the LORENZETTI. Also known as the Ovile Master (and the Master of the Fogg *Nativity*), he has been tentatively identified with Bartolommeo Bulgarini (active *c.*1347–*d.*1378), who is known to have been a painter.

UNDERPAINTING is the preliminary lay-in, usually in GRISAILLE, in which the drawing, composition and tone values of a picture are worked out. It may sometimes include an indication of colour, but the purpose of underpainting is to get the design and tonal values established before tackling the colouristic problems, particularly if many GLAZES are envisaged. The underpainting of a specific area can mean, in a narrower sense, the preparation for a glaze – e.g. a solid yellow which is to be glazed with red and purple to get a richer effect of shot colours and in shadows (*see also* ALLA PRIMA).

UTRECHT SCHOOL. This is a fairly precisely defined moment in Dutch painting, early in the 17th century, when the influence of CARAVAGGIO made its impact on a whole circle of Utrecht painters, of whom the most important were BABUREN, HONTHORST and TERBRUGGHEN. All three were in Rome in the period 1610/20, at the moment immediately after Caravaggio's death when his influence was at its highest and was being exploited by MANFREDI. All three returned to Utrecht by the 1620s. They painted religious pictures – Utrecht is a Catholic centre – and also genre scenes of the Five Senses and brothel pictures, like Manfredi's work, but unlike Caravaggio's though stemming from his relentless realism. Towards the end of the 1620s the effect began to wear off and Terbrugghen in particular began to lighten his palette (e.g. *Jacob and Laban*, 1627, London, NG) and to study light effects in a totally un-Caravaggesque way. BYLERT, BOR and STOMER were more or less influenced by Utrecht ideas, although Bylert changed his style and Stomer remained in Italy. The spread of Caravaggism in Holland through the Utrecht School was such that even Hals, Vermeer and Rembrandt were affected by it.

UTRILLO, Maurice (1883–1955), was the son of Suzanne VALADON, herself a talented painter who was encouraged by Renoir, Degas and Toulouse-Lautrec, for whom she posed as a model. He early developed into a confirmed drunkard and drug addict, spent many years in clinics and sanatoria, and his drinking bouts often ended in the police station. His mother made him learn to paint in 1902 as a distraction and a form of therapy. He met MODIGLIANI about 1905/7 and remained his life-long friend. His art shows nothing of this wild and melodramatic background. His paintings are almost all views of Paris, often painted from picture-postcards; they show a sensitive understanding of tone, and are delicate and almost monochromatic in colour, with precise drawing and a strange feeling for the atmosphere of a particular street or building. To reproduce the crumbling stucco of Montmartre he often mixed plaster or sand with his paint. His best works were produced between 1908 and 1916: success made him repeat himself and there are numerous fakes. The *Place du Tertre* and *Porte St-Martin* (London, Tate) are good examples of his feeling for the texture of brick and stone, representing the end of the TOWNSCAPE tradition going back to SAENREDAM and van der HEYDEN. Other works are in Berne, Boston, Bremen, Buffalo NY, Glasgow, Kansas City, Newport RI, New York (Met. Mus., M of MA and Brooklyn), Paris (Mus. d'Art Mod.), Washington (NG and Phillips) and Zurich.

UYTEWAEL *see* WTEWAEL.

V

VALADON, Suzanne (1867 [or 1865?]–1938), was an artists' model in the 1880s and began to draw out of curiosity. Degas, who never employed her as a model, bought her drawings and helped her to make engravings. Her paintings show his influence, with that of Gauguin and Cloisonnisme, and above all that of MATISSE. Her son, UTRILLO, whose father may have been the Spanish painter Miguel Utrillo y Molins, was born in 1883. There are works by her in Paris (Mus. d'Art Moderne) and other French museums.

VALDÉS LEAL, Juan de (1622–90), was a painter active in Seville where he helped to found the Academy in 1660. He was President 1663–6, but his difficult temperament made it impossible for him to get on with his fellow-artists. His style is dramatic and emotional to the point of morbidity and is seen at its best in VANITAS subjects such as the *Triumph of Death* and the *Sic Transit Gloria Mundi*, with their decomposing corpses. There are works by him in Cordova and Seville, and in Amherst Mass. (one of his rare portraits), Ann Arbor Mich., Barnard Castle (Bowes Mus.), Castres, Dresden, Dublin, Grenoble, Hartford Conn., Kansas City, London (NG), Madrid (Prado), New York (Met. Mus. and Hispanic Soc.), Paris (Louvre), Washington (NG), Yale and York.

VALENTIN, Le (Moïse Valentin, Valentin de Boullogne) (1591–1632), was a French painter, born at Coulommiers, but was perhaps the son of an Italian (neither his Christian name Moïse nor the de Boullogne seems to be correct); certainly he was, like FINSONIUS, more of an Italian painter than a Northern one. He was in Rome by 1612 and again from 1620 to his death. He was strongly influenced by VOUET, whose pupil he may have been, and even more by MANFREDI and the Caravaggismo he represents. Valentin was a friend of Poussin, and his only documented work, the *Martyrdom of SS. Processus and Martinian* (1629/30, Vatican), was a pendant to Poussin's *St Erasmus* in St Peter's. In 1973 two other *Saints* turned up in Camerino (S.M. in Via). There are works attributed to him in Besançon, Cambridge Mass. (Fogg), Cleveland Ohio, Cologne, Copenhagen, Dresden, Gateshead, Indianapolis, Leningrad, London (NG), Madrid (Prado), Malibu Cal. (Getty), Montreal, Munich, Paris (Louvre), Perugia, Poughkeepsie NY (Vassar Coll.), Rome (Gall. Naz.), Toledo Ohio, Toulouse, Valletta Malta, Venice (Accad.), Versailles, Vienna and Wellesley Coll. Mass.

VALLAYER-COSTER, Anne (1744–1818), was a French painter, mainly of still-life and flowers, although some portraits, genre pieces and miniatures also exist. She became a member of the Académie in 1770, and most of her works date between 1769 and 1787, since her career was seriously interrupted by the Revolution. She was regarded in her own day as a still-life painter second only to CHARDIN and OUDRY. There are works in Barnard Castle (Bowes Mus.), Berlin, Cambridge (Fitzwm), Paris (Louvre), Toledo Ohio, San Francisco and elsewhere.

VALORI PLASTICI (Ital. plastic values), was a magazine started in 1918 which supported PITTURA METAFISICA and the artists associated with it: CARRÀ, CHIRICO and SEVERINI.

VALUES (Fr. *valeurs*) are the gradations of tone from light to dark observable in any solid object under the play of light. Tone values are independent of local colour and are best perceived by half-closing the eyes so that colour effects are diminished (a black and white photograph is an example of pure tonal effect). Since it is impossible to match the range from light to dark in nature with pigments ranging only from white to black, great judgement is needed to determine where the transitional tones must be modified, suppressed, or exaggerated so as to maintain pictorial unity. The problem is complicated by colour values, when the relative importance to the composition as a whole of each patch of colour has to be determined simultaneously with its tonal value, one often interacting on the other. Cézanne expressed this perfectly when he told BERNARD: 'When colour is at its richest, form is at its fullest', and his works are proof of this. 'Keeping' is an old-fashioned word, frequent in 18th-century criticism, signifying success in this operation.

VANAKEN *see* DRAPERYMAN.

VANDERBANK, John (1694–1739), was an English painter, born in London, who might have succeeded Kneller, but was less successful than his contemporary HOGARTH. Like Hogarth, he ran an academy in St Martin's Lane (1720), but VERTUE, recording his death, wrote: 'ailments perhaps occasiond by his irregular living (of women and wine) . . . after the death of Sr. Godfry Kneller – he might have carried all before him . . .'. He painted some murals, e.g. in a house in Bedford Row, London, but most of his works were portraits: a good example is in London, Dulwich (1736).

VANDERLYN, John (1775–1852), was an American Romantic painter, who was trained in Paris from 1796, instead of in London under WEST. He remained in Europe until 1815, except for brief visits to America, and became a follower of the Neoclassical ideals of DAVID and INGRES. He also worked in Rome with ALLSTON (1805–8). His classical nude, *Ariadne* (1812–14, Philadelphia), was not well received and he was reduced to painting portraits. There are works in several US museums, including New York (Met. Mus.), Philadelphia and Washington (Corcoran).

VANDYKE *see* DYCK.

VANISHING POINT *see* PERSPECTIVE.

VANITAS *see* STILL-LIFE.

VAN LOO *see* LOO.

VANSOMER *see* SOMER.

VANTONGERLOO, Georges (1886–1965), was a Belgian painter and sculptor who, in 1914, realized that he wanted to 'express space' and that subject matter was therefore irrelevant. He was interned in Holland during the 1914–18 War and joined the DE STIJL group in 1917. He settled in France in the 1920s, evolving a style more austere even than that of MONDRIAN, and experimenting with plexiglass rather than painting. His sculpture had considerable influence on the BAUHAUS. London (Tate) has examples.

VANVITELLI *see* van WITTEL.

VARIANT. Generally used to mean a version of a picture which has slight differences, perhaps intended by the artist. The assumption is that a variant is at least from the studio of the painter of the prime original, but it is often a convenient euphemism for a copy.

VARLEY, John (1778–1842), was an English watercolour painter of the transitional period between topographical drawing and painting in watercolours.

He was helped at the beginning of his career by Dr MONRO, and in his turn helped and taught many other artists. He was also a close friend of BLAKE and knew PALMER. He seems to have been very credulous and he wrote on astrology, in which he firmly believed. There are works in London (BM, Tate and V&A). His brothers Cornelius (1781–1873) and William (*c*.1785–1856) were also painters and are represented in the V&A.

VARNISHING DAY. A custom, once widespread in Academies, of allowing painters into the exhibition after it was hung, but before it opened to the public, so that they could nominally varnish (but actually retouch) their pictures. The custom often led to extensive repainting to outdo one's neighbours: Turner was notorious for submitting his pictures only part-finished and then completing them on the Academy walls. From this custom arose another, that of inviting one's best patrons to see the pictures before the rest of the world, and this Private View (Fr. *vernissage*) is now an established habit among commercial galleries and an excuse for a party.

VASARELY, Victor (*b*.1908), is a French painter of Hungarian origin, who has lived in France since 1930. He is the originator of OP ART, which he has exploited in painting and in sculpture, although his forms are far more geometrical than those used by, for instance, Bridget RILEY. There are works in Paris (public monuments), Buffalo NY, Caracas (a mural honouring MALEVICH), Jerusalem, New York (M of MA and Guggenheim) and elsewhere.

VASARI, Giorgio (1511–74), was born in Arezzo and trained in Florence, in the circle of Andrea del Sarto and his pupils Rosso and Pontormo, where, above all, he became a Michelangelo idolater. He spent his busy and productive life as a painter between Florence and Rome, but he was really a superb impresario rather than a painter himself, and perhaps because of his gifts in this direction his work as an architect ranks much higher than his painting. His principal paintings are in Florence (Pal. Vecchio frescoes and in galleries) and Rome (Sala Regia in the Vatican and the so-called 100 days fresco in the Cancelleria), as well as in his own house in Arezzo, which is now a museum. He was, however, important in the development of Counter-Reformation iconography, as in his *Immaculate Conception* (Florence, SS. Apostoli; sketch in Oxford, Ashmolean), and in elaborate allegories glorifying the Medici Grand Dukes. Above all, however, his fame rests solidly on his book, 'Le Vite de' più eccellenti Architetti, Pittori, et Scultori Italiani . . .', first published in 1550 and issued in a second, much enlarged, edition in 1568. This 1568 edition has been translated into most languages and is perhaps the most important book on the history of art ever written, both as a source-book and as an example for all the later Italian historiographers. By comparison the 1550 edition is little-known, but the differences between it and the second edition are not all in the latter's favour; in the first edition the plan is much clearer, for in it Vasari's intention is plain – to show how the arts died in the Dark Ages, after having been brought to a high pitch in Ancient Rome, and were then revived under Giotto the Tuscan, to progress in a steady rise in Tuscany, until ultimate perfection was reached in his own day in the hands of the Tuscan Michelangelo. In the 1550 edition MICHELANGELO is the climax of the story and his is the only biography of a living artist. The later edition is less sure in design and includes a number of living artists, including Vasari's own autobiography.

VECCHIETTA (1412–80) was a Sienese sculptor who also worked as a painter and architect. He was a pupil of SASSETTA and the teacher of MATTEO di Giovanni. His style is expressive, naturalistic and linear, with strong Florentine influences. His works are mostly in Siena (Mus., and especially Hospital), but there are others in Florence (Uffizi), Liverpool, New York (Frick Coll.), Paris (Louvre and Cluny Mus.), Pienza (Cath.) and Rome (S.M. del Popolo).

VEDUTA (Ital. view). A painting or drawing of a place, usually a town e.g. Venice or Rome (*see* TOWNSCAPE). The accuracy of the delineation varies greatly: a *veduta ideata* is an imaginary view, while a CAPRICCIO is often architecturally accurate but fantastic in its juxtapositions. PANINI and PIRANESI, CANALETTO and GUARDI are the best-known *vedutisti*, but the genre was probably invented by Northern artists working in Italy, e.g. BRIL. *See also* BERCKHEYDE and van WITTEL.

VEHICLE is synonymous with MEDIUM, as something to bind pigment or to thin stiff paint.

VELÁZQUEZ, Diego Rodriguez da Silva (1599–1660), who always signed Velasquez, was born in Seville but was of Portuguese origin. Any training he may have had before entering PACHECO's Academy in Seville in 1613 may be disregarded; in 1617 he became an independent master and in 1618 married Pacheco's daughter. It is now known that both the BODEGÓN scenes in Edinburgh and London are dated 1618, and the Prado *Adoration* is dated 1619: his Caravaggesque period is thus rendered less obscure. The early *Immaculate Conception* (London, NG) also owes much to Pacheco's book. He worked in Seville until 1622 and his early paintings show his interest in the naturalistic representation of things seen in strong light. In 1622 he visited Madrid, and in 1623 returned there to become Court Painter. He was a slow worker, with a deliberate technique without bravura, and sober colour rather low in tone, and he used a plain background for many of his portraits so that the figure stands out as a silhouette. His court appointment gave him few opportunities for religious painting, mythologies were rare in Spain, and only occasionally did he execute subject pictures, except during his Italian journeys. He was little influenced by other artists, though he profited from the Titians in the Spanish Royal Coll. and the visit of Rubens in 1628, which was his first contact with a great living painter, who was also a Court Painter, though one with an entirely different vision, temperament and artistic education. Whether or not it was Rubens who inspired him to visit Italy, it was due to Rubens's influence that he obtained permission to go. He left in August 1629, visited Genoa, Venice, Rome and Naples (where he met RIBERA) and returned to Madrid in 1631. The *Topers* (*'Los Borrachos'*: in the Spanish Royal Coll. by July 1629), with its character heads and still-life detail, suggests the influence of Ribera's realism, and the subject pictures painted in Italy (*Joseph's Coat brought to Jacob*, Escorial, and the *Forge of Vulcan*, Prado) show his preoccupation with the male nude and his fuller range of colour. The main effect of his Italian journey was to increase his breadth of vision, but without affecting its fundamentally realistic basis.

The surrender of Breda – an incident in the Dutch Wars of Independence – took place in 1625. In 1634, Velázquez recorded the moment when the Marchese Spinola (whom he had known in Italy in 1629) received the surrender from Justin of Nassau, as one of a series of victory pictures (others were by MAINO and ZURBARÁN) intended to accompany his equestrian portraits of Philip, his Queen and his heir, Don Balthasar Carlos. Velázquez's composition may owe something to Tempesta's engravings after van Veen in the 'Bataviorum cum Romanis Bellum' of Tacitus, published in Antwerp in 1612, but his brilliant colour, panoramic landscape background and heightened realism transcend any derivation. Portraits painted after his return possibly owe their more brilliant colour to their being the record of the only joyous years in the King's dreary reign – the portrait of the King called *The Fraga Philip* (1644, Frick Coll., New York: *see* MAZO) has a richness reminiscent of Rubens.

In 1648 Velázquez accompanied the embassy travelling to Italy to escort the new Queen, Marianna of Austria. He again visited Genoa, Venice, Rome and Naples, and returned to Madrid in June 1651. His object had been to buy pictures for the Royal Coll., and he also executed several works during his stay: the portrait of Pope Innocent X (Doria Coll., Rome), and his only known female nude, the *Rokeby Venus* (London, NG), were the most outstanding. The finest of the portraits painted after the second Italian journey is that of the little Infanta Margareta Teresa with her retinue of ladies and dwarfs, called *Las Meninas* (1656, Prado), and in this work he reaches perhaps his highest point in the blending of realism with atmosphere and a deeply sensitive appreciation of character. During the 1630s and 1640s he had painted a series of portraits of the court dwarfs, playmates of the Royal children, for they interested him as character studies, much as old age, wrinkles and rags interested him in his imaginary portraits of *Aesop* and *Menippus* (both in the Prado), and as did, too, the ageing face of his sick and gloomy King, whom he painted all through his long reign, and who acknowledged the greatness of his painter by making him a Knight of the Order of Santiago in 1659. His chief assistant was his son-in-law Mazo, but he was far from his equal, and after Velázquez's death his position at Court was held by a succession of dim foreigners, mostly French, until, late in the 18th century, Mengs and Tiepolo were followed by Goya.

There are unrivalled collections in Spain – in the Prado in Madrid and in the Escorial – but most major galleries have an example including Berlin, Boston (Mus. and Gardner Mus.), Budapest, Chicago, Cincinnati, Cleveland Ohio, Detroit, Dresden, Dublin (NG), Edinburgh (NG), Florence (Pitti), Fort Worth Texas, Kansas City, London (NG, Wallace Coll. and Wellington Mus.), Montreal, New York (Met. Mus., Hispanic Soc. and Frick Coll.), Paris (Louvre), Rouen, São Paulo, San Diego Cal., Toledo Ohio, Vienna and Washington (NG).

VELDE, Adriaen van de (1636–72), was the son of Willem I van de Velde, the brother of Willem II, and probably the nephew of Esaias. He was trained under his father and under WYNANTS and POTTER. It is doubtful whether he ever went to Italy, but he used Italian motives and landscapes (e.g. in the Wallace Coll. *Jacob and Laban*); he also painted a few religious subjects without landscape (e.g. the *Annunciation* in Amsterdam), but most of his works are pastoral landscapes with figures, or simply the figures in the landscapes of other painters. He painted figures for his elder brother Willem II, for his master Wynants, and for Ruisdael, Hobbema and others, especially van der Heyden. This last died in 1712, yet nearly all his works are described as having Adriaen's figures, although dated pictures painted after Adriaen's early death prove that van der Heyden was quite capable of adding his own figures. There are pictures in the Royal Coll. and in Amsterdam, Antwerp, Berlin, Boston, Cambridge (Fitzwm), Dresden, Edinburgh, Florence (Uffizi), Frankfurt, Glasgow, The Hague, Leipzig, London (NG, Wallace Coll. and Dulwich), Manchester, Munich, New York (Hist. Soc.), Oxford, Paris (Louvre), Philadelphia, Rotterdam, Vienna and Washington.

VELDE, Esaias van de (1587–1630), was a painter of genre and battle pictures, but is best known for his realistic landscapes which presage those of his great pupil Jan van GOYEN. He may have been a pupil of Coninxloo, who was a religious refugee to Amsterdam, and may therefore be the link between BRUEGEL and the Dutch: van de Velde's *Winter Landscape* (1623, London, NG) is a half-way house between Bruegel and van Goyen. He worked in Haarlem 1610–18 and then in The Hague, where he was Court Painter to the Princes Maurits and Frederik Hendrik, until his death. There are pictures in Amsterdam (Rijksmus.), Berlin, Brighton, Cambridge (Fitzwm), The Hague, Leipzig, London (NG), Manchester, Minneapolis, Munich, Rotterdam, Stockholm and elsewhere.

VELDE, Willem I van de (1611–93), and his son Willem II (1633–1707), both arrived in London in 1672 and remained there as official marine artists. It is extremely difficult to separate the works of the two, and a document of 1674 which provides for regular payment to the father for drawing sea-fights and to his son for colouring them suggests that they worked together. There are, however, some elaborate *grisaille* drawings on a large scale that are certainly the elder man's work, while there are over 600 pictures of marine subjects attributed to the younger, who is generally recognized as the greatest marine painter of the Dutch School as well as the father of all English marine painting. Most of their records of sea-fights were done from drawings made under fire from a small boat in the thick of the action: there is a very large and important collection of these in the Nat. Marit. Mus., London, which also has paintings, including Willem II's earliest signed and dated work, of 1651. His early style was influenced by VLIEGER and then by BACKHUYSEN. Other paintings are in the Royal Coll. and in Amsterdam (Rijksmus.), and in London (NG, Wallace Coll., Kenwood, Dulwich and Ham House).

VENEZIANO, Domenico, *see* DOMENICO.

VERISMO is the Italian form of REALISM. Though chiefly used of opera (Puccini, Mascagni), it has been applied to painters like SIGNORINI.

VERMEER, Jan (1632–75), of Delft, was the most calm and peaceful of all the Dutch masters and the recognition of his greatness has been long delayed. Very little is known of his life and his pictures were completely forgotten until the mid-19th century. He was certainly influenced by Carel FABRITIUS, and may have been his pupil before becoming a Master himself in the Delft Guild in 1653, although he was certainly influenced by Leonard Bramer (1596–1674), a Delft history painter. He married in the same year, was Dean of the Guild in 1663 and later, and died in 1675, leaving a widow and eleven children and an enormous debt to the baker, who held two pictures of his. In 1676 his widow tried to get them back, offering to pay off the debt over twelve years. Later that year she was declared bankrupt. It is certain that she and the children were Catholics, and this may explain the relative obscurity in which Vermeer lived. He was obviously a very slow worker, for only about thirty-five pictures are generally accepted as his and most of them are quite small. Only two (or perhaps four) are dated – 1655, 1656, 1668 and 1669 (see below). They mostly represent domestic interiors with one or two figures writing, doing housework or playing musical instruments; in reproduction they look exactly like works by Maes or Pieter de HOOCH, but in the originals the splendour of the colour and the play of light, falling in little pearls of paint on everything in the picture, transform the everyday scenes into poetry totally unlike the sober prose of the average Dutch master. There are, however, others which are quite different: what are thought to be his early works are larger and represent religious, historical or mythological scenes in a manner close to the Utrecht School. One of these, *The Procuress* (Dresden), is dated 1656. (Recently, a painting signed and dated 1655 – the earliest known – has been discovered. It represents the very unusual subject of *St Praxedis mopping up the Blood of the Martyrs* (New York, private coll.), but it has still to win general acceptance.) This reluctance is partly due to the notorious forgery by H. van Meegeren (*d.*1947) of the *Supper at Emmaus*, sold to Rotterdam just before World War II. The *Christ in the House of Martha and Mary* (Edinburgh, NG), signed but not dated, is also thought to be early. The last of this group, *Diana and Her Companions* (The Hague, Mauritshuis) is slightly different again, and may be the earliest of all. The signature, legible in 1895, is now unreadable, and for this reason it is sometimes ascribed to another Vermeer, a Utrecht painter (*c.*1630–88), who had been in Italy. The best-known work by Jan Vermeer, the *View of Delft* (The Hague), is again different in character, resembling the town-views of van der HEYDEN, and another similar scene, the *Street in Delft* (Amsterdam) very closely resembles the same subject by Pieter de Hooch (1658, London, NG) – de Hooch was in Delft *c.*1653 until the 1660s. Finally, there are some pictures, such as the *Allegory of Faith* (New York, Met. Mus.) or the *Allegory of Painting* (Vienna, K-H Mus.), which represents the painter in his studio, that go beyond the domestic interior. *The Astronomer*, dated 1668 (Paris, Louvre), and *The Geographer*, perhaps dated 1669 (Frankfurt, Städel), are half-way between allegory and genre. There are pictures by him in the Royal Coll., and in Amsterdam (Rijksmus.), Berlin, Boston (Gardner), Brunswick, Dresden, Edinburgh, Frankfurt (Städel), The Hague, London (NG and Kenwood), New York (Met. Mus. and Frick Coll.), Paris (Louvre), Vienna (K-H Mus.) and Washington (NG).

Yet another Vermeer was Jan II (son of Jan I and father of Jan III), a Haarlem landscape painter (1628–91), whose works are very like those of J. van Ruisdael or P. Koninck: examples are in The Hague and Rotterdam as well as London (Wellington Mus.), Oxford (Ch. Ch.) and Paris (Louvre).

VERMEYEN, Jan Cornelisz. (*c.*1500–59), was a Dutch painter and tapestry designer who was probably a pupil of MABUSE. About 1525 he became Court Painter to Margaret of Austria, Regent of the Netherlands, at Malines and in 1535 he accompanied the Emperor Charles V to Tunis. This journey supplied him with scenes for later works, including tapestries designed 1545/8 for the Regent, Mary of Hungary. At present many portraits are ascribed to him on very little evidence, as an alternative to SCOREL, HEEMSKERCK or LUCAS van Leyden. There are pictures in Amsterdam, Brussels, Florence, Haarlem, Karlsruhe, New York and Vienna (tapestry designs), and (as 'Style of Vermeyen') London and elsewhere.

VERNET. A family of French painters of whom the best known is (Claude) Joseph (1714–89), who painted landscapes in a sub-CLAUDE manner and worked for many years in Italy, where he was a friend of WILSON. He was in Rome in 1734, where he was influenced by Claude and Gaspar POUSSIN, as well as by Salvator ROSA in his slightly melodramatic shipwreck scenes. He returned to France in 1753 and spent the next ten years working on a series of the Ports of France, commissioned by Louis XV, of which he executed sixteen. The *Italian Landscape* of 1738 (London, Dulwich) is a good example of his early, Italianate, landscape style. He also painted dramatic shipwrecks of a highly romantic and rather theatrical kind. His father Antoine (1689–1753) and brothers François and Jean were also painters. Carle (1758–1836), son of Joseph, specialized in horses, racing, and battle scenes, the latter principally for Napoleon. Horace (1789–1863), son of Carle, also painted horses and battle scenes, as popular and facile as his father's. He remained an ardent Bonapartist, and his chief work was the huge Gallery of Battles at Versailles, painted for Louis Philippe. His sister married the costume-history painter Paul DELAROCHE.

VERNISSAGE *see* VARNISHING DAY.

VERONA, Stefano da, *see* STEFANO.

VERONESE, Bonifazio, *see* BONIFAZIO.

VERONESE, Paolo (*c*.1528–88), was born in Verona and trained under several minor artists. The chief influence on him was Titian, although such diverse artists as Michelangelo, Giulio Romano and Parmigianino all contributed to his formation. He worked in Venice, probably from 1553 onwards, when he began his ceilings for the Doge's Palace, with daring SOTTO IN SÙ perspective and Mannerist nude figures in complicated poses filling up the picture space. He is thought to have gone to Rome for the first time in 1560, and it was probably after this that he painted the frescoes in the Villa Maser (near Treviso), with their brilliant mixture of illusionism with Palladio's simple architecture. They are also important in the history of Venetian landscape painting.

He specialized mainly in huge pictures of Biblical, allegorical or historical subjects which allowed him to introduce vast crowds of accessory figures, filling the scene with light and colour, with splendid golden-haired women dressed in the height of fashion, with horses, dogs, apes, courtiers, musicians, soldiers and magnificent buildings, but almost devoid of religious or dramatic content. His gorgeous pageantry is redolent of the magnificence and luxury of 16th-century Venice; but the licence he took with sacred subjects (e.g. the *Feast in the House of Levi*, 1573, Venice, Accad.) got him into trouble with the Inquisition, which called him to account for the profane incidents – dogs, German soldiers and such improprieties – introduced into a religious picture. It seems to have been a *Last Supper*, but, because of the objections of the tribunal, it was renamed. The concept of decorum is fundamental to all Counter-Reformation art, and may be summed up in the exchange between Veronese and the Inquisitor:

Veronese: I paint my pictures with such judgement as I have and as seems fitting.

Inquisitor: And does it seem fitting to represent the Last Supper with buffoons, drunkards, German soldiers, dwarfs, and similar scurrilities?

His repudiation of any indecorum and his claim to an absolute right of pictorial licence has remained one of the classic defences of the artist against the Philistine (even though the Inquisitor seems to have out-argued him). Most of his works are in Venice, but other examples are in the Royal Coll. and Amsterdam, Baltimore (Mus. and Walters Gall.), Berlin, Boston (Mus. and Gardner Mus.), Brussels, Budapest, Caen, Cambridge (Fitzwm), Cambridge Mass. (Fogg), Chicago, Cleveland Ohio, Detroit, Dresden, Dublin, Edinburgh, the Escorial, Florence (Pitti and Uffizi), Greenville SC, Hartford Conn., Kansas City, Kingston Lacy Dorset (National Trust), Leningrad, London (NG, Courtauld Inst., Dulwich and Westminster Hospital), Los Angeles Cal., Madrid, Melbourne, Milan (Brera), Modena, Munich, New York (Met. Mus. and Frick Coll.), Ottawa, Oxford (Ashmolean and Ch. Ch.), Padua, Paris (Louvre), Philadelphia, Prague, Rome (Borghese and Capitoline), San Francisco, St Louis, Sarasota Fla (Ringling), Toledo Ohio, Verona, Vicenza, Vienna, Washington (NG) and elsewhere.

VERRIO, Antonio (1639–1707), was a Neapolitan painter who was an Agréé of the French Academy in 1671, and probably came to England in the next year. From about 1675 to 1684 he worked at Windsor and Whitehall (though little survives), and followed Lely as Court Painter in 1684. After 1688 he worked chiefly at Chatsworth and Burghley, but from 1699 he was employed extensively at Hampton Court and Windsor by William III. His decorations are gaudy and banal; they represent the tail-end of a Baroque tradition sufficiently novel in England to impress through pretentiousness, and blatant enough to dazzle eyes ignorant of the real thing. His greatest immortality is in Pope:

'On painted ceilings you devoutly stare,
Where sprawl the saints of Verrio and LAGUERRE'.

VERROCCHIO, Andrea del (*c*.1435–88), was a Florentine painter, goldsmith and sculptor. He may have been a pupil of Donatello, after whose death he ranked as the principal sculptor in the city. He executed many works for the Medici. His style as a sculptor is clearly established and is markedly different from that of Donatello, for Verrocchio is intent upon lightness, grace, elegance of pose, and highly finished craftsmanship, completely missing the tragic power of Donatello. The *David* (before 1476, Florence, Bargello), if compared with Donatello's bronze *David*, shows this difference; even more is it visible in Verrocchio's last work, the equestrian monument to Bartolommeo Colleone in Venice (commissioned *c*.1479, completed after Verroccchio's death by the bronze-founder Leopardi in 1495), where all his effort has been directed to the rendering of movement and of a sense of strain and energy. The Donatello monument to Gattamelata in Padua was obviously the model he sought to surpass, but he misses the air of calm command. Verrocchio ran a large and prosperous shop, accepting orders for paintings as well as sculpture and goldsmith's work. In later years his principal assistant in painting was Lorenzo di CREDI, but he was also the master (and probably employer) of LEONARDO da Vinci, who is supposed to have painted an angel in his *Baptism* (Florence, Uffizi). There are works by him, in painting or sculpture, in Berlin, Budapest, Edinburgh (NG), Florence (Bargello, Cathedral Mus., Orsanmichele, S. Lorenzo and Pal. della Signoria), London (NG, V&A and Courtauld Inst.), New York (Met. Mus.), Paris (Louvre), Pistoia (Cath.), Toledo Ohio and Washington (NG).

VERTUE, George (1684–1756), was an engraver and antiquary who is now remembered as the father of English art history.

> With manners gentle, and a grateful heart,
> And all the genius of the graphic art,
> His fame shall each succeeding artist own
> Longer by far than monuments of stone.

His voluminous, ill-written, and rambling notes on the arts in England, especially on his immediate predecessors and contemporaries, are our principal source and have now been published *in extenso*. They were originally bought by Horace Walpole, and, reduced to order, served as the basis of his 'Anecdotes of Painting in England' (1762–71).

VESPERBILD *see* PIETÀ.

VIEIRA da Silva, Maria Elena (*b*.1908), was born in Lisbon, but became French and lived in Paris. From 1927, she studied sculpture with Bourdelle and Despiau, print-making with Hayter, and painting with Léger and Friesz. From Expressionist beginnings, she developed, during the 1930s, into an abstract painter, creating elaborate expanding linear patterns which seem to be based on intricate town plans or the intersecting wires of a suspension bridge.

VIEN, Joseph (1716–1809), was a French painter who was in Rome 1743–50 under de TROY; he probably knew the young MENGS at that time, when all Rome was excited by the antique Roman paintings newly discovered in Herculaneum and Pompeii, and by Greek classical architecture at Paestum. This revival of interest in the antique made him the more receptive to Winckelmann's Neoclassicist ideas on their publication in 1755 and 1764, an influence reinforced by his long and close association with the amateur archaeologist, the Comte de Caylus. He returned to Rome as Director of the French Academy there 1775–81. His cold, prim, classical genre subjects depict Greek maidens of whom Diderot remarked that they induced 'no desire to be their lover, only their father or brother', yet he achieved enormous prestige, and was the chief teacher of the period; his most celebrated pupil was DAVID. Diderot probably had in mind his *Marchande d'Amours* (1763, Fontainebleau), which is based on a rediscovered wall-painting in Pompeii. Many of his works are in Montpellier, but a fine portrait, of 1757 and not at all Neoclassic, is in Rome (Doria).

VIGÉE-LEBRUN, Louise Élisabeth (1755–1842), one of the most successful of all women painters, was the daughter of a pastellist named Vigée and married the dealer Lebrun, who was consistently unfaithful and stole most of her earnings. She was trained by her father and influenced by GREUZE, and got her great chance when she was summoned to Versailles in 1779 to paint Marie Antoinette. She became her friend, as well as Painter to the Queen, was elected to the Academy in 1783, and kept a famous Salon. She was in fact a charming woman. She left France in 1789, at the outbreak of the Revolution, and went to Italy, Vienna, Prague and Dresden, and was in Russia 1795–1800 before returning to Berlin and, in 1802, to Paris. She had received permission to return, but disliked society under Napoleon and left at once for England, where she stayed until 1805, before going to Switzerland and so back to France. In all these countries she had great success as a portraitist, excelling in portraits of women and children. She wrote her Memoirs, which give a picture of the times as well as an account of her works (they were first published in

1835–7; two English translations exist). Her portraits may be found in most of the places she worked in, and there are other examples in London (Wallace Coll. and NG) and in Brighton, Kansas City, New York (Met. Mus.), Toledo Ohio and Waddesdon Bucks. (National Trust).

VILLON, Jacques (1875–1963). His full name was Gaston Duchamp-Villon, and he was the brother of Marcel DUCHAMP and Raymond DUCHAMP-VILLON. He went to Paris in 1895 and became a friend of Toulouse-Lautrec, making satirical drawings for illustrated papers (later he earned his living as an engraver). He became a Cubist in 1911 and in 1912 organized the SECTION D'OR exhibition with GLEIZES, METZINGER, LÉGER and La Fresnaye. He visited the USA in 1935 and began gradually to make a name, but in 1940, when he fled to the Tarn in southern France, he began painting landscapes which, though abstract, have a feeling for locality. Big exhibitions in 1951 and 1961 in Paris established his reputation. There are works in Paris (Mus. d'Art Moderne).

VILLON, Raymond Duchamp-, *see* DUCHAMP-VILLON.

VINCENT, George (1796–1832), *see* NORWICH SCHOOL.

VINCI, Leonardo da, *see* LEONARDO.

VINGT, Les (Les XX), were twenty painters, including ENSOR, who formed an exhibiting society in Brussels in 1884 which lasted for ten years and showed non-Belgian artists such as Seurat (1887, *Grande Jatte*), Gauguin (1889), Cézanne and van Gogh (1890), but rejected Ensor himself in 1889.

VIRGO Master, *see* MASTER OF THE VIRGO INTER VIRGINES.

VISCHER. A Nuremberg family of bronzeworkers and sculptors, the most celebrated of whom, Peter I and II, were Dürer's contemporaries. The family workshop was started by Hermann (*d.*1488), who was the father of Peter I (*c.*1460–1529). Peter was trained by his father and became a Master in 1489, after which he travelled to Heidelberg and Cracow, but not to Italy, although the influence of Renaissance ideas can be seen in his work, even if far less powerfully than in Dürer. The real problem concerns the exact shares of the various members of the family in their masterpiece, the Shrine of S. Sebaldus in Nuremberg. The first design (now in Vienna, Akad.) is signed by Peter I and dated 1488, but the actual work was begun, on a new design, in 1508, worked on for four years and then completed 1514–19. After 1512, Peter I was working on a Tomb at Innsbruck for the Emperor Maximilian, and it is likely that his sons, Hermann and Peter II, took an increasing share of the Sebaldus Shrine, especially in the second phase: nevertheless, the *Apostles* may be by him. The most important of his sons was Peter II (1487–1528), who may have visited Italy, and who made the statuettes on the Sebaldus Shrine.

VITTORIA, Alessandro (1525–1608), became the greatest 16th-century Venetian sculptor, the equal of his master Jacopo SANSOVINO, and the peer of his friends Titian, Tintoretto, Veronese and Palladio. Born in Trento, he learned there a style dependent on a Donatellesque tradition, but in 1543 he was sent to Venice to the Sansovino shop. Their difficult relations were exacerbated by Vittoria's discovery of Mannerism, inspired by AMMANATI as well as by Michelangelo and Parmigianino (whose drawings he bought). In 1547 he left Venice and worked in Vicenza until, in 1553, Titian and Aretino reconciled him with Sansovino and he returned to collaborate with him on decorations in the Doge's Palace and Sansovino's Library, both of which show influences from GIULIO Romano's Palazzo del Tè and from FONTAINEBLEAU. From 1557 until his partial retirement in 1599 he ran a large workshop in Venice with many pupils: his most important works are the vivid but dignified portrait-busts of Venetian notables, one of the best of which is the self-portrait on his tomb in S. Zaccaria (begun 1602). There are many works in Venetian churches, palaces and galleries: others are in Berlin, Chicago, Florence (Bargello), London (NG and V&A), New York (Met. Mus.), Padua, Rome (Pal. Venezia), Rotterdam, Vienna and Washington. The Villa Maser, near Treviso, is a splendid example of collaboration between Palladio, Veronese and Vittoria.

VIVARINI. A family of Venetian painters, consisting of Antonio (active 1440?–*d.*1476/84), his brother Bartolommeo (active 1450–99), and Antonio's son Alvise (alive in 1457–*d.*1503/5). Antonio was the partner of his brother-in-law, Giovanni d'Alemagna, whose name may imply that he was a German. Antonio signed a picture in 1440 (Parenzo, now called Poreč, nr Trieste) by himself, but he seems to have worked with Giovanni until 1450 (when Giovanni probably died), and then he went into partnership with his brother Bartolommeo. The pictures produced by both partnerships were influenced first by Gentile da Fabriano and then by Mantegna and Giovanni Bellini – i.e. the successive leaders of Venetian painting. There is a picture signed by Antonio alone and dated 1464 in the Vatican; one signed by Bartolommeo and dated 1459 in Paris (Louvre), as well as others up to 1491: it is doubtful whether it is worth the trouble to distinguish further. Alvise was the son of Antonio but perhaps the pupil of Bartolommeo: the important influences on him were ANTONELLO da Messina and Giovanni BELLINI. He was a child in 1457, but the earliest signed and dated work is of 1475 (a polyptych in Urbino). In 1488 he offered to paint a ceiling in the Doge's Palace for nothing. His offer was accepted and two other pictures were commissioned from him, but the first two were never completed and the third was never begun. In 1507 Giovanni Bellini's shop carried out the completion of the first two and painted the third. An altarpiece in S.M. de' Frari, Venice, was completed after Alvise's death in 1503/5 by another Bellinesque, Marco Basaiti. There are examples of one or more of the family in London (NG and Courtauld Inst.), New York (Met. Mus.), Tours, Washington (NG) and Yale, as well as in the Accademia and the churches of Venice.

VIVIN, Louis (1861–1936), was a French modern primitive who worked in the Post Office, 1879–1922, and first exhibited at the Post Office Art Club in 1889. He was – like SÉRAPHINE – discovered by the German critic Uhde in 1925. His works consist largely of naively realist townscapes, and often seem to be inspired by picture-postcard views (cf. UTRILLO). There are works in Paris (Mus. d'Art Moderne).

VLAMINCK, Maurice (1876–1958), was one of the FAUVE group, and shared a studio with Derain. He wrote, played the violin, was a racing cyclist, and loved speed, crowds and popular amusements. He admired van Gogh in 1901, Negro sculpture about 1904 and Cézanne in 1907, and denounced CUBISM as over-intellectual and sterile. He painted chiefly landscapes of stormy weather, where the feeling is Expressionist and the dark shadows, strong light effects and wild skies are rendered in a technique in which the slashing brush-stroke and heavy impasto are largely derived from Courbet – an artist whom he resembled in some ways. Most museums of modern art have examples.

VLIEGER, Simon de (1600/1–53), was one of the leading Dutch marine painters of the first half of the 17th century. He was a pupil of W. van de VELDE the Elder and the teacher of W. van de VELDE the Younger, and he also exerted a great influence on CAPPELLE, who owned 1,300 drawings and nine paintings by him. His principal paintings are of the sea and are representative of the period of Dutch marine painting which concentrated on the rendering of light effects in subdued local colours. He also made twenty etchings of landscapes and animals. He painted a great many pictures, and is well represented in museums.

VORTICISM. A variety of CUBISM, peculiar to England, invented by Wyndham LEWIS.

VOS, Cornelis de (1584–1651), was an Antwerp portrait painter who occasionally worked for Rubens; some of his portraits have been mistaken for those of Rubens or van Dyck. He also painted large historical and allegorical works. There are examples in Antwerp, Berlin, Birmingham, Brussels, London (Wallace Coll.), Madrid, Munich, Philadelphia (Mus.), San Francisco (Legion of Honor), Vienna, York and elsewhere.

His brother Paul (1596–1678), was a painter of lively hunting scenes and large still-life subjects with dead game, fruit and live birds and animals. Their sister married SNYDERS, with whose art Paul's has much in common, and they were close friends of van DYCK.

VOS, Marten de (1531/2–1603), was an Antwerp painter of the last generation of Italianizers (*see* SPRANGER). He spent six years in Italy, in Rome and then in Venice, where he is said to have worked as a landscape assistant to Tintoretto. He brought the Venetian style back to Antwerp, where he returned in 1558, and painted many altarpieces there (especially after the destruction caused in the Spanish Fury of 1576), as well as some portraits. There are works in Amsterdam, Antwerp, Berlin, Brussels, Florence (Uffizi), The Hague, Paris (Louvre), Rouen, Stockholm and Vienna.

VOUET, Simon (1590–1649), was in Italy between 1612 and 1627. Between 1624 and 1627 he was Principe of the Accademia di S. Luca in Rome, until he returned to France to enjoy a successful career as a painter of large decorations and smaller, highly decorative, religious and allegorical works. He derived from his years in Rome, and his visits to Venice, Naples, Genoa and elsewhere, a form of temperate and classicized Baroque which he infused into French painting, and he also adapted to his own uses the cool colour of CHAMPAIGNE, the classical composition of POUSSIN and the richness of Venetian handling. Poussin's return to Paris in 1640 put him on his mettle (particularly in view of Louis XIII's malicious remark which Poussin records with disingenuous satisfaction, and which may be freely translated as 'Here's one in the eye for Vouet'), but after 1642 his position remained unchallenged, except by LEBRUN. There are works in the Royal Coll. and Arles, Berlin, Brussels, Cambridge (Fitzwm), Chatsworth, Cincinnati, Cleveland Ohio, Dresden, Dublin, Florence (Uffizi), Fontainebleau, Genoa, Glasgow, Greenville SC, Hartford Conn., Leningrad, London (NG), Los Angeles, Madrid, Munich, Naples, Ottawa, Oxford, Paris (Louvre and many churches), Rome (S. Francesco a Ripa, S. Lorenzo in Lucina and Corsini), Rouen, Sarasota Fla, Tours, Versailles, Vienna, Washington (NG) and many French provincial museums.

Simon's younger brother Aubin (1595–1641), worked with him in Rome 1619/20–2. He painted three MAIS (1632, 1639 and 1640) for Notre-Dame, Paris.

VRIES, Adriaen de (*c.*1560–1626), was one of the leading Late Mannerist sculptors whose career well exemplifies the internationalism of the period: he was born in The Hague, trained in Italy, and worked mainly in Prague. He was trained as a bronzeworker under Giovanni BOLOGNA (a Fleming in spite of his name) and, from 1593, he worked for the Emperor Rudolf II in Prague, but he also made two Fountains in Augsburg (*Mercury*, completed 1599, and *Hercules*, 1602) and works for Bückeburg and Stadthagen. There are also examples in Edinburgh, London (NG and V&A), Paris (Louvre), Stockholm and Vienna.

VROOM, Hendrick Cornelisz. (1566–1640), was born in Haarlem and became one of the founders of Dutch marine painting. He travelled a great deal (and became very rich), spending two years in Rome, where he met Paul BRIL, before returning to Haarlem and then being shipwrecked off the coast of Portugal, *c.*1590. According to van MANDER, the local inhabitants had suffered much from English pirates and Vroom's life was in danger until he showed his ability as an artist; whereupon it was decided that he was 'not an Englishman, but a Christian'. His pupils included VLIEGER, who in turn was the teacher of the greatest of Dutch marine painters, Willem II van de VELDE. Works by Vroom are in Amsterdam, Haarlem and London (Nat. Marit. Mus.).

His son, Cornelis (1591/2–1661), may have worked in England for Charles I in 1627. He painted little, but his works were marines, like his father's, and, later, landscapes, the earliest of which is dated 1622. There is one of 1626 in London (NG).

VUILLARD, Édouard (1868–1940), was a NABI and an Intimist painter and decorator whose career closely paralleled that of his friend BONNARD, but who, in many ways, is closer to SICKERT. He experimented with mixed media and also made colour lithographs. There are pictures by him in Birmingham, Boston, Bristol, Cambridge Mass. (Fogg), Cleveland Ohio, Edinburgh (NG), Glasgow, Liverpool, London (NG, Tate and Courtauld Inst.), Manchester (Whitworth), New York (M of MA), Northampton Mass., Paris (Mus. d'Orsay and Mus. d'Art Moderne), Toronto and Washington (Phillips), and decorations in Paris (Comédie des Champs-Élysées and Pal. de Chaillot) and Geneva (League of Nations).

W

WALDMÜLLER, Ferdinand Georg (1793–1865), was the leading Austrian artist of the early 19th century, painting BIEDERMEIER portraits (often compared with INGRES's) and landscapes, which later approached the *plein-air* works of the BARBIZON group. He was trained at the Vienna Academy, and from 1829 was a professor there, but he was bitterly opposed to the teaching methods of his colleagues and wrote many pamphlets on the subject. For a time he was put on half-pay. He visited Italy in 1829 (the first of many visits), Paris in 1830, and in 1856 he started out for Philadelphia, but stopped in London, where, through the intervention of the British Ambassador in Vienna, he succeeded in selling thirty-one pictures to Queen Victoria, Prince Albert and the Court. The best collection of his works is in Vienna (Oesterreichische Gal.), but many other Austrian and German galleries have examples; the pictures sold in London seem to have disappeared, except for two in Osborne House (Royal Coll.).

WALKER, Robert (*c.*1605/10–56/8), is chiefly known for his portraits of Cromwell and his circle. The usual way of putting it is that DOBSON painted the Royalists and Walker the Parliamentarians. There are works in Huntingdon (Cromwell Mus.), Leeds (Temple Newsam, a *Cromwell*), London (NPG), Oxford (Ashmolean) and elsewhere.

WALL-PAINTING, or mural, is a term used to describe any kind of wall decoration: it is not interchangeable with FRESCO.

WALL-TOMB. A form of funerary monument with a particularly significant development in Italy. It seems first to appear during the Dugento as a product of the COSMATI workshops: a ciborium or aedicule enclosing a sarcophagus (often antique) raised upon a Cosmatesque base (Cardinal Fieschi, *d.*1256: Rome, S. Lorenzo Fuori). During the late Dugento, the classical type of aedicule was replaced by a Gothic tabernacle (Clement IV, *c.*1270, Viterbo, by Pietro di Oderisio), and then further sculpture was added, as in the de Braye Monument (*d.*1282: S. Domenico, Orvieto) by ARNOLFO di Cambio, where the Virgin and Child and patron saints are in niches above the sarcophagus with angels drawing aside curtains to reveal the effigy: or the Petroni Monument (Siena, *c.*1319–20) by TINO di Camaino, where the sarcophagus is borne on figures of Virtues and surmounted by pinnacled niches enclosing further statues. During the Quattrocento, the type was used by DONATELLO and MICHELOZZO for the tomb of the Antipope John XXIII (Baptistry, Florence, 1427) and received its greatest elaboration at the hands of Bernardo ROSSELLINO (Bruni Tomb: Sta Croce, 1444/50), DESIDERIO da Settignano (Marsuppini Tomb, *d.*1453: Sta Croce), Antonio ROSSELLINO (Cardinal of Portugal: S. Miniato, 1461–6), and MINO da Fiesole (Count Ugo: Badia, Florence, 1469–81). In Rome, the tomb of Innocent VIII by POLLAIUOLO (St Peter's, 1492–8) set a new pattern for papal tombs by including a statue of the living pope enthroned and blessing, together with his recumbent effigy on the sarcophagus. In Venice, the type was varied by being raised above ground level as in the Foscari Monument (Frari, *c.*1457) by Antonio BREGNO, but examples such as the Tron Monument by Antonio RIZZO (Frari, 1476–82) consist of a vast edifice peopled by saints, virtues, the Risen Christ, effigies of the Doge living and dead, and decorative reliefs, all in an elaborate architectural framework. In Rome, during the Cinquecento, Andrea SANSOVINO continued with ever more elaborate and intricate examples, such as those in S.M. del Popolo commissioned by Julius II (finished by 1509), while in Florence the culmination was reached by MICHELANGELO in the Medici Tombs in S. Lorenzo, and by the final form of the Julius Monument in S. Pietro in Vincoli in Rome. During the late Cinquecento, the enormous tombs of Pius V (1586–7) and Sixtus V (1589–90), orchestrated rather than merely assembled by the architect Domenico Fontana in S.M. Maggiore in Rome, pushed the type to its extreme, whole chapel walls being covered by a medley of sarcophagus, effigy, statue, reliefs of incidents from the pontiff's life, attendant figures of saints and virtues and decorative adjuncts. Finally, during the Baroque era, although the wall-tomb was still used, as for example BERNINI's Monument to the Countess Matilda (St Peter's, mid-1630s), the trend was towards deep niches filled with free-standing sarcophagus and statues, although the original inspiration of the wall-tomb survives in, for instance, CANOVA's Stuart Monument in St Peter's (1819).

WANDERJAHRE (Ger. wander years). In the North of Europe it was common for a young artist to complete his apprenticeship in his home town and then to spend several years as a JOURNEYMAN, wandering from one famous master's shop to another and working for a while in each until he returned home, submitted his masterpiece (in the literal sense) to his GUILD, married and settled down. Reade's novel 'The Cloister and the Hearth' gives a picture of this life and Dürer's career affords another.

WARD, James (1769–1859), was a British landscape and animal painter whose early work was influenced by that of his brother-in-law George MORLAND. In 1803 his style was much affected by Rubens's *Château de Steen* (London, NG). His best work is the vast *Gordale Scar, Yorkshire*, which is one of many works by him in the Tate, London. Others are in Bradford, Cardiff, Edinburgh (NG), Leeds and Yale (CBA).

WARHOL (Warhola), Andy (1928/31, probably 1930–87), was born in Chicago to immigrant Ruthenian parents. He started as a commercial artist, but by the 1960s was recognized as a leader of New York POP, along with WESSELMANN and LICHTENSTEIN. He used the commercial technique of SERIGRAPHY to make multiple images of e.g. Marilyn Monroe, and paintings of *100 Soup Cans* (Darmstadt) and *Green Coca-Cola Bottles* (New York, Whitney), but he soon turned over production to 'The Factory', a collection of hangers-on who also served as actors in his films, which included an unchanging eight-hour view of the Empire State Building. One of these young women shot and seriously wounded him in 1968. He claimed that 'everyone should be famous for 15 minutes' and 'everybody should be a machine', art being a mechanical process. His personal life was quite different from his extravagant public image. London (Tate), New York (M of MA) and other modern museums have examples.

WARM COLOUR, TONE. Those colours and tones which are red, orange or purplish in general effect. Not necessarily HOT, but the opposite of COLD.

WASTE-MOULD *see* PLASTER CASTING.

WATERCOLOUR. The technique of painting with colour ground up with water-soluble gums (gum arabic, etc.). When moistened with plain water a transparent stain is obtained which is then applied in washes to white or tinted paper. The classical English method – and pure watercolour is almost an English monopoly, although DÜRER and many Dutch 17th-century painters were first in the field – is to use the white paper as the highest lights and to apply transparent washes one over another to obtain gradations of colour and of tone: to the purists of this school the use of any form of BODY COLOUR is Frenchified and anathema. Nevertheless, the four greatest practitioners – J. R. COZENS, GIRTIN, COTMAN and TURNER – all used procedures which vary from the norm defined above. The watercolours of Cozens are perhaps nearest to this norm, but he retained the monochromatic underpainting used by the earliest exponents as a legacy from oil technique. Turner not only used body colour freely, but also wiped partially dry colour with rags and sponges and scratched the surface of the paper with a knife to get extra lights: this last practice is now regarded with peculiar horror, but is triumphantly vindicated by his late Venetian scenes.

WATTEAU, (Jean) Antoine (1684–1721), was born in Valenciennes, a Flemish town which had recently become French. To a contemporary Watteau was *Vato, peintre flamand*, and his Flemish background probably explains his admiration for (and obscure affinity with) Rubens, whose healthy vitality expressed everything Watteau could only envy. He went to Paris *c.*1702 and worked as a hack painter before going to Gillot, a painter of theatrical scenes, in 1704/5. By then he had probably already contracted tuberculosis and was already exhibiting the symptoms of chronic restlessness which dominated the rest of his short life. By 1707/8 he had moved on to the decorative painter Claude Audran, who, as Keeper of the Luxembourg Palace, was able to give him access to the great Rubens cycle of the *Life of Marie de' Medici*: this was the main influence in the formation of his style, and the drawings he then made were used over and over again. In 1709 he revisited Valenciennes and painted a few military scenes in a Flemish manner, but on his return to Paris he was able to study the great Venetians, especially Veronese, and he then merged all these influences into a completely personal form of RUBÉNISME. In 1712 he was made an Agréé of the Academy and he should then have submitted a Diploma Work, but he delayed this until 1717 when he presented the *Embarkation for the Island of Cythera* (now in the Louvre; a later version in Berlin) and was received as a painter of *fêtes galantes*, the first to be so described. The difficulty felt by the Academy in classifying him is understandable, for, like Giorgione's, his pictures have a mood for a subject, a fleeting and melancholy sense of the transitoriness of all pleasure and all life. Indeed, it has been suggested that the *Embarkation* is *from*, rather than *for*, Cythera, and the reluctance of the ladies is due to a desire to prolong the pleasures of love. In 1719–20 Watteau was in London, perhaps to seek medical advice, but a London winter completed the ruin of his constitution and he returned to Paris to die. One of the last pictures he painted, the *Halt in the Chase* (London, Wallace Coll.), is in the same style as his previous works, but the shop-sign he painted in 1720–1 for his friend the dealer Gersaint (known as the *Enseigne de Gersaint*, now in Berlin) shows a new stylistic trend. The sign is bigger (3 m. wide) than his usual small size, and it represents the interior of Gersaint's shop, full of customers and assistants, with a greater degree of realism than was usual with Watteau. The new style was in fact a return to Flemish naturalism, owing much to TENIERS (who had also influenced his early military scenes), but his death prevented any further development along these lines. His theatrical subjects are far less realistic, although they derive from the painstaking representations of Gillot. They usually show figures from the Italian or French Comedy in more or less melancholy and reflective attitudes. All Watteau's pictures – except the *Enseigne* – were composed by taking the required number of figures from the big bound volumes in which he kept hundreds of his superb drawings. Studies of figures, heads, hands, draperies, were made *à TROIS CRAYONS* – black, red and white for the highlights – and were then used when needed. Many hundreds of these still exist, usually in better condition than most of his paintings, which have suffered badly from his atrocious technique. Because the same drawing may have been used over and over again all his pictures have a strong family likeness, increasing the sense of half-attained intimacy. LANCRET and PATER were his principal imitators, but neither was gifted with his exquisite sensibility, and his tender amorousness coarsens under their hands. There are several pictures by Watteau in the Wallace Coll., and others in Berlin, Birmingham (Barber Inst.), Boston, Chantilly, Cleveland Ohio, Dresden, Edinburgh (NG), Glasgow, Hartford Conn., Leningrad, London (NG, Soane Mus. and Dulwich), Madrid, New York (Met. Mus.), Paris (Louvre), Stockholm, Toledo Ohio, Troyes, Waddesdon Bucks. (National Trust) and Washington (NG).

His nephew and great-nephew, Louis Joseph (1731–98) and François Louis Joseph (1758–1823), were both known as 'Watteau de Lille'. Louis was born in Valenciennes but went to Lille in 1755 and taught drawing from the nude there: this caused such scandal that he had to resign and did not return until 1775. He did not always imitate his uncle's works, often painting histories or religious pictures. His son worked in a style closer to his great-uncle's, and, like him, was influenced by Teniers. Lille has examples of both men.

WATTS, George Frederic (1817–1904), first exhibited, with success, at the RA in 1837, and in 1843 won a £300 prize in one of the competitions for the decoration of the Houses of Parliament. He left at once for Florence, where he stayed until 1847, leading the sheltered life of a tame genius in the household of the British Minister at the Tuscan Court, Lord Holland. In 1847 he again won a prize in a Houses of Parliament competition, this time for £500, and he started to paint large allegorical pictures while earning his living as a portraitist. His portraits of beauties and celebrities make a real attempt at more than a successful superficial likeness; in his series of famous men he strove to portray the whole man – character, personality and appearance – and for this reason would only paint men he could like or admire. His decorations are either frankly decorative stories, such as his *Tales from Boccaccio* (1843–4, Tate), with areas of crude, warring colour, applied flatly within a strongly marked contour, or huge turgid allegories, expressing in trite, rather literary, symbolism such moral imponderables as *Mammon*, *Progress*, *Destiny*, *Chaos*, *Love and Death*. The best known of these is probably *Hope*, which, it has been objected, could as easily portray *Despair*. He attempted to revive fresco painting, of which he had no proper knowledge, and in his allegories often used appalling technical methods which have resulted in considerable deterioration. He also executed some large pieces of sculpture; the best known are the *Physical Energy* in Kensington Gardens, and the huge *Tennyson* monument at

Lincoln. He became an RA in 1867, twice refused a baronetcy, but accepted the Order of Merit in 1902. Watts was one of the last grand allegorical history painters in the Haydon tradition of 'High Art': a type of picture based on high-minded generalities or abstractions, expressed with idealized forms, and a striving for sublime feeling that results in a numbing divorce from reality, physical and intellectual. There are examples in the Royal Coll., Bristol, Compton nr Guildford (Watts Mus. in his former house), Dublin (Municipal Gall.), Edinburgh (NG), Leicester, Liverpool (Walker), London (Tate, NPG, V&A and Leighton House), Manchester, Munich, New York (Met. Mus.), Northampton, Ottawa, Oxford (Ashmolean), Paris (Louvre) and elsewhere. A large mural, *Justice*, is in London, The New Hall, Lincoln's Inn (1853–9).

WEENIX, Jan Baptist (1621–before November 1663), was a pupil of BLOEMAERT who was in Italy 1642–6 and returned, calling himself 'Giovanni Battista', to Holland to paint Italianate landscapes with ruins of ancient buildings and figures in modern dress, very reminiscent of the work of BERCHEM. Later in life he changed his style entirely and painted still-life and some portraits, his very detailed style being continued by his son Jan. There are typical works in Amsterdam, Antwerp, Berlin, Brighton, Dresden, Edinburgh, Glasgow, Hartford Conn., London (NG, Wallace Coll. and Kenwood), New York (Met. Mus.), Paris (Louvre), Rotterdam, Utrecht (including a *Descartes*) and Vienna.

WEENIX, Jan (1642?–1719), was the son of Jan Baptist Weenix, and was his father's pupil with his cousin HONDECOETER. He never visited Italy, but he painted Italianate scenes like his father's and pursued more single-mindedly the still-life with flowers, animals and dead game subjects which he also took over from his father. He worked mainly in Amsterdam, but also at Bensberg and Düsseldorf for the Elector Palatine, for whom he executed a huge series of still-lifes (1702–12). There are works in Amsterdam (Rijksmus.), Augsburg, Barnsley, Cape Town, Dresden, The Hague, London (NG, Dulwich and sixteen still-lifes in the Wallace Coll.), Munich, New York (Met. Mus.), Oxford, Paris (Petit Pal.), Toronto and elsewhere.

WEEPERS. Small mourning figures on a tomb.

WEICHER STIL *see* SOFT STYLE.

WERFF, Adriaen van der (1659–1722), was, according to Houbraken, his contemporary, the greatest of all Dutch painters. He worked in Rotterdam for most of his life, but his great patron, the Elector Palatine at Düsseldorf, took most of his output. His highly detailed style was a mixture of the *fijnschilder* tradition of DOU with 17th-century French classicism, consisting mainly of allegories and mythologies with highly-polished female nudes – *Diana*, *Venus* and so on. There are examples in Amsterdam (Rijksmus.), London (NG, Wallace Coll. and Dulwich) and Paris (Louvre).

WERVE, Claus de, *see* SLUTER.

WESSELMANN, Tom (*b.*1931), like WARHOL, is a representative of American POP ART. Most of his work consists of highly erotic nudes (or details of female anatomy) which, in a long series called *Great American Nude*, treat women as commercialized sex packages.

WEST, Benjamin (1728–1820), came of Pennsylvania Quaker stock, and learned to paint in America. In 1760 he went to Italy, and spent three years in Rome, Florence, Bologna and Venice. He enjoyed the prestige of novelty – American painters were unknown and the blind Cardinal Albani asked if he were not a Red Indian? He was much influenced by the Neoclassical style of MENGS and Gavin HAMILTON and evolved, partly through them and partly because of his lack of academic training, history pictures on a smallish scale (what Haydon dubbed 'Poussin size'). He set up as a portrait painter in London in 1763, working in a style close to Mengs, was a Founder-Member of the RA, and in 1769 began his long, and highly profitable, association with George III. His *Death of Wolfe* (RA 1771: Ottawa and many versions) marked a turning-point in the painting of modern history pieces in England, since West, whose picture is, in fact, historically inaccurate, imposed a classical composition on figures in contemporary dress. He carried the idea further in his pictures of medieval history subjects, and established a fashion not only popular in England but widely imitated in France. Such was his prestige and his favour with George III that he succeeded Reynolds as President of the RA in 1792, but refused a knighthood because of his Quaker principles (or, as his biographer suggested, because it was not good enough).

Seven of his series on Revealed Religion, commissioned by George III for his chapel, but returned to West when the king went mad, are now in Greenville SC (Bob Jones Univ.).

He was very kind and helpful to other American painters – e.g. STUART, ALLSTON, COPLEY, DUNLAP, MORSE, the PEALES, SULLY and TRUMBULL – and thus really founded the American School, in spite of the fact that he was born a British subject, left America at 21, and remained a Loyalist.

There are many works in the Royal Coll., and in Glasgow, Leeds, Lincoln, Liverpool, London (Tate, RA, V&A, Coram Fdn, Nat. Marit. Mus. and Dulwich), Wakefield and a great number of American museums.

WESTMACOTT, Sir Richard (1775–1856), was the son of a sculptor, whose pupil he was before he went to Rome, where he worked under CANOVA. He was in Italy from 1793 to 1797, and on his way home was robbed and wounded by bandits. He enjoyed a large and successful practice in London, working for Queen Charlotte and at Brighton Pavilion for the Prince Regent, executing panels for the Marble Arch, the *Achilles* in Hyde Park as a memorial to Wellington, and the pediment of the British Museum. He became an RA in 1811, succeeded Flaxman as professor of sculpture at the RA Schools, and was knighted in 1837. He made a number of tombs in Westminster Abbey, including those of Fox (1810), which included the figure of a negro, highly praised by Canova, and Pitt the Elder, and in many parish churches all over England.

WEYDEN, Roger van der, or Rogier de le Pasture (1399/1400–1464), was the major artist of the mid-15th century in Flanders. He was almost certainly a pupil of Robert CAMPIN in Tournai, 1427–32, at the same time as DARET. Like Daret, he seems to have been older than most apprentices, since there is a record in 1426 of the Town Council of Tournai making a gift of wine to 'Master Roger'. One possible explanation for the fact that both he and Daret seemed to have started their apprenticeships at a much later age than usual may be found in the conservative and strict rules of the Tournai Guild. It is known that in 1432, immediately after he became a Master in the Guild, Daret was made Provost so it is possible that both men were apprenticed only in a technical sense. Nevertheless, the identification of Campin with the MASTER

OF FLÉMALLE is fundamentally due to the close stylistic similarity between the work of Flémalle and the one documented altarpiece by Daret. This has led some scholars to assume that the stylistic similarity between the work of Flémalle and the work of Roger is to be explained by the fact that both men were one and the same person. More common, however, is the view that Roger's early work resembles the Flémalle group for the same reason as Daret's does – namely, that Roger and Daret were both Campin's pupils.

The problem would be greatly simplified if we had any real knowledge of Roger's early style, but in fact there are no works by him which are certainly documented. What is generally considered to be his masterpiece is the *Deposition* (Madrid, Prado) which is one of the great masterpieces of Northern 15th-century painting. It is quite unlike the work of Jan van EYCK and has a depth of religious feeling, expressed in linear terms, quite different from the dispassionate realism of Jan: Roger's more emotional style was far more influential in Flanders and in Germany in the second half of the 15th century. Nevertheless, the *Deposition* is believed to be Roger's solely on the strength of a 16th-century attribution, and its date is put at about 1435 on rather slender evidence. There are, however, a few pictures generally attributed to him – the *Braque Triptych* in Paris, the Bladelin altarpiece in Berlin, the *Last Judgement* in the Hospice at Beaune in Burgundy – which can be given approximate dates in the 1440s and 1450s. The general feeling of this group of works is far more refined and sensitive than that associated with the realistic but rather plebeian style of Campin/Flémalle, so that there seems little reason to try to fuse the two groups of works. Equally, Roger's works are more concerned with human emotion than those of Jan van Eyck, which tend to concentrate on naturalistic detail in the creation of a miniature world. Roger's colour sense is also highly personal, with a tendency towards the use of gold and pale, bright colours which, in the 15th century, may already have seemed slightly old-fashioned.

Roger married a Brussels woman *c.*1426, and after completing his apprenticeship with Campin, settled in Brussels. He became, before 1436, the City Painter, and achieved a great reputation and a solid fortune. In 1450, the year of the Jubilee, he probably visited Rome and also Florence, since the *Entombment* (Uffizi), once in the Medici Coll., has strong affinities not only with Italian art generally but with Fra Angelico specifically, and the *Madonna with four Saints* (Frankfurt, Städel) not only bears the arms of Florence and contains the Medici patron saints, Cosmas and Damian, and SS. John Baptist and Peter, name-saints of Cosimo's two sons, but also reflects in its composition the Italian SACRA CONVERSAZIONE type of Domenico Veneziano's St Lucy Altar. Roger never held a Court appointment, as Jan did, but he nevertheless worked for many members of the Burgundian Court, such as Chancellor Rolin, for whose foundation, the Hospice de Beaune, he painted the *Last Judgement*, *c.*1446 (still there); Peter Bladelin, Duke Philip's controller of finances and founder of Middelburg, for whose church the triptych of the *Nativity* (*c.*1452, Berlin) was painted; Jean Chevrot, Bishop of Tournai (*The Seven Sacraments*, Antwerp, *c.*1453). He also painted superb and sensitive portraits, such as *Charles the Bold* (Berlin), *Le Grand Bâtard* of Burgundy (Brussels), *Francisque d'Este* (New York, Met. Mus.). He appears to have invented the type of diptych with a Madonna and Child on one wing facing a praying donor portrait on the other, and though none survives intact, the *Philippe de Croy* (Antwerp) and *Madonna* (San Marino Cal., Huntington) and *Laurent Froiment* (Brussels) and *Madonna* (Caen) may be cited. This type of diptych became very popular and perhaps the best surviving complete example is that by his pupil MEMLINC of Martin Nieuwenhove, while many others were executed in the BOUTS workshop. His most closely datable work is the unusual *Braque Triptych* (*c.*1452, Louvre), which displays all his characteristics of colour, feeling and technique.

Other works are in Berlin, Boston, Brussels, Chicago, Detroit, Granada (Capilla Real), London (NG, and two silverpoint drawings in the BM), Munich, Paris (Louvre), Philadelphia (Johnson), Turin, Washington (NG) and elsewhere.

WHEATLEY, Francis (1747–1801), may have been a pupil of Zoffany, and began as a painter of small portraits and conversation pieces. From 1779 to 1783 he worked in Dublin (Leeds has the *Irish House of Commons*, 1780), to escape from his London creditors. He also ran off with another artist's wife. After his return to London he gave up his small group portraits in favour of adaptations to the English taste of GREUZE's type of genre subject, with overtones of the picturesque and deserving poor. His *Mr Howard relieving Prisoners* (1787) and his celebrated *Cries of London*, engraved in 1793–7, are instances of this skilful blend of moral feeling and popular sentiment, and also show his clear, rather pale colour and his free, sensitive handling. His first portrait, *Mrs Pearce* (1786, Wolverhampton) also shows Greuze's influence. There are several works in Dublin, and in the Royal Coll. and Birmingham, Brighton, Cambridge (Fitzwm), Detroit, London (NPG, Tate, Nat. Marit. Mus., V&A and RA), Manchester, Norwich, Nottingham, Ontario, Philadelphia, San Marino Cal., Southampton, Yale (CBA) and York.

WHISTLER, James Abbott McNeill (1834–1903), was born in Lowell, Mass., and attended West Point Military Academy, 1851–4. Failing there, he worked as a Navy cartographer, which at least taught him the technique of etching, before going to Paris to study painting in 1855. There he worked in GLEYRE's studio (1856), met Fantin-Latour and Degas and was influenced by COURBET, as may be seen in *Au Piano*, rejected by the Salon in 1859 and exhibited privately by Whistler, following Courbet's example. In 1859 he moved to London, but he continued to visit Paris frequently as well as going – for no known reason – to Valparaiso in 1866. In 1876/7 he had a quarrel (in which he was entirely in the wrong) over the decoration of the 'Peacock Room' in a London house (now in Washington, Freer Gall.), and in 1877 Ruskin wrote of his *Nocturne in Black and Gold* (now in Detroit) that it was 'flinging a pot of paint in the public's face'. Whistler sued him and won, in 1878, damages of a farthing (the smallest of all coins) but his own costs ruined him and he went to Venice in 1879 and 1880 to make a series of etchings; since his mastery of etching was never disputed even by bitter critics of his paintings, he hoped to recoup himself in this way. He lived as a dandy and had a deserved reputation as a mordant wit, well able to keep up with his friend Oscar Wilde: after one sally Wilde is supposed to have said admiringly 'I wish I had said that'. Whistler replied 'You will, Oscar, you will!'

The early influence of Fantin-Latour and Courbet was succeeded to some extent by that of Manet, who was one of Whistler's fellow-exhibitors in the

Salon des Refusés of 1863, but an even more marked influence in the 1860s was that of Japanese art, then finding its way to Europe and being discovered by the more advanced Parisians. Strangely, there is also some influence discernible from English academic painters like Albert Moore, particularly in the colour 'arrangements' which are really studies in the juxtaposition of closely related tones and colours. Whistler liked to emphasize the aesthetic nature of his pictures in conscious reaction against the domination of the subject in Victorian painting, hence his choice of titles like *Symphony* or *Nocturne*. The best collections of his work are in Washington (Freer Gall.) and Glasgow (University); other pictures are in Cardiff, Glasgow (Gall.), London (Tate), Ottawa, Paris (Mus. d'Orsay: the famous portrait of his mother (1871), officially entitled *Arrangement in Gray and Black: the Artist's Mother*), and several American museums. His etchings are well represented in the Royal Coll. and London (BM and V&A).

WILHELM, Master (active 1358–*d.*1372/8), was a Cologne painter whose works are lost, but who has been built up into a legendary figure to whom even LOCHNER's *Dombild* has been ascribed. He may have been identical with a painter named Wilhelm von Herle, but the legend was begun in the German Romantic era, and, though now dead in Germany, is still active in British and American auction rooms and elsewhere.

WILIGELMO was the sculptor responsible for most of the decoration of Modena Cathedral, in a very classical style, between *c.*1099 and *c.*1106. An inscription dated 1099, on the façade, names him as the principal sculptor and probably relates to the figures on the lower part of the façade, the *Genesis*, and the jambs of the portal. His work is in the mainstream of southern Romanesque sculpture, with stocky, expressive figures of great narrative force. Similar sculpture at Cremona Cathedral is probably by his workshop, and the influence of his style can be traced as far as northern Spain and Bari in south Italy, where the Bishop's throne in S. Nicola, of *c.*1098, is usually connected with him.

WILKIE, Sir David (1785–1841), was the son of the minister of Cults, Fifeshire, and studied in Edinburgh. His first important work, painted when he was 19, was *Pitlessie Fair* (1804, Edinburgh, NG) which is a remarkably accomplished essay in the manner of TENIERS. In 1805 he entered the RA Schools in London and exhibited his *Village Politicians* in the RA of 1806. This made his name and led to his treating similar subjects in the style of Ostade or Teniers for some twenty years. These 'Dutch' genre scenes had great influence in Germany: he received a commission from the King of Bavaria in 1819 for *Reading the Will* (Munich). He was elected ARA in 1809, RA in 1811, succeeded Lawrence as Painter to the King in 1830, and was knighted in 1836. He was a friend of HAYDON – although he had the sense not to attempt Haydon's High Art – and they went to Paris together in 1814 to see the pictures looted by Napoleon. He was most impressed by Rubens and by Rembrandt, especially in his drawings. To commemorate the defeat of Napoleon the Duke of Wellington commissioned Wilkie in 1816 to paint *Chelsea Pensioners reading the Gazette of the Battle of Waterloo* (1822, London, Wellington Mus.), which was a huge success at the RA of 1822. Because of ill-health he spent 1825–8 in Italy, Austria, Germany and Spain, and his new experience of Italian and Spanish art led to a great style change; Velázquez and Murillo being the principal influences on the new, broader manner and change of subject-matter, which included several histories. He showed some drawings to Delacroix in Paris in 1825, who noted that Wilkie was 'unsettled by the paintings he had seen', and he seems to have been the first British artist to see the Spanish masterpieces in the Prado. His change in style was not universally approved, and even Haydon said that Italy had been the ruin of him. In 1840 he went to the Holy Land and died at sea on the way home: his burial at sea is the subject of an imaginative composition by Turner. There are examples in the Royal Coll. and in Aberdeen, Berlin, Birmingham, Cupar Fife (Town Hall), Dublin, Edinburgh (NG, SNPG and United Services Mus.), Leicester, London (Tate and Wallace Coll.), New York (Met. Mus.), Riga, Toledo Ohio, Yale (CBA) and elsewhere.

WILSON, Benjamin (1721–88), was an English portrait painter, whose chief claim to fame lies in the easy confusion of his name with Richard Wilson's, who also painted some portraits: Benjamin's are more Rembrandtesque. ZOFFANY may have worked for him until *c.*1762, perhaps on theatrical scenes. From about 1770 Wilson seems to have devoted himself principally to science. There are examples in Brighton, Leeds, London (NPG and Dulwich) and Manchester.

WILSON, Richard (1713/14–82), was born in Wales and, like Reynolds, was the son of a clergyman who gave him a good classical education. This feeling for antiquity was probably decisive in his approach to landscape painting, which, for Wilson, has the classic overtones of the Italy of CLAUDE and Gaspar POUSSIN. These two, together with CUYP, were acknowledged by Wilson as his inspiration. He is now known to have been in London by 1737, when he painted *The Inner Temple After a Fire* (1737, Tate), his earliest dated work and first recorded landscape, although he was certainly active as a landscape painter by 1746, when he painted two for the Foundling Hospital, which are still there; however, he was also building up a practice as a portrait painter in London (examples in Edinburgh and London, NPG, Tate – *Zuccarelli*, 1751 – and Nat. Marit. Mus.). The real turning point in his career was his Italian period, when he decided to devote himself exclusively to landscape; a decision which may have been influenced by ZUCCARELLI and C.-J. VERNET. He was in Venice in 1750 and spent most of his Italian years in Rome and the Campagna, which left its mark on him as on so many other landscapists from Claude and Gaspar Poussin onwards. He left Rome in 1756 and returned to England, probably in 1757, and continued to paint Italian landscapes, which, considering their classicism of subject as well as of handling, should have been much more popular among the Grand Tourists than they were. The remainder of his output consisted of views in England and Wales treated in a markedly Italian and classical way (so much so, that it is not always possible to be sure what the scene represented is), and of commissioned views of country houses. His *Niobe* was exhibited at the Society of Artists in 1760, and during the 1760s he seems to have painted a series of Grand Manner mythologies, perhaps as an equivalent to the Grand Manner portrait then being introduced by Reynolds, whose success was in marked contrast to Wilson's neglect. He was one of the Founder-Members of the Royal Academy in 1768 and was appointed Librarian in 1776, when he had almost ceased to paint and was in need. At his best, in such designs as the *Snowdon* (Liverpool and Nottingham), Wilson achieved a pure classicism which depends on the austere beauty of the design and informs it with a glow of light learned from the Dutch as well as from Claude. These designs are of such nobility that they can stand numerous repetitions, which they often received, and their poetry is indeed Roman in inspiration: there could hardly be a greater contrast to the naturalness of Constable. Wilson's pictures often exist in many versions, so that most British galleries have at least one. The largest collection is in Cardiff; other works are in Adelaide, Auckland NZ, Baltimore, Berlin, Birmingham (Barber Inst.), Boston, Bournemouth, Bristol, Buffalo, Cambridge (Fitzwm), Cambridge Mass. (Harvard Univ.), Chicago, Detroit, Dublin, Dunedin, Edinburgh (NG and SNPG), Exeter, Glasgow, Hanover, Leicester, London (NG, NPG, Marble Hill, Tate, V&A, RA, Nat. Marit. Mus. and Dulwich), Manchester (Gall. and Whitworth), Melbourne, Minneapolis, Montreal, Munich, New York (Met. Mus.), Northampton Mass., Ottawa, Philadelphia, San Marino Cal., Stockholm, Swansea, Toledo Ohio, Vancouver, Washington (Nat. Coll.), Worcester Mass. and Yale (CBA). Wolverhampton has an unusual large *Niagara*, 1768, from drawings by an army officer.

WILTON, Joseph (1722–1803), was the son of a prosperous maker of ornamental plasterwork and *papier-mâché*, which enabled him to study under DELVAUX in Flanders and PIGALLE in Paris. In 1747 he went to Italy, working in Rome (where he met ROUBILIAC in 1752) and Florence until 1755. His *Dr Cocchi* (1755, London, V&A) is a very early example of the Neoclassical type of bust, with neither wig nor drapery, in the ancient Roman manner, but Wilton never developed these new ideas. He returned to London with Chambers the architect in 1755 and soon had a considerable practice, in which he was helped by Chambers, who often employed him to carve the ornamental detail and chimney pieces in his buildings (notably at Somerset House). Wilton was a Founder-Member of the RA. He retired in 1786, and was appointed Keeper of the RA in 1790, having dissipated the large fortune inherited from his father, as well as that won by his own work. There are several tombs by him in Westminster Abbey (including General Wolfe's), and works in Edinburgh (SNPG), London (V&A), New York (Hist. Soc.) and Yale (CBA).

WINCKELMANN, Johann Joachim (1717–68), was the first of the great German art historians and one of the founders of NEOCLASSICISM. He published his 'Gedanken über die Nachahmung der griechischen Werke ...' ('On the Imitation of Greek Works ...') in 1755, and later that year he moved from Dresden to Rome. The 'Gedanken' contains the phrase which sums up all his teachings about Greek art (which he scarcely knew from the originals, most of them being still undiscovered): *edle Einfalt und stille Grösse*, noble simplicity and calm grandeur. The 'Gedanken' was translated into English by FUSELI. In 1764 he published his very influential history of ancient art, soon translated into French and English, and in 1768 he was murdered in Trieste, ostensibly for some medals he carried. His theories profoundly influenced many artists, but the one closest to him was MENGS.

WINT, Peter De, *see* DE WINT.

WINTERHALTER, Franz Xaver (1805–73), was a German portrait painter who became the favourite of European royalty in the mid-19th century, especially the Empress Eugénie of France and Queen Victoria. His smooth, Ingres-like handling, and elaborate rendering of *haute couture*, combined with an occasional dash of LAWRENCE's bravura, made him admirably suited to portraying great ladies in fine dresses. He went to Karlsruhe in 1830, becoming Court Painter in 1834, after a stay in Italy (1833–4), but moved to Paris, where he soon became known at Louis-Philippe's Court. He fled from Paris after the 1848 Revolution, and again in 1871, during the Franco-Prussian War, when he returned to Karlsruhe. He received his first commission from Queen Victoria in 1841, and there are many works by him in the Royal Coll. Others are in Baltimore (Walters), Cleveland Ohio, Florence (Uffizi), Karlsruhe, London (NPG), Malibu Cal. (Getty), Munich, New York (Met. Mus.), Paris (Mus. d'Orsay and Jacquemart-André) and Versailles. A picture in London (Wallace Coll.) is now known to be signed by his brother Hermann (1808–91), his life-long assistant and manager.

WITTE, Emanuel de (*c.*1617–91/2), was a Dutch painter of church and house interiors and market scenes. His interiors usually stress shafts of light falling on pillars, tombs, or parquetry floors, and his open-air scenes have still-life detail in the foreground, as in his various fish-market pictures. He entered the Guild at Alkmaar in 1636 (apparently aged 19), and moved *c.*1650 to Amsterdam, where he married his second wife. Despite the beauty of his interiors they brought him little success, while his second wife caused him great trouble – she and their daughter were convicted of theft – and he ended his own life. There are works in Amsterdam (Rijksmus.), Berlin, Birmingham (Barber Inst.), Boston, Brussels, Cape Town, Dublin, Edinburgh, The Hague, Hartford Conn., Lille, London (NG and Wallace Coll.), Oberlin Ohio, Rotterdam, Toledo Ohio and elsewhere.

WITTEL, Gaspar (Caspar) van (1653–1736), known in Italy as Vanvitelli, was born at Amersfoort in Holland and received his first training there, although he was in Rome by the time of the Jubilee of 1675. He worked as a draughtsman on a scheme for regulating the Tiber and this probably gave him the idea of making large and very accurate topographical drawings which could be worked up into VEDUTE; he may therefore be the link between Dutch topographical painters like van der HEYDEN and later Italian *vedutisti.* He is now recognized as an extremely important forerunner of painters like CARLEVARIS, CANALETTO and PANINI, since there are dated Roman *vedute* by him of 1681 (Rome, Gall. Naz. and Pal. Colonna). He went to Venice in the 1690s and there is a dated *veduta* of 1697 (Madrid, Prado), which antedates Carlevaris. He was in Naples in 1700, when his son Luigi, later the great Neapolitan architect, was born. He spent his last years in Naples and Rome, where he died. He was nicknamed 'Gaspare degli Occhiali' (Gaspar with the spectacles) from at least 1712, and his short sight may have prevented his working after *c.*1730. Old sale-catalogues often refer to e.g. 'Two landskips by Ochiali'. There are also pictures in Florence (Pitti) and Hartford Conn.

WITZ, Konrad (1400/10–44/6), was the greatest Swiss painter before Holbein. He entered the Basle Guild in 1434, but he came from Germany and may have been attracted to Basle by the Church Council which convened there in 1431. About 1435 he probably began his major work, the large altarpiece of the Redemption (*Heilspiegelaltar*), parts of which have survived. His only signed and dated work is the *Christ walking on the Water* (1444, Geneva), which contains one of the earliest certainly datable views in modern art. The landscape is recognizably that of a particular point on the Lake of Geneva, not just a Swiss scene. His extremely realistic style shows that he must have been in contact with his immediate predecessors in Flanders, Jan van EYCK and the Master of Flémalle, and with them he substituted a strongly realistic style for the SOFT STYLE hitherto practised in Germany. His few known works are in Basle (Mus. and Mus. of History), Berlin, Dijon, Geneva, Naples, Nuremberg and Strasbourg.

WOLGEMUT, Michael (1434–1519), a Nuremberg painter and designer of woodcut book-illustrations, was the master of DÜRER. He probably went to Flanders *c.*1450, as the influence of BOUTS and Roger van der WEYDEN seems to have come to Nuremberg through him. He married PLEYDENWURFF's widow and took over his shop. Very few paintings can be given to him with any certainty: the altarpieces in Zwickau (1476–9), Nuremberg (1485–8), and the one in Schwabach (1506–8). The central panel of a triptych in Brighton is signed MW. He also designed the woodcuts for two of the most famous 15th-century books, the 'Schatzbehalter' of 1491 and Schedel's 'Weltchronik' (1491–3).

WOLS (i.e. Alfred Otto Wolfgang Schulze) (1913–51) was born in Berlin and studied at the Bauhaus under MOHOLY-NAGY before going to Paris in 1933. He made a living as a photographer until he was interned in 1939, when he began to paint. He lived in desperate poverty in the South of France, 1940–5, and began to paint in oils only in 1946. His spiky abstractions are Tachiste, and he was one of the founders of the style.

WOODCUT (Wood Engraving) *see* ENGRAVING.

WOOTTON, John (*c.*1682–1764), was one of the earliest English exponents of landscape in the style of Claude and Gaspar POUSSIN: Vertue said that he 'perfectly entered into his [Gaspar's] Manner'. He was a pupil of J. Wyck, and may have been to Italy before 1710, and introduced Gaspar's style into England, but there is no contemporary evidence for this. He combined his landscapes – which are often very large – with horse portraits, hunting scenes and sporting conversation pieces, and occasionally he even represented battles, all of which appealed to country gentry. From *c.*1720, as Vertue noted, the influence of Gaspar Poussin became stronger. There are works in the Royal Coll., including two huge *Sieges* of 1742, and in Barnsley, Exeter (a *Landscape with Angelica and Medoro*), London (Tate and Nat. Army Mus.: *Battle of Dettingen* and *Blenheim*), Longleat Wilts. (very large *Hunts*), Manchester (Gall. and Whitworth) and Yale (CBA).

WORKSHOP PRODUCTION or 'Shop Work' are descriptions of works of art which are produced by relatively unskilled or insensitive assistants from drawings or cartoons by a major artist, but more or less under his supervision. There are, for example, two *tondi* of the *Madonna and Child*, one in the NG, London, and one in the Pallavicini Gall., Rome, which are painted from the same cartoon by Botticelli – but which nevertheless betray the hands of two men, neither of whom was Botticelli.

WOTRUBA, Fritz (1907–75), was a Viennese sculptor whose work was based on the human figure, but treated in an abstract way. He usually employed coarse stone and carved direct, but some of his work is in lead or bronze. He emigrated to Switzerland, 1939–45, but later taught at the Vienna Academy. There are works by him in London (Tate), Vienna (City and State Galleries), Winterthur and Zurich, and a large relief in Marburg University.

WOUTERS, Rik (1882–1916), was a leading Belgian FAUVE. He began as a sculptor, e.g. *Ensor* (1913), but painted from 1904, and by 1911 was principally a painter, using very thin glazes of oil paint, leaving patches of bare canvas, much influenced by Cézanne. He was interned in Holland in 1914 and died in Amsterdam. There are works in Antwerp, Brussels, Paris (Mus. d'Art Mod.) and Rotterdam.

WOUWERMAN(S), Philips (1619–68), was a Haarlem painter who was a pupil of Hals, but who painted genre scenes of horsemen, battles, and camp life much more akin to BAMBOCCIATE. He frequently disposed dozens, even hundreds, of small figures in his canvases and he had a special fondness for white horses. He often painted figures in the landscapes of other painters – e.g. Wynants and Ruisdael. There are about 1,200 pictures recorded, some of the largest collections being the Royal Coll., Dresden, Leningrad, London (NG and Dulwich), Paris (Louvre) and Vienna. There is a large *Battle* dated 1646 in London (NG), which is one of the few dated works. His brothers Jan (1629–66) and Pieter (1623–82) were also landscape painters: Pieter imitated Philips and used a confusingly similar PW monogram.

WPA (Works Progress Administration) was a Federal Art Project in the US, encouraged by President Roosevelt 1933/43, to relieve artists in the depression of the 1930s by giving them public buildings to decorate. Over 1,100 murals resulted, as well as many other works of art.

WRIGHT, John Michael (1617–94). Wright, whose first name is uncertain, was born in London, but apprenticed to JAMESONE in Edinburgh in 1636. He seems to have gone to Italy by 1644, the approximate date of his first known painting, *Robert Bruce*. In 1648 he became a member of the Roman Academy of St Luke ('Michele Rita inglese'), the only British member in the 17th century. In Rome he became an antiquarian and later (*c.*1653/4) worked as such for the great patron of the arts, the Archduke Leopold Wilhelm, Governor of the Netherlands. It is clear that he was a Catholic, yet he returned to Commonwealth England in 1655 and 1656 and painted many portraits in a Dobsonesque manner, the most important being a series (of which only two survive) for the City of London; of which Evelyn observed in 1673 that 'Most of them are very like the persons they represent, though I never took Wright to be any considerable artist' and Pepys had earlier (1662) compared him with Lely, remarking 'Lord! the difference': Wright was, nevertheless, Painter to Charles II, and James II 'had a particular kindness for him'. He returned to Rome with Lord Castlemaine's Embassy to the Pope in 1686–7 and published an account of it in Italian (1687) and English (1688). While he was away KNELLER built up his practice. In 1679/80 he was in Dublin – the Tate Gallery has *The Irish Chief O'Neill*. There are pictures by him in the Royal Coll., and in Aberdeen (Univ.), Dublin, Edinburgh (SNPG), Glasgow (Univ.), London (Tate, NPG, Guildhall, Tower of London and Ham House), Manchester, Nottingham (part of the ceiling of Charles II's bedroom, from Whitehall Pal.), Oxford (Magdalen and Ch. Ch.), Wolverhampton and Yale (CBA).

WRIGHT, Joseph (1734–97), usually called Wright of Derby, was a pupil of HUDSON. He established himself at Derby where, except for a visit to Liverpool in 1769, he remained until he travelled in Italy in 1773–5. All his life he specialized in lighting effects and his candlelight pictures show affinities with those of Honthorst and others of the Utrecht School, and his moonlit landscapes recall Aert van der Neer as well as his contemporary VERNET. In Derby he found admirers among the pioneers of science allied to industry: Wedgwood and Arkwright were his patrons, and among his completely new subjects were representations of experiments made by candlelight, such as the *Orrery* (1766, Derby) and the *Experiment with an Air Pump* (1768, London, Tate).

In Italy he was not interested in the grandest art, but was deeply impressed by a fireworks display at Castel S. Angelo and an eruption of Vesuvius, both of which he painted on his return. He also evolved moonlit landscapes, first of Vesuvius, then of the Derbyshire countryside, his main interest being as much in the quality of the light as in the picturesque effect. He tried to replace Gainsborough at Bath in 1775, but in 1777 returned to Derby where he had a prosperous portrait connection and opportunities for painting landscapes and subject pictures which eventually decline into sentimental genre. His best portraits were painted in the early 1780s, and *Sir Brooke Boothby* (1781, London, Tate), lying reading Rousseau in a woody glade, is an adroit but sympathetic blend of Batoni with the new literary influences from France. He was elected ARA in 1781 and RA in 1784, but declined to accept the promotion. He is well represented in British galleries (especially Derby), and there are also works in Hartford Conn., Paris (Louvre) and Yale (CBA).

WTEWAEL, (Uytewael) Joachim (1566–1638), was one of the leading Mannerists in Utrecht at the time of BLOEMAERT. He spent four years in Italy and France (St Malo 1588–90). On his return to Utrecht he practised the style known as Haarlem Mannerism, based on the works of SPRANGER, but represented in Haarlem by CORNELISZ. van Haarlem, GOLTZIUS and van MANDER. His religious pictures and portraits are well represented in Amsterdam (Rijksmus.) and Utrecht, and there are others in Gateshead, Kansas City, London (NG), Malibu Cal., Ottawa, Oxford, Vienna, Waddesdon Bucks. (National Trust) and Yale.

WYNANTS, Johannes (active 1643–84), was a Haarlem landscape painter who also kept an inn, but was still always in debt. His rather limited art consisted of landscapes with dunes in the background and a sandy road in the foreground winding past trees in the middle distance. There is usually a dead tree in the foreground as well as a figure group. These figures are not by Wynants himself, but usually by WOUWERMANS (whose own works are very similar), Lingelbach or Wynants' own pupil Adriaen van de VELDE. Some of his early works were painted in collaboration with a specialist in wildfowl, and it is a nice point whether they are landscapes or animal pieces: otherwise, his charming views run to type and were much collected in the 18th and 19th centuries so that most galleries have one or more. They were a profound influence on many English landscape painters, notably Gainsborough (who may even have restored/forged some).

X

XX, LES, *see* VINGT, LES.
XYLOGRAPHY *see* ENGRAVING.

Y

YEATS, Jack B. (1871–1957), was the son of a painter and brother of the poet W. B. Yeats. He began his career as a watercolour painter and illustrator for the family press (later known as the Cuala Press). He exhibited at the ARMORY SHOW (1913), but did not begin to paint in oil until about 1915, evolving an intensely romantic, occasionally rather slapdash, landscape style which, in his last works, approaches ABSTRACT IMPRESSIONISM. It has been said that 'Irish romance is not easily exportable', but Yeats' works have been admired by painters like KOKOSCHKA (who was a close friend). There are examples in Belfast, Cork, Dublin (NG, Municipal Gall.) and London (Tate).
YSENBRANDT *see* ISENBRANDT.

Z

ZADKINE, Ossip (1890–1967), was born in Russia, came to London in 1907 and studied in Paris from 1909, where he met and was influenced by the Cubists. His works, in wood and stone, usually deal with figures from Greek mythology and are quasi-representational. Many of his wooden figures are very large, and have ingenious effects of silhouette obtained by cut-out shapes. Other works include a monument to van Gogh at Auvers-sur-Oise, and a bronze memorial to the destruction of Rotterdam (*The Destroyed City*, 1951–3) which 'touched the imagination of the world'. There are examples in Antwerp, Edinburgh, Glasgow, London (Tate), Norwich (Univ.), Paris (Mus. d'Art Moderne) and Philadelphia. He wrote an account of how he became a sculptor, and also published poems illustrated by himself.

ZAIS, Giuseppe (1709–84), was a Rococo landscape painter active in Venice. His early style was probably influenced by Marco RICCI, but his later landscapes have the brightness and prettiness of the style usually associated with ZUCCARELLI. There are characteristic examples in Venice and London (NG).

ZANDOMENEGHI, Federigo (1841–1917), was born in Venice, the son of a sculptor. He was in Sicily with Garibaldi in 1860, but from 1862 to 1866 was in Florence in contact with the MACCHIATOLI. From 1874 until his death he lived in Paris, often exhibiting with the Impressionists, although he was closest to DEGAS and the works of the two men have occasionally been confused. There are pictures by him in Florence, Milan, Piacenza, Philadelphia (Drexel Inst.) and Venice.

ZEVIO, Stefano da, *see* STEFANO.

ZICK, Januarius (1730–97), was one of the leading German painters in the period of transition from ROCOCO to NEOCLASSICISM. He was trained in Munich and then went to Paris, where he copied WATTEAU, after which (rather inappropriately) he went to Rome and worked in MENGS's studio (1757–8). In 1758 he returned to Germany and began his prolific career as a painter of altarpieces and decorative frescoes, the best of them being those at Mainz, Coblenz and Wiblingen (1778–80) in the Klosterkirche. Many German museums have works and there is one in Kansas (Univ.). His father, Johann Zick (1702–62), painted frescoes at Würzburg, but was replaced by TIEPOLO.

ZOFFANY, Johann (1733–1810), was a painter of portraits, conversation pieces and theatrical scenes, who was born in Germany, studied in Italy, 1750–7, where he was influenced by MENGS, and arrived in London *c.*1760, where he worked as a hack for B. WILSON. He attracted the notice of George III, who made him an RA in 1769, and paid for him to go to Florence. He arrived in 1772 and painted *The Tribuna of the Uffizi* (1772–80, Royal Coll.), staying in Florence until 1778 and then returning, via Parma, to London in 1779. Before this he had created a novel type of theatrical picture, usually representing an actual moment in a play, frequently starring Garrick – his first success was *Garrick in 'The Farmer's Return'* (1762), although he was probably following HOGARTH whose *Garrick as Richard III* was painted in 1746. On his return to London in 1779 he found that taste had changed, and he went to India (1783–9) to paint the English and the native princes. Only about a dozen of these pictures survive (half of them in Calcutta Mus.), but his *Col. Blair and*

Family with an Ayah has three landscapes represented on the wall, the only record of the landscapes Zoffany is known to have painted in India. He made a fortune in India and stopped painting in 1800. There are works in Aberdeen, Birmingham, Bordeaux, Brighton, Burnley, Detroit, Dublin, Edinburgh (NG), Glasgow, Liverpool, London (NG, NPG and Tate), Manchester, Newcastle, Ottawa, Oxford (Ashmolean: a fine portrait of his second wife), Springfield Mass., Vienna (K-H Mus.), Wolverhampton and Yale (CBA).

ZOPPO, Marco (*c.*1433–*c.*1478), was a Bolognese painter who was probably originally a pupil of TURA, but went, at the age of 21, to work for SQUARCIONE whose adopted son he became in 1455. In the same year he went to Venice and subsequently to Bologna. His style is a slightly softer version of the angular manner of both his masters and may reflect the influence of Giovanni Bellini. His main works are in Berlin and Bologna (San Clemente), but there are others in London (NG and Courtauld Inst.), Oxford and Washington (NG).

ZUCCARELLI, Francesco (1702–88), was a Florentine landscape painter who worked principally in Venice and England. He met Richard Wilson in Venice in 1751 and they exchanged paintings; in 1752 he went to London and remained until 1762. He returned to London in 1765 and stayed until 1771, being elected a Founder-Member of the Royal Academy in 1768. His light and facile style of landscape painting, with picturesque peasantry, was very popular in England and was preferred to the graver style of Wilson. There are several examples in the Royal Coll., and others in Cambridge (Fitzwm), Glasgow, London (NG and Dulwich), Manchester, Oxford (Ch. Ch.), Venice and elsewhere. London (Tate) has his grand historical landscape, *Cadmus Killing the Dragon* (1765).

ZUCCARO (Zuccari, Zuccheri), Taddeo (1529–66) and Federico (*c.*1540/3–1609), were brothers and represent the end of the MANNERIST tradition in Rome. Taddeo was the chief exponent of the style of the mid-16th century and his principal works were the fresco cycles in the Sala Regia of the Vatican and the *Farnese Deeds*, in the Villa Farnese at Caprarola, near Viterbo. Almost no oil-paintings by him are known to survive, but there is a fine *Adoration* in Cambridge (Fitzwm). The two fresco cycles were completed by his younger brother, after which Federico went, in 1574, to France and Antwerp and, late in the year, to England. There he certainly made two drawings, one of Queen Elizabeth (both are in London, BM), but he was back in Italy by October 1575, so he cannot have painted all (or perhaps even any) of the portraits attributed to him in English houses. The *Queen Elizabeth* in Siena had a claim to be his, and was also attributed to KETEL, but the signature and date (1583) of Quentin MASSYS II have recently been disclosed by cleaning. Federico also worked in the Vatican, completed the frescoes of the dome of Florence Cathedral left incomplete by Vasari in 1574, and went to Spain in 1585, remaining until 1589, but finding little favour at the hands of Philip II, who was accustomed to the works of Titian. In 1593 he established the ACADEMY of St Luke in his own palazzo in Rome, becoming Principe of it in 1598, and devoting much thought in his last years to the theory of art and particularly of DISEGNO. He made a series of decorations for his own house, only six of which survive (Rome, Pal. Venezia). Like the Cavaliere d'ARPINO, he was an eclectic Mannerist who lived on into a new era. Among the many pictures attributed to him are those in Florence (Uffizi and Pitti), Glasgow, London (NPG: the *'Darnley' Elizabeth* is now thought to be a copy of a lost Zuccaro); Minneapolis, Milan (Brera), New York (Hist. Soc.), Rome (Borghese) and Vienna. His treatise 'L'Idea de' Scultori, Pittori e Architetti' was published in 1607, and his collected writings in 1961.

ZURBARÁN, Francisco de (1598–1664), was born near Bádajoz and was apprenticed in Seville in 1614 to a craftsman-painter of devotional images. By 1617 he had settled in Llerena in southern Spain, but established himself in Seville at the invitation of the City Council in 1629. In 1634 he visited Madrid to paint a *Siege of Cadiz* for the King, to hang with Velázquez's *Surrender of Breda* and Maino's *Recovery of the Bay of S. Salvador*. He was back in Seville in 1635 to enter on his most productive and successful decade, during which he worked for monasteries and churches all over the south-west of Spain. He also painted pictures, some in long series, for religious houses in the Spanish colonies in the New World, and exported them as articles of trade, possibly through members of his second wife's family, established in Peru. Much of this production was shop work, but the argosies were not always successful, for there are many records of his difficulties in collecting the monies due to him. In 1658 he moved to Madrid in search of business, and renewed contact with Velázquez, for whom he was a witness in the proceedings that admitted him to the Order of Santiago. He died in Madrid.

The bleak, austere piety of his early pictures of saints, painted for the more severe religious orders, made him the ideal painter of simple doctrinal altarpieces, expressed in clear, sober colour, with figures of massive solidity and solemnity, and with a Tenebrism owing little to Caravaggio or Ribera, but developed straight out of southern Spanish traditions of unidealized representation, e.g. the *Crucified Christ* (1627, Chicago) and *S. Serapion* (1628, Hartford Conn.). For the same reason, he was one of the finest of all STILL-LIFE painters. He probably never saw a painting by Ribera until the mid-1630s, but he certainly knew his etchings. His ability to portray rather arid scenes from saintly lives, with a perfect union of the mystical and the realistic, accords well with Counter-Reformation theories of the purpose of paintings in churches and with the importance of subjects expressing the 'witness' aspect of a saint's life. The first journey to Madrid opened his eyes to other styles, and shows in something of a stronger feeling for Baroque magnificence. He still retained his hold on pure realism, but the splendour of his colour and the clarity and solidity of the masses in, for example, the *Adoration of the Shepherds* (1638, Grenoble) show how well he absorbed lessons learnt from Italian art. The rise of MURILLO in the 1640s forced Zurbarán to compete with his softer, sweeter expression and more fused, smooth technique, and to abandon his own austerity of vision and colour, and impasted handling. His saints become more romantic in their devotion, his Madonnas ape the sentiment of Italian Mannerist painting, and in this competition with something entirely alien to him his own personality and individuality were lost.

Many of his works are in the churches and religious houses of Spain and Spanish America for which they were painted, but there are twelve in the Bishop's Palace, Bishop Auckland (Durham), and museums in Barcelona, Barnard Castle (Bowes), Berlin, Birmingham (Barber Inst.), Boston (Mus.

and Gardner), Budapest, Cadiz, Cincinnati, Cleveland Ohio, Dresden, Dublin (NG), Edinburgh (NG), Indianapolis, Lisbon, Los Angeles, London (NG), Madrid (Prado and Acad.), Munich, New York (Hispanic Soc. and Met. Mus.), Paris (Louvre), Philadelphia, St Louis, San Diego, São Paulo, Seville, Toledo Ohio and Washington (NG) also have examples.

His son, Juan (1620–49), was also a fine painter of still-life, similar to contemporary Neapolitan works. He is known from three signed and dated pictures: 1639 and 1645 in private collections and one of 1640 in Kiev (Mus.). Attributed works are in Barcelona and Chicago.